JIHAD'S NEW HEARTLANDS

Why The West Has Failed To Contain Islamic Fundamentalism

GABRIEL G. TABARANI

authorHOUSE®

AuthorHouse™ UK Ltd.
500 Avebury Boulevard
Central Milton Keynes, MK9 2BE
www.authorhouse.co.uk
Phone: 08001974150

First published by AuthorHouse 8/9/2011

ISBN: 978-1-4567-7771-5 (sc)

To my two sisters who have always been gifts to my heart, friends to my spirit, and golden threads to the meaning of life.

To Ellen & Nadia

ABOUT THE AUTHOR

Gabriel G Tabarani is an expert on Middle East and North African affairs. He graduated from "l'Universite Saint Joseph de Beyrouth", (Lebanon) specialising in Political and Economic Sciences. He started his working life in 1973 as a reporter and journalist for the pan-Arab magazine "Al-Hawadess" in Lebanon later becoming its Washington, D.C. correspondent. He subsequently moved to London in 1979 joining "Al-Majallah" magazine as its Deputy Managing Editor. In 1984 joined "Assayad" magazine in London initially as its Managing Editor and later as Editor-in-Chief. Following this, in 1990 he joined "Al-Wasat" magazine (part of the Dar-Al-Hayat Group) in London as a Managing Editor.

He has already authored four books: "The Tears of the Horizon" a romantic novel, "The Winter of Discontent in The Gulf" (1991) about the first Gulf War when Saddam Hussein took over Kuwait, "Israeli-Palestinian Conflict: From Balfour Promise To Bush Declaration – The Complications and The Road For a Lasting Peace" (2008), and "How Iran Plans To Fight America And Dominate The Middle East"(2008).

Furthermore, he wrote the memoirs of national security advisor to US President Ronald Reagan, Mr Robert McFarlane, serializing them in "Al-Wasat" magazine over 14 episodes in 1992.

CONTENTS

INTRODUCTION

ISLAMIC TRUTHS AND BIN LADEN'S FALLACY

Since 1993 Islamic terrorists are waging war against the west, they bombed the World Trade Centre in New York City for the first time in that year, killing 6 people and injuring more than 1,000. They bombed U.S. embassies in Kenya and Tanzania simultaneously in 1998, killing 223 (212 in Nairobi & 11 in Dar Assalam) and wounding more than 4,000. They attacked the USS Cole at a Yemen port in 2000 killing seventeen American servicemen. They hijacked four U.S. airliners in 2001 and crashed them into the World Trade Centre towers in New York City, the Pentagon, and rural Pennsylvania, killing more than 3,000 people. A cell related to al-Qa'ida blew up a commuter train in Madrid in 2004, killing 191 and wounding about 1,800. In 2005 a terrorist Islamic militant cell committed a series of coordinated suicide attacks on London's public transport system, killing 52 and injuring more than 700. In December 2010 a suicide bomber blew himself in Stockholm killing one people and damaged several properties.

These attacks and other terrorist incidents have led to growing debates about an emerging new form of terrorism which contribute, perhaps understandably, to a Western perception that all Muslims are anti-American and anti-west terrorists. As we know violent attacks receive enormous media attention, and most Westerners in can not help but have their view of Muslims affected by stories they hear on Televison or read in the Newspapers. Many research studies, scholars' essays and press reports confirmed that most Westerners are unaware of Muslim customs and ideologies, except for what they learn from the media. Nevertheless it is important to acknowledge that not all Muslims are fundamentalists, and not all fundamentalists are terrorists. However, fundamentalism, by its very nature, carries sometimes the threat of extremism, and extremism can easily morph into violence. Islamic fundamentalists can therefore pose a terrorist threat to their enemies. Unfortunately, many Middle Easterners and Muslims perceive America and the West as an enemy. Knowing the principles of Islam is the first step toward understanding how Islamic fundamentalism can sometimes lead to terrorism.

Most statistics and polls confirm that Islam is the fastest growing religion in the world and is second only to Christianity in number of adherents. Muslims live in all parts of the world, but the majority of Muslims are concentrated in the Middle East and Asia. "Islam has two meanings: Peace, and submission to Allah (God). Muslims believe that Islam is the only true religion and that it was revealed by the prophet Muhammad in Arabia in the seventh century. Pious Muslims adhere to the five pillars of Islam: acknowledging that there is no true god except God and that Muhammad is the prophet of God; praying five times a day toward Mecca; giving alms to the poor; fasting during the month of Ramadan (the ninth month of the lunar year); and for those who are financially and physically able, making an annual pilgrimage to Mecca. Islam also requires belief in six articles of faith, which are belief in God, belief in the messengers and prophets of God, belief in the Revelations and the Koran (the Islamic holy book), belief in angels, belief in Judgment Day, and belief in the ultimate power of God or God's decree. Other precepts of Islam are concerned with matters such as diet, clothing, personal hygiene, business ethics, responsibilities toward parents, spouses, and children, marriage, divorce, inheritance, civil and criminal law, fighting in defence of Islam, relations with non-Muslims, and much more." *(See Ref 1)*

The American scholar Auriana Ojeda point out that, all Muslims believe in the six articles of faith which are and adhere to the five pillars of Islam, but they differ in how they interpret the Koran and the shari'a (Islamic law). Several Islamic scholars, such as B.S. Burmeister, who in his essay "The Rise of Islamic Fundamentalism," identified two major divisions within Islam, the modernists and the revivalists. He argues that modernists believe in the inerrancy of the Koran, but they interpret its strictures in a modern context. Modernists accept secular governments, religious diversity, and the emancipation of women. Most Muslim modernists condemn terrorism and advocate individual relationships with God. On the other hand, revivalists favour a literal interpretation of the Koran and a return to traditional Islamic ideas (In Arabic they are referred to as Salafists or Salafis). These Muslims are extremely pious and closely follow the teachings of the Koran and Prophet Muhammad. Their aim is to recreate a true Islamic society, not simply by imposing the shari'a, but by establishing first an Islamic state through political action. Those Muslims see Islam not as a mere religion, but as a political ideology which should be integrated into all aspects of society (politics, law, economy, social justice, foreign policy, etc.). The traditional idea of Islam as an all-encompassing religion is extended to the complexity of a modern society. In fact they acknowledge the modernity of the society in terms of education, technology, changes in family structure, and so forth.Revivalists are frequently referred to as Islamic extremists, Islamic radicals, Islamists, or Islamic fundamentalists.

Religious fundamentalists believe in the absolute inerrancy of their sacred texts and religious leaders. Their beliefs do not automatically translate into terrorism, but the passion and conviction that are inherent in fundamentalism teeter on the edge of extremism. Extremism or radicalism in any belief system often leads some groups to violence because its adherents dogmatically adhere to their beliefs and consider conflicting beliefs threatening. For example, America has witnessed several acts of terrorism in the name of Christian fundamentalism, such as the bombings of abortion clinics and shootings of abortion providers. Jewish extremists in Israel also have committed acts of terrorism because they believed some people are threatening their existence. Islamic extremists manifest the same conviction and self-assurance as Christian and Jewish extremists.

Furthermore, since Islamic fundamentalists maintain that Islam is the one true religion, extremists advocate overthrowing powerful secular governments and replacing them with a single Islamic authority. According to Bassam Tibi, a well-known specialist on Islamic fundamentalism, "The goal of Islamic fundamentalists is to abolish the Western secular world order and replace it with a new Islamist divine order. . .The goal of Islamists is a new imperial, absolutist Islamic world power." *(See Ref 1)*

The specter of radical Islamists dominating the secular world is frightening, especially in light of recent terrorist attacks, but it is important to remember that most Muslims are not radical and that most espouse a modernist interpretation of the Koran and Islamic traditions. Islamic militant extremists represent a small faction of Muslims who, although influential, are probably not powerful enough to overthrow world superpowers. The majority of Muslims in the Middle East and over the world, especially those who live in the West, are moderate, and they accept and value secular societies. These Muslims represent a compromise between Western and Islamic customs that celebrates cultural identity and tolerance.

Furthermore, the idea of Islam as separate from a Judeo-Christian West is as false as it is influential. According to Professor Tariq Modood the author of "Radical Reform", Islam, with its faith in the revelations of Abraham, Moses, Jesus and Muhammad, belongs to the same tradition as Christianity and Judaism. It is, in its monotheism, legalism and communitarianism, not to mention specific rules of life, such as dietary prohibitions, which are particularly close to Judaism. In the Crusades of Christendom and at other times, Jews were slaughtered by Christians and their secular descendents and protected by Muslims. Jewish historians remember Muslim Spain as a "Golden Age". Islam, indeed, then was a civilisation, a "superpower" and a genuine geopolitical rival to the West. Yet even in that period Islam and Christendom were neither discrete nor they were competitors. They borrowed and learned from each other, whether it was in relation to scholarship, philosophy and scientific enquiry, or medicine, architecture and technology. Indeed, the classical learning from Athens and Rome, which was lost to Christendom, was preserved by the Arabs and reintroduced to Western Europe - like the institution of the university - via Muslims. That Europe came to define its civilisation as a renaissance of Greece and Rome and eviscerated from memory the Arab and Muslims contribution to its foundations and subsequent well-being is an example of racist myth-making that has much relevance today. *(See Ref 2)*

However, today in the West the words - 'Islamic fundamentalism' - conjure up images of bearded men with turbans and women covered in black shrouds. Whilst, some Islamist movements do indeed contain reactionary and violent elements, we should not let stereotypes blind us to the fact that there are also powerful modernising forces at work within these movements. According to Graham Fuller, the author of "The Future of Political Islam", "Political Islam is about change. In this sense, modern Islamist movements may be the main vehicle for bringing about change in the Muslim world and the break-up of the old "dinosaur" regimes. What will come in their stead is less clear." *(See Ref 3)*

Fuller argues that Islamists look at the status quo in the Muslim world today and do not like it. In place of good governance, they see authoritarianism, repression, corruption, incompetence, social and economic hardship - an unacceptable situation that calls out for change. But change based on what?

The norms of Western government derive from the English Magna Carta, the French Revolution, or the principles of the American Declaration of Independence; but in Islam they are derived from ideas in the Koran and the sayings and the doings of the Prophet (Hadith). It is therefore quite normal for Islamists to speak in non-Western terms. They look to the past as a philosophical model, not as a mode of daily life to be emulated today. And they differ about what to do, other than honour the basic principles of Islam. *(See Ref 3)*

Islamists have striven to accomplish an Islamic way of life off their own version of an Islamic state, struggling against the socio-economic and political objectives of governments. While autocratic governments have used religion to ensure their legitimacy, Islamic resurgence has professed to have as its objective the establishment of an Islamic dispensation. Resurgent movements aspire towards a greater unity of religion and politics, domains that cannot be separated. Religion provides them with a framework for the transformation.

Islamists are also modern in their heavy emphasis on grass roots organisation. Their parties (such as Hezbollah and Hamas) are in close touch with their constituents and are closely attuned to local interests. Many Islamist parties run local social welfare programmes independently of governments, and provide social services such as clinics, especially for women, housing in university cities for students from rural backgrounds, recreational facilities for youths, legal advice, educational support, and other forms of social assistance. These activities are, often far more responsive than the state to social needs and are generally funded from religious donations, or from large Islamist-run banks and businesses. As a result, Islamists are closer to the needs of poorer neighbourhoods than their political rivals, a resource which can be utilised to great effect.

Islam is solidly rooted in traditions of mercantilism and private enterprise according to Graham Fuller. He argues that the Prophet was a merchant, as was his first wife. Islam does not glorify the role of the state in the economy, or in general. If the state plays an important role in Iran, it is mainly a legacy from the days of the Shah. In principle, however, Islam is quite compatible with modern ideas of a limited state role in the economy. It has regularly opposed the introduction of socialist measures in the Muslim world and expresses its preference for market principles, as long as they are consistent with "social justice". The Islamists' attack on "capitalism" is usually a reference to "consumerism" or intense materialism that they see as a negative characteristic of the West. Islamists want laxer-borders among Muslim states and see the European Union as a potential model. *(See Ref 3)*

The role of women is one of the features most frequently criticised in the West, sometimes with good reason. For instance, the Taliban view on women in Afghanistan is particularly primitive and is rejected as non-Islamic by many Muslims, who are currently engaged in a great debate about the role of women in society. They have a conservative vision that places emphasis on the special place of women as guardians of the home, rearing the children and transmitting moral values. There is a fear of the perceived corruption of Western societies in which women turn into "sexual objects" or are commercially exploited, leading to a breakdown of social and family values. It is only in Afghanistan, however, that women are not permitted to work. In fact millions of Muslim women are today being brought into politics through the women's branches of Islamist parties.

Part of the dilemma of women's positions in Muslim society stems not so much from the principles of Islam itself, but from extremely conservative salafist interpretations of Islam or from the practice of traditional customs considered to be "Islamic". A new breed of Islamist feminist is emerging in many countries including Iran that demands "real" Islam, not tradition. Women are studying the Koran and Islamic law in order to challenge conservative, male-dominated interpretations, reject tradition and demand application of true Islamic norms.

Where does it say in the Koran that women cannot drive cars? Or that women's face must be covered? Or that they may not work? Muslim women are boldly challenging these traditions in many parts of the Muslim world, provoking a split between Islamic modernists and traditionalists on their place in society.

In one sense, fundamentalism can mean getting back to the root meaning of Islam. Islamist modernists say that what matters is not the text but the context: many laws from the time of the Prophet were appropriate for those times, and to understand Islamic law, one must look at the context in which they were formed. Today, they say, one must reinterpret those laws (through what's they call Al-Ijtihad or rational and creative interpretation) and rulings in light of contemporary circumstances.

Interestingly, Fuller argues that "one of the key centres of Islamic modernism is in the West itself where Muslims now have complete freedom for the first time to research and discuss a whole variety of ideas about Islam and propagate them via books, television, conferences and Internet - all impossible or forbidden at home. Today's Islamist leaders are not usually clerics; often they are Western-educated scholars, engineers and doctors whose vision of an Islam-oriented future includes modernism and technology." *(See Ref 3)*

It is through these individuals that a reformation of Islam is underway and there is much lively debate. There is no agreement about what an Islamic state really means or what it should look like. But moderate Islamists are determined to derive meaning for contemporary society from Islamic texts and law.

Islamic reformation will be a long-term process, but in today's accelerated world it will not take as long as the West's own reformation. Islamist thinking today is not about preserving the status quo, but about change. The debate is about what kind of change, and how to bring it about. Visions of what Islam means in contemporary life often differ sharply. Different Islamists seek different goals via different means. No one has a monopoly on Islam and what it means. But the chances are that the Islamic framework of the debate will be with us for a long time to come and few Muslim states will remain outside its influence or reach.

However, and as Graham Fuller wrote in his 1999 article in Le Monde Diplomatique "Islam, A Force For Change", "the mantra that the war on terrorism is not a war on Islam ignores one crucial fact: Islam and politics are inextricably linked throughout the Muslim world. Islamism includes Osama bin Laden and the Taliban but also moderates and liberals. In fact, due to the all encapsulating nature of the Islamic faith – perhaps in a way those in the West can not comprehend, it can be whatever Muslims want it to be. Rather than push secularism, the West should help empower the silent Muslim majority that rejects radicalism and violence. The result could be political systems that are both truly Islamist and truly democratic."

Whilst moderate Islamists look to change their countries through the dialogue and pacifist means, al-Qa'ida and its affiliates radicals seek to change the world by fighting and killing through war and jihad. For this reason there are now new cradles for Jihad, which inflame the world, and threaten the peace. It is these centres, which have lately become new heartlands for radical and militant Islamic movements, where a new generation of Islamists are trained in the use of a variety of weapons to become combatants, with the aim of attacking the West and its allies across the globe.

This begs the question: why has the west continually failed to contain Islamic extremism?

It is the answer to this question that I will attempt to evolve in the coming chapters, step by step through a thorough explanation of the roots of the Islamic fundamentalism, the difference between old-form and new-form terrorism, and al-Qa'ida. Subsequently I will cover examples of Islamic radicals in Egypt, Saudi Arabia, Afghanistan, Pakistan, Yemen, Somalia, the Levant, and the Maghreb. After which I will then discuss the challenge of Islam in Europe, Russia and USA. Finally I will discuss why the west has failed to contain the Islamic radicals and what it must do to contain them.

Throughout this book, I have tried to apply impartial analysis and interpretations of the facts from which I have subsequently come with what I believe are balanced and reasonable conclusions. All I can do is hope that I have succeeded in my attempts.

Gabriel G Tabarani

CHAPTER ONE

THE ROOTS OF ISLAMIC FUNDAMENTALISM

Islamic fundamentalism (in Arabic al-Ousouliyya) is a term used to describe religious ideologies seen as advocating a return to the "fundamentals" (al-Ousoul) of Islam: the Koran, the Hadith and the Sunnah. Definitions of the term vary. It is deemed problematic by those who suggest that Islamic belief requires all Muslims to be fundamentalists and by others as a term used by outsiders to describe perceived trends within Islam. Exemplary figures of Islamic fundamentalism who are also termed Islamists are the Egyptian Sayyid Qutb and the Pakistani Abul Ala Mawdudi. Economist Eli Berman argues that Radical Islam is a better term for many post-1920s movements starting with The Muslim Brotherhood, because these movements are seen to practice "unprecedented extremism", thus not qualifying as return to historic fundamentals.

Most Islamic experts and scholars believe that the Koran and Hadith, which are the original Islamic sources, had very little to say on matters of government and the state. And as Nazih Ayoubi in his 1982 book "Political Islam, Religion and Politics in The Arab World" pointed out, the guidance regarding the original political dispensations in the Muslim world were derived from linguistic explanation (bayan) and reasoning by analogy (qiyas) provided by the juridical elite who had written on political subjects. In this manner jurisprudence and a formal theory of the caliphate became institutionalised. With the expansion of Islam to non-Islamic regions, the institutionalisation of Islam and state met with opposition from groups that had been subjected and but were not of the same religion and culture. These groups usually came from minor or peripheral Arabian tribes, which formed the first religious-political opposition movement against the state. *(See Ref 4)*

1

However, the rise of opposition movements, "the Kharijites" or "al-Khawarej" [The Outsiders] under the fourth Caliph Ali who opposed the caliphate and also inspired later movements, was caused by the lack of a central political system. The Kharijites refused to establish leadership on any ethnic, class or even educational (theological) basis, according to Mehdi Mozaffari, and instead of the Kharijites who justified their actions based on the concepts of God's absolute sovereignty and ruler-ship. They judged the infidel and espoused excommunication (takfir) as well as the assassination of not just those who had blasphemed, but also those who had simply sinned. The comparison of present-day Islamists to the Kharijites can therefore be seen in the sense of exclusion that had inspired the Kharijites. Similarly, the sense of exclusion has been seen as the driving force of present-day Islamists. The historical period of the Kharijites can therefore not be ignored. *(See Ref 5 and 6)*

The main course of legitimacy of the rulers after the 12th century was based on defending the domain of Islam against foreign invaders. However, under the threat from the Mongols and the Crusaders, ideologists of that period, such as Ibn Taymiyya (1263-1328), limited their arguments and actions in order not to destabilise the state of siege. Also, the civil Muslim community of Ibn Taymiyya's time "could not imagine their rulers deviating from the way set by Allah in the systematic and comprehensive manner we witness today. Nor was it conceivable to the Muslim community that rulers would dispense with the shari'a altogether, conspire against Islam, maltreat Muslims, and form alliances with the enemies of God, as happens quite often today". Therefore, the message of Ibn Taymiyya was more moderate than that of present-day Islamists, even if they claim that they have derived their justification from the theories of Ibn Taymiyya. *(See Ref 7)*

Under the Abbasid dynasty the caliphate as an institution had deteriorated which led to the appearance of more than one caliph in different Muslim cities. When the Islamic dynasties disintegrated and separate dynasties ruled over the various Muslim communities, the legitimacy of both the government and the state was questioned. The causes of decadence and deterioration were attributed by ideologists to the Mamluk and Ottoman empires and kingdoms during the 18th and 19th centuries. They also denied the existence of any religious clergy in Islam, and believed that the foundation of political power was civil and derived from the state. Even though they did not establish a theoretical or intellectual framework for reform, they emphasised that Islam was open to and receptive of modern civilisation. During this time Jamal al-Din al- Afghani (1838-1897) became prominent in Egypt. He was a major catalyst and reformer and professed that the causes of the Muslims' decline vis-à-vis the West were Muslim societies' blind imitation (taqlid) of Westernism. Instead, Islam should be seen as a rational religion, capable of rational and creative interpretation "Ijtihad", rather than blind imitation (taqlid). This idealistic view was seen as the best instrument to counter the onslaught of the West and would be revived by later generations in Egypt. Reviving the spirit of the Koran meant a return to the origin of the religion as well as a rejection of distortions brought about through traditions. Through rational and creative interpretation "Ijtihad" it would be possible to use the Koran to extract the abstract principles of the faith and adapt the stipulations of the religion to their own modern ideas. Already at this stage Jamal al-Din al-Afghani warned against political authoritarianism, as he regarded it as one of the main reasons for the decline in the Islamic world. His views that, "science and philosophy had been stifled by our ... fanaticism and tyranny by religion and despotism." *(See Ref 5, 8)*

After al-Afghani came his most effective follower, Muhammad Abdu (1845-1905) who had focused on expanding the scope of "Ijtihad" and argued that Islamic doctrine does not determine the political organisation which can be determined according to circumstances of time and place together with consultation within the Muslim community. He also promoted the Salafiyya (Salafist) movement that would have an impact on Egypt and the Arab world. However the Salafiyya, under Abdu, was an essentially modernist movement explicitly opposed to the principal forces of conservatism in the Muslim world. It sought to promote a renewal of Islamic civilisation on the basis of a selective adoption of Western science and European political ideas, including constitutional government and democracy, while simultaneously modernising Islamic law.

Nina Voges argues in her 2006 essay, that the reformers wanted to overcome the divisions in the Muslim world between Sunni and Shia and also to transcend the distinctions within Sunni Islam between the four legal schools or rites, namely Hanafi, Hanbali, Maliki and Shafi'i, in order to modernise Islamic law in general. At the same time, they identified the leaders of official Islam, the doctors of law or the civil Muslim community as a main force of conservatism. The reformers' insistence on the need for interpretative reasoning or "Ijtihad" in law threatened the civil Muslim community's traditional authority in that domain. The movement's reference to the venerable ancestors (al-salaf al-saleh) thus emphasised the era of Islam before the differentiation into rites or schools had occurred and the Sufi orders had been founded, in order to surpass the conservative religious establishment without incurring the charge of profanation. *(See Ref 5)*

In the same era of Muhammad Abdu came Rashid Rida, who saw that the consultation is the base of the true Islamic movement, while the role of guardian interpreter of Islamic law must be fulfilled by the civil Muslim community. His value for Egypt was his inspiration to tanzimat and Salafiyya movements in Africa and the Middle East. While the tanzimat was present in the Ottoman Empire, the reformists or Salafiyya and secular movements were present in Egypt. The Salafiyya (salaf or ancestor) movements referred to a return to the ancestors in order to address the backwardness of Muslims. *(See Ref 5, 9)*

The origins of Salafists (or Salafis) were not clerical and remained traditional; however, the Salafiyya reform or "Islah" did not entail adopting modernity, but emphasised returning to the tradition of the Prophet. It rejected common law and the tradition of the civil Muslim community of "tafsir" or textual commentary and explanation. The traditional civil Muslim community's monopoly of the religious corpus was targeted, as it represented part of "the dead and deadening systems." Salafism … "demanded the right to individual creative interpretation or "Ijtihad" of the founding text (Koran and the Sunnah) without regard to previous commentaries." In this manner they would have been able to develop a new political and cultural activism, where the only role of the government was to implement the shari'a and restore the caliphate. *(See Ref 10)*

However, these attempts at religious reform which was promoted by Muhammad Abdu and others appeared by the 1930s that they had failed. In addition the Salafiyya teachings of Rashid Rida at this stage reflected more of the influence of Ibn Taymiyya and Muhammad Abd al-Wahhab. These movements influenced Hassan al-Banna and the Muslim Brotherhood with whom they shared the goal to end British rule in Egypt. Al-Banna had as goal the establishment of an Islamic government and a return to the shari'a to counter colonialism. This movement and its fundamentalist ideas later were flourished in the Arab World which sometimes took another violent ways. *(See Ref 5)*

On the other hand, the social movement of Islamic fundamentalism have witnessed a growth in the last three decades. It is associated with the media, militants, terrorists and violent upheavals, such as the bloody conflict occurring in Algeria, the killing of foreign tourists in Egypt and the September 11, 2001 events in USA. However, I must emphasise that the vast majority of Muslims point out that Islam teaches peace, justice and tolerance, not violence and intolerance.

There is no single explanation as to why Islamic fundamentalist movements have spread in recent years, but some general factors are clear. In some states, fundamentalism reflects a failure of existing regimes to meet the aspirations of the masses.In part, it is a response to the social pressures created in traditional Islamic societies by the move towards modernization and by the influence of Western ideas, such as liberal democracy, materialism, equal rights for women as well as attitudes towards sex, marriage and alcohol. Lisa Farhamy argues in her 2009 essay that modernization in many Muslim countries has resulted in a gap between a rich urban minority and an impoverished urban and rural majority. Furthermore modernization has offered little in terms of economic progress in exchange for the Western values encroaching on the traditional value system. Many feel that Western values are a threat to their identity, so Islamic fundamentalism becomes a cultural anchor. *(See Ref 11)*

Broader cultural issues clearly have an effect on the appeal of fundamentalism, too. Different religions offer diverse responses to the alienation people experience at various times in the modern world. Islamic fundamentalists demand a rigid commitment to traditional religious beliefs and rituals. In Muslim countries where symbolic gestures confirm Islamic fundamentalist values are strong, women have resumed wearing floor-length and long sleeve chadors, covering their hair, wrists and ankles. Furthermore religious studies and the publication of religious tracts and orations have increased. The sentiments of Islamic fundamentalists are also increasingly anti-Western. *(See Ref 12)*

Fundamentalists have gained political power in several Muslim countries and have tried to establish "shari'a" or Islamic law. In Islam, there is no separation of church and state. Islam is the source of law, a guide to statecraft and social behaviour. Muslims believe that every aspect of life is within the purview of the faith. Islamic fundamentalists have been most successful in Iran, where they have established an Islamic Republic since 1979. However, Islamic fundamentalism has also influenced Algeria, Afghanistan (with the Taliban until 2002), Egypt, Pakistan, Sudan and Saudi Arabia.

Some explicit economic principles were established in the Koran, many of which are pro-free enterprise, but when matters regard profits, Islam's concern is mainly with social justice. Islam is critical of those who earn profit through the exploitation of others. This critique had being a key factor as to why Islamic fundamentalists resent the Western values of democracy and free markets. Another economic principle of Islam prohibits the payment or receipt of interest or usury. This is not just a matter of theology but is now becoming a matter of law. In 1992, Pakistan's Federal "Shari'a" Court pronounced interest to be un-Islamic and therefore illegal and demanded that the government amend all financial laws accordingly. *(See Ref 11)*

By definition, Islam means submission and a Muslim is one who submits to Allah or God. Islamic fundamentalists ideally want Muslim countries to become Islamist, in line with the guidance of the "shari'a". In addition, they want to subvert the influence and perhaps the existence of infidels or non-believers in the world (because the infidel's influence is wide reaching and encroaching in the Islamic sphere.) Shari'a or Islamic law is derived from the Koran and the Hadith or sayings of the Prophet Muhammad and provides a foundation for a common identity for Muslims around the world. Islamic fundamentalists believe that these pillars of the faith should direct and govern the Islamic "umma" (the global Islamic community), however the "umma" does not represent one religiously homogenous group and is split between various sects. *(See Ref 13)*

The expansion of Islam, the influence of the Ottoman Turks and the Mogul empires, along with European powers led to the dilution of Islam and the rise of Sufism, resulting in revivalist orthodoxy movements or the purification of Islam. These movements paved the way for Islamic reformers and pan-Islamism with Jamal ed-din al-Afghani.

The origins of orthodox Islam and Sufism in the Ummayyad era of 661-750 are evident. Muslims wanted Islamic solutions to the problems they encountered in the conquest of non-Arab peoples; however, the Ummayyad caliphs adopted the practices of the conquered non-Muslim Byzantine and Sassanids emperors. The caliphate's failure to meet the need for solutions in line with Islam led to the development of Islam as a social system more than a means of governance. The intermingling of religion, society and jurisprudence was embedded in Islam at that time. The fundamentalist Ahmad bin Hanbal (780-855) and the liberal Hanifa al Numan (699-767) created parameters for "ijtihad" [the creative interpretation of Koran and Hadith texts]. *(See Ref 13)*

These boundaries would lead to the rigid status quo and intractability of Islam to progress. At the same time, Western development created a bigger rift between the Ottoman Empire and the European powers in the second millennium.

The Islamisation that took place through conquests and conversions carried with it strict observance of Koranic edicts and the pursuit of political power. Attempts to synthesise Islam and Hinduism were unsuccessful over the implementation of the shari'a. Policies were enacted to purify the Muslim community by prohibiting prostitution, hashish cultivation, and music. In 1744, Muhammad ibn Abdul Wahhab set out to purify and revive early Islam, waging jihad against idolatry, injustice, adultery, and apostates and prohibiting music, dance, and jewellery. Western influences of secular ideas, practices, and political models were seen as threatening and corrupting for Islam. This belief and threat perception led to the strengthening of Islam due to Wahhabi teachings (which became a branch in Islam and especially in Saudi Arabia) countering Western influences. *(See Ref 13)*

The Ottoman caliphs, with the decline of their Empire, were forced to secure power through suppressing independent thinking for fear that it would lead to opposition and result in chaos. This was to be avoided at all costs because it would in turn threaten the caliphate. Despite this the caliphate wanted some reform and modernism. Western influences imbuing the Muslim community were also facilitating modernism. One such effort was the enactment of "tanzimat", reorganisation or modernisation of the military, by the Janissaries or the military class. However, Sultan Abdul Hamid II realized that "tanzimat" has failed to deter the European powers from interfering in the affairs of the Ottoman Empire. As such in 1878, he denounced modernism and turned to traditional Islamic values. Here again we see the revival and bolstering of Islamic fundamentalism. The ulama (clergy) maintained that they had "nothing spiritual to learn from the West," a position they still maintain. This allowed Abdul Hamid to rally the Muslim community around religious beliefs. *(See Ref 11, 13)*

Jamal ed-Din al-Afghani, a supporter of Abdul Hamid, saw the "tanzimat" as undermining the society, so he called for another reform, back to the fundamentals. Al- Afghani, an Iranian born Shia of Afghan origin, claimed to have a Sunni background in order to reach a wider audience. His rhetoric set Islam against the West, calling for arms and to learn the secrets of their strengths. He also encouraged resistance to British and French influence in Egyptian affairs. First World War brought about the end of the Ottoman Empire and the caliphate. The Islamic state was now to be guided by the shari'a, as the dominant authority in legislation. Muhammad Rashid Rida (1865-1935), an acolyte to al-Afghani, called for women to be treated on a par with men, except in heading households, leading prayers or holding office. [The reformers blamed these figures for the decay in Islam.]*(See Ref 11, 14)*

However, the reformers eventually advocated that Islam should confront the West because they saw Western secular ideas as having undermined Islamic ideology. This along with the abolishment of the caliphate strengthened religion. Furthermore, the desire for reform backfired because the political and social aspect of life was subordinated to religion.

If the above are the roots of the old-form of fundamentalism one must ask: what are the roots of the new-form of fundamentalism we currently face which is inspiring the contemporary radical Islamists and jihadists?

In the aftermath of the Arab defeat in June 1967 war with Israel the radicalization of a small segment of the Global Islamic Movement appears to have taken place. This event along with the general suppression of the fundamentalist group "Ikhwan al-Muslimeen" (Muslims Brotherhood) by the Egyptian government in the 50s and 60s were the catalysts that facilitated the resorting to armed insurrection by certain individuals and groups as a means to establishing an Islamic state. These individuals and groups incorporated the Islamic concept of jihad into the body of their political discourse to justify their new militant approach. Consequently, the world has witnessed during the course of the last three decades the emergence of a new variant of Islamic political groups that have been identified as jihadist movements. *(See Ref 15, 16)*

However, we can trace the roots of "jihadism"'s ideology back to its cradle in post-1948 Egypt. The Arab defeat in the 1948 war coupled with the growing anti-British sentiment led to widespread civil unrest in Egypt. In

8

response to the loss of Palestine and the humiliating defeat in the first Arab-Israeli war the "Ikhwan al-Muslimeen" launched a campaign in an effort to develop support against the government. The Muslims Brotherhood, led by its founder Hassan al-Banna gained immense respect amongst the masses for their active participation in the 1948 war, and subsequently emerged as a powerful political force in Egypt. The government at the time fearing a revolutionary takeover of the state by the "Ikhwan", which was exacerbated by its ability to stage huge demonstrations against the government in major cities, decided to curtail the movement. *(See Ref 17, 18)*

In early December 1948 the prime minister of Egypt at the time, Nokrashi Pasha, ordered the dissolution of the "Muslims Brotherhood", which led to his assassination, allegedly, by a member of this organisation on December 28, 1948. A member of the breakaway Sa'adist faction of the Wafd party, Ibrahim Abdul Hadi, succeeded Pasha as Egypt's premier, who upon consolidating his power, also made a desperate attempt at crushing the "Ikhwan". He had thousands of the organisation members, workers, and supporters arrested, tortured and held in desert camps without trial. However, undoubtedly the single most devastating blow to the Brotherhood movement was the assassination of its leader Hassan al-Banna on February 12, 1949. It is generally believed that he was eliminated by the police or by mercenaries hired by Nokrashi's friends and/or family members. *(See Ref 18)*

The goodwill movement drove to underground after the assassination of al-Banna and undergone a radical change. However, the vacuum created by the passing of the organisation founder had more ideological than administrative repercussions. While Hasan al-Hudaybi took over as the Supreme Guide of the "Brotherhood", a number of ideologues (such as Abdel Qadir Audah, Muhammad Al-Ghazalli, and Sayyid Qutb) also took to writing, all of who were seen as carrying the ideological torch of their predecessors. Clearly, it was Sayyid Qutb who would have the most enduring influence on future generations of Islamists. It was in the midst of all this chaos that the Free Officers Committee in the Egyptian military led by Colonel Gamal Abdel Nasser ousted the monarchy of King Farouk in a coup on July 23, 1952.

From day one the relations between the regime of Abdel Nasser and the "Brotherhood" had been uneasy. However, the alleged attempt, on October 26, 1954, on the President's life by a member of the "Ikhwan", provided pretext for Egyptian state's brutal crackdown on this Islamic movement. This was the second phase of the suppression of this party whose members experienced arrest, torture, and executions.

Whilst imprisoned in Egypt in the early 1960s, Sayyid Qutb wrote a book that has inspired succeeding generations of radical Islamists. He has come to be seen as the evil genius who inspired today's global jihad. As John Calvert argues in a persuasive biography, Qutb's reputation is not entirely undeserved, but it does less than justice to a complex and enigmatic figure. *(See Ref 19)*

One of the challenges any biographer faces is to explain Qutb's evolution from romantic nationalist to mainstream Islamist, and finally to ardent revolutionary. Calvert's answer is to place his subject firmly on Egyptian soil. Like countless others in the years that followed the First World War, Qutb was a child of rural Egypt who migrated to Cairo as a young man to join the swelling ranks of the "effendiyya", the new urban educated class. An intense, proud, rather melancholy man, he worked as a civil servant and in his spare time he struggled to establish himself as a writer of poetry, fiction and literary criticism.

Calvert pointed out that in this early phase Qutb, a Muslim who had come under the spell of Sufism, subscribed to the essentially secular nationalism of the day, the focus of which was opposition to British rule in Egypt and to Zionist colonisation in Palestine. But by the late 1940s, disillusioned with the failings of the nationalist parties, he had become an Islamist and - as exemplified in his first important book, "Social Justice in Islam" - an Islamist of originality and power. *(See Ref 19)*

Shortly after finishing the manuscript, Qutb set off for the United States on a visit that was to last almost two years. According to Calvert, the trip affected him deeply. Although he was impressed by America's material accomplishments (and confessed to liking "Gone with the Wind"), he felt an abiding contempt for the materialism, racism and sexual promiscuity of what he saw as a debased Western culture. Was the encounter with America, as some have argued, the turning-point in Qutb's radicalisation? Did the sight of scantily-clad women on the dance floors of Greeley, Colorado, turn the sexually repressed Egyptian into an Islamist zealot? Calvert doubts it; the visit, he believes, confirmed the radical turn in Qutb's thinking, rather than inspiring it. *(See Ref 19)*

On his return home, Qutb openly identified with Egypt's main Islamist movement, the Muslims Brotherhood, but he did not formally join it until 1953. Two years after his homecoming, nationalist army officers led by Gamal Abdel Nasser seized power, overthrowing the British-backed monarchy. Qutb and the Brotherhood initially welcomed the coup and worked enthusiastically with its leaders. But after an assassination attempt against him in 1954, Nasser cracked down on the Brotherhood as I mentioned above, and Qutb was caught up in the mass arrests that followed.

Imprisonment and torture turned him into an impassioned and embittered revolutionary. His book "Milestones", written in prison to chart a future course for his crushed and demoralised movement, became an internationally influential manifesto of the Islamic revolution - not least because in 1966, two years after it was published, Qutb was hanged for treason, becoming a martyr for the cause.

Part of the originality of "Milestones" was Qutb's use of the term "jahiliyya" to depict the abject condition of the Muslim world. Literally meaning ignorance, the term was originally used to describe the benighted condition of Arabia prior to the advent of Islam. But Qutb used it to condemn Muslim governments and societies which, in his eyes, had been corrupted by Western culture and secularism to the point where they had abandoned Islam.

Calvert does not disguise the crudely Manichean character of Qutb's worldview. He believed in an all-out global struggle between a noble vanguard of true Muslims and the massed ranks of "jahiliyya". He depicted Islam's external enemies as an insidious alliance of "Crusaders and Jews" - the same phrase that is used by al-Qa'ida and the global jihadists of today. But he was not, as has been suggested, an "Islamo-fascist" or an advocate of indiscriminate violence. Qutb opposed the killing of innocents and would have been appalled by what his followers, from the Egyptian radicals of the 1970s through 1980s to the current generation jihadists, have carried out in his name. Calvert rich and carefully researched biography sets Qutb for the first time in his Egyptian context, rescuing him from caricature without whitewashing his radicalism. *(See Ref 19)*

The Brotherhood's suppression and the hanging of Qutb were followed by the third Arab-Israeli war in June of 1967, in which the combined forces of Egypt, Syria, and Jordan, suffered a humiliating defeat at the hands of the Israeli military.

These events ultimately gave the way to the emergence of proto-jihadist groups "Gama'a al-Islamiyyah", "Attakfeer wa al-Hijrah", "Tanzeem al-Jihad". However, the single most important event that provided the major boost to revolutionary Islamists of all shades throughout the Muslim world was the Islamic revolution in Iran in 1979. With the ousting of the pro-western monarchy of Shah Muhammad Rida Pahlavi, and the subsequent establishment of an Islamic republic led by Ayatollah Khomeini, Iran became the champion of the worldwide Islamic cause by providing support for a variety of groups across the globe, including Egypt, Lebanon, Syria, Palestine, and Jordan. In that same year, the Islamic insurgency began in Afghanistan against a fledgling communist stratocracy, supported by Soviet troops. This proxy war attracted thousands upon thousands of Islamist volunteers from all over the world to join the 'jihad' against godless communism, which was funded by Saudi and Arab Gulf states money, armed with American weaponry, and furnished with Pakistani logistics acting in consortium. It was the war in Afghanistan in the 1980s during which major jihadist figures such as Abdallah Azzam, Omar Abdel Rehman, Osama bin Laden and Ayman al-Zawahiri gained prominence as leaders gathering volunteers from all over the Muslim world to partake in the jihad against the Soviets. *(See Ref 18)*

So this begs the question: when some Islamic extremists call for Jihad on what basis do they make their claims and accordingly what are the true definition, significance and explanation of Jihad?

Like any other political discourse, the Islamist's one is full of plastic concepts and ideas that are meant to serve politically utilitarian and instrumental purposes. But what is important to remember is that the instrumental use of such plastic concepts (including "democracy", "human rights", "justice", etc.) invariably leads to their contestation as well, as they come to serve as tools for political mobilisation.

The word Jihad has now entered the space of international political and media discourse, along with those other well-known favourites, "Fatwa", "Mullah" and "Shari'a". Yet this entry, according to Farish Noor, has also been a disabling one that has robbed the word of some of its meaning while stretching the limits of its signification even further. He argues in his 2001 article that "Fatwa" for instance, has now come to mean "death penalty" thanks to the "fatwa" against the British Muslim author Salman Rushdie. But those who have some knowledge of Islamic jurisprudence will tell you that "Fatwa" really means "judicial ruling"- and these rulings can range from grave matters like the death penalty to mundane everyday concerns like the proper price of sheep in the market. The latest casualty in the war over meaning is the word Jihad which has become such a plastic concept is hardly surprising. Plasticity is, after all, a normal feature of language and signifiers invariably lose their roots as they find themselves translated from one context to another. *(See Ref 20)*

But without falling into the trap of narrow essentialism, it is nonetheless useful for us to get to grips with the concept of Jihad itself and understand how it came into being even if only to see just how far the term has been abused of late.

Jihad can be loosely translated as "to struggle" or "to expend effort" towards a particular cause. Farish Noor pointed out that the term was originally used to refer to one's personal struggle against one's own mortal failings and weaknesses, which would include battling against one's pride, fears, anxieties and prejudices. He argues that Prophet Muhammad himself was reported in "Hadith" to have described this personal existential struggle as the "Jihad Akbar" (Greater Jihad). Alongside this notion of the Jihad Akbar was the concept of "Jihad Asghar" or "Lesser Jihad". This refers to the struggle for self-preservation and self-defence - which has always been regulated by a host of ethical sanctions and prerogatives. *(See Ref 20)*

Noor stated that, the Koran does stipulate clearly that Muslims have to engage in a Jihad when they are under attack, but the conditions for such a Jihad are clearly laid out and are strictly defined within certain ethical prerogatives. Furthermore he argues that Muslims cannot engage in conflict for the sake of mere territorial expansion for instance (which brings into question the legal status of the early Arab conquests which were motivated mainly by considerations of realpolitik). Muslims also cannot engage in acts of terror and indiscriminate violence where civilians are targeted. (In fact, numerous Muslim leaders like the early Caliphs even warned their troops not to burn the fields of their enemies or kill their livestock). A proper Jihad for the sake of self-defence was therefore a complicated and highly regulated matter - and the rulers had to consult the jurists as well as their own populations before such an enterprise was undertaken. *(See Ref 20)*

But Islam also happens to be a faith that does not possess a clerical class or a supreme leader like the Pope. On the positive side, some experts like Noor think that, this lends the creed an egalitarian outlook which puts all Muslims on par with each other. But on the negative side the absence of a centralised hierarchy also means that the Muslim world is full of self-proclaimed "leaders of the faith" like the Taliban and their unwanted guest, Osama bin Laden.

It is this absence of a clerical order as well as the piecemeal education received in many parts of the Islamic world that have allowed the manipilation of religious discourse and concepts such as Jihad to be hijacked by what are effectively self-appointed defenders of orthodoxy. This coupled with the predicament of a Muslim world that feels itself increasingly threatened and marginalised by the forces of globalisation, has lead to the defensive posture being adopted by many Muslim leaders themselves.

Jihad has now been taken - by Muslims and non-Muslims alike - to refer to an aggressive attitude that is rooted in a reactionary discourse of authenticity and purity, giving it a militant edge that it did not possess. While it is true that the international media has done some damage to the understanding of "Jihad", it is also important for Muslims to realise that the term itself has been used and abused by the very same people who have resorted to the use of violence in their name.

Furthermore, in contemporary times, there has been an increasing tendency among both non-Muslims as well as Muslims to misunderstand the concept of Jihad. A vast majority of non-Muslims incorrectly take it to mean "holy war" waged by "Islamic fundamentalists" in an effort to forcibly convert them to Islam. Muslims on the other hand increasingly have come to view it as a legitimate means to establishing an Islamic state. Both are equally misconceptions of what Jihad really means. A rather controversial Islamist activist Omar Bakri Muhammad (who was convicted in Lebanon in November 2010) hailing from the inter-actionist strand of Islamism states: "There is no doubt that jihad is a complicated and dangerous topic. It is dangerous because it involves taking life and property. It is complex because, just like a delicate surgical operation, the slightest of mistakes could be very destructive." *(See Ref 20, 21)*

However, while the Islamic militants used force of arms and the violent acts to reach their aims and legitamised it by debasing the term "Jihad", the rest of the world gave to their actions another name: terrorism.

So what is terrorism and is it only Islamic violent act or it is a global phenomenon of which the Islamic variety is only part of a broader issue?

CHAPTER TWO

TERRORISM: IS IT ISLAMIC OR A GLOBAL PHENOMENON?

Terrorism is a phenomenon with a long history and the international variety has been shaped by larger historical events. While it has existed in one form or another for centuries, no universal definition for the word has been readily agreed upon. One approach, and perhaps the easiest one, is to use the definition of terrorism found in The New Oxford American Dictionary: "Terrorism: the use of violence and intimidation in the pursuit of political aims." Despite having a history longer than the modern nation-state, the use of terror by governments and those that contest their powers remains poorly understood. While the meaning of the word terror itself is clear, when it is applied to acts and actors in the real world it becomes confused. Part of this is due to the use of terror tactics by actors at all levels in the social and political environment. Example, is the unabomber with his solo campaign of terror, a criminal, terrorist, or revolutionary?

One of the most unsettling developments of our time was the increase in the power and reach of terrorist threats in recent years, a multidimensional phenomenon with global ramifications. Evolving over the last century, terrorism has left almost no area of the world untouched. It has been used as a tool by both left-wing and right-wing causes and by groups of every conceivable stripe – anarchists, fascists, nationalists seeking independence, communists, extreme right-wing militias, and eco-terrorists - in places ranging from Europe to Asia, from South America to the Middle East, from the US to Africa. Indeed, depending on particular political affiliations and aspirations, one nation's "terrorist" may be another's "freedom fighter" and the terrorist's actions, rather than regarded as reprehensible, are justified as part of the heroic struggle for a noble cause.

Most scholars believe that the roots of terrorism stem from regional and local conflicts, socio-economic conditions and political instability within states. These forces include "political repression, a lack of self-determination and depravity of rulers." *(See Ref 22)*

However, the majority of Americans view terrorism as a rather new concept, perhaps driven by the September 11, 2001, terrorist attacks on the World Trade Centre and the Pentagon. For Europeans, and most of the rest of the world for that matter, terrorism is not a new phenomenon; rather the use of terrorism has been employed throughout history. The age of modern terrorism might be said to have begun in 1968 when the Popular Front for the Liberation of Palestine (PFLP) hijacked an El Al airliner en route from Tel Aviv to Rome. While hijackings of airliners had occurred before, this was the first time that the nationality of the carrier (Israeli) and its symbolic value was a specific operational aim. Also a first was the deliberate use of the passengers as hostages for demands made publicly against the Israeli government. The combination of these unique events, added to the international scope of the operation, gained significant media attention. The founder of PFLP, Dr. George Habash observed that the level of coverage was tremendously greater than battles with Israeli soldiers in their previous area of operations. "At least the world is talking about us now." *(See Ref 23)*

Furthermore, 1968 marked the advent of international terrorism from another side according to Bruce Hoffman. This was the period in which there was overwhelming opposition to U.S. involvement in Vietnam. Terrorism, in late 1960's and 1970's, was primarily hierarchical and centralised, revolutionary and anti-colonialist leftist, and generally Kremlin-orchestrated in nature. Throughout the Cold War, the Soviet Union provided direct and indirect assistance to revolutionary movements around the world. Many anti-colonial movements found the revolutionary extremism of communism attractive. Leaders of these "wars of national liberation" saw the advantage of free weapons and training. They also realised that the assistance and patronage of the Eastern Bloc meant increased international legitimacy. Many of these organisations and individuals utilised terrorism in support of their political and military objectives. The policy of the Soviet Union to support revolutionary struggles everywhere, and to export revolution to non-communist countries, provided extremists willing to employ violence and terror as the means to realise their ambitions. However, the hierarchical aspect of the old-form terrorism involves clearly defined, unified groups and leaders, with a centralised infrastructure, base or country, as the command and control centre. One watermark event was the 1972 massacre of eleven Israeli athletes at the Munich Olympics by the Palestinian Liberation Organisation's affiliate "Black September." Terrorist acts were more calculated with specific targets against government organisations and entities. This is markedly different from the more random and discriminate targeting features of the new-form terrorism. *(See Ref 11, 23, 24)*

In his 2006 book "Terrorism", David Rapoport has described four waves in the history of modern terrorism: anarchism, anti-colonialism, left-wing radicalism and religious terrorism. The anarchists believed that the state was the source of all evil, and they carried out the murder of Archduke Franz Ferdinand, which triggered First World War. The anti-colonialists believed that independence from the Western powers would lead to economic and political success. The end of Second World War brought about their movement. Imperial constituencies in colonialist countries no longer wanted military repression abroad. On the other hand, the leftist revolutionaries believed that capitalism formed the essence of evil in society and as such their goal was to eliminate capitalism and bring about communism and the redistribution of wealth. Even though Islamism and jihadism may portray themselves as apolitical and puritan, they are similar to nationalists and leftists. We are now, according to Lisa Farhamy, experiencing the fourth wave of terrorism, which is religiously driven, built on the belief that the world has decayed into a morass of greed and moral depravity. As mentioned previously, the Islamic version of the revivalist ideology is known as Salafism. These Salafis [or radical Islamist movement] are composed of a wide variety of movements and views that offer Islam as a total way of life and as a viable alternative to Western secular ideologies. They aim at bringing all of contemporary society under God's sovereignty, rule and law as revealed in scripture. The restoration of Islamic glory will be achieved by purifying society from un-Islamic teachings and practices, by a return to Islam's original pure sources (the Koran--God's written revelation through Muhammad, and Hadith, the divinely inspired traditions of the Prophet's sayings and deeds) as the only authority, and by the establishment of an ideal Islamic state modeled on that of the Prophet and his Companions. Groups such as al-Qa'ida are willing to sacrifice themselves in pursuit of their utopia and conduct terrorist tactics to bring this about. Mark Sageman says they are essentially "chasing a dream." *(See Ref 11, 24, 25)*

The radical Islamist movement is a fairly modern phenomenon, part of a wider resurgence of religion sweeping across the Muslim world, and existing in a symbiotic relationship with other trends. It is rooted in the recurring cycles of revivals characteristic of Muslim history and is also a reaction to the severe crisis of modernity converging with the rise of charismatic prophetic leaders. It constitutes a religious reform movement and a political ideology that includes a social element of protest and a search for identity by the have-nots of the Muslim world against an oppressive world order. Fundamentalism is the spearhead of religion engaging in a counterattack on the secularism which had reduced its power during recent decades. *(See Ref 30)*

According to Russell Howard, "new-form terrorism" is clearly different from "old-form terrorism" in six very distinguishable ways:

1- "New terrorism" is more violent. Terrorists previously wanted attention, not mass casualties. Now terrorists want both.

2- "Old terrorism" was primarily directed at effecting change in local politics, but today's "new terrorists" are transnational, non-state actors operating globally to destroy the West and all Islamic secular state systems.

3- "New terrorists" are much better financed than previous terrorists, utilizing not only illegal but legal income sources to finance their operations.

4- "New terrorists" are better trained in the arts of war and black arts than terrorists of the past.

5- "New terrorists", particularly the religious extremists, are much more difficult to penetrate than previous generations of terrorists. The use of networked, cellular command structures used by al-Qaida pose serious security challenges to the U.S and its allies.

6- The availability of weapons of mass destruction. Terrorism in the 1980s was characterised by the use of small arms, plastic explosives, rocket-propelled grenades, and anti-aircraft missiles. Today's terrorist groups have access to nuclear, radiological, biological, and chemical weapons. *(See Ref 31)*

The features of this new form of terrorism are different from the older one. Its structures are far more difficult to grasp. They are often described as networks rather than as organisations, because formal hierarchies which had characterised the old-form of terrorism have been replaced with personal relationships. Peter R Newman argues in his 2009 book "Old and New Terrorism", that what matters is not someone's formal rank but whom they know and what connections they can facilitate. Although truly 'leaderless resistance' continues to be quite rare, the difficulty in tracing terrorist attacks such as al-Qa'ida's bombings in Madrid and London to any conventional 'leadership' illustrates quite how messy and confused terrorist group structures have become in recent years. Furthermore the National Commission on Terrorism (U.S.A.) found that terrorism is increasingly based on religious fanaticism, where political interests are subordinated to religion. David Rapaport referred to religiously motivated modern terrorism as the "fourth wave of vulnerability," evolving out of the terrorism associated with the breakup of empires, decolonization and lingering anti-Western sentiment. The Soviet test of the atomic bomb in 1949 and nuclear proliferation were cited as the first and second waves with chemical, biological, radiological or nuclear (CBRN) terrorism as the "third wave" starting in 1995. *(See Ref 22, 25, 26)*

However, old form and new form of terrorism share a common theme, which is the anti-Western sentiment. In the past, this emanated as if by reflex from the Soviet Union, but has since been transferred to the tenets of Islamic fundamentalism. The Soviet implosion and the end of the Cold War changed the nature of international terrorism by transferring the placeholder to Islamic fundamentalism. The threat that once stemmed from communism has been now replaced by the rise of Islamic fundamentalism in the Greater Middle East.

Olivier Roy, in his book "Globalised Islam: The search for a new Umma and Islamist Network: The Pakistan-Afghan Connection", discussed "Islam's border-less." He pointed out that Islam has long been a driving force in world politics, but the bulk of its influence was localised. Now, the reach of Islamic fundamentalism has expanded into the West and has affected the global political climate. The theory of the lack of borders and territoriality of Islam ties into another characteristic of new-form terrorism which is the lack of formal sponsorship, a major feature of old- form of terrorism.

New-form terrorism's lack of borders is charcterised by this decentralisation and lack of non-state sponsorship of terrorism. There are several facets to this aspect of non-state sponsorship, such as the absence of a central command headquarters, base or infrastructure. Furthermore, new-form Terrorism's effects are not necessarily aimed at the victims of terrorist violence. Victims are usually objects to be exploited by the terrorists for their effect on a third party. In order to produce this effect, information of the attack must reach the target audience. So any terrorist organisation plans for exploitation of available media to get the message to the right audiences. Victims are simply the first medium that transmits the psychological impact to the larger target audience. The next step in transmission will depend on what media is available, but it will be planned, and it will frequently be the responsibility of a specific organisation within the terrorist group to do nothing else but exploit and control the news cycle. However, Non-state sponsorship is multi-dimensional. First, non-state sponsorship means that there is not a single country sponsoring or funding terrorism. Terrorism is sponsored by individuals in the form of jihadists, wealthy individuals and again by some "rogue states." Second, terrorist attacks and methods are more diffuse, scattered and random in nature. Terrorism is predominately committed by Islamic fundamentalists and its reach expands worldwide, indiscriminate to countries with Muslim populations, or Westerners. *(See Ref 11, 23)*

However, new-form terrorism is fluid and lacks a central theme, specific target, or central rational or justification for its actions. The only consistency is its inconsistency and variable nature as to where, why, when and how. This is in stark contrast with older, traditional or conventional terrorism, which was more targeted, regionally focused and centralised in nature. The magnitude of terrorism in recent years has become global. This enlarged "breadth of audience" means that the "targets and the conspiratorial networks of the forms of religious terrorism in the last decade have been global and transnational." Terrorist acts are no longer a vehicle aimed to damage and affect government or political institutions, but rather use ordinary people as pawns. The nature of attacks goes beyond the discriminate and conventional attacks on hard targets such as embassies, military installations and personnel armed and with built in defences. *(See Ref 27)*

Finally, the religious motive is an overriding factor in new-form terrorism. According to the Rand Corporation, in 1994 religious groups accounted for sixteen of the forty-nine active terrorist groups at the time. However, by the turn of the century this had risen to twenty-six from fifty-six groups.

It is evident that terrorism has become increasingly linked with Islam. "Religion has supplied not only the ideology, but also the motivation and the organisational structure for the perpetrators." This theme is best summed up from an interview with veteran New York Times journalist and author Stephen Kinzer, where he confirmed that, "Passionate religious beliefs often lead people to believe that they are acting on behalf of God. Once someone believes that, all forms of violence, including terror, becomes easy to justify." *(See Ref 27, 29)*

In the last few decades terrorists have increasingly invoked religion as a pretext or even as a duty to carry out acts of terror. They use religion to justify terrorism for socio-political purposes. The rational for terrorism has been to protect the Islamic faith and the Muslim umma, against Western power and its influence, and to create a new sense of social order based on an established Islamic state. Legitimacy is conferred on religious violence because Islamists want to "adopt Islamic law in order to facilitate the return of El-Mahdi to Earth as the Messiah." *(See Ref 11, 23)*

To obtain their aims the Islamic radicals used new tools and ideas. One of them was self-sacrifice or martyrdom which also has religious roots. "Martyr" comes from a Greek term which means "witness to one's faith." However, in Arabic – Islam's sacred language - several words refer to variations on the concept of the martyr. "Shahada", often translated as "martyrdom", literally stands for the act of "witnessing", and depending on context, it can mean the "confession of one's submission to God" or "death for God's sake ". "Istishhad" literally refers to the act of martyrdom. "Shahada" then refers to incidental death during jihad (i.e., a soldier falling in battle) whereas "istishhad" indicates deliberate death during jihad. The former connotes a "willingness to die", the latter an explicit "eagerness to die". Martyrdom is viewed as a religious act and the proof or demonstration of one's commitment to one's faith. Suicide bombings are demonstrations of martyrdom that have become increasingly prevalent in international terrorism. *(See Ref 32, 33)*

With the success of the Sunni mujahideen's resistance in Afghanistan to the Soviets in the 1980s after the 1979 Shia Iranian revolution, acts of violence committed in the name of Islam have risen sharply, and the number of Islamic groups committed acts of violence using martyrdom as a central position have increased. Furthermore, the suicide bomber has become the ideal of Islamic martyrdom, and simultaneously appalling Western audiences and captivating Islamic ones.

23

In Islamic history, martyrdom has taken on a variety of shapes and relied on numerous contexts for justification and implementation. However, new strains of martyrdom have moved across the global Islamic societies over the last century from Mandatory Palestine, French Algeria, and revolutionary Iran to everywhere between Morocco and Indonesia. Evolutions in martyrdom's place within Islamic thought expose shifts within Muslims' own sense of self as well as changes in culture.

In his 2010 article in Middle East quarterly, Benjamin T Acosta pointed out that one major trajectory for martyrdom's importance within the Muslim tradition derives from the Shia narrative that developed following the death of Prophet Muhammad's grandson al-Hussein in 680. He argues that al-Hussein and his followers did not choose martyrdom at the Battle of Karbala in the manner of most other Islamic martyrs in successive generations. Nevertheless, Shia tradition embellishes his death with prophetic foreknowledge of the outcome. It also embodies the model of a woefully small force of true believers arrayed against an overwhelming army of "evil-doers". As a result of his death, the role of martyrdom would forever serve as a basis for the distinction of Shi'ism from Sunni orthodoxy. Al- Hussein's death has since demonstrated the extent to which martyrdom proves one's commitment to an Islamic cause. This gives it a capability like no other in political Islam: the power to affect ideological change from within. *(See Ref 32)*

A second significant trajectory, stated by Acosta in his article, is that of the dominant Sunni perspective on jihad and corresponding understanding of martyrdom. He argues that while always present, Sunni martyrdom within the framework of jihad remained mostly stagnant for hundreds of years as Sunnis largely enjoyed the power of the majority. This began to change in the eighteenth and nineteenth centuries with Western dominance over territory formally under Islamic control (Dar al-Islam) and most significantly with the influx of mainly European Jews into Palestine. Their arrival was often perceived as a challenge to Muslim hegemony by local Sunni leaders. *(See Ref 32)*

Although suicide terrorism has become a major feature of modern jihad, it has its roots in earlier concepts of the "shahid" who goes into battle determined to kill as many of the enemy as possible in the knowledge that he will die. The martyr's death is constantly presented as the perfect way for a Muslim to die, and this conviction has, in the modern period, given rise to the phenomenon of a self-detonating "shahid", especially among Palestinian fighters.

Palestinian groups, throughout the 1950s and 1960s, sat at the forefront of modern terrorism, and their "Feda'iyeen" martyrs remained central to their strategy of political extortion. The term jihad, however, seemed to disappear from the framework. This was not a particularly Palestinian phenomenon. Historian David Cook notes that "the muted use of jihad held throughout the Muslim world until the rise of political Islam after the Six-Day War with Israel in 1967." *(See Ref 34)*

The Muslim world woke up in the 1970s to a new era. Secularist alternatives to tradition, such as pan-Arabism, had either been found wanting or were associated, like Baathism, with repressive regimes. Israel had roundly defeated Arab states in war, particularly in 1967. Most significantly, a revolution in Iran in 1979 resulted in the rise of a religiously-oriented regime that showed itself able to confront the "Great Satan", represented by the United States. This did not go unnoticed in the larger, Sunni world: by the mid-1980s, a coalition of Sunni warriors from several countries was fighting and eventually defeating Soviet forces in Afghanistan. *(See Ref 32)*

On the other hand, the use of "shahada" (martyrdom) by the Khomeini's regime within the Iranian revolution and the Iran-Iraq war demonstrated the ability of martyrdom to advance an Islamic cause. Without the thousands of volunteers who blew themselves up clearing Iraqi minefields, one can never know with certainty if Iran could have staved off Iraq's mechanized encroachments. Soon thereafter, Iran's ally in Lebanon, Hezbollah, advanced notions of Shia martyrdom in its own right, perhaps more significantly than revolutionary Iran did. Hezbollah's superimposition of "shahid" onto the figure of a suicide-bomber completely altered the contemporary direction in the uses of Islamic martyrdom. The act of an individual directly killing him or herself while killing others, whether U.S. troops in Beirut or Israeli troops in southern Lebanon, reinvigorated Islamic martyrdom. Moreover, this evolution was to have an immeasurable effect on political Islam within both Shia and Sunni spheres. This tactic proved so successful at driving the United States and, later, Israel out of Lebanon that most lingering religious concerns were set aside.

However, as to the permissibility of suicide bombings specifically, the scholars have differed. And according to the "Salafi Manhaj" (2007), the majority of senior orthodox Sunni scholars, such as Imam Ibn Uthaymeen, hold suicide bombing to be "haram" (i.e. forbidden) in absolute terms, because the tactic rests upon something which is itself "haram" in absolute terms (i.e. suicide). This is why Sheikh Abdul-Muhsin al- Abbaad, the author of "According to which Intellect and Religion is Suicide Bombings and Destruction Considered Jihad?", is under no obligation to judge suicide bombings on a case-by-case basis: as far as he is concerned, suicide can never be permissible in any application or intention. Then we have Imam al-Albani who is the most notable exception amongst the orthodox Sunni scholars to have permitted suicide bombing or so-called "martyrdom operations" under certain circumstances and prerequisites. However, because those prerequisites are absent - most notably, a single temporal Islamic authority or Khalifah over all the Muslims – Albani also held suicide bombing to be "haram" in this day and age; that is, he held suicide bombing to be "haram" in relative terms, something the poster of the essay, "The Islamic Ruling on the Permissibility of Martyrdom Operations", failed to mention. In any case, none of the scholars permit any act of suicidal violence against non-military targets. This is in sharp contrast to the most vociferous proponents of suicide bombing, such as al-Qa'ida and other takfeeri-jihadis, who almost exclusively encourage and justify the murder of non-combatants, regardless of their religion, age or gender. *(See Ref 35)*

Nevertheless, the Suicide bombings tactic was introduced into Palestinian areas only gradually. In 1988 Fathi Shiqaqi, the founder of the Palestinian Islamic Jihad (PIJ), wrote a set of guidelines (aimed at countering religious objections to the truck bombings of the 1980s) for the use of explosives in individual bombings; he characterised operations calling for martyrdom as "exceptional." However, because "intihar" (i.e. suicide) is a highly problematic concept in Islamic theology often categorised by jurists as "haram", as we mentioned previously, Hamas consciously and systematically circumvents this theological pitfall by terming its suicide attacks "amaliyat istish-hadiyya" (i.e.'martyrdom operation'). This is because the notion of self-sacrifice (istish-had) has been extolled through the Koranic teachings, commentaries and fatwas as not only permitted (halal) but also desirable. The shahid, unlike the suicide, is honoured and guaranteed a place in paradise for all eternity. The Hamas emphatically stresses this difference between "intihar" and "istish-had." Suicide is a shameful path adopted by the weak, despairing and depressed but martyrdom is the beginning of hope and deliverance and is a path chosen only by the strong-willed, noble individual who is therefore worth emulating. For example, according to the former second-in-command of Hamas's political wing Abdel Aziz al-Rantissi (killed on 17 April 2004), if a Muslim wants to "kill himself because he's sick of being alive, that's suicide. But if he wants to sacrifice his soul in order to defeat the enemy and for God's sake – well, then he's a martyr." The Hamas further substantiates its position on martyrdom by referring to the numerous hadith and commentaries that venerate the martyr. The medieval Sunni theologian Al-Bukhari describes how Allah bestows heavenly awards upon the martyr and describes how "nobody in Paradise would wish to return to earth, with the exception of the martyr, who died in battle for God's cause. He would return to earth to be killed again ten times over after all the salutes accorded to him in Paradise." *(See Ref 38, 39, 40)*

But by the mid-1990s Hamas was using suicide bombers as a way of derailing the Oslo peace process. The assassination of the master Palestinian bomb maker Yahya Ayyash, presumably by Israeli agents, in January of 1996, set off a series of suicide bombings in retaliation. Suicide bombings nonetheless remained relatively unusual until 10 years ago, after the Palestinian leader Yasir Arafat walked out of the peace conference with former Israeli Prime Minister Ehud Barak at Camp David - a conference which was held under the auspices of former US President Bill Clinton. However, the Sunni adoption of a Shia form of martyrdom has led to a hybrid version that takes the most virulent components of each. Superimposing the jihadi martyrdom of Sunni tradition onto the self-annihilating Shia version has contributed to the brutality and audaciousness of acts of martyrdom committed by Palestinians and the international jihadi movement.

Despite the Sunni scholars rulings and opinions, which consider the suicide bomber "haram", the growing importance of the Palestinian cause to the Sunni world, at least on a popular level, Palestinian promotion of Hezbollah's virulent shahid/suicide-bomber modus operandi received support and inspired others. The structure of the Israeli-Palestinian conflict, framed as one between Jews and Muslims, helped foster international support for the new type of martyr. In turn, widespread support for this type of attack, against civilians and on a mass scale, led to the construction of a new Sunni culture of martyrdom across the global Islamic community. Though neither the Afghan mujahideen nor their Arab partners used any form of suicide attack during the jihad against the Soviets, Palestinians did inspire Al-Qa'ida and others within the international jihadi movement to adopt not only the suicide-terror tactic but also the complementary "istishhad" strategy. *(See Ref 36, 37)*

The Economist, in its 8/1/2004 article "Martyrdom and Murder", argues that a better way to understand the popularity of suicide attacks may be to focus on their advantages for the groups who commission them. Such operations are rarely, if ever, the work of lone lunatics. Hamas, PIJ and the other Palestinian groups who practise suicide terrorism recruit, indoctrinate and train their bombers. They write the texts for the video testaments filmed shortly before each self-immolation (making them unreliable records of the true motives of the "martyr"), which the bombers themselves watch to redouble their resolve. They take the photographs that will later appear on propaganda posters. Then they deliver their foot-soldiers to pre-identified targets. Al-Qa'ida is remarkable for the expertise and independence of its agents, but they too are trained and primed for their missions. However, terrorists have embraced suicide attacks mainly for their advantages in this world, rather than their rewards in the next.

The international jihadi movement has to a degree restructured the relationship between the Islamic community and its spiritual and temporal leaders, incorporating Muslims into a bottom-up political movement of martyrdom operations, in which they can decide to actively participate at any time. Perhaps not since the death of al-Hussein has notion of martyrdom caused as drastic an evolution in political Islam as has the suicide-bomber. Martyrdom has become a central concept within contemporary political Muslim discourse and has assumed the role of the dominant cause rather than the consequential effect in its relationship with political Islam. *(See Ref 32)*

However, Islam in modern times has become stronger and more revivalist. It has felt the need to defend itself against the influences of Western-Christian political and commercial power. The Ottoman Turkish Empire in Istanbul and the Mogul Empire in Delhi succumbed to the strength of the Western powers. Islam's defensive position has skewed religion to the far right and taken on a fundamentalist nature. Case studies show Islamic fundamentalism has been building since the 1930's in Egypt, Saudi Arabia, Afghanistan, and later in Pakistan, all of which are discussed in subsequent chapters.

CHAPTER THREE

EGYPT: BETWEEN TWO FIRES

The history of Egypt extends back thousands of years. It is one of the richest, oldest and most varied of any country in the world and the country's place in the Middle East is as central now as it was in the fourth millennium BC. The unification of the Lower and the Upper Kingdoms, in about 3180 BC, marks a convenient starting point for Egyptian history. However people settled and lived along the Nile River since early 6,000 BC, where slowly developing into small villages. These villages were eventually organised into a system of government, with the lack of forests and mountains making them easily governable. The subsequent rise of the Egyptian nation over several thousand years produced one of the greatest civilisations of the ancient world. By the time of Jesus Christ, even though past its glory, Egypt was still a centre of Greek and Roman learning and culture. In subsequent years, Egypt also became a centre of Christianity as the birthplace of the Coptic Christian faith. When the Islamic armies from Arabia overran Egypt in 642, the Coptic community welcomed the Muslims, as they were accorded higher status than under the former "pagan" culture and were not forced to convert to Islam. Over the centuries they were generally tolerated by Islamic governments and, though clearly inferior in status to Muslims, proved to be useful in Islamic society due to their skills and education. Although the Fatamids gained control of the country in the late 10th century but their power declined after a century or so. The subsequent revival of Muslim fortunes and the reawakening of the spirit of "Jihad" was largely associated with the career of Salahuddine al-Ayyubi (i.e. Saladin), whose control of Egypt enabled him to reunite much of the Muslim world. *(**Most of historical information in this chapter comes from Ref 41, 42, 43 and 46)**

However, over the years many foreign forces came and went but the external influences in modern Egypt initially came from the French, specifically from Napoleon who saw himself as Egypt's great liberator.

He disguised the policies which would be later followed during Egypt's modernisation as Islamic. This was done by introducing an administration for the Islamic religion in 1798. As such the way was prepared for the subsequent introduction of Muhammad Ali's modernity in Egypt.

After the British and French evacuations, Muhammad Ali (1805-1849) became Egypt's ruler under the Ottoman Empire. He imported Western concepts and ideas such as military technology, but made no attempt to modernise society in general. Even though some historians and scholars such as Mahmud A Faksh and Bernard Lewis were of the opinion that the continuing expansion of government functions and the centralisation of authority, as well as the disruptive nature of socio-economic change and the spread of Western political concepts among the new political elite, increased modernisation, it is more than likely that these processes served to exacerbate resurgence in future generations. The reason for this is that modernisation created a new generation of bourgeois that formed a future elite class that became the basis for autocratic governments. In addition, these elite groups would form an exclusive political and socio-economic class from which the rest of society was excluded. This in turn would lead to increased alienation of the masses and their joining of resurgent movements. Muhammad Ali introduced a history of autocracy into Egyptian politics in a manner that was set to continue in the 20th and the first decade of 21st centuries. *(See Ref 44, 45, 46)*

After Muhammad Ali's death in 1849, his son Ibrahim and his grandson Abbas succeeded him. However, Egypt's economy and social life declined into a state of bankruptcy and corruption. As a result, international economic control and British occupation of Egypt took place in 1882. These foreign interferences, together with economic and political decline in 1879, led to the emergence of four political groups, namely small wealthy landowners that were favourable to foreign intervention for the protection of their interests, Islamic modernists opposed to foreigners and led by Muhammad Abdu (disciple of Jamal ad-Din al-Afghani), wealthy landowners seeking independence and an army clique of anti-foreign junior officers supporting nationalism and led by Colonel Ahmad Arabi (or Arabi Pasha).These societal divisions would lead not only to the 1952 rebellion by these officers but also to nationalist movements in the 20th century. *(See Ref 46)*

Two events took place at that period that would have a significant impact on the future development of resurgent Islamic movements in Egypt. The first event was the impact of British rule in Egypt from 1882 to 1922. This period of British rule led to a struggle for independence and feelings of anti-Westernism. In the early 1900s, an Egyptian nationalist movement started under the influence of Western-educated officials and Islamic religious leaders. This movement was further strengthened when Egyptians fought on the British side in First World War with British assurances of post-war independence. Consequently, following the fall of the Ottomans, Britain formally abolished the protectorate and established a constitutional monarchy under King Ahmad Fouad in 1922. However, Egyptian independence was ephemeral as the British kept control of foreign policy, communications, and defence, causing great resentment among the Egyptians. With the abolishment of the caliphate in 1924 the internal political climate in Egypt consisted of those who favoured the secularist-West, those who were more supportive of religion, a more conservative group that was anti-Western supporting a return to Islam, as well as a pan-Arab nationalist current. These currents were to survive in Egypt's political development and become entrenched in both Islamic resurgent and formal politics. *(See Ref 45, 47)*

The second event that had an impact on Egypt during this period was Hassan al- Banna's founding of the Muslim Brotherhood (al-Ikhwan al-Muslimeen) in 1928, to promote the implementation of traditional Islamic shari'a law and a social renewal based on an Islamic ethos of altruism and civic duty, in opposition to political and social injustice and to British imperial rule. Born in 1906 within the providence of Buhrya in Egypt, Hassan al-Banna was raised in a strict religious setting. Despite the fact that his father was an Imam, al-Banna held an early interest in Sufism and was a member of the "Dhikr" circle as well as the Hasafiyyah Sufi Order until his departure for Cairo in the year 1923. He saw there that the Islamic community at a critical crossroads and insisted that Muslims would find strength in the total self-sufficiency of Islam. The Brotherhood in its early stages focused on educational and charitable work, but quickly grew to become a major political force as well, by championing the cause of disenfranchised classes, playing a prominent role in the Egyptian nationalist movement, and promoting a conception of Islam that attempted to restore broken links between tradition and modernity. Initially the Muslim Brotherhood grew from within the lower-middle classes that had recently been urbanised. This organisation became the first Islamic resurgent movement of the modern era and also formed the basis for subsequent movements. Prior to the formation of the Muslim Brotherhood, apart from the "Salafiyya" (Salafis) movements, the most important and active organisation in Egypt was the Young Men's Muslim Association (YMMA) that was founded by Abdul Hamid Sa'id in 1927. Together with the Society for Islamic Preaching and Propaganda the YMMA embarked on an extensive programme of countering Christian missionary activities by means of evening classes and public lectures. Throughout the 1930s the Isalmic movements in Egypt, agitated against foreign schools and the activities of Christian missionaries and acted against the work of European orientalists. *(See Ref 48)*

However, the "al-Ikhwan al-Muslimeen" kept at the beginning a low profile, and emphasised only its purely religious reformist orientation. It began becoming involved in politics only after 1938. It published a weekly magazine, al Nadhir, on the first of May of that year, in which the organisation set out its national action or political struggle. It had three aims, namely supporting the Palestinians, acting against Britain and gaining Egypt's independence.Both the Association of Young Egypt and the Muslim Brotherhood called for closer cooperation among Arabs against Israel as well as Christians. Because of propaganda by the Association of Young Egypt many followers and members of both the Association of Young Egypt and the Muslim Brotherhood were later found in the radical ranks of the Egyptian army. They were motivated by the goals of Egyptian independence and extending Egypt's influence in the Arab Middle East and Africa. *(See Ref 46)*

Some elements in the army who had the objective of an independent Egypt were involved with the Muslim Brotherhood which shares the same goal. At this stage al-Banna formed a close friendship with the commander-in-chief of the armed forces. In addition, another officer, "Abd al-Munim Abd al-Ra'uf", became a member of the Muslim Brotherhood and subsequently assumed a leading role both within the organisation and the army, which had become dissatisfied with the political situation. Furthermore army officers, some of whom had connections with those in the army calling themselves the Free Officers, help the Muslim Brotherhood trained its battalions at universities in public camps as well as privately. They also provided the Muslim Brotherhood with arms that were used to harass British personnel and positions.These clashes with the British resulted in the banning of meetings as well as any references to the organisation in 1941. *(See Ref 49)*

During the Second World War, the Brotherhood's links to the Nazis, which were began in the 1930s, became close, involving agitation against the British, espionage and sabotage, as well as support for terrorist activities orchestrated by Haj Amin el-Husseini in British Mandate Palestine, as a wide range of declassified documents from the British, American and Nazi German governmental archives, as well as from personal accounts and memoires from that period, confirm. Reflecting this connection the Muslim Brotherhood also disseminated Hitler's "Mein Kampf" and "The Protocols of the Elders of Zion" widely in Arab translations, helping to deepen and extend already existing hostile views about Jews and Western societies generally. *(See Ref 50, 51, 52)*

In response to intense pressure from the Brotherhood's younger members, al-Banna formed in 1937 the battalion or Katiba "to generate a total physical, mental, and spiritual absorption in and dedication to the Society". But this system was a failure and in 1943 the family system was established instead.The primary function of this subsequent system of families was indoctrination of members into the Muslim Brotherhood. Al-Banna referred to the system used within the families as the pillars: familiarity, understanding and responsibility. The form of recruiting that the Muslim Brotherhood most frequently utilised was intimacy. By reaching out to friends and family structures, a foundation of familiarity was established. Islamic recruitment is based on pre-existing societal ties while at the same time fostering a new kind of solidarity based on shared values. Such values were propagated through individual attention and recruitment, and were used to establish a parallel means of involvement through the use of Islamic institutions. The Muslim Brotherhood spread Islamism through lectures, lessons and various media, including books, newspapers, magazines and tapes. The most important source of effective transmission, though, remained the Islamic mosque. The Brotherhood highlights that the religion of Islam calls for individuals to assume responsibility for the condition of the umma. The mosque was viewed as the ideal setting to establish the belief that the full application of Islam is possible only through the establishment of an Islamic state. While this system initially had an external role, ensuring the unity and the preservation of order within the Muslim Brotherhood, it became an active instrument for social welfare and services. This aspect resulted in entrenching the role and function of the Muslim Brotherhood in society as a whole. *(See Ref 46, 49)*

The Resistance to pro-British sentiments became very prominent during the time leading to 1952, which was marked by disorder, destruction and violence. In 1948 the Palestinian war led to the Muslim Brotherhood calling for a complete revision of the established system of government. In November 1948 police seized an automobile containing the documents and plans of what is thought to be the Brotherhood's 'secret apparatus' [secret militant wing] with names of its members. The seizure was preceded by a variety of bombings and assassination attempts by the apparatus. Subsequently 32 of its leaders were arrested and its offices raided. The next month the Egyptian Prime Minister, Mahmud Fahmi Nokrashi, ordered the dissolution of the Brotherhood. A series of terrorist attacks took place, while the Chief of Police in Cairo was killed on 4 December 1948, followed by the assassination of the Egyptian Premier Nokrashi on the 28 of the same month by Brotherhood member and veterinary student Abdel Meguid Ahmed Hassan, in what is thought to have been retaliation for the government crackdown. A month and half later, on 12 February, al-Banna himself was killed in Cairo by men believed to be government agents and/or supporters of the murdered premier, which led the organisation to keep a low profile until the 1952 revolution. Al-Banna was succeeded as head [General Guide] of the Brotherhood by Hassan Isma'il al-Hudaybi, a former judge, who attempted to abolish the secret apparatus, but it continued to operate without the leadership's knowledge. However, the new leader of the organisation could not fill the vacuum left by al-Banna. He claimed allegiance to al-Banna's doctrinal legacy, but interpreted it differently. After al-Banna many members of the Muslim Brotherhood would become disillusioned with lack of activity and the failure of their leaders to take a firm stance and would distance themselves from the group to form their own rival organisations. *(See Ref 53, 54, 55)*

On 25 and 26 January 1952 violence escalated with "massive rejection of the British, the West, the foreigner, the wealthy and the ruler – King and Pasha alike". Richard Mitchell states that while the Muslim Brotherhood supported the revolution as most Egyptians did, little if any evidence indicates that its members were involved in the coup. It is stated that an agreement was reached with the Muslim Brotherhood to protect foreigners, minorities and strategic centres of communications on the day of the revolution.

The Free Officer movement led by Colonel Gamal Abdul Nasser overthrew Egypt's constitutional monarchy in a military coup on July 23, 1952 and put at first General Muhammad Nagib as President who was succeeded by Nasser in 1954. The Free Officer's movement opposed the British occupation and called for the end of foreign domination that controlled Egyptian politics, economy, and culture. The Muslim Brotherhood provided a considerable amount of support to the revolutionary current running through the country. The movement was originally welcomed into the revolution due to the prominence al-Banna placed on liberating the country from the quagmire of humiliation established through Egypt's suppression. Based on its efforts the Brotherhood soon began exerting pressure on Nasser's regime to implement Islamic order and uplift society from the morass of indignity and subjugation that were the vested interests of the imperialism from which they successfully seceded. The organisation was expected the newly independent government to introduce long-awaited Islamic reforms into the government. However, the opposite took place. The Nasser government did not honour its agreement with the Muslim Brotherhood by introducing a more Islamic-based government. Instead it introduced radical political, economic and social changes and introduced effective control measures against any possible opposition it might experience. This involved economic strategies of land confiscation from large landowners and nationalisation of domestic and foreign enterprises in 1956. These measures would have a far-reaching impact on Islamic resurgence. *(See Ref 46)*

However, the exclusion of the Brotherhood from the government, as well as its disillusionment, led to the deterioration of the relationship between the authority and the organisation. The government introduced stricter control over the Muslim Brotherhood's activities to the extent that on 13 January 1952 it decided to dissolve the movement. This resulted in the Communist Party seeking the co-operation of the Muslim Brotherhood against the government. In 1953 all political parties were dissolved, even though the Muslim Brotherhood was initially exempted from this process and still represented the largest organised popular force in the country. Therefore, it was initially allowed to function in order not to alienate a large segment of society in these early stages of the new government. However the group became one of the revolution's main victims after being officially outlawed as an opposition party when a member of the Brotherhood attempted to assassinate Nasser in the year 1954. This single action was the first significant challenge the group faced, thus providing the Brotherhood with momentum in order to propel the movement into the forefront of the political landscape.

However, by the mid 1950s all independent political groups were prohibited. Those that survived the repression were forced underground, limiting their access to the general public. The result of this government decision led to an increased role of the armed forces as the vanguard and base of the revolution. Afterwards the armed forces formed the major source of Nasser active support which their members became the new elites. The defence force was Western in orientation because it had received Western training and equipment and was used in conjunction with the administrative apparatus to exercise control rather than represent the people. When the government adopted harsh methods to curb acts of opposition in general, this had an impact on the Muslim Brotherhood and exacerbated hostilities between the two. This method of dealing with opposition has continued up to the present. *(See Ref 56, 57)*

In his book "The Transformation of Egypt" Mark Cooper stated, that the Egyptian army had "expertise in the disciplined use of violence [that] is more developed, permitting a greater sense of professionalism among officers", their exclusiveness and violent methods under President Nasser in particular added to the radicalisation of resurgent movements to a level never experienced before. *(See Ref 58)*

The hostilities between the government and the Brotherhood even resulted in allegations that a member of the organisation had attempted to assassinate President Nasser on 26 October 1954. Subsequently 1000 Muslim Brotherhood members were arrested, of whom 15 were hanged. At this stage Sayyid Qutb, the future ideologue of Islamic radicalism, came to prominence as the head of the Muslim Brotherhood's propaganda department and the editor-in-chief of the official journal of the Brotherhood called "Al-Ikhwan al-Muslimoon". Utilising his position as editor, he insisted on an exclusive Islamic party based on the constitution and teachings of the Muslim Brotherhood. However, the government resisted the request for an Islamic constitution and employed a two-fold method of attack, using new strategies such as imprisonment and concentration camps to suppress opposition. These measures, as well as the additional use of violence in the aformantioned prisons and concentration camps, served to radicalise those who were imprisoned and subsequently provided

Sayyid Qutb with ideological justification for opposing the government. *(See Ref 46)*

Sayyid Qutb was arrested in 1955 and sentenced to fifteen years in prison where he wrote some of his most influential works including "Fi Zilal al-Koran" (Under the Shade of the Koran). However, at the request of the former president of Iraq, Abdul Salam Arif, he was released in late 1964 only to be imprisoned again. He was hanged on August 29, 1966, along with two other prominent Muslim Brotherhood leaders, Muhammad Yusef Awash and Abd al-Fattah Ismail. Qutb's hanging occurred shortly before the publication of his book "Ma Alim Fi al-Tareeq" (Milestones or Signposts), which is still read as an invitation, calling the people to a revolution in the name of "Allah" (i.e. God) against all of those who suppress His will. Qutb's death together with the conditions under which the Islamists were imprisoned caused many Islamists to adopt the concept of "takfir", or judging somebody as being infidel (or excommunicated). *(See Ref 56, 58, 59, 61)*

If Hassan al-Banna is considered as the founder of the Muslim Brotherhood, Sayyid Qutb is viewed to have been the creator of its dogma. Qutb influenced the minds of the peoples through his writings, which are considered to be essential reading to discuss any aspect concerning the organisation and Islamic radicalism. According to Giles Kepel, "in 1954 the Muslim Brotherhood had been unable to analyse the Nasser regime or to understand why confrontation was inevitable ... in 1965, after Sayyid Qutb's Signposts [Milestones] book, they had a theoretical tool that provided them with an analysis of the state they were opposing". The development and prominence of this theoretical tool would be the most significant aspect emerging from the Nasser era that would be inherited by subsequent generations. Both Qutb, and subsequently, Egyptian Islamists in general, justified their level of violence and retaliation by referring to the treatment they had received at the hands of the government. Qutb's treatment in prison formed the basis of an important deviation from the path espoused by al-Banna. While al-Banna recommended reform of Egyptian legal and political systems by the implementation of the shari'a, Qutb declared the government as "jahiliyya" (i.e. ignorance). *(See Ref 54, 59)*

The 1967 defeat of Egypt at the hands of Israel was another historical event that would radicalise the Islamic resurgence further. This humiliating defeat caused a legitimacy crisis for the Arab governments. The argument which was spreading at the time that their political systems had led to political crisis instead of growing to political maturity, as had happened in Israel. Therefore the answer for many was a return to Islam as an indigenous cultural heritage and political framework. Furthermore, the student uprising in 1968 made the situation even worse. It created a more militant student movement. After 1968, anti-government violence became a common occurrence and can be seen as a form of communication process, conveying dissatisfaction with repressive measures. While most demonstrations were held by students and workers, the middle classes also took part. This situation continued till after the death of President Nasser. Although the tangible entity of the Brotherhood was purged by Nasser, the ideology of the movement remained. Not to be annihilated by the means of torture, imprisonments and executions, the members of the Muslim Brotherhood endured.

Muhammad Anwar Sadat succeeded Nasser on September 1970 and he had inherited not only the legacy of his predecessor's era to deal with, but also the problems from previous regimes. He reversed several of Nasser's policies. This included the act of solidifying his hold on the popular power by reaching out to Islamists by releasing many from prison. The Brotherhood acted on its temporary freedom and in its attempt to unify the nation created a new slogan: "Religion is for God and the Nation is for all." This statement concentrated on the movement's upward mobility and functioned to aid Sadat in his quest to utilise religion as a means toward reaching the people. Nevertheless, the Muslim Brotherhood would remain illegal, but individual members were granted limited access to the public sector if they agreed to renounce the violent overthrow of the regime. This included the ability to form Islamic Societies and the right to run for election to parliament. *(See Ref 62)*

However the Muslim Brotherhood tried to consolidate its position and had embarked upon a phenomenal reemergence that Sadat continued to use to his advantage, thus beginning a process of "de-Nasserisation." In trying to establish his own power base and to eliminate any opposition against him, President Sadat undertook to remove the Nasserite elements from the government. In the process, he empowered the Islamists by providing structures that facilitated their funding and administration. However, these strategies had disastrous results, as the empowering of politically active Islamists would pose a considerable threat to the Sadat regime.

Furthermore he declared Nasser's rule as "the reign of materialism and atheism." Regardless of the fact that Sadat was as opposed to the Islamic movement as his predecessor, he sought the help of the Brotherhood to legitimise his rule in order to combat the left-wing opposition and pro-Nasser groups. He had adopted a strategy of reconciliation with the Islamists. He embraced Islamic symbols to legitimise his position and adopted a pious reputation as the Believer-President (Al-Ra'is al-Mu'emen), beginning all official pronouncements with the traditional religious invocation of "in the name of God, the Merciful and the Compassionate". The shari'a was also declared a principal source of legalisation in Egypt in 1971 and Islamic symbols such as the "Al-Azhar", an Islamic institution of higher learning and jurisprudence, were used to bestow a semblance of Islamic legitimacy on the government. Islamic programmes in schools, media and universities were increased and more mosques were built. President Sadat also cultivated relationships with the religious leaders as well as Sufi orders. However, by 1972, tremendous pressure had been placed on Sadat by the Brotherhood for the Islamisation of Egypt. The Islamic movement coveted the imposition of shari'a penalties in cases of crimes such as adultery and the rising tide of Islam could no longer be contained. Fearful of losing power, Sadat began to arrest and ban official publications, such as "al-Dawa", for publicly criticizing his regime. The government proceeded to take control of over 40,000 privately owned mosques; all prayer leaders were required to register with the state, which prohibited Friday sermon without clearance from Ministry of "Awqaf" (i.e. Religious Affairs). *(See Ref 59)*

While In 1973 Saudi Arabia became prominent as a result of the rising price of oil, which made it possible for this country to exert a more authoritative role in the Islamic world, the Islamists in Egypt were provoked by couple of important events, during the late 1960s to the late 1970s, which proved to be a turning point in the spread of religious revivalism. Religion became a visible force for several reasons; Muslims began to experience a loss of identity powered by a sense of failure. Exemplified through the 1967 war, and followed by the Camp David Accord between Egypt and Israel in 1979 - which delegitimised both the Egyptian state and President Sadat personally in the eyes of Islamists as well as nationalists - the Middle East was in a state of decline despite its independence from colonial rule. "What has gone wrong in Islam?" it was asked; and in searching for an answer, it was concluded that Islam had not abandoned Muslims, but it was the

Muslim people who had failed Islam. Muslims must return to Islam, to the straight path that Prophet Muhammad had established in the seventh century. The newfound sense of pride and power that developed from the 1973 Arab-Israeli War, the oil embargo, and the Iranian Revolution of 1979, [which encouraged Islamists elsewhere to believe they could gain power and prompted the Saudi authorities to promote Sunni Islamic ideas in the Middle East, North Africa and South Asia (notably Pakistan) to counter Iran's Shia revolutionary efforts], and the Soviet invasion of Afghanistan in January 1979 and the ensuing mobilisation for Jihad, in which thousands of young men from across the Arab world took part alongside the Afghan resistance movements, led to a quest for a more authentic identity rooted in an Islamic past. Correspondingly, the demand from the Islamists to introduce an Islamic based government rose to new heights. *(See Ref 46, 61)*

On the other side Sadat government tried to appease the Islamists on both the foreign and economic policies but instead to containing them it fostered an Islamic resurgence. An example is President Sadat's "Infitah" (i.e. open-door policy). Mark Cooper argues that this policy was aimed at encouraging economic growth because Nasser's centralised approach towards the economy had not been successful. However, the uneven distribution of wealth and the social disruption caused by the "infitah", as well as its associations with the West, created fertile ground for Islamist values in the face of an increase in the influx of Western values. The outcome of this open-door policy led to a growth in Western investment as well as the integration of the Islamic world into the systems of multi-nationals. This integration resulted in the introduction of system totally alien to the Muslim world's concept of interest, insurance and taxation. In addition, investment brought an influx of foreign tourists as well as their values and way of life, such as commercialism and individualistic life style in addition to increased consumerism and industrialisation. *(See Ref 58, 63)*

President Sadat deviated too from Nasser's strategy by adopting a more liberal attitude towards the Islamic groups at universities. He encouraged the formation of Islamic student societies and formed the General Union of Egyptian Students to regulate student movements and to deepen religious values among students. Groups such as the "al-Jama'a al-Islamiya" managed to establish cells in the Student Union; as such recruiting more members for their cause. The Muslim Brotherhood called for Muslim youths to place themselves in an atmosphere where they will be constantly reminded of the rewards and punishments of the afterlife. This was accomplished through evening prayer and Friday services. Furthermore, they managed to gain control of the information and publishing committees at a national level enabling them to use government funding for pamphlets advocating their cause. The thirty to sixty pages of Islamic rhetoric were designed to be read in a single sitting. These brochures employed Hassan al-Banna's original speeches and passages from Sayyid Qutb's books, which combined the concept of how a full commitment to Islam would translate into practice and would reform society. The pamphlet called "Sawt al-Haqq" (Voice of The Truth) contained passages from books of Qutb as well as from other Islamist authors. And "Duties of the Muslim Youth", a pamphlet by Dr. Magdi al-Hilali, echoed the organisation's message on afterlife, wrote: "the afterlife will influence his world and concentrate our concerns into one united concern, and that is the fear of the Day of Judgment". However, after 1972 the Islamists found the key to success, namely discreet and tactical collaboration with the government to break the left's domination of the campuses. Their dominance over the leftists would consolidate the president's political power against those who had ties with and supported the Soviet Union. Therefore, a close associate of President Sadat, Muhammad Uthman Isma'il, acted as "al-Jama'a al-Islamiya" godfather from 1972 to 1982 and encouraged them to fight against the communists in a classic example of "my enemy's enemy is my ally". *(See Ref 46, 57)*

Many Islamic groups such as the Muslim Brotherhood continued on a peaceful course centred on working within a legal framework and co-operating with other political forces. It established social welfare, economic, educational and medical services and increasingly penetrated university bodies and professional associations. However, the more radical movements, especially those that had been inspired by Qutb and his ideologies, increased in number and prominence. Already in 1974 a group called Muhammad's Youth or the Islamic Liberation Organisation attempted to assassinate President Sadat. The guilty were caught and executed, but the movement went underground and became active together with other groups such as the "Jund Allah" (Soldiers of God) and "Jama'at al-Jihad".

However, the regime was monitoring closely the activity of the legal opposition parties, preventing them from developing into effective vehicles of political representation and thus challenging the existing power. For this reason, Sadat implemented the 1977 Political Parties Law, excluding parties based on class, religious or regional affiliation. This action was performed with the unstated intention to curb the two groups with the greatest capacity for political mobilisation and the greatest capacity to be overwhelming threats to his regime, the Nasserists and the Muslim Brotherhood. The populace's reaction demonstrated in response to this ruling is accredited with Egypt's transition to a multiparty system. Consequently, from 1977 onwards, Islamic opposition to President Sadat increased, with most of the power bases established in Islamic student organisations. These organisations increasingly began to exert their independence and condemn President Sadat's opportunistic use of Islam. In response Sadat became more autocratic and after the 1977 food riots in Cairo he clamped down on the leftist and Islamist groups, such as the "Jama'at al-Muslimeen", also known as the "Takfir wa al-Hijra". *(See Ref 46, 57)*

However, in late 1970s President Sadat conducted several political steps which shocked the Islamic movements in Egypt and in the Arab World. He visited Israel in 1977, which followed by the 1978 Camp David Peace Accord and the 1979 Egyptian-Israeli Peace Treaty, and led to Egypt's ostracism from the Arab world.This new political strategy proved to be a turning point in increasing Islamic opposition and resurgent in the country, which led to protests and demonstrations. During subsequent arrests of "al-Jama'a al-Islamiya" members who had protested against the government, they were accused of receiving foreign funding.

The government decided to break Muslim solidarity by taken steps directed at the "al-Jama'a al-Islamiya" as the centrifugal force even though this organisation had been unable to persuade Egyptian masses to fight alongside it for the victory of the umma. Therefore, the "al-Jama'a al-Islamiya" banned anything unacceptable to its norms from the universities and tried to enforce its ideas on university campuses. Its control was more prominent than that which the government had in the past by means of the General Union of Students. Members of the organisation expressed their thoughts in the monthly bulletin it distributed at the University of Alexandria. The content of their articles centred on the decadence of the lands of Islam, their occupation by infidels and the Islamic awakening. Furthermore, the "al-Jama'a al-Islamiya" focused on the evolution of an Islamic society by emphasising the wearing of the veil, an untrimmed beard, the wearing of a white "gallabiye" (Arab dress) and the attendance of Friday prayers. The assassination of President Sadat by Khalid Islambuli on 6 October 1981 (during a military parade celebrating the anniversary of the 1973 war) brought to the fore the significance of such radical Islamic groups in present-day Egypt. *(See Ref 46, 64)*

The Muslim Brotherhood during the 1970s has presented a changed strategy, namely accommodation of, not struggle against, the political system. They also had as an objective the reformation of the system. Qutb's calls of "Jihad" against the "jahiliyya" had been supplanted by calls for the enactment of political change through co-operation with the ruling regime. Therefore, under President Sadat the Muslim Brotherhood became an active partner of government and in turn made demands for governmental support. On the other front, while the Muslim Brotherhood previously supported Arab nationalism, it ceased doing so. The Palestinian issue was now seen an Islamic issue which deserved its support. However, two groups emanated from the Muslim Brotherhood. The first school is associated with those who regarded Qutb's idea of separation as referring to spiritual detachment and thus practised "takfir" (excommunication) from the "jahiliyya" society secretly. Those who preached total separation physically withdrew from the "jahiliyya" society. The second school which called "Jama'at al-Muslimeen" by its members and "Al-Takfir Wa al-Hijra" by the government, was founded by Shukri Mustafa (1942-1977) in 1971. This group pushed Qutb's theories to their limits because it justified the excommunication of other Muslims. It believed in violent change but argued that this step had to be delayed until the group was strong enough to act. The concept of "jahiliyya" supported the activity of this group. Extremist in doctrine, the group was apolitical and initially non-violent in behaviour. At first it did not support confrontation with the government, but believed true Muslims should denounce the then social order as infidel hence (al-Takfir) but then withdraw from it as the Prophet withdrew from Mecca hence (al-Hijra) and constitute a new community which would enlarge itself by energetic but peaceful proselytising. This would lead to the elimination of the infidel and the establishment of an Islamic state. Initially the group's activities were directed against the Sadat government's pro-U.S. policies and demanded that a pure Islamic state practising shari'a law be established in Egypt. It endorsed the standard Islamic notion that sin and crime were synonymous, extending these conclusions to the Sadat government. *(See Ref 46, 65)*

When President Muhammad Hosni Mubarak assumed power on 6 October 1981, he had no particular political vision that was uniquely his own. His immediate concern was to contain the crisis in the aftermath of the death of President Sadat. He continued with late President's Camp David accords.He followed a more conciliatory tone than his predecessor had done. He released political prisoners and reinvigorated the political liberalisation that was started in 1976 but aborted by President Sadat. He also tried to defuse the crisis in the government. While he continued supporting the Camp David process he emphasised Egypt's Arab, Islamic and African affiliation. The media also enjoyed an improved working relationship with the government and were granted unprecedented freedom of expression. Mubarak set out to create a broad national front against the threat posed by Islamist extremists. This he did by tolerating the moderate Muslim Brotherhood and other political forces. As a consequence social spaces, such as syndicates, university campuses, charitable and voluntary organisations, and so on, were given a considerable degree of autonomy. The Brotherhood took control of such spaces and, by providing its constituencies with services that superseded and surpassed those supplied by the state, was able gradually to gain the support of these constituencies and to build up an informal legitimacy. The legitimacy of the Islamists was thus derived from society rather than from the state, which continued to deny them official recognition. Ironically, the spaces that had been initiated and maintained to legitimise the regime had turned into a source of legitimacy for its competitors. This eventually led the regime to reverse its policies later and to launch an aggressive campaign against the Islamists. Furthermore, President Mubarak reintroduced a wide range of opposition forces consisting of the Arab Socialist Party (ASP), leftist National Progressive Union Party (NPUP) and rightist Liberal Socialist Party (LSP) and exhibited the commitment of 1977 Political Parties Law toward expanding the freedom of opposition parties, whose number expanded to thirteen by the mid-1980s. Despite remaining banned, the Muslim Brotherhood was allowed to partake in the 1984 and 1987 elections under the Wafd and Labour parties or as independent candidates. Nonetheless, the multiparty system created by Nasser's successors did not generate the extent of freedom necessary for the Brotherhood to enhance its political ideologies through the current regime. Due to the stipulations and restrictions that the party continued to endure, it turned to an extensive list of professional associations to stimulate its political advance. *(See Ref 62)*

However, the multiparty system that was created by Nasser's successors could not offer effective representation of the country's educated youth in contrast to the valuable advantages which were made available by the

Brotherhood. Most graduates did not become involved in political affairs. In contrast to the dominant pattern of political attention, a surprising majority of graduates became active in the minority wing of the Islamic movement. The Muslim Brotherhood possessed the ability to aggregate citizens' newfound sympathies and channels them into electoral campaigns at national-level organisations. The Professional Associations gave the Brotherhood activists an opportunity to hone their leadership skills and broaden their base of support. *(See Ref 57)*

Nevertheless, the Brotherhood infiltrated the country's political system in 1984 through what it referred to as the "Islamic Trend" which is a comprehensive group that represents the overarching political and social philosophy of the religion.The Brotherhood began entering a series of elections as an organised bloc beginning with the Doctors' Association election. Shortly thereafter, the group ran a list of candidates in the Engineers', Dentists', Scientists', Pharmacists' and Journalists' Association elections, among others. The growing support for the Islamic Trend was not the simple result of election-day maneuvers. Its successes were primarily due to the new relationships forged by Islamists on the periphery and then sustained by Muslim Brotherhood leaders as elected association officials. The proliferation of these grassroots societies attempted to institutionalise the Islamic movement through legal and formal organisations. *(See Ref 57, 61, 66, 67)*

On the other hand the military had acquired substantial economic resources under President Mubarak that enhanced its organisational resources as well as its power. This formed an almost entirely autonomous enclave of middle-class modernity in an increasingly impoverished and marginalised Third World economy. Its influence expanded into areas of manufacturing weapons, agriculture and land reclamation as well as construction and service industries. The military has had an elevated standing in society that provided it with access to housing, educational, health, consumer and recreational facilities. The military is also provided with subsidised electricity and petroleum, while branching out into other areas of industry. Furthermore, the influence of the military has been enhanced by its use to contain domestic dissent, a campaign undertaken together with the Ministry of the Interior. However, military intelligence has encroached on the civilian security and intelligence service. Therefore, the role of the military is indicative of the manner in which the government exerts power. *(See Ref 46)*

However, while Mubarak's government has focused its socio-economic development on Cairo, the rest of the country has not benefited. This governmental attitude resulted in Cairo's domination over the south in Egypt's existing political structure. Therefore the south has little effective political power over its own affairs as well as no independent media outlet such as newspapers or radio and television broadcasts. This governmental concentration on the capital led to the emergence of "al-Jama'a al-Islamiya" in southern Egypt. Violence that had broken out under the government of Presidents Nasser and Sadat continued under President Mubarak and several government officials and security officers have been killed. Tourists have become targets. The Islamists have established strongholds in poor Cairo neighbourhoods such as Ein Shams, Inbaba, Umraniya, as well as in Upper Egypt. They imposed their own social and moral code, ran their own mosques with their own preachers, provided social services, settled disputes and applied the Koranic text. Stricter governmental measures were met with fierce counter-actions. Those measures included mass arrests, entire neighbourhoods being put under siege, a systematic campaign to decapitate the "al-Jama'a al-Islamiya" by means of military courts and the imposition of the death penalty. *(See Ref 46, 68)*

Mubarak tried to facilitate the process of political expression, when he took over the presidency, by encouraging political debate and authorising opposition parties and press freedom. By giving more freedom of expression to the Islamists in general, the government deprived the radical Islamists of acting as the surrogate for civil society versus the government. Furthermore after the 1984 elections President Mubarak adopted a different approach by allowing outspoken Islamic opposition members such as Sheikh Muhammad Mitwali Al-Shaarawi and Sheikh al-Hamid Kishk to appear on television regularly, while the Muslim Brotherhood was still denied the right to form a political party. Up to that time the Muslim Brotherhood had operated by means of having its own candidates run as independents. This created a sense of control by the government over resurgent movements and the radical resurgent movements assumed a low profile until 1987. *(See Ref 46)*

However, Egypt's professional associations remained among the major sites of Islamic political experimentation in the early 1990's. The continual, overt support of the populace enabled the Muslim Brotherhood to reach its height in 1994. The growing trend of political moderation began to be displayed through the government's attempt to channel the movement rather than repress it. Mubarak's regime began taking tentative steps necessary to permit the growth of Islamisation and its permeation into the country's legal and educational systems.Remaining true in form to the constant changing values that characterise the delicate relationship between the government and the movement, Mubarak's regime detained 81 of the Muslim Brotherhood's leading activists in 1995. This increased risk involved with Islamic activity created a powerful deterrent to the movement, which enabled the government to once again monitor the movement and manipulate the group's activity within the state. *(See Ref 57, 62)*

The government took the opportunity of the 1995 event and tried to change the image of the Muslim Brotherhood by attempting to transform it from that of a moderate and responsible group pursuing the greater good of humanity to that of a radical, violent organisation by televising the court trials of the accused members of the movement. Also acting as an obstacle was that the arrests prevented some of the group's most prominent members from running in the ongoing local elections. Despite the obstacles involved with the government's negative media campaign to repress the Brotherhood, the movement demonstrated its force by winning seventeen seats in the lower parliament in the 2000 parliamentary elections. Coincidently, this happened to be the same number of seats won by all other opposition political parties combined. *(See Ref 57)*

To counter the government attempt, the Muslim Brotherhood, after being propelled from the working relationship with the government in May 1995, released a statement in response to President Mubarak's accusation that "violence is always an integral part" of the movement's methods.The Muslim Brotherhood insisted that it "is in no way involved in violence and denounces all forms of terrorism, calling on those who commit the sin to return to the correct path of Islam." The Brotherhood has made extreme efforts to obtain legitimacy as a peaceful political actor within the state. This peaceful means of control provides an explanation for the successes of Islamic outreach. The organisation stressed the idea of change by persuasion, through the acquisition of a cohesive force of passionate individuals committed to the development of Islam as a means of change. *(See Ref 62, 69)*

The Mubarak regime faced strong domestic challenges throughout the 1990s, which undoubtedly led it to pursue more repressive policies at the level of both legislation and political practice. The government increasingly applied stricter measures, including mass arrests, while entire neighbourhoods were put under siege. Thus a systematic campaign was launched to decapitate the resurgent movements. Military courts were used to convict and sentence the accused by applying the death penalty. In response to the authorities' repressive policies, the "al-Jama'a al-Islamiya" pursued a new strategy from 1992 onwards aiming to damage Egypt's tourist trade and to affect the economy as a whole. Repression, however, could not prevent the further increase of political violence in the country. The victims of Islamic resurgent movements were mostly members of the security apparatus, but an increasing number were Copts (Egyptian Christians) and tourists as well. Attacks against Copts undermined national unity, while those against tourists threatened one of the country's major sources of revenue as well as its reputation abroad.

The 1992 Act, which defined terrorism as "any use of force, violence, threats or scare tactics used by the criminal to execute a ... crime that aims to disrupt public order or endanger social security", was introduced. The introduction of Act no 97/1992, section 2, added a new section (86) to the penal code, which defined terrorism as force or threat of force in disrupting public order, any act that actually or potentially harmed individuals or damaged the environment, financial assets, transport or communication, the physical occupation of sites and places as well as obstruction of the application of the law. The maximum penalty for establishing a terrorist group was changed from 15 years in prison to the death penalty and the penalty for joining such a group was increased from five to 15 years. *(See Ref 70)*

Following its strategy on tracking down terrorists, the government decided to pursue other steps aiming to marginalise and exclude those whom the state could present as the terrorists' allies or sympathisers from representation and participation. This attempt was applied in particular to the Muslim Brotherhood, which was accused of creating a front organisation for armed Islamist groups. It was even applied to human rights organisations, which the regime repeatedly lumped together with "terrorist organisations". However, the impact of strict government security measures resulted in many members relocating abroad in order to evade arrest and hence diverting them from focusing on the group's activities. In July 1997, Muhammad Amir Abd al-Ali, the leading "al-Jama'a al-Islamiya" defendant in a trial of militants involved in bomb attacks on banks, announced a cease-fire in a court statement, but the government refused to take this seriously. Nevertheless the authorities released 8000 Islamist prisoners in 1997 as reward for positive behaviour while "al-Jihad" organisation members were convicted and put to death. This step showed confidence from the government in its ability to contain the Islamists. After a cease-fire was declared in 1999 a subsequent re-organisation of the "al-Jama'a al-Islamiya" leadership abroad resulted in the marginalisation of extremist elements and gave more prominence to a new collective "Shura" (consultation) supporting the ceasefire. The government also succeeded in convincing other governments to hand over individuals who were wanted by the Egyptian authorities. *(See Ref 46)*

In 2003 the government made several steps to ease some restrictions on the Islamic movements. It abolished the controversial state security courts on 16 June, while outlawing forced labour in the country's prisons. Human rights groups welcomed the reforms by President Mubarak. However, citizens' rights are still under curtailment by the state of emergency declared in 1981, and extended every three years. The latest extension was on 11 May 2010 lasting two more years, and ensuring the continuation of military courts. The government released Karam Zuhdi from jail on 22 September, and two other leaders, Fuad Al-Dawalibi and Issam Abd Al-Mageed on 29 September, which followed on 30 September by releasing nearly 1000 other "al-Jama'a al-Islamiya" activists and another senior figure, Mamduh Al-Yussef. On 6 October some 2400 Egyptian prisoners, including 400 members of a militant group that had helped plot the murder of President Sadat, were set free to mark a national holiday. Analysts are of the opinion that Egypt has released more than 5000 "al-Jama'a al-Islamiya" members since 1981; although human rights groups have estimated that more than 10,000 have remained behind bars. *(See Ref 46a)*

The state has proven adept at thwarting the foes that challenge the rule of Hosni Mubarak, the Muslim Brotherhood – regime's main surviving opponent - and it remained firm in its stance on the organisation which has been criticized for failing to provide an audit of its administrative and financial agencies in the country and for failing to apply its strict membership criteria to new members. In addition, Brotherhood members were banned from travelling and seeking employment. It is argued that the government is seeking to contain the Muslim Brotherhood and prevent it from expanding. The Islamic organisation thus still poses a political threat rather than a security threat. However, on 20 January 2004 the ex- leader of the Muslim Brotherhood, former General Guide Muhammad Mahdi Akef, indicated that he requested unconditional dialogue with the Egyptian government. However, in January 2010 the shura Council of the Muslim Brotherhood elected a new conservative leader named Muhammad Badie who sent a clear moderate message to the government when he said to his members: "show the world the true Islam, the Islam of moderation and forgiveness that respects pluralism in the whole world". However, while the Mubarak government was thwarting the Islamists it has, at the same time, supported the growth of the religious infrastructure by increasing religious broadcasts. Civil Muslim leaders or community leaders like Sheik Metwali el-Sha'rawi and Sheik Muhammad al-Ghazali saw themselves as the "state's ideological rampart against religious extremism". By portraying itself as the bastion of Islam, the government was able to gain respect. *(See Ref 46, 71)*

The events of 11 September 2001 once again proved to be a turning point in relations between the government and Islamists, which has led Egypt to participate in the US-led war on terrorism. This participation gave the government the cause to take more strict measures such as the banning of certain sermons. According to an article published in the Opposition Arab Democratic Party magazine of 7 September 2003, the 114 religious scholars banned by security orders from preaching in Egyptian mosques can be placed in three categories: (i) preachers who had refused to co-operate directly with security bodies and had attacked the USA; (ii) members affiliated to the ruling National Democratic Party (NDP); and (iii) preachers who had refused to deliver sermons prescribed by the Ministry of Awqafs. In addition, orders were given that mosques in which preachers delivered sermons without the necessary permission would be closed. It was also reported that video cameras are used in mosques on Fridays and during major events and ceremonies to monitor the sermons *(See Ref 72)*

If security measures and laws were produced by the authorities to make some pressure on Islamists to thwart them, general elections have been used as platforms for anti-government actions because all governments in Egypt since independence have failed to provide for free and fair elections. An example is the 2010 elections, which were influenced by the decision of most opposition parties to boycott them. These elections, instead of broadening the spectrum of political forces in the Egyptian parliament, resulted in a larger majority for the ruling National Democratic Party

(NDP) than the party had had in 2005. The Islamist group who had 20% of the seats in the outgoing parliament or 88 seats failed even to get one seat in the first round of the elections on 28 November 2010, which it claims has been hit by fraud. Consequently, the Brotherhood which fields its candidates as independents, decided to boycott the second round of the elections on 5 December 2010. However, it was not the first time that this happened, the same also occurred with 1990, 2000 and 2005 elections. *(See Ref 73)*

However, a new generation of Islamists emerged under the Mubarak government that can be divided into two sections. The first comprises those who hailed from the Sadat era, while the second section has became prominent after the 1997 Luxor attacks, and is in turn divided into a faction led by Lieutenant Abd al-Zomour (ex-intelligence army officer) and Ayman al-Zawahiri who formed "Egyptian Islamic al-Jihad" known too as "al-Jihad". These two believed that the "al-Jihad" would only succeed if they were able to destroy the nerve-centre of the "impious regime" that even controlled preaching by violence. *(See Ref 54)*

When the Mubarak regime imprisoned several leaders of "al-Jihad" including Abd al-Zomour after the hanging of Abdel Salam Faraj and Khaled al-Islambouli, the organisation survived, only to split over an internal dispute when the Upper Egyptian wing, Karam Zuhdi's Jihadi Islamic Group, seceded in 1984. Thereafter, "al-Jihad" proved unable to maintain an effective campaign and local Jihadi groups developed outside its control. Its remaining members occasionally attempted to assassinate government leaders in 1990 and 1993, for example the speaker of the People's Assembly, Rif'at Al-Mahgoub, was assassinated in October 1990. Some sources attribute this to "al-Jihad", however, this is not universally believed. In 1993, unsuccessful attempts were made to assassinate the Information Minister Safwat Al-Sharif in April, the Interior Minister Atef Sidqi in August and the Prime Minister in November. These groups were increasingly drawn into international activities through their connection from 1989 onwards with Osama Bin Laden's al-Qa'ida network, with which they formally merged in 1998. This re-orientation of "al-Jihad" to the external and international sphere has been largely associated with Ayman al-Zawahiri, who since 11 September 2001 has attained international notoriety as bin Laden's principal lieutenant. *(See Ref 74, 76)*

Meanwhile, what was left of "al-Jihad" inside Egypt had been largely dismantled. Over 300 suspected members had been put on trial following the arrest of the organisation's membership director, Ismaïl Nassir, in early 1993; a further 280 were arrested and six sentenced to death after the assassination attempt on the prime minister in Cairo the following November. Following the capture by American intelligence agents of senior "al-Jihad" figures in Baku and Tirana in 1998, over 100 members went on trial in Cairo and al-Zawahiri and his brother Muhammad were sentenced to death in absentia. By then, "al-Jihad" had long since been eclipsed inside the country by "al-Jama'a al-Islamiya". When the latter decided to end its campaign in 1999, most "al-Jihad" members still in Egypt accepted its cease-fire and abandoned their violence activities.

The faction under the leadership of the "al-Jama'a al-Islamiya" believed that jihad should be fought by means of preaching within the society itself. However it increasingly became more violent up to 1992 when in that year the so-called five-year war between the government and the "al-Jama'a al-Islamiya" took place. The organisation also managed to broaden its power base by bringing together the Islamic intellectuals, the graduates who had returned from the Gulf in the 1970s, the students from the universities and the local or traditional godfathers of gangs. This mix of Islamists and violent criminals created conditions conducive to violence. In these areas the Islamists organised sports, schools and militias. Thus the "al-Jama'a al-Islamiya" managed to replace traditional institutions in settling disputes, mediating in vendettas and establishing charity organisations to take care of the needy. *(See Ref 75)*

By "1996 al-Jama'a al-Islamiya" was beginning to show signs of fatigue and could not always replace those who killed or arrested. In addition, the closure of the borders and the clampdown on Islamists internationally restricted its movements and prevented it from recruiting new members. Furthermore the imprisonment of Sheikh Omar Abdel Rahman in the USA in 1996 and the disappearance of the European co-ordinator of the organisation disrupted the international support networks responsible for supplies. Money transfers stopped and the organisation had to resort to crime. The government managed to cause internal division and in 1996 the "al-Jama'a al-Islamiya" called for a cease-fire. This did not prevent attacks on tourists. Their attacks on tourists in 1997 were conducted with the minimum expense, but were very effective in reducing much-needed revenue for the government, derived from tourism. It also served to show the government's ineffectiveness in dealing with the situation. In addition, it alienated the more moderate segment of society from the cause of the Islamists, especially those whose livelihood depended on tourism. *(See Ref 75)*

Since then a new generation of Islamists especially in the Muslim Brotherhood has come forward that is engaged and focused on working within the system and that is thoroughly modernised, although not westernised. Another reason for the social engagement of the Brotherhood was the presence of a new breed of activists, whose attitude towards state and society was more open and conciliatory. Religious identity and religious attitudes were no longer expressed in the strict segregationist terms of Sayyid Qutb and the generation influenced by him, but were redefined and negotiated to adapt to new realities and developments. This change in religious identity and discourse was particularly obvious on university campuses. According to Hilmi al-Jazzar, former President of the Cairo University Students' Union, and an active Islamist in the medical syndicate: "In the 1970s we used to have beards and wear julbab [the long, flowing garments traditionally worn by Egyptian men], and our discourse was visibly and directly Islamic. We focused on issues like Islamic dress and spreading Islamic awareness through books and exhibitions. In the 1980s hardly any "Ikhwan" students had beards and all wore Western clothes and suits. We focused on issues related to democracy and on serving the needs of the students by providing them with cheap reference books and revision manuals. I see this as a positive rather than a negative development, since in any social group the individual who is supposed to represent it is the one who is able to serve it." *(See Ref 77)*

However despite being forced underground, the Muslim Brotherhood has continued to expand its power base by appealing to widespread sympathies toward Islamist ideology and, more importantly, by filling the socio-economic gap unaddressed by the government - which, despite the billions it receives from abroad, invests more in its own survival than in the well-being of its people. By financing various social services ranging from health care and education to food drives and the establishment of community centres, the Brotherhood is perceived to be true to its populist platform.

The Islamic party's popularity is by no means limited to the urban masses living in poverty. Young professionals who work as accountants, engineers, or even paralegals, demonstrate that the movement is becoming increasingly middle class (although many Egyptians deny, perhaps rightfully, that their country can even boast a middle class). Nevertheless, the Brotherhood remains highly popular with students at major universities, in large part because post-graduate opportunities for work and prosperity are often uninspiring, if they exist at all. While middle-aged and older citizens tend to shed their idealism and accept the status quo, universities and even high schools are proving to be important arenas for political and social activism.

Although the Muslim Brotherhood would probably win a parliamentary majority if allowed to compete on equal footing, not all Egyptians welcome the idea of a Muslim Brotherhood-led government. The big question is whether, once in power, the Brotherhood would adhere to the ideals of consensual democracy and pluralism or would instead, as an AUC political science student put it, "be like the Nazis in 1933 and betray the system"? *(See Ref 78)*

The fact that the Brotherhood has opted to work from within the system by adopting social and democratic approaches has been seen by authors such as Olivier Roy as an indication that Islamists have adopted new strategies. However, there is still an element in Egypt that resorts to violence. While the traditionalists regarded the Koran as absolute knowledge, the radicals espoused a creative interpretation or "Ijtihad" of its texts. The deconstruction of the written word is set to increase and continue. The possible outcome of this is more diversity in opinions, and groups and intense verbal attacks on government and opponents that will contribute to the marginalisation of governments. It is foreseen that the new generation of so-called Islamists will continue to question those aspects that they disagree with, but their methodology has changed. *(See Ref 79)*

However, on the 12 February 2011, Hosni Mubarak has stepped down as president of Egypt, after weeks of protests and popular uprising in Cairo and other cities.

Announcing Mr Mubarak's resignation, Vice-President Omar Suleiman (who was promoted by Mubarak to this post on 29 January 2011) said the president had handed power to the army.

Mr Suleiman said on state TV that the high command of the armed forces had taken over.

"In the name of God the merciful, the compassionate, citizens, during these very difficult circumstances Egypt is going through, President Hosni Mubarak has decided to step down from the office of president of the republic and has charged the high council of the armed forces to administer the affairs of the country," he said.

Later an army officer read out a statement paying tribute to Mr Mubarak for "what he has given" to Egypt but acknowledging popular power.

"There is no legitimacy other than that of the people," the statement said.

With the end of the Mubarak era, speculation has turned to whether the Muslim Brotherhood will dominate the new Egyptian political landscape. As the largest, most popular, and most effective opposition group in Egypt, it will undoubtedly seek a role in creating a new government, but the consequences of this are uncertain. Those who emphasise the risk of "Islamic tyranny" aptly note that the Muslim Brotherhood originated as an anti-system group dedicated to the establishment of shari'a rule; committed acts of violence against its opponents in the pre-1952 era; and continues to use anti-Western, anti-Zionist, and anti-Semitic rhetoric. But portraying the Brotherhood as eager and able to seize power and impose its version of shari'a on an unwilling citizenry is a caricature that exaggerates certain features of the Brotherhood while ignoring others, and underestimates the extent to which the group has changed over time.

Individuals affiliated with the reformist faction of the Brotherhood, whether still active in the group or not, appear to be the most involved in leading 2011 Egypt's popular uprising. It is not surprising, for example, that the reformist blogger Mustafa Naggar is one of the chief spokesman for Muhammad El Baradei's National Coalition for Change. Still, the Brotherhood's participation has been low profile. It did not officially mobilise until 28 January 2011, days after the protests began. And unlike in previous demonstrations, when members of the Brotherhood held up copies of the Koran and shouted slogans such as "Islam is the solution," religious symbols have been conspicuously absent this time.

The Brotherhood knows from experience that the greater its role, the higher the risk of a violent crackdown - as indicated by the harsh wave of repression that followed its strong showing in the 2005 parliamentary elections. The Brotherhood also knows that a smooth transition to a democratic system will require an interim government palatable to the military and the West, so it has indicated that it would not seek positions in the new government itself. The Brotherhood is too savvy, too pragmatic, and too cautious to squander its hard-earned reputation among Egyptians as a responsible political actor or invite the risk of a military coup by attempting to seize power on its own.

Although the organisation Secretary General Muhammad Badie declared on 21 February 2011 that the Brotherhood decided to form a political party in the new post-Mubarak era under the name of "Party of Liberty and Justice" to enter the Egyptian political arena officially, and he will present the official request to the government soon, still, it is unclear whether the group will continue to exercise pragmatic self-restraint down the road or whether its more progressive leaders will prevail. Such reformers were most welcomed among the other opposition groups in the committee which was formed to make the necessary changes in the Constitution and establish the framework for new elections, but they do not necessarily speak for the group's senior leadership or the majority of its rank and file. It remains to be seen whether the Brotherhood as an organisation - not only individual members - will accept a constitution that does not at least refer to shari'a; respect the rights of all Egyptians to express their ideas and form parties; clarify its ambiguous positions on the rights of women and non-Muslims; develop concrete programs to address the nation's toughest social and economic problems; and apply the same pragmatism it has shown in the domestic arena to issues of foreign policy, including relations with Israel and the West. Over time, other parties - including others with an Islamist orientation - may provide the Brotherhood with some healthy competition and an impetus to further reform itself.

The Brotherhood has demonstrated that it is capable of evolving over time, and the best way to strengthen its democratic commitments is to include it in the political process, making sure there are checks and balances in place to ensure that no group can monopolise state power and that all citizens are guaranteed certain freedoms under the law. In the foreign policy domain, the Brotherhood rails against "U.S. and Zionist domination," demands the recognition of Palestinians rights, and may one day seek to revise the terms of Egypt's relationship with Israel through constitutional channels. The Brotherhood will likely never be as supportive of U.S. and Israeli interests in the region as Mubarak was. Yet here too, the best way for the United States to minimise the risk associated with the likely increase in its power is to encourage and reward judiciousness and pragmatism. With a track record of nearly 30 years of responsible behaviour (if not rhetoric) and a strong base of support, the Muslim Brotherhood has earned a place at the table in the post-Mubarak era. No democratic transition can succeed without it.

However, in the current global environment the battle is fought on a different level. The outcome of the war in Iraq, Afghanistan and the prominence of the use of the media and the Internet to address an ever-increasing audience is proof of this. It is foreseen that till governmental changes provide for equal socio-economic progress and the development of a government system inclusive of all, a segment of society that has been left behind will either seek inclusion or act aggressively on its exclusion. However the evolution of political and socio-economic dispensations will have to be inclusive of Islam because it is a way of life providing a political as well as socio-economic paradigm. As long as religious relevance remains a central point of view in the Muslim world, those in political power as well as those opposing it will justify their arguments on the tenets of Islam. Therefore, imposing a foreign system will not have the desired results compared to systems that have evolved from within or at grass-roots level. It is doubtful if any Western system would be the answer. The Islamic resurgent movement have been seeking a voice in their own government, but this does not mean that the so-called democratic systems are the answer. It should be clear by now that any system that is externally generated and imposed but not internalised by the Islamic world (or any non-Western society for that matter), is not the answer. An internally generated and fully representative system is the only self-sustaining solution.

Finally, regardless of which faction prevails in the post-Mubarak scuffle for power, the army, as well as major contingents from the business community can be expected to usher in a candidate who will protect their current status and political interests. This is not to say, however, that democracy will never take hold in Egypt. If the next president comes from civilian rather than a military background, popular opposition groups like the Muslim Brotherhood may gradually see their parliamentary presence more accurately reflect the level of their support, as happened in the 2005 parliamentary elections. History suggests, in fact, that it is gradual rather than revolutionary change that usually proves more effective, long-lasting and just in reforming society and its political system. If this indeed is the case, Egypt might not be on such a dark path after all.

CHAPTER FOUR

SAUDI ARABIA: FIRST STEPS TOWARD CHANGE

The history of Arabia can be traced to 1000 B.C., when a confederation of states was formed in its southern region, called Arabia Felix, to control the trade between India and Africa. It had a relatively high level of development. The civilisation there evolved rapidly because it had steady contact with the outside world via the trade routes that spanned the region. Exports in frankincense and myrrh brought wealth and global connections to present-day Bahrain, Yemen, Oman, and southern Saudi Arabia. While the Persians and Romans fought to control the Near East, Arabic society benefited from the exchange of ideas that came with the camel caravans. Multiple religions were present in the region, including Christianity, Judaism, and various polytheistic paganisms. However, the birth of the Prophet Muhammad in Mecca in 570 A.D. changed Arabia (present-day Saudi Arabia) forever. Today, many Arabs refer to the time before the introduction and spread of Islam as "Asr al-jahiliyya" (i.e. the time of ignorance.) *(Most of the historic information in this chapter came from Ref 80, 81, 82, 85, 89)*

If the history of Arabia is very old the Saudi state's history began in central Arabia cerca 1744 A.D., when a local ruler, Muhammad Ibn Al Saud, joined forces with an Islamic reformer, Muhammad Ibn Abd al-Wahhab, in an alliance to create and establish a new religious-political entity determined to cleanse the Arabian Peninsula of perceived heretical practices and deviations from orthodox Islam. Over the next 160 years, the fortunes of the Saud family rose and fell several times as Saudi rulers contended with Egypt, the Ottoman Empire, and other rival families for control on the Arabian Peninsula. However, the modern Saudi state was founded by Abdul Aziz Ibn Abd al-Rahman Al Saud (commonly referred to as Ibn Saud). He rose to prominence in the early twentieth century, when his armies recaptured Najd, the traditional homeland of the Al Saud, and later the Islamic shrine cities of Mecca and Medina during 1920s, and declared in 1932 that the area under his control would be known as the Kingdom of Saudi Arabia.

At first Abdul Aziz's realm was a very poor one. It was a desert kingdom with few known natural resources and a largely uneducated population. There were few cities and virtually no industry. Although the shrines at Mecca and Medina earned income from the Muslim pilgrims who visited them every year, this revenue was insufficient to lift the rest of the kingdom out of its near subsistence level. All this changed, however, when United States geologists discovered oil in the kingdom during the 1930s. Saudi Arabia's exploitation of its oil resources transformed the country into a nation synonymous with great wealth, which brought with it enormous material and social change - so much change - that Saudi Arabia became an exaggerated paradigm of possibilities for development in the Third World. The transformation was staggering: in a few years the Saudis had gone from herding camels to moving billions of dollars around the world with electronic transfers. *(See Ref 82)*

History and origins were very important to Saudi Arabia perhaps due to the great upheaval of the last 80 years. However, Saudis tended to view life in more traditional terms, despite that the country owed its prominence to modern economic realities. Nevertheless the state in 21st century remained organised largely along tribal lines. The Muslim religion continued to be a vital element in Saudi statecraft. Moreover, many Muslims considered the form of Islam practiced most widely in Saudi Arabia, Wahhabi Islam, to be reactionary because it sought its inspiration from the past (al-salaf). The basic text of this form of Islam is the "Kitab at-tawhid" (i.e. "Book of Unity"). Central to its founder Muhammad ibn Abd al-Wahhab's message was the essential oneness of God (tawhid). The movement is therefore known by its adherents as "ad-da'wa lil tawhid" (the call to unity), and those who follow the call are known as "ahl at-tawhid" (the people of unity) or "muwahhidoon" (unitarians). "[Ibn Abd al-Wahhab] and his followers believe that they have a religious obligation to spread the call (da'wa) for a restoration of pure monotheistic worship. Thus, the mission's devotees contend that 'Wahhabism' is a misnomer for their efforts to revive correct Islamic belief and practice. Instead of the Wahhabi label, they prefer either "salafi", one who follows the ways of the first Muslim ancestors (salaf), or "muwahhid", one who professes God's unity." So they believe that ultimate authority rests with God (Allah). The Saudi ruler is

Allah's secular representative and bases political legitimacy on his religious credentials. *(See Ref 83)*

Saudi Arabia is the largest country on the Arabian Peninsula. It shares with the Arab Gulf states, Yemen, Jordan, and Iraq the Persian Gulf and the Red Sea coasts, so there are cultural and historical overlaps with its neighbours. Many of these countries rely on the authority of a single family, whether the ruler calls himself a king, as in Saudi Arabia, Bahrain and Jordan, or an emir (prince), as in the other Gulf States. Tribal loyalties also play an important role in these countries, and large portions of their populations have only recently stopped living as nomads. However Saudi Arabia distinguishes from its neighbours because it has never been under direct control of a European power unlike other states in the area. Moreover, the Wahhabi movement that began in Saudi Arabia has had a greater impact on Saudi history than on any other country. Although the religious fervour of Wahhabism affected populations of neighbouring countries such as present-day Qatar, only in Saudi Arabia it was an essential element in the formation of the modern state. *(See Ref 80, 82)*

The Al Saud family origins can be traced to "Ad-Diriyah" town in Najd, near Riyadh, beginning in about 1500. The ancestors of Saud ibn Muhammad settled in the region and began harvesting dates. As a small town developed, the Al Saud came to be recognised as its leaders, and the clan's power and influence grew. The rise of the Al Saud coincided with that of the Muslim scholar Muhammad ibn Abd al Wahhab (1703–87), who wrote and preached against leaders and traditions that he deemed contradictory to the idea of a unitary god. Unlike other religious leaders who preached unitarianism, Muhammad ibn Abd al Wahhab demanded that political power be used to implement his theology. In 1744 he found the political partner that he had been searching for, and he and Muhammad ibn Saud swore a traditional oath to work together in order to establish a state ruled according to Islamic principles. The alliance was based on Muhammad ibn Abd al Wahhab's claim of religious legitimacy and Muhammad ibn Saud's readiness to undertake jihad in defence of such principles. Some scholars have cited this partnership as the "original religio-political movement." Muhammad ibn Abd al-Wahhab offered the Al Saud a clearly defined religious mission to which to contribute their leadership and upon which they might base their political authority. This sense of religious purpose remained evident in the political ideology of Saudi Arabia in the 21st century. *(See Ref 80, 84)*

When Muhammad ibn Saud began leading his armies into Najdi towns and villages to eradicate various popular and Shia practices, the towns and tribes of Najd which liked this movement, rally to the Al Saud-Wahhabi standard. By the time Muhammad ibn Saud died in 1765 his forces had established Wahhabism - and with it the Al Saud political authority - over most of Najd. However, his son, Abdul Aziz after him, continued the Wahhabi advance. In 1801 the Al Saud-Wahhabi armies attacked and sacked Karbala, the Shia shrine in eastern Iraq that commemorates the death of al-Hussein. In 1803 Wahhabi forces moved on to Mecca and Medina. These holy cities were spared the destruction that met Karbala, but the Wahhabis did destroy monuments and markers established for prayer to Muslim saints, which Wahhabi theology deemed to be acts of polytheism. With the assault on the Hijaz, the region of pilgrimage, the Al Saud invited conflict with much of the rest of the Islamic world. Recognising the symbolic importance of the region, the Ottoman sultan ordered the recapture of the Hijaz. At the beginning of the nineteenth century, the Ottomans were not in a position to recover the Hijaz, because the empire had been in decline for more than two centuries, and its forces were weak and overextended. Accordingly, the sultan delegated the recapture of that region to his most ambitious client, Muhammad Ali Pasha, the semi-independent ruler in Egypt. In 1816 Egyptian forces, fighting on behalf of the sultan, regained control of Mecca and Medina. Meanwhile, Muhammad ibn Abd al Wahhab had died in 1792, and Abdul Aziz died shortly before the capture of Mecca. *(Ref 82, 85)*

Saud succeeded his father Abdul Aziz until 1814 when he died, his son, Abdallah, ruled after him. Accordingly, it was Abdallah who faced the invading Egyptian army, which took Mecca and Medina almost immediately. Abdallah chose this time to retreat to the family's strongholds in Najd. Muhammad Ali Pasha decided to pursue him there, sending out another army under the command of his son, Ibrahim. The Wahhabis made their stand at the traditional Al Saud capital of Ad-Diriyah, where they managed to hold out for two years against superior Egyptian forces and weaponry. In the end, however, the Wahhabis proved no match for a modern army, and Ad-Diriyah - and Abdallah with it - fell in 1818. *(See Ref 80, 82, 85)*

Following a six-year period of Egyptian interference, the Al Saud reestablished political control of the Najd region in 1824 under Turki ibn Abdallah, who rebuilt Riyadh and established it as the new centre of Al Saud power. The sphere of influence for Turki and his successors had extended to the regions north and south of Najd, and also along the western coast of the Persian Gulf. Although they did not control a centralised state, the Al Saud successfully controlled military resources, collected tribute, and resisted Egyptian attempts to regain a foothold in the region. *(See Ref 80)*

The Al Saud maintained power and protected Arabia's autonomy between 1830 and 1891, by playing the British and Ottomans against each other. External threats were largely kept at bay, but internal strife plagued the Al Saud throughout much of the century. After the assassination of Turki in 1834, the family devolved into a series of competing factions. The infighting and constant civil war ultimately led to the decline of the Al Saud and the rise of the rival Al Rashid family. In 1891 Muhammad ibn Rashid placed Riyadh under the nominal control of Al Saud leader Abd al-Rahman, but effective control of the city was in the hands of his own garrison commander. When Abd al-Rahman attempted to exert true authority, he and the remainder of the Al Saud, along with young Abdul Aziz, were driven out of Riyadh and forced to take refuge in Kuwait. *(See Ref 80, 82, 85)*

Despite that the founder of the modern state of Saudi Arabia, Abdul Aziz (the eldest son of Abd al-Rahman), lived much of his early life in exile, he succeeded in the end not only to recover the territory of the first Al Saud Empire, but made a state out of it. He began laying the groundwork for the modern state of Saudi Arabia while exiled in Kuwait. In 1902 he led a small force in a raid against the Al Rashid garrison in Riyadh, successfully gaining a foothold in the Najd. From there, he cultivated his Wahhabi connections, establishing himself as the Al Saud leader and as a Wahhabi imam. By forging agreements with tribes around Riyadh, Abdul Aziz strengthened his position so that the Al Rashid garrison was unable to evict him. During the next 25 years, Abdul Aziz gradually extended his authority and in doing so, laid the foundation for the Saudi state. It was a slow process, highlighted by three milestones. In 1905 Abdul Aziz retook control of Najd. In 1921 he led Wahhabi forces to defeat the Al Rashid at Ha'il. In culmination, Abdul Aziz conquered the Hijaz in 1924. Thus, after nearly 40 years the Al Saud again controlled Islam's most holy land. *(See Ref 80, 82, 85)*

During his struggle to establish the Kingdom of Saudi Arabia, Abdul Aziz armies were formed from several groups, tribes and militants including "al-Ikhwan al-Muslimeen" (i.e.the Muslim Brotherhood) movement which began to emerge and to flourish among the bedouin. This organisation spread Wahhabi Islam among the nomads. Stressing the same strict adherence to religious law that Muhammad ibn Abd al-Wahhab had preached, Muslim Brotherhood bedouin members abandoned their traditional way of life in the desert and move to an agricultural settlement called a "hijra". The word hijra was related to the term for the Prophet Muhammad's emigration from Mecca to Medina in 622, conveying the sense that one who settles in a hijra moves from a place of unbelief to a place of belief. By moving to the hijra the Muslim Brotherhood members intended to take up a new way of life and dedicate themselves to enforcing a rigid Islamic orthodoxy. Once in the hijra the Brotherhood bedouins became extremely militant in enforcing upon themselves what they believed to be correct "Sunnah" (custom) of the Prophet, enjoining public prayer, mosque attendance, and gender segregation and condemning music, smoking, alcohol, and technology unknown at the time of the Prophet. They attacked those who refused to conform to Wahhabi interpretations of correct Islamic practice and tried to convert Muslims by force to their version of Wahhabism. *(See Ref 82)*

Once Abdul Aziz controlled the Hijaz, he became a significant leader, not just for Saudi Arabia but for all Islamic peoples. Unlike most other Arab countries, Saudi Arabia existed independent of Western control. That autonomy had been achieved in large part because of the military strength of the radical Muslim Brotherhood forces, desert warriors organised by Abdul Aziz and dedicated to promoting Wahhabi Islam. This militant group looked eagerly for the opportunity to fight non-Wahhabi Muslims. With victory achieved, the Brotherhood expected a strictly Wahhabi state.

In establishing his state, Abdul Aziz had to consider the various constituencies that he served. He made some effort to gain world Muslim approval before he moved into the Hijaz. Once the Hijaz was under his control, he submitted to the world Muslim community, even if only rhetorically, the question of how the area should be ruled. When he received no response, he held an informal referendum in which the notables of the Hijaz chose him as their king. In the Hijaz, Abdul Aziz restrained the more fanatical of his Wahhabi followers and eventually won the support of the local religious authorities, the " ulama" (clergy). *(See Ref 80, 82)*

Other Muslim countries were not at the time in a position to challenge Abdul Aziz. Most of the states lived under foreign rule or mandate, and two of the countries that did not, Iran and Turkey, were in the midst of secular reforms.

However, Abdul Aziz had problems at home. The first and most serious of these was the Muslim Brotherhood. This organisation had no tolerance for the concessions to life in the twentieth century that Abdul Aziz was forced to make. They objected to machines, particularly those used for communication, such as the telegraph, as well as to the increasing presence of non-Muslim foreigners in the country. They also continued to object to some of the practices of non-Wahhabi Muslims. Most important, the Brotherhood remained eager to force their message on who ever did not accept it. This led them to attack non-Wahhabi Muslims, and sometimes Wahhabi Muslims as well, within Saudi Arabia and to push beyond its borders into Iraq. Whereas the first sort of attack challenged Abdul Aziz's authority, the second caused him problems with the British, who would not tolerate the violation of borders that they had set up after First World War. It was largely because of this second concern that Abdul Aziz found himself obliged to take on the Brotherhood militarily. When the fundamentalist militant forces continued to ignore his authority, he waged a pitched battle and defeated them in 1929. He then assembled a diverse and committed political coalition and was able to maintain a delicate political balance between religion and modernisation. The Kingdom of Saudi Arabia became official in 1932 and subsequently faced severe economic constriction in the 1930s. Fortunately, however, following the worldwide depression, geologists made a discovery that significantly buoyed the region's economic outlook - enormous and easy-to-access deposits of oil. *(See Ref 80, 82, 85)*

Following Abd al Aziz's death in 1953, Saud succeeded his father as a king in a reign largely characterised by wasteful state expenditures and the polarisation of wealth. The new monarch did not prove to be a leader equal to the challenges of the next two decades. He was a spendthrift even when he was crown prince before he became king, and this became a more crucial issue when he controlled the Kingdom's purse strings. He paid huge sums to maintain tribal acquiescence to his rule in return for recruits for an immense palace guard, the White Army, so-called because they wore traditional Arab dress rather than military uniforms. Revenues could not match Saud's expenditures for the tribes, subsidies to various foreign groups, and his personal follies. By 1958 the riyal had to be devalued nearly

80 percent, despite annual oil revenues in excess of US$300 million. *(See Ref 82, 85)*

During his reign, Saud had largely cut himself off from the citizenry, relying heavily on his advisers, many of whom were primarily concerned with acquiring personal wealth and power. His half- brother Faisal, in contrast, despite working long hours on affairs of state, made himself available to the public daily in the traditional "majlis" (Arabic for place of sitting where the leader opens up his residence to the citizens to enter and petition him), followed by a meal open to anyone. During the times he had acted as prime minister for Saud, Faisal had strengthened the power of the Council of Ministers and in 1954 had been primarily responsible for the creation of the ministries of commerce, industry and of health. *(See Ref 82)*

Responding to public discontent, the royal family and the ulama deposed Saud in 1964 and appointed his half-brother, Faisal, as king. The new Saudi monarch set for himself the task of modernising the kingdom. His first two official acts were protective, directed toward safeguarding the nation from potential internal and external threats that could thwart development. In the first month of Faisal's reign, his half-brother Khalid was designated crown prince, thus ensuring that the succession would not be disturbed by the kind of family power politics that had nearly destroyed Saudi hegemony in the past. Sultan, another half-brother serving as the minister of defence and aviation, was charged with modernising the army and establishing an air defence system to protect the nation and its petroleum reserves from potential external and internal threats. *(See Ref 80, 82, 89)*

The spread of republicanism in the Arab world had troubled Faisal because it challenged the legitimacy of the Al Saud, for this reason he called an Islamic summit conference in 1965 to reaffirm Islamic principles against the rising tide of modern ideologies. Faisal was dedicated to Islamic ideals that he had learned in the house of his maternal grandfather, a direct descendant of Muhammad ibn Abd al-Wahhab. He was raised in a spartan atmosphere, unlike that of most of his half-brothers, and was encouraged by his mother to develop values consonant with tribal leadership. Faisal's religious idealism did not diminish his secular effectiveness. For him, political functioning was a religious act that demanded thoughtfulness, dignity, and integrity. Respect for Faisal increased in the Arab world based on the remarkable changes within Saudi Arabia, his excellent management of the Islamic holy cities, his reputation as a stalwart enemy of Israel, and his rapidly increasing financial power. His main foreign policy themes were pan-Islamism, anti-Communism, and anti-Zionism. *(See Ref 80, 82)*

The region saw numerous coups d'état during 1950s and 1960s. Muammar al-Gaddafi's coup that overthrew the monarchy in oil-rich Libya in 1969 was especially ominous for Saudi Arabia due the similarity between the two sparsely-populated desert countries. As a result, Faisal undertook to build a sophisticated security apparatus and cracked down firmly on dissent. As in all affairs, he justified these policies in Islamic terms. Early in his reign, when faced by demands for a written constitution for the country, Faisal responded that "our constitution is the Koran." In 1969, he ordered the arrest of hundreds of military officers, including some generals, alleging that a military coup was being planned. The arrests were possibly based on a tip from American intelligence, but it is unclear how serious the threat actually was. *(See Ref 89, 90, 91)*

Faisal proceeded cautiously but emphatically to introduce Western technology. He was continually forced to deal with the insistent demands of his Westernised associates to move faster and the equally vociferous urgings of the ulama to move not at all. He chose the middle ground not merely in a spirit of compromise to assuage the two forces but because he earnestly believed that the correct religious orientation would mitigate the adverse effects of modernisation. In 1963, Faisal established the country's first television station, though actual broadcasts would not begin for another two years. When in 1965 the first television broadcasts, one of Faisal's nephews went so far as to lead an assault on one of the new studios and was later killed in a shoot-out with the police. Such a family tragedy did not, however, cause Faisal to withdraw his support for the television project. As with many of his other policies, the move aroused strong objections from the religious and conservative sections of the country Faisal assured them, however, that Islamic principles of modesty would be strictly observed, and made sure that the broadcasts contained a large amount of religious programming. *(See Ref 82, 87)*

Furthermore, under Faisal's reign a massive educational program was initiated. Expenditures for education increased to an annual level of approximately 10 percent of the budget. Vocational training centres and institutes of higher education were built in addition to the more than

125 elementary and secondary schools built annually. Women's demands, increasingly vocalised, led to the establishment of elementary schools for girls. These were placed under religious control to pacify the many who were opposed to education for women. Health centers also multiplied. *(See Ref 82, 88)*

Faisal was assassinated on March 25, 1975 by his half-brother's son, Faisal bin Musa'id, who had just come back from the United States, Crown Prince Khalid immediately succeeded to the throne and received the oaths, formal pledges of support from the family , tribal leaders and the ulama, within the traditional three days. Fahd, the minister of interior, was named crown prince, as expected.

The new king's first diplomatic coup was the conclusion in April 1975 of a demarcation agreement concerning the Al Buraymi Oasis, where the frontiers of Abu Dhabi, Oman, and Saudi Arabia meet. Claims and counterclaims over this frontier area had exacerbated relations among the three states for years. The successful conclusion of negotiations under Khalid's aegis added to his stature as a statesman among knowledgeable observers of the peninsula political scene. Following this diplomatic success and in a reorganisation of the Council of Ministers in late 1975, Khalid named Crown Prince Fahd deputy prime minister and designated Abdallah (another half-brother and the commander of the Saudi Arabian National Guard) as second deputy prime minister. However, Fahd, who had already participated in major decisions, became chief spokesman for the kingdom and a major architect of Saudi modernisation, foreign affairs, and oil policy. *(See Ref 92)*

Many of the kingdom's ideas about its own stability and its relations concerning its neighbours and allies were shattered on March 26, 1979, when Khalid broke relations with Sadat regime and led in seeking Arab economic sanctions against Egypt as a result of the Egypt-Israeli peace treaty. Furthermore on November 20 of that year at least 500 dissidents invaded and seized the Grand Mosque in Mecca. The leader of the dissidents, Juhaiman ibn Muhammad ibn Saif al-Utaiba, a Sunni, was from one of the foremost families of Najd. His grandfather had ridden with Abdul Aziz in the early decades of the century, and other family members were among the foremost of the Muslim Brotherhood. Juhaiman said that his justification was that the Al Saud had lost its legitimacy through corruption, ostentation, and mindless imitation of the West (virtually an echo of his grandfather's charge in 1921 against Abdul Aziz). Juhaiman's accusations against the Saudi monarchy closely resembled Ayatollah Ruhollah Khomeini's diatribes against the shah. *(See Ref 82, 89)*

This takeover took the Saudi leadership by surprise and the government was stunned and appeared initially as paralised. The Grand Mosque surrounds the Kaaba, symbol of the oneness of God and believed by Muslims to have been built by the Prophet Abraham. The courtyard is one of the sites where the hajj, the fifth pillar of Islam, is enacted. Because of the holiness of the place, no non-Muslims may enter the city of Mecca. Furthermore, all holy places come under a special injunction in Islam. It is forbidden to shed blood there or to deface or to pollute them in any way. Despite careful planning on Juhaiman's part, a guard was shot dead by one of the nervous dissidents. Such a desecration is a major violation under Islamic law and merits crucifixion for the convicted offender. However, on the the government side, its initial attempts to rout the dissidents were stymied. Before any military move could be authorised, the ulama had to issue a dispensation to allow the bearing of arms in a holy place. When the religious problems were solved by announcement of the ulama's ruling, logistical problems bogged down the efforts of the military and the National Guard for several days. Finally, two weeks later the military effort succeeded, and the dissidents were dislodged. All the surviving males were eventually beheaded in the squares of four Saudi cities. However, the event was a turning point in the Islamic Awakening's evolution. Rather than use the opportunity to initiate long overdue political and social change, the regime chose to strengthen the religious establishment and pour additional money into religious institutions as a means of co-opting its critics and bolstering its legitimacy. The unintentional result was to strengthen the Islamists, which used their strong presence in the educational sector to take advantage of the increased funds. *(See Ref 82, 97)*

After two weeks on the siege of the Grand Mosque another event happened, that worried the regime most. Shia riots in al-Qatif in the Eastern Province errupted with many of the rioters bore posters with Khomeini's picture. Although these were not the first Shia protests in the kingdom (others had occurred in 1970 and 1978), the December rioters had become emboldened by Khomeini's triumphal return to Iran in early 1979. Up to 20,000 National Guard troops were immediately moved into the Eastern Province. Several demonstrators were killed and hundreds reportedly arrested.

In response to those events the Saudi leadership announced that a consultative assembly (majlis ash- shura) would soon be formed. The Shia disturbances in the Eastern Province encouraged the government to take a closer look at conditions there. Although it was clear that the Shia had been radicalised by Khomeini, it was also obvious that repression and imprisonment were stop-gap solutions and as likely to promote further resistance as to quell it. However, another violent Shia demonstration occurred in February 1980, and, although they were as harshly repressed as the previous ones, the Deputy Minister of Interior, Prince Ahmad ibn Abdul Aziz, was directed to draw up a comprehensive plan to improve the standard of living in Shia areas. His recommendations, which were immediately accepted and implemented, included an electrification project, swamp drainage, the construction of schools and a hospital, street lighting, and loans for home construction. *(See Ref 82, 89)*

The Saudi leadership began to take a more assertive role in the world after the troubles of 1979 and 1980. It obtained agreement in January 1981 for the kingdom to be the site of the meeting of the Organisation of the Islamic Conference. Hosting the conference of thirty-eight Muslim heads of state was seen as a vehicle for refurbishing the Saudi image of "guardian of the Islamic Holy Places." Shortly after the conference the Saudi leadership announced the formation of the Gulf Cooperation Council (GCC) project long favoured by Khalid who had been with Fahd campaigning actively for such an organisation for some time. The GCC included the six states of the peninsula that have similar political institutions, social conditions, and economic resources: Bahrain, Kuwait, Oman, Qatar, Saudi Arabia, and the United Arab Emirates. The aim of the GCC, as it was formally announced at its first summit in May 1981, was to coordinate and unify economic, industrial, and defence policies. *(See Ref 82, 89)*

In December 1981, following the GCC second summit meeting in Riyadh, Iranian-trained Shia attempted a coup d'état in Bahrain. Most of the insurgents, who were Shia from Kuwait and Saudi Arabia, were captured, reminding the Saudis of one of their worst-case scenarios. Work was speeded up on a causeway to connect Bahrain to the Saudi mainland, completed in 1986. The Saudis believed that given an emergency that the Bahrainis could not contain, the Saudi National Guard could use the causeway to provide support.

The strict financial policies of Khalid's predecessor, coupled with the aftermath of the 1973 oil crisis, created a financial windfall that fueled development and led to a commercial and economic boom in the country. Notable achievements included the institution of the second "Five-Year Plan" in Saudi history, which aimed to build up Saudi infrastructure and health care. King Khalid International Airport in Riyadh and King Khalid Military City were both named after him, and his reign is remembered fondly by Saudi citizens for the economic prosperity inaugurated during his reign. Unlike other Saudi kings, his children have assumed a low profile and hold no notable political positions.

Already the major spokesman for the Saudi regime, Fahd became even more active as Khalid's health steadily deteriorated. This visibility and experience stood him in good stead when Khalid died after a brief illness on June 14, 1982; he immediately assumed power and Abdallah, head of the National Guard, became crown prince. In 1986 he adopted the title of "Custodian of the two Holy Mosques", to signify an Islamic than secular authority. One of the first problems that the new king faced was a 20 percent drop in oil revenues, as a result of a world oil surplus that developed by 1982. Despite the fall in revenues, until the oil price crash of 1986 Saudi Arabia did not make significant changes in the oil policies that it had followed since the oil boom years of 1974 onward. However, the reduction in Saudi Arabia's wealth has not decreased its influence in the Arab world. The Kingdom and Fahd in particular, came to play a mediating role in inter-Arab conflicts. They continued, for instance, their efforts to stop the fighting in Lebanon. In 1989 King Fahd brought the entire Lebanese National Assembly, both Christian and Muslim deputies, to the Saudi resort city of At-Taif. At the time, the assembly had been unable to meet in Lebanon because of military clashes and political violence. Once in At-Taif, however, the Lebanese deputies voted on a plan for reform and were eventually able to elect a new president. Fahd's actions did not solve the problems in Lebanon, but they helped to end a particular stage of the conflict. *(See Ref 82, 89)*

Whilst Riyad has not been so fortunate in its relations with Tehran since Iran's Islamic Revolution in 1979, Fahd made a historic step toward Cairo when in November 1987, he re-established diplomatic relations with Egypt, and visited it in March 1989 where he was received an enthusiastic welcome on the streets of Cairo. His visit signified the end of Egypt's temporary isolation within the Arab world, but it demonstrated at the same time the important position that Saudi Arabia had achieved. Although Egypt was the country of Nasser, one of the most charismatic figures of the modern Arab world, it was the visit of a Saudi king that provided the ritual event to symbolise Egypt's return to the Arab family.

Although the king in Saudi Arabia is the only person who has the power to take big decisions, Fahd was very cautious to make any move concerning the liberalisation of the country, because at the other end of the political spectrum were the religious extremists, who opposed the import of Western institutions and Western values and resisted the liberals' idea of democracy. However despite these difficult circumstances, Fahd took several important decisions: for example, to invite Western forces into the kingdom to deal with the Kuwait crisis in 1990; to establish in 1993 the "Majlis ash-Shura" (consultative council), a step, however modest, towards the sharing of power; to issue warnings and even dismiss some of the more vehement religious officials. In these and other matters Fahd followed the policy of his predecessor and mentor, King Faisal: never get too far ahead of public opinion. He knew that the Saudi people are deeply conservative and, although his own instincts were probably more liberal, he believed that change must be gradual. A step could be taken, but then there must be a pause while the waters are tested. *(See Ref 80, 82, 89)*

Fahd was a good listener to his advisors, but he had a shrewdness of his own and a judgement acquired by the experience of conducting business at the highest level over a period of 40 years. However, he did not win the reverence that was granted to Faisal, nor had the warm affection in which Khalid was widely held. But he was affable and his authority was unchallenged until in recent years his health grew increasingly frail and he was obliged to withdraw from active administration. His half-brother Crown Prince Abdallah became in effect the regent after Fahd suffered a stroke in 1995, but deference to Fahd's kingship continued and all important decisions were referred to him for formal approval.

However, the problems posed by the Islamic extremists (which now include terrorist violence, stimulated by the Iraq affair, Afghanistan and by Osama bin Laden) have become more severe and are continued under the new king. Crown Prince Abdallah (who is only two years younger than Fahd) has taken over without dispute when Fahd died on 5 August 2005 and Prince Sultan, Minister of Defence and Fahd's full brother, became the new Crown Prince.

King Abdallah inherited a nation torn between fundamentalist Islamists and modernising reformers. The fundamentalists sometimes use terrorist acts (such as bombing and kidnapping) to express their anger. The modernisers increasingly use blogs and international pressure groups to call for increased women's rights, reform of shari'a-based laws, and greater press and religious freedoms.

So, why has Islamic extremism returned to Saudi Arabia and how is the Kingdom facing up to this challenge?

It has become clear to most political observers, after 11 September 2001, that the situation in Saudi Arabia had something wrong. It appeared that the house of Al Saud since early 1990s is at pains to address its profound crisis of legitimacy and performance, the overwhelming crisis of identity associated with modernity, the internal and external pressures for socio-economic reforms, and the complex and multi-faceted phenomenon of religious extremism. The Saudi monarchy is making efforts to navigate between the forces of reform and the conservative religious and cultural forces on which its legitimacy depends. However, Saudi society remains deeply conservative and the house of Al Saud seems to recognise the formidable challenge of reforming the state's religious institutions and its rigid politico-ideological agenda without alienating the conservative constituency.

According to the West, the Saudi's troubles are largely of the regime own making. It was its support for the Islamic fundamentalism since early 1980s that laid the groundwork for the surge of modern global terrorism. The state provided the Islamists with overall political guidance, and training for their activities. The Saudis funded mosques, Islamic study centres, universities and madrasas across the globe, to propagate their own Wahhabi version of Islam. Some experts believe that this policy was entrenched after the dangerous challenges of the Khomeini's Islamic Revolution in 1979. Afraid of suffering the same fate as the Pahlavi monarchy in Iran, the royal Saudi family empowered the religious establishment, granting it further financial incentives, significant concessions in social and religious matters, and a mandate to propagate Wahhabi ideology abroad, consequently the clerics enjoyed censorship power over the media. They successfully lobbied for more religious education in the schools and universities, and effectively barred women from TV, prohibited music in any media, and marginalised Shiites and other minorities. Furthermore, the state granted excessive powers to the "mutawa'a" (religious police), [the agents of the Committee for the Propagation of Virtue and the Prevention of Vice], whose main job is to patrol the streets and public settings to ensure compliance with Wahhabi prescriptions. *(See Ref 93)*

The Saudi royal family had little room for manoeuvre after 11 September, 2001. The involvement of 15 Saudis in the attacks on the World Trade Centre and the Pentagon, shook US public opinion and provoked accusations against Saudi Arabia, seen as the main exporter of Islamic terrorism, and consequently put the Kingdom into the spotlight. In the United States, a torrent of articles, books, television shows, documentaries, and congressional speeches vilified the Saudis' religious beliefs, social mores, cultural traditions, and every other conceivable aspect of their life. US journalists discovered to their amazement that the kingdom was not a democracy: that human rights were flouted and women were forced to wear veils. Influential voices in neo-conservative and Christian fundamentalist circles called for Saudi Arabia to be targeted after Iraq, and even for the country to be broken up, and for a Shia republic to be established in the eastern oil region. However, it is important to recognise that, though puritanical, contemptuous of modernity, and amenable to producing terrorists like bin Laden, Wahhabism is not terroristic in and of itself. Anwar Boukhari argues that depicting Wahhabism alone as the godfather of the new global terrorism is false and does not help much in tracing the deep roots of bin Ladenism. Calling Hezbollah and the Taliban "Wahhabised fringe groups," as some American critics do (such as Stephen Schwartz), is wrong. Furthermore as Anthony Cordesman put it, "Blaming Saudi beliefs, or Wahhabism, for the views and actions of most of today's Salafi extremists is a little like blaming Calvin for today's Christian extremists or Elijah for today's Jewish extremists." *(See Ref 93, 94, 96)*

However, the roots of the Islamic Awakening that gripped Saudi universities in the 1970s and 1980s, and the phenomenon of bin Ladenism since the 1990s lie deep. From the 1960s onwards, Saudi Arabia gradually expanded its contacts with the outside world, exposing its citizens to broader political debates at a time of regional radicalisation and politicisation. Moreover, Saudi Arabia became at that time home to elements of the radical Muslim Brotherhood of Egypt, Sudan, Jordan, and Syria. Seeking to shore up its Islamic credentials, the Saudi monarchy championed Islamic causes worldwide without seeming to appreciate that such a stance risked diluting its monopoly on Islamic interpretation. Far too often, the Saudis paid little attention to the radical brand of Islam advanced by legions of teachers coming from Egypt. Fleeing political persecution at home, Muslim Brotherhood members found refuge in the Saudi educational system and large Saudi charities, like the Muslim World League, where they built up strength, laying the groundwork for the development of a new hybrid, best exemplified by Sayyid Qutb. He fled to Saudi Arabia and along with Abdallah Azzam, one of the heads of the Muslim Brotherhood from Jordan (but of Palestinian origin), taught at King Abdul Aziz University in Jeddah, where Osama bin Laden was their student at the time. For regional geopolitical reasons, Saudi Arabia welcomed these Islamic scholars to foster religious education and help offset the ideological assaults of Arab nationalism, communism, socialism, and leftism. *(See Ref 93, 97, 98)*

Since its creation Saudi Arabia's legitimacy was built on Islam. Any challenges emerging that could threaten that legitimacy would lead to a quick counteract by the monarchy in advocating pan-Islamism. Riyadh used the Muslim Brotherhood's politicised version of Islam as a weapon in its political-ideological dispute with Nasserist and Baa'thist neighbours. According to a Saudi Islamist who was then a student, "most of the books that could be found in bookshops in the 1970s were written by members of the Brotherhood". However, the challenge to Saudi Islamic credibility in the late 1970s was of a different kind to that posed by Baa'thist and Nasserist Arab nationalism, and once again the Saudi monarchy reacted, perhaps unwittingly, by accelerating radical religious and Islamic awakening. This Saudi policy helped spur a boom in a new generation of sheikhs, professors, and students influenced by Egyptian Muslim Brotherhood's ideology to counter the menace of Shiism coming from neighbouring Iran where the Islamic revolution posed a direct challenge to the house of Al Saud. Ayatollah Khomeini challenged the Islamic credentials of the Saudi monarchy, accusing it of being an agent for the enemies of Islam and stirring the Shiite minority to rebel against the regime. As has been the case since the founding of the modern Saudi state in 1932, the regime has rebuffed threats to its stability by proving itself to be more Islamic than its detractors, but in the process it helped produce, though unintentionally, a radical, non-official, Saudi Islam even while making efforts to suppress it. *(See Ref 93, 97)*

The Salafist doctrine in Saudi Arabia entered a new stage with the Jihad against the Soviet Union in Afghanistan in 1980s, which was actively encouraged and facilitated by the regime at that time, because it sought to deflect its homegrown militants from domestic agitation by sending them off to fight the Soviets.In addition to logistical and financial assistance offered by the government to prospective mujahideen - for example, subsidised flights to Pakistan - the official religious establishment declared it a collective duty (fard kifayah) for Muslims to fight in Afghanistan. For most of them - typically teenagers - participation was purely symbolic; the trip seldom lasted more than the summer holidays, and many never made it across the border from Pakistan to Afghanistan. But for those who stayed, the experience was profoundly transformative, as they became part of the romanticised culture of violent resistance that flourished within the Arab contingent of the Afghan mujahideen war.It is there that Osama bin Laden became well versed with the Muslim Brotherhood ideology that would transform the concept of jihad in the modern world. In Afghanistan bin Laden and other Saudi mujahideen fought alongside jihadists inspired by the ideologies of al- Mawdudi, Qutb, and their intellectual heirs, Palestinian-Jordanian scholar, Abdallah Azzam, Dr. Ayman al-Zawahiri, and the blind sheikh Omar Abdul Rahman. Abdallah Azzam dubbed the "gatekeeper of the Jihad" and the "Emir of Jihad" had a PhD in fiqh (Islamic jurisprudence) and was credited with being a masterful guerrilla organiser. He recruited Arab mujahideen and built the international network that Osama bin Laden, the late Mohammad Atef, and Ayman al-Zawahiri would turn into al-Qa'ida. *(See Ref 93, 97)*

Two consequences resulted from the jihad in Afghanistan. First, these militants developed a highly militaristic, violent worldview; secondly, they experienced their initial political awakening outside their country. Once the fighting was over and it was time to go back to Saudi Arabia. Some veterans got on with their lives, but others returned home brainwashed by a militaristic ideology steeped in an international jihadist culture that is hostile to Western-influenced Arab governments. Unlike their Egyptian and Syrian counterparts who had their religious or political awakening grafted from inside their countries long before they landed in Afghanistan, most Saudi veterans had their formative years in Afghanistan where their political, social, and religious views were molded. These foreign-born views stood in sharp contrast to the ones promoted by the retrograde but non-political Wahhabi religious school.

The 1990-91 Gulf War which brought American and other Coalition troops to stand guard over Islam's holiest sites, was the most critical event in the history of Saudi Islamism and helps explain subsequent domestic politics. Riyadh responded to Iraq's August 1990 invasion of Kuwait by inviting a U.S.-led multinational force to be stationed on its territory which was a cataclysmic event for a number of Saudis who were shocked by the kingdom's inability to protect itself after having spent billions of dollars on arms. The Jihad Movement epitomised by the Afghan veterans and "the Islamic Awakening" (al-Sahwa al-Islamiya) faction led by Salman al-Awda and Safar al-Hawali delivered fervent sermons criticising the state for allowing an army of infidels on Saudi soil; consequently their popularity skyrocketed and huge numbers of their tapes circulated throughout the Kingdom. For both groups the Gulf War laid bare the incompetence of a corrupt regime that was subservient to the United States. But while the Afghan veterans called for armed struggle against the monarchy and its security forces, the al-Sahwa leaders never openly advocated the overthrow of the Saudi regime. *(See Ref 93, 97)*

However, In March 1991, the two Sheikhs al-Awdah and al-Hawali played a major role in formulating a 12-point "Letter of Demands", [which was made public contrary to the established norm in the Kingdom, and signed by over 400 of prominent religious scholars, judges, and intellectuals], was presented to king Fahd through the late Sheikh Abdul Aziz Bin Baz, the kingdom's grand mufti.This extraordinary manifesto of radical change called for a broad reform program, including the reform of religious institutions, the formation of a consultative council, the creation of an independent judiciary, and the enforcement of accountability rules for all officials. In July 1992, the al-Sahwa leaders and 107 religious scholars drafted an even bolder and comprehensive 46-page "Memorandum of Advice." Islamists formulated two sets of demands: for rule of law, political participation and respect of human rights (as defined by the shari'a); and for strengthened control by religious institutions over state and society. The official clerical establishment and the national media were quick to denounce the memorandum and those who refused to do so were dismissed. *(See Ref 93, 97)*

The Gulf war triggered a process whereby Islamists, especially jihadists (led by Osama bin Laden who was Sahwist at the begining), were both more critical of the Saudi regime and more openly hostile to the U.S. They became more organised than ever before, and their demands became bolder and more far-reaching. King Fahd's hesitant, conciliatory gestures did not help quell the mounting challenge to the regime. The formation of an appointed non-legislative consultative council and the delegation of more power to provincial governments only intensified the Islamists' drive for radical change. However, Some Islamists used violence to make their voices heard, the most spectacular signs of such acts occurred in the mid-1990s with attacks on U.S. targets. On 13 November 1995, a car bomb exploded at a Saudi National Guard facility in central Riyadh, killing five Americans and two Indians and injuring 60. On 22 April 1996, four suspects confessed on Saudi television; they were executed a month later. To date, there is no hard evidence of bin Laden's involvement; the widespread assumption that al-Qa'ida was involved appears to be based essentially on the fact that he praised the militants in subsequent interviews. However, the June 1996 bombing of the U.S. barracks in Khobar that killed nineteen Americans and injured almost 400 people of various nationalities is shrouded in even greater mystery. Although Saudi authorities claim to have sentenced several individuals in connection with it, the perpetrators' identities have never been established, and a considerable debate remains over whether it was carried out by an al-Qa'ida affiliate or an Iranian-sponsored Shiite group. *(See Ref 93, 97)*

To respond to Islamists' violent acts and political pressure the Saudi authorities follow a two-track strategy of repression and division. They targeted dissenting forces, utilising a policy of divide and rule along with inducements to groups willing to repent and cooperate. This assault on rebel Islamists, coupled with selective harassment of political opponents, became the order of the day, creating further political instability and a huge potential for mischief. By mid-1990s, virtually all the most influential sahwist leaders had been imprisoned or forced into exile in the UK. The "London-based Opposition" maintained some influence on politics, distributing leaflets and books through an underground network; over time, however, it suffered from internal wrangling and its distance from the country. With all the major "sahwist" leaders behind bars or in exile, the debate over the politics of compromise shifted dramatically toward the extreme fringe. By the mid 1995, the radicals seemed poised to impose their militaristic platform and revolutionary, "takfiri" (excommunication) ideology. A number of "al-Sahwa" leaders and followers joined the trend of Salafist Jihad though many others did not. The new converts to the jihadists' ideology joined the battle set by Osama bin Laden. Many went to Afghanistan, the Balkans, Central Asia, and Chechnya to join a jihadi contingent recruited by al-Qa'ida-aligned operatives in Jordan, Syria, Egypt, and other countries in the Middle East and beyond. Other Saudi jihadists sympathetic to al-Qa'ida remained at home devising their own set of goals that linked broadly with the supreme military and political goal of the wider multinational network of jihadists, they launched the al-Qa'ida in the Arabian Peninsula (AQAP). As a homegrown terror network, they drew inspiration from the global ideology of hatred, and that is where the connection probably ends between international and local jihadists. The latter's support comes mainly from a variety of local sources brainwashed by the ideology of militant Islam and/or disenchanted with the regime's failure to deliver economic opportunity or political freedom. *(See Ref 93, 97)*

The Saudi regime continued its strategy which was revolved around aggressive law enforcement, deterrence, and antiterrorism operations. Many of those suspected of being involved were arrested or killed in clashes with Saudi police and security forces. And on the other side a steps of change and liberalisation were taken by the new monarch.

Shortly after assuming the throne six years ago, King Abdallah declared that henceforth September 23rd, the anniversary of Saudi Arabia's unification in 1932 would be an official holiday. The move proved wildly popular with ordinary Saudis, and not only because it gives them a rare excuse to do silly things in public, like sporting neon wigs and cruising about noisily in green-painted cars decked with the Saudi flag. Conservatives had long banned secular festivities such as birthdays, insisting that Islam forbids anything but religious holidays. The king's defiance of this view seemed to augur a break from decades of deference by the ruling Al Saud dynasty to killjoy puritans.

Furthermore, in March 2009 the king has moved to show the ultra-conservative Saudi religious establishment quite literally who is in charge. He made reshuffle in his government which was a full-scale assault on those Islamists who have locked up the country's education and justice systems. More than three years after becoming king, Abdallah has moved to confront the challenge of a huge youth demographic that, if not provided with modern schooling and jobs, could become tinder for movements like Al-Qa'ida.

"These are radical and fundamental changes, which the Saudis have hoped for for a long time," said Abdallah Al-Oteibi, a specialist on Islamist groups. In his sweeping shake-up which was announced on February 14,

2009, the king replaced four cabinet ministers, notably those for justice and education, and the head of nearly every key justice-related body. These institutions included the Supreme Judicial Council, the Ulama Council of the highest clerics, the consultative Shura Council, the Supreme Court, and Umm al-Qura, the Islamic university in Mecca. *(See Ref 103)*

While sacking the feared chief of the religious police and naming Saudi Arabia's first-ever woman to ministerial rank grabbed the headlines, analysts say his education and justice changes were far more important. "What the king has done is pretty amazing," said Christopher Boucek, an expert on Saudi Arabia at the Carnegie Endowment for International Peace in Washington. "The king has been trying to force his will, the government's will on institutions that had been working independently". However his education appointments show Abdallah's seriousness in reforming a bureaucracy where conservatives had stymied efforts to bring curriculums into the 21st century, rid textbooks of passages demonising non-Muslims, and provide ample opportunities for women. According to The Saudi political scientist Turki al-Hamad, the education system "had been dominated by radicals who were responsible for ideas of intolerance and extremism being taught to students". *(See Ref 103)*

The new Education Minister Prince Faisal is the king's son-in-law, whose previous job was number two in the intelligence directorate. His wife is Princess Adila, a leading force for women's rights and opportunities, modern education and health services and protection of children. Named Deputy Minister Faisal bin Mu'ammar was royal adviser, who ran the Centre for National Dialogue which the king has cannily used to raise and debate reform issues and thus identify capable reformers and points of resistance. And the new Deputy Education Minister, Norah Al-Fayez, who became the highest-ranking female official in the country's history, is a veteran educationalist who has also fostered some of the agenda identified with Princess Adila. All of them have years of experience dealing with the education system, a western expert in Riyadh said. "Now they know the structure and what are the problems" he added. Ultimately, experts believe, Abdallah is completely conscious of the challenge of providing livings to a growing population that in 2006 was 33 percent aged 15 or less, and that requires education and jobs in modern industries to ensure future stability. *(See Ref 103)*

The king also took drastic measures to change the justice system that was almost completely controlled by clerics with free rein to interpret Islamic texts and tradition. This left the system with no formal body of precedents, inconsistent definitions of crime and inconsistent punishments. It also allowed judges to ignore recently drafted laws on court procedure and defendants' rights.The main replacement was of Sheikh Saleh Al-Luhaidan, head of the Supreme Judicial Council for more than four decades. The new head of the Council is the outgoing leader of the legislature-like Shura Council Saleh bin Humaid who played a big role to advance the king's program. The new Shura leader is the outgoing Justice Minister Sheikh Abdullah Al-Sheikh, another royal confidant whose job is to guide the council in crafting legal reforms.

Meanwhile a relative progressive was named to lead the Ulama Council, which will also include, for the first time, representatives of all four Sunni schools of religious law. Previously only the ultra-conservative Hanbali's school which dominates the Saudi version of Islam was represented. Analysts believe the abruptness of Abdallah's shake-up came only after years of cautious study of what he wanted to do, and after making his general agenda known and watching what happened. The king is "attacking rigidity of thought" in the government, said one westerner who has followed Saudi politics for years. "He wanted to change the policies and the people did not do it for him." *(See Ref 103)*

Saudi Arabia has certainly grown less grim in the reign of King Abdallah. Reforms in state administration, education and law have loosened arcane strictures. Some arch-conservative clerics have been ousted from top posts and forbidden from proclaiming obscurantist fatwas. The notoriously intrusive religious police have been told to curb their enthusiasm. Women have won slightly more freedom. The large Shia minority feels a little less shunned than it was under previous kings. The press is also allowed marginally more freedom.

Many of these changes are subtle, reflecting shifts in society as much as in policy. The Economist reported on September 30, 2010 that last Ramadan (2010) for instance, "Tash Ma Tash," a top-rated Saudi television comedy, took a dig at national hypocrisies towards sex and religion. One sketch showed a fictional wife behaving like a pampered Saudi man, deciding to dump one of her four husbands because she wanted a sexier new one. Another portrayed two brothers meeting a long-lost Lebanese relative and being shocked to find that he was not only a Christian priest, but actually a nice guy. Some conservatives attacked the show as insidious infidel propaganda, and threatened to prosecute its makers. But most public reactions were enthusiastic, and the fact that the show received no official reprimand, as it had done in previous years, is a sign of progress. *(See Ref 101)*

Yet the changes remain, in many ways, cosmetic. King Abdallah has championed international dialogue between religions, for instance. But when Saudi schools reopened in September (2010), parents were surprised to find that in the new, "reformed" religion curriculum, supposedly purged of bigotry as part of a post-September 11th initiative to promote a more tolerant Islam, still taught students that it is wrong to greet non-Muslims. Furthermore, a recent report on political reform in Saudi Arabia by Human Rights Watch, a New York-based lobby group, argues that although gradual changes are welcome, unless they are properly institutionalised the kingdom risks sliding backwards again, as it has done many times before. "Newly gained freedoms are, for the most part, neither extensive nor firmly grounded," the report concludes. "The limited reform that has taken place suggests the elite are still floating trial balloons, undecided about the type of government and society it wants to steer towards." *(See Ref 102)*

On some specific human-rights issues, the report praises the kingdom's progress: reform of the justice system, women's rights and freedom of expression. Yet it notes with concern that, whereas legal reform is one of the areas where changes are under way, new courts have yet to materialise, and new, transparent procedures have yet to be put into practice. Greater freedom of speech is not codified, and so remains subject to arbitrary intervention by the state. Earlier this year, a newspaper editor made the mistake of printing a blunt critique of puritan religious beliefs, and was summarily fired. As for women's rights, an official loosening of the ban against the mixing of the sexes in public places has not been widely implemented. The same goes for an ostensible liberalisation of rules that require women to have a male "guardian". Women are still forbidden to drive.

As for other issues, the report discerns no real progress either in ending religious discrimination against the Shia minority or in improving the position of Saudi Arabia's estimated 8m immigrant labourers. Gestures of tolerance to the Shia by the king himself have not been matched by a relaxation of restrictions on Shia worship. Shia dissidents still face harsh, systematic repression. Most foreign workers lack basic rights and, unlike many other Gulf countries, Saudi Arabia has taken no steps to abolish the onerous kafala or sponsorship system, whereby Saudi employers take possession of expatriates' passports, and can deny them the right to travel.

King Abdallah understands the urgency of reforms, but he is mindful of the regime's religious base and the hardliners within the monarchy who are more adverse to change. Prince Naif Ibn Abdul Aziz, Minister of Interior, and his supporters seem to favour a militaristic solution to the jihadist problem. They see political and social reforms as too risky to implement at this stage of national mobilisation as they may antagonise their conservative power base and detract from the regime's main priority of defeating the terrorists. There is some truth to this viewpoint and its advocates might feel vindicated by their relative successes on the battlefield and the support they drew from unofficial but popular religious critics. There is also some truth to the fact that an opening of the system might most benefit the radical Islamists. After all, there is considerable support for bin Laden's ideas, though not necessarily for his methods or designs, throughout the kingdom. Yet, while there is disagreement as to how far to go with change within the socio-cultural realm, there is an emerging consensus among a wide spectrum of society, including the religious conservatives, on the necessity of moving quickly and aggressively to reform governance issues.

Notwithstanding their differences of view and approach, most if not all senior members of the royal family agree on the need to implement some reforms and most of all eliminate zealous jihadists in the same fashion that the country's founder, King Abdul Aziz, battled the zealous warrior Muslim Brotherhood and crushed their rebellion in 1929. Now, as then, the state has to enforce its will and thus break the forces of extremism. However, the monarchy understands that to lead effectively it needs to bring harmony and balance to the desparate voices and needs of the kingdom's natural constituencies. The majority of Saudis remain attached to conservative religious values and the Saudi regime realises that any opening of the system entails marginalising radical, violent forces without simultaneously alienating the broader conservative constituency. There is a general awareness of the role the religious establishment can play as a veritable bulwark against jihadism and the forces supporting it. In times of crisis the country's religious establishment rose to the challenge and bolstered the regime's response to radical threats to the kingdom's stability.

However, contemporary Saudi Arabia is grappling with fundamental issues of religion and modernity, development and dependency, political oppression and cultural turmoil, social frustration and institution building. There is a battle under way in Saudi Arabia; a battle for social, political, and religious reforms. Whether the country can come together to reconcile the principles of tradition with modernity is still difficult to tell but the failure to develop stable religious and political institutions capable of dealing with the challenges of development and economic changes could be disatrous. Like any other society under attack with heavy domestic and international pressure to reform, the regime is at pains to advance social and political reforms without undermining domestic stability. As it is engaged in a fight against a violent, radical Islamic movement that accuses it of deviation from the path of Islam, the regime is loathe to threaten its relations with religious forces that both oppose violence and enjoy popular legitimacy. The challenge, therefore, would appear to be to marginalise the more radical, violent forces without simultaneously alienating the broader conservative constituency.

The road to reforms is fraught with dangers. The house of Al Saud has waited so long to initiate the most basic of reforms that any path they take entails substantial risk. The rulers' advanced age certainly complicates succession matters. Furthermore, they must find it extremely difficult to break with their life long inertia and engage in these necessary but radical reforms. However, maybe the last demonstrations in Saudi Eastern provinces and the uprisings in neighbouring Bahrain, Yemen, and other Arab countries will give king Abdallah the necessary incentive and the urgency to make the needed reforms.

CHAPTER FIVE

AFGHANISTAN: THE "GREAT GAME"

The strategic location of Afghanistan has played a very important role in shaping its history. Its position astride the land routes between the Indian subcontinent, Iran, and central Asia has always enticed conquerors. Its high mountains, although hindering unity, helped the hill tribes to preserve their independence. Although the archeological records are not clear, some historians believe that, it is probable there were well-developed civilisations in South Afghanistan in prehistoric times.Excavation of ancient sites by Louis Dupree, the University of Pennsylvania, the Smithsonian Institution and others suggests that humans were living in what is now Afghanistan at least 5,000 years ago, and that farming communities of the area were among the earliest in the world.Certainly cultures had flourished in the north and east before the Persian king Darius I (c.500 B.C.) conquered these areas. Later, Alexander the Great (329-323 B.C.) conquered them on his way to India. After Alexander's death the region at first was part of the Seleucid Empire. In the north, Bactria became independent, and the south was acquired by the Maurya dynasty. Bactria expanded southward but fell (mid-2nd century B.C.) to the Parthians and rebellious tribes (notably the Saka). Buddhism was introduced from the east by the Yüechi, who founded the Kushan dynasty (early 2nd century B.C.). Their capital was Peshawar. The Kushans declined (3rd century A.D.) and were supplanted by the Sassanids, the Ephthalites, and the Turkish Tu-Kuie. *(Most historic information in this chapter came from Ref 104, 105, 106, 107, 108)*

In the 7th Century the Muslims conquered Afghanistan and several short-lived Muslim dynasties were founded. The most powerful of them had its capital at Ghazna. Mahmoud of Ghazna, who conquered the lands from Khorasan in Iran to the Punjab in India early in the 11th century, was the greatest of Afghanistan's rulers. Jenghiz Khan (1220) and Timur (late 14th century) were subsequent conquerors of renown. Babur, a descendant of Timur, used Kabul as the base for his conquest of India and the establishment of the Mughal Empire in the 16th century. In the 18th century the Persian Nadir Shah extended his rule to North of the Hindu Kush. After his death (1747) his lieutenant, Ahmad Shah, an Afghan tribal leader, established a united state covering most of present-day Afghanistan. His dynasty, the Durrani, gave the Afghans the name (Durrani) that they themselves frequently use.

Collision between the expanding British and Russian Empires significantly influenced Afghanistan during the 19th century in what was termed "The Great Game". British concern over Russian advances in Central Asia and growing influence in Persia culminated in two Anglo-Afghan wars and "The Siege of Herat" 1837–1838, in which the Persians, trying to retake Afghanistan and throw out the British and Russians, sent armies into the country and fought the British mostly around and in the city of Herat. The first war (1839–1842) resulted in the destruction of a British army; it is remembered as an example of the ferocity of Afghan resistance to foreign rule. The second Anglo-Afghan war (1878–1880) was sparked by Emir Shir Ali's refusal to accept a British mission in Kabul. This conflict brought Emir Abdul Rahman Shah to the Afghan throne. During his reign (1880–1901), the British and Russians officially established the boundaries of what would become modern Afghanistan in 1881. The borders of the nation cut through the ancestral territories of almost all the ethnic groups concerned. The ground work for endless ethnic strife and porous borders was thus set up from the beginning. The question of legitimacy of Durand Line agreement is the root cause of the fears about borders in both Pakistan and Afghanistan. The Pashtun nation is divided between the two states, Afghanistan and Pakistan as per historical account given by Christian Parenti. He further explained that the foundation was laid in 1893, when Afghanistan was separated from British India by a Durand Line, drawn up by Morimer Drand and forced upon Abdul Rahman Khan, the "Iron Emir" of Afghnistan. The Durand Line's main political impact was to divide "Pashtunistan" and thus give it an imaginary life in the minds of the Pashtun nationalists. In Afghanistan Pashtuns are the dominant ethnic group while on the other side of the border, in Pakistan, Pashtuns are minority representing about 16 percent of the population. The last thing for Pakistan was to see the linkage of Pakistani minority Pashtuns with strong Afghani Pashtun rulers, as Pakistan always wanted Afghanistan to remain weak to dominate Afghan consumer markets and to receive water from Afghanistan's Kabul and Kunar rivers. *(See Ref 106)*

Afghanistan is a heterogeneous nation with a population estimated at 29 million, in which there are four major ethnic groups: The Pashtuns - from whom Afghanistan's traditional rulers have come - constitute 52 percent of the population. The Hazaras are 19 percent of the population. The Tajiks in the north constitute 21 percent; Uzbeks, also in the north, 5 percent. Numerous other minor ethnic groups (Nuristanis, Baluchis, Turkmens, Arabs, etc.) also call Afghanistan their home. While the majority of Afghans (99%) belong to the Islamic faith from which about 85 percent are Sunni Muslim, there are also small pockets of Sikhs, Hindus and even some Jews. The official languages of the country are Pashtu and Dari (Afghan Persian). The capital of Afghanistan is Kabul, which throughout history, was admired by many great figures, such as the great Central Asian conqueror, Zahirudeen Babur. Unfortunately, due to many years of war, this great city has been shattered and nearly destroyed. *(See Ref 106, 111)*

However, Afghanistan survived as a medieval island in the modern world, characterised by backwardness and extreme poverty. In the postwar period, some changes began to occur as a result of foreign aid from the USSR and, to a lesser extent, the U.S., which were vying for influence during the Cold War. Power shifted toward the state, and an educated middle class began to emerge. But industry still barely existed.

In the early 1970s the country was beset by serious economic problems, particularly a severe long-term drought in the center and north. Maintaining that King Muhammad Zahir Shah - who succeeded his father Muhammad Nadir Khan (1929-1933) when he was 19 years old - had mishandled the economic crisis and in addition was stifling political reform, Lieutenant General Sardar Muhammad Daud Khan, the king's cousin seized power in a non-violent coup on July 17, 1973, while Zahir Shah was receiving treatment for eye problems and therapy for lumbago in Italy. Daoud abolished the monarchy, abrogated the 1964 constitution, and declared Afghanistan a republic with himself as its first President and Prime Minister. His attempts to carry out badly-needed economic and social reforms met with little success, and the new constitution promulgated in February 1977 failed to quell chronic political instability. Meanwhile, Daud began to collaborate more closely with the Shah of Iran. Lower-level officials and members of the middle class grew increasingly discontented. On 27 April 1978, the pro-Soviet People's Democratic Party of Afghanistan (PDPA), led by Nur Mohammad Taraki, Babrak Karmal and Amin Taha overthrew the government of Muhammad Daoud, who was assassinated along with all his family members in a bloody military coup. The coup became known as the Saur Revolution. On May the first, the well-known novelist Taraki became President, Prime Minister and General Secretary of the PDPA. The country was then renamed the Democratic Republic of Afghanistan (DRA), and the PDPA regime lasted, in some form or another, until April 1992.

Within a few months following the coup, a broad ruling coalition was set up, controlled by the "Khalqi" the radical group of the PDPA's two factions. Khalqi pushed Babrak Karmal and other members of the rival Parcham faction in PDPA out of the government. Karmal was made ambassador to Prague, and other Parchami were also given diplomatic posts. The new government lacked any social base outside Kabul, and its program of reforms soon provoked a popular backlash. The Kabul regime was completely isolated from the bulk of the population who lived in the countryside causing substantial political disconnect. *(See Ref 114)*

In March 1979, Hafizullah Amin took over as prime minister, retaining the position of field marshal and becoming vice-president of the Supreme Defence Council. Taraki remained President and in control of the Army. On 14 September, Amin overthrew Taraki, who was killed. Amin stated that "the Afghans recognise only crude force." Afghanistan expert Amin Saikal writes: "As his powers grew, so apparently did his gravings for personal dictatorship ... and his vision of the revolutionary process based on terror." *(See Ref 115)*

Once in power, the PDPA implemented a liberal and marxist-leninist agenda. It moved to replace religious and traditional laws with secular and marxist-leninist ones. Men were obliged to cut their beards, women couldn't wear a chador, and mosques were placed off limits. The PDPA made a number of reforms on women's rights, banning forced marriages, giving state recognition of women's right to vote, and introducing women to political life. However, the Marxist-leninist and secular nature of the government as well as its heavy dependence on the Soviet Union made it unpopular with a majority of the Afghan population. Repressions plunged large parts of the country, especially the rural areas, into open revolt against the new Marxist-leninist government. By spring 1979 unrests had reached 24 out of the 28 Afghan provinces including major urban areas. Over half of the Afghan army would either desert or join the insurrection. Although the resistance was spontaneous, but soon came to be led by an alliance of conservative Islamic groups who referred to themselves as "mujahideen" (Islamic warriors). On March 24, 1979 a garrison of soldiers in Herat killed a group of Soviet advisers (and their families) who were responsible for ordering Afghan troops to fire on anti-government demonstrators. From this point, the regime was no longer merely isolated from peasants in the countryside, but divided by open hostility from an overwhelming majority of the people in general. The regime had no choice now but to crush much of the population... Prime Minister Hafizullah Amin's secret police and a repressive civilian police force went into action across Afghanistan, and army troops were sent into the countryside to subdue "feudal" villagers. *(See Ref 114)*

Government repression was severe. "Mass arrests were commonly followed by torture and execution without trial. Police terror was common in the city as well as the countryside, where virtually all social groups joined in the rebellion." The rebels' tactics were equally brutal. The "Washington Post" reported that the mujahideen liked to "torture victims by first cutting off their noses, ears, and genitals, then removing one slice of skin after another." *(See Ref 116)*

In the meantime, the United States saw the situation as a prime opportunity to weaken the Soviet Union. As part of a Cold War strategy, in July 1979 the United States government (under President Jimmy Carter and National Security Advisor Zbigniew Brezinski) began to covertly fund and train anti-government Mujahideen forces through the Pakistani secret service known as Inter Services Intelligence (ISI).

As the situation got out of control, the Soviets advised President Taraki to dismiss Prime Minister Hafizullah Amin, reunite with Parcham (the moderate faction of the PDPA, which became later in 1992 Watan Party), and adopt a policy of "democratic nationalism." But Amin got wind of the plan and arrested Taraki in September, assassinating him soon afterward. Amin was now in the position of publicly accusing the Russians of plotting to overthrow the Afghan government while being totally dependent on Soviet military and economic support. *(See Ref 114)*

However, the hard-liners in Moscow who did not like the Afghani Prime Minister's action decided that Amin had to go. They believed that he could be removed by a dramatic show of force and quietly replaced by Babrak Karmal. The Soviet Union decided to intervene on December 24, 1979, when the Red Army invaded its southern neighbour with a force of 5,000 Soviet troops which advanced on Kabul, but Amin refused to leave office quietly and fought back. On December 28, "after twelve hours of bitter combat with Soviet forces at the presidential palace, Amin was killed, along with 2,000 loyal members of his armed forces." Having killed the man whom they claimed had invited them into the country the Russians proclaimed Karmal to be president and flew him back from Moscow. Within a few days, the number of Soviet troops in Afghanistan had reached 80,000. The figure later climbed to more than 100,000. What was to be nearly a decade of Russian occupation had begun. However, On May 4, 1986, under pressure from the Soviet Union, Babrak Karmal resigned as secretary general of the PDPA and was replaced by Dr. Muhammed Najibullah. Karmal retained the presidency for a while, but power had shifted to Najibullah who became president in November 1986. *(See Ref 115)*

President Jimmy Carter immediately declared that the invasion had jeopardized vital U.S. interests, because the Persian Gulf area was "now threatened by Soviet troops in Afghanistan". But the Carter administration's public outrage at Russian intervention in Afghanistan was doubly duplicitous. Not only it was used as an excuse for a program of increased military expenditure that had in fact already begun, but the U.S. had in fact been aiding the mujahideen for at least the previous six months, with precisely the hope of provoking a Soviet response. Former CIA director Robert Gates (now Obama's Secretary of Defence) later admitted in his memoirs "From the Shadows" (1996) that aid to the rebels began in June 1979. In a candid 1998 interview, Zbigniew Brezinski, Carter's national security adviser, confirmed that U.S. aid to the rebels began before the invasion: "According to the official version of history, CIA aid to the mujahideen began during 1980, that is to say, after the Soviet army invaded Afghanistan in December 1979. But the reality, secretly guarded until now, is completely otherwise: indeed, it was July 3, 1979, that President Carter signed the first directive for secret aid to the opponents of the pro-Soviet regime in Kabul. And that very day, I wrote a note to the president in which I explained to him that in my opinion this aid was going to induce a Soviet military intervention... We didn't push the Russians to intervene, but we knowingly increased of drawing the Russians into the Afghan trap... The day that the Soviets officially crossed the border, I wrote to

President Carter: We now have the opportunity of giving to the USSR its Vietnam War." *(See Ref 114, 117)*

However, the Russian invasion in December was the signal for U.S. support to the Afghan rebels to increase dramatically. So, Three weeks later after Soviet tanks rolled into Kabul, Carter's secretary of defence, Harold Brown, was in Beijing arranging for a weapons transfer from the Chinese to the ClA-backed Afghani troops mustered in Pakistan. The Chinese, who were generously compensated for the deal, agreed and even consented to send military advisers. Brown worked out a similar arrangement with Egypt to buy $15 million worth of weapons. "The U.S. contacted me," then-Egyptian president Anwar Sadat recalled shortly before his assassination in 1981. "They told me, Please open your stores for us so that we can give the Afghans the armaments they need to fight. And I gave them the armaments. The transport of arms to the Afghans started from Cairo on U.S. planes." By February 1980, the "Washington Post" reported that the mujahideen was receiving arms courtesy of the U.S. government. *(See Ref 114, 118)*

The mujahideen consisted of at least seven factions, who often fought amongst themselves in their battle for territory and control of the opium trade. To hurt the Russians, the U.S. deliberately chose to give the most support to the most extreme groups. A disproportionate share of U.S. arms went to Gulbuddin Hekmatyar, "a particularly fanatical Islamic fundamentalist extremist and woman-hater." According to journalist Tim Weiner, "Hekmatyar's followers first gained attention by throwing acid in the faces of women who refused to wear the veil. CIA and State Department officials I have spoken with call him scary, vicious, a fascist, definite dictatorship material." However, there was, though, some method to the madness: Brezinski hoped not only to drive the Russians out of Afghanistan, but to ferment unrest within the Soviet Union itself. His plan, says author Dilip Hiro, was "to export a composite ideology of nationalism and Islam to the Muslim-majority in Central Asian states and Soviet Republics with a view to destroying the Soviet order." Looking back in 1998, Brezinski had no regrets. "What was more important in the world view of history? A few stirred-up Muslims or the liberation of Central Europe and the end of the Cold War?" *(See Ref 119)*

The U.S. began recruiting and training mujahideen fighters, with the support of Pakistan's military dictator, General Zia-ul-Haq, from the 3 million Afghan refugees in Pakistan and large numbers of mercenaries from other Islamic countries. Estimates of how much money the U.S. government channeled to the Afghan rebels over the next decade vary, but most sources put the figure between $3 billion and $6 billion, but potentially more. Whatever the exact amount, this was "the largest covert action program since World War II" - much bigger, for example, than Washington's intervention in Central America at the same time, which received considerably more publicity. Furthermore the CIA, according to one report, became the grand coordinator: purchasing or arranging the manufacture of Soviet-style weapons from Egypt, China, Poland, Israel and elsewhere, or supplying their own; arranging for military training by Americans, Egyptians, Chinese and Iranians; soliciting Middle-Eastern countries for donations, notably Saudi Arabia which gave many hundreds of millions of dollars in aid each year, totaling probably more than a billion; presuring and bribing Pakistan to rent out its country as a military staging area and sanctuary. This reached the extent that the former Pakistani Director of Military Operations, Brigadier Mian Muhammad Afzal, was put onto the CIA payroll to ensure Pakistani cooperation. *(See Ref 114)*

When Ronald Reagan became president in 1981, he found the Democratic-controlled Congress eager to help the mujahideen and increase spending on the Afghan war. As such aid to the mujahideen, who Reagan praised as "freedom fighters," increased however initially Afghanistan was not a priority.

In the first years after the Reagan administration inherited the Carter program, the covert Afghan war "tended to be handled out of CIA director William Casey's back pocket," Essentially, under Bill Casey, the CIA created a three-part intelligence alliance to fund and arm the mujahideen, initially to harass Soviet occupation forces and eventually they embraced the goal of driving them out. The three-way alliance in each of the parties had a distinct role to play. The Saudi, their intelligence service primarily provided cash. Each year the congress would secretly allocate a certain amount of money to support the CIA's program. After that allocation was complete, the US Intelligence liaison would fly to Riyadh and the Saudis would write a matching check. The US role was to provide logistics and technological support as well as money. The Saudis collaborated with Pakistan's intelligence service, ISI, to really run the war on the front lines. It was the Pakistani army, in particular the ISI, that picked the political winners and losers in the jihad, and who favoured radical Islamist factions because it suited the Pakistan's army goal of pacifying Afghanistan, a long-time unruly neighbour to the west, whose ethnic Pashtun nationalism the army feared. The ISI saw Islam not only as a motivating force in the anti-Soviet jihad, but as an instrument of Pakistan's regional policy to control Afghanistan. The US acquiesced with all of this in part because they thought that the only purpose that brought them to the region was to drive the Soviets out, and they didn't really care about local politics. But also because, after Vietnam, the generation of CIA officers involved in this program, were scarred by their experiences in Southeast Asia, and they essentially operated under a mantra of no more hearts and minds for us. We're not good at picking winners and losers in a developing world. Let's let the Pakistanis decide who carries this jihad forward. That's how the favouritism of the radical Islamic factions was born and nurtured. Accordingly, Pakistani journalist Ahmed Rashid reports: "between 1982 and 1992, some 35,000 Muslim radicals from 43 Islamic countries in the Middle East, North and East Africa, Central Asia and the Far East would pass their baptism under fire with the Afghan mujahideen. Tens of thousands more foreign Muslim radicals came to study in the hundreds of new madrassas (Islamic religious schools) that Zia ul-Haq's military government began to fund in Pakistan and along the Afghan border. Eventually more than 100,000 Muslim radicals were to have direct contact with Pakistan and Afghanistan and be influenced by the jihad against the USSR". *(See Ref 120)*

These radicals met each other for the first time in camps near Peshawar and in Afghanistan where they studied, trained and fought together. It was the first opportunity for most of them to learn about Islamic movements in other countries, and they forged tactical and ideological links that would serve them well in the future. The camps became virtual universities for future Islamic radicalism. However, one of the first non-Afghan volunteers to join the ranks of the mujahideen was Osama bin Laden, a civil engineer and businessman from a wealthy construction family in Saudi Arabia. Bin Laden recruited 4,000 volunteers from his own country and the Arab World and developed close relations with the most radical mujahideen leaders. He also worked closely with the CIA, raising money from private Saudi citizens. By 1984, he was running the "Maktab al-Khidma" (Service Office), an organisation set up by Abdallah Azzam with the help of ISI to funnel money, arms, and fighters from the outside world in the Afghan war. Since September 11, CIA officials have been claiming they had no direct link to bin Laden. These denials lack credibility. Earlier in 2001, the trial of defendants accused of the 1998 U.S. embassy bombing in Kenya disclosed that the CIA shipped high-powered sniper rifles directly to bin Laden's operation in 1989. Even the Tennessee-based manufacturer of the rifles confirmed this. According to the Boston Globe: "some military analysts and specialists on the weapons trade say the CIA has spent years covering its tracks on its early ties to the Afghan forces... Despite the CIA's denials, these experts say it was inevitable that the military training in guerrilla tactics and the vast reservoir of money and arms that the CIA provided in Afghanistan would have ended up helping bin Laden and his forces during the 1980s". *(See Ref 121)*

In the meantime, with U.S. knowledge, bin Laden created al-Qa'ida (The Base) in 1988: a conglomerate of quasi independent Islamic terrorist cells spread across at least 26 countries. Washington turned a blind eye to the new organisation, confident that it would not directly impinge on the U.S.

However, bin Laden and thousands of other volunteers returned to their own countries after the Soviet withdrawal in early 1989: their heightened political thinking made them believe that countries like Saudi Arabia and Egypt were just as much client regimes of the United States and the West as the Najibullah regime in Afghanistan has been of Moscow. In their home countries they built a formidable constituency - popularly known as "Afghanis" - who combined strong ideological convictions with the guerrilla skills they had acquired in Pakistan and Afghanistan under CIA supervision.

When the Russians withdrew from Afghanistan the country itself collapsed into virtual anarchy. Almost a quarter of the population was living in refugee camps and most of the country was in ruins. Different factions of the mujahideen struggled for power in the countryside, while the government of Muhammed Najibullah, the last Soviet-installed president controlled Kabul. However, after the fall of the Najibullah-regime in 1992, several Afghan political parties agreed on a peace and power-sharing agreement (the Peshawar Accords). This Agreement created the Islamic State of Afghanistan and appointed an interim government for a transitional period with Burhannudin Rabbani as President. According to Human Rights Watch: "The sovereignty of Afghanistan was vested formally in the Islamic State of Afghanistan, an entity created in April

1992, after the fall of the Soviet-backed Najibullah government. [...] With the exception of Gulbuddin Hekmatyar's Hezb-e Islami, all of the parties [...] were ostensibly unified under this government in April 1992. [...] Hekmatyar's Hezb-e Islami, for its part, refused to recognise the government for most of the period discussed in this report and launched attacks against government forces and Kabul generally. [...] Shells and rockets fell everywhere." *(See Ref 122)*

Gulbuddin Hekmatyar received operational, financial and military support from Pakistan. Afghanistan expert Amin Saikal concludes that "Pakistan was keen to gear up for a breakthrough in Central Asia. [...] Islamabad could not possibly expect the new Islamic government leaders [...] to subordinate their own nationalist objectives in order to help Pakistan realise its regional ambitions. [...] Had it not been for the ISI's logistic support and supply of a large number of rockets, Hekmatyar's forces would not have been able to target and destroy half of Kabul. *(See Ref 115)*

In 1994 a new group, the Taliban (a Pashtun translation meaning students), emerged. These were from a generation who had never seen their country at peace. They had no attachment to their historic tribes, elders, and neighbours. Neither did they appreciate the complex ethnic mix of peoples that made up their villages and their homeland Afghanistan. They were literally the orphans of war, the rootless and restless, the jobless and the economically deprived with little self-knowledge. They admired war because it was the only occupation they could possibly adapt to. Their simple belief in a messianic, puritan Islam which had been drummed into them by simple village mullahs was the only prop they could hold on to, and which gave their lives some meaning. Untrained for anything, even the traditional occupations of their forefathers such as farming, herding or the making of "handcrafts", they were what Karl Marx would have termed Afghanistan's lumpen proletariat.

So who are the Taliban and what are their origins in Afghanistan?

Due to the sudden outbreak of the war neither working government departments, police units nor even an accountable system of justice had been formed for the newly-created Islamic State of Afghanistan. Horrific crimes were committed by individuals from various factions. The country's decentralised former anti-occupation fighters turned against each other in a battle for power. These competing militias formed along the country's ethnic divisions, and were led by rapacious and predatory warlords who had survived the long war with the Soviets. Many of these commanders had developed an appetite for sexually abusing women and children, and reports of widespread ethno-genocidal rape campaigns at the hands of these militias during the civil war period indicate that militias specifically targeted women and children from rival ethnic groups as psychological tactic of war. All ethnic groups, all communities, and all regions of Afghanistan were directly affected by ethnically motivated conflict, including sexual violence.

While the diverse capital city of Kabul became the main stage of these turf battles, the entire countryside was divided into private warlord fiefdoms with bloody borders.

Meanwhile southern Afghanistan was neither under the control of foreign-backed militias nor the government in Kabul, but was ruled by local leaders such as Gul Agha Sherzai and their militias. In 1994, the Taliban (a movement originating from Jamiat "Ulema-e-Islam" run religious schools for Afghan refugees in Pakistan) was created in Afghanistan as a politico-religious force, reportedly in opposition to the tyranny of the local governor. The former mujahideen commander Mullah Muhammad Omar started his movement with fewer than 50 armed "madrasas" students in his hometown of Kandahar. However, in fall of that year, he led a group of armed men to help the Pakistanis to wrest control of the area near Kandahar from recalcitrant warlords after some of their men had attacked a convoy of Pakistani trucks carrying goods for export. General Nasirullah Babar, the Pakistani Minister of Interior in Benazir Bhutto's government was impressed by Mullah Omar's operation and began efforts to organise his group as a political and military force. *(See Ref 123, 125)*

General Babar and his allies in the Pakistani military set out to turn the Taliban into Pakistan's main ally and instrument for establishing their influence in Afghanistan. They encouraged Mullah Omar and his allies to begin recruiting fighters from fundamentalist religious schools (madrasas) located in Pashtun and Baluch populated areas of the Pakistan-Afghanistan border regions. During this period, Benazir Bhutto's Pakistan People's Party was allied to a fundamentalist political party known as the "Jamiat ul-Ulema", which had developed an extensive network of fundamentalist Islamic religious schools, especially in the border region between Pakistan and Afghanistan. The other major Islamic political party, the Jama'at-e Islami led by Qazi Hussein Ahmad was opposed to Benazir Bhutto's government and along with many operatives of the Pakistani ISI supported the Hezb-e Islami of Golbuddin Hekmatyar in his efforts to overthrow the Tajik-led Afghan government of Burhanuddin Rabbani. *(See Ref 125,126, 127)*

On the initiative of General Babar, the Pakistani government was soon providing weaponry and training to the Taliban's new political and military force. In addition to religious students from the madrassas, the Pakistanis recruited former officers and NCOs from the Pashtun dominated Khalqi wing of the army from pro-Soviet regime era in Afghanistan as well as former mujahideen commanders a number of whom had been members of Yunus Khales's Hezb-e Islami party. The latter was a separate Afghan political party created by Khales after a split with the party of the same name led by Golbuddin Hekmatyar. *(See Ref 125, 126, 128)*

In the fall and winter of 1994-1995, the Taliban achieved some major military successes, first wresting control of the Kandahar region from a group of warlords nominally allied with the Rabbani government. From their base around Kandahar in southeastern Afghanistan, the Taliban first began attacking the positions of Golbuddin Hekmatyar and the Shiite Hezb-e Wahdat in central Afghanistan. The Taliban presented themselves as an uncorruptable force of strict traditionalist Muslims whose goal was to right the wrongs of Afghanistan's warlords and fractious mujahideen whom they accused of having betrayed the original ideals of the anti-Soviet jihad.

Furthermore, Saudi Arabia joined Pakistan in an effort to secure the success of the Taliban. Saudi Arabia provided money while Pakistan provided weapons, training, expertise, and logistical assistance for the Taliban military offensive. Saudi Arabia's motive for supporting the Taliban was to counter the influence of Iran and its Shiite allies in Afghanistan as well as to establish a stake in a proposed natural gas pipeline through Afghanistan which would link Pakistan to natural gas fields in Turkmenistan. *(See Ref 127)*

When the Taliban took over Kabul from Rabbani regime, Pakistan was able to convince the United States government that the Taliban were simply a traditionalist Muslim group with no geopolitical or ideological ambitions outside of Afghanistan. Islamabad also convinced the Americans that the Taliban could establish stability in Afghanistan, stamp out the drug trade, suppress Afghan Arab terrorist groups, and act as a counterweight to Iran.

The Taliban movement was developed as a direct response to the identity politics and sexual violence of the Afghan civil war. Despite the fact that the movement emerged out of Pashtun southern provinces, the message and mandate of the Taliban were characteristically "Islamist, and not ethnic". Importantly, while the Taliban espoused religious rather than ethnic credentials, ethnic competition did not go quietly in the face of rising Islamism. On the contrary, the Taliban takeover of southern and eastern Afghanistan, which is predominantly Pashtun in ethnic composition, received far more uncontested local political support than it did in the ethnically diverse northern provinces. While the Taliban took the city of Kandahar without firing a shot, their capture of Kabul in 1996 and of Mazar-e-Sharif in 1998 were extremely violent, the latter involving the brutal massacre of the civilian population.Therefore, even though the Taliban were consistent in their message of religious identity over ethnic divisions, the strongest support for the movement was very rooted in the rural Pashtun south. *(See Ref 124, 129)*

However, it was by unifying the previously divided Pashtun regions under the blanket of Islamism that the Taliban were able to turn the tides in their favour. Pashtuns are the largest ethnic group in Afghanistan, making up about 52 percent of the population, and therefore consolidating Pashtun support under one leader and one movement tipped the balance in the civil war stalemate. Moreover, there were many mid-level commanders that accepted and supported the Taliban takeover, such as Muhammad Yunus Khalis of Nangarhar, who allowed the Taliban to take his territory in 1996. These commanders were either bought off with bribes to switch sides, or joined the movement for strategic or ideological purposes. However, no high-level commander with a history of human rights abuses, especially rape, was considered for political inclusion.Momentum and potential of this movement placed its bets in supporting the Taliban over all other groups for control of the country.By draining the support bases of other fragmented, rival Pashtun militias in the south and east, the Taliban generated sufficient military momentum to push west and north successfully. Importantly, by framing the movement on religious identity rather than ethnic identity, the Taliban movement also created the possibility of inclusion for other ethnic groups that were willing to sign on to the Islamist mandate. Therefore, despite its overwhelmingly violent character in its western and northern offensives, the Taliban ushered forth a new configuration of identity politics in Afghanistan, characterised by religiosity rather than ethnic identities. *(See Ref 130)*

The Taliban appeared on the verge of taking over the whole country in August 1998 when U.S. missiles destroyed what was described by the Pentagon as an extensive terrorist training complex near Kabul run by Osama bin Laden, accused of masterminding the 1998 bombings of the American embassies in Kenya and Tanzania. In March 1999, a UN-brokered peace agreement was reached between the Taliban and their major remaining foe, the forces of the Northern Alliance, under Ahmed Shah Massoud, an ethnic Tajik and former mujahideen leader, but fighting broke out again in July. In November, the United Nations imposed economic sanctions on Afghanistan; this action and the 1998 U.S. missile attacks were related to the Afghani refusal to turn over Osama bin Laden. Additional UN sanctions, including a ban on arms sales to Taliban forces, were imposed in December 2000.

Although the Taliban controlled some 90 percent of the country by 2000 which they governed according to the shari'a, their government was not generally recognised by the international community (the United Nations recognised President Burhanuddin Rabbani and the Northern Alliance, only Pakistan, Saudi Arabia and United Arab Emirates recognised Taliban government). Continued warfare had caused over a million deaths, while 3 million Afghans remained in Pakistan and Iran as refugees. Adding to the nation's woe, a drought in West and central Asia that began in the late 1990s was most severe in Afghanistan.

In early 2001 the Taliban militia destroyed all statues in the nation, including two ancient giant Buddhas in Bamian, outside Kabul. The destruction was ordered by religious leaders, who regarded the figures as idolatrous and un-Islamic; the action was met with widespread international dismay and condemnation, even from other Islamic nations. On 7 September, in a severe blow to the Northern Alliance, Massoud died as a result of a suicide bomb attack by assassins posing as Arab journalists. Two days after that attack, devastating terrorist assaults on the World Trade Center in New York and the Pentagon near Washington, which bin Laden was allegedly involved in planning, prompted new demands by then-U.S. President George W Bush for his arrest.

On 7 October 2001, when the Taliban refused to hand bin Laden over, the United States launched "Operation Enduring Freedom" by attacking Taliban and al-Qa'ida positions and forces in Afghanistan. Washington also began providing financial aid and other assistance to the Northern Alliance and other opposition groups. Assisted by U.S. air strikes, opposition forces ousted Taliban and al-Qa'ida forces from Afghanistan's major urban areas in November and December, often aided by the defection of forces allied with the Taliban. Several thousand U.S. troops began entering the country in November, mainly to concentrate on the search for bin Laden and Taliban leader Mullah Muhammad Omar and to deal with the remaining pockets of their forces.

In early December a pan-Afghan conference in Bonn, Germany, appointed Hamid Karzai, a Pashtun with ties to the former king, as the nation's interim leader, replacing President Rabbani. By January 2002, the Taliban and al-Qa'ida were largely defeated, although most of their leaders and an unknown number of their combatants remained at large. Fighting continued on a sporadic basis, with occasional pitched battles.

The former king, Muhammad Zahir Shah, returned to the country from exile to convene (June, 2002) a loya jirga (a traditional Afghan grand council) to establish a transitional government. Karzai was elected president (for a two-year term), and the king was declared the "father of the nation." Karzai and his cabinet, faced many challenges, was confirmed violently in the following months when one of his Vice Presidents was assassinated and an attempt was made on Karzai's life. Nonetheless, by the end of 2002 the country had achieved a measure of stability.

Sporadic, generally small-scale fighting with various guerrillas has continued, particularly in the southeast, with the Taliban regaining some strength and even control in certain districts. There also has been fighting between rival factions in various parts of the country. Reconstruction has proceeded slowly, and central governmental control outside Kabul remained almost non-existent. A return to economic health also was hindered by a persistent drought that continued through 2004.

In August 2003, NATO assumed command of the international security force in the Kabul area. A new constitution was approved in January 2004, by a loya jirga. It provides for a strong executive presidency and contains some concessions to minorities, but tensions between the dominant

Pashtuns and other ethnic groups were evident. In early 2004 the United States and NATO both announced increases in the number of troops deployed in the country. The U.S. move coincided with new operations against the Taliban and al-Qa'ida, while the NATO forces were slated to be used to provide security and in reconstruction efforts. Further increases in NATO forces, to nearly 9,000, were announced in early 2005.

By mid-2004 little of the aid that the United Nations had estimated the country would need had reached Afghanistan, while a new Afghani-proposed development plan called for $28.5 billion over seven years. Although foreign nations pledged to provide substantial monies for three years, necessary forces and funding for Afghan security were not included.

In the country's first democratic elections, Karzai was elected to the presidency in October 2004. The vote, which generally split along ethnic lines, was peaceful, but marred by some minor difficulties. Several losing candidates accused Karzai of fraud, but an international review panel said the irregularities that had occurred were not significant enough to have affected the outcome. Karzai's new cabinet consisted largely of technocrats and was ethnically balanced, although Pashtuns generally held the more important posts.

National and provincial legislative elections were held in September 2005; in some locales the balloting was marred by fraud. Supporters of Karzai won a substantial number of seats in the lower house (Wolesi Jirga); religious conservatives, former mujahideen and Taliban, women, and Pashtuns (which are overlapping groups) were all elected in significant numbers to the body. Tensions with Pakistan increased in early 2006, as members of the Afghan government increasingly accused Pakistan of failing to control Taliban and al-Qa'ida camps in areas bordering Afghanistan; by the end of the year President Karzai had accused elements of the Pakistani government of directly supporting the Taliban. In January 2006, a U.S. airstrike destroyed several houses in East Pakistan where al-Qa'ida leaders were believed to be meeting.

May, 2006, saw the U.S.-led coalition launch its largest campaign against Taliban forces since 2001; some 11,000 troops undertook a summer offensive in four South Afghan provinces, where the Taliban had become increasingly stronger and entrenched. Also in May a deadly traffic accident in Kabul involving a U.S. convoy sparked anti-American and anti-government demonstrations and riots in the city. In July, NATO assumed responsibility for peacekeeping in South Afghanistan, taking over from the coalition. NATO troops subsequently found themselves engaged in significant battles with the Taliban, particularly in Kandahar province. At the time NATO had command of all peacekeeping forces in the country, including some 11,000 American troops. By October; some 8,000 U.S. troops remained part of Operation Enduring Freedom, assigned to fighting Taliban and al-Qa'ida forces in mountainous areas bordering Pakistan.

In the second half of 2006, as NATO casualties mounted, commanders encountered difficulties when their call for reinforcements failing to raise the necessary support. NATO also joined Afghan leaders in criticising Pakistan for failing to end the Taliban's use of areas bordering Afghanistan, especially in Baluchistan, as safe havens. In March 2007, NATO forces launched a new offensive in Helmand province against the Taliban and al-Qa'ida. The same month the National Assembly passed a law granting many Afghans amnesty for human-rights violations committed during the past two-and-a-half decades of civil war. Later in the spring, Pakistan's construction of a fence along the border with Afghanistan led to protests from Kabul, and sparked several border clashes between two countries' forces. (Currently Afghanistan does not officially recognise the modern Pakistan-Afghanistan border.) In May NATO forces killed the top Taliban field commander Mullah Dadullah. However Taliban was still able to mount guerrilla attacks on the outskirts of the capital and in the north. Significant, if sporadic, fighting with insurgents continued into 2008. Also in 2007, Afghan civilian casualties during military operations became a source of anger and concern among Afghans, concerns which continued into 2008. In April 2008, President Karzai escaped an assassination attempt unhurt. And in July, he accused Pakistani agents of being behind insurgent attacks in Afghanistan, among them a suicide bombing of the Indian embassy in Kabul.

Although the majority of the Afghan refugees abroad have been repatriated since the overthrow of the Taliban, at the beginning of 2007 it was estimated that some 2.1 million Afghanis were still refugees, with most of those in Pakistan and Iran. On the other hand, Afghanistan continues to suffer from a fragile central government and weak economy, which have exacerbated the insurgency and led to an increase in illegal drug production. The lack of strong, credible government has contributed to the shortfall in international development aid to Afghanistan. By early 2008, some $25 billion had been pledged, but only three fifths of that actually delivered. The effectiveness of the aid was greatly reduced by government corruption, spending on foreign consultants and companies (sometimes required under the terms of the aid), wasteful spending practices, and sharp imbalances nationally in aid distribution.

When Barack Obama came to power in January 20, 2009, he promised to withdraw American forces from Iraq, a war he spoke against before he became senator in 2005. He did recognise, however, that Afghanistan would be more complicated. He could not just walk away. The new president was determined to ensure the US was not drawn into an interminable, Vietnam-style conflict – a conflict he fully understood could quickly become known as "Obama's War".

However, President Obama was awaiting the presidential election in Kabul in hope that the result will give him a reliable partner in Afghanistan, thereby allowing him to reveal and roll out his plan. The result was not what he had hoped for.

The 2009 presidential election in Afghanistan was characterised by lack of security, low voter turnout, widespread ballot stuffing, intimidation, and other electoral fraud. The vote, along with elections for 420 provincial council seats, took place on August 20, 2009, but remained unresolved during a lengthy vote counting process and subsequent fraud investigation.

Two months later, under heavy U.S. and ally pressure, a second round run-off vote between incumbent President Hamid Karzai and his main rival Abdullah Abdullah was announced for November 7, 2009. On November 1, however, Abdullah announced that he would no longer be participating in the run-off because his demands for changes in the electoral commission had not been met, and a "transparent election is not possible." A day later, on November 2, 2009, officials of the election commission cancelled the run-off and declared Hamid Karzai as President of Afghanistan for another 5-year term.

NATO officials announced in March 2009 that 15.6 million voters had registered to vote, and that 35 to 38 percent of registered voters were women. Those registration numbers were disputed by the Free and Fair Election Foundation of Afghanistan and media reports, which suggested widespread fraudulent activity in the election process.

The Taliban called for a boycott of the election, denouncing it as the "program of the crusaders" and "this American process".

However, in his 2010 book "Obama's Wars", Bob Woodward lays bare the president's decision to get out of Afghanistan while appearing to continue fighting. It was a policy that met with opposition from the military and led to bitter infighting between the security establishment and top White House political strategists, Simultaneously, President Obama also grappled with an unreliable ally in the Afghan president, Hamid Karzai as well as there was what the US president would later call "the cancer in Pakistan".

What emerges from Woodward's book is a picture of a deeply divided administration, at times appearing to be at war with itself, and of a President who is sometimes as scheming and politically calculating as those who opposed him. However, the only thing those in the Obama administration appear to have in common is a quiet acknowledgement that the war in Afghanistan can never be won. Woodward describes Obama around the time of the 2008 presidential election grasping some of the realities of Afghanistan: "I've been worried about losing this election," the future President tells an adviser. "After talking to you guys, I'm worried about winning this election."

Later the president would say that "We were dealt a very bad hand." This would prove truer than he realised.

Furthermore, Woodward's book quotes the president as telling the Chairman of the Joint Chiefs of Staff Admiral Michael Mullen, the Commander of US forces in Afghanistan General David Petraeus and Secretary of Defence Gates: "In 2010, we will not be having a conversation about how to do more. I will not want to hear, we're doing fine Mr President, but we'd be better if we just do more. We're not going to be having a conversation about how to change [the mission] … unless we're talking about how to draw down faster than anticipated in 2011."

General Petraeus is now reluctantly being forced to follow White House policy, even if he occasionally seeks to subvert it in public by continuing to caution against an early withdrawal from Afghanistan. However, Petraeus will replace Leon Panetta, as head of the CIA, when Panetta will move to the Pentagon to replace Robert Gates, as Secretary of Defense, who is leaving to retirement by the end of June 2011. The top commander in Afghanistan then will be Lt General John Allen.

Given the context we have discussed, one must ask why the situation continues to deteriorate and is there any solution in sight?

The underlying causes of this continued decline in Afghanistan are many fold. In the first instance there has been a broad Taliban resurgence in the north, which the coalition had believed would be stable since it does not have a majority Pashtun population. However, there are pockets of Pashtun in the region which can provide a constituency for the Taliban. Furthermore, an increasing number of non-Pashtun Afghans have begun joining the Taliban, either for ideological reasons or because they anticipate an eventual coalition defeat and are working to ingratiate themselves with the Taliban.

Furthermore, there has been substantial resistance from America's European allies.

European coalition forces have tended to focus on protecting themselves or their convoys rather than attempting to engage Taliban ambushes or pursue enemy forces. Even if they were to stay in Afghanistan, European troops are becoming less and less relevant.

The U.S. military have also made strategic mistakes most notably the decision to concentrate forces in the south was a significant error. In the near term, there is no realistic chance of significant improvement in the south, and the movement of troops out of the north leaves the rest of the country vulnerable to the Taliban. Had the United States maintained or increased its forces in the north and focused on securing urban centres, notably Kabul, a real opportunity for progress could have existed. Instead, it has been wasted.

The final, major cog in the Afghanistan problem is that of corruption. It is one of the primary reasons why the Afghan people are losing faith in their government. But, the real question now revolves around the shrinking footprint of the Afghan government outside Kabul causing the fledgling Afghan state to disintegrate.

Given the deteriorating security situation and lack of viable alternatives, the United States has no real choice but to begin dialogue with the

Taliban who, despite their advantageous position, are likely to come to the negotiating table for two reasons:

The first is that of survival: The coalition has been able to inflict casualties on the Taliban, especially in their middle ranks. As such some Taliban members may feel the need to negotiate for their own personal security, although this is unlikely to motivate a large number of Taliban leaders.

An additional basis for the initiation of talks is that the Pakistani military is effectively in control of the Taliban's leadership. Pakistan will pressure the Taliban to negotiate because it is in its interest to have a peaceful resolution and a pro-Pakistani government in Kabul.

These negotiations, at best would result in the formation of a coalition government. Ensuring the return of the Taliban to Afghanistan and they would no longer need to depend on the Pakistani military for survival. Any negotiated settlement would also require a guarantee that al-Qa'ida and other terrorist organisations would not be able to use Afghanistan as a safe haven. Although negotiating with the Taliban is not an appealing concept, they are near impossible to defeat whilst Pakistan continues to provide them sanctuary. The United States must act now to reach a reasonable settlement that would leave the West secure. Otherwise, it appears that progress from the current predicament will never occur.

CHAPTER SIX

PAKISTAN: NEW CENTRE OF FEAR

The rising number of terrorist attacks launched upon Pakistan's major cities recently, have raised alarm bells concerning the country's security. In the last decade, many new terrorist groups have appeared on the scene, several existing groups have reorganised themselves, and a new kind of militants has emerged, more violent and less conducive to political solutions than their predecessors. Relations between many of these new and existing groups became close and their links have strengthened giving fresh concerns for stability. A failed bombing attempt in New York's Times Square in May 2010 with links to Pakistan also exposed the growing ambitions of many of these groups that had previously focused only on the region. The Pakistan-born U.S. citizen Faisal Shahzad who confessed to the bombing attempt was sentenced to life imprisonment by a U.S. court in October 2010.

The ties between authorities and Islamic militant groups in Pakistan are close and have a multifaceted and deeply complex history. Although the two sides mostly focused their efforts in Afghanistan and India they have cooperated also to curb the growing influence of Iran-backed Shi'a forces in the country. But with Pakistan joining the United States as an ally in its "war on terrorism" since September 11, 2001, experts say Islamabad has seen harsh blowback on its policy of backing militants operating abroad. Leadership elements of al-Qa'ida and Afghani-Taliban, along with other terrorist groups, have made Pakistan's tribal areas (the semi-autonomous region along the Afghan border) their home and now work closely with a wide variety of Pakistani militant groups. The security concerns of this have reverberated beyond Pakistan. For example in April 2009, U.S. Secretary of State Hillary Clinton said deteriorating security in nuclear-armed Pakistan "poses a mortal threat" to the United States and the world. *(See Ref 132)*

According to the British government's estimates, 70 percent of the terror plots it has uncovered in the past decade can be traced back to Pakistan, which remains a terrorist hothouse even as jihadism is losing favour elsewhere in the Muslim world. From Egypt to Jordan to Malaysia to Indonesia, radical Islamic groups have been weakened militarily and have lost much of the support they had politically. But why not in Pakistan? The answer, according to the International Newsweek's editor Fareed Zakaria, is simple: "from its founding, the Pakistani government has supported and encouraged jihadi groups, creating an atmosphere that has allowed them to flourish. It appears to have partially reversed course in recent years, but the rot is deep". Furthermore the Pakistani scholar-politician (Pakistan ambassador in Washington) Husain Haqqani confirms that, when he explains in his book, "Pakistan: Between Mosque and Military", how the government's jihadist connections go back to the country's creation as an ideological, Islamic state and the decision by successive governments to use jihad both to gain domestic support and to hurt its perennial rival, India. Describing the military's distinction between terrorists and "freedom fighters," he notes that the problem is systemic. "This duality is a structural problem, rooted in history and a consistent policy of the state. It is not just the inadvertent outcome of decisions by some governments." *(See Ref 133, 134)*

Thus, to understand the situation better and why the Islamic fundamentalism had spread and became a force to be reckoned with in Pakistan, a review of its political history will be helpful in that matter as Haqqani mentioned above.

The first known inhabitants of the modern-day Pakistan region are believed to have been the Soanian - Homo erectus, who settled in the Soan Valley and Riwat almost 2 million years ago. Over the next several thousand years, the region would develop into various civilisations like Mehrgarh and the Indus Valley Civilisation. Prior to the creation of Pakistan in 1947, modern-day Pakistan was part of the medieval and subsequently of colonial India. Throughout its history, the region has also been a part of various other kingdoms like Greek, Persian, Turkic, Islamic and Mauryan. The region's ancient history also includes some of the oldest empires from the subcontinent and some of its major civilisations. The political history of the nation began with the birth of the All India Muslim League in 1906 to protect Muslim interests, amid fears of neglect and under-representation of Muslims, in case the British Raj decided to grant local self-rule. On the

29 December 1930, Muhammad Iqbal called for an autonomous state in "northwestern India for Indian Muslims". The Muslim League rose to popularity in the late 1930s. Muhammad Ali Jinnah espoused the Two Nation Theory and led the Muslim League to adopt the Lahore Resolution of 1940, demanding the formation of independent states for Muslims in the East and the West of British India. Eventually, a united Pakistan with two wings - West Pakistan and East Pakistan - gained independence from the British, on 14 August 1947. Modern-day Pakistan came in existence in 1971, after a civil war in the distant East Pakistan and emergence of an independent Bangladesh. Moreover, Pakistan was created as a homeland for Muslims living in the subcontinent but more Muslims have chosen to live outside Pakistan (in India and Bangladesh) than in Pakistan! *(See Ref 156, 157, 158, 159, 160)*

However, events that took place in the early 1980s shaped and transformed Pakistan as a nation and put it at the front line of what we now call the war on Islamic militants. The Pakistani military, during the 1980s and 1990s, deliberately chose to follow a policy of encouraging and supporting jihadi terrorism as part of a grand strategy to neutralise the severe threat that it perceived was posed to the state by Pakistan's immediate neighbours: Afghanistan, Iran and India. The policy of encouraging and supporting jihadi terrorism had three constituent parts. First, the Pakistani military encouraged and supported domestic Sunni fundamentalist organisations mainly to curb the growing influence of Iran-backed Shia forces in the country. Second, they provided (along with American and Saudi military and intelligence agencies) covert support to the fundamentalist Afghan mujahideen fighting the Soviet occupation forces in Afghanistan. After the Soviets withdrew, support was given to various Pashtun warlords. Eventually, the Pakistani military created the Taliban and helped to install it in power in Kabul in 1996 (as discussed in greater depth in the previous chapter). Finally, the Pakistani military sponsored and trained jihadi insurgent groups to carry out terrorist attacks in Indian Kashmir, where a Muslim secessionist insurgency had broken out in the late 1980s. The domestic and international repercussions of the policy were significant. Domestically, it contributed to the radicalisation and militarisation of Pakistani society, rise in sectarian violence and deterioration of law and order, and further emasculation of political institutions and moderate-democratic forces. It also contributed in large measure to growing Islamicisation within the military itself.

Furthermore, Pakistan's haunting security nightmare since its creation has been "economic and political disintegration culminating in an Indo-Iranian-Afghan arrangement to divide up the country". If this should ever happen, many Pakistanis believe that Iran would occupy the western parts of Baluchistan, Afghanistan would incorporate the rest of Baluchistan along with the Pashtun dominated Northwest Frontier Province and the Federally Administered Tribal Areas (FATA), leaving India to absorb the Punjab and Sindh provinces. In the early eighties, the collective threat posed by Afghanistan, Iran and India was perceived by Zia ul-Haq's military regime to be real and extremely severe. *(See Ref 135, 136)*

A region called "Pashtunistan" by the Afghanistan government, and by those among the local population who aspire for independence from Islamabad, lies on the high up in the mountain ranges of the Hindu Kush in the north-western corner of Pakistan. This area is bordered on the north and west by the Durand Line and by the Indus River in the south and east. It includes the Tribal Areas (FATA), the North West Frontier Province (NWFP) proper, and Northeastern Baluchistan. Historically, the controversy over Pashtunistan marked the political relations between British India and Afghanistan. The Afghan government challenged the right of the British to control this area and claimed that the region should rightfully belong to Afghanistan since the Pashtun people of this region were ethnically similar to the dominant ethnic group in Afghanistan, the Pashtuns. The Afghan irredenta was further strengthened by the fact that the Pashtun tribes of this region were fiercely independent and hence the British Indian government was unable to exercise strong political control over them. With the withdrawal of British power from the subcontinent in 1947, this area's incorporation into the newly created state of Pakistan caused a tremendous political controversy. The Pashtun population, led by a popular political movement, refused to be incorporated into Pakistan and opted for independence. However, the issue played right into the hands of the Afghanistan government (which was not under direct colonial rule) and provided it with an opportunity to denounce the Treaty of 1893 and assert territorial claims vis-a-vis Pakistan. The British, on the other hand, were unwilling to support the creation of an independent Pashtunistan and the area was forcibly incorporated into Pakistan. *(See Ref 171, 172)*

As Pakistani leaders were aware that during the freedom struggle, Mahatma Gandhi had promised the Pashtuns that India would not abandon them and was keen to promote "a new frontier nationalism cutting across the Province's communal and political solidarity with Pakistan", the forcible incorporation of the NWFP and the FATA into Pakistan did not significantly reduce Islamabad's threat perception as the possibility of a plot between New Delhi and Kabul to dismember Pakistan remained high. Moreover, Indian Prime Minister Jawaharlal Nehru (1947-1964) had also sounded optimistic about the future accession of the NWFP to the Union of India. Pakistan was also aware that Pashtun leaders had approached Afghanistan for support for the creation of an independent "Pashtunistan". *(See Ref 137)*

The Afghan support to Baluch insurgents on the other hand had further exacerbated the threat from Afghanistan. The Baluch were hoping to create an independent Greater Baluchistan "that embraced the Baluch areas of Iran as well as Kalat and the other Baluch principalities of Pakistan, British Baluchistan, Dera Ghazi Khan (a Baluch-claimed district in the Punjab), and the province of Sind." Apart from putting pressure on Pakistan over the issue of "Pashtunistan", access to the sea was an important consideration for the Afghan government and an independent state of Baluchistan with a natural harbor at Gwadar, created with Afghan help and having cordial relations with Kabul, would suit very well. *(See Ref 135)*

The political status of the Baluch was left undecided at the time of the partition of the subcontinent in August 1947, due to the unsuccessful attempt by the Cabinet Mission to arrive at an acceptable compromise between the Baluch leaders and the leaders of the Muslim League, who wanted unconditional accession of the Baluch to Pakistan. However, in keeping with the stated desire of the Baluch leaders, the Khan of Kalat (Khan is the title of former rulers of the state of Kalat) formally declared independence twenty-four hours after the creation of Pakistan. The Muslim League rejected the independence declaration and asserted that this decision was not shared by a majority of the Baluch people. Matters came to a head in April 1948, when the Pakistani army occupied Kalat and forced its Khan to sign the accession papers. When the Khan of Kalat capitulated under military pressure from Pakistan, his younger brother, Prince Abdul Karim, led a band of followers across the border to Afghanistan and declared an armed revolt against the Pakistani government. Karim's movement was short-lived and was eventually defeated by the Pakistani military.

Aiming to amalgamate the four provinces in the Western Wing into one administrative unit, Pakistani government introduced the "One Unit" plan in 1954, which was opposed by the Baluch as they suspected this move to be a ploy on the part of the Punjabi elite to consolidate their dominance over the other minorities in Pakistan. This led to a renewal of the Baluch insurgency, which was supported by Kabul. The Afghan government was still adamant about the issue of Pashtunistan and it interpreted the "One Unit" plan as being initiated by Pakistan in an effort to deprive the Pashtuns of their independence. As tension between the two countries mounted, relations were severed, and Pakistan feared that its close alliance with the Western bloc might induce Moscow to take advantage of this opportunity and support the Afghan claim on the issue of Pashtunistan. However, under the mediation of the Shah of Iran, Pakistan and Afghanistan signed the Tehran Accord in May 1963 whereby diplomatic relations between the two states re-established. With Afghan support dwindling after 1963, it was fairly easy for the Ayub Khan regime to crush the Baluch insurgency by force. *(See Ref 138)*

In the elections to the provincial assembly of 1970, the Baluch had overwhelmingly elected Ghaus Bux Bizenjo as governor and Ataullah Mengal as chief minister of Baluchistan. Despite that the government of Zulfikar Ali Bhutto enjoyed a solid majority in the Baluchistan Assembly, he decided suddenly in February 1973 to dismiss the Baluch provincial government. As justification for his actions, Bhutto not only criticised Bizenjo and Mengal for exceeding their constitutional authority but also accused them of hatching a sinister plot to dismember both Pakistan and Iran with the help of Iraq and the Soviet Union. To lend credence to his arguments Bhutto disclosed that a huge cache of Soviet-made arms and ammunition had been discovered in the Iraqi Embassy in Islamabad. These weapons, according to the Pakistani government, were earmarked for Baluch rebels in Pakistan. In response, however, insurgency broke out in Baluchistan in 1973 to which the afghan government of Mohammed Daud provided some help to the Baluch militants, but the Pakistani military eventually crushed it by 1977. *[Iraqi officials later claimed that the weapons were meant for the Iranian Baluch in retaliation for the Iranian support for the Kurdish minority in Iraq. This fact was never publicised by the Bhutto Administration] (See Ref 136)*

When the Soviet Union moved troops into Afghanistan in December 1979, Islamabad reacted with alarm, due to the turbulent history of Pakistani-Afghan relations and the consistent presence of strong secessionist sentiments among the Pashtun and Baluch populations in Pakistan.The

Muhammad Zia ul-Haq military regime, which had seized power in a coup in 1977, was still hurting from the Bengali rebellion in East Pakistan and the Indo-Pakistani war of 1971 that had led to a humiliating loss and the dismemberment of the country with the birth of an independent Bangladesh. Therefore the Zia regime was quick to accept the view of many Western experts that the Soviet invasion of Afghanistan was part of a wider plan by Moscow (acting perhaps in concert with pro-Soviet regimes in Kabul and New Delhi) to further dismember Pakistan by encouraging and supporting Pashtun and Baluch secession.

Furthermore, an influx of more than four million Afghan/Pashtun refugees with their three million livestock into the Pakistan controlled Tribal Areas and NWFP, was also another result of the Soviet invasion of Afghanistan. These refugees often displayed anger towards the Pakistani government mainly because of the economic hardship they had to endure in the refugee camps and the failure of the Zia regime to protect them from reprisal attacks from Afghan and Soviet security forces. Additionally the security environment in the NWFP and Tribal Areas worsened as massive amounts of arms and ammunition moved into the region. Local crime also increased as a result of the Afghan drug trade. The Zia regime quickly became aware that Pashtun anger was growing rapidly as a result of the deterioration in the security and economic environments in the NWFP and Tribal Areas. The situation, however, was prevented from exploding largely because of the huge influx of cash from the heroin trade, US refugee aid, and sympathetic feelings in certain quarters among the Pakistani Pashtuns for the Afghan refugees with whom they shared ties of ethnic kinship. *(See Ref 136)*

On the other side, since its creation in 1947, Pakistan's relations with Iran were not always good. Although Tehran has clearly preferred over the years a stable Pakistan as a buffer against India, an unstable Pakistan was another matter. Iranian officials gave the impression, in early 1980s, that they would not mind an excuse to take over some of the Pakistani Baluch areas immediately adjacent to the Iranian border. Rather than wait until separatism in Pakistan became unmanageable and Kabul/Moscow intervened, they cautiously suggested working out a military arrangement with Islamabad which would give Tehran responsibility for the western end of Pakistani Baluchistan. Iran therefore began "to treat Pakistani Baluchistan as a quasi-protectorate" and to show an eagerness to intervene there militarily, which increased the threat perception in Pakistan. *(See Ref 139)*

Furthermore, the Balush minority's situation, which Iran perceived as an internal threat, was exacerbated by two external developments. The first was the rise of hostilities between Iran and Iraq. Baghdad started accusing Tehran of meddling in its internal affairs by providing covert military aid to the Iraqi Kurds who wanted to secede from Iraq. Though these charges were hotly denied by Tehran, the Iraqi government retaliated by covertly providing arms and ammunition to the Iranian Baluch. The second development which worried Tehran was the growing hostility of the Soviet Union towards Pakistan in the wake of the successful secession of Bangladesh in 1971 and its support to the Baluch insurgency. Moscow had geostrategic reasons in wanting to support Baluch independence. An independent and friendly Baluchistan would not only have provided the Soviet Union with access to the warm water port of Gwadar (a historic Soviet objective) and a foothold in the Persian Gulf region (thereby changing the balance of power in the Indian Ocean region), but it would have also enabled the Soviet Union (along with its ally Iraq) to destabilise Iran and extend its influence in the Middle East. This was a potentially dangerous situation for Iran and therefore Tehran was vehement in its opposition to the secessionist movement in Baluchistan.

If Tehran had its causes to act against the Pakistani Baluch, Islamabad perceived that Iranian position as a cause for concern. However, during the 1970s, the Zulfikar Ali Bhutto regime regularly consulted the Shah of Iran in forming policy towards the Pakistani Baluch. In this context, immediately upon his return from Tehran, Bhutto dismissed the provincial assembly and ordered the Pakistani military to crack down in Baluchistan with the help of the Iranian military. Bhutto also had prominent Baluch politicians arrested and imprisoned (as we mentioned above). However, this policy changed course after Zia Ul-Haq ousted Bhutto. Immediately after assuming the presidency, Zia released the Baluch political prisoners and entered into an uneasy truce with the Baluch. But the damage caused by the brutal army crackdown in Baluchistan from 1973 to 1977 was irreparable with even moderate Baluch leaders like Bizenjo and Mengal starting to believe that political accommodation with the central authorities in Pakistan was no longer possible. Hence, in the 1980s Baluch nationalism moved towards the more hard-line position of secession. Furthermore, in the aftermath of the Islamic Revolution in 1979, the growing Iranian support to the Shi'a minority in Pakistan began to surface which did not go down well with the Sunni majority. Consequently, sectarian clashes between Shi'a and Sunni began to rise, which further alarmed the Zia government.

On the other side there is also the Indian threat. The roots of that threat lies in the hostility between Hindus and Muslims and, initially, in the disposition of self-governing princely states. They can be traced specifically back to the Indian freedom movement, which was a struggle between two rival ideologies. One vision, championed by the Indian National Congress, believed that India's diverse religious, linguistic, and ethnic groups could co-exist together in a single secular and democratic state. In contrast, the Indian Muslim League regarded Hindus and Muslims as forming two separate nations with distinct social customs and practices, philosophies and ways of life, which precluded peaceful co-existence between the two communities in an undivided India. When a Congress-League compromise proved elusive, a complex formula was devised to partition the subcontinent into two states-India and Pakistan. Under the partition plan, contiguous Muslim majority provinces of British India were to become Pakistan, with the border provinces of Bengal and Punjab (with nearly equal number of Hindus-Sikhs and Muslims) to be divided. *(See Ref 140)*

However, the Partition of India came about in the aftermath of World War II, when both Great Britain and British India were dealing with the economic stresses caused by the war and its demobilisation. It was the intention of those who wished for a Muslim state to come from British India to have a clean partition between independent and equal "Pakistan" and "Hindustan" once independence came. The partition itself, according to leading politicians such as Mohammed Ali Jinnah, leader of the All India Muslim League, and Jawaharlal Nehru, leader of the Indian National Congress, should have resulted in peaceful relations. However, the partition of British India into India and Pakistan in 1947 did not divide the nations cleanly along religious lines. Nearly 50 percent of the Muslim population of British India remained in India. Inter-communal violence between Hindus, Sikhs, and Muslims resulted in between 500,000 to one million casualties. *(See Ref 141, 142, 143)*

On the other hand, the partition of the subcontinent resulted in a massive population migration accompanied by severe communal violence and rioting. Millions died from communal slaughter, dislocation, hunger,

115

hardship and disease. In this highly polarised and vitriolic environment, Congress and Muslim League leaders also squabbled bitterly over the division of public assets between the two new states. A further arena of fierce competition between the two new states was regarding the status of the 565 princely states, which were controlled by the British under the doctrine of paramountcy. British disengagement from the subcontinent meant that the doctrine of paramountcy was to lapse and, hence, the princely states could technically become independent. This was vehemently opposed by both the Congress and the Muslim League; intense political pressure was therefore brought on the princes to join either India or Pakistan, keeping in mind the issues of geographical contiguity and the communal allegiance of the population of the princely state. All the princely states, with the exceptions of Hyderabad, Junagadh, and Jammu and Kashmir (hereafter referred to as Kashmir), joined India or Pakistan by the time the British transferred power. While Junagadh and Hyderabad, located deep within the India but wanting to join Pakistan, were forcibly annexed by New Delhi, Kashmir posed a problem. The state had a Hindu ruler but an overwhelming majority of its population was Muslim; it was also contiguous to both India and Pakistan. Kashmir, therefore, was claimed by both sides on the basis of ideology. From their very inception, therefore, India and Pakistan were locked in a bitter zero-sum ideological struggle over Kashmir. *(See Ref 144)*

In 1947 the first war between Pakistan and India arose over Kashmir, when Muslim subjects revolted and were supported by Pakistani troops. The Hindu ruler of Kashmir, Maharaja Hari Singh, appealed to India for aid, agreeing to cede the state to New Delhi in return, a move that was supported by Sheikh Abdullah, the leader of a popular, secular and democratic political movement in Kashmir. India moved quickly to consolidate its position in Kashmir, pushing Pakistan's "volunteers" and its army back. Conflicts also arose in the Punjab and in Bengal. However, the undeclared war in Kashmir continued until January 1, 1949, when a truce was arranged through UN mediation; negotiations between New Delhi and Islamabad began and lasted until 1954 without resolving the Kashmir problem. Pakistan controlled part of the area, Azad (Free) Kashmir and the Northern Areas (about the third of Kashmir), while India held most of the territory (about two thirds), which it annexed in 1957. Over the next twenty years, both India and Pakistan sought to absorb their respective portions of Kashmir and the 1949 Cease-Fire Line (CFL) gradually became the de facto border between the two states. *(See Ref 145)*

A second war began in April 1965 between India and Pakistan, when fighting between their two armies broke out in the Rann of Kachh, a sparsely inhabited region along the West Pakistan–India border. The causes which encouraged Pakistan and led it to launch a military offensive to seize Indian Kashmir by force were Pakistan's confidence in its military ability, which was stemmed from the massive weapons procurement program that it had undertaken ever since it joined the Central Treaty Organisation (CENTO), an American-led military alliance, and on the assumptions that India was militarily vulnerable after the Sino-Indian war of 1962, and that widespread popular discontent existed in Indian Kashmir against New Delhi. In August, fighting spread to Kashmir and to the Punjab. In September Pakistani and Indian troops crossed the partition line between the two countries and launched air assaults on each other's cities. After threats of intervention by China had been successfully opposed by the United States and Britain, Pakistan and India agreed to a UN-sponsored cease-fire and withdrew to the pre-August lines. Thereafter, under Soviet Prime Minister Alexei Kosygin's initiative, Prime Minister Shri Lal Bahadur Shastri of India and President Ayub Khan of Pakistan met in Tashkent, USSR (now in Uzbekistan), in January 1966, and signed an agreement pledging continued negotiations and respect for the cease-fire conditions. After the Tashkent Declaration another period of relative peace ensued. *(See Ref 145)*

A third Indo-Pakistani War, which broke out in December 1971, was fought over the secession of the Bangali "autonomous" East Pakistan. Despite a majority Muslim population, East Pakistan was also the subject of Pakistani aggressions. As ten million Hindu refugees flooded into India, fleeing atrocities in East Pakistan, Prime Minister Indira Gandhi asked for US support but was rebuffed. She later requested, and received, Russian military aid. As the Pakistani military's offensive continued in East Pakistan, New Delhi, however, calculated that it was cheaper to go to war against Pakistan on behalf of the Bengali secessionists than to absorb the six million Bengali refugees who had taken shelter in the province of West Bengal. East Pakistan, separated from West Pakistan by 1200 miles of Indian territories, was militarily indefensible for the Pakistani arm forces; hence, when the Indian army attacked East Pakistan, the Yahya Khan regime in Pakistan countered by attacking Indian Kashmir. The war in the Kashmir sector proved to be of short duration, however, since the Indian military offensive in East Pakistan lasted only two weeks and led to the creation of the independent state of Bangladesh. India won a decisive military victory in this third declared Indo-Pakistani war, which led to a significant diplomatic victory by New Delhi on the Kashmir issue in the post-war peace agreement that was signed between Prime Ministers Indira Gandhi and Zulfikar Ali Bhutto at Simla on July 2, 1972. The second paragraph of the Simla Agreement stated that India and Pakistan "are resolved to settle their differences by peaceful means through bilateral negotiations or by any other peaceful means mutually agreed upon between them", excluding the UN and all other parties. Both sides also agreed the modified Cease-Fire Line which was renamed as the Line-of-Control or LOC. *(See Ref 146, 147, 148, 149)*

India's nuclear test in 1974 generated great uncertainty in Pakistan and is generally acknowledged to have been the impetus for Pakistan's nuclear weapons development program. In 1983, the Pakistani and Indian governments accused each other of aiding separatists in their respective countries, i.e., Sikhs in India's Punjab state and Sindhis in Pakistan's Sindh province. In April 1984, tensions erupted after troops were deployed to the Siachen Glacier, a high-altitude desolate area close to the China border left undemarcated by the cease-fire agreement (Karachi Agreement) signed by Pakistan and India in 1949. However, the situation improved after Rajiv Gandhi became Prime Minister in November 1984 and after a group of Sikh hijackers was brought to trial by Pakistan in March 1985. In December 1985, President Zia and Prime Minister Gandhi pledged not to attack each other's nuclear facilities. In early 1986, the Indian and Pakistani governments began high-level talks to resolve the Siachen Glacier border dispute and to improve trade.

After the Soviet Union invaded Afghanistan in December 1979, the United States (and also Saudi Arabia) used the services of Pakistan's military and intelligence agencies to traine, to channel millions of dollars and large quantities of weapons and ammunition to the Afghan mujahideen (as we mentioned in more details in chapter 5). Being elevated to the status of a frontline ally of the US suited Pakistan well since it allowed access to millions of dollars in American aid and sophisticated weapons; Washington also turned a blind eye towards Pakistan's covert nuclear weapons and missiles programs, which were being developed with assistance from China and North Korea. Some of the weapons that Pakistan received from the Americans earmarked for the Afghan mujahideen were diverted by Pakistan military intelligence services to insurgent groups operating in India's Punjab province. India responded to Pakistan's massive military spending by undertaking its own military modernisation program. A destructive and destabilising arms race thus erupted in the region and tensions remained high. *(See Ref 144)*

Bilateral tensions increased again between New Delhi and Islamabad in early 1990s, when Kashmiri militants began a campaign of violence against Indian Government authority in Jammu and Kashmir. The main reason for this was the outbreak of a widely popular secessionist insurgency in Indian Kashmir in the late 1980s, which was actively encouraged and supported by Pakistan. From its inception, the secessionist insurgency in Indian Kashmir split into two factions based upon ideology and objective. One faction, represented by the nationalist Jammu and Kashmir Liberation Front (JKLF), advocated the formation of an independent and secular Kashmir state comprising of the five main regions of the former princely state; this was to be achieved by the secession of Indian and Pakistani parts of Kashmir followed by a merger of these two areas. A second and more dominant faction within the secessionist movement, represented by Pakistan-based and -backed Islamic fundamentalist groups such as "Hizb-ul Mujahideen", "Lashkar-e-Taiba" and "Jaish-i-Mohammad", advocated Indian Kashmir's secession from India followed by either a merger with Pakistan or, at the very least, the creation of an independent Islamic state with close ties with Pakistan. These groups endorsed the ethnic cleansing of the minority Hindu Pandit community from the Valley and Tibetan Buddhist community from Ladakh. Massacres of Hindu and Sikh families were also carried out in the Jammu region. Pakistan-backed Islamic militants even carried out terrorist attacks in other parts of India, often with help from international terrorist organisations like Al-Qa'ida, disgruntled domestic groups such as the Student's Islamic Movement of India (SIMI) and the criminal underworld. However, subsequent high-level bilateral meetings relieved the tensions between India and Pakistan, but relations worsened again after the destruction of the Ayodhya Masjid by Hindu extremists in December 1992 and terrorist's bombings in Bombay in March 1993. Talks between the Foreign Secretaries of both countries in January 1994 resulted in deadlock.

The Pakistani military decided to follow discreet set of objectives in order to neutralise the three threats from Afghanistan, Iran and India. To pursue those objectives, Zia-ul Haq banned all political parties and decided to build a new Pakistan along Islamic moulds. He deliberately set about to increase the power and influence of the Islamic parties. Large sums of money started to flow into the coffers of the Islamic parties and madrasas or Islamic seminaries began to proliferate. These groups gained prominence and also began to have more say in the foreign and security policies of the country. Furthermore on December 2, 1978, Zia-ul-Haq delivered a nationwide address on the occasion of the first day of the Islamic (Hijra) calendar. He did this in order to usher in an Islamic system to Pakistan. In the speech, he accused politicians of exploiting the name of Islam, saying that "many rulers did what they pleased in the name of Islam." As a preliminary measure to establish an Islamic society in Pakistan, Zia announced the establishment of Shari'a Benches. Speaking about its jurisdiction, he remarked, "Every citizen will have the right to present any law enforced by the government before the 'Sharia Bench' and obtain its verdict whether the law is wholly or partly Islamic or un-Islamic." However, Zia's Islamicisation drive was also a reaction to events unfolding in neighbouring Iran and Afghanistan. Alarmed at the growing influence of the Shi'a in the country in the wake of the Iranian Revolution of 1979 the Zia regime gave its blessings to the formation of the militant Sunni Islamist organisation, the "Sipah-e-Sahaba Pakistan" (SSP), which carried out numerous attacks on Shi'a groups and even directed violence towards Iranian diplomatic personnel stationed in Pakistan. *(See Ref 140)*

Pakistan also became the main staging ground for the Afghan mujahideen in its jihad against the occupying Soviet forces throughout the 1980s. Radical Islamic parties and organisations in Pakistan opened many madrasas, particularly in the Tribal Areas, where children of Afghan refugees were imparted education and training in Islamic theology and ideology. These madrasas provided a fertile recruiting ground for the mujahideen. The Pakistani army's Inter Services Intelligence (ISI) (along with American and Saudi military and intelligence agencies) further provided covert support to the fundamentalist mujahideen fighting the Soviet occupation forces in Afghanistan. Consequently, the ISI came to develop very close ties with the mujahideen and eventually, the ISI created the Taliban and helped to install it in power in Kabul in 1996. *(See Ref 150)*

The ISI turned its attention to Kashmir when the Afghan war was over, where a secessionist insurgency had broken out in the late 1980s. Indian intelligence reports have suggested that initially nearly thirty thousand members of the fundamentalist Hizb-ul-Mujahideen along with members of the Jammu and Kashmir Liberation Front (JKLF) received training in bases located in Azad Kashmir and in the NWFP. Further, in the aftermath of the Afghan war, large quantities of highly sophisticated weapons, including Stinger anti-aircraft missiles and automatic rifles, which the U.S. had poured into Pakistan to be used by the Afghan mujahideen, were diverted to Kashmiri insurgents by Pakistan through bases in Azad Kashmir. The ISI has also encouraged veteran guerrillas of the Afghan war, who were left aimless after the Soviets withdrew from Afghanistan, to infiltrate into Kashmir to carry out a jihad against India. To facilitate the infiltration of insurgents across the LOC, the Pakistani military periodically fired upon and shelled Indian forward positions and border villages. The Pakistan government also lost no opportunity to internationalise the Kashmiri dispute by highlighting in international forums New Delhi's corrupt rule in Indian Kashmir and the human rights abuses committed by the Indian counterinsurgency forces against the Kashmiri people. Islamabad also consistently demanded international mediation in the Kashmir dispute and called for the holding of an UN-sponsored plebiscite to ascertain the wishes of the Kashmiri people regarding the state's future political status. *(See Ref 151, 152, 153, 154)*

However, Zia ul-Haq's death in a mysterious plane crash in August 1988 did little to curb the growing clout of the radical Islamic forces in Pakistan. Ghulam Eshaq Khan became the President after General Zia. In the ensuing elections the Pakistan People Party (PPP) emerged victorious and its leader Benazir Bhutto was sworn in as Prime Minister. Although the military grudgingly gave in to the liberals' demand for the restoration of democracy in Pakistan, it did so after retaining complete veto powers in policy matters. Over the next ten years, Pakistan went through a series of governments, none of which were able to govern effectively. Corruption became rampant and together with a moribund economy generated much popular anger towards the mainstream political parties. The internal security situation also became dire. The military however continued to aid religious fundamentalists at home and abroad. Along with the Talibanisation of Afghanistan, religious extremism in Pakistan also progressed rapidly during the second half of the 1990s. Radical new groups such as Lashkar-e-Taiba (LeT), Hizb-ul Mujahideen (HuM) and Jaish-e-Mohammad (JeM) were formed to wage jihad in Indian Kashmir where popular discontent had given rise to a mass insurgency in the late-1980s. *(See Ref 153)*

The restoration of democracy in Pakistan in 1988 did little to advance the cause of regional autonomy, the most coveted goal of Baluch leaders, since the central government continued to maintain almost total control over power, resources, and revenues. This led to ethnic agitation in the provinces. In Baluchistan, the ruling and opposition parties in the provincial assembly demanded more autonomy especially in the economic sphere and appealed to the Pakistani President to oversee that the province receives its rightful share of federally allocated funds. The Baluchistan Assembly also warned the federal government of dire consequences if it tried to meddle in the internal affairs of Baluchistan. *(See Ref 173)*

However, an undeclared border war broke out in May 1999 when local insurgents and foreign volunteers, backed by regular Pakistani soldiers in civilian garb, crossed the LOC in the Kargil sector in Kashmir and occupied large tracts of land and several unmanned peaks and ridges on the Indian side. Though initially stunned by the suddenness and scope of the border incursion, New Delhi responded militarily with vigour and determination. The real question during this war was whether it would escalate into a bigger showdown, perhaps even involving nuclear weapons. Thankfully, in July 1999, the status quo ante was restored after Pakistan was forced, by a massive Indian counter-offensive and intense American diplomatic pressure, to withdraw its soldiers and the insurgent forces under its control from the Indian side of the LOC. *(See Ref 155)*

The Kargil war was followed by a military coup d'etat in Pakistan in October 1999. The military government under General Parvez Musharraf that took power in Islamabad tried to overcome the frustrations of the Kargil fiasco by referring to the possibility of a real catastrophic nuclear war in South Asia if the Kashmir dispute wasn't resolved quickly. In the aftermath of the 11 September 2001 terrorist attacks in the United States, when Pakistan was elevated to the status of a frontline ally by the Bush administration in return for joining the American-led war on terror, the Musharraf regime stepped up its support to terrorist organisations operating against India. In late-2001 and early-2002, a series of spectacular terrorist attacks were carried out by Lashkar-e-Taiba in different parts of India, including an attack on the Indian Parliament in New Delhi that had led to a nuclear standoff. In reaction to this, serious diplomatic tensions developed and India and Pakistan deployed 500,000 and 120,000 troops to the border respectively. While the Indo-Pakistani peace process has since made progress, it is sometimes stalled by infrequent insurgent activity in India, such as the 26 November 2008 Mumbai attacks. Pakistan also has been accused of contributing to nuclear proliferation; its leading nuclear scientist, Abdul Qadeer Khan, admitted to selling nuclear secrets, though he denied government knowledge of his activities. *(See Ref 161)*

By the time Pervez Musharraf seized power in a coup d'etat in October 1999, the liberal democratic establishment and the mainstream political parties had already become thoroughly discredited and Islamic fundamentalist groups that openly advocated the full implementation of Shari'a law in Pakistan and the waging of jihad in Indian Kashmir operated freely. This suited the Musharraf regime perfectly. Like Zia before him, Musharraf was deeply suspicious of the liberal-democratic elements and sought to take advantage of the regime's close ties with religious fanatics to neutralise political opponents like Benazir Bhutto and Nawaz Sharif (both were implicated on corruption charges and sent into exile). With the encouragement of the regime, an alliance of six Islamic parties called the Muttahida Majlis-e-Amal (MMA) was also formed. In the October 2002 elections, the MMA secured 58 seats in the National Assembly, an absolute majority in the North West Frontier Province and second position in Baluchistan.

The islamicisation of Pakistan has come back to haunt the Musharraf regime after September 11, 2001. As part of the US-led global war on terrorism, the Pakistani military was asked to capture or eliminate suspected Taliban and al-Qa'ida personnel who had fled Afghanistan and were hiding in the Federally Administered Tribal Areas (FATA) under protection from the fiercely independent and fundamentalist Pashtun tribes. The Americans also put pressure to clamp down on fundamentalist groups within Pakistan. The Musharraf regime's decision to cooperate with the Americans and take military action against the Pashtun tribes and the Taleban and al-Qa'ida fighters led to fierce fighting in the tribal areas. It also led to clashes between the government and hardline Islamic clerics and their supporters. A major flashpoint occurred after Ghazi Abdul Rashid, a radical cleric, and his supporters barricaded themselves inside Islamabad's Lal Masjid (Red Mosque). After failing to persuade the cleric to surrender, President Musharraf ordered the military to flush out the fundamentalists from inside the mosque. In the military operation, Ghazi Abdul Rashid and around seventy of his supporters were killed. This immediately led to retaliatory suicide bomb attacks against Pakistani military and government personnel in which hundreds of soldiers died.

Finding itself poorly positioned with the religious fundamentalists in the aftermath of September 11 and actively prodded by the United States, the Musharraf regime grudgingly tried to mend fences with the liberal-democratic forces and work out a power-sharing agreement. But what complicated the picture was the refusal of the military to hand over power to a democratically elected civilian government and return to the barracks. Instead the regime tried to manipulate the constitution and intimidate key institutions like the parliament and the judiciary so that Musharraf could stay on as a "civilian" president (after he recently got himself re-elected in a dubious presidential election), thereby giving the military a firm hold over political power. This has brought President Musharraf into direct confrontation with the main political parties and an activist judiciary.

For Pakistan's liberal-democratic forces, the military's fallout with the fundamentalists offered a window of opportunity to return to power and both Nawaz Sharif and Benazir Bhutto were keen to grab it. And so, former Prime Minister Nawaz Sharif attempted to return from exile on 10 September 2007 against the military's wishes, but was arrested on corruption charges after landing at Islamabad International Airport. Sharif was then put on a plane bound for Jeddah, Saudi Arabia, whilst outside the airport there were violent confrontations between Sharif's supporters and the police. This did not deter another former Prime Minister, Benazir Bhutto, from returning on 18 October 2007 after an eight year exile in Dubai and London, to prepare for the parliamentary elections to be held in 2008. However, on the same day, two suicide bombers attempted to kill Bhutto as she travelled towards a rally in Karachi. Bhutto escaped unharmed but there were 136 casualties and at least 450 people were injured. On 27 December 2007, Benazir Bhutto was leaving an election rally in Rawalpindi when she was assassinated by a gunman who shot her in the neck and set off a bomb, killing 20 other people and injuring several more. The exact sequence of the events and cause of death became points of political debate and controversy, because, although early reports indicated that Bhutto was hit by shrapnel or the gunshots, the Pakistani Interior Ministry stated that she died from a skull fracture sustained when the explosion threw Bhutto against the sunroof of her vehicle. Bhutto's aides rejected this claim and insisted that she suffered two gunshots prior to the bomb detonation.The Interior Ministry subsequently backtracked from its previous claim. However, a subsequent investigation, aided by the Scotland Yard of U.K., supported the "hitting the sun-roof" as the cause of her death. The Election Commission, after a meeting in Islamabad, announced that, due to the assassination of Benazir Bhutto, the elections, which had been scheduled for 8 January 2008, would take place on 18 February 2008.

Facing a rapidly deteriorating law-and-order situation and also alarmed by rumours that the Supreme Court was about to declare his dubious re-election to the office of president unconstitutional, Musharraf declared a state of emergency in the country on 3 November 2007. The regime also cracked down on demonstrators demanding an end to military rule and arrested prominent political leaders (including Benazir Bhutto) and activists. However, the net effect of the emergency has been to further strengthen the opposition to the Musharraf regime, from both the liberal-democratic and the fundamentalist camps. Already Benazir Bhutto has called for the military to relinquish power and allow democratic elections to take place; this could be an indication that if a deal between Benazir and Musharraf existed before, it no longer existed after the declaration of emergency. Nawaz Sharif, who has returned to Pakistan on 25 November 2007, has also indicated that he is willing to bury his differences with Benazir and work jointly with her and other pro-democracy leaders to restore democratic rule in Pakistan. On their part, radical Islamic groups in Pakistan have vowed to avenge the "martyrdom" of Ghazi Abdul Rashid and carry out more terrorist attacks against the regime and the security forces. They have also vowed to attack the liberal-democratic forces, who they suspect of secretly negotiating with Musharraf for a slice of power. This has reached the extent that Osama bin Laden's deputy within al-Qa'ida, Ayman al-Zawahiri, has even called upon Pakistanis to rise up in revolt against President Musharraf for giving in to American pressure and launching attacks on domestic Islamic groups and the Taliban and al-Qa'ida fighters in the FATA.

Despite the return to democracy and the general elections which occurred on the 18th of February 2008 and were won by late Benezir Bhutto's People's Party in which her husband Asif Ali Zardari was elected president, the threat of domestic terrorism and civil war is therefore greatly magnified in Pakistan. If Pakistan descends into further anarchy and if fundamentalist forces gain more ground, the command and control of the country's nuclear weapons could be at risk.

However, the question here: who is magnifying the extent of domestic terrorism and potential civil war and what kind of Islamic militant and radical organisations are currently at work in Pakistan?

Many experts agree that it is difficult to determine how many terrorist groups are operating out of Pakistan. Most of these groups have tended to fall into one of the five distinct categories laid out by Ashley J. Tellis, a senior associate at Carnegie Endowment for International Peace, in January 2008 testimony before a U.S. House Foreign Affairs subcommittee:

- Sectarian: Groups such as the Sunni Sipah-e-Sahaba and the Shi'a Tehrik-e-Jafria, are engaged in violence within Pakistan;

- Anti-Indian: Terrorist groups that operate with the alleged support of the Pakistani military and ISI, such as Lashkar-e-Taiba, Jaish-e-Muhammad, and Harakat ul-Mujahideen;

- Afghan Taliban: The original Taliban movement and especially its Kandahari leadership centred around Mullah Muhammad Omar, believed to be now living in Quetta;

- Al-Qa'ida and its affiliates: The organisation led by Osama bin Laden and other non-South Asian terrorists believed to be ensconced in the Federally Administered Tribal Areas (FATA). Rohan Gunaratna of the International Centre for Political Violence and Terrorism Research in Singapore says other foreign militant groups such as the Islamic Movement of Uzbekistan, Islamic Jihad group, the Libyan Islamic Fighters Group and the Eastern Turkistan Islamic Movement are also located in FATA;

- The Pakistani Taliban: Groups consisting of extremist outfits in the FATA, led by individuals such as Hakimullah Mehsud, of the Mehsud tribe in South Waziristan, Maulana Faqir Muhammad of Bajaur, and Maulana Qazi Fazlullah of the Tehrik-e-Nafaz-e-Shariat-e-Mohammad.

There are some other militant groups that do not fit into any of the above categories. For instance, secessionist groups such as the Baluchistan Liberation Army (BLA) in the southwest Baluchistan. The BLA was declared a terrorist organisation by Pakistan in 2006. Also, a new militant network, often labeled the Punjabi Taliban, has gained prominence after the major 2008 and 2009 attacks in the Punjabi cities of Lahore, Islamabad, and Rawalpindi.

Hassan Abbas, a fellow at the Asia Society, writes that the Punjabi Taliban network is a loose conglomeration of members of banned militant groups of Punjabi origin-sectarian as well as those focused on Kashmir-that have developed strong connections with the Pakistani Taliban, Afghan Taliban, and other militant groups based in FATA and the North-West Frontier Province. The Punjabi Taliban provide logistical support for attacks on cities in Punjab province and include individuals or factions of groups such as "Jaish-e-Mohammed", "Sipah-i-Sahaba Pakistan", and "Lashkar-i-Jhangvi" and their various splinter groups, along with small cells unaffiliated with any large group. Abbas writes that many of these militants "directly benefited from state patronage in the 1990s and were professionally trained in asymmetrical warfare, guerrilla tactics, and sabotage." The Punjabi Taliban are distinct from the traditional Pashtun Taliban, experts say. They are usually more educated and more technologically savvy. *(See Ref 162)*

Since there is also greater coordination between all these groups, say experts, lines have blurred regarding which category a militant group fits in. For instance, the Pakistani Taliban, which were committed to fighting against the Pakistani state, are now increasingly joining insurgents fighting U.S. and international troops across the border in Afghanistan. U.S.-NATO Chief in Afghanistan General David H. Petraeus, in a Council on Foreign Relations (CFR) interview, says the groups have long shared a symbiotic relationship. "They support each other, they coordinate with each other, sometimes they compete with each other, [and] sometimes they even fight each other", making it difficult to distinguish between them. *(See Ref 163)*

Supporters of the Afghan Taliban in the tribal areas transitioned into a mainstream Taliban force of their own as a reaction to the Pakistani army's incursion into the tribal areas, which began in 2002, to hunt down the militants. In December 2007, about thirteen disparate militant groups coalesced under the umbrella of "Tehrik-i-Taliban Pakistan" (TTP), also known as the Pakistani Taliban, with militant commander Baitullah Mehsud from South Waziristan as the leader. After Mehsud was killed in August 2009 in a U.S. missile strike, his cousin and deputy Hakimullah

Mehsud took over as leader of the TTP. Experts say most adult men in Pakistan's tribal areas grew up carrying arms but it is only in the last few years that they have begun to organise themselves around a Taliban-style Islamic ideology pursuing an agenda much similar to that of the Afghan Taliban in Afghanistan. Hassan Abbas writes in a January 2008 article that "the Pakistani Taliban killed approximately two hundred tribal leaders and effectively established themselves as an alternative." *(See Ref 164)*

TTP not only has representation from all of FATA's seven agencies but also from several settled districts of the NWFP. According to some estimates, the Pakistani Talibans collectively have around 30,000 to 35,000 members. Among their other objectives, they have announced a defensive jihad against the Pakistani army, enforcement of shari'a, and a plan to unite against NATO forces in Afghanistan. Pakistani authorities accused the group's former leader, Baitullah Mehsud, of assassinating former Prime Minister Benazir Bhutto in December 2007. Some experts have questioned the ability of the different groups working under the Pakistani Taliban umbrella to stay united given the rivalries between the various tribes. However, the group has proved since its inception, through a string of suicide attacks, that it poses a serious threat to the country's stability. TTP also expressed transnational ambitions when it claimed responsibility for a failed bomb attack in New York in May 2010.

Besides providing militant groups in Pakistan with technical expertise and capabilities, al-Qa'ida is also promoting cooperation among a variety of them, say some experts. Don Rassler, an associate at the Combating Terrorism Center, an independent research institution based at the U.S. military academy at West Point, writes that al-Qa'ida "has assumed a role as mediator and coalition builder among various Pakistani militant group factions by promoting the unification of entities that have opposed one another or had conflicting ideas about whether to target the Pakistani state." Al-Qa'ida's greatest strength today, says counterterrorism expert Brian Fishman, is its "ability to infiltrate and co-opt other militant groups that have existing operational capability." In Pakistan, he says, "There's this whole milieu of militant groups, and individuals within those groups, that have come together ideologically and decided that they want to embark on this mission that al-Qa'ida has set forth for them." *(See Ref 165, 166)*

Carnegie's Asheley J. Tellis says the coordination between these different militant groups is ad-hoc and is driven by necessity. "The important point is that such coordination takes place through the entire spectrum of jihadi groups," he says. "They are much more flexible in their cooperation now than they ever were historically."

Bruce Riedel, the original coordinator of President Barak Obama's policy on the Afghanistan-Pakistan region, in an interview to the Council of Foreign Relations also stressed al-Qa'ida's growing cooperation with groups like the Afghan Taliban, the Pakistani Taliban, Lashkar-e-Taiba, and others. "The notion that you can somehow selectively resolve the al-Qa'ida problem while ignoring the larger jihadist sea in which [al-Qa'ida] swims has failed in the past and will fail in the future," he said. *(See Ref 167)*

However, some experts believe that Pakistani Taliban's attacks against the government and the security establishment may have strained their relations with the Afghan Taliban who enjoy close relationship with the army and the ISI, the country's premier intelligence agency. Richard Barrett, a former British intelligence officer who tracks al-Qa'ida and the Taliban for the United Nations told the New York Times in October 2009 that the Afghan Taliban "don't like the way that the Pakistan Taliban has been fighting the Pakistan government and causing a whole load of problems there."

Experts say militants have also expanded their control over other parts of Pakistan such as in South Punjab, some settled areas of NWFP, and as far south as Karachi. Military analyst Ayesha Siddiqa writes "South Punjab has become the hub of jihadism". She argues South Punjabi jihadists have been connected with the Afghan jihad since the 1980s and the majority is still engaged in fighting in Afghanistan. According to some estimates, she says about 5,000 to 9,000 youth from South Punjab are fighting in Afghanistan and Waziristan. *(See Ref 168)*

Pakistan's security forces are struggling to confront these domestic militants. Efforts are underway to reform the forces but challenges remain both in terms of willingness to fight some of these militant groups as well as capabilities. Security forces, especially the army and the police, have increasingly become the target for the militant groups. In October 2009, militants attacked the army headquarters in Rawalpindi and held around forty people hostage for over 20 hours much to the army's embarrassment.

These attacks have heralded a new period in army and ISI relations with many of these militant groups, say analysts. Steve Coll, president of the New America Foundation, a Washington-based think tank, says since the bloody encounter between Pakistan's security forces and militant Islamic students in Islamabad's Red Mosque in 2007, there has been a pattern of some of these groups previously under state patronage, breaking away from the state. He says Pakistan's security establishment is currently trying to figure out how to control them. However, most analysts believe that even though the Pakistani army and the ISI are now more willing to go after militant groups, they continue some form of alliance with groups they want to use as a strategic hedge against India and Afghanistan. But Pakistan's security establishment denies these charges. In October 2009, ISI Chief Ahmad Shuja Pasha said: "The ISI is a professional agency and does not have links with any militant outfit including the Taliban." *(See Ref 169, 170)*

In particular, U.S. officials would like Pakistan to crackdown on the leadership of the Afghan Taliban believed to be based in Quetta and two major factions of the Afghan insurgency led by veteran Afghan warlords, Jalaluddin Haqqani and Gulbuddin Hekmatyar. These, U.S. officials believe, are actively engaged in supplying fighters in Afghanistan. Analysts believe these groups do not engage in direct attacks against the Pakistani state in lieu of political cover inside Pakistan. Islamabad denies these charges. However, journalist Steve Coll, who visited Pakistan several times, believes that there is some shift in Pakistan's strategy of supporting groups against India and to project influence in Afghanistan. "There are more debate and more ambivalence," he says. "Overall, the Pakistani establishment is moving in the right direction but it will take a very long time to undo the pattern that has been established so far." *(See Ref 170)*

However, until the Pakistani military truly takes on a more holistic view of the country's national interests - one that sees economic development, not strategic gamesmanship against Afghanistan and India, as the key to Pakistan's security - terrorists will continue to find Pakistan as an ideal place to establish themselves.

Over the past four decades, much Islamic terrorism has been traced back to two countries: Saudi Arabia and Pakistan. Both countries were founded as ideological, Islamic states; over the years the governments sought legitimacy by reinforcing that religious ideology, with the effect of making those countries hothouses of militancy, fundamentalism, and jihad. That trend is slowly being reversed in Saudi Arabia, However, given its weaker central government and intrinsic nature it may not be so easy for Pakistan to overcome its jihadist past.

CHAPTER SEVEN

AL-QA'IDA: THE BASE OF THE NEW TERRORISM

In the nineteenth and early twenty centuries, terrorism was most often premised on secular ideology – anarchism, communism, nationalism or the like. And, the tactic of choice was the assassination of a highly visible political leader - Tzar Alexander II of Russia in 1881, President William McKinley of the United States in 1901 and Archduke Franz Ferdinand, heir to the Austro-Hungarian Throne in 1914, are three more prominent examples. At that time, terrorism was largely seen as a violent tool of communication that allowed small, regional political movements sufficient resources to bring attention to their cause and more broadly promote their secular agenda. In more recent years the world has witnessed the emergence of a unique and innovative form of political violence. In stark contrast to the older form, scholars have identified a "new terrorism" grounded largely in non-secular ideology; more specifically, an ideology of sacred proportions that traces its roots to traditional culture and fundamental religious beliefs rather than secular ideas.

The term "new terrorism," came into the scene after the September 11, 2001 attacks, but it is itself not new. In 1986, the Canadian news magazine, Macleans, published "The Menacing Face of the New Terrorism," identifying it as a war against the "perceived decadence and immorality of the West" by Middle Eastern, "mobile, well-trained, suicidal and savagely unpredictable" "Islamic fundamentalists." More frequently, "new" terrorism has been focused on a perceived new threat of mass casualties caused by chemical, biological or other agents. Discussions of "new terrorism" are often highly alarmist: it is described by Dore Gold in the American Spectator (March 2003), as "far more lethal than anything that has come before it," "a terrorism that seeks the total collapse of its opponents". *(See Ref 174)*

So, in contrast to the limited agenda of the older forms, new terrorist groups want much more than merely bringing attention to their movement and their secular agenda. Their objectives are far broader. They seek nothing less than to hasten the onset of a new and idealised age. And, they strive to do so by stirring up a world-ending devastation on a global scale. As a result, this "new-form-terrorism" differs from the old- form along two important dimensions: source of ideology (secularism versus religious millenarianism) and scope (modest, regionalised goals versus worldwide, massive devastation). The Tupac Amaru Revolutionary Movement (MRTA) in Peru, Aum Shinrikyo in Japan and al-Qa'ida, have all been identified as prominent examples of the "new-form-terrorism" phenomenon. It has been estimated that the potential adherents to such movements numbers in the millions worldwide. *(See Ref 175, 176)*

The role of religion was virtually ignored by scholars of International Relations during the Cold War and, in particular, by those who studied international conflict. In fact, until rather recently, Western academic circles considered religion to be a declining force in politics in general. No one could have predicted that "religion" in its many forms would become an alternative to the competing secular ideologies that had previously dominated world affairs. During this period, insufficient attention was placed on cultural variables. In particular, the developing world was viewed largely within the context of a broader struggle between East and West.

Nonetheless, in the aftermath of World War II the developing world has emerged as a culturally fragmented, frequently political unstable, economically diverse group of states, with rapidly growing populations and substantial structural problems. Collectively, these new states had no particular affinity with the international status quo, which they were obliged to accept upon assuming political independence. As a result, ordinary people in the developing world found themselves caught up in the desires of their governments to modernise their societies along Western lines, while at the same time attempting to retain their long held cultural and religious beliefs. Over time, the realisation became altogether clear that this model of a modernising, national, secular state existing in complete harmony with powerful cultural institutions and local traditions was a failure. The two notions were simply incompatible. Leaving many populations feeling their traditional ways were being threatened. They quickly came to realise that in the modern world secularism abounds and comes at the expense of cultural pluralism, and satisfying the human need for sacred authenticity. Many concluded that modernisation impinges on traditional culture and can lead to its eventual destruction.

To many in the Islamic community, this threat was characterised along two dimensions. First, was a strictly religious one in which Christianity, often portrayed as in collusion with "Zionism," was seen as an agent seeking to restrict the power of Islam in a modern world. More importantly, this was perceived as merely a first step toward the elimination of Islam altogether. According to Sayyid Qutb: "We are aware of the strenuous efforts which have been exerted for some time in an effort to confine Islam to the emotional and ritual circles, and to bar it from participating in the activities of life... this is a Christian offensive against the Muslim Nation in its Realm of Islam. They were as well the cause of the exhaustion suffered by a scheming international Zionism for a long time. Both had no alternative but to combine their prodigious efforts to attempt to restrict this religion to emotional belief and ritualism, so as to end its intervention in the systems of actual life in the first step, or first offensive, of a battle of ultimate annihilation". *(See Ref 177)*

Second, was a "sacred versus secular dichotomy," through which modern leaders, such as Kemal Attaturk of Turkey, Gamal Abdel Nasser of Egypt, or the Pahlavi family in Iran, sought to transform the power of the state from within the community in order to incorporate a more "modern" Islam into their larger, secular socio-political and economic agenda. The goal was to dislodge the Islamic Shari'a from its place as the only source of legislation, to replace it with European codes of law and to corner Islamic legislation in a limited, narrow circle called status "personalis", or personal law. *(See Ref 177)*

However, the government legitimacy in the developing world started to decline in the 1970s due to a combination of factors: cultural invasion, corruption, economic failure, and political repression. In response, ordinary people turned to others to champion their interests. In the process, ethnicity and religion became intertwined into a cultural and political worldview. As ruling elites failed to deliver the developmental goods in the overwhelming majority of developing states, their own legitimacy was called into question by religious and /or ethnic leaders, who often framed their criticisms in religious doctrinal or sub-nationalist terms.

The world currently finds itself in the midst of a global resurgence of religion and cultural pluralism in international affairs. This resurgence is part of a larger crisis of modernity. It reflects a very deep and rather pervasive disillusionment with a western style of modernisation that many see as largely reducing one's world to what can be perceived and controlled through reason, science, technology, and bureaucratic rationality and leaves out considerations of the religious, the spiritual, or the sacred. In particular, this resurgence is directly related to a search for authenticity in the developing world. Nowhere is this resurgence more salient than in Islamic communities and it has been cast in an authentic and powerful messianic context. . It is within this context that al-Qa'ida was launched.

The origins of al-Qa'ida (meaning the base in Arabic), as a network inspiring Islamic terrorism around the world and training operatives, can be traced to the movements of Islamic resistance to the Soviet war in Afghanistan. The United States viewed the conflict in Afghanistan, with the Afghan Marxists and allied Soviet troops on one side and the native Afghan "mujahideen" radical Islamic militants on the other, as a blatant case of Soviet expansionism and aggression. As previously discussed the U.S. channelled funds through Pakistan's Inter-Services Intelligence agency to the Afghan mujahideen fighting the Soviet occupation in a CIA program called Operation Cyclone. *(See Ref 178)*

At the same time, a growing number of Arab mujahideen joined the jihad against the Afghan Marxist regime, facilitated by international Muslim organisations, particularly the "Maktab al-Khidmat li al-Mujahideen al-'Arab" (the Arab Mujahideen Service Bureau or Office), whose funds came from some of the $600 million a year donated to the charity organisations and jihad by the Saudi Arabia government and individual Muslims – particularly independent Saudi businessmen who were approached by Osama bin Laden. *(See Ref 179)*

Maktab al-Khidmat (MAK) was established by Abdallah Azzam and Osama bin Laden in Peshawar, Pakistan, in 1984. From 1986 it began to set up a network of recruiting offices in the United States, the hub of which was the "al-Kifah Refugee Centre" at the Farouq Mosque in Brooklyn's Atlantic Avenue. Among notable figures at the Brooklyn centre were "double agent" Ali Mohamed, whom FBI special agent Jack Cloonan called "bin Laden's first trainer," and "Blind Sheikh" Omar Abdel-Rahman, a leading recruiter of mujahideen for Afghanistan. (*See Ref 180*))

Al-Qa'ida evolved from "Maktab al-Khidmat", a Muslim organisation founded to raise and channel funds and recruit foreign "mujahideen" for the war against the Soviets in Afghanistan. It was founded by Abdallah Yussef Azzam, a Jordanian-Palestinian Islamic scholar and member of the Muslim Brotherhood and joined later by Osama bin Laden. Furthermore MAK organised guest houses in Peshawar, near the Afghan border, and gathered supplies for the construction of paramilitary training camps to prepare foreign recruits for the Afghan war. Bin Laden became a "major financier" of the mujahideen, spending his own money and using his connections with "the Saudi and the petro-billionaires of the Gulf" in order to improve public opinion of the war and raise more funds. Beginning in 1987, Azzam and bin Laden started creating camps inside Afghanistan. *(See Ref 181)*

U.S. government financial support for the Afghan Islamic militants was substantial. Aid to Gulbuddin Hekmatyar, (an Afghan Mujahideen commander and leader of the "Hezb-e Islami" radical Islamic militant faction), alone amounted "by the most conservative estimates" to $600 million. Hekmatyar "worked closely" with Osama bin Laden in early 1990s. In addition to hundreds of millions of dollars of American aid, Hekmatyar also received the lion's share of aid from the Saudis. There is evidence that the CIA supported Hekmatyar's drug trade activities by giving him immunity for his opium trafficking that financed operation of his militant faction. *(See Ref 182, 183)*

The MAK and foreign "mujahideen" volunteers, including "Afghan Arabs," did not play a major role in the war. While over 250,000 Afghan "mujahideen" fought the Soviets and the communist Afghan government, it is estimated that were never more than 2,000 foreign "mujahideen" in the field at any one time. Nonetheless, foreign volunteers came from 43 countries and the total number that participated in the Afghan movement between 1982 and 1992 is reported to have been about 35,000. *(See Ref 184)*

The Soviet Union finally withdrew from Afghanistan in 1989. To the surprise of many, Mohammed Najibullah's communist Afghan government hung on for three more years before being overrun by elements of the "mujahideen". However, with "mujahideen" leaders unable to agree on a structure for governance, chaos ensued, with constantly reorganising alliances fighting for control of ill-defined territories, leaving the country devastated.

Toward the end of the Soviet military mission in Afghanistan, some "mujahideen" wanted to expand their operations to include Islamist struggles in other parts of the world, such as Israel and Kashmir. A number of overlapping and interrelated organisations were formed to further those aspirations. One such organisation that would eventually be called al-Qa'ida, formed by Osama bin Laden with an initial meeting held on 11 August 1988. Bin Laden wished to establish non-military operations in other parts of the world; Azzam, in contrast, wanted to remain focused on military campaigns. After Azzam was assassinated in 1989 in Pakistan, the MAK split, with a significant number joining bin Laden's organisation. Furthermore in November 1989, Ali Muhammad, a former special forces Sergeant stationed at Fort Bragg, North Carolina, left military service and moved to Santa Clara, California. He travelled to Afghanistan and Pakistan and became "deeply involved with bin Laden's plans." *(See Ref 179)*

A year later, on 8 November 1990, the FBI raided the New Jersey home of Muhammad's associate Sayyid Nosair, discovering a great deal of evidence of terrorist plots, including plans to blow up New York City skyscrapers. Nosair was eventually convicted in connection to the 1993 World Trade Centre bombing, and for the murder of Rabbi Meir Kahane on November 5, 1990. In 1991, Ali Muhammad is said to have helped orchestrate Osama bin Laden's relocation to Sudan. *(See Ref 178)*

While he was in Afghanistan bin Laden established close cooperation with a group of Egyptian Islamists, the most important of whom was Ayman al-Zawahiri, who had been implicated in the assassination of President Anwar Sadat. After Abdallah Azzam's death, members of the Egyptian group took over key positions in the al-Qa'ida leadership. Al-Zawahiri, who returned to Egypt to head the Islamic Jihad organisation at the beginning of the 1990s, became the leading ideologue for the organisation and was instrumental in al-Qa'ida's move towards terrorism on a global scale and for attacks on United States interests.

Following the Soviet Union's withdrawal from Afghanistan in February 1989, Osama bin Laden returned to Saudi Arabia. The Iraqi invasion of Kuwait in August 1990 had put the kingdom and its ruling House of

Saud at risk. The world's most valuable oil fields were within easy striking distance of Iraqi forces in Kuwait, and Saddam Hussein's call to pan-Arab-Islamism could potentially rally internal dissent. Moreover, in the face of a seemingly massive Iraqi military presence, Saudi Arabia's own forces were well armed but far outnumbered. Bin Laden offered the services of his mujahideen to the Saudi government to protect the country from the Iraqi army. The Saudis refused bin Laden's offer, opting instead to allow U.S. and allied forces to deploy troops into Saudi territory. *(See Ref 185, 186)*

The deployment angered bin Laden, as he believed the presence of foreign troops in the "land of the two holy mosques" profaned sacred soil. After speaking publicly against the Saudi government for harbouring American troops, he was banished and forced to live in exile in Sudan.

Bin Laden and his organisation were headquartered in Sudan, between 1991 and May 1996, where he has received the support and protection of the country's leaders General Omar al-Bashir and Hassan al-Turabi who was the regime's leading ideologue at that time, aspired to turn Sudan into the centre of world Islamic revolution. However, according to an arrangement worked out between Osama bin Laden and al-Turabi, al-Qa'ida set up camps and provided training in guerrilla warfare to the militias of the Sudanese National Islamic Front (NIF), which was fighting a war in southern Sudan with the Sudanese People's Liberation Front. By the end of 1991 most of bin Laden's trained militants had moved from Afghanistan to Sudan. *(See Ref 182)*

On the other hand, bin Laden invested a large part of his substantial inheritance, while he was in Sudan, in business and financial ventures which he intended to use to finance the expansion of the al-Qa'ida and its operations around the world. Bin Laden's "Al Hijra" construction company obtained contracts from the Sudanese government to build roads, bridges, and government buildings. Other bin Laden enterprises in Sudan included Laden International, the "al-Thema" agricultural company, and the "Wadi Al-Aqiq" trading company. At the same time, bin Laden also invested in a variety of businesses in Africa, Asia, and elsewhere and he opened bank accounts in many countries. These businesses and investments became an important pillar in the financing of al-Qa'ida's terrorist activities around the world. *(See Ref 182, 187)*

Furthermore, many terrorist organisations, other than al-Qa'ida, were also allowed by the Sudanese government to set up offices, bases, and training facilities on its territory. Among these were the Algerian Islamic Salvation Front, Tunisia's al-Nahda, the Egyptian Islamic Group (al-Gama'a al-Islamiya) and Egyptian Islamic Jihad. During bin Laden's stay in Sudan he developed a closer relationship with the Egyptian and North African Islamist organisations and helped finance the dispatching of fighters to Bosnia, Chechnya, Kashmir and elsewhere while continuing to maintain al-Qa'ida safe houses, bases and training facilities in Pakistan and Afghanistan. *(See Ref 178)*

Following the first World Trade Centre (WTC) Bombing in March1993, the Pakistani government, under pressure from Washington, expelled some of the Arab Afghans, and bin Laden paid for their tickets out of the country. Many of these fighters came to Sudan to participate in bin Laden's training camps there. Additional training facilities were also moved across the Pakistan-Afghan border into Afghanistan. *(See Ref 188,189)*

The first bombing of the World Trade Centre took place in New York City when bin Laden was in Sudan. Among the participants in that WTC bombing were members of a mosque headed by Sheikh Omar Abdul Rahman, a radical Islamist cleric and leader of the Egyptian Islamic Group, who had entered the United States from Sudan and had been granted political asylum. Sheikh Omar and a number of his associates were implicated in a parallel attempt to bomb the United Nations and the Holland Tunnel, an act which, if successful, would have led to massive casualties of innocent civilians. Among those implicated in the United Nations bombing plot were two Sudanese diplomats who had been attached to the Sudanese United Nations mission in New York City. In August 1993, the US State Department placed Sudan on its list of state sponsors of terrorist activity. *(See Ref 190)*

The role, which al-Qa'ida had played in the first World Trade Centre bombing, still not clear.In 1993, bin Laden had yet to formalise ties with organisations and factions that by the end of the decade were to form part of the al-Qa'ida. What is clear is that the Egyptian Islamic Group headed by Sheikh Omar Abdul Rahman had links to al-Qa'ida going back to the late 1980s and later became one of the main components of the al-Qa'ida led alliance of radical Islamic terrorist organisations. Two of Sheikh Omar's sons joined Osama Bin Laden in Afghanistan, where they remained until after the September 11 attacks. However, the mastermind of the 1993 WTC plot, Ramzi Yusef, is believed to have had links to Islamic extremist groups associated with al-Qa'ida in Pakistan and Afghanistan before the 1993 bombing. After his flight from the United States the same day the bombing occurred he developed a closer association with al-Qa'ida supported groups in Pakistan, the Philippines, and Southeast Asia. Some investigators believe that Ramzi Yusef became al-Qa'ida's chief representative for Southeast Asia. *(See Ref 191)*

While his relations with Khartoum were strong and good, Osama bin Laden's relationship with Riyad deteriorated further during his stay in Sudan. The Saudis made several unsuccessful attempts to convince bin Laden to return to the Kingdom. In response to those attempts he intensified his efforts to undermine the royal government and encouraged the "Sahwa" group to found the "Advice and Reformation Committee" which issued an anti-regime manifesto known as the Memorandum of Advice in 1992. The Saudi government responded to Osama's anti-regime moves by freezing his assets in the kingdom and in 1994 revoked his citizenship. In March 1994, the bin Laden family in Saudi Arabia issued a press statement denouncing and condemning Osama's political activities. *(See Ref 182, 187)*

Islamic extremists stepped up their violence against the Mubarak government in 1995. They organised an assassination attempt against the Egyptian President on 26 June 1995 at the Addis Ababa summit in Ethiopia and bombed the Egyptian embassy in Islamabad on November 19 of that year. In response to these actions by the bin Laden-allied Egyptian groups, the United States and Eygpt began putting intense pressure on Sudan to expel Osama bin Laden and his entourage from the country while the Saudi government continued its efforts to induce the Sudanese to end their support for bin Laden. In spring of 1996, Sudan was no longer able to resist the continued international pressure, asked bin Laden and his fighters to leave the country. *(See Ref 192, 193, 194)*

According to Pakistani-American businessman Mansoor Ijaz, the Sudanese government offered the Clinton Administration numerous opportunities to arrest bin Laden. Those opportunities were met positively by Secretary of State Madeleine Albright but spurned when Susan Rice and counter-terrorism tzar Richard Clarke persuaded National Security Advisor Sandy Berger to overrule Albright. Ijaz's claims in this regard appeared in numerous Op-Ed pieces including one in the Los Angeles Times and one in The Washington Post co-written with former US Ambassador to Sudan Timothy Carney. Similar allegations have been made by Vanity Fair contributing Editor David Rose and Richard Miniter, author of Losing bin Laden, in a November 2003 interview with World. *(See Ref 195, 196, 197)*

Several sources dispute Ijaz's claim, including the National Commission on Terrorist Attacks on the United States (more commonly known as the 9/11 Commission) which concluded in part that "Sudan's Minister of Defence, Fatih Erwa, has claimed that Sudan offered to hand bin Laden over to the United States. The Commission has found no credible evidence that this was so. Ambassador Carney had instructions only to push the Sudanese to expel bin Laden. Ambassador Carney had no legal basis to ask for more from the Sudanese since, at the time, there was no indictment out-standing." *(See Ref 198)*

As we discussed previously, following the Soviet withdrawal, Afghanistan was effectively ungoverned for seven years and plagued by constant infighting between former allies and various "mujahideen" groups.

During the 1990s, the Taliban began to emerge. According to the Journalist Ahmed Rashid, five leaders of the Taliban were graduates of "Darul Uloom Haqqania", a madrasa in the small town of Akora Khattak. The town is situated near Peshawar in Pakistan but largely attended by Afghan refugees. This institution reflected Salafi beliefs in its teachings, and much of its funding came from private donations from wealthy Arabs. Bin Laden's contacts were still laundering most of these donations, using "unscrupulous" Islamic banks to transfer the money to an "array" of charities which serve as front groups for al-Qa'ida or transporting cash-filled suitcases straight into Pakistan. Another four of the Taliban's leaders attended a similarly funded and influenced madrasa in Kandahar, Afghanistan. *(See Ref 199)*

The continuing internecine strife between various factions, and accompanying lawlessness following the Soviet withdrawal, enabled the growing and comparatively well-disciplined Taliban to expand their control over territory in Afghanistan, and they came to establish an enclave which it called the Islamic Emirate of Afghanistan. In 1994, they captured the regional centre of Kandahar, and after making rapid territorial gains thereafter, conquered the capital city Kabul in September 1996.

After the Sudanese made it clear, in May 1996, that bin Laden would never be welcomed to return, Taliban-controlled Afghanistan - with previously established connections between the groups, administered with a shared militancy, and largely isolated from American political influence and military power- provided a perfect location for al-Qa'ida to relocate its headquarters. Al-Qa'ida enjoyed the Taliban's protection and a measure of legitimacy as part of their Ministry of Defence, although only Pakistan, Saudi Arabia, and the United Arab Emirates recognised the Taliban as the legitimate government of Afghanistan.

After establishing al-Qa'ida's headquarters in Taliban controlled Afghanistan and cementing a close relationship with Mullah Omar and other Taliban leaders, bin Laden increased the scope and intensity of the organisation's activities world-wide. In 1996, al-Qa'ida announced its jihad to expel foreign troops and interests from what they considered Islamic lands. Bin Laden issued a fatwa, which amounted to a public declaration of war against the United States of America and any of its allies, and began to refocus al-Qa'ida's resources towards large-scale, propagandist strikes. Furthermore, on 23 February 1998, Osama bin Laden, Ayman al-Zawahiri, a leader of Egyptian Islamic Jihad, along the leader Rifai Ahmed Taha of the Egyptian Islamic Group (Gama'a al-Islamiya), and leaders of several other extremist organisations in Pakistan and Bangladesh, co-signed and issued a "fatwa" calling on Muslims to kill Americans and their allies where they can, when they can. Under the banner of the "World Islamic Front for Combat against the Jews and Crusaders" they declared: "[T]he ruling to kill the Americans and their allies -civilians and military-is an individual duty for every Muslim who can do it in any country in which it is possible to do it, in order to liberate the al-Aqsa Mosque [in Jerusalem] and the holy mosque [in Mecca] from their grip, and in order for their armies to move out of all the lands of Islam, defeated and unable to threaten any Muslim. This is in accordance with the words of Almighty Allah, 'and fight the pagans all together as they fight you all together', and 'fight them until there is no more tumult or oppression, and there prevail justice and faith in Allah'". *(See Ref 178, 200)*

Neither bin Laden nor al-Zawahiri possessed the traditional Islamic scholarly qualifications to issue a fatwa of any kind; however, they rejected the authority of the contemporary "ulama" who they seen as the paid servants of religiously vacuous rulers and took it upon themselves to take up the mantle.

Until 1998, most of the violence unleashed by al-Qa'ida and its allies had been against military or civilian supporters of Middle Eastern governments that had been declared apostates or supporters of governments fighting Muslim insurgencies in places like Bosnia, Chechnya, the Central Asian republics of the former Soviet Union, Xinxiang province of China, and the Philippines. The new World Islamic Front soon showed that it was ready to strike directly at United States and other Western targets. On 7 August 1998 al-Qa'ida operatives launched powerful bomb attacks on the United States Embassies in Nairobi, Kenya and Dar Es-Salam, Tanzania. On September 20, 1998, the United States responded to the embassy bombing with missile strikes against several al-Qa'ida training camps in Afghanistan and a chemicals factory in Sudan. The strikes failed to kill bin Laden or any of the top al-Qa'ida leaders or the owner of the chemical factory, who denied any links to al-Qa'ida and sued the US government for damages. On 14 December 1999, police arrested Ahmed Ressam, an Algerian with ties to the "Groupe Islamique Arme" (GIA) whose vehicle contained explosives with which he planned to blow up Los Angeles international airport, LAX. On 5 October 2000, Yemeni terrorists belonging to an al-Qa'ida cell launched a suicide bombing from a small boat against the USS Cole in Aden harbour in Yemen, killing 17 seamen and wounding 39 others. After the US embassy and Cole bombings, the United States tried unsuccessfully to influence Pakistan to force the Taliban to shut down terrorist training camps in Afghanistan and to hand over bin Laden for trial in the United States. It was only after the September 11 attacks, that the United States was able to make the Pakistani leadership stop shielding the Taliban and take measures to crack down on extremist groups in Pakistan itself. *(See Ref 201)*

However, to understand the specific circumstances that led to the ideological transformation of al-Qaida during and after the jihad against the Soviet occupation of Afghanistan in the 1980s, we must examine the influence of the Egyptians Islamists on bin Laden himself.

The Arabs who came in to join the Afghan mujahideen fell into two main camps, Yemeni and Egyptian. These zealots inspired by their local clerics, were mostly from the Yemeni camp. In breaks from fighting they spent their days drilling and cooking their food, before going straight to sleep after the isha (last prayer of the day). As the Afghan jihad tailed off, they went home or melted into the population in Afghanistan or Pakistan,

144

where many married. In al-Qa'ida circles, they were called "drawish" or easy-going.

The Egyptian camp was more politically minded and ideologically motivated. Though most belonged to the Muslim Brotherhood, they opposed its commitment to elections and the democratic process. The Afghan jihad cohered these like-minded, often educated individuals, many of them doctors and engineers or former soldiers associated with the Egyptian Islamic Jihad under Ayman al-Zawahiri now bin Laden's deputy. This group had been responsible for the assassination of President Anwar Sadat in 1981 after he signed a peace deal with Israel at Camp David. All agreed that the US and its puppet governments in the Middle East were responsible for the decline of the Arab world. In contrast to the Yemenis, after the "isha" the Egyptian camp would discuss contemporary issues. Their leaders reiterated the message that members should invest their resources in the armies of their countries, and cultivate the best brains.

During an interview in Amman, Abdallah Azzam's son Hudayfa, who has spent almost 20 years among Arab militants in Afghanistan and Pakistan, told the French monthly Le Monde Diplomatique: "Most Yemeni fighters, simple minded warriors whose only ambition was martyrdom, left Afghanistan after the fall of the Communist government. The Egyptians stayed because they had other ambitions as yet unfulfilled. When Osama bin Laden joined them, after he left Sudan in 1996, they focused on shifting his basic thinking from opposition to American hegemony in the Middle East towards a Takfirist perspective."

Hudayfa continued: "When I met Osama bin Laden in 1997 in Islamabad, he was flanked by three members of the Egyptian camp: the Somali Abu Obaida, and the Egyptians Abu Haf and Saiful Adil. I realised how successfully they had instilled their extremist ideas into him. When my father asked him to go to Afghanistan in 1985, he had replied that he would only do so if King Fahd personally granted permission. At that time Osama still referred to Fahd as wali al-amr (supreme authority). After 9/11, when he denounced the rulers of Saudi Arabia, I could see how much the Egyptian camp had influenced him". *(See Ref 202)*

However, while al-Qa'ida was still in Afghanistan, its ideologues instructed the network's recruiters to look for Jihadists internationally, Muslims who believed that jihad must be fought on a global level. The concept of a "global Salafi jihad" had been around since at least the early 1980s. Several groups had formed for the explicit purpose of driving non-Muslims out of every Muslim land at the same time with maximum carnage. This was, however, a fundamentally defensive strategy. So, al-Qa'ida sought to open a new "offensive phase". Now for example, Bosnian Islamists today call for "solidarity with Islamic causes around the world", and they supported the insurgents in Kashmir and Iraq as well as the groups fighting for a Palestinian state. *(See Ref 203, 204)*

While al-Qa'ida retreated to Pakistan-Afghanistan borders region with Taliban forces after they were defeated in Afghanistan, the percentage of terrorist attacks in the West, according to the Russian sources, originating from that area have declined considerably from almost a 100 percent to 75 percent in 2007 and to 50 percent in 2010, as al-Qa'ida has shifted to Somalia and Yemen. However, whilst al-Qa'ida leaders continue to hide in the tribal areas along the Afghanistan-Pakistan border, the middle-tier of the extremist movement display heightened activity in Somalia and Yemen. "We know that South Asia is no longer their primary base," a source in the US defence agency said to the Washington Times. "They are looking for a hide-out in other parts of the world and continue to expand their organisation". *(See Ref 205)*

In Somalia, al Qa'ida agents closely collaborate with the Islamic a-Shabab Movement, actively recruit children for suicide-bomber training and export young people to participate in military actions against Americans at the Afghanistan-Pakistan border. In January 2009, al-Qa'ida's division in Saudi Arabia merged with its Yemeni wing to form al-Qa'ida in the Arabian Peninsula. Centred in Yemen, the group takes advantage of the country's poor economy, demography and domestic security. In August 2009, for the first time in decades, they made an assassination attempt against a member of the Saudi royal dynasty. President Obama in a letter asked his Yemen counterpart Ali Abdallah Saleh to ensure closer cooperation with the USA in the struggle against the growing activity of al-Qa'ida within Yemen's borders, and promised to send additional international aid. However, due to the wars in Iraq and Afghanistan, and the uprisings in the Arab World, the United States is unable to pay sufficient attention to Somalia and Yemen, which may cause the U.S. serious problems in the near future. Al-Qa'ida in the Arabian Peninsula claimed responsibility for the 2009 failed bombing attack on Northwest Airlines Flight 253 by the Nigerian Omar Farouk Abdulmutalleb. The group released later photos of Omar smiling in a white shirt and white Islamic skullcap with the al-Qa'ida in Arabian Peninsula banner in the background. *(See Ref 206)*

Now that we have an historic context for its creation as well as knowledge of its means of operation, one must ask: what does al-Qa'ida want?

Modern Islamic militancy is varied and complex. According to Jason Burke, al-Qa'ida is as much an ideology or a set of values as a single organisation led by a single leader. In fact, the values and ideas, the 'wants', of militants are very varied. Recent Islamic militants have shown many different motivations. Ramzi Yousef, who tried to destroy the World Trade Centre in 1993, was driven more by a lust for notoriety than religious fervour. He did not pray and flirted with female lawyers while on trial. Muhammad Atta, the leader of the 11 September hijackers, acted because he felt, with absolute certainty, that he had no option but to wage a jihad. He was obliged to fulfil his religious duty. One of the men who organised the bombing of a night club in Bali in October 2002 said he had been disgusted by the 'dirty adulterous behaviour' of the 'whites' there. Another said he was angered by the war in Afghanistan. *(See Ref 212)*

However, al-Qa'ida's objectives surprisingly remain in dispute amongst experts and pundists, particularly with regard to the United States. Two camps have emerged according to Council on Foreign Relations' expert Daniel L Byman. Some maintain that al-Qa'ida's aims are bound up in U.S. policy in the Middle East, in particular the U.S. security presence in the Persian Gulf and U.S. support for Israel. According to this view, al-Qa'ida is using terrorism to achieve concrete (though ambitious) goals. Others portray an existential struggle, with al-Qa'ida hating the Western way of life and its values. As former President George W Bush noted in his address to U.S. Congress on 21 September 2001, "They hate our freedoms: our freedom of religion, our freedom of speech, our freedom to vote and assemble and disagree with each other … These terrorists kill not merely to end lives, but to disrupt and end a way of life." *(See Ref 207, 208)*

If pundits and experts remain in dispute concerning al-Qa'ida aims and objectives, they all agree that resolving this debate is crucial and vital for informed policy. On the one hand, a hatred born of U.S. policy implies that often-suggested changes – a withdrawal of U.S. forces from Saudi Arabia (which was happened given their withdrawal to Qatar and other Gulf States), a strong push for a Palestinian-Israeli peace, and so on – could take the wind out of al-Qa'ida's sails. On the other hand, according to Daniel Byman, "if al-Qa'ida can never be appeased, then there is little incentive to change U.S. policies and the struggle becomes existential." *(See Ref 208)*

Al-Qa'ida's rage is deep, but not inchoate. All the authors agree that al-Qa'ida objects to numerous elements of American foreign policy (and West in general) – though some see the movement's grievances as much deeper. However, despite this variety, there are certain universal themes. To understand them we have to redraft our question. 'What do they want?' implies a Western concept of acting to achieve specific goals. Instead we should be asking: 'Why do they feel that they have to act in the way that they do?' The answer is that, from their twisted standpoint, they believe they have no choice. In fact, constructing a list of supposed Western (in particular U.S.) offenses is instructive:

+ A blasphemous military presence. The stationing of U.S. and other Western forces in the Middle East, particularly in the Arabian Peninsula near Muslim holy sites, is the ultimate American sin, trespassing on the heart of the holy land and demonstrating America's desire to subjugate Islam;

+ A blinding bias toward Israel. The United States is seen as creating and nurturing the Jewish state as part of a modern-day colonial venture;

+ Support for a range of corrupt regimes in the Muslim and Arab world. Regimes seen to oppress and impoverish their people;

+ The destruction and enslavement of Iraq. The United States sought to crush Iraq in order, according to bin Laden's 1998 statement, "to destroy Iraq, the most powerful neighbouring Arab state"; *(See Ref 182)*

+ Subordination of the Muslim world. In general, the United States seeks to undermine any effort by a Muslim nation to gain strength. In bin Laden's words, the West seeks to "keep Muslims weak and incapable of defending themselves"; *(See Ref 209)*

+ Forcing Saudi Arabia and other Muslim oil producers to sell out their oil under artificially low prices;

+ A willingness to tolerate, or even inflict, Muslim deaths in struggles around the world. Al-Qa'ida's list would include Chechnya, Kashmir,

Indonesia, Nigeria, Uzbekistan, the Philippines, and the Xinjiang province in China, among others.

It is also worth recognising what is not on this list. As Peter Bergen notes, these grievances are political. Bin Laden "does not rail against the pernicious effects of Hollywood movies, or against Madonna's midriff, or against the pornography protected by the U.S Constitution. Nor does he inveigh against the drug and alcohol culture of the West, or its tolerance for homosexuals. He leaves that kind of material to the American Christian fundamentalist Jerry Falwell...". Bin Laden's grievances are focused on power – who possesses it, why it is used, and (in his judgment) how it is abused. *(See Ref 182)*

At times, however, al-Qa'ida's views go from the extreme to the delusional. For example, Daniel Byman notes that bin Laden saw the U.S. intervention in Somalia as the first step in a broader occupation of Africa and the overthrow of the Islamist regime in Sudan. Australia's intervention in East Timor was merely a Christian land-grab. Serbs acted as America's henchmen to kill Muslims in the Balkans. As if this long list of offenses were not enough, these specific grievances are tied to a broader agenda, that al-Qaida shares with the broad Islamist movement of restoring Muslim dignity and re-establishing God's rule. America, the superpower, is resented for its "cultural hegemony, global political influence, and overwhelming conventional military power". The ubiquitous presence of American popular culture only fuels the anger of Islamists. *(See Ref 208, 210)*

This perception that a belligerent West is set on the humiliation, division and eventual conquest of the Islamic world is at the root of most Muslim violence. Al-Qa'ida militants believe they are fighting a last-ditch battle for the survival of their society, culture, religion and way of life. They are fighting in self-defence and understand, as the West also believes, that self-defence can justify using tactics that might be frowned on in other circumstances.

In fact, this hatred toward the West goes beyond current disagreements and is directed at, in the words of Sayyid Qutb, the "Crusader spirit which runs in the blood of all Westerners". Radical Islamists are combining this view of an eternal conflict with the West with virulent anti-Semitism (historically rare in the Muslim world). They then interpret all current events as part of a broader conspiracy against Islam and, armed with these "facts," contend that the United States is truly evil rather than merely misguided.

Al-Qa'ida's grievances, while shared by many Muslims, are a departure from the traditional agendas of most Islamist groups, even violent ones. For much of recent history, radical Islamist groups sought to overthrow the "near enemy" –secular and repressive Arab regimes– first. Only then, radical Islamists declared, should the "far enemy" –Israel and the United States– be confronted. Bin Laden turns this idea on its head. Ending U.S. hegemony, he argues, will produce the collapse of pro-Western regimes in the Muslim world. As bin Laden remarked, "If we cut off the head of America, the kingdoms in the Arab world will cease to exist". *(See Ref 209)*

Jihad is a central concept in this struggle. Radical Islamists reject the claim that jihad is primarily an individual's spiritual struggle against one's more base instincts, instead interpreting it as actual warfare – a view that appears to have strong historical support. In their eyes, jihad is as much a pillar of faith as fasting during Ramadan or praying five times a day. Indeed, the radicals take this concept to new heights, arguing that jihad can be declared against Muslims who are insufficiently pious, particularly Muslim rulers. For example, bin Laden's teacher, Abdallah Azzam, declared "jihad is every man's duty" if foreigners seize Muslim lands. Furthermore, in a video that circulated in the Middle East in the months before September, 2001, bin Laden declared, "If you don't fight you will be punished by God". *(See Ref 211)*

Because of the scope of its grievances, its broader agenda of rectifying perceived humiliation and its poisoned worldview that glorifies jihad as a solution, appeasing al-Qa'ida is difficult in theory, and impossible in practice. It is hard to imagine what would suffice al-Qa'ida. So many U.S. interests are involved that even significant policy changes would only be the tip of the iceberg. In essence, al-Qa'ida seeks America's unconditional surrender, interpreted to mean a withdrawal of all forms of U.S. influence – including cultural - from the Muslim world. Any concessions regarding Israel, troops in the Arabian Peninsula and so on, would simply be milestones on al-Qa'ida's path to victory. In fact, according to Daniel Byman, "al-Qa'ida regards attacking as a goal in and of itself, demonstrating the movement's strength and determination." *(See Ref 208)*

Given this mix of aims and objectives, it is not surprising that al-Qa'ida's attacks go beyond seeking political or strategic advantage in an attempt to advance its cause. It concentrates heavily on symbolic targets, striking Embassies, military forces and facilities, and other symbols of American hegemony. Yet the attacks are not just moves in a global game of chess, designed to provoke a particular move from the United States. In Daniel Benjamin and Steven Simon's words, al-Qa'ida's attacks are "to humiliate and slaughter those who defied the hegemony and God". Indeed, mass casualties serve both a strategic and redemptive purpose, forcing the West to take note of al-Qa'ida's position and, at the same time, bringing the suffering of the Muslim world home to otherwise oblivious Americans. *(See Ref 210)*

Although its aims and objectives are mixed and complex al-Qa'ida structure seems also unclear and mixed to most experts. So, how is it structured?

In fact, what exactly al-Qa'ida is, or was, remains in dispute. Author and journalist Adam Curtis contends that the idea of al-Qa'ida as a formal organisation is primarily an American invention. Curtis contends the name "al-Qa'ida" was first brought to the attention of the public in the 2001 trial of bin Laden and the four men accused of the 1998 U.S. embassy bombings in East Africa:

"The reality was that bin Laden and Ayman al-Zawahiri had become the focus of a loose association of disillusioned Islamist militants who were attracted by the new strategy. But there was no organisation. These were militants who mostly planned their own operations and looked to bin Laden for funding and assistance. He was not their commander. There is also no evidence that bin Laden used the term "al-Qa'ida" to refer to the name of a group until after September the 11th, when he realised that this was the term the Americans had given it." *(See Ref 178, 214)*

As a matter of law, the U.S. Department of Justice needed to show that bin Laden was the leader of a criminal organisation in order to charge him in absentia under the Racketeer Influenced and Corrupt Organisations Act, also known as the RICO statutes. The name of the organisation and details of its structure were provided in the testimony of Jamal al-Fadl, who said he was a founding member of the organisation and a former employee of bin Laden.Questions about the reliability of al-Fadl's testimony have been raised by a number of sources because of his history of dishonesty, and because he was delivering it as part of a plea bargain agreement after being convicted of conspiring to attack U.S. military establishments *(See Ref 215,216)*

Most experts believe that, unlike many radical groups, al-Qa'ida's members carry out many functions, and its organisational structure reflects its multi-purpose nature. It is loose, making it both hard to attack, as well as harder to find crucial evidence for its terrorist involvement. However, the organisation has demonstrated a capability for exceptionally lethal terrorist attacks on a global scale, but terrorism is not only, nor necessarily, its primary function. For many years, the bulk of al-Qa'ida's energy went into training and supporting guerrilla fighters who fought with the Taliban against their opponents. Similarly, al-Qa'ida backs Islamist insurgencies in the Philippines, Chechnya, Indonesia, Georgia, Algeria, and elsewhere in the world, acting, in Benjamin and Simon's words, as the "quartermaster for jihad". Al-Qa'ida also sees itself as a missionary organisation, trying to spread its own interpretation of Islam and issue propaganda against the Al Saud and other Arab regimes.Thus it seeks to influence the agendas of other, autonomous, terrorist groups, making them more anti-American and less inclined toward any compromise with secular states. In addition, its propaganda is intended to raise the consciousness of Muslims worldwide. *(See Ref 208,210)*

However, information mostly acquired from Jamal al-Fadl provided American authorities with a rough picture of how the group was organised and structured. While the veracity of the information provided by al-Fadl and the motivation for his cooperation are both disputed, American authorities base much of their current knowledge of al-Qa'ida on his testimony. *(See Ref 217)*

Osama bin Laden used to be the emir, or commander, and was the Senior Operations Chief of al-Qaeda (though originally this role may have been filled by Abu Ayoub al-Iraqi). As of August 6, 2010, the chief of operations was considered to be Adnan Gulshair el Shukrijumah, replacing Khalid Sheikh Mohammed. *(See Ref 218)*

Bin Laden used to be advised by a Shura Council, which consists of senior al-Qa'ida members, estimated by Western officials at about 20–30 people. Ayman al-Zawahiri is al-Qa'ida's Deputy Operations Chief. The organisation's network was built from scratch as a conspiratorial network that draws on leaders of all its regional nodes "as and when necessary to serve as an integral part of its high command." *(See Ref 213)*

- The Military Committee is responsible for training operatives, acquiring weapons, and planning attacks.

- The Money/Business Committee funds the recruitment and training of operatives through the hawala banking system. U.S-led efforts to eradicate the sources of terrorist financing were most successful in the year immediately following September 11; al-Qa'ida continues to operate through unregulated banks, such as the 1,000 or so hawaladars in Pakistan, some of which can handle deals of up to $10 million. It also provides air tickets and false passports, pays the organisation members, and oversees profit-driven businesses. In The 9/11 Commission Report, it was estimated that al-Qa'ida required $30 million-per-year to conduct its operations. *(See Ref 213, 219, 220, 221)*

- The Law Committee reviews Islamic law, and decides whether particular courses of action conform to the law.

- The Islamic Study/Fatwa Committee issues religious edicts, such as an edict in 1998 telling Muslims to kill Americans.

- In the late 1990s there was a publicly known Media Committee, which ran the now-defunct newspaper "Nashrat al Akhbar" (Newscast) and handled public relations. In 2005, al-Qa'ida formed "As-Sahab", a media production house, to supply its video and audio materials.

However, this unusual structure leads to confusion about its size – a judgment that can only be reached after carefully parsing out what, exactly, is al-Qa'ida. Rohan Gunaratna estimates that between 100,000 and 110,000 fighters trained in al-Qa'ida camps but – reflecting the high-quality recruits it seeks - that the organisation only asked 3,000 to join its elite ranks. In addition, the organisation draws on the support of over six million more radicals. However, even the figure of 3,000 may be something of an overstatement if al-Qa'ida's insurgency-related activities are excluded. The organisation core devoted to terrorism or skilled operations beyond simple participation in guerrilla war may be far smaller than is generally realised. The group of individuals who have sworn loyalty to Osama bin Laden focused on terrorism, most of whose members are highly skilled and dedicated, probably numbers in the hundreds.

What makes precise numbers so elusive, however, is that al-Qa'ida is both a small core group and a broader network linking various Islamist groups and causes. It has successfully spun a web of relationships with Islamist groups that espouse similar, though not always, identical goals. Gunaratna argues: "It is neither a single group nor a coalition of groups: it comprised a core base or bases in Afghanistan, satellite terrorist cells worldwide, a conglomerate of Islamist political parties, and other largely independent terrorist groups that it draws on for offensive actions and other responsibilities". *(See Ref 182, 213)*

The core group of al-Qa'ida guerrillas and terrorists is in turn connected with like-minded groups such as the Egyptian Islamic Jihad, the Islamic Movement of Uzbekistan, and literally dozens of other radical organisations. The "anonymous" U.S. intelligence officer claims that al-Qa'ida is active in Sudan, Somalia, Morocco, South Africa, Libya, Algeria, Mauritania, Nigeria, Madagascar, Uganda, Ethiopia, and Eritrea. Peter Bergen uses the analogy of al-Qa'ida as a holding company, exercising near-complete or partial control over a range of other groups. When these groups are added in, al-Qa'ida's manpower increases dramatically – a conclusion that requires to dramatically expand our estimate for the size and appeal of the adversary. *(See Ref 182, 209)*

The objectives or at least the priorities of many of these organisations differ from al-Qa'ida. For example, the Islamic Movement of Uzbekistan is focused largely on Uzbekistan, and to a lesser degree Central Asia – not the struggle against America. The Taliban in Afghanistan and Jemaat Islamiyyah in Indonesia are concerned about the penetration of Western popular culture, as suggested by its attack on the Bali nightclub. For them, in contrast to bin Laden, Madonna's midriff is a fighting issue. Nevertheless, even when it does not exercise direct control or have identical objectives, al-Qa'ida has tried to weave various jihadist elements together into a broader network that while hardly unified, is capable of working together for common goals. It assists groups with logistics and skilled personnel to encourage cooperation and unity of purpose. For example, bin Laden reconciled two leading Egyptian groups, the Egyptian Islamic Jihad and the Islamic Group, that had long been bitter rivals despite their overall shared agenda. *(See Ref 213)*

The conceptual key is to see al-Qa'ida not only as a terrorist group, but instead that in the light that bin Laden is promoting (and at times directing) a "worldwide, religiously inspired, and professionally guided

Islamist insurgency". Although the spectacular terrorist attacks are what garner the most U.S. attention, these grinding low-intensity conflicts are what cause the most suffering and have the potential for the most dramatic change.In addition, many of these causes are seen as legitimate liberation struggles by Muslims who reject terrorism, expanding the jihadists' appeal. *(See Ref 209)*

Given the publicity which the organisation had over the last decade and especially after the events of 11 September 2001, the question which comes to mind: how influential is al-Qa'ida?

Although the organisation has ties to a range of insurgencies and Islamic local groups, a key question is identifying where the al-Qa'ida's influence stops. Do other radical groups and ideologues share al-Qa'ida's objectives and worldview? Speaking to U.S.Congress and the nation in the immediate aftermath of the September 11 attacks, former President Bush declared: "The terrorists practice a fringe form of Islamic extremism that has been rejected by Muslim scholars and the vast majority of Muslim clerics - a fringe movement that perverts the peaceful teachings of Islam." This view is comforting, for if al-Qa'ida's views are indeed on the fringe, then the organisation's ability to recruit, raise money, and sustain itself in the face of a worldview manhunt are diminished. But if many Muslims share al-Qa'ida's vision, then the organisation, or a successor, can count on continued support and sympathy. *(See Ref 222)*

In fact, through its sponsor to the various struggles al-Qa'ida has expanded its appeal. For example by organising and training jihadists, the organisation makes local conflicts more deadly and gains a venue for pressing its own worldview. These conflicts, in turn, produce a pool of alumni who give al-Qa'ida greater reach and increase the attractiveness of the broader jihadist cause. To broaden this pool further, the organisation taps into more than 35,000 Arabs who fought in Afghanistan against the Soviets in the 1980s. Most of these individuals returned to their homes and became enmeshed in society at large. The problem, as former CIA officer Milton Beardon noted, was that "they didn't die in great numbers. They died in tiny numbers, and they did come back". *(See Ref 209)*

Daniel L Byman notes that violent movements are also linked to an even broader network that includes charities supporting relief in Chechnya, Islamic education efforts in Southeast Asia, and fundraising in Europe. The non-government organisation (NGO) network is particularly important. NGOs are a means of raising money, but they also are valuable for giving activist jobs, channelling money, and acquiring necessary documents. In addition, Western police and security forces often hesitate (particularly before September 11) before investigating any charity. *(See Ref 208)*

However, going beyond the world of active Islamists, the picture remains gloomy. Bin Laden was not a voice in the wilderness. Bergen notes that while "only a tiny minority [of Muslims] are committed to violence against American citizens," many are angry at U.S. policies in the Middle East. The radical view that Muslim governments that collaborate with the West are illegitimate appears to be gaining ground, particularly as these governments rely on repression while failing to deliver economically. Although power remains concentrated in the hands of secular elite, the foundation of their rule is increasingly thin. *(See Ref 182)*

Many Muslims, particularly Arabs, share al-Qa'ida's resentment of and disdain for the United States and its values. Poll results of the Pew Charitable Trusts released after the end of the war in Iraq indicated that, "People in most predominantly Muslim countries remain overwhelmingly opposed to the U.S., and in several cases these negative feelings have increased dramatically." The result is a bias against U.S. efforts to counter al-Qa'ida. Increasingly, claims that the United States is denigrating Islam and endangering Muslim children are gaining credence. *(See Ref 209)*

Al-Qa'ida's appeal goes beyond the Arab world. Many new babies in Muslim parts of Nigeria are named "Osama," and only 38 percent of Nigeria Muslims have a favourable opinion of the United States, a decline from 71 percent in 2008. Jihadist appeal is very strong in Europe as well. Benjamin and Simon cite a Sunday Times (London) poll that found that an astonishing 40 percent of British Muslims supported bin Ladin's attacks on the United States. *(See Ref 210)*

The picture is ominous, suggesting al-Qa'ida's appeal, or at least that of its ideology, runs deep. Indeed, al-Qa'ida's railing against modern-day Crusaders and talk of the subjugation of Islam raises the issue of the much-maligned "clash of civilisations." Political scientist Samuel Huntington has famously argued that the problem is Islam, not Islamic fundamentalism: "It is Islam, a different civilisation which its people are convinced of the superiority of their culture and are obsessed with the inferiority of their power." *(See Ref 223)*

Following al-Qa'ida's defeat and lost of its safe haven in Afghanistan, government officials, scholars and analysts started to debate about the role of al-Qa'ida's central leadership and they asked: is it still relevant especially after the death of bin Laden by the CIA on May the 1st, 2011?

In fact, many experts argued that al-Qa'ida had transformed into a decentralised organisation with little vertical hierarchy that it had become "more of an ideology than an organisation." In the words of one analyst, al-Qa'ida was seen as "a fragmented terrorist group living on the run in the caves of Afghanistan." This description may have been true in the months following the overthrow of the Taliban, but the notion of a scattered and ineffective al-Qa'ida central leadership has been overplayed over the past several years. Many analysts have exaggerated the capabilities that the terror group's top leaders require to remain relevant and so have overlooked the fact that even during its nadir from 2002 through 2004, al-Qa'ida's senior leadership was able to develop terrorist plots for regional nodes to execute. Now that al-Qa'ida's senior leadership has gained a safe haven in the tribal regions of Pakistan, the organisation's power and relevance grow even greater. Today, even after the death of bin Laden, the Al-Qa'ida network – has a resilient central leadership – is still considered the most dangerous terrorist adversary that the United States faces, possessing a lethal combination of capability and, unlike Hezbollah, a demonstrated desire to carry out mass-casualty attacks on U.S. soil. *(See Ref 224, 225)*

Furthermore, about ten years after the tragic events of 11 September 2001, al-Qa'ida has lost much of its top leadership, commands just a few hundred fighters and is strapped for cash. Paradoxically enough, it also probably exercises more power than at any point in the past.

From the north-western Himalayas to the deserts that surround Timbuktu, al-Qa'ida's message has been taken up by a new generation of jihadist leaders which some experts call 'Baby bin Ladens'. In the main, the new al-Qa'ida subsidiaries are led by Islamists who participated in the anti-Soviet Union jihad in Afghanistan, and went on to found jihadist movements in their own countries. They successfully tapped local issues and political grievances to build a political base for the jihadist movement – and are now expanding their constituency in the West.

Muhammad Illyas Kashmiri, a Pakistan-based jihadist who commands several hundred fighters, is thought to be responsible for an operation to attack British airports that has sparked off a nationwide alert.

The turn of the decade has seen a string of similar jihadist operations targeting the West: British resident Taimur Abdelwahab al-Abdaly's suicide attack in Sweden; Somali-born Mohamed Usman Mahmoud conspiracy to bomb Christmas festivities in Portland. Police in Denmark stopped a plot to stage a Mumbai-style attack, and Pittsburgh college student Emmerson Begolly was charged with being a top online jihad propagandist.

Each has been linked to one or the other of the 'Baby bin Ladens.'

However, terrorist networks considered by most analysts to be centralised when there is a principal command exercising control over the network, making operational decisions, and guiding its ideology. Decisions filter from top to bottom, and levels do not mix: There is a clear separation between the leadership and lower ranking operatives. A central command joins terrorists with specific skill sets across regions, tasks smaller cells, and provides financial and logistical resources. A prime example of such a centralised structure was pre-September-11 al-Qa'ida, which had a supreme leader (Osama bin Laden), a shura (consultation) council, various committees, and a cadre of lieutenants in charge of regions or cells. Although some analysts assume that youths can self-radicalise and train themselves via the Internet, training camps produce the most capable terrorists. Graduates of terrorist training camps have conducted the deadliest post-9-11 attacks: in Bali, Madrid, London, Sharm el-Sheikh, and Mumbai. U.S. officials are fortunate that both the group that plotted to bomb the John Kennedy airport in 2007 and the cell arrested in Miami in 2006 were untrained and apparently isolated from global jihadist networks. *(See Ref 213, 226, 227)*

While there are clear advantages for terror groups to centralisation and hierarchy, decentralisation does offer some benefits: Bureaucratic intelligence agencies have trouble keeping up with cells that are disconnected and on the move, making it almost impossible to uproot an entire decentralised network. Regional terrorist groups can also act with greater spontaneity absent the need to coordinate their operations through hierarchical channels. But on balance, centralised terrorist groups pose the greater threat to the United States. Marc Sageman, a clinical psychiatrist who previously worked for the CIA, has observed that small-scale operations "may be lethal," but "they will not result in mass carnage, which requires coordination, skills, and resources". *(See Ref 203)*

Analysts differ on the question of al-Qa'ida's centralisation. On one end of the spectrum are people such as Jason Burke. Arguing that al-Qa'ida has been significantly degraded since it lost its sanctuary in Afghanistan, Burke claims that the "nearest thing to 'al-Qa'ida', as popularly understood, existed for a short period between 1996 and 2001. Its base had been Afghanistan, and what I had seen at Tora Bora were the final scenes of its destruction. What we have currently is a broad and diverse movement of radical Islamic militancy". *(See Ref 228, 229)*

At the other end of the spectrum is Peter Bergen, the author of two books about bin Laden and his terror network. Bergen argues that al-Qa'ida's leadership has regrouped in the border region between Afghanistan and Pakistan and has established new terrorist training camps in Pakistan's Federally Administered Tribal Areas. Al-Qa'ida's propaganda campaign is expanding, as are its affiliations with regional terrorist groups. For example, the Algeria-based "Groupe Salafiste pour la Predication et le Combat" (Salafist group for preaching and combat, GSPC) recently changed its name to al-Qa'ida in the Islamic Maghreb, signalling incorporation into al-Qa'ida's global network. Since January 2005, some forty different organisations in countries that include Afghanistan, Egypt, Iraq, Lebanon, Morocco, Pakistan, Saudi Arabia, Syria, and Yemen "have announced their formation and pledged allegiance to bin Laden, al-Qa'ida, and their strategic objectives." While the April 2006 National Intelligence Estimate assessed that "the global jihadist movement is decentralised, lacks a coherent strategy, and is becoming more diffuse," the July 2007 National Intelligence Estimate supports the view that al-Qa'ida "has protected or regenerated key elements of its Homeland attack capability". *(See Ref 230, 231, 232, 233)*

If the experts have different views concerning al-Qa'ida leadership relevancy, the same debate is happening within the organisation about the group's future. Most members favour a strong central leadership. Abu Musab al-Suri, one of the most prolific jihadist ideologues, in recent years has argued for a decentralised combat model. In contrast, Abu Bakr Naji, another prominent jihadist ideologue, calls for a more centralised model.

Suri's 1,600-page manifesto, "The Call for Global Islamic Resistance," argues that the centralised, hierarchical model of jihadism cannot overcome the U.S.'s technologically advanced military, and that regional security cooperation-such as the alliance between Washington and Islamabad-makes a hierarchical structure dangerous. He suggests that decentralisation immunises terrorist cells from detection through the capture and interrogation of members of other cells. Suri's prescription for decentralisation would mean replacing the old training camp model with one in which fighters are trained "in homes and mobile camps". *(See Ref 234)*

In contrast, Abu Bakr Naji's "The Management of Savagery" argues that once the jihadists hold territory, they should erect a governing apparatus to enforce Islamic law and provide security, food, and medical care. A high command would ensure that efforts are not needlessly duplicated and would prioritise actions against various groups or nations. Naji has carried the day within al-Qa'ida's hierarchy, especially as al-Qa'ida has gained new safe havens in Pakistan. *(See Ref 235)*

The preference of al-Qa'ida's leadership for Naji's approach rather than Suri's reflects the long-standing inclination for centralisation. Bin Laden originally formed al-Qa'ida to keep the vanguard of jihad alive after the defeat of the Soviet Union in Afghanistan. He maintained his Afghanistan and Pakistan training camps and established new ones. Al-Qa'ida forged relationships with other, more established terrorist groups, while maintaining a corporation-like structure. West Point's Combating Terrorism Center has translated a number of documents captured during the Afghan and Iraq campaigns that the Department of Defence has declassified from its Harmony Database. These documents depict a clear al-Qa'ida hierarchy dating back to bin Laden's residence in Sudan. One document, entitled "Interior Organisation," delineates al-Qa'ida's hierarchical structure, from the commander and ruling council down to the organisational committees. It explains that the commander must have been a member of al-Qa'ida for at least seven years, have a sufficient understanding of Islamic law and jihad, and "have operational experience from jihad." Below the commander are a deputy who must share the same qualifications, a secretary whom the commander appoints, and then a command council. The document also enumerates five separate committees: military, political, administrative and financial, security, and surveillance. *(See Ref 236)*

Although the U.S. military intervention in Afghanistan devastated al-

Qa'ida's safe haven, the group's core leadership survived. Abdel Bari Atwan, editor in chief of the London-based Al-Quds al-Arabi newspaper, wrote that U.S. forces may have destroyed "more than 80 percent of al-Qa'ida's military capabilities and infrastructure," but the group's senior leadership fled. A few-such as Saif al-Adl, Saad bin Laden, and Sulaiman Abu Ghaith-fled to Iran, but most of them relocated to Pakistan. *(See Ref 237, 238)*

With the benefit of hindsight, it is clear that in this period analysts and media commentators underestimated the extent to which al-Qa'ida's central leadership remained able to organise terror attacks. Al-Qa'ida's leadership formulated the Madrid plot, even though a regional node implemented the operation: The police traced the mobile phone detonators used in that plot to Jamal Zougam, a Moroccan who owned a cell phone shop in Madrid. Spanish authorities monitored a call between Zougam and Imad Eddin Barakat Yarkus, the now-jailed head of al-Qa'ida's node in Spain. Zougam said that Mohamed Fizazi, spiritual leader of the Moroccan extremist group Salafia Jihadia convicted for his part in the May 2003 Casablanca suicide bombings, offered him financial aid. Zougam also visited Mullah Krekar, an Iraqi Kurd based in Norway who founded the Ansar al-Islam terrorist organisation. The ringleader of the Madrid cell, Sarhane Ben Abdelmajid Fakhet, was friendly with senior al-Qa'ida operative Amer Azizi. But the most salient connection is the fact that the Centre of Mujahideen Services, an internal al-Qa'ida "think tank" and linear descendant of the Maktab al-Khidmat (Service Office), a non-governmental organisation formed in the mid-1980s to provide services during the Afghan-Soviet war, developed the political strategy behind the attack. The Centre of Mujahideen Services, formed to provide the same kind of services to Iraqi mujahideen that Maktab al-Khidmat provided to Afghan fighters, published a book entitled Iraq al-Jihad, which concluded that "the Spanish government will not endure two or three attacks" and argued that a coordinated terrorist assault could turn the Spanish public against the government, forcing it to withdraw. *(See Ref 239, 240, 241, 242)*

Al-Qa'ida's senior leadership also played a crucial role in the July 7, 2005 attacks on London's transit system. British police reports were hesitant to link the bombers to al-Qa'ida, believing the terror cell to be autonomous and self-actuating. But as the official account of the 7-7 attacks hit the British press, terrorism analysts Dan Darling and Steve Schippert enumerated a number of problems with the early conclusion that the broader al-Qa'ida network was largely irrelevant to the London cell that executed the bombings *(See Ref 243, 244)*

The connections between al-Qa'ida's senior leadership and the attacks in Madrid and London demonstrate that the group's top command was not as isolated and irrelevant during this period as some suggested. Still, it would gain more strength over time.

Analysts declared al-Qa'ida's central leadership defeated before it had been dealt a death blow. Its regional nodes and ambitious newcomers stepped to the fore while the group's senior leadership fought to gain control of territory - thus helping to reinforce the idea that the senior leadership was marginalised and irrelevant. Even at the time, the fallacy of this view should have been apparent: As Bergen points out, "the existence of al-Qa'ida imitators does not prove the obsolescence of the real thing." Now, as al-Qa'ida's vitality approaches pre-9-11 levels, many analysts still do not have their eye on the central network-and fewer yet understand how it regained its strength after losing Afghanistan. *(See Ref 182)*

However the scene in Europe last September and October (2010) called to mind the heyday of the IRA in the 1970s or of Algerian terrorism in the 1990s: Buckingham Palace and Trafalgar Square were teeming with police, the Eiffel Tower was repeatedly evacuated, and everywhere, tourists were on edge. The threat, however, involved a newer brand of terrorist: The CIA and its European counterparts warned of an al-Qa'ida plot to kill civilians in France, Germany and Britain, and alerted travellers, especially Americans, to be extra-vigilant.

Few operational details were released. But unlike many thwarted al-Qa'ida operations of days gone by - such as the 2006 Heathrow plot, in which several airliners bound from London to America were to be blown up at coordinated intervals - it was clear from news reports that the European plan called for less spectacular, smaller-scale attacks, perhaps using machine guns to strafe clusters of tourists near public landmarks.

Has al-Qa'ida become dispirited? No.

Recent plots, including the Mumbai raid in November 2008, the Times Square car bomb attempt in May 2010 and in November that year the plot in Europe and the explosive materials which found in planes in Dubai, Britain and Chicago, show that al-Qa'ida is not only operationally alive and well, but has transformed its post-Afghanistan tactical retreat into a formidable new strategy. In the early part of the last decade, al-Qa'ida had no choice but to use conventional explosives and old-fashioned terrorist tactics to hit soft targets, the 2002 bombing of nightclubs in Bali being perhaps the best example. With its leadership under siege in Pakistan, it lacked the capacity to mount sophisticated and coordinated attacks that would match, let alone exceed, the innovation or shock value on display on Sept. 11, 2001, or even in the USS Cole operation the year before.

Watching this shift, the tacit assumption of most counterterrorism officials and analysts, was that al-Qa'ida was simply biding its time and trying to rebuild its capacity to stage unprecedented, apocalyptic attacks on the United States and Europe. But even if that was once the group's intention, it appears to have been side-lined.

The new al-Qa'ida seems to understand its limitations and appears to be adopting more realistic means of achieving its grand objectives. There is no reason to think that al-Qa'ida has abandoned its all-out jihad to defend Islam against what it sees as centuries of repression and humiliation at the hands of the West. But instead of fomenting revolutionary outrage with spectacular gestures, it is slowly raising a new army designed to wage traditional urban warfare.

Some members of this second-generation army have been seasoned by the classical insurgencies in Iraq and Afghanistan; others are Western members of the Muslim diaspora or converts to Islam. Although many of them have attended al-Qa'ida training camps, a large number of them lack traditional terrorist pedigrees and have no criminal records.

With the help of these so-called "clean-skins," who are difficult for Western security services to detect, al-Qa'ida's opportunistic, pragmatic leadership has embraced urban warfare of the sort pioneered by terrorists decades ago: low-intensity, IRA-style operations in densely populated areas, using both conventional military weapons (such as assault rifles and rocket-propelled grenades) and standard terrorist weapons (such as improvised explosive devices). This, not simultaneously blowing up airliners or destroying skyscrapers, was the mode of jihad envisioned by Abd al-Aziz al-Muqrin, the late leader of the jihad in Saudi Arabia and the author of the appropriately named turn-of-the-century al-Qa'ida combat manual "The War Against Cities."

This vision of a close-quarters confrontation with the general population is at least as disconcerting as the more novel style of apocalyptic terrorism that the strikes against the Pentagon and the World Trade Centre appeared to herald. For one thing, it could eventually bring about an on-going, direct, ground-level armed engagement of Western security forces - think of Belfast or Beirut in the 1970s and 1980s. That sort of campaign could ultimately shake the public's confidence in the state to a greater extent than have less frequent, larger-scale operations such as the 11 September 2001 attacks.

The most vivid evidence to date of urban warfare's ascendancy was the Mumbai operation, which ranks as the third most lethal jihadist attack since 11 September 2001. Pakistani terrorists functioned like commandos, making an amphibious landing near Mumbai, infiltrating the city, converging on a set of pre-established targets and killing at least 173 people, mainly with AK-47s. Subsequently thwarted plots in Germany, Denmark and Britain reflected similar tactics. The Times Square operation and the European conspiracy have now confirmed the movement toward old-style terrorism, but on a new, more internationally coordinated basis.

Urban warfare has great appeal for al-Qa'ida insofar as it gives perpetrators the opportunity to identify individual targets, as they did in Mumbai, where they purposefully killed Hindus and Jews. In this way, it is consistent with the core al-Qa'ida leadership's growing interest in avoiding Muslim casualties, an objective that has come largely at the behest of respected jihadist dissenters such as the Egyptian cleric Sayyid Imam al-Sharif (also known as Dr. Fadl).

In addition, urban warfare is relatively easy to execute, involving fewer and cheaper resources, less exacting planning and coordination, relatively inconspicuous preparation (requiring mainly readily concealable small arms and dual-use items such as fertilizer) and fewer operatives.

Keeping the west under sustained pressure is the key to al-Qa'ida's new strategy. It seeks to do that without relying on an expensive – and relatively easy to target – central infrastructure, of the kind the September 11 attacks needed.

The new generation of terrorits or "Baby bin-Ladens" have been adroit in using the internet to recruit cadre in the West, and meeting their logistical needs. Last December (2010), jihadist websites released an

English-language book called The Explosives Course, offering illustrated, step-by-step instructions for assembling improvised explosive devices from things you could buy in some drug stores.

The book's introduction states that it has been written by students of 'Shabab al-Masri' – the pseudonym of al-Qa'ida's top explosives expert, Midhat Mursi al-Sayyid Umar. Before his death in a 2008 U.S. drone strike, Umar was a key figure in al-Qa'ida's pursuit of weapons of mass destruction. He ran the notorious Derunta complex of camps, where al-Qa'ida tested chemical weapons on dogs, and also wrote the explosives manual used by the organisation's operatives.

Experts agree that even if the new jihadists have been unable to successfully stage a major attack in the West, they impose costs disproportionate to the actual threat they hold out. Each terror alert is, in al-Qa'ida's view, a small victory, because it costs its adversaries millions and sows fear.

This sustained war of attrition, al-Qa'ida hopes, will undermine public support for the West's increasingly-unpopular military commitments against Islamist movements in Asia and Africa – and thus give jihadists a crack at the big prize: seizing control of a nation-state.

The long-range implications of this evolution are sobering. Al-Qa'ida's leaders are realising that they can panic and disrupt Western society the old-fashioned way-but on a global level. If they succeed their new strategy will inspire increasingly rigid security measures and rising paranoia, which will almost inevitably drive a wedge between Muslim and non-Muslim in The West. Given the Western increasingly rancorous, polarised politics and the politicisation of counterterrorism, al-Qa'ida's foray into urban warfare could make effective governance and the preservation of constitutional norms much tougher propositions than they have been so far in the age of terror.

Al-Qa'ida is fighting a new war. Its adversaries must stop fighting the old one.

However, the strike on bin Laden's compound in Pakistan on the 1st day of May raises lots of questions. Here are seven:

1. Does Bin Laden's death cripple al-Qa'ida and jihadist terrorism more broadly? Probably not. Al-Qa'ida long ago ceased to be a centralised

operation. For the last decade bin Laden has been a figurehead than a mastermind. Terrorist attacks, like the bomb plot that German authorities broke up last April (2011), have been planned and carried out by largely independent al-Qa'ida "affiliates." Nonetheless, U.S. Special Forces might have picked up valuable intelligence as they scoured bin Laden's command post that could help uncover terrorist cells and plots.

2. Can you kill a symbol? In announcing bin Laden's death on the 1st of May, President Obama noted that "For over two decades, bin Laden has been al-Qa'ida's leader and symbol." Men die, symbols don't. In death, bin Laden will continue to inspire jihadists as much as he did in life. The biggest threat to bin Ladenism comes not from American bullets but from the prospect that the Arab spring will remake the political order in the Middle East.

3. Where is Ayman al-Zawahiri? With bin Laden dead, his chief lieutenant and the man frequently described as al-Qa'ida's "brains" goes to the top of the most wanted listed. Al-Zawahiri reportedly was gravely injured in a missile strike in Pakistan in 2008. Given his deep operational experience and cunning, the Egyptian-born al-Zawahiri is more than capable of plotting major terrorist attacks on his own.

4. Is Pakistan a reliable partner for the United States? President Obama said on the 1st of May 2011 that "our cooperation with Pakistan helped lead us to bin Laden." But the White House didn't notify the Pakistani government in advance and Pakistani troops did not participate in the attack. Bin Laden's compound was located just forty miles north of the Pakistani capital of Islamabad - or about the distance from Washington to Baltimore - in a city that hosts a Pakistani military base and military academy. Expect to hear more doubts inside the Washington Beltway about the value and viability of the U.S.-Pakistani partnership.

5. Can NATO forces leave Afghanistan now? Sometime in the next several months, President Obama will decide whether and how fast to draw down U.S. troop levels in Afghanistan. Last April the Pentagon reported mildly optimistic news about progress in the Afghan War. Bin Laden's death gives the US president the political opening to order the sizable draw-down that public opinion polls show that most Americans want. He has always justified the war in Afghanistan in terms of defeating and dismantling

al-Qa'ida, and he can say that with bin Laden's death that goal has been achieved.

6. Will Obama benefit politically from bin Laden's death? The president's public approval ratings have slipped recently after enjoying a modest bump earlier in the year. Expect another bump in the coming weeks as the public gives the White House credit for a job well done. But if past "rally-'round-the-flag" dynamics hold true, the boost that Obama gets from bin Laden's death will be short-lived.

7. The final question is perhaps the most important. What will the effects be on the ideology? Here the situation is less clear. Bin Laden's greatest success was to make his particular interpretation of radical Islamism globally known. There were other strands of militant thinking and strategy around in the late 1990s but 20 years of "propaganda by deed" made bin Laden's the dominant one. A thriving "Jihadi" subculture has emerged. Al-Qa'ida has become, in many ways, a social movement. Bin Laden's death means the removal of the iconic figure at the centre of this construct. This is undoubtedly important.

Asking these questions does not diminish the significance of what the Obama administration accomplished in the 1st of May. Killing bin Laden brings closure to the families who lost loved ones on 9/11. It shows that terrorists will pay for their crimes. Justice was done.

But killing Bin Laden is still only one step in the fight against terror. Bin Laden has had over 20 years to build a substantial international organisation, which is all the more dangerous as it is a loose alliance of like-minded people in many countries, ready to help and cooperate whenever needed , but without one central control.

This makes al Qa'ida very hard to eliminate. The most important part of its activity is in south and south west Asia and it would be a great mistake to think that is going to stop any time soon. Its members are very deeply entrenched there, they are still recruiting large numbers of suicide bombers and they are still carrying out mass casualty attacks.

So, it would be very dangerous to assume that the death of bin Laden means that journalists can write the obituary of al-Qa'ida.

CHAPTER EIGHT

YEMEN: AL-QA'IDA'S NEW SAFE HAVEN

The more than two-year-old merger of Saudi and Yemeni jihadists into a Yemen-based al-Qa'ida in the Arabian Peninsula (AQAP) seems to have been a success. Certainly, that is what the suspect packages, including mobile phone technology, on board two cargo planes which found in October 2010 suggests. The Saudis have brought funds, the Yemenis manpower. In January 2010, Secretary of State Hillary Clinton called Yemen "an urgent national security priority." On 25 August 2010 the Washington Post reported that CIA sources believe that al-Qa'ida in the Arabian Peninsula now represents a greater threat to the U.S. security than al-Qa'ida in Pakistan. Furthermore, AQAP was described on 28 October 2010 by the chief of Britain's Foreign Intelligence Service, Sir John Sawers, as posing a threat comparable to that emanating from Pakistan or Afghanistan.

Although it's impossible to say whether it was a Saudi or a Yemeni national, who provided the technical know-how, it is not the first time AQAP has employed mobile phone technology. Barely reported in the west, AQAP road-tested a first mobile phone-enabled bomb in August 2009, at an elegant Ramadan party in Jeddah hosted by Saudi Arabia's chief of counter-terrorism, Prince Mohammad bin Nayef, followed later by the failed 2009 Christmas Day attack on a U.S. passenger jet, which was tied to al-Qa'ida elements in Yemen. Those events and others prompted questions of whether the fractious Arab state might give rise to a Taliban-style regime.

Surprisingly, it took 2009 December's failed plane bombing to concentrate Western minds on Yemen. The poorest country in the Middle East, a terrifyingly dysfunctional state stranded among some of the richest states in the world, including Saudi Arabia, looked ideally suited to providing the world's Islamic jihadists with a welcoming safe haven as Pakistan's tribal areas. In January 2010, the then-British Prime Minister Gordon Brown hurriedly added a forum to discuss Yemen to the end of a London meeting about Afghanistan. But what, precisely, could be done?

Yemen is one of the oldest centres of civilisation in the Near East. Its relatively fertile land and adequate rainfall in a moister climate helped sustain a stable population, a feature recognised by the ancient "Roman-Greek" geographer Claudius Ptolemy, who described Yemen as Eudaimon Arabia (better known in its Latin translation, Arabia Felix) meaning "Fortunate Arabia" or Happy Arabia. Between the 12th century BCE and the 6th century CE, it was dominated by six successive civilisations which rivaled each other, or were allied with each other and controlled the lucrative spice trade: M'ain, Qataban, Hadhramaut, Awsan, Saba and Himyarite. Islam arrived in 630 CE during the Islamic prophet Muhammad's lifetime, and Yemen became part of the Muslim realm. At that time the Persian governor Badhan was ruling. Thereafter Yemen was ruled as part of Arab-Islamic caliphates, and Yemen became a province in the Islamic empire. *(Most historic information in this chapter came from Ref 249, 250, 251, 252, 253, 254)*

The former North Yemen came under control of Imams of various dynasties usually of the Zaidi sect, who established a theocratic political structure that survived until modern times. In 897, a Zaidi ruler, Yahya al-Hadi Ila al-Haqq, founded a line of Imams, whose Shiite dynasty survived until the second half of the 20th century. Nevertheless, Yemen's medieval history is a tangled chronicle of contesting local Imams. The Fatimids of Egypt helped the Isma'ilis maintain dominance in the 11th century. Saladin (Salahuddine al-Ayubi) annexed Yemen in 1173. The Rasulid dynasty ruled Yemen, with Zabid as its capital, from about 1230 to the 15th century. In 1516, the Mamluks of Egypt annexed Yemen; but in the following year, the Mamluk governor surrendered to the Ottomans, and Turkish armies subsequently overran the country. They were challenged by the Zaidi Imam, Qasim the Great (ruled from 1597 to 1620), and were expelled from the interior around 1630. From then until the 19th century, the Ottomans retained control only of isolated coastal areas, while the highlands generally were ruled by the Zaidi Imams.

As the Zaidi Imamate collapsed in the 19th century due to internal division, the Ottomans moved south along the west coast of Arabia back into Northern Yemen in the 1830s, and eventually even took San'a making it the Yemeni district capital in 1872.

The British conquered Aden in 1839 and it was then known as the Aden Protectorate. The British also made a series of treaties with local tribal rulers, in a move to colonies the entire area of Southern Yemen. British influence extended to Hadhramaut by the 1950s and a boundary line, known as the 'violet line' was drawn between Turkish Arabia in the North and the South Arabian Protectorate of Great Britain, as it was then known. (This line later formed the boundary between Northern and Southern Yemeni states in the 1960s.)

In 1849 the Turks returned to Yemen and their power extended throughout the whole of that region not under British rule. Local insurrection against the Turks followed and autonomy was finally granted to the Zaidi Imam in 1911. By 1919 the Turks had retreated from Yemen for the last time and the country was left in the hands of Imam Yahya, who became the country's king. Yemen's independence was recognised by Britain in 1925.

Meanwhile, Aden was ruled as part of British India until 1937, when the city of Aden became the Colony of Aden, a crown colony in its own right. The Aden hinterland and Hadhramaut to the east formed the remainder of what would become South Yemen and were not administered directly by Aden, but were tied to Britain by treaties of protection. Economic development was largely centred in Aden, and while the city flourished partly due to the discovery of crude oil on the Arabian Peninsula in the 1930s, the states of the Aden Protectorate stagnated.

Imam Yayha ruled Yemen from 1918 until his assassination in the 1948 failed revolution, and was succeeded by his son Ahmad (1948-1962). Clashes with the British over Aden were characteristic of Ahmad's rule, and he sought protection from Cairo, resulting in a short-lived pact between Yemen, Egypt and Syria.

After Ahmad death in 1962, his son, Muhammed al-Badr, ruled for only one week before the 26th September Revolution, led by Colonel Abdallah al-Sallal, proclaimed the Yemen Arab Republic (YAR).

The deposed Imam fled to the mountains of the North and his Royalist forces, backed by Saudi Arabia, and waged a civil war against the YAR, which lasted for eight years. Egypt gave aid to the Republican army and a meeting between Egyptian President Gamal Abdel Nasser and King Faisal of Saudi Arabia in 1965 led to an agreement to end the involvement of both countries in the civil war. Arrangements were made to hold a plebiscite to allow the people of YAR to choose their own form of government, but this never happened and fighting resumed in 1966.

In the late 1960s, British presence in Southern Yemen was minimal outside Aden itself. Intense guerrilla fighting throughout the mid-sixties resulted in a British withdrawal from Aden in 1967. With the closure of the Suez Canal, Yemen's economy was on the verge of ruin, and the new People's Republic of South Yemen, which came into being on 30 November 1967, relied heavily on economic support from Communist countries. It became, in effect, the first and only Arab Marxist State. In 1970 the Republic's name was changed to the People's Democratic Republic of Yemen (PDRY).

Mutual distrust between the two Yemenis characterised the seventies, and tensions flared into a series of short border wars in 1972, 1978 and 1979. Two presidents of the YAR (Ibrahim al-Hamidi and Ahmad al Ghashmi) were assassinated during this period. However, under the Presidency of Ali Abdallah Saleh of the Hashid tribe, in the late seventies and early eighties, the stability of the YAR steadily improved.

By the end of 1981 a constitution had been drafted in order to implement a merger between the two states. Attempts to consolidate this, however, were delayed by political instability in the PDRY and it was not until 22 May 1990 that the merger was made official.

The new country was named the Republic of Yemen. The border was opened and demilitarised and currencies were declared valid in both of the former countries. A referendum sealed the unification of the Yemen, and today's Yemen is probably more accessible than it has ever been throughout its history. Nevertheless, the unification left much of Yemen's periphery currently under tribes leaders' dominance, without effective formal state-administered governance, but this does not mean that these regions are ungoverned – or there for the taking, particularly by outsiders to the area.

While the history is essential to understand the contemporary Yemen, one must look to another factor to have the full picture of the situation: the tribes and their historic role in the state governance.

The tribe is the primary social unit of the Arabian Peninsula's countries including Yemen. The Qahtan tribal confederation - believed to be the descendants from Qahtan, one of Noah's sons - are common in the south of the Peninsula, especially in Yemen and parts of Oman.Their life style is different from their nomadic counterparts in the northern parts of the Arabian peninsula. They are peasants who settled and established themselves in certain areas - a feature that allowed them to create the ancient agricultural civilisation of South Arabia. *(See Ref 264, 265)*

In fact, the tribes in ancient Yemen constituted the structural foundation of the state, at the time in the form of kingdoms. These kingdoms, such as Ma'ien, Shiebah, and Himiar, were not only named after certain tribes. Some historians have even asserted that in certain cases the leaders of particularly powerful tribes were able to unify the tribes into a confederation and could become kings themselves.

In Yemen's contemporary political history two distinct periods may highlight the relationship between the state and the tribes in the North of Yemen: the period before and after the 1962 watershed. The character of this relationship ranged from the state's confrontation with the tribes to incorporation. During the Mutawakiliat Kingdom 1911-1962, the state was, generally speaking, strong enough to control the tribes. Its methods in dealing with the tribes, however, were insufficient to effectively integrate the tribes into the political system. Only the establishment of the Yemen Arab Republic in 1962 marked the beginning of the state's embodiment of the tribes, but tribal influence enhanced political instability of the system.

During the Yemen Arab Republic rule (1962-1990), tribes play a major role in the war between republicans and royalists. Eventually the war ended in the late 1960s the republicans being victorious. The major outcome of the war, however, was that the previous separation between the state and the tribal institution no longer existed. In fact, the state became virtually an embodiment of the tribes. During the civil war, some tribes aligned with the royalists against the republicans while others supported the republicans against the royalists. Again, the war was seen primarily as an opportunity for financial gains. Both Egypt and Saudi Arabia, who had a strong political stake in this war, were more than willing to pay the tribes, in money and weapons, to secure their support. As a result, the war continued for years because the tribes readily switched sides for profit. By the end of the war, the tribes, having large sums of money and weapons, emerged as an economically independent social force, powerful enough to actively influence the political system. *(See Ref 265, 266)*

On the other side, under the British rule which started from 1839, the role of the tribes in the political system in South Yemen was different compared to that in the North. Mainly among left wing scholars exploring the political history of the pre-independent South, there was a tendency to merge the concepts of feudalism and tribalism in a unified unit of analysis and to criticise the tribal structure of the society claiming that it was the main source of the South's problems. In reality, however, this perception is farfetched. According to Paul K. Dresch "ethnographically that is simply wrong. Those areas that are, or were, in any way feudal are not very tribal. The tribal areas are not feudal. What sense the equation made derived solely from the modernist assumption that both are 'backward'." However the tribal role in the South in some scholar opinions requires the differentiation between (a) Aden and the Hinterland and (b) the social structure and the political structure of the Hinterland. In Aden the tribal role was virtually non existent. Education, the media, and commerce facilitated the emergence of an influential and substantial middle class. It was this segment of the society which has provided the seeds for the development of political parties, labour unions and later led the opposition movement against the British occupation. The tribal role in the Hinterland, by contrast, was more apparent, in that the social structure was based on the tribal unit. However, the various tribes did not exercise political influence as in the North. In fact, the Hinterland was itself divided into several Emirates and Sultanates each of which were ruled by a Sultan or an Emir. These rulers practically owned their region. *(See Ref 261, 266)*

However, in the united Yemen, the tribe in the southern parts, who were subdued previously, started to meet again prompting the Socialist party to warn of 're-tribalisation'. However, quite contrary to this claim, the underlying motive was limited "to mediate the disputes of others and, as with the northern tribes (though in a different setting), to preserve themselves from dangers produced by non-tribal politics." There was a growing belief among Southern as well as Northern tribes alike that the state was setting one tribe against another.Although this can hardly be true given the chaotic political situation in the centre, this conviction facilitated the organising of formal tribal conferences between 1990 and 1994. The objective was to set their differences aside, and more importantly, to emphasise the tribal identity of Yemen. "Yemen is the Tribes and the Tribes are Yemen" said the slogan of one conference. *(See Ref 261, 266)*

If the tribes were and are important to Yemen governance, religion, in fact, has been closely associated with political power in the Yemeni highlands and coastal areas since the beginnings of Islam. After having ruled for over a millennium, it was only in 1962 that the fall of the Zaidi imam's monarchy gave way to a more direct separation between politics and religion in the country. This occurred through the establishment of the republican regime, once inspired by Gamal Abdel Nasser's model in Egypt. The modernisation of the state and society in North Yemen and in Marxist South Yemen did not really undermine the influence of the religious political actors. The same can be said of the May 1990 unification of North and South Yemen. *(See Ref 248)*

Historically, Yemeni society has been divided along two main Islamic religious identities: 52 percent of the population are Sunni and 47 percent are Shi'a. Sunnis are primarily Shafi'i, but also include significant groups of Malikis and Hanbalis. Shi'as are primarily Zaidis, and also have significant minorities of Twelver Shias and Musta'ali Western Isma'ili Shias. *(See Ref 255, 256)*

The Sunnis are predominantly in the South and Southeast. The Zaidis are predominantly in the North and Northwest whilst the Ja'faris and Ismailis are in the main centres such as Sana'a and Ma'rib. There are mixed communities in the larger cities. Less than 1% of Yemenis are non-Muslim, adhering to Hinduism, Christianity, Judaism and atheism. *(See Ref 257)*

Although Zaidis are constituents of a Shi'a sect, they often described as moderate in its jurisprudence, distinct from the Twelver Shi'as found in Iran, and close to Sunnism in many aspects. "Shafi'is" are Sunnis. Yet throughout the twentieth century, the divide eroded considerably, and consequently it does not appear to be as important as in the past, when Zaidi imams ruled North Yemen. No accurate and reliable statistics exist, but "Shafi'is" are usually considered to be the significant majority among a population of 28 million in Yemen (2005 estimates), while Zaidis represent around 35 percent of the population. *(See Ref 258)*

In fact, most Yemenis now consider the divide as merely symbolic, because of recent changes, particularly internal and external migrations, individualisation and marketisation of religious identities, as well as the improvement of education levels. Recent difficulties due to a brutal conflict in the North of the country opposing the army and an armed Zaidi revivalist group called the Believing Youth (a-Shabab al-Mu'emin) do not seem to have had a significant effect on the structure of the convergence of religious identities. In fact, despite episodes of violent stigmatisation orchestrated by certain radical groups, the vast majority of the population is at times indirectly (and most of the time passively) involved in the convergence. For instance, the president is himself of Zaidi origin but never refers to his primary identity. At the grassroots level, many Sunnis do not mind praying in Zaidi mosques and vice versa. Consequently, the religious divide only marginally structures political affiliations and adherence to specific Islamist groups. *(See Ref 259)*

However, one of the most remarkable features of the contemporary Yemeni political formula has been its capacity to deal with the various Islamist ideal groups through integration and cooptation rather than repression. Muslim Brothers, Salafists, violent "jihadi" fringes, Sufis, and Zaidi revivalists have all at some point collaborated with the state to a certain extent. Since the 1970s, such an equalibrium has proved rather functional, as it has reduced the level of political violence, allowed the participation of most, and maintained government stability. Yet due to internal developments and external pressures after September 11, 2001 events in U.S.A., this system has increasingly been placed in jeopardy with still unknown consequences.

The plurality of Islamism in Yemeni context is expressed through five distinct Islamist ideal groups: the Muslim Brothers, violent "jihadi" fringes, Salafis (or Salafists), Sufis, and Zaidi revivalists. All five are rooted in the country's complex, rich, and ancient history, but are also products of contemporary international and transnational dynamics. Groups may also overlap and situations change quickly due to shifting alliances. Nevertheless, each of these groups is structured in a specific way and distinguishes itself from the others through a number of key issues: participation in party politics, loyalty to the ruler, significant episodes of confrontation with the state, and overt stigmatisation of other religious and political identities.

The most prevalent in the wide spectrum of Yemeni Islamism are The Muslim Brothers which inspired by the teachings of the Muslim Brotherhood. As early as the 1940s, the reformist and revolutionary movements opposed to the Zaidi monarchy were closely associated with Islamist intellectuals.

While studying in Cairo, many reformists - including Muhammad Ahmad Nu'man (of Shafi'i origin) and Muhammad Mahmood al-Zubayri (of Zaidi origin) - became acquainted with the ideas of Hassan al-Banna, although it seems that most of them were never formally Muslim Brothers. Both the failed 1948 revolution against the Zaidi imam Yahya, and the successful 1962 revolution against his grandson Imam Muhammad al-Badr, were at least in part inspired by the teachings of the Muslim Brothers. *(See Ref 248)*

Following the 26 September 1962 revolution to overthrow the Zaidi imamate, which had united nationalists, Nasserists, Muslim Brothers and modernists, disagreements quickly emerged among the new leaders. Through the creation of the Hezbollah (Party of God) in 1964, Zubayri, who felt that the new Egyptian-backed regime lacked legitimacy, intended to draw together different segments of society, the intellectuals (many of whom could be labeled as Islamist) and the tribal elements in particular. While Zubayri was assassinated in 1965, his project of reconciliation and integration of all parties became a founding principle of the republic. In that framework, Muslim Brothers were brought into various institutions, especially the education system and the security forces. *(See Ref 260)*

However, in September 1990 "al-Islah" (Reform) party was created, bringing together Islamist figures, tribal leaders and businessmen, which permitted to this successful association to live on through it, and for that reason it was generally described as the Yemeni branch of the Muslim Brotherhood.From its foundation until late 2007 it was headed by Sheikh Abdallah al-Ahmar, chief of the most prominent tribal confederation (the Hashid, of which Ali Abdallah Saleh's tribe, Sanhan, itself is a member) and speaker of parliament.More than a 3 years after Sheikh Abdallah al-Ahmar's death on December 29, 2007, the tribal and political consequences are still unclear. *(See Ref 261, 262, 263)*

Al-Islah has succeeded to bring individuals with different agendas together and has proven its ability to adapt to the internal and international changing context. In fact, it has taken part in the democratisation process since its inception, competing in free elections and participating in the parliament. While debate over whether the democratic system holds religious legitimacy may exist inside the party, al-Islah overtly accepts the multiparty system and has never supported direct armed confrontation with the government. It collaborates with the regime and could even be considered an integral part of it. During the secession war opposing Southern elites to the North in 1994, militias supported by al-Islah assisted the government in defeating the socialist-led secessionists. Today, al-Islah is well-implanted in numerous regions of the country (including in the former Marxist South, where anti-socialist reaction is strong and favours Islamist candidates and platforms). Nationally, it won an average of 18 percent of the vote during the 1993, 1997, and 2003 parliamentary elections (though the elections' lack of transparency reduces the significance of this data). *(See Ref 267, 268)*

To meet the challenges that occurred in the late 1990s, the al-Islah's leadership follow a new strategy in the new millennium based on alliance and collaboration with other opposition movement - particularly with its former enemy, the Yemeni Socialist Party (YSP), which headed South Yemen. A common platform was composed, which not necessarily popular among all activists, and Faysal bin Shamlan (a former oil minister) was designated as the main opposition candidate against Ali Abdallah Saleh in the September 2006 presidential election. Shamlan won 22 percent of the votes. His relative success (considering the means monopolised by the president to ensure his reelection) has opened new horizons for the opposition and for the Islamists. The April 2009 parliamentary elections were postponed until 27 April 2011, but because of the rioting and the demonstrations across the country to oust President Saleh which started in February 2011, this date was postponed. *(See Ref 269, 270)*

On the other hand, the violent fringes labeled as jihadis, although a small number, have played an important role in Yemen's recent history, often putting the country on the map of international terrorism. Since the 1990s, they have become increasingly visible in the media, a fact that often obscures other versions of Islamism. The participation of Yemenis in the Afghan War in the 1980s and the subsequent "jihads" in Bosnia, Chechnya, and Iraq have affected internal politics. In 1994, during the war against the socialist-led secessionists in the South, militias (some comprised of former "Afghan Arabs") assisted the national army, murdered socialists, and sacked Aden. Some were integrated into the security forces or local tribal institutions. An example is Tariq al-Fadli, heir of the sultan of Abyan and one of the leaders of the mujahideen in Afghanistan, who later was appointed by the president to the "Majlis al-Shura", the upper house of the parliament. *(See Ref 259, 271, 272)*

While some Jihadis were working with the government, others created cells with transnational links (such as the Aden-Abyan Islamic Army or other groups affiliated with al-Qa'ida that eventually turned against government interests and explicitly targeted Westerners). These took part in the 1998 kidnapping of tourists; in the bombing of the USS Cole in 2000; and since September 2001 in various assassinations or (often failed) bombing plots throughout the country, including against infrastructure. In November 2002, a missile shot by an American drone in the central desert of Yemen near the city of Ma'rib killed Abu Ali al-Harithi, alleged to be the leader of al-Qa'ida in Yemen. Some other activists were arrested and tried by the authorities. Nevertheless, the level of security controls has been considered insufficient by the new U.S. ally. In February 2006, the escape of 23 al-Qa'ida militants, including a leading operative, Jamal al-Badawi, from a high-security prison raised questions about infiltration into the state apparatus. In 2008, after a campaign of low level (and often unsuccessful) attacks on state and Western interests, including in the capital and the bombing of the American embassy on September - in which a total of 19 people died- symbolised a new strategic phase. In July of the same year, the attack in Say'un (east of the country) against the buildings of security services and the subsequent claim by the attackers showed that the Yemeni regime was becoming a target of jihadi groups more than ever. *(See Ref 273)*

The Yemeni version of Salafis is the third Islamic group. They are labelled sometimes by their opponents as "Wahhabis" due to their real or supposed links to Saudi Arabia. Furthermore they often inaccurately associated with the jihadi groups. Although they have connections with other Islamist groups, significant differences exist between them. However, the Salafi movement emerged in Yemen in the early 1980s around the figure of Muqbil al-Wadi'i, who was educated in Saudi Arabia in the 1960s and 1970s, and maintained links with that country's rulers and religious elites until his death in 2001. The Salafis' principals include a claim of complete loyalty to the ruler, even if he is corrupt and unjust, as well as a will to transcend local and national contexts by delivering a universal message. Salafis, then, aim to preserve all Muslims from chaos (fitna) by not engaging in any kind of politics and not participating in elections, demonstrations, or revolutions. Instead, they believe they can play a role in orienting state policies through secret advice given to the ruler. They usually condemn violence and have long been critical of terrorist operations targeting civilians. In fact, the Salafi leader al-Wadi'i remained very critical of the jihadists' strategy at the global level as well as inside Yemen from the early 1990s onward. At the time, he accused Osama bin Laden of preferring to invest in weapons rather than in mosques. He even botched some of his plans for jihad against the socialist elites of South Yemen. *(See Ref 274, 275, 276, 277)*

In fact, the Salafis in Yemen play a very political role and have received indirect assistance and benevolent tolerance from the government. Their doctrine is convenient, as it helps undermine support for more political Islamist groups such as the Muslim Brothers and the Zaidi revivalists, as well as to socialists in former South Yemen. The mainstream Salafi doctrine indeed helps keep certain segments of the population out of politics and considers all opposition to the ruler to be illegitimate. Consequently, abstention during local or national elections favours candidates of the ruling party. The division of its opponents has long been a strategy of Ali Abdallah Saleh's regime, and it appears to have been rather successful until last February when the new uprising started.

Like the Salafis, the Sufis, which constitute the fourth Islamic ideal group in contemporary Yemen, played an important role in Yemeni politics. Popular in former South Yemen and especially in the eastern province of Hadhramout, they suffered from intense repression under the socialist regime, and many clerics then found refuge in Saudi Arabia and North Yemen. After unification, the support by some of their leaders for the Southern secessionist movement in 1994 continued to undermine their position. After the war and the defeat of the secessionists, the government even turned a blind eye toward the destruction of their shrines in Aden and Hadhramout by the Salafis and some radical Muslim Brothers.However, since late 1990s, the Sufi movement has experienced a significant revival, symbolised by the Dar al-Mustafa institute in Tarim. Headed by two internationally renowned figures, al-Habib Umar bin Hafidh and al-Habib Ali al-Jiffri (the son of Abd al-Rahman al-Jiffri, a prominent leader of the 1994 secession), this religious teaching institute has received much attention and support from the government. In return, local candidates of the ruling Congress party were granted support during the 2003 parliamentary elections against candidates of al-Islah. While Sufis have been described by many analysts as a group threatened on all sides by government policies and by other Islamist groups, this is no longer entirely the case. Despite his small following, in 2003, al-Habib Umar was appointed to be the national television anchorman for religious programs during Ramadan. As a sign of the new link between this Islamist group and the state, President Ali Abdallah Saleh has also paid numerous visits to Dar al-Mustafa, benefiting from the groups historic transnational connections. *(See Ref 278, 279)*

The Sufi doctrine appears, like that of the Salafis, to be politically useful. It does indeed help weaken government support for other Islamist groups while broadcasting a supposedly more tolerant, peaceful, and moderate version of Islam. Indeed, the Sufi doctrine taught in their various institutions apparently tends to focus more on individual spirituality and personal development than on politics.

The Zaidi revivalists represent the fifth Islamic ideal group .It is the only one of all the five groups that is specifically Yemeni, but nevertheless has created transnational links. It finds its roots in an intellectually based reaction to the fall of the Zaidi imamate in 1962. Most of its supporters can be found among a specific segment of the population: the sayyids who are descendants of Prophet Muhammad. In fact, they have begun to organise themselves during the 1980s when a small minority turned toward Iranian Shi'ism, abandoning much of the Zaidi dogma and admiring the 1979 Iranian Revolution. Others are eager to portray Zaidism as a modernist religious doctrine with potential for reform and enlightenment, as liberal intellectuals who present the most severe critiques of the government. Another group - which remains loyal to the Zaidi doctrine - creates religious institutions, publishes many books, and in 1990 even established a political party, the Party of Truth (Hizb al-Haqq). In 1993, two of its leaders were elected to parliament, and in 1997, the secretary general of al-Haqq was chosen to head the Ministry of Religious Affairs. *(See Ref 280)*

However, in the mid-1990s a split in "Hizb al-Haqq" party led to the creation of a more radical fringe called the Believing Youth (a-Shabab al-Mu'min), headed by Husayn Badr al-Din al-Huthi, a former al-Haqq member of parliament. The objective of this group, backed by intellectuals in the region of Sa'da, was to oppose the rise of the Salafi movement which they perceive as the cradle of Zaidism. At first, they received support from the government, but in the post-September 11 context, tensions began to rise. Huthi and his supporters were very critical of the regime's new strategy and its cooperation in the U.S. led War on Terror. In June 2004, the government sought to arrest Husayn al-Huthi, who was accused of receiving aid from Iran and from the Lebanese Hezbollah and of wanting to restore the Zaidi imamate (which he denied). He and his supporters resisted. What started as a police operation quickly turned into a full-scale war that left thousands dead or injured. In May 2005, the prime minister admitted on television that 525 soldiers of the Yemeni army had perished in the operations, but he never provided estimates of civilian or rebel casualties. Despite the massive violence - this war, which by all means cannot be considered a legitimate operation of the War on Terror-drew little criticism from Western powers and scarce media attention. It is nevertheless started to destabilise a political and sectarian equilibrium that had until recently proved effective. *(See Ref 281)*

While some experts have long portrayed Yemen as on the brink of collapse, it has in fact remained surprisingly stable. Despite strong internal opposition (by political and tribal actors) and frequent hostility from neighbours, especially Saudi Arabia, the republican regime and Ali Abdallah Saleh's rule have resisted and managed to overcome numerous periods of crisis: wars between antagonistic Yemeni regimes, clashes with Saudi Arabia and Eritrea, the unification of the two Yemens, the Gulf War and the subsequent eviction of around 800,000 Yemeni workers from Saudi Arabia and Kuwait, as well as the post-September 11 crisis.

In fact, the relationship between the state and the various political groups, especially Islamist ones, and their integration into public institutions (army, police, universities, and so forth) are likely the key to understanding such stability. While it may have been maintained over the years by the regime out of self-interest (weakening its enemies, dividing political and religious groups) or due to its own incapacity - for better and for worse - power-sharing has long been one of the main features of the system. The presence of a strong traditional "civil society" in the form of tribal and religious groups, most of them armed or capable of opposing the state, has undermined the regime's capacity to monopolise all the levers of power and to fulfill any totalitarian dreams. Unfortunately, it appears that internal dynamics as well as external pressures have wrecked the equilibrium rather than tried to preserve it.

Despite that unification was initially built on a partnership between the two former ruling parties of North and South Yemen, Northern elites were eager to find new allies. Accordingly, the power-sharing between Ali Abdallah Saleh with the Islamists became more directly political during the 1990s. Following the first multiparty general elections in 1993, Abd al-Majid al-Zindani became part of the five-man presidential council, while

Abdallah al-Ahmar, head of al-Islah, was elected as speaker of parliament benefiting from the voices of the ruling Congress party MPs. As tensions rose with the socialist leaders in the coalition, Ali Abdallah Saleh agreed to govern with al-Islah. The Muslim Brothers directly participated in government between 1993 and 1997, playing an even greater role after the 1994 war and the complete demise of the socialists. Abd al-Wahhab al-Anisi was named deputy prime minister, and al-Islah members held important ministries (justice, education, trade, and religious affairs). *(See Ref 259)*

Although the crisis following the 11 September 2001 attacks in U.S.A. affected these political arrangements, it has not yet threatened their existence. With pressure coming from both its own society and from its new American ally, the Yemeni government has tried to show its involvement in the War on Terror while also remaining eager to prove its independence from Western powers.

Nevertheless, growing international pressure and criticism is slowly leading to change.This trend is furthered by elites inside the government in order to enhance their own power. Since 2004, repression in the form of arrests, closure of religious institutes (including those controlled by al-Islah), army raids, torture, and imprisonment have seemed to go in tandem with rising instability and violence from Islamists affiliated with or inspired by al-Qa'ida rhetoric. The September 2006 bombings against oil facilities, the July 2007 suicide bombings against Spanish tourists that left 10 dead, fighting between militants and the army in August 2007, and the September 2008 attack on the American embassy illustrate these tensions. In this context, it appears as if the government is actually losing touch with the violent groups it once largely managed to control through political and economic integration. *(See Ref 282, 283)*

However, while the government lost its equilibrium with the Yemeni Islamists another factor came to increase the uncertainty to the state, it is of al-Qa'ida in The Arabian Peninsula (AQAP).

Al-Qa'ida in the Arabian Peninsula (AQAP) was formed in January 2009 by a merger between two regional offshoots of the international Islamist militant network in neighbouring Yemen and Saudi Arabia. Led by a former aide to Osama bin Laden, the group has vowed to attack oil facilities, foreigners and security forces as it seeks to topple the Saudi monarchy and Yemeni government, and establish an Islamic caliphate.

It has claimed responsibility for a number of attacks in the two countries over the past 12 months, and has been blamed by President Barack Obama for attempting to blow up a U.S. passenger jet as it flew into Detroit on 2009 Christmas Day.

A Nigerian man charged in relation to the incident, Omar Farouk Abdulmutallab, has allegedly told investigators that AQAP operatives trained him in Yemen, equipped him with a powerful explosive device and told him what to do. He also warned there were others like him who would strike soon. *(See Ref 284)*

In fact this organisation first came to prominence in Saudi Arabia in May 2003, when it claimed responsibility for simultaneous suicide bombing attacks on three Western housing compounds in Riyadh, which left 29 dead. These attacks followed by a subsequent crackdown on Islamist militants and radicals by the Saudi security forces, however the group was able to mount another attack on the Muhayyah residential compound in the capital in November of that year, killing 17 people.

Nevertheless, it suffered a major blow in 2004 when its leader, Khaled Ali Hajj - a Yemeni and former bodyguard of bin Laden - was ambushed and killed by Saudi troops. However, the group soon recovered under the guidance of a veteran Saudi militant, Abdul Aziz al-Muqrin, and launched a series of spectacular attacks.

On 1 May 2004, militants shot dead five Western workers at a petrochemical complex in the north-western Red Sea city of Yanbu. On 29 May, more than 20 foreign and Saudi nationals were killed in attacks on three sites in the city of al-Khobar, increasing fears of political instability and pushing up global oil prices. The following month, members of AQAP abducted and beheaded a 49-year old American aerospace worker named Paul Johnson. *(See Ref 284)*

The triumph was short-lived, however, as when security forces stormed a hideout in Riyadh looking for Johnson's murderers, Muqrin was shot dead.

Although militants killed at least nine people in a raid on the US consulate in Jeddah in December 2004, al-Qa'ida in the Arabian Peninsula enjoyed notably less success under Muqrin's successor, Salih al-Awfi.

The Saudi security services gradually gained the upper hand, and succeed in preventing any major attacks the following year, when Awfi was himself killed during a police raid in the holy city of Medina.

In spite of the large numbers of Saudis who then travelled to militant training camps and gained experience fighting in places such as Iraq, the group found it increasingly difficult to organise operational cells inside the kingdom. Its last attempt a significant attack was at the Abqaiq oil facility in February 2006.

Meanwhile in Yemen - the ancestral home of bin Laden - Sunni militants took advantage of the weak central government, whose authority does not extend far outside the capital Sana'a, and established strongholds in its largely autonomous tribal regions. Although al-Qa'ida cells were held responsible for several attacks inside Yemen since the suicide boat attack on the USS Cole near the port of Aden in 2000 that killed 17 U.S. sailors, it was not until the second half of the decade that a fully-functioning affiliated group was formed.

According to Gregory Johnsen of Princeton University, between 2002 and 2003 the Yemeni government co-operated closely with the U.S. to fight al-Qa'ida. By the end of that period - which included one leader being killed in a controversial strike by a CIA drone aircraft - al-Qa'ida appeared to be substantially weakened and so both countries shifted focus. *(See Ref 284)*

The policy appeared to have worked until February 2006, Mr Johnsen says, when 23 suspected al-Qa'ida members managed to escape from a prison in San'a , including Jamal al-Badawi, the alleged mastermind of the USS Cole bombing.

Most were eventually either recaptured or killed, but two of the lesser-known escapees eluded the authorities, including Nasser Abdul Karim al-Wahayshi, a former personal assistant to bin Laden in Afghanistan, and Qasim al-Raymi.

Al-Wahayshi, a 33-year-old from the southern governorate of al-Baida, spent time in religious institutions in Yemen before travelling to Afghanistan in the late 1990s. He fought at the battle of Tora Bora in December 2001, before escaping over the border into Iran, where he was eventually arrested. He was extradited to Yemen in 2003.

Al-Wahayshi, al-Raymi and others within the organisation have proven particularly talented at creating a narrative of events that is designed to appeal to a local audience, something both the U.S. and Yemen have been incapable of doing. In a sense, both the U.S. and Yemeni governments have ceded the field of debate and discussion within Yemen to al-Qa'ida. Within months of the prison break in February of 2006, al-Qa'ida was able to attempt simultaneous attacks on oil and gas facilities in Ma'rib and Hadhramaut.

This early and haphazard attempt was soon eclipsed by more professional operations. In March 2007, the chief criminal investigator in Ma'rib was assassinated. The group also claimed responsibility for two suicide bomb attacks that killed six Western tourists before being linked to the assault on the US embassy in San'a in September 2008, in which terrorists detonated bombs and fired rocket-propelled grenades. Ten Yemeni guards and four civilians were killed, along with six assailants. However, four months later, al-Wahayshi announced in a video the merger of the al-Qa'ida offshoots in Yemen and Saudi Arabia to form "al-Qa'ida of Jihad Organisation in the Arabian Peninsula". Since then, the organisation has only grown stronger as al-Wahayshi and al-Raymi have worked to resurrect al-Qa'ida from the ashes.

Next to al-Wahayshi and al-Raymi in the same video sat the new group's deputy leader, Said Ali al-Shihri, a Saudi national who was released from the US military detention centre at Guantanamo Bay in November 2007. Another former detainee, Mohammed Atiq al-Harbi, also known as Mohammed al-Awfi, appeared alongside them and was described as a field commander. *(See Ref 284)*

Embarrassingly for both Riyadh and Washington, both men had been released from Guantanamo into the custody of the Saudi government's "deradicalisation" programme for militants, which included art therapy. They both left the facility within weeks.

The group's first operation outside Yemen was carried out in Saudi Arabia in August 2009 against the kingdom's security chief, Prince Mohammad bin Nayef, though he survived. The bomber concealed a bomb containing the high-explosive PETN (pentaerythritol) inside his body.

After news of the failed attempt to destroy the Northwest Airlines Airbus A330 emerged, AQAP released a statement saying it had sought to avenge recent raids by Yemeni forces aided by US intelligence, in which dozens of militants are reported to have died.

"We tell the American people that since you support the leaders who kill our women and children... we have come to slaughter you [and] will strike you with no previous [warning], our vengeance is near", the group said.

"We call on all Muslims... to throw out all unbelievers from the Arabian Peninsula by killing crusaders who work in embassies or elsewhere... [in] a total war on all crusaders in the Peninsula of Muhammad". *(See Ref 285)*

Does AQAP have links to al-Qa'ida central?

Experts agree that if there's a connection between AQAP and Al Qa'ida leadership, the command and control communication is minimal. Gregory Johnsen explains that "the strongest connection is ideological." *(See Ref 289)*

Al-Wahayshi, who worked as Bin Laden's personal assistant, formed the group along the lines of the central group's structural and ideological model. "When you see him [al-Wahayshi] in the tapes, it's very much the same sort of personal dynamics of how he carries himself, how he addresses individuals. What he does is what bin Laden did," says Johnsen. "But since there is so little command and control, it's an organisation that really isn't a subsidiary; it's much more of a parallel organisation," he says. *(See Ref 289, 290)*

Reports on al-Qa'ida in the Arabian Peninsula's membership vary wildly - some experts say there are fewer than 100 fighters, while others believe there may be 400 to 500 - but most agree that if it is left unmolested it will soon become a major threat especially since they have another skill other than terrorism the management of the media.

Although, the suicide bombing is an important tool in AQAP arsenal to wage its terrorist attacks against the West, its effective management of the media is one of its key survival tools. Internet technologies such as web mail, instant messenger, email lists, and message boards are skillfully used to spread their propaganda campaign, advance the group's training and operational purposes, and produce the maximum psychological effect. They also use these technologies to recruit followers, raise funds, and engage in psychological warfare tactics. This sophisticated use of the Internet to carry messages, plan attacks, project a false view of events, and launch a campaign of fear through intimidation, propaganda, and psychological warfare has made it difficult for Saudi and Yemeni authorities and its

Western allies to defeat a versatile enemy that masters the art of deception and electronic warfare.

Despite the arrest of high-profile AQAP operatives, the organisation continually puts out several magazines including two, which run from 30 to 50 pages each. "Sawt al-Jihad" (the Voice of Jihad) is devoted to political and ideological matters. Its primary goal is to cement the ideological basis of jihad (as they see it and interpret it), promote theological justifications for martyrdom, and boost fighters' morale. The second online magazine, "Mu'askar al-Battar" ('Al-Battar Training Camp), covers military training.

However, with the U.S. robbing al-Qa'ida of its training facilities, the need arose for the terrorists to find a substitute for this loss. Although new training centres were set in several places, including Pakistan, Yemen, Somalia and Iraq, they could never replace the vast safe havens destroyed in Afghanistan. AQAP had to find other practical venues capable of absorbing and training the growing number of its recruits. It is in this context that the architects behind AQAP explored the Internet as a means to expanding their training operations and launched the monthly magazine, al-Battar in which page after page the reader is introduced to the art of guerrilla warfare and survival tactics, the skills of kidnapping, negotiating, and taping executions, the importance of maintaining operational security, and the value of sports, just to name a few. The regimen of terror lessons is comprehensive. Senior members of al-Qa'ida also contribute to the magazine, the most prominent of which was the Egyptian, Saif al-Adel, the security chief for Osama bin Laden. *(See Ref 256)*

Furthermore, in August 2004, AQAP also launched a new magazine publication on the Internet aimed exclusively at women, advising them on how to reconcile the apparent contradiction of fighting jihad while maintaining family life, how to support their husbands in their conflict with the authorities, and how to bring up their children in the path of jihad. Named after a female Arab poet belonging to the early Islamic era and published by the "Women's Information Office in the Arabian Peninsula," the "al-Khansa" magazine is the first of its kind to reach out to women for terrorist operational support missions. The wife-mother is strongly urged to be in top physical condition, "not overindulge in eating and drinking," and to "ask personal permission neither from her husband nor from her guardian, because she is obligated and none need to ask permission in order to carry out a commandment that everyone must carry out." This is a striking development given the draconian constraints that most jihadists impose or want imposed on women. But this change of heart is driven by cruel though pragmatic reasoning. The effectiveness of female suicide bombers from the occupied territories in Palestine to Chechnya has convinced male jihadists, who could care less about women's rights or equality with men, to elevate women's status in the war against what they perceive as the enemies of Islam. *(See Ref 287)*

Many experts believe that male jihadists were impressed by the shocking suicide operations conducted by the Palestinian Wafa Idris, the first Palestinian woman to successfully penetrate Israeli defences and blow herself up killing scores of Israelis in the process, or Reem Raiyshi, the first Palestinian mother of young children to become a suicide bomber.Those acts were enough to let AQAP leaders engage in a debate about the proper role of women in jihad. Proponents of an active role of women in jihad back their stand with historical examples where women played a tremendous supportive role in the cause of jihad. The stories of those legendary females who joined men in battle in the early days of Islam and celebrated the sacrifices of their sons and husbands for the sake of jihad are recounted endlessly and posted on several extremists' websites. What is also novel in this approach is that the champions of women's rights to participate in jihad are no longer concentrated on opportunistic male extremists. The articles and editorials in "al-Khansa" magazine are seemingly written by women, though it is not clear if they actually are. *(See Ref 288)*

However, incorporating women into al-Qa'ida in the Arabian Peninsula ranks in this new strategy has the ultimate goal of using a hitherto untapped asset as a vehicle for indoctrinating the coming generation into a jihadist mindset. Women can play a major role in altering the social order of society and rebuilding it in conformity with revolutionary jihad. They can contribute to the ideological training of their children, indoctrinating them for martyrdom and "takfiri" (excommunication) thinking. By instilling takfiri indoctrination in children at a younger stage, they can grow up to be "good" jihadis.

On the other hand AQAP also markets training films detailing targets and tactics. Role-playing and scenario type of assassinations, kidnappings, bombings, attack technique at security posts, and small unit raids on various types of targets are shown in fairly good quality produced films.

The production of these films demonstrates the sophisticated infrastructure put in place by the jihadists' media production wing, the Sahab Institute for Media Production.

This effectiveness of the use of the media accounts for AQAP's continued longevity, despite the major setbacks and heavy losses inflicted upon it by the regime's forces. That the online magazines have not been interrupted by the death of AQAP mastermind, Sheikh Yousef al-Ayyiri, known also as al-Battar ("The Cutting Edge"), and such other leaders as Abdel Aziz al-Muqrin, once Saudi Arabia's most-wanted militant, Rakan Muhsin Mohammed Alsaykhan, Nasir Al-Rashid, and Faysal Al-Dakhil, who worked closely and immediately under al-Muqrin, is a sign of the resilience of the organisation. Eliminating the movement's commanders has proven to be less damaging than purging its most important ideologues. Military commanders are much easier to replace than prominent theorisers who provide the ideological support necessary for recruitment, propaganda, and indoctrination.

The organisation has realised how crucial preserving its communications structures is to its survival. Its online journals (especially Sada Al-Malahem which was lauched in January 2008) and printed pamphlets are the movement's Achilles Heel and they have been instrumental in safeguarding its ideological core.

However, given the weakness of the central Yemeni authority of Ali Abdallah Saleh, the question which comes to mind: is al-Qa'ida in the Arabian Peninsula has the capacity and the capability to bring about the collapse of the fragile Yemeni government and usher in a Taliban-style regime? Is Yemen becoming the next base from which al-Qa'ida will target the West?

In fact, most Western policy makers are scrambling to be seen as responding decisively to the crisis, offering increased military assistance, development aid, or some combination thereof. Although foreign intervention presents opportunities for positive change there are limits to what it can accomplish. However, two issues must be taken in consideration before any action in Yemen: the nature of authority in the state, and the complex relationship between its tribal communities and militant jihadis such as AQAP.

Most experts believe that al-Qa'ida benefits from the weakness of the Yemeni regime, but the regime's failure would not necessarily be a win for the militants. Yemenis are not inherently sympathetic to militant jihadism, and AQAP probably benefits more from Yemen's position as a weak state than it would if the state were to fail altogether.

Yemen faces a set of profound political and economic issues. It is the poorest country in the Arab world, with 40 percent living below the poverty line, according to the CIA factbook's analysis of Yemen. Some 50 percent of the country is illiterate, which the government hopes to address with a new fifteen-year education plan. Thirty five percent of the population is unemployed, and the population is expected to double to fourty million over the next two decades. Nevertheless, the process of state-building in Yemen has been rapid, but remains underway. As recently as fifty years ago, the Yemeni imam presided over a country with no local currency, no sewage system, and only three hospitals. Change has been swift since the republican revolution abolished the imamate in 1962, but the country has never settled on the rules of its political game. As in many developing states, negotiations over "who gets what,when, and how" are ongoing. When a state is in the throes of establishing a new domestic political order, other nations must be more constrained in their involvement there than when it has imploded. *(See Ref 291)*

However, to stabilise his regime Ali Abdallah Saleh must control the tribes' leaders, for this reason he created a system of patronage in which the state grants those leaders on yearly basis funds, resources and facilities to buy their cooperations. Furthermore this system became more generous following the Yemen's oil era which began in the 1980s. Nevertheless, this state-sponsored patronage system has distorted the country's traditional mechanisms of dispute resolution and resource distribution. Tribal sheikhs are pillars in both the traditional and the patronage systems, although in the latter the regime detaches them from their communities by offering wealth and status in exchange for political acquiescence. This has resulted in the rapid centralisation of the political system, which was built on the state's capacity to distribute oil wealth to those it deems politically relevant. This centralisation, although artificial, has been transformative. Society does not function as it did only one generation ago; today, tribal leaders are rarely the first among equals and are sometimes rather divorced from their tribes' concerns. *(See Ref 292, 293)*

On the other hand, tribes' people no longer support their sheikhs as tenaciously as they did when the central government enjoyed less power.

Now, as the regime's patronage system buckles under the pressure of reduced oil income, its imprint on Yemen's political ecology is clear: The patronage system has eroded many of Yemen's tribal codes and norms, helping create a vacuum where there is no clear alternative to the current patterns of leadership and in which entrepreneurial radicals such as AQAP have greater room to maneuver *(See Ref 294)*

According to analyst Christopher Boucek, Yemen faces a great and growing number of challenges that endanger its political future and threaten its neighbours on the Arabian Peninsula. War, terrorism, a deepening secessionist movement, and interconnected economic and demographic trends have the potential to overwhelm the Yemeni government, jeopardizing domestic stability and security across the region. Yemen's oil - the source of over 75 percent of its income - is quickly running out, and the country has no apparent way to transition to a post-oil economy. The dire economic situation makes it increasingly difficult for the government to deliver the funds needed to hold the country together. Furthermore, according to "Pulitzer Gateway Fragile States Guide", Yemen is also depleting its water resources, with many predicting San'a will become the first capital city in history to go dry. The resulting population migrations - combined with high unemployment and a bleak post-oil economy - would likely create a swelling population of the disaffected and impoverished. The lack of money in the state's treasury -and the sense of pessimism about the future that this creates- is the most important driver of the country's other political crises. *(See Ref 295)*

As the political situation became very dire during the last three years, the Yemeni regime's capacity to contend with domestic challenges such as AQAP has diminished so much. The radical organisation appeared to no longer regard the regime as a significant obstacle to its ambitions according to the tenth edition of AQAP's online magazine, "Sada al-Malahim", in August 2009. The magazine asserted that the organisation's main goal was now to unseat the regime in Saudi Arabia, noting that Yemeni President Ali Abdallah Saleh's grasp on power was weakening: "We concentrate on Saudi Arabia because the government of Ali Abdallah Saleh is on the verge of collapse [and he is about to] flee the land of Yemen." AQAP's very public assertion that Saleh could not hinder its expansion marks a significant change from earlier editions of the magazine, which had called on Yemenis to fight the regime and hints at AQAP's plans for Yemen. Within a widening political space, the organisation has become more explicit about its domestic political ambitions. In the same edition of Sada al-Malahim, Qassem al-Raymi called for skilled labourers to help "the mujahideen" establish an Islamic state: "A man's value is in what he does for a living.... The jihadi arena needs all powers, skills and abilities [such as] doctors, engineers and electricians. It also requires plumbers, builders, and contractors, just as it needs students, educators, door-to-door salesmen and farmers. It is searching for media specialists from writers and printers [to] photographers and directors. It also needs conscientious Muslim reporters and sportsmen, skilled in martial arts and close combat. It is searching for proficient, methodical, organised administrators, just as it is in need of strong, honest traders who spend their wealth for the sake of their religion without fear or greed...Know my virtuous brother that by following your mujahideen brothers with some of these qualities it will accelerate the pace of achieving our great Islamic project: establishing an Islamic Caliphate". *(See Ref 296)*

From this declaration, which considered by many expert as a political manifesto by al-Raymi, it appears that AQAP is seeking to destroy the existing political system and establish its own. But to do that it must have the cooperation of the tribes to live in their area, where they are currently based, and to convince them that AQAP is not a danger for their existence and their preveleges. However, to succeed in their aims with the tribes the organisation will need to remember that tribal communities are motivated by a lot more than religious ideology; one's social responsibility within the tribe is, for example, an often-heard theme in Friday sermons in tribal areas. *(See Ref 296)*

It seems that the al-Qa'ida's leadership understood that the tribal system is still central to power and authority in large parts of Yemen. This understanding, in fact, was demonstrated in February 2009, when Nasser al-Wahayshi called on the tribes to resist pressure to grant the state control of their territory, and when Ayman al-Zawahiri called on Yemen's tribes to act like the tribes of Pakistan and Afghanistan and support al-Qa'ida: "I call on the noble and defiant tribes of the Yemen and tell them: don't be less than your brothers in the defiant Pushtun and Baluch tribes who aided Allah and His Messenger and made America and the Crusaders dizzy in Afghanistan and Pakistan... noble and defiant tribes of the Yemen ... don't be helpers of Ali Abdallah Saleh, the agent of the Crusaders ... be a help and support to your brothers the Mujahideen". *(See Ref 297)*

These statements played on notions of tribal honour, autonomy and, most important, the tribes' longstanding hostility to the central authorities. Clearly al-Qa'ida intends to capitalise on the tribes' well-founded distrust of the state. *(See Ref 298)*

The radical organisation is attempting to present itself as an alternative to a regime that is decried for selectively delivering wealth to Yemen's sheikhs at the expense of their tribes. In doing so, it seems to assume an organic acceptance of a jihadi political model within grassroots communities. Furthermore, as the state's patronage system continues to unravel, there is less money available to those on the periphery of that system, which is fueling competition over the depleting resources. Smaller sheikhs are becoming more likely to be cut from the state's largesse and might be more inclined to aid al-Qa'ida fugitives to assert their relevance or fill the vacuum created by dwindling state power.

To gain the sympathy of the tribes, AQAP is making use of a tradition which hinges on a tenet of Yemeni tribal culture: Honour requires providing hospitality to an outsider who requests protection, and turning over someone who has sought protection is shameful. So the tenth edition of Sada al-Malahim extolled the duty of sheikhs to give sanctuary to the mujahideen, referencing a story of how tribes offered sanctuary to the Prophet during a crisis. Given the cultural imperatives, and the relative inexpense of offering refuge, a tribe's provision of sanctuary does not necessarily mean it would support a more aggressive phase of the mujahideens' work. *(See Ref 296)*

On the other side Yemen's government must persuade the tribes that it can offer them more than al-Qa'ida can. The radical organisation is making the reasonable assumption that the government will not be willing or able to persuade the tribes that it will offer much. They are likely correct, but unlikely to be able to offer much to the tribes themselves. However, to most tribes, the Yemeni state is an instrument through which a small band of elites exploits and harasses the people. This will not change unless the state delivers benefits and builds trust between itself and grassroots communities.

According to Sarah Philips, "the Yemeni regime has weakened many aspects of the tribal system by co-opting sheikhs with access to wealth and power from the centre, thus severing many from their traditional support bases. Sheikhs now often derive their wealth and status from the political centre, rather than their traditional constituency in their local area. With the vacuum of legitimate authority that these fractured centre-periphery relationships have created, the Yemeni system is poorly equipped to deal with the political and economic crises it faces. AQAP is presenting its credentials in the regime's stead but is offering little more than a lightning rod for entrenched grievances, of which there are many." *(See Ref 296)*

Both AQAP and the Yemeni government have aspirations that clash with those of Yemen's tribes. The gulf between the tribes' local concerns and the internationally focused agenda of al-Qa'ida provides opportunities for the government to solve simple grievances and convince the tribes that the government is a better long-term bet than al-Qa'ida. But, with the Yemeni regime in crisis, this appears a distant hope. The only long-term solution to the question of bolstering the nation's stability - the regime agreeing to include more of Yemeni society - is unlikely to be achieved soon.

The government of President Ali Abdullah Saleh remains weak outside the capital, lacking in resources and credibility, and riddled with corruption. The government's attention and resources are also diverted by a bloody Zaidi Shia rebellion in the northern Saada governorate as well as a deepening secessionist movement in the south. Furthermore, the riots and the demonstrations across the country calling for the resignation of the president, make the situation to President Saleh very difficult to stay in power.

Yemenis have been sympathetic to radical Islam for several decades. Thousands of Yemenis responded to the call for jihad against the Soviets in Afghanistan in the 1980s and were welcomed home afterwards. "There's a reason why Yemenis in Guantanamo make up the largest core contingent; there's a reason why so many Yemenis have gone to Iraq, and now they go to Lebanon," says Barak Barfi, a visiting fellow at the Brookings Doha Centre. "There is a fertile radical environment." *(See Ref 289)*

However analysts say Yemen has been slow to confront the al-Qa'ida threat with the gusto that the U.S. has been pushing for, in large part because going after the Islamist group hasn't always been in the government's best interests. "If the government wants to fight [al-Qa'ida] seriously, they can do it", says Ali Saif Hassan, the director of Yemen's Political Development Forum to Time magazine (22/12/2009). But, he adds: "It's a matter of political decision - how much they will win, and how much they will lose". San'a has recently focused more of its attention on the rebel separatist movement in the south and on the recent Houthi uprising in the north than it has on al-Qa'ida.

While some western analysts say that al-Qa'ida seeks to overthrow Yemen's government, Hassan disagrees, saying that al-Qa'ida only seeks to establish a base there - a link between the Horn of Africa and the rest of the Arabian Peninsula - and that so long as President Saleh leaves al-Qa'ida alone, they will do the same for him. "The government still sometimes thinks it is too costly for it to fight al-Qa'ida. If you ask them to go and fight al-Qa'ida, they say 'Why? And what do I get back?'" says Hassan. Fighting al-Qa'ida would mean losing key fundamentalist support in the country, support that is already falling away. What would compel Saleh to turn it around? "It is business", says Hassan. "If the government gets more support from the Americans, they will change". The Obama administration has requested $65 million to help Yemen battle its resurgent terrorist threat.

However, with the riots and demonstrations spreading through Yemen since February 2011 against the Saleh regime the question now, is that help is sufficient and enough? And furthermore can the President stay in power and protect his regime under these circumstances? Accordingly is the unrest an opening to al-Qa'ida branch?

In the political tumult surrounding Yemen's embattled president, Ali Abdallah Saleh, many Yemeni troops have abandoned their posts or have been summoned to the capital, San'a, to help support the tottering government, the officials said. Al-Qa'ida in the Arabian Peninsula has stepped in to fill this power vacuum, and Yemeni security forces have come under increased attacks in recent weeks.

A small but steadily growing stream of al-Qa'ida fighters and lower-level commanders from other parts of the world, including Pakistan, are making their way to Yemen to join the fight there, although American intelligence officials are divided on whether the political crisis in Yemen is drawing more insurgents than would be traveling there under normal conditions.

Taken together, these developments have raised increasing alarm in the Obama administration, which is in the delicate position of trying to ease Mr. Saleh out of power, but in a way to ensure that counterterrorism operations in Yemen will continue unimpeded. These developments may also help explain why the United States has become less willing to support

Mr. Saleh, a close ally, given that his value in fighting terrorism has been diminished since demonstrations swept his country.

Some experts on Yemen who have observed Mr. Saleh's long domination through political shrewdness speculated that he might be deliberately withdrawing his forces from pursuing al-Qa'ida to worsen the sense of crisis and force the Americans to back him, rather than push him toward the exits.

But a senior American military officer with access to classified intelligence reports discounted those doubts: "This is a reflection of the turmoil in the country, not some political decision to stop."

Mr. Saleh's son and three nephews are in charge of four of Yemen's main security and counterterrorism agencies, including the Republican Guard and the Central Security Forces, which are trained and equipped by the United States. If they were forced to step down as part of any deal to remove Mr. Saleh, American officials acknowledge that the country's counterterrorism efforts would be left in the hands of untested lieutenants.

"We have had a lot of counterterrorism cooperation from President Saleh and Yemeni security services," Defence Secretary Robert M. Gates said on 27 March 2011 on ABC's "This Week." "So if that government collapses or is replaced by one that is dramatically more weak, then I think we'll face some additional challenges out of Yemen. There's no question about it. It's a real problem."

The Yemeni government's already weak reach is withering by the day, as violent convulsions rack several parts of the impoverished country. American officials said they were watching unrest in Shabwa Province, an al-Qa'ida stronghold, as well as in Jaar, a city in the southern province of Abyan where al-Qa'ida is known to have set up a base.

An officer in Yemen's counterterrorism forces said his unit had not been deployed and was on standby, even though much of the south was apparently outside government control and jihadists had apparently declared a separate emirate in Abyan. Yemeni counterterrorism officers would like to respond, but "we are only door-kickers," he said. "We need support from the army, and the army is busy splitting."

However, Yemenis have turned the page on Saleh and looking forward for a new unknown era. Beyond acolytes who benefited from his largesse,

Yemenis today perceive Saleh for what he is, an expert manipulator who craves power. Decent Yemenis no longer wish to be ruled by an official who makes the army of thieves in Ali Baba's legendary story look good.

CHAPTER NINE

SOMALIA: THE HOTBED
OF FUTURE TERROR

President Barack Obama has inherited a dangerous and fast-moving crisis in Somalia - one with profound implications for regional and international security. While some within his administration are continuing to place short-term counterterrorism goals ahead of a more comprehensive strategy approach as was done during the Bush administration, the shortcomings of this approach, according to most experts, are abundantly clear: violent extremism and anti-Americanism are now rife in Somalia due in large part to the blowback from policies that focused too narrowly on counterterrorism objectives.

However, the Somalian crisis during George W Bush administration was pushed to catastrophic dimensions due to his Policy. An Ethiopian military intervention in December 2006 succeeded in ousting an increasingly radical Islamist movement, the Islamic Courts Union (ICU) in Mogadishu, but provoked a brutal cycle of insurgency and counterinsurgency that plunged the country into new depths of misery. As conflict raged and humanitarian conditions spiraled downward, flawed U.S. policies only strengthened the radical "a-Shabaab Islamic Movement" and its commitment to attack Ethiopian, western and United Nations interests, as well as regional governments collaborating with the United States. This homegrown terrorist threat emanating from Somalia has the potential to become even more dangerous than the East Africa al-Qa'ida cell that was responsible for the 1998 terrorist attacks against U.S. embassies in Kenya and Tanzania. And as the recent epidemic of piracy off the Somali coast demonstrates -as did Afghanistan earlier this decade- the cost of ignoring failed states can be very high.

History of Islam in the Horn of Africa is as old as the religion itself. The early persecuted Muslims fled to the Axumite port city of Zeila in Modern Somalia to seek protection from the Quraish at the court of the Axumite Emperor in modern Ethiopia. Some of the Muslims that were granted protection are said to have settled in several parts of the Horn of Africa to promote the religion. The victory of the Muslims over the Quraish in the 7th century had a significant impact on Somalia's merchants and sailors, as their Arab trading partners had now all adopted Islam and the major trading routes in the Mediterranean and the Red Sea now became part of a trade network known as Pax Islamica. Through commerce, Islam spread amongst the Somali population in the coastal cities of Somalia. Instability in the Arabian Peninsula saw several migrations of Arab families to Somalia's coastal cities, who then contributed another significant element to the growing popularity of Islam in the Somali peninsula. *(See Ref 304, 305, 306)*

Somali people in the Horn of Africa are divided among different territories that were artificially and arbitrarily partitioned by the former Imperial powers. Besides Somalia proper, other historically and almost exclusively Somali-inhabited areas of the Horn of Africa now find themselves administered by neighbouring countries, such as the Somali Region in Ethiopia and the North Eastern Province (NFD) in Kenya. Pan Somalism was and is an ideology that advocates the unification of all ethnic Somalis under one flag and one nation. This led to a series of cross border raids by Somali insurgents and violent crackdowns by Ethiopian troops from 1960 to 1964, when open conflict erupted between Ethiopia and Somalia. This lasted a few months until a cease fire was signed in the same year. In the aftermath, Ethiopia and Kenya signed a mutual defence pact to protect their newly acquired territories from the Somali separatists. *(See Ref 307)*

However, modern Somalia was created in July 1960 when the British colony in the North and the Italian one in the South acquired independence and merged to form the Somali Republic with Mogadishu as its capital in which Aden Abdullah Osman was elected President. In 1967 Abdi Rashid Ali Shermake was elected President until October 1969, when General Muhammad Siyad Barre executed a military coup that made him president of the young state, and soon he proclaimed socialism as Somalia's governing political ideology, and established close relations with the Soviet Union until he was overthrew by the opposition in 1991. Some of Barre's draconian tactics for dealing with Somalia's fledgling Islamist movements consolidated the groups and gave them momentum. When Muslim leaders denounced reform of Somali family law, Barre executed ten prominent scholars and prosecuted hundreds more. In response, "underground organisations proliferated in every region in defence of the faith against the Godless socialists" writes Abdurahman M. Abdullahi. *(See Ref 317)*

Though Barre ruled for more than twenty years, by the early 1990s he faced "widespread insurrection initiated by the tribes and powerbrokers." Opponents forced him to flee the country, which collapsed into civil war and prolonged anarchy. *(See Ref 318)*

In these lawless conditions, two Islamist groups that were the progenitors of a-Shabaab became prominent. The first was the Islamic Union (IU). Although there is no firm date for the IU's birth, most credible accounts date this to around 1983. Ken Menkhaus, an associate professor of politics, notes that the IU was originally "comprised mainly of educated, young men who had studied or worked in the Middle East." It received significant funding and support from - and was in turn influenced by- the Salafi/ Wahhabi movement and its Saudi-based charity organisations. Members concluded that political Islam was the only way to rid their country of its corrupt leadership. The group had two goals. First, it sought to defeat Siad Barre's regime and replace it with an Islamic state. Second, it wanted to unify what it regarded as Greater Somalia -Northeastern Kenya, Ethiopia's Ogaden region, and Djibouti- and add them to the existing Somali state. *(See Ref 319, 320)*

After warlord Muhammad Farrah Aidid's rebel forces drove Barre into exile and destroyed his regime in 1991, the IU attempted to seize "targets of opportunity," including "strategic sites such as seaports and commercial crossroads." It managed to hold the seaports of Kismayo and Merka for almost a year but was quickly expelled from Bosaso. Ken Menkhaus notes that even with the prevailing lawlessness, Somalis were "suspicious of politically active Islam and remained attached to the clan as the sole source of protection". *(See Ref 321)*

The IU managed to control one location for a sustained period: the town of Luuq near the border with Ethiopia and Kenya. Consonant with its original aspirations, the IU implemented strict Shari'a there, meting out punishments that included amputations. However, in a pattern that would later work to the advantage of Somali Islamists, rough justice in Luuq made it safer from crime than most other places. *(See Ref 322)*

Luuq's proximity to Ethiopia was significant because of the IU's commitment to a Greater Somalia. In particular, the group focused on Ethiopia's Ogaden, a region inhabited by a majority of Somali speakers. The IU stirred up separatist unrest, and from 1996 to 1997, Ethiopia experienced a "string of assassination attempts and bombings by Al-Ittihad (IU) in Addis Ababa." In response, Ethiopian forces intervened in Luuq and destroyed the IU's safe haven. An American-led military intervention designed to restore order began in 1992. But this venture came to a humiliating end the following year when U.S. troops fought militias in the streets of Mogadishu, killing hundreds and losing 18 of their number in battles later immortalised by the film "Black Hawk Down". *(See Ref 321)*

Questions linger over the degree to which the IU was linked to al-Qa'ida during its heyday. For example, an analysis published by West Point's Combating Terrorism Center finds numerous alleged ties between the IU and al-Qa'ida. *(See Ref 323)*

Against this, Ken Menkhaus argues in his "Adelphi Paper", that there has never been a smoking gun regarding the relationship between the IU and al-Qa'ida since "no Somalis appear in al-Qa'ida's top leadership, and until 2003, no Somali was involved in a terrorist plot against a Western target outside of Somalia."

Despite these divergent views, there are two important points about the IU-al-Qa'ida relationship. First, al-Qa'ida's leadership recognises Somalia's role in one of its first actions, the first time it successfully bloodied America's nose. Al-Qa'ida dispatched a small team of military trainers to Somalia in 1993, which liaised with the IU prior to the battle of Mogadishu. Since then, al-Qa'ida leaders have claimed that they - rather than the forces of Muhammad Farrah Aidid - were the real hand behind the U.S. defeat. Many scholars believe these claims are highly exaggerated. But the true facts behind the battle of Mogadishu are beside the point insofar as al-Qa'ida's perceptions are concerned since the "rosecolored memoirs of Somalia have ... come to embody the 'founding myths' of the core al-Qa'ida methodology". *(See Ref 312, 324, 325, 326)*

Second, it is clear that certain key members of the IU had strong relationships with bin Laden's group. One was Aden Hashi Ayro, who went on to lead a-Shabaab. After Ayro's death, a-Shabaab posted a Somali-language biography of him, claiming the battle of Mogadishu was "the first time he fought under the supervision of al-Qa'ida, and with its logistical support and expertise." The New York Times would report at the time of Ayro's death that he was "long identified as one of al- Qa'ida's top operatives in East Africa."However, following the IU's defeat in Luuq, the group declined in prominence. By 2004, it was regarded as "a spent force, marginal if not defunct as an organisation". *(See Ref 327)*

That "Black Hawk Down"'s searing chapter effectively ended the prospect of international intervention to rebuild Somalia. Since 1993, the country has been divided into a patchwork of fiefdoms, fought over by warlords. The fundamental cause of the conflict lies in Somalia's bitter clan rivalries. Elsewhere in Africa, countries are divided by tribe. In Somalia, by contrast, almost all of the 9.5 million people are from the same tribe. They are ethnic Somalis, sharing a common language and loyalty to Islam. But they are all divided into clans, for example the Hawiye and the Darod. In turn, these large umbrella groups are divided into scores of sub-clans who are then split between hundreds of sub-sub-clans. These groups, each led by a warlord, fight for the scarce resources of an arid country.They form complex alliances, which are made and broken with bewildering speed.

Moreover, outside factors have made this situation still more explosive. Radical Islamists have clearly identified Somalia as a target for expansion.

The revolving-door politics of Somalia brought the country fourteen separate governments between 1991 and 2011. On June 5, 2006, the Islamic Courts Union (ICU) defeated a group of CIA-backed warlords and took control of Mogadishu, instigating what, for the first time, became a period of relative peace. Bronwyn Bruton, working at the time with about fifty local non-governmental organisations (NGOs) in Somalia, says, "Groups operating in Mogadishu were consistently telling me they never had a better operating environment." *(See Ref 300)*

The ICU was a broad umbrella group of Islamic fundamentalists and for a brief period was poised to end Somalia's 16 years of state collapse. After the Somali government fall in 1991, a system of sharia-based Islamic courts became the main judicial system, funded through fees paid by litigants. Over time the courts began to offer other services such as education and health care. The courts also acted as local police forces, being paid by local businesses to reduce crime. The Islamic courts took on the responsibility for halting robberies and drug-dealing, as well as stopping the showing of what it claims to be pornographic films in local movie houses. Somalia is almost entirely Muslim, and the Islamic court institutions initially had wide public support. The early years of the courts include such outfits as Sheikh Ali Dheere's, established in north Mogadishu in 1994 and the Beled Weyene court initiated in 1996. They soon saw the sense in working together through a joint committee to promote security. This move was initiated by four of the courts - Ifka Halan, Circolo, Warshadda and Hararyaale - who formed a committee to co-ordinate their affairs, to exchange criminals from different clans and to integrate security forces. In 1999 the group began to assert its authority. Supporters of the Islamic courts and other institutions united to form the ICU, an armed militia. In April of that year they took control of the main market in Mogadishu and, in July, captured the road from Mogadishu to Afgoi. Their system of government, controlled by judges, is known as a krytocracy. *(See Ref 309)*

In fact, the Islamic Courts Union (ICU) was the next incarnation of the Islamic Union (IU). By the time it caught the attention of Westerners, it was more militarily adept than the old IU had been, more capable of governing, and had more leaders committed to a global jihadist ideology. International attention came in June 2006 when the ICU seized Mogadishu and thereafter won a rapid series of strategic gains. It took control of critical port cities such as Kismayo and met little resistance as it expanded. Typical of the ICU's advance was its seizure of Beletuein on August 9, 2006. The local governor fled to Ethiopia almost immediately after fighting broke out between his forces and ICU militiamen. *(See Ref 328, 329, 330)*

There was international concern during the ICU's rise. Some centered on the ICU's ideology. Writing in the Jamestown Foundation's Terrorism Monitor, Nairobi-based journalist Sunguta West noted that though the ICU's immediate goal was to establish Islamic rule in Somalia, "media reports allege that the Islamic courts are eyeing a bigger Islamic state in the long term carved out of East Africa, similar to the old goals of the IU, which wanted to create an Islamic state out of Somalia and Ethiopia". *(See Ref 331)*

Other concerns focused on the ICU leadership. Sheikh Hassan Dahir Aweys, the most prominent ICU leader as head of its consultative council, had previously been an IU leader. Sunguta West writes that Aweys "has a history of being connected to … al-Qa'ida." Indeed, Washington named

Aweys a specially designated global terrorist in September 2001. *(See Ref 331, 332)*

With U.S. backing, Ethiopia intervened in December 2006 to end the ICU's rule and instated the Transitional Federal Government (TFG). The courts fell in a day; however, the coup drastically stoked extremist flames and catapulted a-Shabaab-previously a mere fringe movement-into a full-blown insurgency. In 2008, alarmed by the prospect of Somalia "deteriorating into an Afghanistan like cauldron of militant Islamism", the United States, the UN, the African Union, the League of Arab States, and other actors endorsed the UN-sponsored Djibouti Peace Process. This led to the election of Sheikh Sharif Sheikh Ahmad, a moderate figure in the ICU, as president of the TFG. However, these efforts backfired. A-Shabaab and other hardliners quickly and successfully labeled Ahmad a Western puppet, and his appointment triggered the creation of a new fundamentalist Islamist group, al- Ittihad al- Islamiyya, led by Sheikh Hassan Dahir Aweys, allied with a-Shabaab but with a more nationalist agenda. *(See Ref 301)*

Ethiopian soldiers withdrew from Somalia in January 2009, leaving behind African Union forces (AMISOM) to help protect the coalition government and enforce its authority. However, the opposition rebels attacked and captured most of the capital of Mogadishu on May 7. AMISOM managed to halt the opposition forces and protect a few square kilometers of government buildings, now the only territory under TFG authority. In June 2009, the TFG government declared a state of emergency and requested immediate international support. *(See Ref 302)*

The TFG is currently organising its last stand. Ethnic Somalis living in Djibouti, Ethiopia, Uganda, Kenya, and Sudan -some reportedly recruited from refugee camps- have been trained abroad and most are now back in the capital, waiting to fight. As many as 6,700 Ugandan and Burundian peacekeepers will reinforce the effort, and the United States is providing funding and some tactical support.

However, the world has grown numb to Somalia's seemingly endless crises – more than 20 years of state collapse, failed peace talks, violent lawlessness and warlordism, internal displacement and refugee flows, chronic underdevelopment, intermittent famine, piracy, regional proxy wars, and Islamic extremism. So it would be easy to conclude that today's disaster is merely a continuation of a long pattern of intractable problems there. So Somalia's in flames again – what's new?

Most experts agree that this time what's happening in Somalia is new. According to Ken Menkhaus, "it would be a dangerous error of judgment to brush off Somalia's current crisis as more of the same. It would be equally dangerous to call for the same tired formulas for U.N. peacekeeping, state-building, and counterterrorism operations that have achieved little since 1990. Seismic political, social, and security changes are occurring in the country, and none bode well for the people of Somalia or the international community." *(See Ref 303)*

In fact, during the past 5 years, Somalia has descended into terrible levels of displacement and humanitarian need, armed conflict and assassinations, political meltdown, radicalisation, and virulent anti-Americanism. Whereas in the past the country's endemic political violence -whether Islamist, clan-based, factional, or criminal in nature - was local and regional in scope, it is now taking on global significance which is the exact opposite of what the United States and its allies sought to promote when they supported the December 2006 Ethiopian military intervention to oust an increasingly bellicose Islamist movement in Mogadishu. Indeed, the situation in Somalia today exceeds the worst-case scenarios conjured up by regional analysts when they first contemplated the possible impact of an Ethiopian military occupation. How did it get to be this bad?

The culmination of a series of developments since 2004 has created the current crisis in Somalia, when national reconciliation talks produced an agreement on a Transitional Federal Government (TFG) which was led by President Abdullahi Yusuf. The TFG was intended to be a government of national unity, tasked with administering a five-year political transition. But the new transitional gevernment was viewed by many Somalis, especially some clans in and around the capital Mogadishu, as a narrow coalition dominated by the clans of the President and his Prime Minister Muhammad Ghedi. It was also derided by its critics as being a puppet of neighbouring Ethiopia. *(See Ref 308)*

It seemed that Yusuf's deep animosity toward any and all forms of political Islam alarmed the increasingly powerful network of Islamists operating schools, hospitals, businesses, and local Islamic courts in Mogadishu. Accordingly, by early 2005, serious splits emerged within the TFG between what became known as the "Mogadishu Group" and Yusuf's supporters. Facing deep opposition in Mogadishu, the TFG was unable to establish itself in the capital, taking up residence instead in two small provincial towns. Weak and dysfunctional, the TFG appeared destined to become yet another stillborn government in Somalia, which has not had an operational central government since 1990.

The coalition of clans, militia leaders, civic groups, and Islamists which formed the Mogadishu Group were themselves divided, however, and war erupted between two wings of the group in early 2006. This war was precipitated by a U.S.-backed effort to create an alliance of clan militia leaders to capture a small number of foreign al-Qa'ida operatives believed to be enjoying safe haven in Mogadishu as guests of the hard-line Somalia Islamists, especially the jihadi militia known as the Youth Islamic Movement [in Arabic Harakat a-Shabaab al-Mujahideen (known as a-Shabaab)].The cynically named Alliance for the Restoration of Peace and Counter-Terrorism (ARPCT) as the U.S.-backed group was called, clashed with local Islamists and within months was decisively defeated. The clan militias' defeat paved the way for the rise of the Islamic Courts Union (ICU), which for seven months in 2006 came to control and govern all of Mogadishu and most of South-Central Somalia. *(See Ref 208)*

The ICU quickly delivered impressive levels of street security and law and order to Mogadishu and South-Central Somalia. It reopened the seaport and international airport and began providing basic government services. In the process, the ICU won widespread support from war-weary Somalis, even those who did not embrace the idea of Islamic rule. To its credit, the U.S. government made a good-faith effort to support negotiations between the ICU and the TFG, with the aim of creating a power-sharing government.

The peaceful atmosphere did not stay for long. A power struggle emerged within the ICU, putting moderates against hardliners. The hardliners, led by Hassan Dahir Aweys (one of only two Somalis designated as a terror suspect by the U.S. government for his leadership role in an earlier group known as al-Ittihad al-Islamiyya), began pushing the ICU into increasingly bellicose and radical positions that alarmed neighbouring Ethiopia and the United States. The ICU declared jihad on Ethiopia, hosted two armed insurgencies opposed to the Ethiopian government, made irredentist claims on Ethiopian territory, and enjoyed extensive support from Ethiopia's enemy Eritrea, which was eager to use the ICU to wage a proxy war. In short, the hardliners in the ICU did everything they could to provoke a war with Ethiopia, and in late December 2006 they got their wish. For its part, the United States understandably grew increasingly frustrated with the ICU's dismissive non-cooperation regarding foreign al-Qa'ida operatives in Mogadishu, and as a result became more receptive to, and supportive of, an Ethiopian military solution. *(See Ref 303, 310)*

Ethiopia's U.S.-backed military offensive against the ICU was a rout. The ICU militias took heavy losses in the first engagements, and when they fell back to Mogadishu angry clan and business leaders forced the ICU to disband and return weapons and militiamen to the clans. While core ICU supporters fled toward the Kenyan border, the Ethiopian military marched into Mogadishu unopposed. Within days the TFG relocated to the capital to govern a shocked and sullen population. It was a scenario no one had foreseen, and it set the stage for the current catastrophe.

The history of Somalia and Ethiopia is littered with distrust, animosity and war. Suspicion of neighbouring expansionism and political extremism is deeply rooted in both states. However, Somalia's disappearance into a political abyss since 1991 opened a new chapter. Nevertheless, the Ethiopian government, its allies, and its enemies all understood that a prolonged Ethiopian military occupation of the Somali capital would be resented by Somalis and was certain to trigger armed resistance. So, the proposed solution was rapid deployment of an African Union peacekeeping force to replace the Ethiopians. But African leaders, not unlike their European and North American counterparts, were reluctant to commit troops to such a dangerous environment, and after long delays were only able to muster a force of 2,000. So Ethiopian forces stayed joined in their efforts by TFG security forces which Ethiopia trained.

But the honeymoon was not to last for long. Within weeks, a complex insurgency - composed of a regrouped a-Shabaab, clan militias, and other armed groups - began a campaign of armed resistance. Since early 2007, attacks on the TFG and the Ethiopian military have been daily, involving mortars, roadside bombs, ambushes, and even suicide bombings.The Ethiopian and TFG response has been extremely heavy-handed, involving attacks on whole neighbourhoods, indiscriminate violence targeting civilians, and widespread arrest and detention.TFG security forces have been especially predatory toward civilians, engaging in looting, assault, and rape. The insurgency and counter-insurgency produced a massive wave of displacement in 2007; over 400,000 of Mogadishu's population of 1.3 million were forced to flee from their homes. *(See Ref 203)*

However, splits have occurred by late 2007 in both the opposition and the TFG. In the opposition, exiled ICU leaders established an umbrella group with non-Islamist Somalis, called the Alliance for the Re-Liberation of Somalia, or ARS. This alliance with secular Somalis prompted the a-Shabaab to publicly break with the "apostate" ARS. In the TFG, the corrupt and deeply divisive Prime Minister Ghedi was finally forced to resign, and a new prime minister, Hassan Hussein Nur "Adde," came to lead a promising moderate wing. He formed a new cabinet, which included many technocrats from the Somali diaspora, and reached out to the opposition, pledging himself to unconditional peace talks. However, his efforts were viewed with deep hostility by the hardliners in the Yusuf camp.

The international community, led by U.N. Special Representative for the Secretary-General Ould Abdullah, sought to forge a centrist coalition of TFG and opposition figures. In June 2008, a U.N.-brokered peace accord was reached in Djibouti between moderate elements in the TFG and moderate leaders in the ARS, the latter led by Sheikh Sharif Sheikh Ahmed and Sharif Hassan (known locally as the "two Sharifs"). The Djibouti Agreement, which was finally signed on August 18, calls for a cessation of hostilities, deployment of a U.N. peacekeeping force, and the subsequent withdrawal of Ethiopian forces. *(See Ref 311)*

Supporters of the agreement see it as a major breakthrough and call for robust international support for its implementation, especially U.N. peacekeeping. Their hope is that any agreement that facilitates the withdrawal of Ethiopian forces will open the door for an end to the insurgency. However, in January 2009 Ethiopia has completed the withdrawal of its troops. Fighters from the radical Islamist a-Shabaab militia took control of the town of Baidoa, formerly a key stronghold of the transitional government.

In the meantime, meeting in neighbouring Djibouti, Somalia's parliament swears in 149 new members from the main opposition Alliance for the Re-Liberation of Somalia. It elected a moderate Islamist, Sheikh Sharif Sheikh Ahmed, president, and extended the transitional government's mandate for another two years.

In February 2009 President Ahmed selected Omar Abdirashid Ali Sharmarke as prime minister. Mr Sharmarke, a former diplomat, is widely seen as a bridge between Islamists within the Somali government and the international community. However, after three month, Islamist insurgents has launched onslaught on Mogadishu, and Somalia's security minister and more than 20 other people were killed in a suicide bombing at a hotel in Beledweyne, north of the capital Mogadishu..

President Ahmed declared a state of emergency as violence intensifies. Somali Officials appealled to neighbouring countries to send troops to Somalia, as government forces continue to battle Islamist insurgents.

In Octobre 2009 a-Shabaab won control over the southern port city of Kismayo after defeating the rival Hizbul-Islam Islamist militia, which withdraws to villages to the West. At least 20 are killed and 70 injured in fighting that threatens to spread to the rest of the Islamist-controlled South.

A-Shabaab declared in February 2010 that it is ready to send fighters to support Islamist rebels in Yemen and formally declared alliance with al-Qa'ida. In the same time it began to concentrate troops in southern Mogadishu for a major offensive to capture the capital. On the other hand in July 2010 a-Shabab said it was behind twin blasts which hit Ugandan capital Kampala, killing 74 people watching the World Cup football final on TV. And later in September, Prime Minister Sharmarke quits to be replaced on October 31, 2010 by Muhammad Abdullah Muhammad.

However, since emerging from an era of colonialism under Italy and Britain, Somalia has passed through military dictatorship, famine, and civil war to regional fragmentation as we explained above. More recently, the hijacking of ships by pirates operating from the Somali coast has attracted considerable attention globally. But the biggest threat emanating from Somalia comes from a different source: An ongoing lack of internal order has left the country vulnerable to the rise of hard-line Islamist groups, of which the latest is a-Shabaab, which rose from obscurity to international prominence in less than two years. A-Shabaab's ideological commitment to global jihadism, its connections to al-Qa'ida, its military capabilities, and its ability to capture and control territory suggest that it will continue to pose a strategic challenge to the U.S., the West and Somalia's neighbours.

Since its creation, a-Shabaab has played a major role in the insurgency that pushed Ethiopian forces out of Somalia; it also received the endorsement of Osama bin Laden and has seen large numbers of Somalis living in the West flock to its camps. Somalia has become, like Pakistan, a significant al-Qa'ida safe haven. Due to the relatively large number of Americans who travel to Somalia for military training, individuals linked to a-Shabaab are among the top U.S. domestic terrorist threats. *(See Ref 246, 313)*

In fact, a-Shabaab emerged from two previous Somali Islamist groups, The Islamic Union (Al-Ittihad al-Islamiyya, IU) and the Islamic Courts Union (Ittihad al-Mahakim al-Islamiyya, ICU). There are three strands of evolution from the IU to the ICU and finally to a-Shabaab. The first is ideological, in which the groups go through a funneling process and slowly become less ideologically diverse. Though all three strove to implement Shari'a (Islamic law), a significant faction of IU and ICU leaders had a vision that focused on the Somali nation itself - that is, inside the borders of Somalia and in neighbouring territories where Somalis are the predominant ethnic group, such as Ethiopia's Ogaden region. In contrast, key a-Shabaab leaders are committed to a global jihadist ideology. They view the group's regional activities as part of a broader struggle.

The second strand lies in the groups' relations with al-Qa'ida. Bin Laden's organisation has long had a presence in Somalia. It dispatched trainers to liaise with the Islamic Union prior to the 1993 battle of Mogadishu when eighteen U.S. soldiers were killed. Despite that connection, some scholars have questioned how deep the ties between al-Qa'ida and the IU really are. In contrast, after a-Shabaab emerged as a distinct entity, its leaders reached out to al-Qa'ida's senior leadership, and its chief military strategist openly declared his allegiance to bin Laden. *(See Ref 314, 315, 316)*

The final strand is the groups' opportunity and ability to govern. Since all three have been dedicated to implementing Shari'a, they would ideally like a governing apparatus through which to apply Islamic law and mete out God's justice. The Islamic Union could not control any territory for a sustained period apart from the town of Luuq. In contrast, the Islamic Courts and a-Shabaab came to control broad swaths of Somalia, and the governing strategies they put in place indicate that both groups thought hard about how to maintain and expand their power.

Given the current bad situation in Somalia and the role of Islamists movement in that country's deterioration, which became a danger in waiting for the region, the West and its allies, the question which comes to mind: what the a-Shabaab movement's threat represents to the region and the West, and accordingly is a-Shabaab a transnational organisation?

The practice of Islam in Somalia has traditionally been dominated by apolitical Sufi orders. Islamist movements did not emerge until the late 1960s when Somalis gained greater exposure to less moderate currents of Islam in Saudi Arabia, Egypt, and elsewhere.

However, a-Shabaab emerged as a distinct force during the course of the insurgency. The break between a-Shabaab and other insurgent groups came in late 2007. That September, the ICU attended a conference of opposition factions in the Eritrean capital, Asmara, and reemerged as the Alliance for the Reliberation of Somalia (ARS). A-Shabaab boycotted the conference, and its leaders launched vitriolic attacks on the ARS for failing to adopt a global jihadist ideology. In late February 2008, fighting between supporters of the ARS and a-Shabaab in Dhobley killed several people. As Ethiopian fighters left Somalia in early 2009, fighters affiliated with a-Shabaab took their place and implemented a strict version of Shari'a in areas they came to control. *(See Ref 342)*

A-Shabaab is nominally led by Sheikh Mohamed Mukhtar Abdirahman "Abu Zubeyr," though experts say a core group of senior leaders guide its actions. The group is divided into three geographical units: Bay and Bokool regions, led by Mukhtar Roobow "Abu Mansur," the group's spokesman; south-central Somalia and Mogadishu; and Puntland and Somaliland. A fourth unit, which controls the Juba Valley, is led by Hassan Abdillahi Hersi "Turki," who is not considered to be a member of a-Shabaab, but is closely aligned with it. These regional units "appear to operate independently of one another, and there is often evidence of friction between them," says a December 2008 UN Monitoring Group report.

Estimates of a-Shabaab's size vary, but analysts generally agree that the group contains several thousand fighters (between 6,000 and 7.000), many of whom are from the Hawiye clan. A-Shabaab is battle-ready, given that Somalia's history is replete with fighters who have experience with asymmetrical warfare, small unit tactics, and a wide array of weaponry. One tactic that a-Shabaab is said to have introduced to Somalia is suicide bombing. They have also carried out assassination attempts against Somali government officials. The group has been able to expand its footprint in Somalia with relatively small numbers for two reasons: Somalia hasn't had a central government since 1991; and many of the clan warlords that filled the power vacuum have proven willing to cooperate with a-Shabaab, at least in Somalia's south. A-Shabaab has engaged in forced recruitment among Somalis, so it's unclear how many members of the group truly believe the organisation's ideology. Experts say the number of rank-and-file members is less important than the number of hardcore ideological believers, which could range between three hundred and eight hundred individuals.

Foreign fighters have traveled to Somalia to fight with a-Shabaab, as have Somalis from the United Kingdom and the United States. "We have seen an increasing number of individuals here in the United States become captivated by extremist ideologies or causes," said White House national security adviser John Brennan in a May 2010 speech, noting, among others, five Somali-Americans that left Minnesota to fight in Somalia. U.S.-born Abu Mansoor Al-Amriki joined a-Shabaab in 2007 and has become the recognisable face of the group, starring in propaganda videos that have helped recruit hundreds of foreign fighters, according to intelligence officials. In June 2010, two U.S. citizens from New Jersey were arrested at New York's JFK Airport after allegations that they planned to travel to Somalia to join a-Shabaab. The arrests came amid a growing trend in which radicalised Americans have become involved in terrorism-related activities.

Some experts say there are deep divisions within a-Shabaab. In a February 2009 report Somalia expert Ken Menkhaus writes that, "The a-Shabaab faces multiple internal divisions - over clan, leadership, tactics, and ideology - which a new unity government can exploit to convince parts of the a-Shabaab to abandon the movement and gradually outmaneuver, marginalise, and defeat the core hardliners." Each unit of a-Shabaab is led by individuals who must combine their ideological aims with pragmatic considerations of different clan-based agendas. It's important to "focus on what they do, not what they say," writes Menkhaus. *(See Ref 299)*

Roland Marchal, senior research fellow of the National Centre for Scientific Research in Paris, says that reports of increasing divisions within a-Shabaab are overstated. They are "based on the assumption that they were once united," he notes. However, he says the organisation must decide "to what extent they want to accommodate the Somali society and to what extent they want to keep the ideology they have developed."

So, what is the a-Shabaab ideology?

A-Shabaab represents a further step toward a global jihadist vision. Like the Islamic Union and Islamic Courts, it believes that religious governance is the solution to Somalia's ills. When addressing a rally in the Southern city of Marka, Sheikh Mukhtar Roobow emphasised the importance of complying with Islamic law. In an effort to show that Shari'a was equitable, Roobow stated that "punishment would be meted out to anyone," including mujahideen, citing a mujahid executed in Waajid as an example. *(See Ref 343, 344)*

One important document explaining a-Shabaab's outlook was written by the American mujahid Abu Mansur al-Amriki. In January 2008, he wrote a document entitled "A Message to the Mujahideen in Particular and Muslims in General" that rapidly made its way around the jihadist web. In it, he reiterated the need to establish Shari'a, citing as exemplars Sayyid Qutb, the leading theoretician of the Muslim Brotherhood, and Abu A'la Maududi, founder of the Islamist Jama'a-i Islami in India and Pakistan, both of whom "refused to accept entering into the "infidel" governments as a solution." He specified commitment to Islamic law as a means of distinguishing a-Shabaab from the Alliance for the Reliberation of Somalia. Al-Amriki explained that a-Shabaab had boycotted the Asmara conference because it refused to work with the non-Muslim Eritrean state. He argued that cooperation with "infidels" would corrupt the jihad because Eritrea would open "the door of politics in order for them to forget armed resistance," leaving "members of the Courts in the lands of the "Kuffaar", underneath their control, sitting in the road of politics which leads to the loss and defeat they were running from." Indeed, al-Amriki's screed underscores the gradations from the IU to the ICU and finally to a-Shabaab. His criticisms of the Islamic Courts emphasise a-Shabaab's global jihadist perspective. He touts a-Shabaab's pan-Islamism in opposition to the ICU's clan-backed politics, saying that "the Courts used to judge over each individual tribe," whereas "a-Shabaab were made up of many different tribes". *(See Ref 342)*

Other a-Shabaab leaders have said that they see the continuation of jihad beyond Somalia as a religious imperative. In early 2009, "Kataaib.net" reported that Sheikh Ali Muhammad Hussein, the group's Banadir region governor, gave a media briefing on Ethiopia's withdrawal. He said that "the fact that the enemy has left Mogadishu does not mean that the mujahideen will not follow him to where he still remains," adding that in compliance with the command of God, "he will be pursued everywhere and more traps will be laid for him." Hussein added that the idea that the jihad had ended with Ethiopia's withdrawal was "in clear contradiction with the statement of Prophet Muhammad … that jihad will continue until Doomsday." *(See Ref 345)*

In early 2008, when the U.S. designated a-Shabaab a global terrorist entity, prominent members struck a celebratory tone. Roobow told the British Broadcasting Corporation (BBC) that he welcomed the designation as an "honour" because "[w]e are good Muslims and the Americans are infidels. We are on the right path." Though Roobow then denied a connection to al-Qa'ida, his position has since changed. In August 2008, he said that a-Shabaab was "negotiating how we can unite into one" with al-Qa'ida. He continued, "We will take our orders from Sheikh Osama bin Laden because we are his students." And Saleh Ali Saleh Nabhan, a-Shabaab's chief military strategist, formally reached out to al-Qa'ida's senior leadership in a 24-minute video entitled "March Forth," which circuited the jihadi web on August 30, 2008. In it, Nabhan offers salutations to bin Laden and pledges allegiance to "the courageous commander and my honourable leader". *(See Ref 346, 347, 348, 349)*

Al-Qa'ida has not ignored a-Shabaab's overtures. They first took note of developments in Somalia in 2006 when the Islamic Courts captured Mogadishu. When Ethiopia intervened to push back the ICU's advance on Baidoa, al-Qa'ida deputy leader Ayman al-Zawahiri soon appeared in a web-based video and called for Muslims to fight the Ethiopians: "I appeal to the lions of Islam in Yemen, the state of faith and wisdom. I appeal to my brothers, the lions of Islam in the Arab Peninsula, the cradle of conquests. And I also appeal to my brothers, the lions of Islam in Egypt, Sudan, the Arab Maghreb, and everywhere in the Muslim world to rise up to aid their Muslim brethren in Somalia". *(See Ref 350)*

On July 5, 2007, he released a new video, describing Somalia as one of the three main theaters for al-Qa'ida's mujahideen, along with Iraq and Afghanistan. The al-Qa'ida propagandist Abu Yahya al-Libi devoted an entire video to urging Muslims to join the Somali mujahideen. *(See Ref 352)*

On November 19, 2008, Ayman al-Zawahiri responded to Nabhan's video with one in which he called a-Shabaab "my brothers, the lions of Islam in Somalia." He urged them to "hold tightly to the truth for which you have given your lives, and don't put down your weapons before the mujahid state of Islam has been established and Tawheed has been set up in Somalia". *(See Ref 353)*

In February 2009, al-Zawahiri released another video that began by praising a-Shabaab's seizure of the Somali town of Baidoa. The group will "engage in Jihad against the American-made government in the same way they engaged in Jihad against the Ethiopians and the warlords before them," al-Zawahiri said. Though al-Qa'ida appears to support a-Shabaab's jihad, it's unclear whether a-Shabaab has ambitions beyond Somalia. According to a report by Chris Harnisch of the American Enterprise Institute, the group's "rhetoric and behaviour" have shifted over the past two years, "reflecting an eagerness to strike internationally.

Bin Laden himself issued a video devoted to a-Shabaab in March 2009, entitled "Fight on, Champions of Somalia," where he addresses "my patient, persevering Muslim brothers in mujahid Somalia." Here, bin Laden explicitly endorses a-Shabaab and denounces the Alliance for the Reliberation of Somalia, saying that when NATO supported former president Abdullahi Yusuf, the mujahideen were not fooled. "They replaced him and brought in a new, revised version," says bin Laden, "similar to Sayyaf, Rabbani, and Ahmed Shah Massoud, who were leaders of the Afghan mujahideen before they turned back on their heels (as apostates)." In bin Laden's view, Sheikh Sharif Sheikh Ahmed -who had been an ICU official before becoming ARS's leader- also falls into this category. *(See Ref 354)*

Bin Laden explains in the same video that in becoming the new president of Somalia, Sharif "agreed to partner infidel positive law with Islamic Shari'a to set up a government of national unity," and in that way apostatised from Islam. He asks, "How can intelligent people believe that yesterday's enemies on the basis of religion can become today's friends? This can only happen if one of the two parties abandons his religion. So look and see which one of them is the one who has abandoned it: Sheikh Sharif or America?"

Today, a-Shabaab is a capable fighting force that implements a strict version of Shari'a in key areas of Somalia. Its range is enhanced by training camps from which many Western Muslims have graduated. This has made a-Shabaab a significant security concern to several countries, including the United States.

Given the relationship noted above between a-Shabaab and al-Qa'ida, which includes ideological affinity and interlocking leadership, there are worries about a-Shabaab's connections to transnational terrorism. These concerns are bolstered by a-Shabaab's operation of terrorist training camps, successors to the ICU camps.

According to Julie Cohn of the Council on Foreign Relations (CFR), a-Shabaab's recruitment of Western operatives, partly through the Internet, heightens the organisation's threat. In late 2009, over twenty Somali-Americans disappeared from Minneapolis, Saint Paul, (USA), and similar disappearances have been reported in Ohio, Oregon, Toronto, and the Netherlands. Director of the National Counterterrorism Centre Michael Leiter reported to Congress in 2009 that a-Shabaab sent "dozens" of Somali Americans and American Muslims through training conducted by al-Qa'ida, and that seven have been killed in fighting so far. These Americans that leave to fight for a-Shabaab are fighting for solely Somali nationalist reasons, and have shown no anti-U.S. sentiment. Andrew Liepman, deputy director for intelligence at the Counterterrorism Centre, affirms this fact, "They are going to Somalia to fight for their homeland, not to join al-Qa'ida's jihad against the United States, so far". Nonetheless, according to a Committee on Foreign Relations report to the US Senate in 2010, Senator John Kerry states that "the prospect that U.S. citizens are being trained at al-Qa'ida camps [in Somalia] deepens our concern and emphasises the need to understand the nature of the evolving dangers". *(See Ref 300, 355)*

The biggest concern is not what these individuals do while in Somalia but what happens when they return to the countries from which they came. It is a concern not only for the United States but also for Britain: The Times of London reports that the British security services believe that "dozens of Islamic extremists have returned to Britain from terror training camps in

Somalia." British intelligence analysts are concerned about possible terror attacks in the U.K., and British television has reported that an October 2007 suicide bombing in Somalia was thought to have been carried out by a U.K.-raised bomber. Peter Neumann of the International Centre for the Study of Radicalisation and Political Violence at King's College, London, told Channel 4 News: "The numbers I hear (going from Britain to Somalia) are 50, 60 or 70, but in reality we don't know. You don't need big numbers for terrorism". *(See Ref 356)*

A-Shabaab's training is both military and ideological. In 2006, Frederick Nzwili, a Nairobi-based journalist, reported that training camps run by Aweys and a-Shabaab founder Aden Hashi Ayro "included indoctrination into fundamentalist ideology aimed at advocating jihad in Islamic states." The Economist notes the fundamentalist environment in which a-Shabaab's training occurs, wherein recruits "are expected to disavow music, videos, cigarettes and qat, the leaf Somali men chew most afternoons to get mildly high". *(See Ref 358)*

A number of governments now look upon a-Shabaab's rise as a major security concern. Its commitment to global jihadism, joint leadership with al-Qa'ida, and military capabilities are likely to make it a problem for some time to come.

Looking ahead, there are several measures that will indicate a-Shabaab's level of strength and internal coherence: first, whether the group is able to maintain its territorial control over parts of Mogadishu and how far it can expand this control in Somalia; second, whether Somalia's business community decides to support the group; third, whether the Somali diaspora continues to fund a-Shabaab through the hawala money transfer system (it is not clear how much money a-Shabaab currently receives from the diaspora or other sources). Finally, analysts are closely watching the extent to which the Somali government, led by Sheikh Sharif Sheikh Ahmed, negotiates with a-Shabaab.

Experts strongly cautioned that there is little the United States can do to weaken a-Shabaab. The United States has launched air strikes to target high-level members of a-Shabaab it believes have links to al-Qa'ida. In April 2010, President Barack Obama issued an executive order aimed at blocking the finances of a-Shabaab's leaders and those who are contributing to the conflict in Somalia. Following the Uganda bombings, the Obama administration also indicated that it would boost its efforts against a-Shabaab, most likely in the form of increased assistance (IPS) to the African Union Mission in Somalia, as well as to the Western-backed Transitional Federal Government (TFG) in Mogadishu.

But experts say these activities have only increased popular support for a-Shabaab. In a March 2010 Council on Foreign Relations (CFR) report, Bronwyn E. Bruton argues that "the open blessing of the TFG by the United States and other Western countries has perversely served to isolate the government and, at the same time, to propel cooperation among previously fractured and quarrelsome extremist groups". She proposes a "constructive disengagement" policy that recognises a-Shabaab's Islamist rule in Somalia as long as it does not engage in regional violence or terrorism.

On January 17, 2007, the Center for Strategic and International Studies (CSIS), in collaboration with the Council on Foreign Relations, the U.S. Institute of Peace, and the Woodrow Wilson International Center, hosted a major conference in Washington, DC, entitled "Somalia's Future: Options for Diplomacy, Assistance, and Peace Operations." The conference brought together observers from Mogadishu, senior U.S. policymakers, representatives from humanitarian assistance organisations, and regional analysts to convey to a U.S. audience the current situation in Somalia and to lay out the challenges facing the United States and the broader international community.

Conference participants agreed that there is a window of opportunity for the United States, in collaboration with Somalis and the broader international community, to effect positive change in Somalia but that this window may close in the near future. After 12 years, then, of policy disengagement that followed the failed U.S. military intervention of 1993, the United States has an opportunity to forge a forward-looking, comprehensive strategy to address immediate security concerns and the longer-term threat of regional instability. In his opening remarks to the conference, former Senator Russell Feingold chairman of the Senate Foreign Relations Africa Subcommittee at that time, summarised the challenge:

"We cannot allow our past to overshadow the pressing security concerns we face in the [Horn of Africa] today. We have an opportunity to help the Somalia people dig themselves out of almost two decades of chaos and to strengthen U.S. national security at the same time. But if our government does not move quickly and aggressively on all fronts, we can be sure Somalia will continue to be a haven for terrorist networks and a source of instability that poses a direct threat to the United States."

Those words which were applicable in 2007 still applicable today. The fact is that U.S. policies have left a legacy of mistakes and missed opportunities. To move forward, policymakers will need to recognise past U.S. mistakes and understand the strategic challenges posed by radical Islamic groups such as a-Shabaab.

CHAPTER TEN

THE LEVANT: AL-QA'IDA'S POTENTIAL NEW FRONTIER

The declaration in early 2009 by an individual believed to be an al-Qa'ida "spokesperson" of the existence of an active branch of the organisation in the Levant falls into the same paradoxical framework of a reality that, while often not tangible or verifiable, nevertheless possesses distinctly lethal potential. The spokesperson in question, a frequent contributor to jihadist online forums whose essays are regularly published and distributed by "official" al-Qa'ida outlets, uses the handle "Assad al-Jihad 2" (AJ2, or the Lion of Jihad 2). "Assad al-Jihad 1" is presumably reserved for Osama bin Laden, whom AJ2 consistently refers to as "[my] father" - using a variant of the Arabic word usually reserved for biological parents (al-walid). AJ2 is probably the most prominent member of a disparate group of writers, bloggers, and contributors - who can be termed "al-Qa'ida ideologues" - who both provide the international jihadist movement with its rationale and point potential recruits to regions of interest. *(The growing "canon" of the al Qa'ida ideologues is maintained by Umm Abi Dharr. Originally posted on the now crippled "al-Ikhlas" forum in summer 2007, this canon is periodically updated and widely distributed on the Internet as an archived collection of hundreds of tracts, fatwas, and books by a select number of authors. Umm Abi Dharr included twenty-four authors in her initial release. By late 2008, her list of authors had grown to thirty-six. Asad al-Jihad 2 made his entry into the list in mid-2008)*

Assad al-Jihad 2 focused on the so-called "al-Qa'ida in the Levant," claiming that this organisation is "well established and firm in the region, like the Levant's mountains. The organisation has studied every inch of the Levant, sent their reports to the leaders of al-Qa'ida, and discussed them with the geniuses of the organisation. Al-Qa'ida has penetrated the Levant states and infiltrated them. I think the reason for the delay in announcing the presence of the organisation is due to waiting for the completion of preparations." *(See Ref 361)*

The ideologist stated that the goal of al-Qa'ida in the region is to fight against Israel, alleging that the organisation was already behind missile strikes on "the north of so-called Israel" on June 17, 2007, and again in January 2008; "one day before [former President] Bush's visit to the region." Assad al-Jihad 2 also claimed that the weapons the Lebanese army announced they discovered stored in the south of the country on December 25, 2008 belonged to al-Qa'ida in the Levant. He claimed that these Russian pattern Grad rockets were stored for use in attacks on Akka (Acre) and the northern Israeli cities of Nahariya and Shlomi. Nahariya was targeted by hundreds of Hezbollah rockets in 2006; Shlomi was struck by Hezbollah rockets in 2005 and 2006. *(See Ref 361)*

AJ2 asserted that al-Qa'ida started to attack Israel from Lebanon in December 2005, when the late leader of al-Qa'ida in Iraq, Abu Mus'ab al-Zarqawi, claimed responsibility for launching missile attacks on northern Israel. Assad al-Jihad 2 also claimed Osama bin Laden has sent some al-Qa'ida leaders to create bases in Lebanon. One of these leaders was Saleh al-Qablawi (Abu Ja'afar al-Maqdesi) from Ain al-Hilwa Palestinian camp, who was the mastermind behind an attack against Israel in 2002. Al-Qablawi later became friends with al-Zarqawi and appeared with him in a video in 2006 before being killed in Iraq the same year.

At the conclusion of the question and answer session, Assad al-Jihad 2 pointed to the increasing importance of Salafi-Jihadis in the Levant region, as indicated by the recent trials in Jordan, Lebanon or Syria of members belonging to al-Qa'ida-affiliated groups, as well as the increasing focus on the region found in the speeches of various jihadi leaders and ideologues. *(See Ref 359, 360)*

However, the "declaration" of the existence of the "al-Qa'ida in Levant" in the question and answer session came in the form of a deliberate revelation at the end of AJ2's February 7, 2009, response to questions submitted online by sympathisers and jihadist forum visitors. Since the beginning of the hostilities in Gaza in December 2008, jihadist forums have been flooded with inquiries about al-Qa'ida's plans in the Palestinian theatre. Most of these messages expressed intense desire for quick, robust al-Qa'ida action. Some, however, expressed disappointment and dismay at al-Qa'ida's failure to secure a leading role, or even to participate, in the uneven confrontation in Gaza, which inflamed sentiments across the Arab Internet community. *(See Ref 361)*

In succession, the global leadership of al-Qa'ida, as well as that of its local affiliates in Iraq, the Arabian Peninsula, and North Africa, released written statements and audio and video messages expressing determined support - all while denouncing the Arab political order for its failure to act in Gaza's defence and urging Muslims worldwide to join the Gaza jihad.What these pronouncements distinctly lacked, though, was any specific indication that al-Qa'ida would support its position with action. *(See Ref 362)*

At the conclusion of his written answers on February 7, 2009, AJ2 addressed a question about who was responsible for the aborted launch of Katyusha rockets into northern Israel on December 25, 2008, just prior to the Israel-Hamas confrontation in Gaza, and for the actual launching of five rockets on January 8, 2009 - actions from which Hezbollah was quick to distance itself. The same query also addressed the whereabouts of "al-Qa'ida fi Bilad a-Sham" (al-Qa'ida in The Levant), a previously unknown organisation that issued a lone communiqué in 2007 following the unexpectedly difficult confrontation between the Lebanese army and Fateh al-Islam. This latter terrorist formation had occupied the Palestinian refugee camp of Nahr al-Barid in northern Lebanon and was increasingly daring in its raids on neighbouring communities and its maneuvers outside of the camp, suggesting plans and designs beyond the Palestinian enclave. Skirmishes between Fateh al-Islam and the Lebanese authorities degenerated on May 20, 2007, into a sudden massacre of Lebanese conscripts in their sleep, prompting the Lebanese armed forces to engage in a full-scale assault on the refugee camp -a battle that lasted until September 2, before Fateh al-Islam's routing and the restoration of the status quo in Nahr al-Barid. *(See Ref 363)*

More significantly, AJ2 linked the communiqué released in the aftermath of the Nahr al-Barid fighting by "al-Qa'ida fi Bilad a-Sham", a then-unknown organisation, to a string of diverse attacks that have occurred in Lebanon since at least 2005 to reveal the prior existence of an organised, al-Qa'ida – sanctioned affiliate in Lebanon. It was indeed al-Qa'ida which was responsible for the Katyusha attacks in December 2008 and January 2009, AJ2 asserted.

With his assertion, the dispute over the existence of an al-Qa'ida affiliate in the Levant is supposed to end. It is an organisation endowed by "a Shura Council, a Shari'a committee, a general command, and experienced field commanders with expertise in all aspects of international Jihad." It is a deeply rooted formation that was sponsored and nurtured by the late Abu Mus'ab al-Zarqawi, the infamous Jordanian-born leader of the al-Qa'ida organisation of Jihad in the Land of the Two Rivers, the most notorious jihadist formation in Iraq. It is an organisation, according to AJ2, with a meticulous long-term plan that has purposely remained underground until now, but whose existence and impending revelation have been alluded to by the leadership of international jihad, including bin Laden and his second in command, Ayman al-Zawahiri. With this revelation, and the group's presumed subsequent actions, AJ2 asserted, "the Jews will have to forget all the wars in which they have engaged; they will have to forget the horrors of Nazism and the wars with Arabs," while jihad supporters worldwide will indeed have reasons to rejoice. *(See Ref 364)*

Al-Qa'ida in the Levant (AQL) has thus emerged as an official affiliate of global jihad through unorthodox means. Jihadist forums, replete with communiqués and multimedia releases from a plethora of jihadist organisations - each studded with a colourful logo and consistent branding - still lack the AQL equivalents: the ever-expanding list of communiqués and releases are attributed to organisations engaged in jihad in Afghanistan, Iraq, Algeria, Somalia, and the Caucasus, but not to AQL. Nonetheless, with the authoritative pronouncement of AJ2, a recognised spokesperson for global jihad in its virtual reality, al- Qa'ida has overcome what seemed to be a vexing obstacle in its quest for real world legitimacy in Arab political culture: a "presence" in Palestine, however symbolic, however fictive. In April 2009, the new appointed AQL's Chief Saleh al-Qaraawi, threatens to loose a fresh wave of attacks on US and Israeli targets as well as UN peace keepers in South Lebanon.

The Muslim world is today the scene of an asymmetrical confrontation between a conventional, pluralistic, lived Islam, expressed diversely in the multitude of societies where Muslims form communities, and aggressive Islamism, a global ideological movement seeking, in its most forceful expressions, to transform the current Muslim reality into one regimented, religion-based, totalitarian ideal. The asymmetry stems from the fact that conventional Muslim cultures, for reasons that are both common across the Muslim world and particular to individual Muslim societies, are largely lagging in generating effective responses to the Islamist challenge. The way in which Islamism might affect the shape and structure of Muslim communities in the current absence of a counterbalancing movement remains an unwritten chapter in world history.

Al-Qa'ida represents the culmination of the Sunni Islamist movement. It combines elements of Salafism with "jihadism"-the religiously based legitimisation of armed action as a means to achieve political ends-against organisational and operational structures that benefit from both twentieth-century totalitarian experiences and turn-of-the millennium globalism. As a universal project, with an explicit vision of world domination, al-Qa'ida is not concerned, in principle, with any particular cause of Muslim populations. Still, the "repertoire" of causes that have emerged in the wake of twentieth-century decolonisation and international conflict have forced al-Qa'ida to construct narratives directed at specific populations.

None of these causes has equaled in its symbolic importance the question of Palestine. Palestine has dominated Arab political culture, virtually since the inception of a common public intellectual space in the Arabic-speaking societies of the Middle East and North Africa in the aftermath of World War I.

Despite that Palestine is still central in Arab popular culture its place in al Qa'ida's doctrine is more nuanced. In fact, in addition to the predominant Salafist-jihadist identification of the United States (rather than Israel) as the main external enemy, the centrality of the question of Palestine is severely undermined by the Salafist-jihadist postulation that the entire Muslim world-with the exception of a few fictive entities, namely the Islamic Emirate of Afghanistan, the Islamic State of Iraq, the Islamic Emirate of the Caucasus, and the a-Shabaab-ruled territory in Somalia-is governed by "Taghut", illegitimate systems not based on true Islam. National and nationalist aspirations are deemed irrelevant in the future global caliphate to which al-Qa'ida aspires. Thus, in theory, there is no particularity for the Palestinian situation. Whether the locale is Palestine, Algeria, or Uzbekistan, the obligation of jihad on true Muslims is one and the same: a struggle that ends only with the imposition of Islamist rule on the totality of the population, Muslim and non-Muslim alike. *(See Ref 365)*

While al Qa'ida has internalised the frequent anti-Jewish bigotry and occasional anti-Jewish racism native to Arab culture, as well as various forms of imported Western anti-Semitism, its main imagery in referring to its existential enemy is inspired by Christianity, not Judaism. Crosses are prominent in al-Qa'ida target practice, rather than Star of David. "Crusader" is the pejorative label of choice applied to enemies, while "Zionist," with its connotations of evil world power, has fallen out of usage in the discourse of many al-Qa'ida ideologues in favour of the contempt-filled generic "Jew." The "massacre of Gaza"- that is, the alarmingly high casualty count suffered by the Palestinian population as a result of the Israeli war on Hamas in December 2008 and January 2009 - is thus not blamed on "the Zionists," as is the inclination in Arab nationalist and leftist circles, but instead is characterised as then–U.S. president-elect Barack Obama's "gift" to the Palestinians. Lest this change of focus be misinterpreted as a softening in the enmity toward Israel and the Jews, al-Qa'ida and sister organisations have standardised the use of a distorted derivation from a Koranic parable of transfiguration, thus making "the progeny of monkeys and swine" an established euphemism for Jews. Another derogatory practice in common use in Salafist-jihadist circles is the application of the word Yahud (Jews), stripped of the definite article as a collective name. This practice, however, is only a supplemental disparagement, since virtually any reference to Jews lacking a positive qualification is, in Arab culture, ipso facto derogatory. *(See Ref 366)*

From a dogmatic point of view, al-Qa'ida's doctrine has often displayed unease about the place of Palestine in Arab political discourse. Centrality, from al-'Qa'ida's perspective, ought to be reserved for the establishment of divine rule on earth; the fetishism of Palestine, as practiced by nationalists, leftists, and human rights advocates alike, endows Palestine with an importance that dilutes or rivals the true purpose of the struggle. Abu Yahya al-Libi, a second-generation leader and spokesperson for al-Qa'ida, underlined in his reaction to the last Gaza confrontation the tension between the generic yet assertive support that al-Qa'ida reserves for the Palestinians in their struggle and the rejection of the Palestinian fetish in Arab discourse. Al-Qa'ida, Libi asserts, recognises Palestine as "ard al-ribat" (the land of confrontation [with the West]). There is, however, no ideological premium on an active role for the network in Palestine. Still, the al-Qa'ida leadership has productively referenced the Palestinian cause in order to elicit public support in the wider Muslim world in general, and in the Arab context in particular. *(See Ref 367)*

In fact, even when al-Qa'ida is silent on the question of Palestine, the current dominant acceptance in the Arab "street" of a dualist nature of global conflict (United States/Israel/the West versus Arabs/ Islam/ Palestine) assigns to its anti-American and anti-Western actions a pro-Palestinian value. Even with the absence of any effective presence of al-Qa'ida in Palestine, and with the apparent lack of any particularism for the struggle in Palestine within al-Qa'ida doctrine, the references to the plight of the Palestinians in al Qa'ida public pronouncements have provided the jihadist network with considerable support among Arabs and Muslims. *(See Ref 368)*

With such a positive predisposition, an engagement by al-Qa'ida on the Palestinian scene would be expected to amplify the support currently received by the jihadist network by an order of magnitude. Yet, the most glaring omission in al-Qa'ida's global operations is the absence of any meaningful action by its operatives in the Palestinian-Israeli conflict. Even if the recent claims by AJ2 attributing responsibility for the sporadic rocket attacks from south Lebanon to AQL are true, al-Qa'ida still lacks credible association with any Palestinian faction, whether in the West Bank and Gaza or in the refugee camps in neighbouring countries. In fact, al Qa'ida's record in the Levant has been mediocre when compared to its actions in adjacent regions, in particular Iraq and the Arabian Peninsula. *(See Ref 369)*

The Levant is not merely another theatre of operations that al-Qa'ida may or may not opt to join. Since the emergence of the post–First World War nation-state system in the Middle East, Levantine society and culture, with the Palestinian cause at the heart of its concerns, have been instrumental in shaping the character and direction of Arab political culture. A framework of reference in political culture in the Middle East has consistently been one in which the Palestinian question is concentrically surrounded by Levantine, Arab, and Muslim layers, with the Levantine backdrop to Palestine serving as an incubator of ideas and movements.

The voracious opportunism of al-Qa'ida naturally suggests that its absence from the Levant is not due to the region being assigned a lower priority. Instead al-Qa'ida has so far failed to take root as a result of multiple factors that have constituted obstacles to its emergence. Al-Qa'ida, in ideology and practice, is still alien to the Levant. Still, from the point of view of Islamists sympathetic to its cause, the prospects of its emergence in the Levant are improving as a result of the attrition of such obstacles.

Al-Qa'ida as an ideology is an outgrowth of the reductionist interpretation of Islam initiated by Muhammad ibn Abd al-Wahhab in eighteenth-century Arabia (as we explained in Chapters 4 and 7). Ibn Abd al-Wahhab promoted a strict intransigence toward interpretations and practices inconsistent with his own reading of the Islamic foundational corpus. To exact greater discipline, he created the kernel of a clerical establishment with enforcement powers and allied himself with a powerful political dynasty. The Wahhabi establishment has remained entrenched ever since. Indeed, today, Wahhabism, with the backing of the current Saudi monarchy-the heir to this arrangement-has become religious orthodoxy and custodian of social norms across the Arabian environment of which it was a product. Prior to the advent of oil wealth, though, its impact beyond its cradle was limited.

Due to the yearly pilgrimage (the Hajj), Arabia- and, in particular, the Hijaz, the western part of the Arabian Peninsula and the location of Islam's two holiest sites in Mecca and Medina-was historically a land of religious immigration and a melting pot for Muslim expressions. While Wahhabism disrupted the inflow to the Hijaz, it created, through persistent attacks on groups that deviated from its orthodoxy, an outflow into neighbouring territories. Thus, for example, Sufi mystics and ascetics who in previous centuries would have settled in the Hijaz occasionally made Egypt and the Levant their final destination. *(See Ref 368)*

By the end of World War I and with the emergence of the new political order, Arabia and the Levant were sharply different in terms of their socio-cultural and religious outlook: the common label of Sunni Islam, though predominant in both, masked substantive differences in religious and social life. In jurisprudence, the more literalist Hanbali school of Islam dominated in Arabia, while in the Levant an interlacing of the Shafi'i and Hanafi schools prevailed-both incorporating more liberal approaches to jurisprudence. In theology, the Wahhabi understanding of the Athari dogma-a literalist school that rejects exegetical tools aimed at rationalising the Islamic belief system-laid the foundation for modern Salafism in Arabia. Levantine scholars, following the lead of their Egyptian counterparts, experimented with rationalist formulations, rooted in the Ash'ari tradition-influenced by and articulated in reaction to Hellenistic philosophy-and informed by the progressive nineteenth-century "Nahdah", or renaissance, approach. And while Sufism, the mystical expression of Islam, continued to find in Egypt and the Levant a warm welcome, it was systematically and forcibly eradicated from Arabian society. *(See Ref 370)*

More significant, the intellectual strata of the Levant, home to a multitude of non-Sunni and non-Muslim communities, adopted nationalism as a basis of its socio-political identity, relegating religion to a theoretical background. Also, it was Cairo's Al-Azhar University, not Mecca or Medina, that graduated the clerical class and defined the general religious identity of Levantine Muslim communities. Levantine Islamism, from Gaza to Aleppo, was inspired by and oriented toward Cairo, where the Muslim Brotherhood had restated Islamic values by replacing quietism with activism and pietism with proselytism. It was indeed these Egyptian reformulations, imported to Arabia in the second half of the twentieth century that combined with Wahhabi absolutism and irredentism to eventually create the potent ideological totalitarianism of al-Qa'ida.

In fact, developments in the second half of the twentieth century began to erode the differences between Arabia and neighbouring regions that had emerged during previous centuries. The advent of oil wealth further empowered the Wahhabi establishment's grip on Saudi education and enabled the funding of new clerical learning centres in the kingdom. In particular, the Islamic University of Medina, a producer of ideological formulations that were increasingly at odds with the evolving political approaches and lifestyle of the Saudi monarchy, nurtured through its scholarship programs a new generation of Arab clerics.

The effect of this new curriculum was considerable. Ample space in the new course of study was allocated to the fourteenth-century scholar-activist Ibn Taymiyyah and his line of disciples who developed the Salafi ideology professed by the Wahhabi establishment. Through both the carefully designed amplification and reduction of the importance and assessed impact of other schools and currents of thought within Islamic history, this curriculum, empowered by the newly elevated status of Saudi Arabia as patron of much of the Muslim world, set the stage for a fundamental transformation of Islamic doctrine-from an explicitly recognised pluralism to an intransigent orthodoxy with Salafism as its unadulterated expression.

Upon their return, the graduates of the new Saudi learning centres had a noticeable effect on the religious landscape of their hometowns.

Traditional forms of religiosity that had already been undermined by the nationalist and leftist challenge of "modernity" were becoming even more emasculated. The most vulnerable of these forms had proven to be the Sufi orders: many cities where Sufism dominated religious life at the beginning of the twentieth century were effectively void of any tangible Sufi presence at the century's close. Even when the social and political order prohibited Sufism's open takeover by militant forms of religious expression, literalist and pietistic movements, such as the Sururiyyah and Qubaysiyyah, emerged, decimating the centuries-long presence of Sufi orders in the Levant.

The impact of Arabia as a new centre of religious learning in the Middle East was compounded by the regression of Al-Azhar University-conventionally the foremost institution of religious learning in the Sunni Muslim world and home to the Islamic revivalist movement that shaped much of Muslim culture worldwide in the nineteenth and twentieth centuries. Al-Azhar in Egypt did not enjoy the same quasi-autonomy from the state accorded to the Wahhabi establishment in Saudi Arabia; nor did it have access to the financial resources that were bestowed on its Saudi counterpart. It instead became a mouthpiece and rubber stamp for the policies of the Egyptian state, losing much credibility in the process and developing a "schizophrenic" ideological outlook-that is to say, compliant with regime demands at the top while maintaining different and occasionally opposing positions at the rank-and-file level. More dramatically, the resulting vulnerability of Al-Azhar allowed a gradual Salafist encroachment, leading to the transformation of the institution, which was traditionally pluralistic and with a considerable Sufi colour, into another Salafist bastion. *(See Ref 368, 371)*

In the ideological competition that began flaring in the mid-twentieth century between the militant forms of Islamic revivalism and Salafism for the mantle of restoring Islam to the centre of Muslim political life, Salafism enjoyed the advantage of oil wealth, giving it the upper hand. Still, activists schooled in the gradualist revivalist approach, as synthesised by the Muslim Brotherhood, continued to thrive.

Indeed, today, while Salafism may be aspiring for supremacy in the Levant, a generational transformation has yet to occur there. And though such a transformation may still be plausible, the texture of Levantine Islam is distinctly different from that of its Arabian expression. This difference

230

remains an impediment to the acceptance of the underlying ideological premises upon which al-Qa'ida jihadism is based. And while the impact of induced change in religious denominational and activist outlooks may be considerable, the resilience of Levantine culture-and the incompatibility of Arabian Salafism, with its evolving socio-cultural patterns- will prove to be a difficult, perhaps even insurmountable, obstacle for the appropriation and replication of al-Qa'ida–style jihadism.

In fact, while the ascendancy of the financial and doctrinal influence of Arabian Salafism on the Levant is noticeable, the aggressive character of Salafi dogma has generated considerable reactions. The battered movement of Sufism has occasionally found in Shiism a refuge, not only in the Levant, but also in Egypt and North Africa. Active Shiite proselytism - from Najaf, Iraq, and Qom, Iran - has been able to gain public converts, both in Palestine and in Syria, often on the basis of its provision of a Sufi-like connection with human spiritual figures (the imams of Shiism thus replacing or being identified with the sheikhs of Sufism). In Lebanon, where the presence of a significant Shiite community and communitarian rivalries preclude the possibility of a meaningful Sunni conversion, open anti-Salafist, post-Sufi formations have emerged, challenging both Salafist dogma and praxis and underlining the resistance to Salafism and jihadism as Arabian imports. For al Qa'ida–style jihadism to take root in the Levant, it will have to adapt to local Levantine concerns and worldviews. In the case of Palestinian society, Hamas might offer a practical balance. *(See Ref 372)*

A product of the Muslim Brotherhood movement, Hamas emerged in Palestinian society during the 1980s as an expression of the growing self-assertiveness of Islamist thought in the Muslim world following the Islamic revolution in Iran and in the midst of the Afghan jihad. Its birth was also a reflection of disillusionment with the many militant factions of the Palestine Liberation Organisation (PLO) - of various national, pan-nationalist, and leftist stripes- prone to infighting, corruption, and lack of a clear ideological program. With the emergence of pragmatic tendencies within the PLO and the ensuing acceptance - however tactical - of the existence of the state of Israel, Hamas was able to inherit the support of the maximalist tendencies within Palestinian society. Hamas benefited from multiple assessments. For the Israelis, at first, it was viewed as a potent rival that could bleed support from Yasser Arafat's Fatah movement, a more imminent threat. For some on the ideological left in the Arab world and elsewhere, Hamas became the true, albeit rough, expression of Palestinian popular resistance to occupation once the PLO's proclivity to compromise was exposed. As a movement native to the Palestinian territories, Hamas was even portrayed as an expression of opposition to the oligarchic and even kleptocratic PLO elite returning from exile in Tunisia to the West Bank and Gaza following the 1993 Oslo Accords.

The truth of these assessments is subject to debate. However, the question of whether Hamas has become the most successful example of an Islamist movement in the Levant is not. In both its electoral success and assumption of executive decision-making power in the Gaza Strip, it represents the first instance of an Islamist movement acquiring political power by nonviolent means. Paradoxically, this nonviolent political success was achieved while the organisation engaged in one of the most virulent, lethal campaigns in the history of jihadism.

Hamas uses a hybrid proposition in which a nationalist argument is layered upon religious foundations, often with apocalyptic dimensions. The conflict in Palestine is no longer a mere struggle for the recovery of lost land and the emancipation of a captive population. Indeed, it is also framed as a preordained mandate to recuperate territory belonging to Islam - as a monolithic religion-from an eternal enemy that embodies evil in this world. While optimistic intellectuals in the Arab world and beyond dismiss such an argument as a mere rhetorical device aimed at mobilising the base in a conflict characterised by rising bitterness, its effects on corroding shared norms of common humanity between Palestinians and Israelis, and Arabs and Jews, are readily visible. Since its assumption of power, Hamas itself appears to have retreated, in its official discourse, from blatantly anti-Jewish statements by qualifying the enmity as one stemming from the occupation. The official retreat, however, is less meaningful in the context of the cultural saturation that the previous discourse had achieved. *(See Ref 374)*

Even if the dogmatically charged proposition is the result of a pragmatic decision on the part of a leadership seeking to maximize both loyalty and willingness to sacrifice, its damage to Palestinian society and to any progress-based vision will outlast any tactical advantage it was meant to generate for Hamas as an organisation. Hamas "moderates" might be willing, in some hypothetical future, to steer a course toward "compromise." The culture that Hamas has amplified and deeply anchored in Palestinian society, however, will constitute a permanent deterrent against such a reversal.

The totalitarian regimentation sought by al-Qa'ida under the guise of religious compliance consists of four major facets: political, military, social, and cultural. Hamas, even by al-Qa'ida's standards, has performed satisfactorily in three out of the four. At the cultural level, Hamas has engaged in a systematic program for the reform of the individual, in pursuit of the Islamist ideal. Its members are provided with strict instructions on obligatory, permissible, and forbidden actions ranging from personal hygiene to speech and thought. At times, the high burden of compliance has hindered Hamas membership drives, even among its ideological supporters, prompting such rules to be adjusted accordingly. The reform of the individual is the first stage in the multiphase program devised by Muslim Brotherhood founder Hassan al-Banna in Egypt in the 1920s. Hamas has been engaged in a diligent implementation of this program, notably at the social level. Gaza under Hamas has far fewer venues for youth and popular culture and is more gender segregated. The main difference between the Hamas approach toward Islamisation and the methods favoured by al-Qa'ida is that Hamas has largely proceeded in incremental steps-at times discretely-that are often phrased as responses to social and cultural demands. The sale of alcoholic beverages and entertainment venues thus gradually disappeared from Hamas's Gaza with little fanfare, through a process of regulation and intimidation that avoided the spotlight favoured by al-Qa'ida in its targeting and elimination of establishments engaged in activities incompatible with its religious understanding. *(See Ref 375)*

Socially, culturally, and militarily, Hamas has won the admiration of al-Qa'ida–style jihadists. Militant forums as well as al-Qa'ida leadership statements are replete with admiration for the "Mujahideen" in Gaza. It is apparent that, while the ideological underpinnings might exhibit theoretical differences, Hamas and al-Qa'ida are in agreement about the practice of jihad. The disagreement between them is fundamentally political.

It has repeatedly been noted in academia and the media that a distinction must be made between Hamas and al-Qa'ida on the basis of the former's national focus versus the latter's global approach. Yet, al-Qa'ida itself, as evidenced by the elaborate critique that its leadership and ideologues have offered, does not view this distinction as a reason for disagreement.

Indeed, al-Qa'ida claims a number of affiliates with localized focus, in Iraq, Afghanistan, the Caucasus, Algeria, and Somalia. Al-Qa'ida ideologues have even stated that allegiance to or identification with the al-Qa'ida network is not a sine qua non for endorsement by the al-Qa'ida leadership. Instead, what is expected of those seeking al-Qa'ida's imprimatur, in addition to the tangible proof of their ability to deliver massive lethal blows to the enemy, is the solemn adherence to "divine rulership" (hakimiyyat Allah) and the Salafist concept of "al-wala wa-l-bara", or allegiance to fellow believers and repudiation of all others. On both accounts, from the al-Qa'ida perspective, Hamas falls short. *(See Ref 368)*

By accepting the political framework of the Palestinian Authority, recognising international law, and seeking power through the electoral system, Hamas has transgressed on divine rulership. And by entering into tacit and explicit alliances with Shiite Iran, Hezbollah, and the Alawi regime in Syria, Hamas has ignored the obligation of repudiating non-believers. Al-Qa'ida ideologues would be satisfied if Hamas were to declare its rejection of all agreed-upon political arrangements and terminate its current alliances; they would be gratified if Hamas were further to declare its allegiance to the global jihad network. Even in the ranks of al-Qa'ida ideologues, however, the realisation exists that, from a practical point of view, these steps are not possible today. The attitude toward Hamas thus ranges from seeing its defaulting from the acceptable political path as a matter of necessity, and thus excusable, to viewing it as a mere reflection of the corrupted thought of the Muslim Brotherhood- a perennial rival, albeit also an incubator, of al-Qa'ida–style jihadism. In its current state, Hamas is thus a group that cannot be granted unqualified al-Qa'ida endorsement; it is, however, a group that satisfies most of the prerequisites for such an endorsement.Thus, the compromise implicitly reached in al-Qa'ida discourse in recent months is to provide unequivocal endorsement and support for the jihad in Palestine as an action, with no reference to Hamas as an organisation or leadership.

In response to Hamas's departure from the al-Qa'ida–approved path, al-Qa'ida leadership and ideologues had first sought to "advise" the group to no avail. With its counsel ignored, al-Qa'ida engaged in a loud denunciation of Hamas, with the hope of intimidating it into compliance. However, bolstered by its strong position in Palestinian society, Hamas responded defiantly. Intimidation did not work.The sidelining of the Hamas leadership in al-Qa'ida discourse constitutes a third approach to dealing with Hamas and is a considerable shift from a previous relationship characterised by anger and animosity. *(See Ref 376)*

Al-Qa'ida ideologues have instead recognised a number of smaller groups in Gaza as endeavoring toward the initiation of Salafist jihadism. The most notable of these groups is Jaysh al-Islam (the Army of Islam), responsible- in partnership with Hamas - for the 2006 raid on Israeli territory and the kidnapping of Israeli soldier Gilad Shalit. Jaysh al-Islam is a clan-based militia that has succeeded in carving out a territory for itself, through measures that combine elements of militancy with organised crime. It provides tactical added value to Hamas, as part of the configuration of militant organisations that shield Hamas from responsibility in problematic operations that are nevertheless consistent with Hamas's vision, such as the targeting of Christian educational and social organisations. Its assertiveness vis-à-vis Hamas's authority, however, led to a confrontation in September 2008 in which Hamas forces raided the Jaysh al-Islam complex, killing and injuring many of its members and their relatives. It was notable that al-Qa'ida ideologues, while deploring the action, called for restraint and refrained from any meaningful denunciation of Hamas. *(See Ref 377)*

Other Palestinian Salafist-jihadist groups claimed presence on the ground and were occasionally highlighted in the jihadist cyberspace, including Jaysh al Ummah, Fateh al-Islam, Kata'ib al-Mujahideen, and Jund Allah. Virtually all are ephemeral in their setup and recruitment capacity, as well as problematic in their composition. While they may engage in sporadic anti-Israeli actions, they also contribute to the state of lawlessness that Hamas has sought to counter. *(See Ref 378)*

Since its confrontation with Jaysh al-Islam, Hamas seems to have moved in the direction of imposing its control over other jihadist groups, with virtually no complaint from al-Qa'ida ideologues.

However, as a largely virtual entity thriving on perception management, al Qa'ida has been bracing for the potential harm it would suffer in the event of a Palestinian battle from which it was excluded. To help mitigate the danger, al-Qa'ida leaders and ideologues have periodically engaged over the last few years in preemptive announcements and analyses designed to underline the fact that al-Qa'ida is a leader, not a laggard, on the issue of Palestine.

The treatment of Hamas over the years has changed considerably. The original al-Qa'ida approach to this predominant Palestinian Islamist formation was one of giving both criticism and advice. Hamas was invited to reform itself along lines consistent with pure doctrinal precepts, as promoted by al-Qa'ida. The list of required actions was lengthy, but it could be best summarized as a renunciation of Hamas's acceptance of the political process and a severing of its questionable regional alliances. The Hamas leadership largely ignored al-Qa'ida's advice. It was clear that al-Qa'ida constituted a further nuisance to a Hamas striving for legitimacy in a generally hostile court of world opinion.

By the end of 2007, with Hamas firmly in control of Gaza and having de facto renounced its recognition of the Palestinian Authority, al-Qa'ida stepped up its pressure for compliance. In fact, Hamas's June 2007 "coup" in Gaza, ouster of its Fateh rivals, and self-appointment as the sole legitimate authority in Gaza - at the exclusion of official Palestinian Authority entities - was a considerable step in the direction proposed by al-Qa'ida. Independent of al-Qa'ida pressure and from a democratic perspective, these moves exposed a major defect in Hamas's acceptance of the electoral process, giving credence to the argument that such an embrace was utilitarian and one-way-that is, Hamas was willing to recognise a democratic process that elevated it to power but was just as prepared to ignore it when it required the surrender of any control it had gained.

Still, allowing its actions to be interpreted as consistent with al-Qa'ida demands would have been disastrous for an already besieged and battered Hamas. Hamas reacted publicly, dismissing al-Qa'ida's advice and underlining that no one was in a position to lecture the Palestinian resistance on its course of action.

The advice approach - the first tactic adopted by al-Qa'ida - was no longer tenable. Al-Qa'ida thus resorted to denunciation. A salvo of al-Qa'ida verbal attacks followed, with contributions from Osama bin Laden, Ayman al Zawahiri, and Abu Umar al-Baghdadi, (real name Hamid al-Zawi), the "commander" of the al-Qa'ida–affiliated Islamic State of Iraq (Killed on 18 April 2010)- a figure about whom little is known with certainty but who at one point was groomed by jihadist media for a potential role in any resurrected caliphate. Al-Baghdadi openly called for a mutiny by the Izziddin al-Qassam Brigades, the military wing of Hamas, and invited all Palestinian factions for jihad training in the "triumphant" Islamic State of Iraq-despite a precipitous decline in al-Qa'ida's ability to maneuver there following the American Forces "surge" and the rise of antiradical Sunni groups. The prominent al-Qa'ida ideologue Asad al-Jihad 2 (AJ2) made a series of contributions placing Hamas's actions and statements in the context of a conspiracy aimed at "liquidating" the Palestinian question by ultimately accepting a compromise that would allow Israel to continue to exist. *(See Ref 379, 380, 381, 382, 383)*

Hamas's response was defiant, unyielding, and dismissive. Al-Zawahiri's elaborate argumentation was discounted as irrelevant by the Hamas leadership, while a blunt and slighting response to al-Baghdadi's offer was given by a young Izziddin al-Qassam field commander, further raising the ire of devoted al-Qa'ida supporters. It was nonetheless clear that, in the battle of words al-Qa'ida had initiated, Hamas had the upper hand. Al-Qa'ida had to yield and effectively abandon its second approach – denunciation - in favour of a new and third approach.

Bin Laden's statement, on the occasion of the sixtieth anniversary of the inception of the state of Israel, epitomised this third approach. Al-Qa'ida would henceforth embrace the Palestinian cause, underlining its primacy as a justification for jihad, but would deliberately avoid any substantive reference to Hamas. Vowing to "continue" the fight against Israel, bin Laden informed the West that "the Palestinian cause is the central cause for my nation". Though the centrality of Palestine in al-Qa'ida discourse had varied over the years, bin Laden realised that it would have been counterproductive to allow this question to drain the credibility and stature of al-Qa'ida. The new "ignore and embrace" approach would thus be justified on the basis of the objective progress Hamas made toward meeting al-Qa'ida's political precepts - in particular, in its resistance to resubmitting to the Palestinian Authority's rule. Al-Qa'ida also realised that there was a need to avoid distractions, given that Gaza was under siege. Abu Yahya al-Libi, one of the most prominent second-generation al-Qa'ida leaders, embodied this approach in his October 2008 'il- Khutbah' (sermon): in it, there were traditional supplications to God to support all al-Qa'ida affiliates, which Libi referenced by name and theatre, including "Palestine and its Mujahideen," but without any specific indication of who they were. *(See Ref 384, 385)*

In March 2008, AJ2 made a prediction that would prove of considerable utility to his standing as an informed source: "Within a year or so, a devastating calamity will be fall Gaza, and a hopeful development will be revealed." It may not have been difficult to anticipate that the reckless behaviour of the Hamas leadership, and the continuous barrage of rockets it persisted in launching, would trigger a confrontation. But this statement and subsequent al-Qa'ida pronouncements were meant to compensate for the effective exclusion of al-Qa'ida from the Palestinian arena. *(See Ref 383)*

Still, almost three weeks had elapsed since the start of the Israeli military confrontation with Hamas in December 2008 before new statements from al-Qa'ida were released, expressing support for Gaza and urging action against Israel, as well as Arab regimes, for their failure to provide aid to the Palestinians.

Two statements were released in tandem by al-Qa'ida's top leadership: one by al-Zawahiri and another by al-Baghdadi, followed shortly by a call by bin Laden himself for jihad on behalf of Gaza. Offerings of support also came from al-Qa'ida affiliates in Arabia and the Maghreb.

In the days prior to the release of these statements, expectations in the jihadist cyberspace ran high amid promises of a major al-Qa'ida announcement. Speculation centered on everything from prospective recipients of a presumed "al-Qa'ida in the Land of al-Aqsa" franchise to talk of a specific announcement of forthcoming al-Qa'ida action and a response to Israel's Gaza incursion. The delay in the release of the statement, many believed, stemmed from the need to complete necessary preparations.

The primary candidates mentioned for an al-Qa'ida endorsement were the Izziddin al-Qassam Brigades, the military wing of Hamas-itself previously courted unsuccessfully by al-Baghdadi - and the al-Nasir Salahuddin Battalions, a group closely associated with Hamas. The absence of a reference to Jaysh al-Islam or other openly Salafist-jihadist formations as contenders indicated a realisation among al-Qa'ida active supporters that al-Qa'ida action in Palestine would have to emerge from within Hamas, not outside it. *(See Ref 386)*

However, upon the circulation of the al-Qa'ida leadership's statements, unease could be felt across the blogs, forums, and websites that propagated them. Jihadist Internet outlets hosted the usual flow of concurring messages, endorsing the content of the statements with supplications for divine help. Some of these messages, however, expressed mild disappointment at the lack of a specific promise for vengeance on the part of al-Qa'ida. Others repeated the demands for al-Qa'ida's entry into the Palestinian scene.

These demands were answered, albeit not in the anticipated way, with the claim of responsibility provided by AJ2 for the Katyusha rocket attack across the Lebanese-Israeli border and the revelation of the existence of an al-Qa'ida affiliate in the Levant (Bilad a-Sham), and not in Palestine (Ard al-Aqsa, the land of the Aqsa) as speculated.

It can indeed be argued that, being content with such meager offerings to its constituency, al-Qa'ida has demonstrated its limitations and failure to achieve a breakthrough on the Palestinian scene. AJ2 himself, in the context of the second approach (denunciation) then adopted by al-Qa'ida toward Hamas, had declared that two opposing and incompatible paths are being offered in Palestine-one being the genuine jihad exemplified by Jaysh al-Islam and the other being a path of corruption and compromise represented by Hamas.In his most recent answers to queries about jihad in Gaza, the previous dichotomy between two opposing camps no longer holds; instead, AJ2 discourses on the importance of unity and cooperation. Is al-Qa'ida conceding the ideological battle? *(See Ref 383)*

Palestine has proven impenetrable to direct al-Qa'ida action. Palestinian society is still dogmatically and ideologically unripe for a pure adoption of the al-Qa'ida vision: Palestinian Salafist-jihadist groups have been lacking in capacity, thwarted by both Israel and Hamas, and unable to establish the logistics of any al-Qa'ida penetration. The implicit rehabilitation of Hamas as a valid expression of jihad may serve the cause of the global jihad, and that of Hamas, but not al-Qa'ida per se. The ambiguous creation of al-Qa'ida in the Levant (AQL) may address this lacuna. It does, however, place a considerable burden on al-Qa'ida to deliver: claiming responsibility for disparate operations in the distant past, and further responsibility for a lone rocket attack that had no impact on the unfolding of the Gaza war, is not sufficient. Al-Qa'ida has promised spectacular operations by its new Levant affiliate. Its ability to deliver, however, depends on the assets it is able to gather and activate.

Looking more broadly at the region, three models of operations are available for AQL states outside of Palestine and Israel: Lebanon, Syria, and Jordan.

In the last few years, particularly after the May 2007 fighting in the

Palestinian refugee camp of Nahr al-Barid, the threat of al-Qa'ida establishing a base in Lebanon from which to wage its global jihad has become a cause for concern for most of the international community.

So the question here: Is there such threat and what are the roots of the Islamic extremism in Lebanon?

The roots of Islamic extremism and, by extension, the Salafi jihadist movement in Lebanon during the 1980s are complex and best analysed on three levels: the local, the systemic and the individual.

At the local level, the rise of Salafi jihadism can be attributed to the nature of Lebanon's socio-political system as defined by the 1943 National Pact. The Pact stipulates that Lebanese Christians will forgo all military alliances with Western powers while Muslims will set aside any forms of nationalism that extend beyond Lebanon's geographical boundaries. The Pact also reinforced the confessional schism that existed by confirming that Lebanese presidents would be Maronite Christians, premiers would be Sunni Muslims and speakers of the Parliament would be Shiite Muslim. Civil service appointments and public funding would also be determined on a confessional basis. In sum, Lebanon's sectarian system has denied the possibility of one group monopolising power and creating an authoritarian state, thus frustrating Lebanon's radical Islamists who aspire to create an Islamic state. It has also greatly polarised the various sects and hampered the growth of a national identity. As a result, Salafi jihadists became more receptive to outside actors and often paved the way for external interventions into Lebanese affairs. *(See Ref 387)*

At the systemic level, the rise of Islamist militancy in the broader Middle East coincided with an identity crisis stemming from the failure of pan-Arabism, the humiliation resulting from successive military defeats to Israel, and a perception among Muslims that the umma was losing the ideological battle to the West. In Lebanon, these frustrations were reinforced by a 15-year civil war that pitted Christians against Muslims and by Israel's 1982 invasion and subsequent 18-year occupation of southern Lebanon. Lebanese militants are also quite affected by ongoing regional conflicts, particularly the Israeli-Palestinian conflict and the sectarian violence in Iraq.

At the individual level, the growth of Salafi jihadism is attributable to the success of local and foreign Salafi jihadist leaders in penetrating Lebanese

Muslim society with their ideology. While nonviolent Salafists are the most likely to be receptive to the ideology due to the common religious foundation, ordinary criminals and alienated individuals with little concern for Islamic thought also make up the pool of recruits. It is no coincidence that the cities in which Salafism and Salafi jihadism emerged and developed - Tripoli, Majdal Anjar, Qarun and Sidon - are characterised by high unemployment and rampant poverty.

Geographically, Lebanon is relatively small and there are few remote areas from which Salafi jihadist organisations can operate freely. The exceptions are the areas surrounding Tripoli and the Palestinian refugee camps that are outside the control of the Lebanese state.While it is possible that small groups have operated in the hinterland surrounding Tripoli, all major Salafi jihadist organisations have thus far used the refugee camps as their bases. Given their centrality to Salafi jihadism in Lebanon, a brief overview of the camps is in order. *(While these are the areas to which Salafi jihadist groups are restricted, other extremist organisations operate more widely within Lebanon. For example, Hezbollah operates independently in southern Lebanon below the Litani River as well as within the Beqaa Valley. However, Salafi Jihadists are not on friendly terms with Hezbollah, and so do not have access to these areas)*

The Palestinian "problem" can be traced back to the First Arab-Israeli War of 1948 and the June 1967 war, during which more than 300,000 Palestinians fled to Lebanon, mainly settling in the South. A further influx of approximately 3,000 Palestinian militants occurred in 1970 in the aftermath of what Palestinians refer to as "Black September," when King Hussein of Jordan evicted the majority of armed Palestinians from his country in three weeks of bloody fighting. Today, according to the United Nations agency for Palestinian refugees (UNRWA), there are between 350,000 and 400,000 refugees in Lebanon, most of them live in 12 camps. *(See Ref 388)*

Conditions within the Palestinian refugee camps slowly improved under the control of the Palestinian Liberation Organisation (PLO) in the1970s due to an influx of money from the Arab Gulf states and strong employment programs. When the PLO was ejected from Lebanon in 1983 by Israeli and Syrian forces, the economies of the camps collapsed, despite UNRWA's continued provision of aid. The refugees suffered yet another blow when the Gulf States cut off funding in response to PLO Chairman Yasser Arafat's siding with Iraq during the first Gulf War in 1991.

Since then, conditions have steadily declined. Palestinians are prevented by law from working in over 60 skilled professions and are not allowed to own property or register companies. Construction around the camps is prohibited, resulting in severe overcrowding and unsanitary conditions, and a large percentage - as high as 27% in some camps - live in abject poverty. *(See Ref 389, 390, 391)*

Each successive Lebanese government has ignored Palestinian issues for fear of appearing to facilitate the naturalisation of the overwhelmingly Sunni refugees, which would upset Lebanon's delicate power balance. As such, feelings of resentment and alienation are common within the camps, making them either ripe ground for recruitment or, at the least, passive supporters of extremist groups targeting the state.

In the 1990s, large-scale crackdowns on Salafists by Lebanese security forces, multiple Israeli aggressions against Lebanon and violent clashes with rival Islamic groups further mobilised Salafi jihadists. However, Salafi jihadist ambitions remained almost exclusively local during that decade and the various groups rarely subscribed to the doctrine of al-Qa'ida's global insurgency. Furthermore, Lebanon's various Salafi groups were not united under a single organisation and so were not considered too great a threat to the state.

From 2003 to 2007 the threat was completely transformed as Lebanon, and the region as a whole, witnessed a number of events that led to the rapid growth of Salafi jihadist movements. The most consequential of these events were the Syrian withdrawal from Lebanon and the U.S. invasion of Iraq.

The political and security void that characterised Lebanon in the aftermath of the 2005 assassination of former Prime Minister Rafik al-Hariri and the subsequent Syrian withdrawal from the country gave radical groups room to maneuver and grow. Syria's effective intelligence and security apparatus had previously kept many of the radical Islamist groups in check, but Lebanese security forces were incapable of rising to the task. At the time the Salafi jihadist movement faced difficulties in many parts of the world, and the lack of security in Lebanon attracted many of its members. Additionally, the withdrawal of the Syrian presence delivered a further blow to the camp economies as it had provided employment to many Palestinians. This sudden job loss resulted in dramatic increases of drug and alcohol abuse which in turn facilitated the encroachment of radical jihadist groups. *(See Ref 392, 393, 394)*

The second major factor in the rapid spread of Salafi jihadism in recent years was the U.S. invasion of Iraq in 2003. Following the invasion, Usbat al-Ansar, a Salafi jihadist group based out of the Ain al-Hilweh camp, sent - with the tactical cooperation of Syrian military intelligence - hundreds of volunteers to join the Iraqi insurgency, where they not only gained combat experience but also strengthened their ties to al-Qa'ida leaders. Such activity subsided upon Syria's 2005 withdrawal; however, Damascus continued to act as a willing conduit for fighters moving to and from Iraq. As Andrew Exum notes, there was a definite correlation between the 'Awakening' in Iraq, which severely limited al- Qa'ida's ability to operate there, and the rise of Lebanon as a base of Salafi jihadist operations. *(See Ref 395, 396, 397)*

However, the extent to which al-Qa'ida has now and in the past maintained a presence in Lebanon is the subject of considerable debate, with Syria and its supporters claiming that al-Qa'ida poses a real threat to Lebanon's national security while the 14 March coalition led by former Prime Minister Saad al-Hariri and parliamentary minority leader Fouaf Siniora believes that Syria fabricates this threat in order to destabilise Lebanon and justify continued intervention. Externally, Swedish, Danish, German, Italian and U.S. intelligence agencies are convinced that al-Qa'ida has a real presence in Lebanon and is set on striking against their respective interests in the country. *(See Ref 398, 399)*

But what does having a "real presence" in Lebanon entail for a group like al-Qa'ida? Since the 2001 U.S. invasion of Afghanistan, al-Qa'ida has ceased to exist as a structured organisation and instead persists as a network of affiliated groups motivated by a common ideology. Terrorism expert Marc Sageman recently took this notion further by arguing that the threat of al-Qa'ida leaders plotting attacks and issuing commands to affiliated groups has transformed into one in which local groups conceive and execute operations independently with little or no guidance from the top. Other analysts take exception to this argument, concluding that while al-Qa'ida has exhibited bottom-up initiatives it still remains capable of top-down operations. Sageman's characterisation of al-Qa'ida would imply that the organisation has established a presence via groups like Fatah al-Islam and Usbat al-Ansar. However, its activities over the last decade seem to

243

indicate that it is attempting to establish a more traditional presence in Lebanon so as to exert more direct control over operations in the area. *(See Ref 400, 401, 402, 403, 404)*

What follows is a brief history detailing al-Qa'ida's involvement in Lebanon which demonstrates that while the threat of al-Qa'ida has often been exaggerated, it is by no means a Syrian myth. The group has repeatedly worked with local Salafi jihadist groups by providing financing, training and ideological guidance. *(See Ref 405)*

Links between al-Qa'ida and Lebanese Salafi groups began to develop in 2000, when a group of possibly Chechen origin and connected to Osama bin Laden asked Bassam Kanj, a veteran from Afghanistan, to set up a Salafi jihadist network in Lebanon. Kanj focused his recruitment efforts in the poor neighbourhoods of Tripoli and in Ain al-Hilweh, a Palestinian refugee camp located outside the city of Sidon in south Lebanon. In January 2000, an Islamic group in the north town of Dinniyeh was involved in a week-long firefight with the Lebanese Armed Forces (LAF) afterwhich the group more or less disbanded with survivors joining Usbat al-Ansar. *(See Ref 387, 406)*

From 2001 to 2005, Usbat al-Ansar was one of the most prominent Salafi jihadist groups in Lebanon. Although it has denied formal links to al-Qa'ida, Usbat al-Ansar is reported to be partly funded and armed by the bin Laden organisation.

During this period other incidents had occurred linking al-Qa'ida to Lebanon. First was the March 2003 car bombing murder in Ain al-Hilweh of Abd al-Sattar Jad (Abu Muhammad al-Masri), identified by Israeli intelligence services as al-Qa'ida's commander in Lebanon.Two months later, in May 2003, was the arrest of a Yemeni, Maamun al-Awami (Abu al-Shahid) for providing military training to a group that was plotting to blow up a McDonalds. Al-Awami was arrested while leaving the Ain al-Hilweh refugee camp and accused of having connections to prominent al-Qa'ida leader Ayman al-Zawahiri who funded his group. At around the same time, Lebanese authorities discovered a cell linked to al-Qa'ida under the supervision of known jihadist Ismail al-Khatib. *(See Ref 408, 409)*

Beginning in 2004, al-Qa'ida's leadership in Iraq decided to use Lebanon as a base where it could hold meetings and plan operations in Iraq. Al-Qa'ida also began to increase funding of certain religious programs and charities including Jund al-Sham, a splinter group of Usbat al-Ansar. Jund al-Sham, during this period at least, was used by al-Qa'ida to directly influence events in Lebanon according to Fida Itani of the Lebanese daily Al Akhbar.In September 2004, twenty al-Qa'ida suspects, including two leaders, were arrested in connection with a plot to attack the Italian embassy in Lebanon. One of the involved networks was based in Ain al-Hilweh and the other was based in West Beqaa. Following these arrests, Lebanese authorities claimed that al-Qa'ida no longer had a network in Lebanon. *(See Ref 406, 410)*

However, one year later - in December 2005 - an al-Qa'ida affiliated organisation claimed responsibility for firing rockets at Israel from the south of Lebanon. Abu Mus'ab al-Zarqawi, at the time leader of al-Qa'ida in Iraq, announced on tape that the attack was "made under direct instructions from Osama bin-Laden" and Lebanese Interior Minister then Ahmad Fatfat confirmed that the attacks were financed directly by al-Qa'ida.In January 2006, Lebanese police announced the capture of 13 al-Qa'ida suspects connected to al-Zarqawi who were in the process of planning suicide attacks in Iraq and possibly Lebanon. *(See Ref 411, 412, 413)*

Later that year, al-Qa'ida's "Human Resources Group" arrived in Lebanon to reinforce the tactical, technical and logistical skills of local groups. The group was led by "Badran Turki Hisham al-Mazidi" known as (Abu Ghadiyah), a Syrian member of al-Qa'ida with training experience in Turkey and Afghanistan.Weeks later, Palestinian-Syrian Abdullah Hadraji, together with seven members of al-Qa'ida, visited Nahr al-Barid with the goal of establishing an official presence in Lebanon.At this point the story of al-Qa'ida in Lebanon becomes inextricably linked to that of Fatah al-Islam. *(See Ref 414)*

Fatah al-Islam was officially formed on 26 November 2006 after splitting from Fatah al-Intifada, a secular pro-Syrian faction that had itself broken away from the mainstream Palestinian Fatah movement in 1983. The group's leader, Shakir al- Absi, has denied all links to al-Qa'ida, claiming "al-Qa'ida has its strategy; we have ours". *(See Ref 415)*

However, investigations into the group indicate that Fatah al-Islam was actively trying to deepen its affiliation with al-Qa'ida. According to Syrian political analyst Sami Moubayed, Fatah al-Islam repeatedly tried to gain al-Qa'ida approval for its operations, but failed each time despite al-Absi's and other group members' strong links to al-Zawahiri and other top al-Qa'ida members. Abdullah al-Binshi, the Saudi "shari'a expert" sent by al-Qa'ida to evaluate Fatah al-Islam, concluded that "Lebanon is not the land of jihad". Abu Abdulrahman al-Afghani, another senior member of al-Qa'ida who evaluated Fatah al-Islam's operations, left unconvinced of their tactics. *(See Ref 416)*

Abu Hamza, a jihadist who has in the past demonstrated key insight into al-Qa'ida operations, wrote on the jihadist forum "Ekhlaas," that Fatah al-Islam continued to attempt serious negotiation to become a formal affiliate until the group was crushed by the Lebanese Armed Forces (LAF) during the May 2007 firefight at Nahr al-Barid. Al-Qa'ida saw fighting against the Lebanese government as counterproductive to jihadist interests and worried about becoming new targets of the LAF, so it severed relations with Fatah al-Islam. *(See Ref 417, 418)*

That al-Qa'ida had personal, financial and ideological connections to the major Salafi jihadist groups in Lebanon should not be taken to mean that it was alone in supporting these groups. Multiple actors have been accused of funding and providing weapons to these groups in order to advance their own agendas. Ultimately, however, the real winner would always be al-Qa'ida and its adherents. For example, there is considerable evidence that at various points in its development, Fatah al-Islam was supported by both Syria and Saad al-Hariri's Future Movement. Al-Hariri is alleged to have funded Fatah al-Islam so that it might act as a counterbalance to Hezbollah, while Syria, which has a history of sponsoring foreign terrorist groups, may have supported Fatah al-Islam to deflect attention from the United Nations al-Hariri tribunal or to use the group to break up any potential al-Hariri-created Islamist coalition that could be used to fight Hezbollah. As both actors quickly learned, however, Fatah al-Islam was following its own program and used the funds it received to recruit dozens of new combatants, organise more training sessions at Ain al-Hilweh and prepare plans for attacking UN peace keepers in the South. As a Hamas official explained, "all sides tried to benefit from [Fatah al-Islam] but no one can control them". By late 2007, al-Qa'ida had developed a vast network throughout Lebanon; however, it remains unclear how the group intends to use it. *(See Ref 419, 420, 421, 422, 423)*

Having suffered strategic defeat in Iraq and Afghanistan, many analysts are concerned that al-Qa'ida is searching for new fronts on which to wage its global jihad. This concern is reinforced by multiple statements made by al-Zawahiri and bin-Laden over the last few years explicitly referring to Lebanon,and by the appointment of al-Saadi Nahed, a Saudi extremist and veteran of the insurgency in Iraq, as the new "emir" for al-Qa'ida in Lebanon.This section will address the likelihood that al-Qa'ida will continue to establish a traditional presence in Lebanon from which to pursue its objectives and, if so, whether it will be successful given the current situation. *(See Ref 424)*

As mentioned earlier, Lebanon's small size and sectarian population greatly limit the ability of extremist groups to freely maneuver within the country. A further limitation, according to a former high-ranking jihadist, is that many Islamic groups and religious leaders have ties to Lebanese intelligence services.As such, should al-Qa'ida choose to settle in Lebanon, it will be compelled to find a home in the Palestinian refugee camps. With Nahr al-Barid completely destroyed after the May 2007 fighting, Ain al-Hilweh, the largest of the 12 Palestinian refugee camps, which hosts Usbat al-Ansar, Jund al-Sham and possibly other unknown Salafi jihadist groups that subscribe to al-Qa'ida's ideology, is the most likely candidate. In fact, according to several sources, al-Qa'ida may have already begun infiltrating the camp. In September 2008, a Jordanian official told London daily based al-Hayat that a group of al-Qa'ida members including 25 Jordanians and a number of Yemenis, Saudis and Europeans had relocated to the camp from Iraq. He also asserted that "al-Qa'ida representatives are in Lebanon at present and they are trying to establish contact with [certain] groups based in Ain al-Hilweh." These "certain groups" would include Jund al-Sham, Usbat al-Ansar and the remnants of Fatah al-Islam. Others doubt that this infiltration is being directed by a central al-Qa'ida authority and refer to what currently exists as a "fake al-Qa'ida". *(See Ref 425, 426)*

Regardless, Ain al-Hilweh is quite different than Nahr al-Barid and it cannot be assumed that-even given al-Qa'ida infiltration - the camp will radicalise at the same astonishingly quick rate that Nahr al-Barid did. Ain al-Hilweh is home to several Palestinian nationalist parties including Fatah and Hamas which, fearing the fate of Nahr al-Barid, are proactively trying to avoid a confrontation with the state. A joint security force involving all the various factions has been formed to create some sense of internal order, and discussions have been held regarding turning over some of the most-wanted jihadists that may be living in the camp.The Salafi jihadist groups are resisting this "moderating" of the camp, however a prominent Fatah commander has been quoted as saying that "all the Palestinian forces are discussing how to get rid of [them]" and that "if a peaceful solution is not found, we will mount a security operation against them and finish them off once and for all". Furthermore, the Lebanese Armed Forces (LAF), and to some extent Syria, has undercover intelligence officers stationed in the camp, thus making large-scale operational planning a challenge. Ain al-Hilweh's external security environment is also quite different from Nahr al-Barid's. Fearing attacks on UN Peace keeping forces stationed nearby, the LAF has encircled the camp, and Hezbollah, which is hostile to al-Qa'ida, is in effective control of south Lebanon. *(See See 427, 428)*

Assuming al-Qa'ida means to exert more direct control over groups in Lebanon, it is still unclear how receptive Lebanese Salafi jihadist groups would be to subordinating themselves to bin-Laden or al-Zawahiri. Although these groups share much of al-Qa'ida's ideology, they have thus far failed to unite under a single organisation due to their dissimilar agendas. Indeed during the Nahr al-Barid fight, no other Salafi jihadist group militarily - much less vocally - aided Fatah al-Islam, as those groups' leaders believe that jihad should be waged against Israel, not Lebanon. Furthermore, Salafi jihadists in Lebanon have to contend with several enemies - the Lebanese government, Israel, Shiite and Christian groups, and UNIFIL - and may thus be unwilling to utilise their limited resources to engage in activities that may upset the prioritisation of their targets. As Bilal Saab and Magnus Ranstrop argue, "each [group] is more concerned about its own survival than about waging an offensive jihad against 'infidels'". *(See Ref 429)*

However, it has been argued that al-Qa'ida recognises the above challenges and indeed has no intention of waging jihad from Lebanon. Instead, al-Qa'ida may settle on using Lebanon as a staging ground for operations in Palestine and Europe. In the past four years numerous groups from Algeria, Saudi Arabia, Kuwait, Iraq, Libya, Egypt and Jordan - most of which have close links to al-Qa'ida-have gone to Lebanon, primarily to Ain al-Hilweh, to train. After training, many of the jihadists either return to their home country or move on to Iraq. It has been reported that a significant number travel to several European countries with considerable ease. The threat to Europe is very real: in September 2009, French police disrupted a Salafist Group for Call and Combat (GSPC) cell allied to the al-Zarqawi network in the suburbs of Paris. Two of the detainees told authorities they had received explosives training at a camp near Tripoli in northern Lebanon. *(See Ref 413, 414)*

If Lebanon will be a possible staging ground for al-Qa'ida's operations in Palestine and Europe, what is the Islamic extrimists situation in Syria?

The Syrian government is the longest-standing member of the U.S. State Department's list of state sponsors of terrorism, having been so designated in 1979.In February 2008, the U.S. Treasury Department underscored the findings in a collection of documents generally known as the Sinjar records.These records provide details of 700 foreign nationals who entered Iraq between August 2006 and August 2007. The records were found in October 2007 by U.S. troops at Sinjar, a small town on the Iraqi-Syrian border. The Sinjar documents identified four members of a key terrorist facilitation and finance network operating out of Syria in support of al-Qa'ida in Iraq (AQI). The Treasury Department reported that the "Abu Ghadiyah" network, named for its leader, Badran Turki Hisham al-Mazidih, known as Abu Ghadiyah, controlled the flow of much of the money, weaponry, personnel, and other materiel that passed through Syria into Iraq for the use of AQI. According to the Treasury Department, the network "obtained false passports for foreign terrorists, provided passports, weapons, guides, safe houses, and allowances to foreign terrorists in Syria and those preparing to cross the border into Iraq." Indeed, Mazidih reportedly received several hundred thousand dollars from his cousin, another member of his network, with which he facilitated travel by AQI foreign fighters and supported insurgent activity targeting the U.S. military. *(See Ref 430)*

The Abu Ghadiyah network and others like to pump money into the local economy through the purchase of food and housing for fighters moving through safe houses. The networks additionally provide business opportunities for the local, smuggling-based economy and for bribes to local officials. The Abu Ghadiyah network reportedly maintained safe houses in Syria in Damascus and Latakia as well, investing in local economies in other parts of the country far from the Iraqi border. *(See Ref 431)*

This has both operational and economic consequences. Foreign fighter networks in Syria, for example, have direct and indirect, and positive and negative economic consequences on the country, the government, and on various elements of the Syrian populace, from the political, social, and religious elites to locals living in towns along the Syrian-Iraqi border. There is also an impact on Iraq, as the destination for foreign fighters, and on other countries in the region as well. Developing realistic strategies to contend with these networks depends first on obtaining a broad picture of what is happening. Such a picture has to include a proper understanding of the economic impact. Countries that host networks that expedite the movement of foreign fighters risk incurring both political and economic consequences because of such activities. Ultimately, violent extremists tolerated and supported by the host country may turn against it and come to pose a threat within the country or to the regime itself.

Following the October 26, 2008 U.S. cross-border raid which resulted in the killing of Abu Ghadiyah, Western journalists reported that the Syrian government cooperated with the United States in this raid. According to "The Sunday Times" of London, the Syrian regime was "complicit" in the raid because "Abu Ghadiyah was feared by the Syrians as an agent of Islamic fundamentalism who was hostile to the secular regime in Damascus." Such cooperation demonstrates the regime's willingness to crack down on foreign fighters when they threaten Syria's internal security. Doing so on an ongoing basis, however, is another matter. *(See Ref 432)*

On the other side, in what might be described as Syria from a jihadist perspective, an article entitled "al-Qa'ida al-Salbah" (the Solid Base) was posted on the jihadi website al-Faloja.com on July 21, 2009, by active al-Faloja contributor Abu Fadil al-Madi. The article urges Salafi-Jihadis to reconsider the importance of the political and strategic changes in Syria. The title of al-Madi's posting is borrowed from a 1988 article by Palestinian jihad ideologue Abdallah Azzam. *(See Ref 433)*

Al-Madi claims there was a kind of agreement between the jihadis and the Syrian regime, an "unannounced agreement to stop mutual hostilities," but the situation has changed since the latter part of 2005. It was then that the regime launched a campaign against "all the components of the Sunnis in Syria; the traditional religious groups (al-Khaznawi Naqshbandiya [a Sufi order] and al-Qubeisyat for example), the Shari'a institutions (al-Fatah Institute and Abu Nur Institute, in particular), and even against those who were considered to be close allies of the regime, working with all their strength as a trumpet [of the regime] (Muhammad Habash, as an example).As well, there is the fierce security campaign against the Salafi-Jihadi movement, which has escalated since [Fall 2005]". *(See Ref 434)*

Al-Madi's post asserts that there is an alliance between the "Syrian Alawite" regime and Ja'afri-dominated Iran.This alliance, based on the religious links of these two branches of Shi'ism (though not all Shiites recognise the Alawis as Shi'a), created the division in the Middle East between "the Shi'a crescent" and the "moderate axis." Despite these ties, the article claims the Syrian regime is pragmatic in terms of its relations with the United States, especially when it comes to coordination against jihadis. Washington's extradition to Syria of jihadi ideologue Abu Mus'ab al-Suri is an indication of the degree of this cooperation, claims the writer. *(Al-Madi refers to the Imami Shi'a's school of jurisprudence, named for its founder, Ja'afar al-Sadiq, the sixth Shi'a imam. The Alawis are a small but powerful minority in Syria, where most of the population is Sunni Muslim. There is also a small Christian community)*

Having concluded that the Syrian regime is working hard against Sunnis in general, the writer asks, "What is the Salafi-Jihadi movement's strategic vision for Syria? Will it remain a potential passage for supplies [to Iraq] or has the time come - or close to it - for a radical strategic change?"

Al-Madi's post states that the jihadi movement has concentrated its efforts on the Iraqi front since 2003 and "developed its political-strategic project by proclaiming the Islamic State of Iraq". However, the geographically sensitive location of Iraq and the international and regional strategic conflict over resources such as oil have pushed both the states of the moderate axis and the Shi'a crescent to try to contain the jihadi movement, penetrate its apparatus and "adapt" it by all means, "each in its own way." Accordingly, the Awakening councils (al-Sahwat) of Iraq were created by exploiting tribal relations with Jordan and Saudi Arabia. The councils also had connections to Syria, benefitting from the latter's close ties with some Iraqi Ba'athist elements. Al-Madi believes that such policies wasted the efforts of the jihadis since 2007 in a battle of attrition instead of a final battle with "the Crusaders and their supporters in Iraq."

Al-Madi continued by saying that "the fall of the Syrian regime or its collapse into chaos will have a direct impact on the neighbouring Sunnis in Iraq and Lebanon, and they will liberate themselves from the constraints on their movement and will find in Syria, a free, important space for movement and supply." In such a scenario the writer thinks that the "fall of Syria" will cut off land transport of Iranian land supplies to Hezbollah in Lebanon. This will equalise the strength of the Lebanese Sunnis with

Lebanon's Shi'a community. According to the author, Syria will serve as a backyard to support the fight against Americans in Iraq. "More importantly, the jihadi project will be in direct contact with Israel in an area which is ideal for guerrilla warfare, namely the occupied Golan Heights, without having to fight a costly battle to overcome the Shiite strongholds in southern Lebanon".

The writer concludes that "material interests" in Syria do not exist as they do in Iraq, meaning that international and regional actors will not become involved in armed conflict in Syria as they did in Iraq because any military invasion would be too costly. He also declared that "the planning for change relies on a solid popular base in Syria which never existed in Iraq. The Sunnis, whose rights are prejudiced, are the majority in Syria, while the dominant and well-armed Rafidah (rejectionist) Shi'a do not form more than a quarter of the Syrian population". *(See Ref 435)*

Despite the "unannounced agreement" between jihadis and the Syrian regime, the enmity between the parties goes back to the early 1980s, when clashes took place between Syrian authorities and the Muslim Brotherhood. The hostility exists not because there is a close relation between the jihadis and the Muslim Brotherhood, but because that era has played a significant role in shaping the way Islamists in the Arab world regard the Syrian regime. The negative perception of the Syrian Alawite regime can be seen in much of the Arab world's Islamist literature, but is particularly visible in the works of Abu Mus'ab al-Suri.

Al-Madi's article shows that the jihadis in the Levant region are concerned about the influence of Iran, based on their religious differences. The increasing numbers of Syrian fighters that have taken part in jihad activities in Iraq or in Lebanon since the invasion of Iraq in 2003 make the ideas presented above crucial.The Salafi-Jihadi movement is in decline in Iraq, but it follows that those jihadis returning to their own countries or new locations could become a potential security problem. *(See Ref 436)*

However, al-Qa'ida in Iraq has long benefited from a network of associates in Syria, which it uses to facilitate travel to Iraq. In a 2003 investigation of foreign fighter recruiters operating out of Italy, prosecutors noted that "Syria has functioned as a hub for an al-Qa'ida network." Transcripts of operatives' conversations "paint a detailed picture of overseers in Syria coordinating the movement of recruits and money" between cells in Europe and training camps in northern Iraq run by al-Qa'ida affiliated, Kurdish Ansar al-Islam.Syrian cell leaders facilitated travel for recruits and provided them with funding while European members gave false travel documents to recruits and fugitives and monitored their travel. Some of the recruits traveling to the Ansar camps stayed at the Ragdan Hotel in Aleppo for some time and later stopped in Damascus. Indeed, the Italian investigation revealed that operatives in Europe who worked for late al-Qa'ida leader Abu Mus'ab al-Zarqawi acted on the instructions of his lieutenants in and around Damascus and Aleppo. These men included Muhammad Majid (also known as Mullah Fuad), described as the "gatekeeper in Syria for volunteers intent on reaching Iraq". *(See Ref 437)*

In 2005, the U.S. Treasury Department designated Sulayman Khalid Darwish, who was operating out of Syria, a specially designated global terrorist for fundraising and recruiting on behalf of Zarqawi's network known then as "Jama'at at-Tawhid wa'l-Jihad" and al-Qa'ida. Described as a member of the Zarqawi organisation's advisory (shura) council and "one of the most prominent members of the Zarqawi network in Syria," Darwish forged documents, recruited and dispatched terrorists, and raised funds for the Zarqawi network. *(See Ref 438)*

Evidence of this network's continued presence in Syria came two years later in 2007. On December 6, the U.S. Treasury Department designated seven individuals, all based in Syria, for providing financial and operational support to the Iraqi insurgency. One individual was a member of AQI and the remaining six were former regime officials representing the Iraqi wing of the Syrian Baath party. Undersecretary of the U.S. Treasury Stuart Levey at that time insisted, "Syria must take action to deny safe haven to those supporting violence from within its borders". *(See Ref 439)*

The benefits of facilitation networks for terrorist and insurgent groups are clear: Without their support, terrorist organisations cannot function. The networks are essential elements of group efforts to finance and resource their expensive activities. As Gen. Raymond T. Odierno, commander of U.S. forces in Iraq, noted when commenting about payments for insurgents, "When we first got here, we believed it was about $100 to conduct an attack against coalition forces, and $500 if you're successful. We now believe it's somewhere between $1,000 and $2,000 if you conduct an attack, and $3,000 to $5,000 if you're successful." Still, it is not the cost of any individual attack but rather the larger infrastructure costs that drive insurgent expenses. A senior intelligence officer from the US Defence Intelligence Agency explained in 2005: "We believe terrorist and insurgent expenses are moderate and pose little significant restraints to armed groups in Iraq. In particular, arms and munitions costs are minimal -leaving us to judge that the bulk of the money likely goes toward international and local travel, food and lodging of fighters and families of dead fighters, bribery and pay - offs of governmental officials, families and clans; and possibly into the personal coffers of critical middle-men and prominent terrorist or insurgent leaders". *(See Ref 440, 441)*

While some facilitators are ideologically driven members of the group or like-minded followers, others are traditional criminal smugglers who do not differentiate between smuggling foodstuffs or foreign fighters across the Syrian-Iraqi border. A West Point review of the Sinjar documents concluded, "Large groups of people-such as foreign fighters-cross the border in remote locations, often using the same tracks and trails as the livestock smugglers. In fact, the same ring of smuggling guides will often move both livestock and human beings." This untidy mix of insurgents, terrorists, professional smugglers, and corrupt government officials provides multiple opportunities for financial gain for all parties involved. *(See Ref 442)*

Consider the case of Fawzi al-Rawi.In late 2007, the U.S. Treasury Department designated al-Rawi -a leader of the Iraqi wing of the Syrian Baath party- for providing financial and material support to al-Zarqawi's al-Qa'ida in Iraq (AQI). The extent of the Syrian role in al-Rawi's activities is noteworthy. Al-Rawi was appointed to his position in the Syrian Baath party by President Bashar al-Assad in 2003. According to U.S. Treasury, the Iraqi wing of the Syrian Baath party "has since provided significant funding to Iraqi insurgents at al-Rawi's direction." Indeed, Treasury noted that al-Rawi "is supported financially by the Syrian government and has close ties to Syrian intelligence." With the authorisation of the Syrian regime, al-Rawi twice met with a former commander of Saddam Hussein's Army of Muhammad (Jaysh Muhammad) in 2004 and told the commander his group would receive material aid from Syria. In 2005, al-Rawi "facilitated the provision of $300,000 to members of AQI" as well as providing AQI vehicle-borne improvised explosive devices (IEDs), rifles, and suicide bombers. In meetings in Iraq with senior AQI representatives in September 2005, al-Rawi and AQI leaders discussed operational issues, including attacks against the U.S. embassy and assaults in the international zone. *(See Ref 443)*

Ultimately, a truly successful insurgency can become such a successful fundraising enterprise that it controls sufficient funds to finance activities beyond the immediate area of operations. Thus, in a July 2005 letter to al-Zarqawi, Ayman al-Zawahiri, al-Qa'ida's second in command, humbly asked the leader of AQI if he could spare "a payment of approximately one hundred thousand" because "many of the lines have been cut off". Additionally, the robust network can be used to transport fighters, money, and goods to other potential jihad locales such as Lebanon, Yemen, and Somalia. The implication, of course, is that AQI was by then very well funded; the result - at least in part - of large subventions arriving via Syria. *(See Ref 444)*

One reason AQI and other insurgents in Iraq have been so successful is because their facilitation networks have successfully raised and transferred funds, recruited and transported fighters, and procured and moved weapons and goods - mostly through Syria. Shutting down these networks and starving the insurgency of its supply of materiel, funds, and manpower is a critical component of any successful counterinsurgency campaign. But convincing and enabling Syria to take the necessary steps to shut down the smuggling pipelines will require something more than just economic sanctions. As the Obama administration pursues its engagement strategy with Syria, closing the pipelines perhaps more than anything else will provide the clearest yardstick by which to measure Syrian reciprocity to the administration's outstretched hand.

To be sure, convincing the Assad regime to forgo sponsorship of insurgent and terrorist groups as part of a policy of engagement will be difficult. Given the relatively strong return on minimal financial investment, Syrian support for insurgents will remain an attractive option for Damascus so long as it continues to be a viable and productive means of furthering the regime's domestic and foreign policy goals. Given the financial interests of local and national officials, cracking down on established smuggling networks (which would threaten the regular payments that supplement officials' income) is no easy task. As part of its engagement strategy, Washington must develop a multifaceted approach to the problem posed by the foreign fighter networks. *(See Ref 445)*

However, Syria may be one of the countries that jihadis could aim to turn into a new front after benefitting from its use as a passage to Iraq for the last seven years, and the uprising which is occurring across the Syrian cities may open the door for the Islamists to play a role to overthrow Assad regime and to get a place on the political table in Damascus.

While Lebanon and Syria have different problems with Islamic salafists what is the situation in Jordan?

The Islamist movement in Jordan has a history and heritage as old as that of the Hashemite regime itself. While Jordan's main Islamist political party-the Islamic Action Front (Jabhat al-Amal al-Islami or IAF)-was not legalised until the early 1990s, Jordan's Muslim Brotherhood (al-Ikhwan al-Muslimun) maintained a functional relationship with the Hashemite monarchy especially throughout the reign of King Hussein (1953-1999), who tolerated the Ikhwan as a loyal opposition. Indeed the relationship between the Muslim Brotherhood and the Hashemite monarchy predates even the reign of King Hussein. Most strikingly, Islamist activism in Jordanian politics has for more than 60 years emphasised reform, moderation, and democratic participation, rather than revolution, radicalism, and militancy.

The Muslim Brotherhood was founded in 1928 in Egypt by the Islamist activist Hasan al-Banna as we mentioned before. The organisation quickly developed branches throughout the Arab world, calling for a reassertion of Islam into public life in both government and society. While the Muslim Brotherhood established a presence in almost every Arab country, the individual organisations remained mainly autonomous, responding to local and national circumstances. In the case of Jordan, the Muslim Brotherhood was established officially in the kingdom in 1945. From the very beginning, the Brotherhood made clear that its agenda was Islamist but not militant, and this drew the recognition of the state itself. In 1946, King Abdallah I officially recognised the Muslim Brotherhood as a charitable society in Jordan, and the king actually presided over the ceremony himself.

King Abdallah I, even included Muslim Brotherhood Secretary Abd al-Hakim al-Din in his governing cabinet, making this early linkage between the Brotherhood and the Hashemites institutionally clear. From the outset, the Muslim Brotherhood established a pattern of loyal opposition to the Hashemite regime. By emphasising reform rather than revolution, the Brotherhood saw itself in partnership with the Jordanian state. As the regime consolidated its rule within Jordan, its moderate political positions, pro-Western foreign policy, and conservative monarchical institutions immediately served as a target for emerging Cold War ideological rifts, as well as emerging regional nationalist and revolutionary tensions. Thus from the perspective of the ruling regime, this de facto, if not de jure, relationship between the monarchy and its Islamist loyal opposition was intended in part to provide a counter to left-leaning secular oppositional trends ranging from Ba'thism to Nasserism to Communism. *(See Ref 446)*

While the regime attempted to curb leftist, secular, and pan-Arabist political tendencies, the monarchy simultaneously permitted its Islamist opposition to flourish. This allowed the Muslim Brotherhood to become by far the best organised group in the Jordanian opposition. *(See Ref 447)*

In doing so, the moderation of the Muslim Brotherhood also acted as a counter to more radical trends within Islamism, such as the Hizb al-Tahrir (Liberation Party) that had espoused a more revolutionary brand of Islamism, particularly in the 1960s and 1970s. In an effort to enhance its own Islamic credentials, the Hashemite regime continuously emphasised the direct lineage of the royal family from that of Prophet Muhammad. The Brotherhood too has at times emphasised this level of Islamic legitimacy, in contrast to the many secular, leftist, or nationalist regimes that emerged in the Arab world in neighbouring Egypt, Iraq, and Syria. *(See Ref 446)*

Beyond more direct political or governmental activism, however, the Muslim Brotherhood has taken very seriously its role as a charitable organisation. With regime approval, the Brotherhood established the Islamic Centre Charity Society in 1963, and was able to tap into funding generated from the oil economies of the wealthy and socially conservative Arab Gulf monarchies. For several decades now, the Brotherhood has presided over a range of non-governmental organisations (NGOs). Indeed, the only organisation that patronises and sponsors more social and charitable organisations is the Hashemite royal family itself. The Brotherhood, meanwhile, established across the country an array of schools and health clinics, including the Islamic Hospital in central Amman. *(See Ref 446)*

While it is clear that relations between the Hashemites and the Brotherhood are almost as old as the Jordanian state itself, this does not mean that the two sides have always agreed. The Muslim Brotherhood did indeed support the monarchy through its wars with Israel, its foiling of various nationalist coup attempts, and even the Jordanian civil war between the Hashemite army and the guerrilla forces of the Palestine Liberation Organisation (PLO) in 1970-1971. The Brotherhood walked a slightly finer line during the various political upheavals triggered by International Monetary Fund (IMF) economic austerity programs, such as the "bread riots" of 1989 and 1996. *(See Ref 448)*

Yet at other times the Brotherhood has directly opposed Hashemite policies, even while maintaining its de facto status as loyal opposition. The Brotherhood adamantly opposed Anwar Sadat's separate peace treaty with Israel, for example, and viewed the Hashemite regime as too mild in its own opposition to Sadat's move. When King Hussein resolutely stood by the shah of Iran in 1979 even as the Iranian Islamic Revolution swept the monarchy away, the Brotherhood again objected to the official Jordanian stance. This rift actually deepened following the 1980 Iraqi invasion of Iran, as Jordan supported Saddam Hussein's Ba'thist Iraq in its war with the Iranian revolutionary regime. For Hussein, the prospect of an Islamist movement successfully toppling a conservative pro-Western monarch was positively chilling. Yet for the brotherhood, opposing the only successful Islamist regime in the region was unconscionable

In more contemporary politics, the major policy rift between the Islamist movement and the Hashemite state has centered on Jordan's own peace treaty with Israel signed in 1994. The Islamist movement adamantly opposed the treaty at the time, and in the years afterward its opposition only grew. The Brotherhood became a leading part of the broader "anti-normalisation" movement in Jordan; if the opposition could not prevent the treaty, it could and did manage largely to prevent normalisation of society-to-society relations. Since Islamists had tended to win democratic elections for the leadership positions within most of Jordan's professional associations (for doctors, engineers, lawyers, and pharmacists, for example), the Islamist movement was institutionally positioned to maintain its self-declared ban on working with Israeli counterparts. *(See Ref 449)*

However, Jordan's program of political liberalisation began in earnest in 1989, as a direct response to widespread political unrest in the kingdom. An International Monetary Fund (IMF) economic austerity program, imposed in an attempt to improve the kingdom's declining economy, had triggered rioting throughout the country. The depth and breadth of the political upheaval had clearly shaken the regime itself, which responded with what amounted to "defensive democratisation." King Hussein fired the unpopular Prime Minister Zayd al-Rifa'i, shuffled the governing cabinet, and announced the return of elections for parliament for the first time since martial law had been declared in the wake of the 1967 War with Israel. Jordan's political liberalisation thereafter included several rounds of democratic parliamentary elections (1989, 1993, 1997, 2003, and 2007), the lifting of martial law (1991), legalisation of political parties (1992), and several rounds of revisions regarding government control of media, press, and publications.Given its longstanding relationship with the regime, and its status as virtually the only officially tolerated form of opposition, the Muslim Brotherhood was perfectly positioned to benefit from the new atmosphere of openness. As parliamentary and electoral life returned to the kingdom, the Brotherhood was able to capitalise on decades-worth of organisation. *(See Ref 478, 479, 480)*

Yet beyond the Brotherhood, Jordan also has a long tradition of independent Islamist activism in addition to that of organised groups such as the Ikhwan, or their contemporary political party : the Islamic Action Front (IAF). Independent Islamists have tended to resist joining organisations like the Muslim Brotherhood, or parties like the IAF, which they often accuse of being co-opted by the regime. Among the most well-known independent Islamist activists is the outspoken Layth Shubaylat, who was among those independents serving in the 1989-1993 Parliament. Shubaylat has argued that "institutional" Islamism is effectively a tool of the regime, which thereby has managed to "tame" the Muslim Brotherhood. *(See Ref 446)*

While the Muslim Brotherhood and the IAF are the best organised, most recognisable faces of Islamism in Jordan, there also remain more subtle and even underground forms. Jordan's Salafiyya movement, for example, has grown steadily since the 1980s.In fact, the rise of Islamism in Jordan was accelerated by mounting economic difficulties and diminishing employment opportunities, the disarray of Arab nationalism following defeat in the 1967 Arab-Israeli war, and the enhanced influence of an increasingly prosperous and proselytising Saudi Arabia. The 1979 Soviet invasion of Afghanistan provided a timely outlet, as devout young Sunni Muslims - encouraged by the success of the recent (Shiite) Islamic revolution in Iran, yet simultaneously keen to keep Shiism itself in check - responded to calls from religious leaders to join the holy war against the Soviets.

One of the leading proponents of this war was a Jordanian of Palestinian origin, Abdallah Azzam, who developed the notion of international participation in jihad as we explained before (Chapter 5). Azzam left his teaching position at a Jeddah university and moved to Pakistan in the early 1980s. There, he founded Maktab al-Khidmat li al-Mujahideen al-'Arab (the Arab Mujahideen Services Bureau or Office), providing assistance to would-be fighters on their way to Afghanistan. He became an increasingly active propagandist for a pan-Islamic jihad, writing books on the subject and travelling around the Arab world to enlist support for the mujahideen. Azzam's efforts - funded and supported by the U.S., UK, Saudi Arabia, China and others - were largely responsible for the influx of foreign (predominantly Muslim Arab) mujahideen into Afghanistan.

Most of the Jordanians who joined the mujahideen appear to have done so more out of economic opportunism than religious conviction. Generally poorly educated, they had few other prospects; becoming a mujahideen reportedly meant receiving monthly stipends of hundreds of dollars, making it a viable and attractive alternative to remaining at home. While Saudi Arabia openly encouraged its young men to go and fight, the Jordanian regime, concerned about growing Islamist influence and happy enough to see its Islamists depart, turned a blind eye to those who left, while keeping watch on those who returned. Unofficial estimates put the number of Jordanians who joined the mujahideen in the 1980s in the low hundreds. *(See Ref 450,451, 452)*

Saudi Arabia became a major transit point for those heading to Afghanistan, simultaneously providing an introduction to the country's fundamentalist Wahhabi culture and religious teachers. But it was the experience in Afghanistan that most profoundly affected the mujahideen, and it is there that they received ideological grounding in a fundamentalist, violent and militaristic worldview. A decade of fighting was enough to create a substantial, well organised and well trained army, a strong network of contacts, and a new way of life. Samih Khreis, a Jordanian defence lawyer for Islamists, explained: "The mujahideen for the most part were supposed to live like warrior monks, cut off from the rest of the world, believing that they were fighting to protect Islam". *(See Ref 453, 454)*

With the withdrawal of Soviet troops and the end of the war in 1989, the fighting factions begun to fragment, and the mujahideen drifted back home. In Jordan, according to Khreis, they "became personae non gratae, without marketable skills. There was no effort to rehabilitate them. Ten years are a long time to be called a mujahid, and suddenly you are a terrorist. These people were poor and simple rather than evil". The returnees included a man who would later gain great notoriety: Ahmad Fadhil Nazzal al-Khalaileh, better known as Abu Mus'ab al-Zarqawi. *(See Ref 455)*

Their return in the early 1990s coincided with one of the most significant shifts in Jordanian society in decades. Some 250,000 Palestinians had recently arrived in the country, having been expelled from Kuwait during the 1991 Gulf War as a result of their leadership's support for the Iraqi invasion.

This influx of refugees triggered a significant societal transformation. Largely due to their conspicuous consumption, behaviour mostly unknown within the traditionally conservative and discreet society, the relative prosperity of many Kuwaiti Palestinians highlighted the already existing gap between rich and poor. They also brought with them more liberal social mores, from more revealing women's clothing to other more relaxed forms of behaviour. According to Abdallah Abu Rumman, a Jordanian journalist, the arrival of liberal, Westernised Kuwaiti Palestinians made the growing wealth of the Jordanian bourgeoisie more visible and shocked the Afghan returnees. "They were disgusted by the decadence they saw when they returned. Is this what they had been fighting a holy war for?" *(See Ref 456)*

Of the 250,000 new arrivals, some 160,000 of the poorer settled in Zarqa, a bleak satellite town east of Amman. Its mix of Trans-Jordanians, Circassians and Palestinians from the al-Ruseifeh refugee camp and from Kuwait, combined with the lack of a strong tribal structure, turned it into an ideal recruitment ground for Salafi-inspired groups that offered a sense of identity and common cause to an uprooted community.

In Jordan, a mainstream Salafi current has existed since the 1960s, introduced by young men who had studied in Syria, Egypt or Lebanon. Its key exponent was a Syrian scholar, Nasr al-Din al-Albani (1909-1999), who inspired many followers in the 1980s. He was a frequent visitor to the Kingdom throughout the 1970s, invited by students he had met in Damascus; in the wake of President Assad's violent 1979 crackdown on the Islamist movement, al-Albani was expelled, and he relocated to Jordan.

Once there, he preached his message of "correcting" Islam from his base in Zarqa, but his ability to draw large crowds quickly led the authorities to ban him from public speaking. Rather than curtail the movement, however, this pushed it underground, spawning an informal network upon which it continues to rely. Jordan's Salafism remains highly unstructured; meetings are normally organised by word of mouth and held in private homes, with most recruitment occurring between close friends and family members. *(See Ref 457, 480)*

In the 1990s, under the combined effect of the growth of Islamist movements region-wide and the mobilisation of jihadi energies for the war in Afghanistan, salafism in Jordan developed into three basic trends: traditionalist (taqlidi), reformist (islahi) and violent (jihadi). The traditionalists, who had their start with al-Albani, were generally hostile to Islamist political activism, adhering to the injunction of obedience even to an unjust Muslim ruler. Theirs was a strictly religious, not political, movement. The jihadis arose in opposition to them with the preachings of Abu Muhammad al-Maqdisi from 1992 onward that emphasised the need to overthrow "impious" regimes through violent means. In 1995-1996, Salafis of a political bent who rejected the use of violence established the reformist branch, espousing peaceful opposition to the secular regime in Jordan. *(See Ref 458)*

American scholar Quintan Wiktorowicz has argued that while the Muslim Brotherhood and IAF rely on formal organisation and participation in political parties, professional associations, and charities, the Salafi movement has instead relied on informal networks for recruitment and activism. He further argues that many of Jordan's religious scholars, the ulama, are themselves Salafists. The informal networks, meanwhile, allow Salafists to at least attempt to continue their activism under the radar of state surveillance. Still, despite the rise in Salafiyya ideas and activity, most of Jordan's Islamist movement remains more mainstream, reformist, and democratic, while the major terrorist threats have come largely from foreign al-Qa'ida militants. *(See Ref 481)*

With the Jordanian government either unable or unwilling to rehabilitate them, and the country's all-pervasive General Intelligence Directory (GID) first detaining and then keeping an eye on them, Afghan Arabs found that they had won their war but lost its aftermath. Facing serious reintegration problems and a still-depressed job market, they often chose one of three options: return to Afghanistan, join the Muslim diaspora in Europe or go underground and try to recreate the networks they had developed in Afghanistan to attack the "al-kuffar" (un-believers) - in this case the Hashemites.

Those who remained in Jordan found fruitful recruitment opportunities. The privatisation drive that followed a 1992 agreement with the International Monetary Fund generated several unintended consequences, especially for Trans-Jordanians, who predominate in the public sector. Cuts in government jobs removed an important safety net, provoked a sharp rise in unemployment and harmed many who once held sought-after bureaucratic positions. Many of the newly unemployed were attracted to preachers who gave voice to their disaffection. Privatisation and job cuts also eroded the power of (Trans-Jordanian) tribal leaders who used to dispense patronage in the form of public sector employment; some of these leaders, together with their followers, also turned to religion. Reduced investment in the public sector, including education, prompted parents who could afford it to send their children to private schools, the least expensive of which offered an Islamic curriculum. *(See Ref 459)*

Other events heightened simmering anger. Iraq's invasion of Kuwait and subsequent defeat at the hands of an alliance of Western and Arab forces was experienced by many Jordanians - who manifested great sympathy for Saddam Hussein - as yet another humiliation. The onset of negotiations between Jordan and Israel, culminating in the 1994 peace treaty, was another blow. As Hazem al-Amin, who conducted an in-depth investigation of jihadi groups in Jordan, put it, normalisation of relations with Israel "crowned the series of Jordanian and Palestinian frustrations". *(See Ref 460)*

Abu Muhammad al-Maqdisi, who had settled in Jordan in 1992, began travelling around the country with a small group of supporters, lecturing against the regime, democracy and elections, as well as distributing copies of his book Mullat Ibrahim (Ibrahim's Creed), which quickly became the seminal work for the country's jihadis. By 1993, small underground militant organisations had appeared, comprised for the most part of Afghan Arabs. They were bolstered by support from some of the country's youth, angered by steps to normalise relations with Israel and feeling abandoned by Jordan's mainstream Muslim Brotherhood, which refused to clash openly with the government over the issue.While these groups began to launch small-scale attacks against "un-Islamic" targets, fire-bombing cinemas and liquor stores, they lacked the logistical or organisational capacity to strike at the regime itself.

Until that time, Jordan had contained the threat of violent Islamist militancy typically by relying on the largely coopted Muslim Brotherhood to recruit politically - inclined Islamists. The Brotherhood in Jordan incorporates all Sunni Muslim schools (madhaheb), including Salafis and Sufis, but, with its middle-class base, it has become a party of peaceful political opposition that may protest government policies (for example, the peace treaty and normalisation with Israel) but fully accepts, and embraces, Hashemite rule. Those seeking to challenge the regime either physically or ideologically first had to confront the Brotherhood and, as of 1989, its political arm, the Islamic Action Front (IAF). As a result, public support was diverted away from more militant groups.

However, the growth of the Salafi movement came at a difficult time for the Brotherhood, which sought to combine its roles as supporter of the regime and opponent of the peace treaty with Israel. Moreover, the Salafis drew support mainly from the lower classes, while the Muslim Brotherhood retained an essentially middle class membership. As one observer put it, the Salafi movement "tends to pick up the dregs of society-people who are schooled in the mosques rather than at the university.While they do not have a strong influence in society as a whole, they maintain a very tight grip on their supporters". *(See Ref 461)*

Despite its proven ideological flexibility and ability to incorporate a wide range of Islamist groups and personalities, the Brotherhood could not bring the Salafis into the fold. The emergence of a militant Islamist grouping that, unlike the Brotherhood, refused to deal with the establishment, led to a schism within the Brotherhood itself. Two competing blocks emerged, one more traditionalist and peaceful, referred to as the doves (Hama'em), the other more militant, known as the hawks (Suqour). The former consisted mostly of Trans-Jordanians, the latter of Jordanians of Palestinian extraction who supported violent resistance to the Israeli occupation and, in this, came closer to the views of al-Maqdisi (himself a Jordanian of Palestinian origin). Despite obvious differences in outlook, however, the legitimacy and resources that membership in the Brotherhood provided kept the two currents inside the movement.

In addition to internal friction, the Brotherhood suffered from its ambiguous political stance. While it participated in elections and has had representatives in two successive parliaments, it has yet to formulate a clear and effective opposition role. Unable to provide a credible alternative to the status quo or articulate a distinct program, the Brotherhood and the Islamic Action Front (IAF) saw their support erode significantly. Young people seeking to challenge the status quo were drawn elsewhere, almost by default. "For those who are disillusioned with the IAF and the Muslim Brotherhood, there is no real alternative. And so they are pushed into the arms of extremist groups". *(See Ref 462)*

Al-Maqdisi's ideology and tactics proved appealing magnets to a growing number of disaffected youth. Adnan Abu Odeh put it this way: "The [Salafi] Islamists offer an active response to the humiliations to which people feel subjected in their own lives or vicariously through the suffering of Palestinians and now also Iraqis. People have no way to react, to stop the insults, the injustice. The Islamist groups offer a form of therapy by doing what the masses cannot or will not do: attack the authorities. And they end up enjoying a lot of silent popular support, even in the face of attacks on innocent people, which are seen as balancing the deaths resulting from Israeli incursions and so forth". *(See Ref 463)*

Although during the early 1990s there had been outbreaks of unrest in southern cities such as Ma'an and Karak over hikes in the price of bread and the cost of fuel (as well as in Palestinian refugee camps over moves to normalise relations with Israel), Amman's largest satellite towns Salt and Zarqa (and to a lesser extent the northern city of Irbid) became focal points for the jihadi Salafi movement. Referred to as the "birthplace and capital of the jihadi Salafi movement in Jordan", Zarqa is an impoverished working-class suburb of 480,000 inhabitants.It is the hometown of al-Zarqawi, Abdallah Azzam and Abu Muhammad al-Maqdisi, and one of its first Salafi preachers was Sheikh Nasr al-Din al-Albani. *(See Ref 464)*

In the late 1990s, more than 500 men from Zarqa and the adjacent al-Ruseifeh refugee camp have joined the Taliban in their fight against the Northern Alliance in Afghanistan. In 1999, after his release from prison, al-Zarqawi followed them. In December 2004, more than 300 fighters from the Zarqa area were said to be in Afghanistan, Iraq or Chechnya, and 63 reportedly were in jail, in the U.S. prison at Guantánamo in Cuba or in Jordan.

Despite Zarqa's role in the development of the jihadi Salafi movement, as of May 2005 more men from Salt than from Zarqa reportedly had been killed, or died in suicide operations, under al-Zarqawi's leadership in Iraq. In March 2005, the town acquired instant notoriety – and caused intense embarrassment to the government – when the family of a suicide bomber reportedly celebrated their son's 28 February attack in Hilla in which some 125 (Shiite) civilians died. *(See Ref 465)*

Since the state's establishment, Salt, a town of roughly 80,000 directly west of Amman and increasingly one of its suburbs, has been the traditional home of the ruling elite, the feeder town for army officers and one of the monarchy's mainstays.Many government leaders and other senior politicians come from there.The introduction of political and economic reforms in the 1990s hit the town hard, however, diminishing the power of the traditional elites and job opportunities in the administration.

The rise in unemployment exacerbated tensions between a powerful Muslim Brotherhood tradition and mores that were highly liberal by Jordanian standards. Salt was considered the country's most liberal town but it was beset by serious alcohol and drug abuse problems.In the mid-1990s, it experienced an about-face, as previously unruly teenagers converted to a conservative and more militant brand of Islam, harassing fellow towns-people with demonstrations of piety rather than drunken antics. As former IAF Secretary-General Abd-al-Latif Arabiyat noted: "they didn't cause less trouble, but they were now attacking people with Islam, which meant it was harder to criticise them". *(See Ref 466)*

This newfound religious fervour initially was sparked by Abd-al-Fatah al-Hiyeri, a Trans-Jordanian cleric who preached against the regime in general and growing Palestinian influence in particular.Given the growing number of disaffected, unemployed young men, his vitriolic statements found a receptive audience.

This cleric's status as Salt's chief agitator was soon usurped by al-Maqdisi and al-Zarqawi, who were transferred to the town's prison in 1997. From that unlikely base, they trumped his narrow vision with the breadth of their agenda and the scope of their anti-regime activities. Al-Zarqawi had been arrested in 1994 on charges of possessing illegal weapons and belonging to a banned organisation and received a fifteen-year sentence; al-Maqdisi was detained in 1996 on similar charges. Already, during their detention in the south, they had substantially increased membership in "Bay'at al-Imam", recruiting especially among "Afghan Jordanians" but also ordinary criminals; Salt prison, with its flexible visiting policy and town-centre location, brought them into contact with many more potential recruits, mostly petty criminals who rotated in and out of jail. Al-Maqdisi was able to publish and distribute his essays from jail, further spreading his message and bolstering recruitment.

Detainees disillusioned by a system they felt had already failed them and was unlikely to welcome them upon their release were ideal targets for a discourse that denounced a corrupt and decadent society. According to Muhammad Abu Rumman, "Salt became the perfect breeding ground. After al-Maqdisi arrived, the refrain [among disaffected youths] became, 'the problem isn't us, it is the situation'". Jihadis also took advantage of the lack of credibility of government-sponsored clerics and the Muslim Brotherhood. According to a local politician, "the Awqaf [religious endowment] sends weak imams with strong Mukhabarat [intelligence service] links but little religious authority", who often read the same sermon throughout Salt on any given friday. *(See Ref 467, 468)*

The authorities eventually clamped down on al-Maqdisi and al-Zarqawi, restricting visiting hours, searching and monitoring anyone who came to see them, then moving them to a small complex in al-Balqa, on the outskirts of Amman, where they separated Islamist prisoners from other detainees.

Al-Maqdisi, al-Zarqawi and some 30 of their new recruits were released from prison in 1999 as part of a general amnesty declared shortly after King Abdallah's accession to the throne (others had already been released, having served out their sentences). Following their discharge, however, many of the group's members found the General Intelligence Directory (GID) pressure combined with censure from their local community unbearable. They left the country, either returning to Afghanistan to fight alongside the Taliban or joining the new jihadi struggle in Chechnya. Al-Zarqawi, unemployed and without other sources of income, went to Pakistan and then Afghanistan. To the authorities, the departure of al-Zarqawi and his group was "a cause for comfort". *(See Ref 469, 470, 471)*

Early allies, al-Zarqawi and al-Maqdisi fell out in jail, reportedly as a result of al-Zarqawi's increased assertiveness as the leader. Once al-Zarqawi was released and left the country, al-Maqdisi began openly to criticise him, alluding in particular to his turn away from support for Palestinian resistance as a jihadi priority, but their differences were first of all personal and doctrinal: al-Maqdisi opposed the use of violence in Jordan, while al-Zarqawi advocated it.

Both retained significant followings, especially after the U.S. invaded Iraq but al-Zarqawi's reputation grew as a result of extensive media coverage and descriptions of him as "America's most wanted man".

While al-Zarqawi returned to Afghanistan in 1999, al-Maqdisi remained in Jordan to capitalise on the work already done but was re-arrested six months later. The scale of the charges against him this time and the size of the group eventually arrested suggested the progress they had made in jail in recruitment, organisation and capability. On 28 March 2000, 28 defendants were put on trial (including thirteen in absentia) on charges of planning attacks against U.S. and Israeli targets in Jordan, dubbed as the Millennium plot. U.S. authorities directly linked the Jordanian plot to two other attacks scheduled to take place on American soil. *(See Ref 472)*

Al-Zarqawi, for his part, believed he could run his jihad by remote control. In Afghanistan he joined forces with Osama bin Laden, but he soon fell out with both the Taliban and al-Qa'ida, whose members in his view "were not sufficiently pious and did not adhere strictly enough to the Islamic laws of punishment. He was more extreme than the Taliban". To avoid damaging debates over doctrinal differences (al-Qa'ida was focused on the "far enemy" -the U.S.- while al-Zarqawi preferred to target the "near enemy"- the Hashemites in Jordan) and to accommodate al-Zarqawi's penchant for independent operations, Taliban leader Mullah Omar asked him to establish a mujahideen camp near the Afghan town of Herat. Here al-Zarqawi blossomed, forming "al-Tawhid wa al-Jihad" and training recruits primarily from the Levant: Syria, Lebanon, Palestine and Jordan.

According to the journalist Hazem al-Amin, it is this camp that al-Zarqawi supporters "repeatedly mention in the historical narrative of their movement" as the place where his jihadi trajectory truly took off and as "the main sinew" in the structure of his current organisation. The camp attracted some 100 recruits and while its initial aim was to overthrow the Jordanian regime and attack Israel, al-Zarqawi broadened his agenda to include attacks on Israeli and Jewish targets in Europe after a number of recruits refused to return to Jordan. *(See Ref 473,474)*

Al-Zarqawi's absence and al-Maqdisi's incarceration led to an apparent downturn in jihadi activity in Jordan over the next two years and a renaissance of the Islah, or reformist, branch of Salafism.However, the events of 11 September 2001, the ensuing U.S. "war on terror" and the invasion and occupation of first Afghanistan and then Iraq effectively acted as a call to arms for jihadi groups. The General Intelligence Directory (GID) had frequently looked to the traditional Salafi movement to curb jihadi tendencies, hoping that militants would follow the religious teachings of leading traditionalist clerics such as Ali al-Halabi, Abu Shaqra or al-Albani. But in the polarised atmosphere that emerged, the strategy appeared to have run its course.Even the founder of the reformist current, Abu Anas al-Shami went to fight in Iraq, where he was killed.

The rivalry between al-Zarqawi and al-Maqdisi continued, fuelled by unresolved doctrinal differences. Following his release from prison in 2005, al-Maqdisi gave an interview to the Qatary TV "Al-Jazeera" in which he criticised al-Zarqawi for the mass killing of fellow Muslims in Iraq, arguing that "the indiscriminate attacks might distort the true jihad". Al-Zarqawi, by contrast, has expressly called for the killing of Shiites, whom he refers to as apostates. *(See Ref 475, 476)*

This debate has come on top of one within jihadi circles over the wisdom of carrying out attacks inside the Kingdom. Al-Maqdisi had already expressed his opposition to attacks inside Jordan, though he appears to have been motivated by concern that jihadi ranks were infiltrated by the GID, following the foiled "chemical" attack in Amman in April 2004, blaming al-Zarqawi who was taking risk of using Jordanians in an operation in the country. As Hazem al-Amin reports, al-Zarqawi's supporters in Jordan "realise that the Jordanian security forces have infiltrated their ranks in a major way.....Many of them say that they are with Abu Mus'ab [al-Zarqawi] in his war in Iraq but do not support operations inside Jordan". A Zarqawi supporter, al-Amin continues, told him that "Abu Mus'ab erred in asking Jayousi [the alleged leader of the thwarted "chemical" attack] to carry out the...operation against Jordanian intelligence [headquarters], because the mujahideen do not have the capability to open additional fronts".

On the 9th of November 2005 a horrifying suicide attacks carried out by al-Zarkawi organisation with Iraqi members against three hotels in Amman-with a toll of 60 dead and over 100 wounded - drove home two important messages. No security apparatus, however efficient, can prevent each and every attack by a person prepared to die as they kill others. And any security response must be complemented by a genuine opening of the political system and more equally shared economic opportunity if Jordan is to minimise the risk of further attacks and instability.

However, on the 7th of June 2006, al-Zarkawi was killed by an American strike near the city of Baquba in Iraq, while the Jordan authority put Abu Muhammad al-Maqdisi in Jail on the 29 of September 2009.

For the time being the Jihadi movement in Jordan became quiet while the Muslim Brotherhood returned to play a big role in the political life. They took the opportunity to press on reform which can open the political system and which was promised by King Abdallah II. Based on that, they boycotted the November 2010 parliamentary elections and put some conditions to move forward to cooperate with the government. But until now it seems that the government is not ready yet to meet their conditions despite the King's meeting with the Brotherhood leadership in early February 2011, after the Tunisian and Egyptian uprisings, in which he promised to make some reforms.

However, Jordanian government officials often argue that any restrictive measures are actually quite moderate (when compared to most other states in the Middle East) and that they are simply prudent given the extreme circumstances in the region. In contrast, many in the Islamist movement feel that the longstanding cooperation between reformist Islamism and the monarchy may be in decline. These vastly different interpretations are a key issue for the future of Jordanian politics, as they will in turn affect the policies and tactics of both government and opposition in Jordan. There is, in short, a danger here that the regime's various deliberalisation moves in recent years (all made in the name of national security) may ultimately serve to alienate the moderates who make up the overwhelming majority of Jordan's Islamist activists, unwittingly empowering the heretofore smaller but more militant alternatives.

CHAPTER ELEVEN

THE MAGHREB: THE ISLAMISTS THREAT

The North African countries of the Maghreb hosts some of the most active and powerful fundamentalist Muslim movements. Indeed, with the exception of the Iran-Tajikistan-Afghanistan-Pakistan area, North Africa may be one of the regions of the world with the greatest potential for the Islamic fundamentalists. In fact, the Maghreb countries encompass a wide spectrum of beliefs in Islam. Since their independence, governments in these countries have not permitted political Islam to expand; instead, they have sought to contain and control Islam in their societies and polities. Nonetheless, in recent years, the growth of Islamic fundamentalism has proved to be a threat to the stability of each of these countries.

The Maghreb consists of Morocco, Algeria, and Tunisia. More than 95 percent of the population of the region is Sunni Muslim, although there are wide variations in belief and practice. Sufi traditions and saints are a prominent feature of the Maghreb, as are syncretic and mystical interpretations of Islam. Culturally, the countries of North Africa are distinguished by their significant Berber populations, and this heritage exerts a strong influence upon their linguistic traditions and political organisation. Berbers form approximately 40 percent of the population in Morocco, 25 percent in Algeria, and more than 5 percent in Tunisia. Morocco also has a small Jewish community. Despite the strong Berber heritage, a large proportion of the Maghreb's population now identifies itself as Arab and is increasingly drawn to Arab culture.

Islam entered the Maghreb in the late seventh century, facing fierce resistance from the nomadic Berber population. The Arab conqueror Uqba Ibn Nafi'h established an encampment at present-day Kairouan, in Tunisia, and expanded throughout North Africa from there. His forces drove the Byzantines from their hold on Carthage and established an Islamic community under the Umayyad dynasty in their place. Uqba Ibn Nafi'h is believed to have spread Islam to Morocco by making a 5,000-kilometer march around the country in 681. Moulay Idriss (788–793), a Shi'ite refugee who traced his lineage to the son-in-law of the prophet Muhammad, later established the existing Alawite monarchy in Morocco. Over the centuries, Islam in the region absorbed traditional local beliefs as well as Islamic trends from abroad, such as Sufism. Islamic beliefs in the Maghreb today span Sufi and syncretic traditions, traditional Sunni doctrine, and more fundamentalist Salafi thought, as well as many other variations in philosophy and practice. Most Berbers belong to the Maliki's school of Islamic jurisprudence, with Sufi orders and interpretations remaining extremely influential. The Maliki's school emphasises the authority of the traditions of the prophet and the Medina Muslim community, but it has been adapted by local communities. In Morocco, the Maliki interpretation of Islamic law has tended to incorporate local traditions, so that traditional Islam and legal interpretation may differ from Maliki communities elsewhere. *(See Ref 489, 490)*

For centuries, traditional practices have been dominant in the society of the Maghreb. The most influential Islamic practice in the region remains Sufism, which emphasises mysticism and the attainment of the highest ideals of the faith. Maliki Sufism is dominant in Morocco, Algeria, and Tunisia. The Sufis are historically organised in "zawiyas", or brotherhoods. These brotherhoods served various societal purposes across the Maghreb, giving religious lectures, preaching, and providing protection for individuals seeking refuge. The "zawiya" provided these benefits to three main segments of society: (1) the general public; (2) urban intellectuals, scholars, and high society; and (3) both the intellectuals and the superstitious in the countryside. Modern zawiyas differ in influence according to the historical context of the country. The zawiya remains a central feature of traditional Islamic practice in Tunisia to the extent that the fundamentalist leader of "Ennahda" Rashid el-Ghannoushi targeted this aspect of Tunisian culture as a major barrier to the growth of fundamentalism. In Algeria, accusations that the zawiyas collaborated with colonial France diminished their influence among the population, whereas their influence has remained strong in Morocco. Thus, Moroccan Sufism and the zawiya there provide the most comprehensive example of Sufism in the Maghreb. *(See Ref 490,491)*

On the other hand, radical Islamic fundamentalism has grown in acceptance throughout the Maghreb since the 1970s. In contrast to the vast majority of traditionalists across the region, fundamentalists are extremely well organised. The groups maintain distinct organisations in each country, but they are not coordinated across national borders and in fact differ substantively in their goals and ideology. Radical fundamentalist groups in the region have pursued the most violent approach through permitting various Salafist individuals and groups to apply at will " takfir" [excommunication], the ability to declare others apostates of Islam. Salafist groups in the Maghreb have used this authority to label various governments, supporters of the government, and often innocent civilians as "kuffar" (unbelievers) for opposing, resisting, or not supporting the Salafist movement.

The primary proponents of Sunni fundamentalist thought in the Maghreb are the Salafist groups in Algeria, Ennahda in Tunisia, and "al-Adl Wal Ihsane" in Morocco. All these movements were influenced by earlier fundamentalist movements and thinkers, such as the Egyptian Muslim Brotherhood's Hassan al-Banna, Sayyid Qutb, and The Pakistani Abu al-A'la Mawdudi. However, their religious development and their relationship with the governing institutions of the state differ. The fundamentalist groups in Algeria largely reject traditional practices in the region, decrying them as superstitious, whereas the largest Moroccan fundamentalist movement has its roots in Sufi traditions. The Algerian Salafist groups are the most extreme in belief and practice: Since their failure to take over via the ballot, various factions support violent attacks upon the military or civilians to gain power. The Tunisian movement Ennahda explicitly accepts democracy even if it results in victory for an un-Islamic party. Various observers doubt the sincerity of Ennahda's commitment to democratic practice, however. The largest Moroccan fundamentalist movement, led by "al-Adl Wal Ihsane", accepts some traditional belief and practice but rejects electoral democracy. However, smaller, more violent groups have also become more active in Morocco recently.

However, a proper understanding of the Islamic challenge in Algeria and comparing the Algerian experience to Morocco and Tunisia is urgent. Not only is the Arabian Maghreb different than the Mashreq (Arab East), but experience within the Maghreb itself is highly varied.

In response to growing public frustration with decades of single-party rule, Algerian authorities began opening up the political system in the late 1980s. Algeria's sudden, wholesale adoption of a Western-style political liberalisation program in 1989-91 was unprecedented in the Arab world. It included the unqualified legalisation of explicitly Islamic political parties. No other Arab regime had dared to make such a move. The consequence was the implosion of the Algerian polity. Algeria became a place conforming, ironically, to Moroccan sociologist Fatima Mernissi's definition of the gharb (West): a place where "all terrors are possible." Sweeping victories by the new "Front Islamique du Salut" [Islamic Salvation Front](FIS) in municipal and then the first round of parliamentary elections, triggered a military coup in January 1992 which deposed President Chedli Benjedid, canceled elections before the second round of parliamentary voting, and arrested thousands of Islamist activists. The state quickly descended into chaos. Years of brutal warfare between Algeria's military authorities and armed Islamist groups took an estimated 60,000 lives and ripped the already tattered fabric of Algerian society. However, political and military leaders ended the violence in 2002 and rhetorically committed themselves to democratic principles like political pluralism, free and fair elections and the rule of law. The military has since gradually withdrawn from civilian life and multiparty elections have established local and national assemblies, though deep political divisions remain. *(See Ref 482, 483)*

Despite this progress, the government has increasingly limited the activities of opposition political parties (in particular the Islamists), local and international organisations and the traditionally independent press. Election law reform is needed; many citizens remain deeply skeptical that political change is possible through the ballot box. Legislative and local elections held in 2007 were accompanied by allegations of fraud and record-low voter turnout. President Abdelaziz Bouteflika, in power since 1999, was elected to a third term in 2009 after amending the constitution to abolish term limits.

The occurrence of terrorist attacks in recent years has alarmed Algerian authorities and neighbouring countries. Yet while the security situation has improved considerably in recent years, many Algerians' quality of life has not had the same positive trajectory. Citizens see increasingly little result and face greater frustration in their daily lives as the government struggles to meet expectations on key social issues such as housing, education and unemployment. With limited political freedoms and continued dominance by the same politicians, there is growing apathy to participate in political process. The current situation is an uneasy, unstable stalemate especially after the "Yasmine Revolution" in neighbouring Tunisia and the other uprising in Libya, though the Boutaflika regime still maintains an upper hand.

So, what are the roots of the contemporary crisis?

The ideological roots of modern day Islamic fundamentalism in North Africa are not solely recent: the ideas of the salafiyya current of Islamic reform and purification were present in pre-Protectorate Morocco among both the ulama (clergy) and various sultans (kings), and became widespread in the Maghreb in the era between the two world wars. One can argue that more than in the Mashreq, Islam was one of the core values for Algerian, Moroccan and Tunisian nationalist movements that opposed European domination. In Algeria, the crystallisation of a modern national identity between the two world wars was considerably shaped by the Islamic reformist movement led by Sheikh Abd al-Hamid Bin Badis. The movement promoted both the purification of Islamic practices from "polytheism" (maraboutic practices) and creation of an educational network that would stress that Islam and the Arabic language, and not French culture, are at the core of modern Algerian identity. *(See Ref 484,485)*

Similarly, salafi activity in Morocco played an important role in shaping the nationalist movement, personified in the 1920s by Allal al-Fasi, the religio-nationalist leader of the Istiqlal party. Likewise in Tunisia, Islam "as a component of Tunisian identity and a legitimising value...suffused the first generation nationalist movement [in the decades prior to World War I] and...persisted even into the age of Bourguibist secularism." *(See Ref 484, 485)*

In contrast to the general salafi current, political Islam in North Africa was not a "pan-Maghreb" movement. Nor, again in contrast to the Mashreq, was pan-Arabism a competing ideology. Thus, the legitimacy of the state in North Africa has never been in doubt: "The state appears more as an appropriately adjusted transfer of technology than as an alien institution." *(See Ref 486)*

The Maghreb's proximity to Europe rendered its youthful population (about two-thirds under 35 years of age) especially vulnerable to psychic dislocation, especially since North Africa had already been widely penetrated by the West (primarily France) during the prior 150 years.

The proliferation of satellite dishes and powerful television transmitters brought images of Europe's material glitter into people's living rooms, raising expectations and prompting demands that had no chance of being fulfilled, thus opening the way to profound disillusionment. In Fatima Mernissi's words," [W]hat strikes me as a sociologist (when visiting a Muslim country) is the strong feeling of bitterness in the people - the intellectuals, the young peasants. I see bitterness over blocked ambition, over frustrated desires for consumption - of clothes, commodities, and gadgets, but also of cultural products like books and quality films and performances which give meaning to life and reconcile the individual with his environment and his country...In our country (Morocco) what is unbearable, especially when you listen to the young men and women of the poor class, is the awful waste of talent. "Ana daya'" ("My life is a mess") is a leitmotif that one hears constantly". *(See Ref 482)*

The crisis, which took root during the 1970s and gathered strength during the 1980s, 1990s and through the first decade of 21st century, spawned a new kind of dissent, articulated most forcefully by Islamist movements. They spoke not only on issues or strategies of development but on matters concerned with justice and cultural identity. Given the dual legacy of popular-maraboutic Islamic practice and the Maghreb's penetration by the modern West, it is not surprising that Maghrebi salafis-fundamentalists often found themselves alienated from their own societies and thus sought guidance and inspiration from outside the Maghreb: e.g., the Egyptian-based Muslim Brotherhood, Iran's Islamic Revolution, and Sudan's Hassan al-Turabi and later Usama bin Laden. This interaction marked a departure from pre-modern historical patterns. *(See Ref 487)*

Despite the strongly similar development patterns of their Islamist movements, the specific socio-political and historical circumstances of the three Maghreb states (Morocco, Algeria and Tunisia) varied widely. This produced a disparate state-society/regime-opposition dynamic which, in each case, produced very different political outcomes. Consider Morocco: apart from Saudi Arabia, no other Arab regime has so thoroughly draped itself in Islam's mantle. King Mohammad VI, who has reigned and ruled since July 1999, is constitutionally the "Emir al- Mu'mineen" (the Commander of the Faithful) deputised by virtue of his descent from the Prophet Muhammad to lead the Moroccan Islamic Umma in all matters, both temporal and spiritual. He is the Chairman of the Jerusalem Committee of the Organisation of the Islamic Conference. His own erudition in religious matters, displayed in dialogues with religious scholars on Moroccan television, reinforce this dual role. So it seems reasonable to conclude that the Moroccan regime has been a relatively successful "modernising monarchy" given Moroccan political and socio-cultural traditions. This enabled it to avoid some of the harsher social, political and psychic dislocations of revolutionary Arab regimes. *(See Ref 709)*

One of these realities is the institution of the monarchy itself: the ruling Alawite dynasty is almost 350 years old. At the same time, as I. W. Zartman argues, the monarchy under Hassan II and later under his son Mohammad VI has evolved through interaction with society. Part of this involved Hassan's modification of religious traditions to reinforce his legitimacy and Mohammad's economic and social programs to the poor, women and the young generation, which made him "The People's King". More prosaic factors promoting relative political stability include a liberal economy and multiparty politics. Hassan II has described his political strategy as "homeopathic democracy," a process of controlled, well-managed change that maintains social peace while promoting economic development and the general welfare. His ultimate declared goal is a "bipolarised democracy," in which two parliamentary blocs will alternate in power, with the monarch serving as the ultimate arbiter and source of authority. This political strategy was pursued and evolved with Mohammad VI since he took power.

In Morocco, traditional Islam remains a dominant force, particularly in the countryside. The belief and practice affiliated with traditionalism in Morocco are reinforced by the presence of King Mohammed VI and his base of religio-political authority. The monarch has played a central role in unifying the ethnically diverse country and has gained substantial respect from the citizenry for doing so. However, radical and fundamentalist groups that can challenge the authority of the monarchy have become increasingly powerful. The May 2003 bombing of multiple locations in Casablanca, which killed 42 people and the arrest of 6 men of radical "Jamma'at Mezuak Tetouan" in March 2010, is a reflection of newly aggressive violent Salafist groups working in Morocco. The more nonviolent, yet antimonarchical fundamentalist groups, such as "al- Adl Wal Ihsane", have found unprecedented popularity among the general public.

The Casablanca bombings by radical Salafists sent a message to the monarchy that its religious and political authority was by no means unquestioned. The bombings by radicals were carried out against a Spanish restaurant, a Jewish cultural association, a Jewish-owned Italian restaurant, an international hotel, and a Jewish cemetery. The ultra-radical groups "Salafia Jihadia" and "Assirat Al-Mustaqim", which are believed to be behind the bombing, derive their followers from the uneducated and unemployed in Morocco. Some reports indicate that recruits are even taken from the ranks of the city's alcohol-drinking population, who are indoctrinated before being sent out to perform duties for the groups. The Moroccan Islamic Combatant Group (GICM) has also been connected with the Casablanca bombings. This group comprises Moroccans who were recruited to train and fight in Afghanistan. *(See Ref 492, 493)*

The ultimate goal of the GICM is the establishment of an Islamic state in Morocco, but they are also believed to support the objectives of al-Qa'ida. These terrorist groups support a radical and marginal Salafist ideology that was not well known in Morocco until recently. *(See Ref 494, 495)*

The March 2003 train bombings in Madrid that killed 191 people indicate that Moroccan terrorist groups are active in Europe as well. A group of predominantly Moroccan radicals was suspected in connection with the bombings, possibly under the direction of al-Qa'ida. The Moroccan Islamic Combatant Group was again implicated in the attacks. In the aftermath of the bombings in Spain, Moroccan radical groups have drawn considerable international attention. Although several members of these radical groups were either killed in suicide attacks or intercepted, a number of sleeper cells are believed to still be active in various countries of Europe. *(See Ref 495, 496)*

The Salafist movement in Morocco began among the Koranic and traditional schools of Tangiers. According to Mohamed Tozy, a Moroccan scholar of political Islam, the 1980s saw a flow of Saudi funds into Morocco for religious education. The first Koranic houses were established in Marrakesh, Tangiers, and other urban centres. These schools maintained connections to schools in Saudi Arabia. The authorities did not pay sufficient attention to these groups and trends because the groups were not political and were therefore not viewed as a threat. In addition to the religious schooling, the media was used effectively by Islamists groups. The Arabic-language media and television stations have focused on religious and Islamic issues and have benefited from generous Saudi financing. According to Professor Tozy, the use of the media to relay religious values has the added effect of resolving the contradiction between modernity and Islam. As satellite television becomes increasingly popular, Moroccans are viewing a standardised, global Islam that is practiced by Muslim communities everywhere. The media have helped to popularise non-Moroccan Islamic traditions such as the hijab and chador. *(See Ref 490)*

Despite the high profile of the more violent Islamist groups, the most influential Islamic fundamentalist organisation in Morocco is "al-Adl wal Ihsane" (the Justice and the Charity). This group does not participate in politics and pointedly boycotted the elections of September 2002 and September 2007. The group was formed by Sheikh Abdelsalam Yassine in the early 1970s. Despite having been founded in 1973, the organisation lacks legal recognition, although its activities are still tolerated. But members of the influential organisation say they are regularly subjected to threats, intimidation, and smear campaigns. The media tag them as a group capable of violently overthrowing Morocco's monarchy in order to establish an Islamic republic. Furthermore, Yassine questioned the authority of the monarchy in Morocco, as well as its claim to religious legitimacy. He sent a letter to the late King Hassan II, titled "Islam or the deluge," stating his views and was imprisoned for the next six years. The government also banned his organisation and arrested many of its other leaders. Yassine's philosophy, nonetheless, has been able to draw substantial support from the population. Separate from fundamentalist movements in Algeria or Tunisia, Yassine retains a connection to his Sufi roots and the charismatic authority that he wields through his historical connection to the tariqa (Sufi orders). This difference is substantial, in that the fundamentalist opposition in Morocco clearly is built upon local traditionalism whereas fundamentalist movements elsewhere reflect Arab or pan-Muslim trends. Yassine also carefully expanded the applicability of his ideology by incorporating the arguments of the left. Emphasising social justice and utilising the organisational finesse of leftist groups, he has been able to control much of the political discourse in opposition to the monarchy. Yassine's indigenous fundamentalist movement has thus consolidated its support base; in the face of opposition from the monarchy, the group has continued to grow in popularity. Its membership is estimated to be from 50,000 to a few hundred thousand. *(See Ref 490)*

In response to the rise in influence of "al-Adl Wal Ihsane", the government of Morocco allowed the establishment of a moderate Islamic party, the Party of Justice and Development (PJD) with the intent of drawing away the support base of Yassine. The PJD supports Islamic ideals in governance but is careful not to challenge the authority of the monarchy. Although the PJD has a fundamentalist political ideology, it believes in working within the existing system. By permitting a party with ideals that overlap Yassine's the monarchy believed that it could weaken the Islamic opposition movement and control its direction. In its first five years, the PJD was a peripheral force, unable to muster more than a few seats in parliament. In the 2002 parliamentary elections, however, PJD moved beyond the expectations of most observers, becoming the third-largest political force in Morocco after the nationalist Istiqlal Party and the socialists. In 2007 elections it became the second-largest after the Istiqlal. Support for "al-Adl Wal Ihsane" compared with PJD is difficult to assess, however, because some members of the PJD are known to be members of the banned "al-Adl Wal Ihsane" as well.

Nonetheless, Islamist activities in Morocco, particularly on university campuses where they came to control nearly all the student unions and periodically clashed violently with leftist groups, were publicly acknowledged by several government officials as constituting a worrisome development.

Tunisia's Islamists have enjoyed a higher international profile than their Moroccan counterparts but suffer from even greater repression. As in other cases in the Middle East, the Tunisian Islamists' protests can be seen partly as a response to socio-economic dislocations stemming from the complex processes of modernisation and development. Also contributing is the existence of a clogged political system. However, the most important factor has been the "psycho-social alienation" that has resulted from the predominant Western liberal model of modernity.

This model has been the objective of President Habib Bourguiba since the state became independent in 1956. Notwithstanding Bourguiba's efforts to legitimise his policies in Islamic modernist terms, his initiatives brought more secularisation than in any other Arab country. For example, the Personal Status Code, which guarantees equality between men and women in matters of divorce and forbids polygamy. A second example is the relatively large number of women in managerial and executive positions. President Zine el-Abidin Ben Ali, who assumed power in November 1987, softened some of Bourguiba's strident secularism and put more emphasis on Tunisia's Arab-Islamic heritage. The regime permitted Islamists to run in elections as independents in 1989. Officially, they captured around 14 percent of the vote, came close to winning a majority in several urban areas. Some have claimed that the real percentage attained by Islamist candidates was 30-32 percent. The regime quickly took notice and cracked down harshly, banning the newly formed Islamist Ennahda (the Renaissance) Party and taking advantage of some Islamists' violent acts to imprison thousands of activists. Stern reprimands from international human rights organisations did not deter the regime. *(See Ref 488, 497)*

Ben Ali ruled Tunisia with a firm hand. He also continued the tradition of secular politics in Tunisia, allowing little maneuvering room for Islamist politics in the country. However, the harsh measures used by Bourguiba and Ben Ali prompted Islamists to seek refuge and regroup abroad. Since 11 September 2001, several Tunisian émigrés have been arrested in Italy and France for connection to Islamic terrorist groups and activities.

The Tunisian government is secular and has limited the role of Islam in the state since independence. Under President Ben Ali, the country has focused its efforts on co-opting Islam and Islamic ideology by overseeing mosques and religious education in the country. People are dissuaded from wearing Islamic dress or beards. Nonetheless, Tunisia has had to struggle with Islamic fundamentalism, because of both the organised Ennahda movement and the growth of more radical organisations willing to use violence to attain their goals. Tunisia's recent brush with radical Islamic groups was in 2002, when a Tunisian suicide bomber, Nizar Nawar, assisted by relatives, orchestrated a dramatic attack on a historic synagogue on April 11 in Djerba that killed 21 people, mainly German tourists. A group called the "Islamic Army to Liberate the Holy Places" claimed responsibility in a statement after the attack. They claimed that Nawar's purpose had been to avenge Israeli crimes against the Palestinians. A more troubling trend is the involvement of Tunisians living in Europe in recent terrorist attacks outside Tunisia. A Tunisian national, Sarhane Ben Abdelmajid Fakhet, was suspected to be the leader of the terrorist group that conducted the Madrid train bombing in March 2004 (Fakhet was among four suspects who blew themselves up on 3 April 2004 as police raided their Madrid apartment). Another Tunisian, known as Ihsan G., was arrested for planning multiple bombings in Germany. He is suspected of receiving training in Afghanistan in early 2003 and then attempting to recruit others in Germany to form a terrorist group. The involvement of these key individuals in terrorist activities outside Tunisia is an area of concern that is easily overlooked as a result of the relative calm inside Tunisia. *(See Ref 498, 499, 500)*

The Tunisian government's larger battle, before Ben Ali was deposed on 14 January 2011, has been in the domestic arena with the Islamic fundamentalist group Ennahda which became the largest Islamic organisation in Tunisia after independence. Rashid el-Ghannoushi formed the movement in opposition to President Bourguiba's programs for Tunisia. Resentment was rising against Bourguiba because he was widely perceived as hostile to Islam and unable to address the economic and social problems plaguing Tunisia. His controversial policies included the use of French as the official language, the banning of polygamy, a ban on wearing the veil, and encouraging the public to ignore the fast of Ramadan. In response, el-Ghannoushi and his colleagues Ahmida Enneifer and Abdelfattah Mourou promoted the use of Arabic and the adoption of Islamic values in society.

Like their counterparts elsewhere in North Africa and the Sunni world in general, Tunisia's Islamists have been influenced by Egypt's Muslim Brotherhood and the teachings of Sayyid Qutb and Pakistan's Abu al-Al'a Mawdudi. Nonetheless, there was considerable talk during the 1980s within Islamist circles of developing a specific "Tunisian Islam." Part of the rationale was the rejection of the predominant Islamist view that legitimacy is solely divine and instead supporting the idea of popular will as the source of legitimacy. The Islamic notion of shura (consultation), declared Rashid el-Ghannoushi, legitimises multi-party politics, alternation in power and the protection of human rights. In November 1995, el-Ghannoushi and a group of non-Islamist exiled opposition members, including former Prime Minister Muhammad Mzali, published a joint communique appealing for democracy in Tunisia via the election of a parliament representing a diversity of views and political parties. The problem, el-Ghannoushi stressed, was the repressive Ben Ali regime and most Arab governments, for that matter, which rejected all notions of civil society (al-mujtama` al-madani). El-Ghannoushi's avowed goal to promote a modernist-Islamic synthesis opposing the Tunisian regime's "superficial modernity," makes him one of the more interesting and original of contemporary Islamist thinkers. *(See Ref 501, 502, 503, 504, 505)*

To be sure, el-Ghannoushi views are not entirely congruent with Western liberal values. As he said in one interview, state-building must begin with recognition of the "Arab's Umma" and Islamic identity. Without first agreeing on this central pillar, the "cultural context" of state-society relations, there can be no stable, legitimate authority. Once the identity question is solved, he continued, democracy can be practiced. (He did not address the place in society of those without an Arab-Islamic identity). *(See Ref 727)*

However, the Ennahda movement grew increasingly political in the late 1970s under the name of "el-Jama'ah al-Islamiya", and it undertook a more active program of social and political change with the ultimate goal of establishing an Islamic state. El-Ghannoushi particularly emphasised the necessity of promoting practical social objectives through Islam rather than abstruse philosophical debates. According to former Tunisian Minister of Education Moncer Rouissi, there were three main reasons for the rise of Ennahda's popularity during these years: Bourguiba's harsh methods toward Islam, Ennahda's social activism, and its work in education. Bourguiba's public statements and aggressive pursuit of a secular society were exploited by his Islamist opponents, who portrayed him as an enemy of Islam. Like other Islamist groups, Ennahda was able to gain widespread support among teachers and academics. Through this support group, Ennahda was able to promote Islamisation and Arabisation of the curriculum, changing lessons and textbooks to conform to its ideological vision. *(See Ref 490)*

In a crackdown in 1991, the Tunisian government moved against the fundamentalists, arresting many, including the leaders of Ennahda. In August 1992, el-Ghannoushi fled to London. Many Tunisian commentators view el-Ghannoushi's statements after his exile skeptically, saying that he simply changed the message to fit his more liberal audience in the West after seeking refuge abroad. After the dismantlement of Ennahda, no other fundamentalist group has been able to effectively organise in Tunisia. The Islamic Jihad has most effectively spearheaded the neo-fundamentalist movement, using violence to further its fundamentalist goals. This small group was responsible for bombing four hotels in Tunisia in 1987 in response to the hanging of one of its members by the government. Subsequent arrests weakened the Islamic Jihad further, and its strength is currently unclear.

On 14 January 2011, Ben Ali was ousted and fled the country which led to the return of el-Ghannoushi to Tunisia on 30 January 2011. Upon his arrival he declares that Ennahda will request soon a permission to be an official recognised political party, which was legalised by the new government of unity on on the 1st of March 2011. The question now: what will be the future of Ennahda and other Islamists movement in the Tunisian new era?

As for Algeria, nowhere was the crisis more acutely felt. The socio-economic dimension is obviously crucial in explaining Algeria's slide into this dilemma. A generation of misguided, mismanaged "state capitalist" policies, the worldwide slump in the hydro- carbon sector beginning in the mid-1980s, rampant corruption, rapid population growth and high unemployment all fuelled the breakdown of the ruling FLN (Front de Liberation Nationale) regime and the Islamists' rise. Taken alone, however, a socio-economic explanation for Algeria's woes is insufficient. From a historical perspective, the sudden, dramatic swing to the Islamist camp and resulting war for Algeria's soul is the latest chapter in a pattern of extreme changes and dislocations marking Algerian history: the general absence in pre-colonial times of a relatively strong central authority and unified political tradition (as compared to Morocco); the colonial power's thoroughgoing destruction of existing elites; the terrible bloodletting during the 1954-1962 war of independence, not just between Algerian Muslims and the Europeans, but within the Muslim community as well. Finally, a mobilising, revolutionary ideology and authoritarian leadership in the newly independent state left no room for other visions or political activity.

However, we must emphasise that the independence movement in Algeria started as a violent struggle and was integrally connected to the religious reform movement. These linkages laid the foundation for a tradition of religiously based war in the country. Algerian reformism was influenced by the thought of Muhammad Abdu, the Egyptian thinker who stressed the need to purify Islam from the corrupt ideas and superstitions that had weakened it by returning to the Koran and the sunna. Abdu had visited Algeria in 1903, spreading modernist ideals and inspiring Abdelhamid Ben Badis, later to be a leading reformist in Algeria's movement. In 1931 Ben Badis organised a group of Islamic reformists called the Association of Algerian Muslim Ulama (AUMA). Ben Badis and the AUMA focused on cleansing society of alcoholism, gambling, and other vices and also established educational establishments to spread their teachings. A primary goal of the organisation was the elimination of popular forms of Islamic practice, such as the Sufi traditions of mysticism and veneration of the marabout. It was also involved in lobbying for equal status of Algerians with the French and for the recognition of Arabic as an official language, and it sought to work cooperatively with the French authorities. However, AUMA's actions resulted in French attempts to control its activities and arrest its members, and relations between the AUMA and the French authorities became increasingly hostile. *(See Ref 513)*

In 1954, a new independence movement under the Front de Libération Nationale (FLN) began attacks on the French administration in Algeria and found support for its activities among the leaders of the AUMA. With this critical support, the FLN absorbed the AUMA in 1957, giving the nationalist fight for independence an aura of religious legitimacy. Using terrorist methods in order to gain independence from France, the rebels of the FLN took on the title of mujahideen and stated as a goal, "the restoration of the sovereign, democratic and social Algerian state within the framework of Islamic principles." Despite the deep influence of Islam upon the independence struggle, socialism quickly became the dominant philosophy in the FLN during the war. The primary proponent of socialist thought was Ahmed Ben Bella, a senior FLN leader. Stating that socialism and Islam are compatible, Ben Bella became the first president of Algeria and attempted to follow a socialist path despite great support for a more Islamic form of governance. *(See Ref 513)*

Throughout the post-independence years, the ruling authorities in Algiers, like counterparts elsewhere in the Maghreb and Mashreq, sought to manipulate Islam in the regime's service. Measures were taken included the enactment of a personal status code in 1984, adhering closely to Islamic precepts, banning alcohol in some cities, making Friday the day of rest, promoting religious education in schools and implementing an Arabisation program in schools and public institutions. At the same time, the FLN regime, under Houari Boumedienne and then Chedli Benjedid, sought to wed Islam to the governing socialist revolutionary ideology and block any independent Islamic political activity whether urban-reformist or rural-popular. Algerian Islamists had to go to Tunisia, Morocco or Cairo for proper Islamic training because Algeria lacked an Islamic institution of high calibre. It is thus not surprising that Algeria has not produced Islamist theoreticians comparable to el-Khomeyni, at-Turabi, or el-Ghannoushi. Indeed, the "thinness" of Islamist clerics in numbers and learnedness, might make it tougher for Islamists to govern effectively should they gain power. This scenario is quite different from Iran, where the religious classes were able to establish sophisticated networks of power quickly, even down to the neighbourhood level book. Notwithstanding the regime's efforts to monopolise and manipulate Islam, signs of an Islamic revival outside of authorised state structures were widespread during the 1970s, 1980s and early 1990s. Violent clashes between leftists and radical Islamists occurred on university campuses; Mustafa Bouyali, an ex-FLN fighter in the war of independence, attempted to promote an armed insurrection in the countryside between 1984 and 1987; and the regime placed hundreds of activists in detention, including a number of the future founders of the FIS. Islamists also expanded their activities in the social welfare sphere at the neighbourhood level. Nonetheless, nearly all observers believed that the authorities had matters well in hand. The literature analysing Algeria during the period is devoid of any reference to 'Abbasi Madani, the most prominent personage of the soon to be established FIS, or any sense that the Islamists had reached a critical mass. To be sure, one cannot demand clairvoyance, and the situation did become increasingly more dynamic and fluid after 1988. Nonetheless, it is a fact that scholars and observers, many of them "secular-modern" Algerians, were slow to recognise the budding power of the Islamists. In 1989, Abbasi Madani and Ali Belhadj established an Islamist party named the Islamic Salvation Front (FIS). *(See Ref 507, 508, 509, 510)*

The FIS began as many other political opposition movements in 1970s and 1980s. Following the legalisation of independent political parties in 1989, the FIS won most seats in Algeria's first multi-party municipal elections in 1990. It then won 188 out of 483 national assembly seats in Algeria's first round multi-party general elections in December 1991. The FLN had come in a weak third place with only a handful of votes. Fearing a potentially obliterating loss versus the FIS, the nation's military cancelled the second round of elections, and effectively took control over the government via its High State Council. After the resignation of President Chezli Benjedid, the FLN was dissolved, The FIS was banned by the military and thousands of its members were arrested. Four years since its legalisation, though, the FIS had established such strong bonds of trust between communities, activists and party loyalists that Islamists has to lose, if they did not fight back.

As a social movement, the FIS had politically mobilised hundreds of communities leaders, organised various trade union, and funded municipal and social services such as sanitation pickup, school and hospital construction, market co-ops, and mosque-related activities. FIS also established youth associations such as the league of Islamic Universities and Intellectuels, which developed political mobilisation and participation, as well as links with potential recruits (community youths). As a political movement, FIS quickly permeated and entrenched itself in Algerian society. These links provided crucial support from hundreds of thousands in communities throughout the country that, when repression finally came, FIS was able to mobilise many in a short amount of time. For example, during demonstration in the spring of 1991 in central Algiers, the FIS was able to mobilise more than 30,000 supporters in twenty-four hours.

Many sought to explain away the movement's successes as a mere protest against a discredited and corrupt FLN regime, which to a large extent it was, or as the result of voter apathy or the boycott of municipal elections by other political parties. But what in the end stands out as most salient was the FIS's ability to repeatedly mobilise large-scale support in competitive, highly-charged electoral contests, even after its top echelon was imprisoned in June 1991, and then in its capability to mount a sustained armed uprising beginning in January 1992. The two more moderate, "gradualist" Islamist parties, Hamas, led by Mahfoud Nahnah, and al-Nahda, headed by Sheikh Abdallah Djaballah, were completely overwhelmed by the FIS and won only minimal support in the 1990 and 1991 elections.

One keen observer of Algeria, Hugh Roberts, explains the FIS's appeal in the context of modern Algerian history. In ideological terms, he states, the FIS has developed the Islamic aspect of the FLN's governing vision, rather than repudiating it entirely. In fact, the FIS explicitly claims to be the new bearers of the FLN's torch, and the authentic inheritors of the FLN's legacy. The FIS-FLN connection is further strengthened by the fact that Sheikh Abbasi Madani, first among equals of the FIS leadership, was an early member of the FLN, and was even imprisoned for his activities for most of the 1954-1962's period. Also like the FLN, the FIS maintains a sort of collective leadership, befitting its status as a "front" and helping it to gather together a number of streams and groups belonging to Algerian Islamism. But what is most important is that the FIS constituted a political body which gave primacy to political action over religious activities. *(See Ref 511,512)*

After the FIS was banned in 1992, Islamic groups took up arms in the face of a closed political system to reclaim what they considered their rightful role as the political leaders of the nation. Islamists insurgents, many of whom had just returned from the long-decade Afghan war versus the

Soviet Union, emerged to rapidly begin an armed campaign against the government and its supporter. These violent radical fundamentalist groups were made up of individuals who had rejected the feasibility of democratic means to establish an Islamic state. The Islamic Armed Movement (MIA), The Armed Islamic Group (GIA) and the Salafist Group for Preaching and Combat (GSPC) were at the forefront of a campaign of terrorism, leading to the death of approximately 100,000 in the decade after the banning of the FIS. Some of the Islamists in the GIA and GSPC had originally supported the FIS electoral attempt but saw the cancellation of elections as a sign to move forward with a militant strategy. The GIA in particular has been notable in its use of indiscriminate violence against both military and civilian targets, including villagers, the media, schools, and foreign nationals. Its approach has been to label all those who do not rise in its support as kuffar (unbelievers), thereby legitimising the killing of such individuals. The GSPC, alternatively, arose as a more moderate jihadist movement, decrying the use of such indiscriminate violence against civilian populations. This group has adopted a far more limited definition of kafir (unbeliever). It permits violence against the regime and military but does not promote attacks against civilians. However, other splinter movements reflect this divide in their interpretation of takfir (excommunication) and have generated further violence by labelling each other as kafir and engaging in intra-Salafist jihad. *(See Ref 513)*

The GIA was founded by one of these returning mujahideen from Afghanistan Abdelrahim Zarghouli known as Qari Sa'id. Sa'id like many Algerians returning home soon focused his energies on the brewing civil war. He also made a pact with Abu Mus'ab al-Suri (Mustafa bin Abd al-Qadir Sitt Maryam Nassar), the so called the architect of the global jihad in al-Qa'ida, that he planned to build a jihad organisation in Algeria after his involvement in Afghanistan ended. Al-Suri obliged in pledging to fight alongside him: "…Should Sa'id be able to establish jihad in Algeria, and there is needed for me there, I will go to Algeria like I went to Afghanistan". Al-Suri's role in supporting jihad in Algeria had an indirect, yet very crucial importance for not only GIA in the 1990s, but for the current GSPC/AQIM (al-Qa'ida in Islamic Maghreb) alliance. Although he never fought directly in the civil war, al-Suri used connections from Afghanistan to establish vital network between the Afghan tested-jihadi community in Europe and the fighters in Algeria. "I arrived in London and got to know some of the brothers, and discovered that several of the brothers who supported the jihad in Algeria, and who had been with us in Afghanistan, were present in a number of European countries." These connections only solidified over time as Sa'id's GIA became bolder and more successful in their terrorist tactics. *(See Ref 515)*

The insurgents originally targeted military and government facilities, but soon began attacking civilians. In 1994, as negotiations between the government and the FIS's imprisoned leadership reached their height, the GIA declared war on FIS and its supporters, while the MIA and smaller groups regrouped, becoming the FIS-loyalist Islamic Salvation Army (AIS). Thus began a three-way battle between the Army, the AIS, and the GIA. All the while, al-Suri criss-crossed Europe, gathering financial support in Spain, France and Belgium, training militants in Bosnia and Italy, and meeting with GIA supporters in Turkey and Holland. Although he has never managed to fight in Algeria, his contribution in linking the European jihadi diaspora as the central support line to the GIA's sustenance against the AIS and the Army was critical and long lasting. North African insurgents and their European supporters use those same lines of support and communications today. Al-Suri continued his Jihadi writing throughout the 1990s, and even today, he is held in high regards by GSPC/AQIM as a great jihadist thinker and strategist. *(See Ref 515)*

In 1994 General Liamine Zeroual was elected as President after which a conflict and bloodshed between GIA and AIS intensified. From 1994 to 1998 the GIA began a series of massacres targeting entire neighbourhoods and villages, although some evidence also suggests the involvement of government forces for the purpose of framing the GIA. Few were spared by the GIA's ultra-violence. The political demonstrations and moderation of years past yielded to terror tactics such as assassinations, armed attacks, bombings, sabotage...mutilations and throat-cutting.

In 1998 The GIA splintered as some members objected to its massacre policy on ordinary civilians. Following the election of the Alliance presidential candidate Abdelaziz Boutaflika in 1999, a new law gave amnesty to most insurgents, motivating large number to leave their Islamist groups and return to normal civilian life. From 1999 to 2002, insurgent violence declined substantially. Presumably due to the government amnesty program, in fighting within the group and the breakaway success of The Salafist Group of Preaching and Combat (GSPC), the remnants of the GIA finally dissolved.

The GSPC, in fact, has ideologically, if not logistically, aligned itself with the global jihad against the West. On 11 September 2006, al-Qa'ida second in command, Ayman al-Zawahiri, announced the "blessed union" between GSPC and al-Qa'ida. He then publicly anointed the group as "al-Qa'ida representative in North Africa" and declared his hopes that the merger will be a "bone in the throat" of its former coloniser, France, and the far enemy of the United States. In January 2007, the group changed officially its name to al-Qa'ida in the Islamic Maghreb (AQIM). On 11 April 2007, an explosion ripped through Algiers' main government building, killing 23 people and injured 118. Seven months later, on December 11, again in Algiers, two more suicide bombs exploded at United Nations offices and another Algerian government building, killing 63. AQIM claimed responsibility for both bombings. Thus began the most recent chapter in Algeria's war against Islamist insurgency. As we expect, the battle now takes on a global perspective: Ideologically, the next battle of Algiers will be fought between Western-backed, pseudo-democratic political constructs that only recently have dipped their toes into multi-party governance versus the supporters of transnational salafi-jihadism and the re-establishment of the Caliphate. *(See Ref 516)*

However, al-Qa'ida organisation and its affiliate AQIM regard the moral authority of North African's political elites invalid and foreign because of its complicity with U.S., Europe, and Israel. "The secular character of the Tunisian, Algerian, and Mauritanian states, and the pro-Western Moroccan monarchy, for them are blights of Islam". In forcing the withdrawal of foreign/secular forces, al-Qa'ida's global jihad ideology would spread and the shari'a law would flourish. These goals have been stipulated by Abu Omar abdul Birr, GSPC's media director: "GSPC is not limited by a narrow regional vision. It is important for us to spread the fragrance of jihad in every country and region and ignite the flames under the feet of the Jews, the Christians and the apostates." *(See Ref 517, 518)*

In firmly couching salafi-jihadism into a global anti-West, anti-globalisation, anti-American vehicle, GSPC tapped the same local nerve in those resentful of perceived Western injustice and hegemony that al-Qa'ida had done on a global level. In discarding its political accoutrements and championing an extreme Islamic vision, GSPC ideologically attuned itself to al-Qa'ida's dogmatic frequency. According to regional experts, John Nomikos and Aya Burweila, the new and improved GSPC/AQIM merger has three main objectives that run parallel to the ideological objectives.

Firstly, AQIM wants to unite jihadists in the region under one al-Qa'ida umbrella; secondly, AQIM must recruit and send suicide bombers to Iraq and Afghanistan; and thirdly, its long-term goal is to carry out attacks in Europe and U.S. However besides their apparent ideological calibration, both groups stood also to gain logistically from the merger.

However, the inability of secular governments in the region to provide sufficient economic progress and equitable distribution of income has given Islamic groups a way to gather public support. As modernisation reaches across the Maghreb, the population is finding that adjustment entails changing traditional modes of thought and ways of working. The result of this challenge has often been a return to the core values in society and religion that have served well over the centuries. Attempts by the governments of Algeria, Tunisia, and Morocco to modernise society and increase national wealth have most often led to increasing disparities in income distribution between urban and rural areas and within communities. Inefficient allocation of national wealth - with little regard for development of infrastructure, education, and employment - leaves much room for improvement. In the Maghreb, particularly Morocco and Tunisia, fundamentalist groups have taken advantage of such lapses by the central government. These groups have expanded their outreach into disadvantaged and poor communities, providing social welfare benefits and education in local madrassas.

The absence of representative governing institutions is yet another critical factor creating support for Islamic fundamentalism in the region. The countries of the Maghreb have not established democratic norms, and authoritarian governments have moved to limit the political space to their advantage. In Tunisia, former President Ben Ali was elected with over 99 percent of the vote, whereas in Algeria, President Bouteflika has maintained tight control over the political process. Neither country allows Islamic parties to participate in national elections. In Tunisia, both Bourguiba and Ben Ali pursued harsh policies meant to suppress the Islamist movement. Banning the popular Ennahda from electoral politics encouraged a movement that could be free of legal restraints on its activities. By arresting thousands and using torture and the death penalty, Tunisia may have also created further discontent. Algeria's repressive actions following the election results of 1991 led to a vicious cycle of violence between the radical fundamentalists and the military. FIS supporters believed the banning of the party and nullification of the election results to be sufficient grounds for violent action. The subsequent arrests and murders by military and police gave them a further rationale for violent methods. Morocco presents a unique case in which the monarchy remains above politics, and moderate Islamic and opposition parties are allowed to participate effectively in parliamentary elections. Nonetheless, the most extreme, and possibly most popular, Islamic opposition movement remains outside Moroccan electoral politics. The various opposition movements have found in Morocco's stifling political atmosphere an argument for more radical methods to implement Islamic political ideals. Absent meaningful methods for political discourse, these groups see violence as an increasingly viable political tool. The Casablanca bombings reflect a new aggressive methodology for radical Islamic groups in Morocco.

Across the Maghreb, political leaders have attempted to contain the threat of Islamic fundamentalism through both authoritarian and more liberal policies. In Algeria, the government has firmly barred the Islamists from taking power at the centre, retaining ultimate authority in the hands of the military. The secular government of Tunisia has similarly, albeit more peacefully, limited the role of Islamic parties in politics. However, substantial numbers of Tunisian fundamentalists who have resorted to working from abroad started to return to the country after the ousting of President Ben Ali on 14 January 2011. In Morocco, the government has faced a dilemma as it attempts to liberalise the political process and incorporate moderate Islamic parties. Although the government allows a legal political avenue for disaffected segments of the population through the PJD, a significant number of Moroccans nevertheless remain attracted to al-Adl Wal Ihsane and radical Salafist groups. Morocco's success in navigating this situation may provide critical insights for other countries in the Middle East and the Maghreb considering political liberalisation and democratisation in the future.

Furthermore, the late Arab uprisings which started in Tunisia, and spread to Egypt and Libya in Northern Africa may affect a lot of things concerning the future of all the countries in the Maghreb.

CHAPTER TWELVE

EUROPE: A CLASH OF CIVILISATIONS?

Over the past two decades, the number of Muslims living in Western Europe has steadily grown rising from less than 10 million in 1990 to approximately 17 million in 2010 as by the American Pew Research Centre. The continuing growth in Europe's Muslim population is raising a host of political and social questions. Tensions have arisen over such issues as the place of religion in European societies, the role of women, the obligations and rights of immigrants, and support for terrorism. These controversies are complicated by the ties that some European Muslims have to religious networks and movements outside of Europe. Fairly or unfairly, these groups are often accused of dissuading Muslims from integrating into European society and, in some cases, of supporting radicalism.

Muslims have been present in Western Europe in large numbers since the 1960s, when immigrants from Muslim-majority areas such as North Africa, Turkey and South Asia began arriving in Britain, France, Germany, Italy, and other European nations, often to take low-wage jobs. Many of the major Muslim networks and movements operating in Western Europe today originated in Muslim-majority countries, including Egypt, Algeria, Morocco, Tunisia, Pakistan, Saudi Arabia and Turkey.

The overseas origins of the groups, and their continuing ties to affiliates abroad, have prompted concerns that by strengthening Muslims' connections to the umma – the world community of Muslim believers – they may be encouraging Muslims to segregate themselves from the rest of European society. In addition, some in the West perceive many Muslim groups as fomenters of radical Islam and, ultimately, terrorism.

It is difficult to generalise about Muslim groups in Western Europe because they vary so widely in their philosophies and purposes. Certain groups, including radical Islamist movements, do work to foster extremist sentiments or to detach Muslims from the European societies in which they live. But other groups focus on different goals, such as helping Muslim communities deal with day-to-day religious issues, improving schools or encouraging personal piety.

NUMBER OF MUSLIMS IN WESTERN EUROPE

Countries	Estimated 2010 Muslim Population	Percentage
Austria	475,000	5.7%
Belgium	638,000	6.0%
Denmark	226,000	4.1%
Finland	042,000	0.8%
France	3,574,000	5.7%
Germany	4,119,000	5.0%
Greece	527,000	4.7%
Ireland	043,000	0.9%
Italy	1,583,000	2.6%
Luxembourg	013,000	2.7%
Netherlands	914,000	5.5%
Norway	144,000	3.0%
Portugal	022,000	0.2%
Spain	1,021,000	2.3%
Sweden	451,000	4.9%
Switzerland	433,000	5.7%
United Kingdom	2,869,000	4.6%
Total	17,094,000 (Source: PEW Research Centre/USA)	

So the question here: what are the most significant cultural, economic, political, religious and security based impediments to the full and enduring integration of Muslim communities into the fabric of Western European society generally and especially into the societies of France, Germany and the United Kingdom at present?

Let us start by the situation of the Muslim communities in France.

The Muslim segment of the population of France is composed principally of individuals and families from the Maghreb region of North Africa, the first generations of who were recruited as guest workers in the 1950s. It also includes communities from sub-Saharan Africa, Middle Eastern states such as Turkey and Lebanon, and a growing segment of French converts. A 2000 estimate by the French High Council on Integration report, for example, classified the number of Muslims in France as follows: Algerians (1.5 million), Moroccans (1 million), Tunisians (500,000), Turks (350,000), other Middle Easterners [Arabs, Iranians and Kurds] (400,000), and Sub-Saharan Africans (250,000) (A reliance on estimates is necessary here because the French census does not include any questions on religion). While Muslims account for no more than eight percent of the French population nationally at present, their numbers are increasing at a 3.7 percent rate annually and they are not evenly dispersed geographically. *(See Ref 519, 520)*

However, Franco-Islamic communities are located almost exclusively in low-rent housing projects in the suburbs (banlieues) that ring major urban centres, most notably Paris, Marseille, Lyon and Lille. The Muslim presence is more pronounced and publicly visible in local banlieues than is the case regionally or nationally. Fueled mainly by the development of the second and third generations since 1973, growth in these banlieues has left some French metropolitan areas with populations that are as high as one-third North African Muslim in ethno-religious orientation. Similarly, the French Interior Ministry estimates that Muslims account for proportions as high as 11 percent in particular regions. *(See Ref 521)*

In Marseille, which is closer than any other major French city to the North African coastline, a quarter of the members of the population - roughly 200,000 - are Muslims. In the La Bricarde housing project north of the city centre, for instance, some 200 satellite dishes spring from rooftops, pointing south across the Mediterranean. More than 85 percent of La Bricarde's residents have roots in the Maghreb. *(See Ref 522)*

Regrettably, Muslims face considerably worse economic circumstances than the majority of others living in France, both natives and immigrants of European ethnic extraction. Although unemployment was a serious national problem throughout the 1990s and 2000s and continues as such today, its impact is markedly greater in Muslim communities. In January 1999, for example, the unemployment rate in France was 10.2 percent nationally. However, among North African Muslims, it stood at 33 percent. Unemployment is even more pronounced in the banlieues (the suburbs).

According to Didier Bonnet, who directs a social-service organisation in Marseille, unemployment in October 2000 was 20 percent in the city overall and 50 percent in La Bricarde. *(See Ref 523, 524)*

In addition to economic marginalisation, Muslim communities have suffered exclusion as a result of the French government's inflexibility vis-à-vis the provision of public funds for the construction of mosques and the maintenance of exclusively Muslim sections in cemeteries in French cities and towns (as stipulated under the tenets of Islam). At the turn of the 21st century, there were a scant nine mosques in France that could accommodate 1,000 or more worshippers - four in the Paris metropolitan area, two in Lille and one each in Lyon, Marseille and Reims. As a result, most Muslims in France are relegated to the hundreds of Islamic prayer rooms that often double as apartments for the Maghrebians residing in a given locale. As French scholar Catherine Wihtol de Wenden explains, it "is the poverty . . . of the prayer rooms [that] strikes the negative image of mosques in the neighbourhood in French public opinion, rather than the challenge to French identity brought by minarets in the French landscape". *(See Ref 525,526)*

While Muslims in France are divided among several distinctive ethnic groups, their communities - whether Algerian, Moroccan, Tunisian or Turkish in orientation - are perceived by most Frenchmen as a monolith, one characterised by Islamic fundamentalism rather than moderation or modernity. In reality, French Muslims are, on the whole, by no means radical in their practice of Islam. While the majority of Muslims tend to eat ritually slaughtered halal meat or at least what they believe is such, most do not pray every day or attend weekly Friday services at a mosque or prayer room. *(See Ref 527)*

Politically, there are two paths leading to representation for Muslims living in France. The first is through election to political office at local, regional or national level. The second is by way of organisations - defined according to ethnicity, religion or both - with the capacity to present the concerns of Muslim communities to government officials and extract concessions ranging from the provision of funds for the construction of mosques to the rights of schoolgirls to wear head scarves (foulards) while attending public school classes. Thus far, what limited success Muslims have achieved on each of these issues has been confined almost exclusively to local level. For example, while no Muslim has ever been elected to the French Parliament, 130 were elected as municipal councilors in 2001. *(See Ref 528)*

Efforts to forge a collective Islamic identity among French Muslims and develop representative bodies to express their communal concerns have unfolded in three general contexts over the past 30 years. First, in the early 1980s, Muslim elites founded the initial national Islamic organisations, most notably the Federation National des Musulmans de France (FNMF) and the Union des Organisations Islamiques de France (UOIF). A similar initiative in the early 2000s resulted in the establishment of the slightly more broad-based Conseil de l'Islam en France (CIF). Second, in 1989, then French Interior Minister Pierre Joxe created the Conseil de Reflexion sur l'Islam en France (CORIF) to act as an interlocutory arm of the state. Similarly, in April 2000, then French Interior Minister Jean-Pierre Chevènement instituted a joint government-Muslim council designed to improve domestic Franco-Muslim relations, the mandate of which was extended by Chevènement's successor, Daniel Vaillant, in May 2001. Third, lay preachers -often connected with international Islamic organisations - have undertaken what French scholar Olivier Roy describes as "a 'grass roots' reconversion of the Islamic community, severing it from French society . . . as a means of ensuring Islam's position as a minority". *(See Ref 524,529,530)*

Organisations in the first two contexts - those associated with Islamic elites and the French government - have thus far proven ineffective, largely because unemployed Muslims in their teens and twenties do not identify comfortably with representatives in either forum. Instead, they have grown more likely to seek and find solac - and a common purpose - in the teachings of foreign Imams who extol the virtues of orthodox Islam and berate the culture and values of a French society from which they feel excluded.

The initial wave of North African migrants to France associated with the guest worker programs of the 1950s and 1960s did not trigger a concurrent need to integrate those individuals into mainstream society. Both the French government and the migrants felt at the time that their reciprocal interactions would not extend beyond the postwar recovery. Once the domestic labour supply increased, the demand for foreign workers would subside, causing the immigrants to return home. For their part, Maghrebian labourers generally did not try to anchor themselves in

French society, preferring instead to return to the hostels after work and send most of what they earned back to North Africa in anticipation of prosperous futures in the communities from which they originated.

The issue of minority integration increased in significance when the government's decision to end foreign labour migration programs in 1974 triggered an unanticipated wave of family reunifications and the resultant entrenchment of Muslim communities in banlieues across France. Historically, the French have integrated foreigners by assimilating individuals rather than incorporating communities with distinctive minority identities based on factors such as class, culture, ethnicity and religion. The logic behind that approach is understandable given the importance of republicanism in the development of the modern French nation. However, the French model of integration based on assimilation was problematic for Muslim guest workers and their families, who wanted to retain their own identities, which were anchored in Islam. In short, the philosophical differences between French secularism and Islam have rendered the integration of Muslims a complex and - thus far - not fully surmountable task. As James Corbett contends, "France has never been a multicultural society. Foreigners are expected to fit into the French mold, French thought processes [and] the French value system". *(See Ref 531)*

The appearance and subsequent growth of younger generations in Islamic communities across France from the mid-1970s to the 1990s increased the proportion of Muslims with citizenship to approximately 50 percent by 2000. It also intensified the need to develop a more inclusive model to equitably integrate Muslims - particularly those born in France - into mainstream society. French scholar Jocelyn Cesari argues that such a model must bridge the gap separating multiculturalism from assimilation and the unequivocal acceptance of Muslim identity through full communal integration, stressing that "Islam has changed the balance between the three major 'pillars' of French political life: unity, respect for political pluralism and liberty. If pluralism is linked with democracy, it no longer refers to the integration of dominated groups or to the representation of the diversity of citizens, but to the balance between multiculturalism and communities". *(See Ref 529)*

While successive French governments have made superficial attempts to mitigate the marginalisation of Muslim communities over the past two decades, a comprehensive national framework to achieve substantial progress toward that end has yet to emerge. Following the wave of family reunifications in the late 1970s, for example, government officials shifted their rhetoric, replacing the historical emphasis on assimilation to a more accommodating "insertion" of minority communities into the majority. Similarly, late President François Mitterand's Socialist Party (PS) focused on improvements in human rights accorded to immigrant groups in the 1980s and early 1990s.In addition, former President Jacques Chirac and former Prime Minister Jean-Pierre Raffarin have both encouraged more open dialogue between the government officials and Muslim communal representatives after the 2002 presidential and parliamentary elections. On a particularly positive note, Raffarin backed his rhetoric with concrete political action by naming two North African Muslims to national cabinet posts. Additionally, then French Interior Minister Nicolas Sarkozy, who was elected President in May 2007, established a French Muslim Council in an effort to facilitate more effective communication between Islamic communal leaders and governmental officials. *(See Ref 528)*

If France is moving toward accommodating its Mulims communities what is the situation of Muslims in Germany?

Muslim communities in Germany are composed of groups from a wide range of ethnic backgrounds. Three-quarters of Muslims living in the Federal Republic are of Turkish national origin, including more than 400,000 Kurds. However, Germany is also home to Muslims with ancestry - whether immediate or one or two generations removed - in countries as geographically wide ranging as Bosnia-Herzegovina, Iran, Morocco and Afghanistan. One widely accepted study, for instance, listed the following breakdown of German residents possessing roots in Muslim-majority states (Turkey is excluded): 167,690 Bosnians, 116,446 Iranians, 81,450 Moroccans, 71,955 Afghans, 55,600 Central Asians from Azerbaijan, Kazakstan, Kyrgystan, Tajikistan, Turkmenistan and Uzbekistan, 40,000 Syrians, 10,000 Palestinians, 10,000 Egyptians, 54,211 Lebanese, 51,211 Iraqis, 38,257 Pakistanis, 24,260 Tunisians, 17,186 Algerians, 12,107 Albanians and 8,350 Somalis. Among these groups, only the size of the Bosnian community is on the decline, having fallen by nearly 50 percent since 1997. *(See Ref 532)*

As is true of the French and British contexts, Muslim communities in Germany are prevalent in low-rent housing zones on the peripheries of major to mid-size cities such as Berlin, Munich, Frankfurt-am-Main,

Duisberg and Cologne. More than three-quarters of Turks residing in the Federal Republic, for instance, are concentrated in urban areas, including 136,400 in the Berlin district of Kreuzberg. Regionally, 35 percent of Turks live in North Rhine-Westphalia, which houses most of the industrial plants that attracted guest workers during the 1960s. This Länd includes the cities of Cologne and Duisberg, each of which houses Turkish enclaves of at least 30,000 residents. *(See Ref 533)*

Most Muslims of other ethnic groups living in Germany - Bosnians in particular - are similarely situated in urban rather than rural areas.

Among the most significant demographic differences between these esoteric communities and the societal majority are those associated with age, culture, and the related issues of linguistic proficiency and educational attainment.One 1990 study, for example, found that just five percent of ethnic Turks in Germany were aged 65 and older compared with 17 percent of the population overall.Similarly, birth rates in Turkish communities are substantially higher than is the case nationally,which helps to explain why nearly 70 percent of individuals in the former context are under 30 years of age.These figures suggest the likelihood if not certainty of further increases in the proportion of Turks both among minorities in Germany and in the national population in the future. *(See Ref 534,535, 536)*

A general lack of proficiency of the German language permeates Turkish communities in cities across Germany. According to Ali Ucar, "most third-generation Turks in Germany do not have a sufficient knowledge of German even though most of them have been born and raised here". A 2001 study conducted in Berlin's Kreuzberg district is demonstrative of this trend. Among a sample group of 273 pre-school children from Turkish families living in Kreuzberg, Ucar found that 63 percent spoke little or no German and thus failed to "meet the linguistic requirements for primary school". Such linguistic deficiencies have contributed to striking gaps between Turks and ethnic Germans regarding educational and vocational qualifications. One 1999 report found that Turks had 4.5 years less of schooling than Germans on average and that twice as many members of the latter group had high school degrees than was true of the former. *(See Ref 534,537)*

The inability to communicate effectively in German, and related deficiencies of educational attainment and vocational training among most Muslims in the Federal Republic have had markedly negative effects on their economic status. As guest workers, for example, Turks were limited all but exclusively to unskilled jobs in the industrial sector of the economy, where the need for extensive interaction with German-speakers was minimal if it existed at all. However, the decline in demand for unskilled labourers in the wake of the 1973 oil crisis, followed by the gradual modernisation of the German economy with concurrent shifts in emphasis to the technology and service sectors in the 1980s and 1990s, had profound effects on Turkish job seekers. Influxes of migrants from Eastern and Central Europe and the Balkans, triggered by the collapse of the Soviet empire in 1989-90 and the civil wars of 1992-95 in Bosnia and 1998-99 in Kosovo, only exacerbated matters by increasing the supply of idle blue collar labour. As a result of these factors - in part if not fully - the jobless rate among Turks in Germany is substantially higher than the national average. One 2006 study, for instance, cited that rate among Turks as 20 percent. *(See Ref 538)*

Economic shortcomings among Muslims are also related in part to the socio-religious characteristics of their communities. The growth of Turkish-owned enterprises is itself a product of the significance of religion and culture in the lives of Muslims in contemporary Germany, particularly with respect to members of the first generation. As Zehra Onder asserts, the "identity of a Muslim family is widely determined by Islam. The passage into a foreign culture occurs via a social change. Many of the still dominant traditions in Turkish behaviour take their origin from religion. Some families can overcome the norms and values of traditions, especially if from large Turkish cities. But, for the majority, the Islamic norm-value system keeps its validity". *(See Ref 502)*

Prior to the family reunifications of the 1970s and 1980s, Islam did not play a significant role in the lives of guest workers residing in government-provided housing complexes in the Federal Republic's central and northern industrial centres. The reunification sparked an increase in the desire among Muslims to place an emphasis on their cultural and religious traditions. As a result, Islamic communities increasingly pressed for the construction of mosques and the establishment of accompanying social associations across Germany in the 1980s and 1990s. According to Germany's Central Islam Institute Archive, for example, the number of mosque associations has grown from single figures to more than 2,200 over the past two decades. *(See Ref 540)*

301

Initially, virtually all of the mosques administered by these associations were situated in contexts ranging from abandoned factories to temporarily converted Turkish apartment buildings. This was related both to a lack of funds for the construction of traditional mosques with prominent domes and minarets, and opposition by the societal majority to accept the existence of these structures in German cities. Take Berlin, where construction of the German capital's first cathedral mosque did not commence until 2000. The hurdles the Turks of Berlin had to overcome before moving forward with construction of their first cathedral mosque was attributable in part to a German misperception of Islam as a monolith whose adherents share fundamentalist Islamic beliefs. Yet, in reality, Muslim communities in Germany are diverse in ethnic extraction as well as in the particulars of religious denomination and practice. Ethnically, such communities are predominantly Turkish in national origin. But nearly one quarter of these enclaves are composed of Kurds, who left Turkey because of government repression and generally shun interaction with Turks. Similarly, while the majority of Muslims living in the Federal Republic practice Sunni Islam, sizable Iranian and Iraqi communities in that state are composed predominantly of members of the Shia strain of the faith. Further divisions are evident vis-à-vis orthodox (salafists) versus modernist interpretations of Islam among Turks and other ethnic minorities. *(See Ref 541,542)*

The lack of socio-religious homogeneity has complicated the efforts of Islamic communities to achieve political representation to a degree proportionate to the Muslims' share of the German population, glaringly so when broken down nationally. In order to examine the roles of Muslims in the political life of the Federal Republic accurately but incisively, brief analyses of two types of representation are necessary. First, the endeavours of individual politicians catering to the needs of Muslim communities, whether through seeking - and at times achieving election to - office in the national parliament or on a local council. Second, the pursuit of Islamic communal objectives by political parties and organisations, some sponsored internally and others externally.

Muslim communities in Germany are severely limited in terms of formal political representation - at the Länd and national levels. Of 82 million inhabitants in Germany, about fifteen million have a so-called "migration background", among them roughly 2.5 million people with Turkish ancestry. But their presence is hardly reflected in the composition of the newly elected German Bundestag. However, the majority of Muslims in

Germany have no German citizenship and are therefore excluded from the right to vote and actively participate in the political sphere—the basis of real integration into German society.

Today, approximately 608,000 Muslims in Germany are German citizens. The number of Muslims taking up German citizenship is decreasing despite the creation of German citizenship laws that are characterised by aspects of a ius soli (territory based law), moving beyond the traditional ius sanguinis (derivation-based law) in 2000. Now children can be born as German citizens, even if their parents do not have German citizenship.

In fact, if people with immigrant backgrounds were to be proportionately represented in the German parliament, more than 100 out of 622 members of the Bundestag would have foreign roots. But the new German Parliament, elected in September 2009, has 20 members with a migration background.Nine of them have a Muslim family background, of which again three explicitly state their Muslim religion on the official website of the Bundestag. The others do not wish to state it, or are secular or Christian. Three of the 20 MPs with a migration background have an Indian parent, whose religion is not stated, but two of them state to be Christians. *(See Ref 543)*

The ex- Berlin Green state senator Ismail Kosan in the upper house (Bundesrat), the 39-year-old son of guest workers who settled near Stuttgart in the 1960s, has been particularly outspoken on minority issues since first gaining a Bundestag seat in 1993. His lobbying was instrumental to the eventual passage of the 2000 law reducing hurdles to citizenship for foreigners born in Germany. The measure rendered 40 percent of Turks - principally those of the second and third generations - eligible for immediate citizenship and thus qualified to run for political office. Ozdemir, who was re-elected in 1998 and stepped down to focus on better facilitating Muslim communal integration in 2002, notes that these "babies born today won't experience what I went through. They will grow up as citizens, and it will change the future of the country. . . There are going to be Ozdemirs at every level, local, state and federal. That's for sure, because the law will change the attitudes of the society and because there could soon be two million new voters, enough to swing an election. One day it will be very normal for a non-German like myself to be a member of the government". *(See Ref 544)*

Yet, notwithstanding such electoral advances, there remains a relative dearth of effective cross-ethnic political advocacy groups among the Muslims in the Federal Republic. A 1999 study of minority behaviour in Western Europe, for example, found that ethnicity - not religion - is the primary motivating factor in the establishment of political organisations by foreigners residing in Germany. According to the study, 82.5 percent of minority claims filed with the German government from 1990-95 came on behalf of groups identifying themselves by ethnicity or nationality rather than religious denomination. Specifically, of those claims, 33, 15 and 4 percent were made by individuals referring to themselves as Kurds, Turks and Muslims, respectively. Additionally, among all minority claims made during the above period, 41.5 percent were related to contemporary issues in their countries of origin as opposed to just 6.3 percent associated with the integration and civil rights of foreigners in Germany. *(See Ref 545)*

The initial appearance, subsequent growth and eventual entrenchment of Muslim communities in the Federal Republic over the latter half of the 20th century left the German national and regional political establishments with a dilemma. Successive governments whether SPD or CDU-CSU in party affiliation, had to determine how to respond to the presence of then unfamiliar minority groups domestically. They have employed three distinct strategies to that end over the past four decades. First, the government employed the recruitment of temporary foreign guest workers to boost industrial expansion in the 1950s and 1960s, and segregation of those minorities from mainstream society during their stays in Germany. Second, it made efforts to reduce the flow of new migrants to the Federal Republic and encouraged the departure of those already residing there between the early 1970s and the reunification of Germany in 1990. Third, it made gradual acceptance of the need to fully integrate minority groups through a series of inclusive initiatives in the 1990s and 2000s.

Since the end of World War II, governments of the left and right alike have proclaimed unabatedly that the Federal Republic is not "a country of immigration," a demographically inaccurate rhetorical stance belying the fact that foreigners account for 80 percent of Germany's population growth over the last 50 years. The government's approach to the recruitment and subsequent use and treatment of foreign workers in the 1950s and 1960s was illustrative of this philosophy. From the outset of the guest worker programs, Germany officials viewed immigrants as a temporary solution to the shortages of labour caused by the loss of domestic manpower that occurred during the war. Theoretically, as soon as the native German labour pool was once again sufficient to satisfy the demand for blue-collar jobs, the guest workers would return to their countries of origin. Thus, there was no reason to develop a model for the integration of foreign minority groups. *(See Ref 546)*

However, when declining labour demand in the 1970s sparked a wave of family reunifications rather than an exodus of foreigners, the Federal Republic was forced to acknowledge and respond to ongoing increases in the number of immigrants and the resultant potential for permanent alterations in the demographics of German society. Over the ensuing two decades, national and Länder government officials did so through a pair of related legal and political strategies. First, they attempted to stem the flow of new migrants to Germany by ending foreign labour recruitment, gradually imposing restrictions on reunification of guest worker families and implementing programs to entice minorities to return home. Second, they sought to entrench clear distinctions between foreigners and Germans in the legal system in order to slow if not fully preclude the development of a multi-ethnic domestic society. *(Germany is made up of sixteen Länder. Singular Land, colloquially but rarely in a legal context also called Bundesland, for "federated state")*

The development of a federal policy vis-à-vis family reunification neither eliminated the need to eventually incorporate foreigners into German society nor ensured uniform treatment of minorities across the Federal Republic. In light of the considerable autonomy accorded to Länd governments in the Basic Law, Länder governments often treat immigrants with differing levels of tolerance. This bifurcation was manifested in a series of legal and political conflicts - particularly after the change in administrations in Bonn in 1982 - among officials at the federal and Länd levels and the minority communities they governed. Examples included an increase of the aforementioned federal family reunification stipulation on marriage from one to three years in Baden-Württemburg and Bavaria, Bremen's refusal to lower from 18 to 16 the maximum age for foreign children to rejoin their parents in Germany and Hesse's lowering of the second-generation marriage requirement from eight to five years. *(See Ref 542)*

Ultimately, such contradictions resulted in a series of attempts to develop a universal policy on minorities, which culminated in the enactment of a new Foreigner Law in April 1990. The measure featured a mixture of old and new ideas vis-à-vis the treatment of foreigners under German law. Positively, it acknowledged that, by 1990, nearly 70 percent of foreigners residing in the Federal Republic were natives, including 1.5 million born there since 1970. It also refrained from the explicit encouragement of return migration. On the negative side, at least from the perspective of Islamic communities, the law retained one overarching element of past dogma: it "replicated the fundamental distinction between Germans and foreigners." However, that distinction in itself served as the basis for the campaign to reduce hurdles to citizenship for foreigners that unfolded over the balance of the decade.

The political debate over the integration of minorities in Germany in the 1990s focused on two questions. First, should the national government concentrate primarily on protecting the rights of foreigners living in the Federal Republic or on easing restrictions on the acquisition of citizenship by members of those minority groups? Second, upon resolution of the initial question, what type of model would prove most useful in building a more inclusive society?

The first question was resolved - albeit not until after the change of government from Helmut Kohl to Gerhard Schröder and even then only after a full year of SPD - Green rule and over strident objections from the opposition CDU-CSU in favour of the reduction of citizenship barriers to foreigners. The 2000 citizenship law included three revolutionary provisions with respect to residents previously defined as foreigners. First, children born in Germany to foreign parents acquired immediate eligibility for citizenship - both in the future and retroactively for those individuals 10 years of age or younger - if at least one parent has lived legally in the Federal Republic for at least eight years. Second, children obtaining citizenship under this provision were also given the right to hold dual passports until the age of 23, at which point they must choose German or foreign nationality. Third, the residency requirement was reduced from 15 to eight years for adult foreigners seeking German citizenship. *(See Ref 547)*

Concurrent with progress toward higher levels of citizenship for foreigners -both preceding and in the time since the enactment of the 2000 law- the resolution of the second question continues to revolve around the development of an effective integration model. Governmental discussions on the issue have been limited to two general options. First,the assimilation of minorities - either as individuals or communities - into mainstream German society. Second, the acknowledgement and gradual acceptance of the co-existence of majority and minority cultures in the Federal Republic. The latter option has proved the most amenable to date, particularly so with respect to the federal and Länder governments and ethnic German population but also to a large extent among minority groups. As Christian Joppke explains: in "both nationally exclusive and post-nationally inclusive perspectives, immigrants are not expected to assimilate. The rejection of assimilation is the one continuity in the unprincipled, wavering German approach to immigrant integration". *(See Ref 546)*

What is the situation of the Muslim communities in the United Kingdom?

Islamic communities in the United Kingdom are composed of groups from a wide range of ethnic backgrounds. The majority of Muslims residing in Britain are of Pakistani, Indian and Bangladeshi extraction. However, the United Kingdom is also home to Muslims with roots -whether immediate or one or two generations removed - in countries such as Saudi Arabia, Yemen, Iran, Turkey, Malaysia and Nigeria. For example, a variety of statistical estimates, including but not limited to the 2001 census, categorise Muslims inhabitants in the following ethnic and numerical terms: 775,000 Pakistanis, 395,000 Indians, 357,000 Bangladeshis, 450,000 Middle Easterners and North Africans and 280,000 others (most notably Nigerians and Malaysians). These totals, however, do not account for illegal immigration, which is understandably difficult to measure accurately. *(See Ref 538, 548)*

As is true of North Africans in France and Turks in Germany, Pakistani, Bangladeshi and Indian Muslims in the United Kingdom are concentrated in low-rent housing blocks on the peripheries rather than in the city centres of major metropolitan areas such as London, Bradford, Birmingham, Manchester and Glasgow. The communities in which Muslims live are distinguished by a variety of ethnic, religious and social class characteristics, with Pakistanis, Bangladeshis, Indians and Arabs each clustered in distinct neighbourhoods of a particular city. Geographically, for instance, more than two-thirds of British minorities are situated in the Greater London, West Midlands (Birmingham), Greater Manchester and West Yorkshire (Bradford) regions compared with less than one-fifth of whites residing in those environs. *(See Ref 549)*

Pakistani communities in the United Kingdom are located predominantly in north-central England, an industrial region traditionally known for the production of textiles. Nearly 50 percent of British Pakistanis reside in the Greater Manchester, West Midlands and West Yorkshire regions, more than one-third of whom live in Birmingham and Bradford, accounting for four and five percent of the populations of those metropolitan areas, respectively. In each of the latter two cases, Pakistanis are concentrated in a low proportion of municipal wards - eight of 42 in Birmingham and seven of 30 in Bradford - which are culturally and religiously distinct, with mosques and halal butcher shops prevalent in most neighbourhoods. Similarly, almost half of Britain's Bangladeshis reside in London (36,955 in Tower Hamlets alone) and more than three-quarters of its Indian Muslims live in either London or Leicester. *(See Ref 550)*

Economically, Muslims residing in the United Kingdom are forced to subsist at significantly lower levels than is true of the societal majority, in large part because of substandard income levels and high unemployment rates in the Pakistani, Bangladeshi - and to a lesser extent -Indian communities. Figures drawn from a 2004 study, for example, indicated that Muslim men (13 percent) and women (18 percent) had the highest unemployment rates of any groups in the United Kingdom.A 1999 study conducted by the British Board of Health found that among those males 16 and over with jobs, 90 percent of Bangladeshis and 70 percent of Pakistanis earned 10,000 pounds or less per year as opposed to a national average of 28 percent. Similarly, just one percent of Bangladeshis and four percent of Pakistanis earned 30,000 pounds or more, whereas the national average was 23 percent. *(See Ref 538, 551)*

In terms of the role of Islam in British Muslims' lives, the manner in which individuals with different ethnic and denominational backgrounds practice their faith are by no means identical. For example, although Pakistanis and Bangladeshis are predominantly followers of the Sunni strain of Islam and generally more inclined to practice their religion regularly, their dispositions toward inter-faith marriages differ significantly. According to one poll, while 64 percent of Pakistanis view marrying outside of Islam negatively, only 35 percent of Bangladeshis share that viewpoint. Similarly, although nearly three-quarters of Pakistanis and Bangladeshis consider religion "very important" in their lives and nearly 90 percent abstain from the consumption of alcohol as stipulated in the Koran, those living in close proximity rarely worship at the same mosque.

Instead, Muslims of variegated ethnic and ancestral backgrounds often pray at mosques employing imams from the villages to which they trace their familial ancestry. As a result, the points a given imam makes in the course of presiding at Friday services are at times more reflective of political circumstances on the Indian subcontinent than those germane to the contemporary United Kingdom. *(See Ref 552)*

This lack of socio-religious homogeneity has complicated the efforts of Muslim communities to achieve political representation to a degree proportionate to their share of the population, glaringly so at the national level. In order to examine the roles of Muslims in British political life accurately but incisively, brief analyses of two types of representation are necessary.

First, the endeavours of individual politicians catering to the needs of the Muslim communities, whether through seeking - and at times achieving election to - office in the national parliament or on a local council. Second, the pursuit of Islamic communal objectives by political parties and organisations, some sponsored internally and others externally.

Just six Muslims have earned seats in the parliament in 2010 general elections; and Rushanara Ali, was the first Muslim woman and person of Bangladeshi origin to be elected to the British parliament in that election, stood for former Prime Minister Gordon Brown's Labour Party. She won the east London seat of Bethnal Green and Bow.

The initial appearance, subsequent growth and eventual entrenchment of minority Muslim communities in the United Kingdom over the latter half of the 20th century left the British political establishment with a dilemma. Successive governments, whether Labour or Conservative in political orientation, had to determine how to respond to the presence of then unfamiliar minority groups in Britain. As opposed to the French and German cases, the migration of guest workers to the United Kingdom was triggered by a combination of private recruitment and individual initiative rather than formal government sponsorship. London's primary internal policy objective related to the collapse of the British imperial empire was to minimise immigration from former colonies in order to ensure the preservation of domestic homogeneity. As Christian Joppke notes, "Britain rejected immigration because of political boundaries wider than the nation: its immigrants were formal co-nationals without substantive ties of belonging, capitalizing on political boundaries that had too expansively and indistinctly been drawn on the boundaries of the empire". *(See Ref 546)*

In general terms, most legislative measures pertaining to the issue of minorities in the United Kingdom between 1948 and 1981 were designed either to reduce immigration flows or limit the citizenship rights of those migrants who had already settled in major British cities. Examples of this brand of legislation included the British Nationality Act of 1948, the Commonwealth Immigrants Acts of 1962 and 1968, the Immigration Act of 1971 and the British Nationality Act of 1981. The Commonwealth Immigrants Act of 1962 limited citizenship to individuals born in the United Kingdom proper, thus excluding migrants from former colonies in South Asia and Africa. Similarly, the Commonwealth Immigrants Act of 1968 denied entry to 200,000 East African Asians fleeing repression in post-independence Kenya. The 1981 British Nationality Act was even more discriminatory: it redefined the traditional jus soli, which granted automatic citizenship to anyone born in the United Kingdom, in a manner that increased the legal hurdles for migrants' children born in Britain who attempt to obtain citizenship. *(See Ref 542)*

In short, the above measures all served - whether consciously designed as such or not - to postpone if not avoid altogether the daunting challenge of fully integrating minority groups generally and South Asian Muslims specifically into British society. However, notwithstanding government attempts to reduce immigration and thus limit the presence of ethnic, racial and religious minorities, Muslim communities grew and developed distinct cultural identities in a large part through the reunification of families in the 1970s. As a result, it was left to the Conservative and Labour governments of the 1980s and 1990s first to acknowledge and then to attempt to redress the exclusion of minorities from the benefits accompanying acceptance by the societal mainstream. Building on the limited work undertaken by their predecessors - both historically distant and recent - via measures such as the Race Relations Act of 1976, contemporary British leaders have addressed the issue of integration through a general framework that contrasts starkly with that described in the French case study: The recognition of the coexistence of distinctive minority communities as opposed to the assimilation of individuals into an overarching national culture.

The United Kingdom laid the foundation for its present approach to the integration of minority groups through the then Home Secretary Roy Jenkins' formal dismissal of the utility of assimilation as a workable policy in 1966. At that juncture, Jenkins stressed that "I do not think that we need in this country a 'melting pot.' . . . I define integration, therefore, not as a process of flattening uniformity but of cultural diversity coupled with equal opportunity in an atmosphere of mutual tolerance". Essentially, Jenkins' statement implied both that there was room for the existence of myriad distinct cultures in the context of British society and that - irrespective of origin - those minorities not ascribing to the traditional norms of the mainstream were entitled to equal protection under the law. *(See Ref 553)*

Jenkins' formula was the initial public step in a process that continues - but as yet remains incomplete - in present-day Britain. The general rhetoric encapsulated in his multicultural approach was formalised through the Race Relations Acts of 1968 and 1976, the latter of which established a Commission for Racial Equality (CRE) designed to respond to the concerns of the United Kingdom's minority communities. The Race Relations Act of 1976 sought to ameliorate the economic - and by association - class standings of minority groups by prohibiting two types of discrimination. First, direct discrimination on the basis of "colour, race, nationality, ethnic or national origin". Second, indirect discrimination, "in which a 'condition or requirement' is applied that stops persons of a particular race from complying with it equally, is not 'justifiable' on non-racial grounds, and works to the 'detriment of these persons'". *(See Ref 554)*

The United Kingdom's multicultural formula for integration reflects the pragmatic nature of British national identity. Rather than facilitate protection of minority rights through constitutional means similar to those prevalent in the United States and Germany, the United Kingdom - at least in theory - uses multiculturalism to achieve the political flexibility necessary to accommodate minority concerns, whether defined in terms of race, ethnicity, nationality or an admixture of those elements. This flexible construct served as the basis for the CRE's development of two strategies to achieve progress toward the full integration of minority groups in the 1980s and 1990s. First, it pressed for and ultimately obtained government approval of a question on ethnic origin in the 1991 national census in order to more accurately gauge the number and needs of minorities residing in the United Kingdom. Second, it pushed for and has gradually achieved recognition of minority cultural requirements in government administered institutions such as prisons, schools, public services and the military. *(See Ref 546)*

However, notwithstanding the CRE's successful efforts to improve the status of minorities generally, the United Kingdom's multicultural approach has proved less effective vis-à-vis the integration of Muslims in particular. Put simply, while multiculturalism is a noble and often effective means to recognise the relevance of a variety of groups - both majority and minority - possessing distinct and disparate characteristics in a given society, it must include fully all communities that exist within that context. Additionally, even once all those groups are recognised, multiculturalism in and of itself does not ensure that the majority and minority will develop the cooperative multilateral relationships that are required to form an inclusive whole.

The case of Muslims in the United Kingdom is demonstrative both of the daunting challenges associated with the integration of minority groups and the implications of that process.

While the European governments failed to contain and integrate their Muslim communities in their societies other Islamic radicals, especially the Muslim Brotherhood, were working to make from that failure an opportunity to attain other objectives.

Europe has become an incubator for Islamist thought and political development since the early 1960s, when Muslim Brotherhood members and sympathisers have moved to Europe and slowly but steadily established a wide and well-organised network of mosques, charities, and Islamic organisations. Unlike the larger Islamic community, the Muslim Brotherhood's ultimate goal may not be simply "to help Muslims be the best citizens they can be," but rather to extend Islamic law throughout Europe and the United States. *(See Ref 555, 556)*

Four decades of teaching and cultivation have paid off. The student refugees who migrated from the Middle East forty years ago and their descendants now lead organisations that represent the local Muslim communities in their engagement with Europe's political elite. Funded by generous contributors from the Persian Gulf, they preside over a centralised network that spans nearly every European country.

These organisations represent themselves as mainstream, even as they continue to embrace the Brotherhood's radical views and maintain links to terrorists. With moderate rhetoric and well-spoken German, Dutch, Italian, Spanish, English and French, they have gained acceptance among European governments and media alike. Politicians across the political spectrum rush to engage them whenever an issue involving Muslims arises or, more parochially, when they seek the vote of the burgeoning Muslim community.

But, speaking Arabic or Turkish before their fellows Muslims, they drop their facade and embrace radicalism. While their representatives speak about interfaith dialogue and integration on television, their mosques preach hate and warn worshippers about the evils of Western society. While they publicly condemn the murder of commuters in Madrid and school children in Russia, they continue to raise money for Islamic terrorist organisations. Europeans, eager to create a dialogue with their increasingly disaffected Muslim minority, overlook this duplicity. The case is particularly visible in Germany, which retains a place of key importance in Europe, not only because of its location at the heart of Europe, but also because it played host to the first major wave of Muslim Brotherhood immigrants and is host to the best-organised Brotherhood presence. The German government's reaction is also instructive if only to show the dangers of accepting Muslim Brotherhood rhetoric at face value, without looking at the broader scope of its activities. *(See Ref 557)*

The situation in Germany is particularly telling. More than anywhere else in Europe, the Muslim Brotherhood in Germany has gained significant power and political acceptance. Islamist organisations in other European countries now consciously follow the model pioneered by their German peers.

During the 1950s and 1960s, thousands of Muslim students left the Middle East to study at German universities, drawn not only by the German institutions' technical reputations but also by a desire to escape repressive regimes. Egyptian ruler Gamal Abdel Nasser's regime was especially vigorous in its attempts to root out the Islamist opposition. Beginning in 1954, several members of the Muslim Brotherhood fled Egypt to escape arrest or assassination. West Germany provided a welcome refuge. Bonn's motivations were not simply altruistic. As terrorism expert Khalid Durán explained in his studies on jihadism in Europe, the West German government had decided to cut diplomatic relations with countries that recognised East Germany. When Egypt and Syria established diplomatic relations with the communist government, Bonn decided to welcome Syrian and Egyptian political refugees. Often, these dissidents were Islamists. Many members of the Muslim Brotherhood were already familiar with Germany. Several had cooperated with the Nazis before and during World War II. Some had even, reportedly, fought in the infamous Bosnian Handschar division of the Schutzstaffel (SS). *(See Ref 558, 559, 560)*

One of the Muslim Brotherhood's first pioneers in Germany was Sa'id Ramadan, the personal secretary of Muslim Brotherhood founder Hassan al-Banna. Ramadan, an Egyptian who had led the Muslim Brotherhood's irregulars in Palestine in 1948, moved to Geneva in 1958 and attended law school in Cologne. In Germany, he founded what has become one of Germany's three main Muslim organisations, the Islamische Gemeinschaft Deutschland (Islamic Society of Germany, IGD), over which he presided from 1958 to 1968.Ramadan also cofounded the Muslim World League, a well-funded organisation that the Saudi establishment uses to spread its interpretation of Islam throughout the world. The U.S. government closely monitors the activities of the Muslim World League, which it accuses of financing terrorism. In March 2002, a U.S. Treasury Department-led task force raided the group's Northern Virginia offices looking for documents tying the group to al-Qa'ida, Hamas, and Palestinian Islamic Jihad. In January 2004, the Senate Finance Committee asked the Internal Revenue Service for its records on the Muslim World League "as part of an investigation into possible links between non-governmental organisations and terrorist financing networks". This privileged relationship with the oil-rich kingdom granted Ramadan an influx of money, which he used to fund the powerful Islamic Centre of Geneva and to bankroll several financial and religious activities. Hani Ramadan, Sa'id's son, currently runs the Islamic Centre. Among its other board members is Sa'id's other son, Tariq Ramadan, who recently made headlines in the United States when the Department of Homeland Security revoked his visa to teach at Notre Dame University. Sa'id Ramadan's case is not isolated. *(See Ref 561, 562, 563, 564)*

Following Ramadan's ten-year presidency of the IGD, Pakistani national Fazal Yazdani briefly led the IGD before Ghaleb Himmat, a Syrian with Italian citizenship, took the helm. During his long stewardship (1973-2002), Himmat shuttled between Italy, Austria, Germany, Switzerland and the

United States. Intelligence agencies around the world have long scrutinised Himmat's "terrorist connections". He is one of the founders of the Bank al-Taqwa, a powerful conglomerate dubbed by Italian intelligence, "Bank of the Muslim Brotherhood," which has financed radical Islamic groups since the mid-1990s if not earlier. Himmat helped Youssef Nada, one of the Muslim Brotherhood's financial masterminds, run Al-Taqwa and a web of companies headquartered in locations such as Switzerland, Liechtenstein, and the Bahamas, which maintain few regulations on monetary origin or destination. Both Himmat and Nada reportedly funneled large sums to groups such as Hamas and the Algerian Islamic Salvation Front (FIS) and set up a secret credit line for a top associate of Osama bin Laden. *(See Ref 565, 566)*

In November 2001, the U.S. Treasury Department designated both Himmat and Nada as terrorism financiers. According to Italian intelligence, the Al-Taqwa network also financed several Islamic centres throughout Europe and many Islamist publications, including "Risalat al-Ikhwan", the official magazine of the Muslim Brotherhood. After the U.S. Treasury Department designation, Himmat resigned from the IGD's presidency. His successor was Ibrahim el-Zayat, a 36-year-old of Egyptian descent and the charismatic leader of numerous student organisations. *(See Ref 565, 566, 567)*

The fact that IGD leaders Ramadan and Himmat are among the most prominent Muslim Brotherhood members of the last half-century suggests the links between the IGD and the Ikhwan. Moreover, reports issued by internal intelligence agencies from various German states openly call the IGD an offshoot of the Muslim Brotherhood. In particular, according to one intelligence report, the Egyptian branch of the Muslim Brotherhood has dominated the IGD since its early days. *(See Ref 568, 569)*

The Muslim Brotherhood -led by Ramadan and Himmat- sponsored the construction of the imposing Islamic Centre of Munich in 1960, aided by large donations from Middle Eastern governments such as Saudi Arabia who, according to a 1967 Sueddeutsche Zeitung article, donated 80,000 marks. The Ministry of Interior of Nordrhein-Westfalen states that the Islamic Centre of Munich has been one of the European headquarters for the Brotherhood since its foundation. The centre publishes a magazine, Al-Islam, whose efforts (according to an Italian intelligence dossier), are financed by the Bank al-Taqwa. According to the interior minister of

Baden-Württemberg, Al-Islam shows explicitly how the German Brothers reject the concept of a secular state. Its February 2002 issue, for example, states: "In the long run, Muslims cannot be satisfied with the acceptance of German family, estate, and trial law. … Muslims should aim at an agreement between the Muslims and the German State with the goal of a separate jurisdiction for Muslims". *(See Ref 571, 572, 573)*

The IGD, of which the Islamic Centre of Munich is one of the most important members, represents the main offshoot of the Egyptian Brotherhood in Germany. But the IGD is also the quintessential example of how the Muslim Brotherhood has gained power in Europe. The IGD has grown significantly over the years, and it now incorporates dozens of Islamic organisations throughout the country. Islamic centres from more than thirty German cities have joined its umbrella.Today, the IGD's real strength lies in its cooperation with and sponsorship of many Islamic youth and student organisations across Germany. *(See Ref 574)*

This focus on youth organisations came after Zayat's succession. He understood the importance of focusing on the next generation of German Muslims and launched recruitment drives to get young Muslims involved in Islamic organisations. But a Meckenheim police report on the sharply dressed Zayat also reveals alarming connections. German authorities openly say he is a member of the Muslim Brotherhood. They also link him to the World Assembly of Muslim Youth (WAMY), a Saudi non-governmental organisation that seeks to spread Wahhabism, the Saudi interpretation of Islam, throughout the world with its literature and schools.WAMY, which falls under the umbrella of the Muslim World League, has the stated goal of "arming the Muslim youth with full confidence in the supremacy of the Islamic system over other systems". It is the largest Muslim youth organisation in the world and can boast unparalleled resources.In 1991 WAMY published a book called "Tawjihat Islamiyya" (Islamic Views) that stated, "Teach our children to love taking revenge on the Jews and the oppressors, and teach them that our youngsters will liberate Palestine and Al-Quds [Jerusalem] when they go back to Islam and make jihad for the sake of Allah". The sentiments in Tawjihat Islamiyya are the rule rather than the exception. Many other WAMY publications are filled with strong anti-Jews and anti-Christian rhetoric. *(See Ref 575, 576)*

Meckenheim police also link Zayat to Institut Européen des Sciences Humaines, a French school that prepares European imams. Several radical clerics lecture at the school and several European intelligence agencies accuse the school of spreading religious hatred. German authorities also highlight the fact that he is involved in several money laundering investigations. Zayat has never been indicted for terrorist activity, but he has dubious financial dealings and maintains associations with many organisations that spread religious hatred. The IGD may have changed leadership after the U.S. Treasury's designation of Himmat, but it did not change direction. *(See Ref 577)*

While the Egyptian branch of the Muslim Brotherhood has chosen Munich as its base of operations in Germany, its Syrian branch is headquartered in Aachen, a German town near the Dutch border. The former Carolingian capital, with its famous university, is now home to a large Muslim population including the prominent Syrian Al-Attar family. The first Attar to move to Aachen was Issam, who fled persecution in his native country in the 1950s when he was leader of the Syrian branch of the Muslim Brotherhood. Other members of the Syrian Muslim Brotherhood soon followed. With time, Islamists from other countries adopted Attar's Bilal mosque in Aachen as their base of operations. From hosting exiled Algerian terrorists to operating a charity designated by the U.S. Department of Treasury as a financial front for Hamas, Aachen is well known to intelligence agencies throughout the world. *(See Ref 558)*

The Syrian Muslim Brotherhood base in Aachen kept close relations with their Egyptian counterparts. For example, confirming the tendency of important Muslim Brotherhood families to close alliance through intermarriage, Issam al-Attar's son married the daughter of Al-Taqwa banker Youssef Nada.Links between the two Muslim Brotherhood branches are more extensive than a single marriage, however. The Aachen Islamic Centre reportedly received funding from Al-Taqwa.Staff members have rotated between the Islamic Centres in Aachen and Munich. For example, Ahmed von Denffer, editor of the Islamic Centre of Munich's Al-Islam magazine, came to Munich from Aachen.Nevertheless, some distance remains. The Syrian Muslim Brotherhood has never joined the IGD, instead preferring to keep some form of independence. *(See Ref 558, 565)*

From all of Zayat's financial activities, the one that has attracted the German authorities' greatest suspicion has been his association with officials of Milli Görüş (National Vision, in Turkish). Milli Görüş, which has more than 30,000 members, and perhaps another 100,000 sympathizers, claims to defend the rights of Germany's immigrant Turkish population, giving them a voice in the democratic political arena while "preserving their Islamic identity". But Milli Görüş has another agenda. While publicly declaring its interest in democratic debate and a willingness to see Turkish immigrants integrated into European societies, some Milli Görüş leaders have expressed contempt for democracy and Western values. The Bundesverfassungsschutz, Germany's domestic intelligence agency, has repeatedly warned about Milli Görüş' activities, describing the group in its annual reports as a "foreign extremist organisation". The agency also reported that "although Milli Görüş, in public statements, pretends to adhere to the basic principles of Western democracies, abolition of the laicist government system in Turkey and the establishment of an Islamic state and social system are, as before, among its goals". *(See Ref 579, 580)*

Milli Görüş' history alone indicates why the group should be considered radical. Former Turkish Prime Minister Nehmettin (Nejmedeen) Erbakan, whose Refah Party was banned by the Turkish Constitutional Court in January of 1998 for "activities against the country's secular regime", was until his death on 27 February 2011, Milli Görüş' undisputed leader, even if his nephew Mehmet Sabri Erbakan is its president. The 2002 European Milli Görüş meeting held in the Dutch city of Arnhem, where Nehmettin Erbakan was the keynote speaker, provides a glimpse into Milli Görüş' ideology. After a tirade against the evils of integration in the West and U.S. policies, Erbakan declared that "after the fall of the wall, the West has found an enemy in Islam." A Bundesverfassungsschutz report reveals Milli Görüş' real aims: "While in recent times, the Milli Görüş has increasingly emphasised the readiness of its members to be integrated into German society and asserts its adherence to the basic law, such statements stem from tactical calculation rather than from any inner change of the organisation". *(See Ref 579, 581, 582)*

Milli Görüş pushes an agenda similar to that of the IGD, even if its target is more limited. Nevertheless, both Milli Görüş and the IGD collaborate on many initiatives. There is also a family connection. El-Zayat married Sabiha Erbakan, the sister of Mehmet Sabri Erbakan. The siblings' mother is also involved in politics and runs an important Islamic women's organisation in Germany. The el-Zayat family is active as well. Ibrahim el-Zayat's father is the imam of the Marburg mosque; other members of his family are involved in Islamic organisations. As Udo Ulfkotte, a political science professor specialising in counter-espionage at the University of Lueneburg and an expert on Islamic terrorism, notes, the Erbakans and the el-Zayats lead networks of organisations that aim at the radicalisation, respectively, of the Turkish and Arab communities in Germany. *(See Ref 557, 583)*

IGD and Milli Görüş are active in their efforts to increase political influence and become the official representatives of the entire German Muslim community. With well-endowed budgets, their mosques provide social services, organise conferences, and distribute literature nationwide. As the Office for the Protection of the Constitution (Landesverfassungsschutz) in Hessen notes: "The threat of Islamism for Germany is posed ... primarily by Milli Görüş and other affiliated groups. They try to spread Islamist views within the boundaries of the law. Then they try to implement ... for all Muslims in Germany a strict interpretation of the Koran and of the Shari'a. ... Their public support of tolerance and religious freedom should be treated with caution". *(See Ref 584)*

It presents a problem that politicians and security services in Germany view the IGD and Milli Görüş so differently. But, as Ulfkotte wrote about el-Zayat in his book, "Der Krieg in unseren Staedten" (The War in Our Cities): "politicians of all colours and parties try to reach out to him". For example, the prestigious Berlin Catholic Academy invited el-Zayat to represent the Muslim point of view in an inter-religious meeting organised by the academy in October 2002. German politicians and Christian institutions regularly partner themselves with Milli Görüş in various initiatives. Milli Gazete, the official journal of Milli Görüş, once stated that "Milli Görüş is a shield protecting our fellow citizens from assimilation into barbaric Europe". Nevertheless, German politicians meet regularly with Milli Görüş officials to discuss immigration and integration issues. The fact that an official like Ahmed al-Khalifah, IGD secretary general, represents Islam before members of parliament, who are discussing religious tolerance, shows the success of Brotherhood-linked organisations' efforts to gain acceptance as the representatives of German Muslims. The Office for the Protection of the Constitution well described these efforts, saying that Milli Görüş (and the IGD) "strives to dominate regional or nationwide federations and umbrella organisations for Muslims which are increasingly gaining importance as interlocutors for state and ecclesiastical authorities and thus to expand its influence within society". *(See Ref 585, 586, 587)*

In 1989, under the auspices of Abdallah at-Turki, dean of Bin Saud University in Riyadh, the Saudis created the Islamische Konzil Deutschland (Islamic Council of Germany). Turki assumed the presidency with other top positions held by Ibrahim el-Zayat, Hasan Özdögan, a high-ranking Milli Görüş official, and Ahmad Khalifa, an officer from the Islamic Centre of Munich. However an official German parliament report describes the Islamische Konzil as just "another Sunni organisation". *(See Ref 557)*

The trend toward consolidation took a step forward in 1994 when German Islamists realised that a united coalition translated into greater political relevance and influence. Nineteen organisations, including the IGD, the Islamic Centre of Munich, and the Islamic Centre of Aachen, created an umbrella organisation, the Zentralrat der Muslime. According to a senior German intelligence official, at least nine out of these nineteen organisations belong to the Muslim Brotherhood.The German press has recently investigated the Zentralrat president, Nadeem Elyas, a German-educated Saudi physician and an official of the Islamic Centre of Aachen. Die Welt linked Elyas to Christian Ganczarski, an al-Qa'ida operative currently jailed as one of the masterminds of the 2002 attack on a synagogue in Tunisia.Ganczarski, a German of Polish descent who converted to Islam, told authorities that al-Qa'ida recruited him at the Islamic University of Medina where Elyas sent him to study. Elyas said he could not remember meeting him but did not deny the possibility that Ganczarski, who never completed high school, might have been one of the many individuals he had sent over the years to radical schools in Saudi Arabia. Saudi donors paid all of Ganczarski's expenses. Ganczarski was not alone. Elyas admitted to having sent hundreds of German Muslims to study at one of the radical Islamic institutions in Saudi Arabia. *(See Ref 588, 589, 590, 591)*

The Zentralrat, which portrays itself as the umbrella organisation for German Muslim organisations, has become, together with the IGD and Milli Görüş, the de facto representative of more than four million German Muslims. Even though the IGD is a member of the Zentralrat, the two organisations often operate independently. Their apparent independence is planned. With many organisations operating under different names, the Muslim Brotherhood fools German politicians who believe they are consulting a spectrum of opinion.The media seek the Zentralrat's officials when they want the Muslim view on everything from the debate about the admissibility of the hijab (headscarf) in public schools, to the war in Iraq, and so forth. Politicians seek the Zentralrat's endorsement when they want to reach out to the Muslim community. Many German politicians are uninformed about Islam and do not understand that the view and the interpretation of Islam that the Zentralrat expresses, as does the IGD and Milli Görüş, is that of the Muslim Brotherhood and not that of traditional Islam. Accordingly, the Zentralrat expresses total opposition to any ban of the hijab, supports Wahhabi-influenced Islamic education in schools, and endorses a radical position on the Middle East situation.While many Muslims endorse these views, the problem is that the Zentralrat neither represents nor tolerates those with divergent views. Moderate German Muslim groups lack the funding and organisation of Muslim Brotherhood-linked groups. In terms of numbers, influence on the Muslim community, and political relevance, the Zentralrat and its two most important constituent parts, the IGD and Milli Görüş, dominate the scene. With ample Islamic governments financing especially from the Gulf countries, the Muslim Brotherhood has managed to become the voice of the Muslims in Germany. *(See Ref 592)*

While the Muslim Brotherhood and their Gulf States financiers especially from Saudi Arabia have worked to cement Islamist influence over Germany's Muslim community, they have not limited their infiltration to Germany. Thanks to generous foreign funding, meticulous organisation, and the naïveté of European elites, Muslim Brotherhood-linked organisations have gained prominent positions throughout Europe. In France, the extremist Union des Organisations Islamiques de France (Union of Islamic Organisations of France) has become the predominant organisation in the government's Islamic Council.In Italy, the extremist Unione delle Comunita' ed Organizzazioni Islamiche in Italia (Union of the Islamic Communities and Organisations in Italy) is the government's prime partner in dialogue regarding Italian Islamic issues. *(See Ref 593, 594)*

In parallel to European Union integration efforts, the Muslim Brotherhood is also seeking to integrate its various European proxies. Over the past twenty years, the Muslim Brotherhood has created a series of pan-European organisations such as the Federation of Islamic Organisations in Europe, in which representatives from national organisations can meet and plan initiatives. Perhaps the Muslim Brotherhood's greatest pan-European impact has, as with the Islamische Gemeinschaft Deutschland, been with its youth organisation. In June 1996, Muslim youth organisations from Sweden, France, and England joined forces with the Federation of Islamic Organisations in Europe and the World Assembly of Muslim Youth to create a European Islamic youth organisation. Three months later, thirty-five delegates from eleven countries met in Leicester and formally launched the Forum of European Muslim Youth and Student Organisations (FEMYSO), which maintains its headquarters in Brussels. *(See Ref 595, 596)*

According to its official publications, FEMYSO is "a network of 42 national and international organisations bringing together youth from over 26 different countries." FEMYSO proudly stated in 2003 that over the preceding four years it had become the de facto voice of the Muslim youth in Europe. It is regularly consulted on issues pertaining to Muslims in Europe. It has also developed useful links with: the European Parliament, the Council of Europe, the United Nations, the European Youth Forum, and numerous relevant NGOs at the European level.

Ibrahim el-Zayat, who held the presidency until his commitments in Germany forced him to step down, even used the FEMYSO perch to address the European Parliament. Because the Muslim Brotherhood provides the bulk of FEMYSO's constituent organisations, it provides the "de facto voice of the Muslim youth in Europe". While FEMYSO claims that it "is committed to fighting prejudices at all the levels, so that the future of Europe is a multicultural, inclusive and respectful one", such statements ring hollow given the position of sponsors like the World Assembly of Muslim Youth which believes that "the Jews are enemies of the faithful, God, and the Angels; the Jews are humanity's enemies. ... Every tragedy that inflicts the Muslims is caused by the Jews". *(See Ref 597, 598, 599)*

The Muslim Brotherhood's ample funds and organisation have contributed to their success in Europe. But their acceptance into mainstream society and their unchallenged rise to power would not have been possible had European elites been more vigilant, valued substance over rhetoric, and understood the motivations of those financing and building these Islamist organisations. Why have Europeans been so naïve? Bassam Tibi, a German professor of Syrian descent and an expert on Islam in Europe, thinks that Europeans - and Germans in particular- fear the accusation of racism. Radicals in sheep's clothing have learned that they can silence almost everybody with the accusation of xenophobia. Any criticism of Muslim Brotherhood-linked organisations is followed by outcries of racism and anti-Muslim persecution. Journalists who are not frightened by these appellatives are swamped with baseless and unsuccessful but expensive lawsuits. *(See Ref 600)*

While the Muslim Brotherhood made the furtile land for the radicals, al-Qa'ida and its affiliates came later to cultivate and take the result.

From the mid-1990s and increasingly after September 11, 2001 and the subsequent invasions of Afghanistan and Iraq, there has been a shift to terrorist violence inside Europe by Islamist radicals residing in the region, or coming from abroad. Between 1994 and 1996 terrorists linked to the Algerian Armed Islamic Group (Groupe Islamique armée or GIA) staged a series of bomb attacks in France killing 8 people and injuring more than 200. Between 1998 and the invasion of Iraq, European security services intercepted several al-Qa'ida linked terrorist cells preparing attacks against US, Israeli, French and Russian targets.After the invasion of Iraq, European nations that joined the Bush Administration's War on Terror became targets for terrorist cells composed of people with varying ties to al-Qa'ida, many of whom were Europeans by citizenship, or ethnicity.

What were the ideological influences and patterns of jihadi terrorism in Europe?

Jihadis in Europe differ greatly from their Muslim world counterparts. First, apart from a few semi-organised groups focused on propaganda and support activities, there exist no clearly defined jihadi organisations in Europe equivalent to, for example, Al-Qa'ida in Iraq, or Al-Qa'ida in the Islamic Maghreb (AQIM), etc., presenting ideological programs and coherent strategies for jihadism in European countries. Secondly, jihadis in Europe live in peaceful societies far away from jihad battlefields in the Muslim world, societies in which there are poor prospects for establishing Islamic states, or causing widespread Islamisation.

Jihadism came to Europe during the 1980s and early 1990s with a critical mass of activists, leaders and ideologues involved in the local jihadi "projects" in the Maghreb and the Levant, and/or the international jihad in Afghanistan.London emerged as the main centre for Islamist militancy referred to as Londonistan by European security officials (because it served as a base and transit place for Islamists going to Afghanistan for training and indoctrination). Because of the concentration of hardliner Islamists and jihadis in London, the capital was a popular destination for jihadis from all over Europe and the Muslim world. Radical Islamists travelled to the UK to interact with militant groups, attend the sermons of radical preachers, and make the contacts necessary to attend training camps and religious schools in the Muslim world. Terrorism investigations revealed that the majority of jihadi terrorists in Europe had attended sermons by radical preachers in London (in addition to training camps). There were militant subcultures, radical mosques and ideological mentors in other European countries as well (Milan, Madrid, Paris, Hamburg etc) as I explained above, but the jihadi community in London stood out as the most vigorous and influential. *(See Ref 601)*

Prominent London based activists who played important roles in setting up and expanding a jihadi networks in Europe include, amongst others, the Palestinian Omar Mahmoud Othman known as Abu Qatada al-Falastini, the Egyptian Mustafa Kamel Mustafa known as Abu Hamza al-Masri, the Syrian Omar Bakri Mohammed, the Syrian Mustafa Setmariam Nasar known as Abu Musab al-Suri and others. Abu Qatada acted as religious mentor for a number of jihadi combat groups formed by Arab Afghans (GIA, Libyan Islamic Fighting Group (LIFG), Tawhid wa'l Jihad etc). Bakri headed the semi-jihadi al-Muhajiroun group from localities in Tottenham, whereas Abu Hamza was the leader of a militant group called Supporters of Shari'a centred on the Finsbury Park mosque (the largest radical mosque in Europe). Abu Musab al-Suri was a more independent activist and thinker with ties to multiple jihadi groups. These jihadi activists and others contributed much to the recruitment, radicalisation and training of two generations of jihadis in Europe. *(See Ref 602)*

The 1st generation of jihadis in Europe was dominated by Maghrebian jihad veterans aiming to ignite Islamic revolutions in their home countries and function as an 'ambulance guerrilla' protecting Muslims under attack from non-Muslims. Abu Qatada was the leading activist and ideologue for the 1st generation (Abu Musab al-Suri was another important figure amongst Afghan veterans in London). The 1st generation of jihadis in turn recruited, radicalised and trained a 2nd generation of jihadis consisting of activists who were born and raised in European countries, and who had no personal experience of jihad in the Muslim world. Abu Hamza and Omar Bakri Mohammed were the charismatic leaders of the 2nd generation of jihadis in Europe within the frameworks of al-Muhajiroun and Supporters of Shari'a, and likeminded groups in other European countries. Recruits from Europe were commonly sent to al-Qa'ida associated training camps in Pakistan/Afghanistan for indoctrination and paramilitary training.

First hand accounts from the camps report that recruits were given special courses in the theorizing of the Egyptian Sayyid Qutb and other ideologues. *(See Ref 604)*

Many activists of Europe's 2nd generation jihadis came from Pakistani backgrounds and thus constituted the Pakistani-European axis of jihadism in Europe. Others came from multiple ethnic backgrounds (including European backgrounds). The 2nd generation jihadis linked to, or inspired by the global jihadi al-Qa'ida, constitute today's main terrorism threat to Europe. Activists of the 2nd generation, some of whom have received training in al-Qa'ida linked training camps in the badlands on the Afghan-Pakistani border, were behind the killing of Theo Van Gogh in Holland, the London bombings, and several high-profile attemptted attacks in the UK, Spain, Denmark, Germany and other European countries that contributed to the War on Terror. After 11 September 2001, the main radical mosques and centres in Europe were closed down, and jihadi preachers went in and out of prisons for supporting terrorism. In the post 11/9/2001 security climate the 2nd generation of jihadis in Europe oriented themselves more towards the Internet as a source of ideology. Online, the activists obtained free and direct access to a wide spectrum of ideological material, translated into multiple languages, something that enabled them to "shop around" for messages resonating with their beliefs and objectives.

What ideological material did Europe's jihadis access?

Information from terrorism investigations (judicial documents, press reporting and correspondence with one expert witness) and secondary literature, suggests Europe's jihadis accessed three main categories of ideological sources: classical jihadi theorists, leaders and ideologues of jihadi networks internationally, and leaders and ideologues of jihadi networks in Europe (mainly in London).They accessed these sources via three main platforms: religious schools and training camps in Pakistan/ Afghanistan, radical mosques and study circles in Europe (primarily in London), and the jihadi Internet (websites and discussion forums). The main topics of interest appear to have been general historical justifications for jihad against the unbelievers, contemporary enemy perceptions and calls for global jihad against the US, Israel and their allies, and religious rulings (fatwas) concerning conduct of jihadism (e.g. the use of martyrdom operations, the use of weapons of mass destruction, etc). *(See Ref 605)*

The GIA-linked terrorists attacking France in 1995 left little evidence of ideological drivers. Leading figures of the network escaped prosecution, or were shot dead by French gendarmeries, and those who went on trial were elusive about their motivations. Moreover, the GIA produced relatively little ideological material of its own. *(See Ref 606)*

Judicial documents from trials of al-Qa'ida linked terrorist cells operating in Europe around the millennium contained only general references to ideological training in radical mosques and study circles in London, and in training camps in Afghanistan, based on the ideology of al-Qa'ida and associated groups (e.g. the Jordanian al-Tawhid movement).Judicial documents rarely referenced concrete ideological texts and statements, although in the verdict against the so-called Frankfurt cell operating in 2000, jihad hymns from Afghanistan (annashid) were quoted. The main indicators of ideological influences were the terrorists' target selection and attack methods, statements or texts by leaders and ideologues of groups they belonged to (e.g. al-Tawhid), and communications by the terrorists themselves (testimonies from trials, transcripts from surveillance material, etc). *(See Ref 607, 608)*

When Spanish investigators recovered files from the computers belonging to members of the Madrid cell they retrieved much ideological material (primarily downloaded from jihadi websites), which included classical theorists (e.g. medieval scholar Ibn Taymiyyah, the founder of Saudi salafism (wahhabism) Mohammed Ibn Abd al-Wahhab, the author of the manifest for modern jihadism"Milestones", the Egyptian Muslim Brother Sayyid Qutb, the main ideologue for the internationalist Arab Afghan movement Abdallah Azzam, etc), as well as contemporary theorists and activists (e.g. the al-Qa'ida leadership 'bin Laden and al-Zawahiri', the Jordanian Abu Muhammad al-Maqdisi, and a number of ideologues and strategists from Saudi Arabia, Morocco, Syria, Kuwait, etc.). Saudi ideologues appear to have been particularly popular amongst operative terrorist cells, because they were very concrete in terms of justifying operational strategies and tactics (weapons, target selection, etc). Notably the material also included texts and audiovisual speeches by the main jihadi theorist in London, Abu Qatada and another salafi preacher named Abu Basir al-Tartousi. Investigations revealed that members of the network maintained close relations with Abu Qatada. The Madrid cell accessed texts concerning the reasons for jihad, and the practical conduct (strategic and tactical advice). *(See Ref 609, 610)*

The killer of Theo Van Gogh, Muhammad Bouyeri, downloaded English translations of Ibn Taymiyyah and Sayyid Qutb and translated them into Dutch. In addition he downloaded a number of works by the London based preacher Abu Hamza, and translated excerpts. According to the expert witness, because of Bouyeri's poor Arabic, Hamza's writings functioned as an entrance into the jihadi ideological universe. According to the expert witness, Taymiyyah's writings on Hadith justifying individual punishment of people mocking the Prophet were important drivers for the murder of Van Gogh. The writings of Abu Hamza were retrieved from the belongings of several terrorist suspects in the UK and abroad, and several British-Pakistanis convicted for terrorism in the UK attended his sermons at the Finsbury Park mosque. Other members of Bouyeri's jihadi cell, the Hofstad group, accessed jihadi texts and propaganda produced in London and uploaded material on the Internet. Bouyeri and his accomplices consulted texts concerning the rejection of un-Islamic societal systems (democracy) and laws, and clarification about the legitimacy of conducting operations in Holland. *(See Ref 611, 612, 613)*

The terrorist cell attempting to execute car bomb attacks in central London in 2007 and at the airport terminal in Glasgow also accessed ideological texts and jihadi propaganda on the Internet. One of the terrorists spent time in Iraq the year before the operation and allegedly met the late leader of al-Qa'ida in Iraq, Abu Mus'ab al-Zarqawi. On a computer retrieved from the burning car in Glasgow, experts retrieved ideological and strategic texts and audio-visual material by al-Qa'ida's leaders bin Laden and al-Zawahiri, head of Iraqi branch at the time, the late Abu Mus'ab al-Zarqawi, and several texts by al-Qa'ida associated preachers and activists in Saudi Arabia (e.g. Sulayman Ibn Nasir Al-Ulwan, Husayn ibn Mahmoud, Hamud Bin Uqla al-Shu'aybi). Several of the texts had been downloaded from al-Tibyan Productions, a jihadi website specialising in translating ideological and strategic texts into English. The ideological material dealt with the whys and hows of jihad, rulings on the conduct of suicide bombings and weapons of mass destruction, ruling on the killing of Americans outside Iraq, etc. *(See Ref 559)*

Apart from what was found on the computers of known terrorists, we have to rely on other indicators of ideological influence, such as organisational ties (the ideology of a specific group), social networks (social interaction with activists and preachers with a known ideological profile), target selection and methods (e.g. Maghrebian terrorists tend to target France, al-Qa'ida tends to execute martyrdom operations), or statements, or testimonies by terrorists justifying their actions.

Umar Abd al-Hakim, in "A Summary of My Testimony on the Holy Struggle in Algeria, 1988-1996" (2004), he wrote "I knew that this game would be dangerous, and that it would be beneficial to us to push the jihadi current forward in a new phase after the Afghanistan-period if we exploited this opening correctly. If we erred in this, it would have fatal consequences. It was almost like a mission by special commandos operating behind the enemy lines, but of a political-security-media [not military] character".

During the 1980s, following the ideological template of Sayyid Qutb, local jihadis from Syria, Egypt, Libya, etc, emigrated (committed hijra) to Europe in order to escape persecution by their regimes. In Europe they mixed with activists shuttling between the Arab world and Afghanistan, engaging in support activities for the anti-Soviet jihad. Ideologically, during the 1990s, before al-Qa'ida declared global jihad in 1998, Europe's jihadis seem to have agreed on the legality and utility of supporting jihad from "behind enemy lines". However, conflicts did emerge over the conduct of local jihadism, especially concerning the excommunication (takfir) and killing of fellow Muslims, as well as over the allocation of resources (which jihadi groups and projects should benefit from fundraising efforts). Moreover, there were fierce conflicts between Europe's jihadis and political Islamists such as the European branches of the Islamic Salvation Front (FIS) and the international Muslim Brotherhood movement. At the forefront of the jihadi mocking of political Islamists was Abu Qatada, who considered the Muslim Brotherhood deviant for "throwing itself on the threshold of the Taghut [tyranny]". The main project and mobilising cause after the consolidation of the European jihadi networks was to support the emerging jihad in Algeria and the GIA. *(See Ref 615)*

The "Groupe Islamique armée" or GIA was formed by Algerian Afghan veterans in concert with local jihadi groups operating in Algeria from the late 1970s. At first, the GIA adopted the Arab Afghan version of jihadism, educating its recruits on the classical jihadism of Qutb and the theorizing of al-Qa'ida associated thinkers such and Abu Mus'ab al-Suri and Ayman al-Zawahiri.The first leaders of the GIA, e.g. Qari Said and al-Sharif Qusumi had close ties to al-Qa'ida and the Arab Afghans in Europe. *(See Ref 616, 617)*

However, when the jihad in Algeria got out of hand under the leaderships of "Emirs" Jamal al-Zaytuni and Antar Zuwabri, and the GIA excommunicated the Algerian people and declared war on fellow Islamists, the group clashed ideologically with al-Qa'ida and the support network in Europe. Abu Qatada was an ardent supporter of the Algerian jihad, and he theologically justified strategies and tactics used by the GIA in the war against the "Tyrants". He even wrote a fatwa defending the killing of the wives and children of the "apostates" (representatives of the Algerian regime). After Zaytuni loyalists killed FIS and Jazara leaders Muhammad Said and Abd al-Rasaq Rajam, and emissaries of the Libyan Islamic Fighting group during 1995 (accusing them of collaborating with the regime and propagating political Islamism), the GIA's main supporters in Europe (London), Abu Qatada, Abu Mus'ab al-Suri, as well as representatives of the Egyptian Islamic Jihad and the Libyan Islamic Fighting Group, withdrew their support for the group on the grounds that the GIA failed to provide evidence that the FIS leaders had been collaborating with the government.Abu Qatada, who had built his reputation and following around supporting the Algerian jihad, was reluctant to denounce the GIA, but had no choice when the group exceeded the limits of extremism and lost popular support. *(See Ref 617, 618, 619)*

A protagonist of local jihadism, Abu Qatada refocused on jihadism in the Levant, in addition to supporting the mujahideen in Chechnya (international jihad). After 11 September's attacks in USA Abu Qatada supported the attacks publicly, but criticised the attacks in front of his personal assistant. In his most popular texts written during the 1990s Abu Qatada stresses that fighting "the groups of apostasy that govern the lands of the Mulims....takes precedence over others besides them from the polytheists and the hypocrites and the people of the book". Abu Qatada's "best pupil", the Egyptian Abu Hamza took over the editing of al-Ansar and continued to support the GIA until the famous communiqué by GIA Emir Antar Zuwabri excommunicating the Algerian people in 1998. Between 1996 and 1999 (when Hamza finally had been presented with the proof he needed to reject the GIA), he gathered a substantial following of North African GIA sympathisers, who previously belonged to the crowd of Abu Qatada. During the 1990s, the main jihadi voices in Europe, Abu Qatada, Abu Hamza and Bakri, competed for resources and followers.The main conflict was over who should control the main radical mosque, Finsbury Park. While Abu Qatada "preached to the congregation"

(Maghrebian Afghans mainly) in Arabic, Abu Hamza and Bakri preached in English targeting second-generation immigrants from North Africa and Asian countries (Pakistan, Bangladesh). *(See Ref 621,622)*

"The un-Islamic regime's oppressive practices which are backed by France were never seen except during the French occupation over 132 years and which is still continuing today. France is now a full partner in Genocide by paying mercenaries and rewarding its agents and financing arms deals". *(See Ref 623)*

The GIA's bombings in France during 1995 were ordered by GIA Emir Jamal Zaytuni and the group's Chief of External Affairs Radwan Abu Basir against the advice of the group's Advisory Council. The ideological driver for the GIA's attacks in France was the enemy perception of the GIA's Emir, seeing the Algerian regime as the main enemy, but France as a "full partner" in the regime's war against the Islamists. As for the use of terrorism tactics, they had been justified by the GIA in Algeria and by ideologues in Europe. The campaign in France was considered an integrated part of and necessary condition for success on the Algerian battlefield. An off-shoot of the Arab Afghan salafi-jihadi movement, the GIA was always fiercely anti-Western, and violently opposed to French interference in Algerian affairs. GIA's "anti-Westernism" was expressed through hateful characterisations of the former colonial power and the US, and accusations that these powers covertly supported the apostate regime in killing Algeria's Muslims. *(See Ref 624)*

According to the GIA, France committed "disgusting crimes" against the Algerian Muslim community (umma), and pressured the tyrannical (taghut) Algerian regime to "slaughter" innocent and unarmed civilians. Emir Zaytuni blamed French colonialism for the "oppressive practices" of the "un-Islamic regime", and characterised France as "a full partner in genocide" by supporting the Algerian government. The GIA gradually stepped up operations against French interests and citizens in Algeria before the group internationalised the conflict. The al-Qa'ida associated jihadi theorist and strategist Abu Mus'ab al-Suri may have planted the seeds of ideas to transfer the battle to French soil. He claimed he advised the third Emir of the GIA Sharif Qusumi that attacks in France, "… would be beneficial to draw France into an openly declared support for the Algerian regime, a support which existed, but only in secrecy. This will unify the Islamic Nation around the jihad in Algeria as it unified the Islamic Nation in Afghanistan against the Soviets". *(See Ref 625)*

The GIA campaign in France was controversial and disputed ideologically and strategically amongst jihadis in Algeria (opposed by the GIA's Advisory Council) and certainly, the attacks in France caused problems for the group's supporters in Europe. The campaign jeopardised the GIA's support cells in France, Belgium, the UK and other countries, and thus stole resources from a GIA with its back against the wall locally, in fierce conflict with GIA defector groups, FIS and its armed wing AIS, in addition to taking military defeats in the war against the Algerian army and security forces. To what extent the perpetrators of the attacks were committed to the ideology of Zaytuni's GIA leadership remains unknown. Members of the terrorist networks had been indoctrinated and received training in Algerian camps in Afghanistan, but the network also included marginalised immigrant youths from French suburbs recruited, socialised and trained by recruiters targeting vulnerable environments. Although GIA's terrorist campaign in France had strong strategic elements to it, and was consistent with the strategic thinking of al-Qa'ida linked ideologues (Abu Mus'ab al-Suri), the extreme beliefs, ambitions and recklessness of one man, Zaytuni, and loyal members of his Green Battalion, probably had a greater impact on the operational network than classical and contemporary jihadi theorists. *(See Ref 626)*

Around the millennium Europe was exposed to terrorism by jihadis seemingly lacking a unified enemy perception and strategic vision. Torn between local and global jihadism, ideologues and activists within Europe's jihadi networks disagreed on the questions of who constituted the most important and prioritised enemies and how to combat them. Moreover, because of the massive crackdown on Algerian support networks in the wake of the GIA's terrorist campaign in France, the strategic value of Europe as a support base had decreased substantially. When jihadis in Europe received more attention from the security services it became problematic for them, ideologically, to justify living in the land of the unbelievers. *(See Ref 627)*

After al-Qa'ida declared jihad against Jews and Crusaders in 1998, European and US intelligence services received information that North African terrorists linked to al-Qa'ida planned attacks against US and Israeli interests in Europe. In December 1998 al-Qa'ida struck a deal with an ex-

GIA member going by the alias Abu Doha. Abu Doha acted as a facilitator and recruiter for Algerian guesthouses and training camps in Pakistan and Afghanistan, and oversaw the shuttling of Maghrebian jihadis between their home countries, Europe and Afghan training camps. In exchange for funding and support, Doha's network in Europe was to execute terrorist attacks within the framework of global jihad in Europe. Little is known about the ideological profile of the al-Qa'ida linked Maghrebian terrorist networks, apart from that their members attended the sermons and study circles of Abu Qatada and Abu Hamza in London, and that they were indoctrinated with classical jihadism and the ideology of al-Qa'ida in training camps and religious schools in Pakistan and Afghanistan. *(See Ref 629)*

Members of the network were linked to salafi defector groups from the GIA in Algeria (such as the GSPC and Protectors of the Salafi Call) pursuing local jihad, al-Qa'ida in Afghanistan pursuing global jihad, and the jihadi subculture of "Londonistan" engaging in the different variants of jihadism (local, international and global). The operational patterns and communication (e.g. target selection and justifications) of the terrorists suggested that their multiple allegiances had caused ideological disarray and confusion.

For example, a cell planning to bomb revellers at a Christmas marketplace in Strasbourg on New Year's Eve 2000 disagreed among themselves and the central leadership over enemy perceptions and target selection. Whereas the original mission of the cell was to bomb US or Israeli targets for al-Qa'ida, they decided instead to bomb French civilians in line with the Maghrebian perception of France as enemy number one. Moreover, although recruits at al-Qa'ida camps in Afghanistan were taught about the virtues of martyrdom, the militants planned remote control attacks and planned to escape to Algeria after the operation (consistent with Algerian jihadi traditions of not using suicide bombers). Another cell linked to the Abu Doha network planning operations against the US embassy in Paris and an American airbase in Belgium prepared suicide bombings. Justifying their actions, members of the cell referred mainly to Israeli injustices in Palestine, but they also complained about French interference in Algeria and persecution of Algerians in France. Another Abu Doha linked cell in France appeared to be even more complicated in terms of organisational and ideological allegiances. Like the Strasbourg plotters, the terrorists had been commissioned by al-Qa'ida to strike US and Israeli targets.

The terrorists were former members of GIA defector groups in Algeria who had trained in al-Qa'ida associated camps in Afghanistan and the Caucasus. Identifying with and supporting Chechen mujahideen they decided to attack the Russian embassy in Paris, indirectly hurting the French arch enemy. In addition to receiving projects from al-Qa'ida, Abu Doha's networks engaged extensively in support activities for Algerian insurgents, something that made them vulnerable to counter-terrorism. Several terrorist cells were brought to the attention of European security services because of weapons smuggling and fundraising for jihad in Algeria. *(See Ref 630, 631, 632)*

Another example of the tension between local and global jihadism is the plan by a terrorist cell linked to the Levantine jihadi organisation al-Tawhid wa'l Jihad (al-Tawhid) to execute terrorist attacks against Jewish targets in Germany. The fact that the cell controlled by al-Zarqawi in Germany planned attacks against Jewish targets in Berlin and Dusseldorf rather than German targets (although Germany had deployed forces to Afghanistan) also suggested a preference for local jihadism (although the Germans would be hurt indirectly). *(See Ref 633)*

Strengthening the impression of ideological disarray and identity crisis amongst Europe's mujahideen, in 1999 Abu Hamza addressed the dilemmas of living in the land of the unbelievers in a speech before his followers in London and foreign guests from Sweden and France. The speech was packed with contradictory and confusing statements about the role of jihadis in Europe. Hamza opened the speech by explaining it was forbidden to stay amongst the unbelievers, and that they had to constantly plan and prepare for leaving.Whereas in interviews with the media Hamza spoke about the concept of the Covenant of Security, implying that Muslims enjoying protection in a country (e.g. political asylum) were not permitted to harm that. *(See Ref 634, 635)*

The main project of militants in Europe (that were not allowed to stay there in the first place) was to safeguard themselves and their families, engage in da'wa (calling) to Islam, prepare for jihad and travel to jihadi battlefields. However, while focusing on da'wa, they also had an obligation to engage in jihad, and were permitted to kill unbelievers for any reasons. In other speeches, Hamza also talked about how to conduct jihad and the permissibility of using any means available. Although Abu Hamza justified jihad in the West he remained focused on supporting jihadism in the Muslim world (mainly Yemen, Chechnya and Kashmir) until he was arrested in 2004. *(See Ref 636)*

Omar Bakri Mohammed, in "the World Is Divided into Two Camps..." in 2004, he wrote: "In the present abnormal situation, where there is no application of the Shari'a laws upon the earth, the Muslims worldwide find themselves scattered living beneath the laws of Kufr from the East of the East's and the West of West's. Since there is no Dar al-Islam for the Muslims to make Hijrah to, each individual Muslim has a specific relationship pertaining to his own security with the country he is residing in. It is important to emphasise that a Muslim either has a contract of security with the nation he is residing in or not. If a person has a contract or covenant of safety ('Aqd Amaan') with the United Kingdom, this does not mean that individual also has a covenant with the United States or with any other Kufr allied country".

Between the invasions of Afghanistan and Iraq, jihadi ideologues and opinion makers in Europe and internationally focused more on European nations as enemies and called for operations in Europe. As rationale for targeting European interests the jihadis did not only point to European warfare in Afghanistan and Iraq, but increasingly to the persecution of Muslims in Europe. At the operational level, cells erupting from the 2nd generation of jihadi networks in Europe planned, prepared and executed attacks against the US's European allies. The justifications of the terrorists in threat communiqués, martyrdom testaments, or during interrogations and trial hearings echoed recent speeches by the al-Qa'ida leadership, accusing Europeans of leading a crusade against Islam. *(See Ref 637, 638)*

Although many European countries contributed to the invasion of Afghanistan after 11 September 2011, Europe had a marginal place in al-Qa'ida's enemy perceptions until 2002. Before 2002 Osama Bin Laden and Ayman al-Zawahiri spoke in general terms about the Europeans' role in the historical crusades and European colonialism (focusing mainly on France, UK and Italy). In addition they condemned the UK and France for contemporary foreign policies in the Muslim world (e.g. France's role in Algeria and the UK's role in the first Gulf War). After European countries joined the War on Terror, al-Qa'ida increasingly began to mention and threaten specific European countries in statements. For example, in October 2002 al-Zawahiri threatened Germany and France (France did not contribute troops in Iraq, but is generally perceived as an enemy by jihadis). In November 2002, bin Laden threatened "the US allies". In May 2003 al-Zawahiri threatened the US, UK, Australia and Norway for military contributions in Afghanistan. In a statement from bin Laden in October 2003, he threatened Spain, UK, Australia, Poland, Japan and Italy, and said that al-Qa'ida would attack the US's allies at the "suitable time and place". However, overall Europe as a collective term was almost non-existent in al-Qa'ida's April 2004 (nearly one month after the Madrid bombings). *(See Ref 639, 640)*

Bin Laden offered a truce to "our neighbours north of the Mediterranean", saying the attacks in Madrid were consequences of European contributions to the invasions of Afghanistan and Iraq. Semi-diplomatically, al-Qa'ida's Emir appealed to "The European people" to pressure their authorities to accept the truce offer within a three-month deadline. The truce would begin the moment the last European soldier left Muslim territories. After the April speech there has been a clear tendency towards al-Qa'ida (especially bin Laden) talking to the Europeans as one entity (although al-Qa'ida still threatens specific countries in the communiqués). In their communications, the terrorists that launched the attacks in Madrid and London identified themselves with al-Qa'ida and echoed al-Qa'ida statements.The Madrid bombers called themselves The Military Wing of The Supporters of al-Qa'ida in Europe, or The Supporters of God (Ansar Allah). The London bombers called themselves soldiers of God and praised al-Qa'ida. *(See Ref 641)*

There has also been a tendency for the al-Qa'ida leadership increasingly to portray local European politics as a manifestation of the global crusade against Islam and Muslims. In February 2004 al-Zawahiri portrayed the banning of veils in French schools as "a new sign of the enmity of the Western crusaders against Muslims even while boasting of freedom, democracy and human rights...", equivalent to "the burning of villages in Afghanistan, the destruction of houses over the heads of their inhabitants in Palestine, the massacre of children and the theft of oil in Iraq". *(See Ref 642)*

In April 2006 al-Qa'ida's media company al-Sahab released an audiotape in which bin Laden condemned the caricatures of Prophet Muhammad and instigated the "youths of Islam" to kill the cartoonists and punish Danish authorities for allowing the publication. During 2006, 2007 and 2008 al-Zawahiri and bin Laden repeatedly threatened European countries because of the cartoons. In November 2007 Bin Laden again appealed to Europeans to pressure their governments to withdraw forces from Muslim lands (specifying Blair, Brown, Berlusconi, Aznar and Sarkozy), or face the consequences. In March 2008 bin Laden warned the EU and portrayed the publication of the "insulting drawings" of the Prophet as "within the framework of new crusade" demanding "punishment", and claiming that "The Pope and the Vatican" had been involved in the crime. He added that the cartoons represented a worse crime than bombings of "villages that collapsed over our women and children". Addressing insults against Islam in Europe al-Qa'ida referred to Ibn Taymiyyah's sunnah based rulings on individual punishment (killing) of whoever insults the Prophet. *(See Ref 643)*

In a parallel development ideological discussions intensified amongst extremist and jihadi opinion makers in the UK and other European countries about the concept of the Covenant of Security (aqd al-amaan). The leader of al-Muhajiroun, Omar Bakri Mohammed, was a proponent of a theologically based security contract between British Muslims and British authorities. As explained by Bakri, a Muslim living in a non-Muslim country enjoying protection for himself, his family and being able to practice his religion, finds himself in dar al-aman (the land of safety). *(See Ref 644)*

According to the Covenant of Security the protected Muslim is forbidden to harm wealth and lives in the country offering protection. However, Bakri explained that this does not hinder the Muslim from participating in jihad in other countries (e.g. the 11/9 bombers coming from Europe and Arab World to the US, and of course participating in jihad in the Muslim world). Bakri focused on two specific factors disqualifying the Covenant of Security between non-Muslim governments and individual Muslim citizens: arrests of Muslims and acts of war against Muslims. By arresting and combating Muslims the protector state becomes "dar al-fitnah", a country in which Muslims no longer enjoy security and the contract is broken (justifying jihad). Omar Bakri portrayed himself and the Covenant of Security as a constraint on terrorism by British Islamists. Reportedly, a group of British-Pakistanis convicted for planning attacks in the UK during the spring of 2004 (linked to the London bombers) left al-Muhajiroun because they disagreed with Bakri over the Covenant, and oriented themselves towards Abu Hamza and al-Qa'ida associates in Pakistan instead. After the invasion of Iraq and police crackdowns of jihadi cells and networks in the UK, Bakri could no longer justify a Covenant of Security and in January 2005, he annulled the pact from exile in Lebanon on the Internet service PalTalk. *(See Ref 645, 646, 647)*

From 2004 Omar Bakri's al-Muhajiroun adopted a more militant position. Members of the group voiced threatening statements to the public. In April 2004 members of the Luton branch claimed they looked forward to and prayed for an attack in London. They added that an attack would occur "because bin Laden has said that it would happen, like in Bali, Turkey and Madrid". One of the activists stated that he would like to see, "mujahideen coming to London and killing thousands, either with nuclear weapons or with germs...if they need a hiding place they can stay with me, and if they need fertilizer (reference to the terrorist cell disrupted in March 2004 planning fertilizer bomb attacks) then I will tell them where to get it". The leader of al-Muhajiroun in Luton, the 24-year-old Ishtiaq Alamgir alias Saif al-Islam (The Sword of Islam), said attacks against the UK were legitimate, as long as they were not executed by Muslims being protected by UK authorities. He said he was radicalised by al-Muhajiroun, and inspired by al-Qa'ida which he supported 100%. He added that the UK had violated the Covenant of Security when the country sent troops to Iraq (he did not mention Afghanistan). In October 2004 al-Muhajiroun was banned after UK authorities sanctioned new terrorism laws, and the group became divided into al-Ghuraba (The Strangers) and The Savior Sect. Spokesmen for the groups (and Bakri's protégés), Anjem Choudary, Abu Izzedin (Trevor Brookes), and Abu Uzair voiced threatening statements to the British press in August 2005, in which they hailed the London bombers and emphasised over and over again that the Covenant was history. All of them have since been arrested for supporting terrorism. Abu Uzair said to the BBC: "We don't live in peace with you anymore, which means the covenant of security no longer exists. That is why those four bombers attacked London. They believed there was no covenant of security and for them, their belief was they were allowed to attack the UK... for them it was allowed, for them it was particularly allowed....Because me myself my belief has not been attacked personally me myself. For them the banner has been raised for jihad in the UK, which means for them it is allowed for them to attack, and they probably have many other cells in the UK". *(See Ref 601)*

Abu Izzedin, said the Europeans and the British had to expect attacks after they rejected bin Laden's truce offer in April 2004; "Osama bin Laden, excuse me, Sheikh Osama bin Laden, he offered to the British public and the European people at large an offer of ceasefire. He said that if they roared up against their governments…brought their troops back home… he promised not to attack them". Izzedin added that suicide operations should be considered legitimate "mujahideen activity" and "completely praiseworthy". Like al-Qa'ida, Bakri's followers' focus linked European (British) foreign policy to persecution of Muslims in the West. *(See Ref 648)*

A popular topic in Islamist extremist websites and discussion forums, the Covenant of Security was commented on by al-Qaida. In an open questions and answers session with al-Zawahiri on the Internet he received the question whether Muslims who have obtained visas in "infidel countries" should consider themselves obligated by the Covenant of Security. Al-Zawahiri said he didn't "believe that the entry visa of the infidels is a security contract, and I explained this opinion in detail in the seventh chapter of the second part of The Exoneration. At the end of that chapter, I said that this is what my brothers and I have chosen, so whoever is at ease with it let him apply it, and whoever is not at ease with it, let him look for other means with which to fight the Crusaders and Jews. But beware; beware of the third way, which is to refrain from the obligatory Jihad against them". In The Exoneration, written as an answer to a critique by former al-Jihad leader Sayyid Imam Sharif (Dr. Fadl), al-Zawahiri presented a series of examples aiming to show that having a visa to a Western country does not imply safety and security for a Muslim, highlighting that Western countries allowed the U.S. to arrest Muslims on their territories (the practice of extraordinary rendition), and that Muslims in the West have been forced to pay taxes that finance warfare in the Muslim world. Also, he emphasised the inability of Muslims in the West to offer their children proper Islamic education, cited that they were prevented from practising their faith, and that Western authorities allowed insults against Islam and Muslims, such as the Muhammad drawings. Al-Zawahiri's extensive discussion suggested that the Covenant is too important to be ignored by al-Qaida, and that the organisation certainly saw the opportunity to make visible violations of the security pact aiming to radicalise Muslims in the West. *(See Ref 649, 650, 651)*

According to French expert Olivier Roy's description of the members of groups and cells that have emerged in the West, most of these militants have not received a religious education, nor are they familiar with either the

Koran or Islam in general. They do not have strong ties with their native community anymore and have mostly broken with the ethnic-religious diaspora community and their family there. Largely westernised, they make the decision to adopt a fundamentalist version of Islam on a purely individual level, similar to the converts who decide to abandon their Christian confession and to become Muslims.

To understand the decision-making process these young people go through, it might be useful to compare them with people who in a comparable exile or diaspora situation become fanatic nationalists. These latter opt for their country of origin in a situation in which they are confronted with two national cultures and identities. They glorify that country, identify with it and become estranged from the host society on a spiritual plane. A young man who becomes a religious fanatic, in contrast, takes a stance above any particular society or culture. Placed between two countries and societies in his case becomes the starting point from which he moves to a higher, more general level of adherence and identification. Superficially, these two processes resemble each other: in both, a situation of ambivalence and existential insecurity is replaced by a firm hold and a clear orientation. But this parallel is misleading. To detach oneself from every concrete culture, territory or society for the sake of a religion is qualitatively different from choosing between two (or more) countries, cultures and traditions. *(See Ref 653)*

The most striking trait of a radical religious attitude, which at the same time distinguishes the global jihadists from their more rooted 'brothers' in South-Lebanon or Gaza militant groups, is the abstract quality of their principles, aims and claims. The supporters of global Islamism preach a faith disconnected from cultural and regional specificities, a faith of abstract principles and norms that can be applied to any society. Their enemies (the US, the West in general, all infidels), the plans they pursue, their supposed followers and supporters are all situated in a nebulous sphere and addressed in a very general language that makes it difficult to identify anything tangible and concrete. *(See Ref 655)*

It is probably because of this very impersonal and abstract orientation –which is sometimes regarded as a general characteristic of monotheism– that these radicals are able, or even feel obliged, to kill innocent civilians in their terrorist attacks, even though these civilians belong to the society in which the radicals themselves have grown up and been socialised.

Enclosed in their little cells, communicating exclusively with one another, the radicals gradually lose contact with reality and end up seeing their world only through the black-and-white glasses of their doctrine. *(See Ref 656)*

This is not a new phenomenon. Fifty years ago an American sociologist of Russian origins, Vladimir Nahirny, coined the term 'ideological group' for militant cells with an abstract and totalising worldview - cells, that is, like those of the present-day global jihad - Nahirny based his concept on the empirical example of 19th century Russian anarchists, especially on those of Narodnaja Volja, but the traits he elaborates are easily applicable to the global jihadists:

"First, an ideological orientation which is total – involving a response to the whole person as nothing but a belief - possessed being. It is total because it is all-inclusive and requires that the individuals empty themselves of all personal interests... that they severe all personal ties... and indeed stand outside all normal social ramifications.

"Second, ideological orientation is dichotomous. This dichotomy... conceives of the social universe in terms of black and white, helplessly divided into two irreconcilable parts - one of it to be collectively saved, another collectively destroyed.

"Third, ideological orientation precludes seeing a human being as a composite of personal ascribed qualities and performances. In other words, ideologists... conceive of themselves as nothing but the carriers of belief ... the most important criterion is commitment.

"Finally, ideological orientation precludes a direct affective disposition toward human beings... At the same time, it is not an affectively neutral orientation. In fact, ideologists channel all personal passions and emotions onto the collective cause they cherish. Human beings share in this displaced and collective affectivity to the extent to which they are vessels of this cause". *(See Ref 652)*

In the case analysed by Nahirny, these impersonal vessels of affectivity and belief were the peasants. He cites a member of the anarchist movement as saying: "Not the concrete and real peasant attracted all our attention, was liked by us, made us ready to sacrifice everything for the sake of improving his life - we wished well to and loved the abstract peasant". The same,

I would argue, holds true for the radicalised young Muslims in today's diaspora communities, who see their brothers in faith suffer in some part of the world and decide to join the global jihad to revenge them.

At the end of his article, Nahirny rises the question of what kind of person is attracted to people who are placed outside normal social relationships and feel alienated and uprooted –people who belong nowhere – "The category of individuals best fitted to join ideological formations would have to be looked for among those who have no personal responsibilities, who have severed for one reason or another all personal attachments and primordial ties and who are not bound, as adults are, by specific obligations to corporate groups and associations". *(See Ref 653)*

Social isolation, no social responsibility, no obligations: these traits lead us back to the differentiation between nationally and globally oriented jihadists. Those militant Islamists who defend a certain territory or claim it for their ethnic-religious group are by no means socially isolated. Mostly, they are embedded into a radical community that supports them and backs their armed attacks, but at the same time prevents them from acting arbitrarily. Excessively brutal acts, and acts that provoke harsh repressive measures without visible or symbolic successes to balance these drawbacks, can cost the terrorists the sympathy of the population on whose supportive attitude they depend. Thus, the terrorists' leaders have to take into account the consequences of their violent acts for the social groups they try to defend and claim to represent. These groups form the social base of their fight, but they also set certain limits on it.

Those jihadists, on the other hand, who are not bound to a territory and its population but follow their abstract religious ideas and principles do not have restraints of this sort. They do not feel accountable to anybody; the only responsibility they accept is to their fundamentalist project itself, which discourages them from making concessions of any kind. They discuss their plans exclusively with comrades who share their intransigent attitude and dichotomic worldview. This is one of the reasons why the network of the global jihadists is particularly dangerous.

CHAPTER THIRTEEN

RUSSIA: THE ISLAMIC CHALLENGE

For over a decade, suicide attacks have been a persistent and macabre feature of Russia's battle with militants in the North Caucasus. The suicide bomber who took the lives of 35 people in the arrival hall of Moscow's Domodedovo airport on 24 January 2011 provided only the latest chapter in a dark history that, for many Russians, is also the history of Chechnya's struggle for national self-determination. In reality, however, the violence is no longer political - for the residents of this troubled region, it has become something much more noxious and potentially unsolvable.

Furthermore, when bombs killed 40 people in Moscow's metro in late March 2010, Russians received another poignant reminder of increasingly likely future. These bombings were preceded by at least six similar outrages since 1996, all targeted at public transportation. All have been blamed on or claimed by Islamic militants. After the latest bombings, President Dmitri Medvedev promised that "We will find and destroy them all," echoing similarly empty promises by his predecessor Vladimir Putin, now Russia's Prime Minister.

But whereas finding and destroying terrorists who profess to operate in the service of Islam was once focused mostly on the independence - minded Chechens on Russia's southern flank, today Islamic awareness has spread throughout the North Caucasus and increasingly into the more populous Muslim regions of Russia along the upper Volga River. It will not be contained easily, least of all by bombastic threats from Moscow, which itself is home to more than 2.5 million Muslims, likely making it Europe's largest Muslim city.

Estimates of the number of Muslim in Russia vary greatly, but their natural growth far outstrips that of Russians, who are in a demographic death spiral. Within a decade, nominally Muslim peoples could comprise as much as 20% of Russia's population. Not every Muslim is a radical or potential terrorist, of course. That said, Russia's policies, like its brutal assault on Chechens and other North Caucasians in recent years, has unquestionably tipped the scales for many Muslims against easy reconciliation with Russian rule.

How different things might have been. In the 19th century, the Russian empire was home to Islamic modernist movements that were the most progressive in the world. But in 1918 the Bolsheviks came to power fearing competition from any force challenging their drive to build a new Russian empire on the ashes of the one they had just destroyed. In virtually every Muslim region of this vast territory Muslim nationalists – many of whom were professed Bolsheviks – sought to escape Russia's grasp on the basis of the Bolsheviks' own insistence that all nations of the empire had a right to self-determination.

Lenin quickly disabused them of this idea through one of his many feats of ideological gymnastics. Self-determination is indeed a right, he argued, but because it would stand as a barrier to the unity of the working class it was in reality a counter-revolutionary act. By 1928 Lenin, then Stalin, had liquidated virtually the entirety of Russia's illustrious Muslim intelligentsia. For the duration of Soviet rule successive Soviet rulers sought to eradicate Islam, though there was a tame official Islamic establishment deftly used to court foreign Muslim states. *(See Ref 654)*

The Soviets' anti-Muslim strategy failed, but its unintended consequences are now obvious. The Chechen struggle for independence was a manifestation of anti-colonialism which in its beginning had very little to do with Islam. Chechens were not fanatic Muslims. Historically speaking, they were late converts to Sufi Islam, less-fanatic than most of the other branches of the faith. They maintained – and continue to maintain - that they were victims of colonial conquest and entitled, like the Georgians, the Uzbeks and the Azerbaijanis who had "union republics", to become automatically independent when the Soviet Union broke up.

Post-communist President Boris Yeltsin launched a war to keep Chechnya part of Russia, but he ended up having to compromise in face of fierce Chechen resistance. Even so, prospects for a settlement in Chechnya did not seem hopeless. The second Chechen war, initiated by President Vladimir Putin, began about 10 years ago; in effect, it has never ended.

Moscow's effort to lure Chechens into support of a Chechen satrapy has continued, but a series of Moscow-appointed rulers in Chechnya have not have been successful. Meanwhile, rebellion has spread across the entire North Caucasus.

The Caucasus is a very diverse mosaic, and it would be a risky business to judge what is happening in the downstream areas of the Sunzha River (which flows down from the Mountain-tops through three of Russia's Caucasian republics), for example, by looking at what is going on upstream.

The North Caucasus is divided into two sub-regions: the eastern sub-region, which includes Dagestan, Chechnya, and Ingushetia; and the western sub-region, which includes the other republics (North Ossetia, Karachaevo - Cherkessia and Adygea). Kabardino-Balkaria is in the middle. Some consider it part of the western sub-region, while others place it in the east, and still others again see it as forming a third "central" sub-region.

Various criteria have been used to categorise the republics of the North Caucasus (the degree of Islamisation is one of the main ones, for example, with the east being considered more Islamised than the west). But the main criterion presently is the political situation that arose out of the collapse of the Soviet Union and continues today. The east is reliably unstable, while the west has periodic flare-ups followed by periods of relative calm. Chechnya, of course, is the champion as far as instability goes. Specialists, however, think that the situation in Dagestan is even more dangerous. This view is shared by Chechen President Ramzan Kadyrov, though he may be boasting to a degree about his own services in pacifying "his" republic.

Kabardino-Balkaria is somewhere in between as far as instability is concerned. The tragic events of October 2005, when Interior Ministry and Federal Security Service (FSB) units spent an entire day in battles with the Islamic opposition (a conventional designation), was more than just an isolated episode (97 rebels, 35 law enforcement officers and 14 civilians were killed in these battles). Rather, these events were the culmination of a cycle of conflict stretching well back into the recent past, while the consequences are still making their effects felt today and will likely remain in people's memories for a long time yet. Many analysts, as a result, increasingly see Kabardino-Balkaria as part of the more restless eastern sub-region. *(See Ref 657)*

To what extent is the instability in the east worsening the situation in the west?

There is a real threat that conflict will indeed spread. Islamist separatism has established strong roots among Muslims in Karachaevo-Cherkessia, Adygea, and North Ossetia, and it can always be sure of finding support among fellow believers in the neighbouring republics. The Ingush-Ossetian conflict, which in the 1990s erupted into outright violence, is not as acute as in past years, but continues to smolder and could spread to other parts of the Caucasus.

The relationship between Chechnya and Russian is long and tumultuous. A review of the historical development of encounters between Chechnya and Russia, as it was defined by religion, helps to explain the process by which the region was fertile for the transplanting of Islamic extremism in the form of Wahhabism. Around the eighth century, the Arabs brought Islam to the Caucasus. The region became an arena for clashing empires as Ivan the Terrible fought the Persians and Ottomans for control of the Caucasus in the sixteenth century. During that time, Russia used Christianity to facilitate its expansion and counter Ottoman imperialism; Islam became an antithesis to Christian Russia in the struggle for empires. As those political religious identities became rigid, the seeds were sown for centuries of antagonism. Later, Peter the Great's invasion in the early 1700's signaled to the Chechens and their neighbours that Russia was intent on destroying their religion and political autonomy.

The emergence of religious nationalism can be traced back to the 1800's, when two religious warriors, Sheikh Mansur and Sheikh Shamil fought Russia with Islam as their rallying cry. Sheikh Mansur led several successful campaigns against Russia. He effectively popularised the Naqshabandi Sufi tariqat in Chechnya and is remembered as a messiah, 'priest, warrior and prophet'. Another heroic figure was found in Sheikh Shamil, who fought the Russian for decades in the mid 1800s. Although Shamil was from neighbouring Dagestan, he was widely supported by the people of Chechnya. Both warriors used Islam and strict interpretations of shari'a to smooth over tribal divisions and mobilize the Caucasus. The legacy of resistance to infidels, enshrined by Mansur and Shamil, remains with the people of Chechnya today. *(See Ref 658, 659, 660, 661)*

Chechnya and the Soviet Union Chechen Islamic nationalism reemerge in the 1920's after the Bolshevik Revolution. During the October Revolution in 1917, the Bolsheviks were initially sympathetic to Chechen calls for autonomy and in May 1918, the independent North Caucasian Republic ('The Mountain Republic') was formed. However, once in power, the Soviet's changed their tune, invaded, usurped control, and imposed an ethnically neutral, atheistic government. The Chechens responded with a call to jihad and were met with harsh suppression. Mosques were demolished, Islamic weddings and funerals outlawed, and religious schools closed. In 1944, Josef Stalin took Chechnya off the Soviet map and ordered the dismantling of all religious buildings and sacred symbols within the Caucasus. To ensure control, the Soviets opened the region to Russian settlers and then deported many Chechens. After Stalin's demise, Khrushchev allowed the repatriation of the Chechens back to the Caucasus; however, they met resistance and confrontation from Russians residing in the region. Both Chechen identity and Islam were suppressed during most of the Soviet regime. One indicator of this decline is found in dramatic decrease in mosques in Chechnya. In 1913, there were 806 mosques, by 1960 only nine remained. *(See Ref 662, 663)*

With the Gorbachev Era and the extraordinary changes in the Soviet Union, particularly those of glasnost (openness), new cultural freedoms sparked an Islamic revival. Islamic schools were built, Korans became available, and 'Lenin Square' in Grozny, (the capital of Chechnya), was renamed 'Sheikh Mansur Square'. Chechens also began making the pilgrimage to Mecca and relearning Islam. Calls for independence were also awakened and by the early 1990s, several nationalist groups organised advocating separation and independence from Russia. *(See Ref 658)*

When Moscow came under siege during an attempted coup, the Chechen secessionists began their move for independence. In November 1990, the Chechen All-National Congress designed an independent Chechen Republic and issued a 'Declaration of State Sovereignty of the Chechen-Ingush Republic.' The following September, Dzhokhar Dudayev, a former Soviet General and Chechen native, forced the Supreme Soviet of the Chechen-Ingush Autonomous Republic to disband and declared Chechnya independent from Russia. A month later, Dudayev became the first president of the Chechen-Ingush Republic.

Problems within the self-declared Chechen government emerged in early 1993 as an internal struggle between Dudayev and his opponents grew.

Dudayev used force to dismantle the Chechen National Congress and suppress his opposition. Preferring a secular state, Dudayev originally rejected incorporating Islam into the institutional structure of the Chechen Republic. However, in 1993, political pressure from Islamic factions within Chechnya - specifically 'Mehk Khel' or the Council of Elders composed of Muslim clergy and chieftains - forced him to adjust this position and embrace Islamic principles and organisations. In February 1993, the Constitution of Chechnya acknowledged Islam as the official state religion. *(See Ref 664)*

To prevent the secession of Chechen, Russian President, Boris Yeltsin ordered a fullscale military invasion of Grozny. Despite Russia's air raids, ground soldiers, and tanks, the invasion was met with fierce resistance. Even after extensive bombing of the capital, the secessionists refused to relinquish the city. Russia's tactics were extensively criticised and many countries - primarily Islamic states - harshly condemned the military invasion.Despite numerous attempts at peace settlements and cease-fires, Russia and Chechnya fought a bloody war from 1994 to 1996. When Russia was unable to regain control over Chechnya, the republic gained de facto autonomy from Russia through a 1997 cease-fire agreement.

Although many portray this conflict as a civil war, such conceptualisation is inaccurate.Much of the fighting power and organisation during the 1994-96 war was facilitated by the presence of volunteers from outside Russia. Beginning in the early 1990s a wave of Islamic missionaries from Saudi Arabia descended on Dagestan and Chechnya with Korans and cash. In fact, between 1991 and 1992, Muslim associations increased from 870 to 4000. Outsiders first came to teach Islam to the Chechen who had been isolated from their religious traditions for seventy years. Then, when the fighting broke out with Russia, Muslim warriors came into Chechnya from Jordan, Pakistan, Turkey, and Afghanistan to fight the 'Russian infidels'. *(See Ref 664)*

Many of those that assisted in the resistance were part of the radical Wahhabi group.Founded in Saudi Arabia in the 18th century Wahhabism is a sect of Sunni Islam. Wahhabism is considered fundamentalist as its founder Muhammad ibn al-Wahhab (1703-91) sought a return to the "essential teaching' of Islam that had been corrupted through time. This spiritual purification includes the rejection of other branches of Islam and the local customs and idol worshiping practices found in the mystical

Sufism of the North Caucasus. Moreover, unlike mainstream branches of Islam, Wahhabism engages in proselytising to realise its agenda. *(As we explained in Chapter 4)*

Both mainstream Muslims and other religions are perceived as threats to 'pure Islam'. Within this interpretation of Islam there is an extremist faction that views the use of violence as part of the purification process. This belief holds that jihad must be fought to address non-believers and Muslims who have strayed. It is important to note that within Dagestan and Chechnya, many reject the term "Wahhabis" and instead refer to themselves as "Salaphists" or 'Muslims of Jama'a'. However, for the purposes of this chapter, the term Wahhabi will be employed as it is generally accepted within academia and the media.Current estimates are that around ten percent of the Chechen population is Wahhabi. *(See Ref 665)*

Although Wahhabi militants became visible during the 1994-95 war, reports indicate that Wahhabis were operating in Chechnya as early as 1992. When Moscow invaded Chechnya in December 1994, Chechen political leaders used religious rhetoric to mobilise the population. The re-Islamisation of Chechnya helped to smooth competing factions. General Dudayev used religious rhetoric to portray Russians as infidels. His political speeches were replete with religious images in describing Russia as riddled with 'satanism' and 'full of sin' ("Dudayev Urges Fight against 'Satanic' Russia", 1994). Paul Henze argues that, for the anti- Russian cause, Islam supplied the Chechen people with an ideology that promoted 'unity of purpose' in transcending tribalism. The Islamic symbols and historical images of Mansur and Shamil provided the needed legitimacy to the secessionist political agenda. The nationalists wanted their cause to have broad popular support and moral justification. In fact, Sebastian Smith argues that the Islamic identity deepened as the conflict progressed. The Islamic historical tradition contributed to the emotional polarisation between Chechens and Russians and gave credence to patriarchy, tradition, and cultural integrity - each important components of nationalism. The Wahhabis were welcomed by the Chechen separatists, they were viewed as part of the Muslim community's fight against the infidels in Moscow. *(See Ref 666, 667, 668)*

An excellent example of such transnational collaboration is found in the Saudi Arabian Emir Khattab, who organised an 'Islamic Battalion'. Khattab was extremely successful in his military campaign against Russia. In an

April 1996 incident that became legendary, Khattab's forces ambushed and wiped out an entire sector of Russian soldiers. The triumph of the Wahhabi fighters inspired many Chechens fighters. One indication of this sentiment was visible in the green bands many Chechen fighters wore on their hats that symbolised their commitment to die in protecting Islam, a custom established in the 1800's with Mansur and Shamil. The Wahhabis were well organised and well trained and eventually, this collaboration was successful in expelling the Russian forces. In August 1996, Russian Prime Minister Alexander Lebed signed the Khasavyurt Accords which agreed on a cease-fire and granted Chechnya de facto independence.In January 1997, presidential elections were held in Chechnya and Aslan Maskhadov (former chief of staff of the Chechen military) was elected President. *(See Ref 669)*

For Chechnya, independence proved challenging. As a territory that was essentially a Russian colony for two centuries tried to build political institutions, conflict emerged. Tensions between the secular Chechens, mainstream Muslim Chechens and the Wahhabis' surfaced. The Wahhabi agenda revealed that, in addition to fighting 'Russian infidels,' their goal was to create a Wahhabi Imamate in Chechnya and Dagestan. Despite the fact that political voices within Chechnya remained full of staunch Islamic rhetoric, there were increasing factional tensions between the rather fervent fundamentalists and more mainstream Muslims. Many local leaders became wary of the Wahhabi movement and the extensive role they believe Islam should play in governing Chechnya. These frictions began to materialise over constitutional questions and the incorporation of the Islamic law of shari'a.

In efforts to placate different factions, the new president adopted a policy of appeasement. However, this was short lived. In September of 1997, a shari'a court in Chechnya sentenced two people to death. They were shot and killed in a public square in Grozny and the executions were broadcast over a local television station. In addition, despite more normal relations between Moscow and Grozny, the Wahhabis continued their mobilisation against Russia. Furthermore, they continued passing out leaflets to recruit supporters. With its continued militantism and attempts to implement the shari'a, by early 1998, much of the popular support for the Wahhabis in Chechnya had diminished. The political leadership began to distance itself from the rhetoric and Wahhabi leadership like Khattab. In addition, there were struggles over the control of local mosques. In July 1998, the situation escalated as the Wahhabis attempted a violent take over of Gudermes. President Maskhadov declared a state of emergency, and in a speech at a local non-Wahhabi mosque affirmed, "The Chechens from time immemorial are Muslims, they have their history, national traditions and customs, and will never become either Arabs or Afghans. We are Chechens and it's no use to impose on us, exploiting the Islamic factor, the Arab, Pakistani or other ideology... Military formations of the Wahhabi stamp will be disarmed and disbanded. Ring-leaders and ideologies of these movements will be held criminally responsible". *(See Ref 670, 671, 672)*

The Chechen officials were able to gain control of the situation and after the fighting subsided in 1998, Chechnya expelled many Wahhabis. In response to these internal battles, in the summer of 1998, President Aslan Maskhadov outlawed the practices of Wahhabism and dissemination of Wahhabi propaganda. In 1999, there were several attempts on Maskhadov's life. The President viewed the Wahhabis as a threat to his own power based as well as the internal stability of Chechnya. In part, this move was a response to the fact that Khattab refused to demilitarise and instead continued fighting. In addition to a rejection from the political and religious establishment, the Wahhabis were also met with a popular rejection. Many Muslims are, in fact, opposed to the incorporation of Islamic law and argue that seventy years of atheism has left the Chechens without the religious training and knowledge or the kadiz (religious judges) to implement the shari'a legal doctrine correctly. The Chairman of the Chechen Constitutional Court Ikhvan Gerikhanov rejected the full adoption of Islamic law in Chechnya and remarked that the people of Chechnya are 'Chechens first and Muslims afterwards,' explaining that the women would refuse to wear the Muslim veil and men would not give up their sheep fur hats for the Muslim turban.Although the Wahhabis were welcomed in battle, they were not so welcomed in peace. *(See Ref 673)*

With the military defeat, lose of popular support, and the closing of political opportunity structures, the Wahhabis again took their show on the road and moved their based of operations into Chechnya's neighbour. Within Dagestan, another resistance movement against Russia was gaining momentum and the opportunities seemed ripe. Together, the Chechen rebel Shamil Bassaev and the Wahhabi commander Emir Khattab entered Dagestan with several hundred fighters. Again, the intention was to establish an Islamic state and Dagestan proved to be more receptive to the Wahhabi agenda. In 1999, the leadership in Dagestan announced the creation of a shari'a court and started broadcasting its own Islamic television stations. One article explains the appeal of the extremist ideology. "Today the authorities have nothing to counterbalance the fundamentalist propaganda because the regime has no ideology. That is why the ideals of 'pure Islam' are attracting new disciples all the time, mostly young people who cannot expect to live a life of comfort in poverty-stricken Dagestan". Once more, the transnational aspect of this situation is revealed as the conflict between Russia and Chechnya spilled over into Dagestan with the Wahhabis serving as a conduit. *(See Ref 674, 675, 676, 677)*

Within Russia, September 1999 witnessed several horrific bombings. First, a car bomb outside Russian army barracks in Buianaksk (Dagestan) killing sixty four soldiers. The second hit an apartment building in Moscow, where ninety four civilians died. This was followed by another killings sixty civilians in Moscow and the last killed seventeen people in Volgadonsk Russia. Moscow immediately blamed Chechen insurgents for the bombing although Chechen militants denied any connection. One Chechen leader, Movladi Udugov, claimed that the insurgents were Wahhabis: "All attempts to blame the Chechen side … are completely unfounded." In response to these attacks and the escalation of fighting in Dagestan, Russia recommitted itself to a military solution within Chechnya. Moscow responded with air strikes and the bombing of an oil producing facility in Djohar. By early October, the Russian government started ground operations in Chechnya and on December 15, 1999, Russian tanks again entered Grozny. In response to the violence, 240,000 fled Chechnya. Many Chechens viewed the Wahhabi actions in Dagestan as a direct threat to their autonomous control of Chechnya. One source claims, "The Chechens already had independence, and the Wahhabis put it at risk". *(See Ref 678, 679)*

In 2000, the Chechen administration banned Wahhabism in the republic. Then, in 2003, the new Chechen President Akhmad Kadyrov condemned Wahhabism and its activities and ordered all associated mosque to be closed. The Spiritual Administration of Muslims of Dagestan and religious leaders throughout the region are now aggressively campaigning against the extremist agenda *(See Ref 680)*

How is it that the Wahhabi ideology was first welcomed and then shunned? How is it that fundamentalist Islam became source of cohesion in the separatist war against Russia in 1994-95, and then a source of conflict within Chechnya and its neighbours?

In fact, there are several reasons why Chechnya was fertile ground for the transplanting of the Wahhabi agenda.

The first influence the Wahhabis had on the situation is their assistance in the consolidation and politicisation of identity. Ethnic and religious identity is the glue that bonds people together in collectivities, creates a sense of 'us' (and 'them') and justifies the need for political action and even violence. So the Islamic identity played a unifying role in the quest for independence and the Wahhabis helped to provide this sense of unity and identity in the early stages of the secessionist movement against Russia. The Muslim heritage of the Chechen people provided a sense of identity that reemerged during the turbulence and uncertainty of the late 1980's and 1990's. The Chechens secessionists and the Wahhabis used the Islamic tradition to mobilise the Chechen populous and propel them in resisting federal troops. Furthermore, this identity was pervasive and popular in the fact that during the 1997 presidential elections each candidate included the incorporation of shari'a law in their platform. Ethnic nationalism when combined with a tradition of Islamic struggle provided an explosive concoction. The appeal of Wahhabi Islam is discussed by Anna Matveeva who wrote that after the fall of the Soviet Union, "In many places official Islamic clergy were co-opted by the ruling regimes, and they effectively became extensions of their respective governments". Many of the local religious leaders supported Boris Yeltsin which backfired into a popular rejection of the local clerics. In turn, many embraced the foreign teachings that did not carry the political baggage associated with the Russian government. Furthermore, Chechnya, like Russia is in transition and in the process of filling the ideological void left after the fall of the Soviet Union. *(See Ref 671)*

"Although the Wahhabi tradition remains marginal, it has consolidated its influence by offering a framework for socialisation to disoriented young people in a devastated country". The Wahhabis have waged a deliberate and structured political campaign. The groups' goals are transnational and go far beyond religious education and Islamic purification. Siyavus Karimov, an Azerbaijani official identifies the Wahhabis' political motives, he claims "They direct all their capacities towards propaganda in the first stage, establish contacts with representatives of the power structures in the second stage and seize power in the country in the third stage". The relationship between the Wahhabis and the Chechens has both fed and defined much of the violence in the 1990s. Islam intensified this struggle, defined it, legitimised it, invigorated it and created international alliances. One author explains, "a Wahhabi was a religious dissident and Wahhabism an alternative worldview, a form of socio-economic and political protest". At the same time, it was nascent and, when confronted with governing together, there was little agreement about the shape and form that religion would play. *(See Ref 681, 682, 683)*

The Wahhabi denunciation of the practices that are pervasive throughout Chechnya and Dagestan in the form of Sufi mysticism created tensions. In fact, since the beginning of the Second Chechen-Russian War, thirty moderate religious leaders and two hundred Chechen government officials have been killed by Islamic militants. The Wahhabis oppose with local religious leaders on several grounds. In addition to the incorporation of Shari'a, the Wahhabi teachings dismiss local customs and Sufi practices of centuries. Finally, there is a rejection of the adoration of saints and idol worshiping pervasive in the Chechen tradition. Ultimately, the Wahhabis, in their efforts to transplant their religious fundamentalist ideas beyond warfare found little encouragement. *(See Ref 684)*

While the Chechnya and its neighbours were welcoming first the Wahhabis and rejecting them later what was the Kremlin doing?

Moscow has attempted to secure order by adding intelligence agents and beefing up the presence of federal border guards, along with redeploying police from elsewhere in Russia, but with a little success. In October 2009, President Dmitry Medvedev told Russia's Security Council that the North Caucasus remains the country's foremost internal political problem.

Confronting the threats to internal security that bubble up from the southern frontier - both real and perceived - had been a constant in Russian history and culture. "Cossack! Do not sleep", Aleksander Pushkin wrote in the 1820s. "In the gloomy dark, the Chechen roams beyond the river". But today, unlike in Pushkin's time, the intrigues and conflicts of the North Caucasus do not stay contained in a remote and restive borderland. They affect the Russian heartland itself.

As the violence has spread, Moscow has responded by relying on the playbook of imperial Russia, buying off provincial officials and deploying the state's substantial repressive apparatus to sweep up suspected subversives. But the success of such a strategy depends on the good faith of local elites and the weakness of their rivals. It merely buys Moscow time without fixing the underlying problems of economic development and governance. Medvedev is encountering the same dilemma that has confronted past Russian rulers: What happens when payoffs and raw power are no longer enough to stop those who seek to break the bargain with the centre?

Particularly after Vladimir Putin became president, in 2000, the Russian government began burnishing its image as the redoubtable guardian of order. The smoldering politics of the North Caucasus - and the seepage of violence north of the Terek and Kuban rivers, which form a natural and symbolic barrier between central Russia and its southern republics - could tarnish this cultivated reputation, potentially eroding the government's legitimacy. If the Kremlin cannot contain the cycle of attacks and counterattacks, then Russian nationalist groups - many of which spew chauvinistic rhetoric demonising Russia's non-Christian minorities - could gain traction in Russian politics. Such groups have already been involved in mob attacks and killings of Muslim migrants from the Caucasus and Central Asia. The possibility of street violence is very real and potentially destabilising - Muslims make up as much as 15 percent of Russia's population, with more than 2.5 million living in Moscow alone. *(See Ref 685)*

However, let's take a look at what the federal authorities have managed to achieve in the decade since Vladimir Putin promised to "wipe out the terrorists in the outhouse."

First, and most importantly, the war in Chechnya has ended from the Kremlin view point. But the first and second Chechen wars were ended less by force than through dialogue with part of the Chechen separatists, and by capitalising on divisions among the separatists themselves. Some of the separatists, taking Akhmat-hajji Kadyrov and his son Ramzan at their word and thus receiving the implicit guarantee of Russia's protection, came over to Moscow's side and began fighting against their erstwhile comrades.

Whether by luck or calculation, the Kremlin put its finger on the most suitable candidates for carrying out its policy of "chechenising" its renewed domination of the republic. The Kadyrovs, father and son, proved successful in becoming national leaders, establishing a stable special relationship with

Moscow, and undertaking Chechnya's reconstruction. They wielded a very heavy hand in doing so, and risked their own lives; Akhmat-hajji Kadyrov was assassinated in 2004.

Second, the idea of outright separatism had exhausted itself. Were the Russian Federation to disintegrate entirely, real separatism in the Caucasus would surely emerge again. But short of that, real – as opposed to rhetorical – separatism has become a non-starter in the North Caucasus. Separatism would inevitably be accompanied by internal inter-ethnic strife and conflicts over Islamism, which would ultimately mean the self-destruction of the local peoples. All politicians with even a modicum of responsibility realise this, as society does at large; the latter, hopefully, has not lost its instinct for self-preservation.

Third, the unpopular ex-presidents rejected by the public have been replaced by new leaders, in whom people have placed their hopes. In some cases, these hopes have been fulfilled, even if only in part. The president of North Ossetia, Teimuraz Mamsurov, for example, has attempted to address the consequences of the Beslan tragedy of 2004. Kabardino-Balkaria's president, Arsen Kanokov, has promised to get to the bottom of what happened in 2005. But the most energetic and efficient of all the new leaders has been Yunus-Bek Yevkurov, the army general who became president of Ingushetia in 2008 and, in trying to build bridges between the authorities and the public in order to restore stability, has "demonstrated a completely un-military, peaceful policy". *(See Ref 686)*

As a result, the federal authorities have managed to achieve at least a fragile peace by offering the local elites an implicit agreement that can be summed up as follows: you give us your loyalty and obedience, and we will not meddle in the way you run your internal affairs.

The authorities' biggest failure has been in institutionalising instability. Events over the course of 2009-2010 have shown just how illusory the "political calm" in the region re- ally is. Intoxicated by its successes in fighting separatism and the early results of its "chechenisation" policy, the Kremlin woke up too late to what was happening in Dagestan, Ingushetia and Kabardino-Balkaria.

Reports from the first two of these republics have long since started to sound more like news from the front lines of a war zone. In Ingushetia alone, 58 armed attacks took place in the first half of 2008, leaving 37 law enforcement and security personnel dead and 79 injured. Militants have suffered even higher casualties. Dagestan's interior minister, Adilgerei Magomedtagirov, was shot in May, Ingushetian president Yevkurov was seriously wounded in an attack in June, and there have been repeated attempts on Ramzan Kadyrov's life. *(See Ref 687)*

One can produce all kinds of elaborate theories on who is behind these attacks, ranging from Islamists and the beneficiaries of corruption to "elusive avengers" (in a region where the traditions of the blood feud have made a comeback). But no matter who is behind the terrorist attacks, their systematic nature, the professionalism with which they are executed, and the authorities' powerlessness to prevent them are evidence of the permanent political crisis in the region and the federal and local authorities' inability to exercise effective control.

The federal authorities' next strategic mistake is that their relations with Russia's Caucasus regions are based on the personalisation of politics, with priority placed on personal relations between regional politicians and their patrons in Moscow. Ramzan Kadyrov is the classic example, but the model also applies to a greater or lesser extent to other republics' former presidents, Murat Zyazikov in Ingushetia, Alexander Dzasokhov in North Ossetia, Mustafa Batdyev in Karachaevo-Cherkessia, as well as to their successors, including Yevkurov. Of course, personal trust between "patrons" and "clients" has some obvious advantages, but at the same time, leaders accountable only to the authorities in Moscow lose the trust of their own people, and this eventually gives rise to mutual dissatisfaction and leads to conflicts. *(See Ref 688)*

Finally, the excessively "private" nature of these relations brings the constant risk of further (or renewed) destabilisation, should the local partner be forced to leave the political stage for one reason or another. This concern has been raised frequently with regard to Ramzan Kadyrov, but it was Yevkurov who was suddenly put out of the action in a bombing, and even just finding someone to replace him while he recovered turned out to be difficult.

Political institutions and parties in the region have seen their real role eviscerated. Both are becoming secondary players, mechanisms in the hands of the executive authorities. In some cases, during local elections, for example, political parties are still called on to play a part, camouflaging clan, ethnic and other private interests, but they are unable to guarantee stability, and no one expects them to do so.

This policy of personal power is combined with a continued emphasis on resolving problems by force. Force is always the simplest solution. There is an undoubted need for a federal military (or para-military) presence in the region, but it only restrains the potential for violence, rather than actually eradicating it at its roots. Furthermore, as copious evidence attests, the federal presence often ends up provoking conflicts. Attempts to curtail the use of force and the lifting in April, 2010 of the regime of the counterterrorist operation in Chechnya (which was akin to martial law) have not brought results.

The spontaneous flare-up in violence in several of the region's republics only confirms that military force is not a panacea.

Despite official declarations, the counterterrorist operation regime remains in place de facto, and even Ramzan Kadyrov, who had demanded its end (in order to transfer more law enforcement authority from Moscow to Grozny), has had to acquiesce. Reliance on force has left the Kremlin aware that it cannot continue to keep its troops in the region and is yet unable to withdraw them. For now, it seems, Moscow is sticking with the status quo.

What next?

Moscow's military solution is being implemented at two levels. The federal agencies are paramount, while local security forces – of which Kadyrov's appear to be most successful and ruthless – act separately and in tandem.

Kadyrov's means of action, his ruthlessness and, most of all, his desire to ensure an exclusive position for himself and his republic within the Russian political structure, were effective during his first years in power. The war had just ended, Kadyrov indeed faced exceptional circumstances and acted as he saw fit, not letting anything stop him. The situation today is different.

Absolute success is no longer possible, the rebels still have considerable reserves, people are getting tired of the total monopolisation of power, and far from everyone is willing to see Islamisation make a return in the republic. Finally, Kadyrov's name has been mentioned in connection to four headline-making murders: those of journalist Anna Politkovskaya, the brothers Ruslan and Sulim Yamadayev and the well known human rights campaigner Natalya Estemirova. This is all gradually starting to irritate the Kremlin.

Meanwhile, what has been done in Chechnya cannot be repeated in the rest of Russia's Caucasus. Imitating Ramzan Kadyrov's tactics in Dagestan, Ingushetia and Kabardino-Balkaria would be not just risky, but unrealistic. That said, there is no clarity about what tactics would work better. President Dmitry Medvedev held a meeting with Russia's security and law enforcement officials at the end of July 2009 in response to the escalation of tension in the region. Such a meeting is in itself evidence that the presidents of the North Caucasus republics on their own are unable to keep their region at peace.

On 8 Februray 2010, Russian President Dmitry Medvedev selected Magomedsalam M Magomedov as new president for the troubled North Caucasus republic of Dagestan. The lead-up to the selection was marked by an uptick in violence, and the political controversy surrounding the choice is likely to lead to even further instability.

While Yunis-Bek Yevkurov has returned to his post in Ingushetia after the fail attempt of assassinate him in June 2009 in which he was hurt badly, it remains an open question whether he will be able (or allowed) to continue his course of bridging the gap between the authorities and public and minimising internal confrontation. But whatever happens, Ingushetia's "experiment" offered an original new alternative that cannot be ignored.

The North Caucasus operates according to the same political model as the rest of Russia. But in the North Caucasus, this model has been grafted onto a semi-traditionalist society characterised by a retreat from modernity and increasingly archaic relationships (a similar situation is taking place in the former Soviet republics of Central Asia). Society is moving imperceptibly backwards. The revival of old traditions is producing a dual effect. On the one hand, it creates a clearer and calmer environment for the local elites, whose only task is to maintain order. On the other hand, the North Caucasus has emerged as an enclave within Russia which lives according to its own laws and seeks to limit Moscow's intrusion in its internal affairs.

Some have compared attempts to limit federal influence in Chechnya to the separatist policies implemented under Dudayev.

The economic crisis is making the North Caucasus even harder to manage. The volume of money coming from the federal budget is slowly shrinking, and local authorities are being asked to draw on internal reserves instead. Kadyrov found one such new revenue source by seeking international status for Grozny's airport.

A recent assessment of the risk of conflict in the North Caucasus made by the International Conflict and Security Consulting Centre reports a minimal risk of armed conflict and of increased violence over the next five years, but a medium risk of increased political violence (i.e., violence to accomplish political goals). The report is cautious, and justifiably so. But this kind of academic assessment should not lull politicians, who see murders and terrorist attacks happening practically every day. Systematic political violence – and in the North Caucasus, political violence is both systematic and well armed – sooner or later leads to military confrontation. This was the case in Ingushetia in 2004 and in Kabardino-Balkaria in 2005, when both republics' capitals witnessed battles lasting hours and involving heavy military equipment. *(See Ref 688, 689)*

Any act of provocation could serve as the pretext for armed conflict, which, given constant tension and public discontent, could end up drawing hundreds and even thousands of people into the fighting. And it is getting ever more difficult to prevent this eventuality from turning into inevitability.

However, Islam has always been part of the potent cocktail containing the nationalist and anti-colonialist ideas powering the Chechen resistance and its neighbours. As Russian brutality increased, so did the adherence of many Caucasian Muslims to an increasingly conservative interpretation of Islam, driven in no small part by Wahhabis radicals from the Arab world who seeped into the North Caucasus to assist the fight against Russia as we explained before.

The attachment of Chechen fighters to the wider community of radical Islam is at least partly to secure solidarity in the face of unremitting Russian opposition. But some have become true believers that Islam offers the answers to their predicament. Not surprisingly, the Russian leadership has embraced "Islamic Fundamentalism" as the explanation for the quagmire they themselves created on their Southern flank.

As the conflict in the North Caucasus has evolved, it has also spread, especially into the republics of Dagestan, Ingushetia, and Kabardino-Balkaria. The Islamist insurgency of today is not a counter-government force, like the Chechen rebel fighters of the 1990s, but something closer to an entire counter-society. The insurgents' main enemies are not the rulers in distant Moscow but local leaders whom they consider immoral, corrupt, and un-Islamic. A growing number of militant attacks have targeted not Russian officials, but local movie theatres and stores that sell alcohol. That said, these militants still consider dramatic, high-profile attacks in Moscow - like January 2011's airport bombing - a legitimate means to strike at the country's political and financial heartland and thus acquire power in the North Caucasus.

Local security forces in the North Caucasus have responded to the rise of militant cells of the Wahhabis with indiscriminate crackdowns, harassing anyone with a long beard or a skullcap. Young men go missing in "disappearances" and wind up dead in extrajudicial executions, further radicalising a population that is already alienated from the state and has a long tradition of blood feuds.

The problem is spreading. Within the Caucasus it has already infected the Daghestanis, a substantial group that occupies a strategic territory bordering Azerbaijan and the Caspian Sea. Tatars (Russia's second-largest titular nationality) and Bashkirs (the Muslim people of the Middle Volga region) are making unprecedented claims for autonomy within Russia, sometimes even for full independence, Islamic clerics are speaking out boldly in ways that challenge Moscow directly.

Will Russia become the next major frontier for Islamic radicalism? Contradictory forces are at work. The Muslims of Russian empire have been predisposed historically to moderation, even modernism. But Russia today has its own Islamic radicals, and it is bordered by Islamic states in Central Asia which host home-grown and foreign Islamic radicals, Russia's young Muslims can no longer be sheltered from trends in the larger Islamic world, as modern media and the internet connect them around the clock. Meanwhile, Russians continue down the well-worn path of thinking of Russia's Muslims as Lenin did, even as they fill their cities.

CHAPTER FOURTEEN

AMERICA: COMBATING ISLAMIC MILITANTS NOT ISLAM

The history of Islam is very long compared to that of the United States. However, from the outset, the U.S. has enjoyed close and valued ties with the Islamic world. Significantly, a Muslim state, Morocco, was the first to recognise American independence. The Bey (Sultan) of Morocco signed a Treaty of Peace and friendship with U.S. in 1787, and thereafter the new republic had a number of dealings with other Muslim countries. During the inter war years, America had a clean image in the Muslim world because of educational and health services organised by American missionaries. The Second World War, the oil industry and the post war developments brought many Americans to the Islamic countries; large number of Muslims also came to America, first as students, then as teachers or businessmen or visitors, and eventually as immigrants.

After the emergence of US as a prominent power, the American policy makers devoted special attention to West Asia which includes greater Middle East. Prompted by the American oil companies, they tried to cultivate Saudi Arabia to ensure access to oil. However, the US role in the creation of the state of Israel resulted in strong anti-American feelings among the Muslim countries. This also resulted in the emergence of radical groups, some of which were able to attain state power. They adopted anti-American postures. It then became an objective of US diplomacy to ensure that a consolidation of such radical Muslim states did not materialise and a corporate relationship was established with the moderate and conservative regimes in the Muslim world. The US found Saudi Arabia's championship of Islam quite a convenient weapon to beat the Arab radicals with. In the wake of Suez Crisis in 1956, which spelled disaster for Britain as a custodian of western interests in the region, President Eisenhower seriously toyed with the idea of promoting King Saud as the "Pope" of Islam. But the project failed to take off. This was also the period when U.S. was striving to contain Soviet expansionism, which also implied similar containment of 'radical' Islamic states that tended to move closer to the Soviet Union. During the cold war period, American ideologies and strategists tended to view positive side of Islam from their own perspective and ironically concluded that "conservative" Islamic regimes were the custodians of Islamic values which held Communism as an atheistic heretical creed and disapproved of it. Therefore, they considered such conservatism a useful impediment to any unacceptable growth of pro-Soviet radical regimes in the Islamic world. *(See Ref 690)*

The U.S. policy in West Asia throughout the cold war era was directed to drive a wedge between the socialist and communist communities and the Muslim national liberation movements and prevent them from establishing friendly relations. Washington was seeking to destroy the very possibility of such relations by arguing that people who supported Marxism could never support Islam. The U.S. tried to impress upon Muslims that there were incompatibilities between the Islamic world and the Soviet Communism. In Washington's view, Islam could play the role of a "barrier" blocking the spread of socialist ideology in the Muslim countries. By and large, American diplomacy achieved considerable success, notwithstanding the occasional setbacks. From the second half of 1970's Washington began to evince special interest in Islam. It was chiefly due to world energy crisis. The Muslim countries of the Middle East and North Africa at that time provided as much as fifty five percent of oil requirement in the western world and exported as much as seventy five percent of its oil.

Another important factor was that these oil exporting Muslim countries had built up huge financial strength which enabled their ruling classes to exert even greater influence on the world economy. The U.S. also took note of the growing political and economic weight of the Muslim oil producing countries in the non-aligned movement among developing countries in general and international organisations in particular.

All these factors resulted in an increasing interest in Islam in the U.S. In January 1979, Zbignew Brzesinski, then the President's National Security Advisor, instructed the relevant departments to arrange for an intensive study of Islam and its political role in the world and prepare a detailed report on the situation in various Muslim countries. So, at the turn of Seventies, the issues related to Islam came to figure prominently in the activities of U.S. policy-making bodies. Washington began to view these issues as important components of its foreign policy. In order to legitimise its concern, US extended support to the movements like the one which was going on in Afghanistan against the Soviet Union in the eighties, which according to its perception would be appreciated by the Muslims in other countries.

The "Islamic factor" was also strategically used by U.S. to keep the Soviet Union out of any possible Middle East settlement. According to the reasoning of American diplomats, the "religious affinity" of two sides, i.e.: the Muslims and the Jews, which was affirmed in the Camp David Accord, should help in enhancing the hostility of the Middle East Muslim countries towards the 'atheist' Soviet Union.

The end of the cold war also witnessed the rise of religious fervour in Muslim countries. All over the Muslim world, from Algeria, Morocco, Tunisia, Libya, Sudan, Egypt, Lebanon, to Iran, Pakistan and Indonesia, a persistent undercurrent of religious revival, taking the form of political ideology is being observed now. In media and among the academic circles, this has been referred to as "Islamic Fundamentalism". The Islamic current is not novelty of 1990s although it is gaining new heights now. The new burst of activism has reached such proportions that with the demise of International Communism, Islam is increasingly being perceived as one of the future ideological rivals to the West, led by the U.S. After the cold war, Americans are turning in increasing number towards a new enemy: Islam. The American mass media has started sounding alarming signals: Beware of Islamic Fundamentalism, the Muslims are coming, the Roots of Muslim Rage, Islamic Fundamentalists call for a Holy war etc.

These headlines are symbolic of the prevailing negative images of Islam and Muslims in America. It is argued that with the demise of International Communism, Islam's militant strain is on the verge of replacing Communism as the principal adversary of western liberal democracy and the values in en-shrines. Some American strategic thinkers view Islamic fundamentalism as a far more serious threat than international communism since Islam is more deeply embedded in the psyche of its adherents than Communism. To many in America, Islam is seen in terms of killing and bombing by extremist groups. Explicitly and implicitly, Islam is depicted in the media and even in academic literature as the religion of war, vengeance, hatred and destruction, and a force that is inimical to the orderly conduct of international relations and the progress of society and politics. Islam as a world civilisation has been reduced to Islamic fundamentalism. Thus, with the end of the cold war, the new focus for American policy makers is on Islamic fundamentalism. For the American power-elite that is the challenge in the new century. Jean Kirkpatrick, former U.S. ambassador to the UN had said on the CNN as she watched the hammer and sickle go down last time on Kremlin: The next enemy is "Islamic Fundamentalism". *(See Ref 690, 691)*

The American phobia of Islam has some justification. A whole succession of memories starting with the Crusades and coming down to the bombing of U.S. embassies in Kenya and Tanzania, USS Cole bombing in Yemen,... the 11 September 2001 events and a huge cultural divide keeps the U.S. and Islam apart. The divide was never that deep and wide between the Americans and the Russians. Both culturally and civilisation-ally, they were similar even if they were ideologically apart at the political level. In contrast, Islam had confronted the Christianity off and on for centuries. From the battle of Ajnadayn in 634 A.D, military hostility has always defined the crux of Christian-Muslim relationship. Many Americans see the acts of terrorism and the ubiquitous Muslim diatribes against the West as part of a deepening conflict between an aggressive Islam and a defensive Christian civilisation. According to Bernard Lewis, "the struggle between Islam and the West has now lasted 14 centuries. It has consisted to a long series of attacks and counter-attacks, Jihads and Crusades, conquests and re-conquests. Today, much of the Muslim world is again seized by intense and violent indictment of the West. Recently, America had become the enemy, the incarnation of diabolic opponent of all and specifically for Islam. Explosive headline events and acts of violence make it tempting to view Islam through the prism of religious extremism and terrorism." *(See Ref 693)*

Thus, political Islam has become one of the hottest, nastiest themes for debates in academic circles today, mirroring the well-organised and monolithic debate that was going on between Communism and Liberal Democracy. Muslim phobia that took off in 1989 was a by product of the orgy of speculation that accompanied the fall of Soviet Union and the liberation of Central Europe. During the cold war period the US had an "enemy". Now it has to create an enemy to instill national purpose into a tottering economy. The end of the cold war sparked off a kind of intellectual exercise to identify the biggest and the most credible new enemy. One threat has crystallised well in the public mind: Islamic Fundamentalism. *(See Ref 694)*

Apart from such historical and cultural divides, there are more recent geo-strategic interests that keep the U.S. and Islam apart. The new antithesis of the West is specially designed to replace communism with Islamic Fundamentalism in popular perception, which would make it easy on the part of the whole American nation to redefine its national and security concerns in terms of this new menace. The strategic thinkers might be speculating that such a redefinition could bring about a new surcharged national solidarity that would serve national interests well in an era of economic crises. Thus, with the end of the cold war, the new focus for the American policy makers is on Islamic nations and movements. As Professor Ahmad Dallal rightly argues that "there is now an all-out effort to drive a wedge between the U.S. and Muslim world". *(See Ref 695)*

The evidence is clear that Islam is the new enemy and the major flash-points all over the world involve Islamic people and movements. The threat from the Islamic world is perceived at various levels. At one level Iran, Iraq, Syria, Libya…and now al-Qa'ida and affiliates are perceived as military forces bent on waging Jihad. At the other level, the overwhelming migration from the Islamic countries to the West during the post-Cold War period, in the event of the rising tide of socio-political upheavals in the Islamic world, has given rise to the fear that the Muslim immigrants may play havoc with the cultural system of the West and subvert the western civilisation from within.

So, are the Muslim Americans a danger within?

Before answering this question let us learn first, who are the American Muslims and what is their history in the U.S.A.

The history of Islam in the United States can be divided into two significant periods: the post World War I period, and the last few decades, although some members of the Islamic faith are known to have visited or lived in the United States during the colonial era.

From the 1880s to 1914, several thousand Muslims immigrated to the United States from the Ottoman Empire, and from parts of South Asia; they did not form distinctive settlements, and probably most assimilated into the wider society. *(See Ref 696)*

Once very small, the Muslim population of the US increased greatly in the 20th century, with much of the growth driven by rising immigration and conversion. In 2005, more people from Islamic countries became legal permanent United States residents - nearly 96,000- than in any year in the previous two decades. *(See Ref 697)*

Recent immigrant Muslims make up the majority of the total Muslim population. South Asians Muslims from India and Pakistan and Arabs make up the biggest group of Muslims in America at 60–65% of the population. Native-born American Muslims are mainly African Americans who make up a quarter of the total Muslim population. Many of these have converted to Islam during the last seventy years. Conversion to Islam in prison, and in large urban areas has also contributed to its growth over the years. American Muslims come from various backgrounds, and are one of the most racially diverse religious group in the United States according to a 2009 Gallup poll. *(See Ref 698)*

A Pew report released in 2009 noted that nearly six-in-ten American adults see Muslims as being subject to discrimination, more than Mormons, Atheists, or Jews.While Muslims comprise less than two percent of the American population, they accounted for approximately one quarter of the religious discrimination claims filed with the Equal Employment Opportunity Commission during 2009. *(See Ref 699)*

The Ahmadiyya Muslim Community has claimed to be the oldest Muslim community in the United States, settling in 1921 before the existence of Nation of Islam. However, the two major branches of Islam do not consider Ahmadiyyas to be Muslims.

American views of Islam affected debates regarding freedom of religion during the drafting of the state constitution of Pennsylvania in 1776. Constitutionalists promoted religious toleration while Anticonstitutionalists called for reliance on Protestant values in the formation of the state's republican government. The former group won out, and inserted a clause for religious liberty in the new state constitution. American views of Islam were influenced by favourable Enlightenment writings from Europe, as well as Europeans who had long warned that Islam was a threat to Christianity and republicanism. *(See Ref 700)*

When Benjamin Franklin helped establish a non-denominational religious meeting house in Philadelphia, he emphasised its non-sectarian nature by stating that "even if the Mufti of Constantinople were to send a missionary to preach Mohammedanism to us, he would find a pulpit at his service". Franklin also wrote an anti-slavery parody piece claiming to be translation of the response of a government official at Algiers to a 17th-century petition to banish slavery there; the piece develops the theme that Europeans are specially suited for enslavement on cultural and religious grounds, and that there would be practical problems with abolishing slavery in North Africa; this satirises similar arguments that were then made about the enslavement of Blacks in North America. *(See Ref 701)*

Between 1785 and 1815, over a hundred American sailors were captive in Algiers for ransom. Several wrote captivity narratives of their experiences that gave most Americans their first view of North Africa, Middle East, and Muslim ways, and newspapers often commented on them. The result was a collage of misinformation and ugly stereotypes. Royall Tyler wrote The Algerine Captive (1797), an early American novel depicting the life of an American doctor employed in the slave trade who becomes himself enslaved by Barbary pirates. Finally Washington sent in the Navy to confront the pirates, and ended the threat in 1815. *(See Ref 702)*

In 1776, John Adams published "Thoughts on Government", in which he praises Prophet Muhammad as a "sober inquirer after truth" alongside Confucius, Zoroaster, Socrates, and other "pagan and Christian" thinkers. In 1785, George Washington stated a willingness to hire "Mahometans," as well as people of any nation or religion, to work on his private estate at Mount Vernon if they were "good workmen." *(See Ref 703)*

In 1790, the South Carolina legislative body granted special legal status to a community of Moroccans, twelve years after the Bey (Sultan) of Morocco became the first foreign head of state to formally recognise the United States.In 1797, President John Adams signed a treaty declaring the United States had no "character of enmity against the laws, religion, or tranquillity of Mussulmen". *(See Ref 704)*

Thomas Jefferson defended religious freedom in America including those of Muslims. Jefferson explicitly mentioned Muslims when writing about the movement for religious freedom in Virginia. In his autobiography Jefferson wrote "[When] the [Virginia] bill for establishing religious freedom... was finally passed ... a singular proposition proved that its protection of opinion was meant to be universal. Where the preamble declares that coercion is a departure from the plan of the holy author of our religion, an amendment was proposed, by inserting the word 'Jesus Christ', so that it should read 'a departure from the plan of Jesus Christ, the holy author of our religion.' The insertion was rejected by a great majority, in proof that they meant to comprehend within the mantle of its protection the Jew and the Gentile, the Christian and Mahometan, the Hindoo and infidel of every denomination". And President Jefferson also participated in a "Ramadan iftar" with the Ambassador of Tunisia in 1809. *(See Ref 705)*

However, not all politicians were pleased with the religious neutrality of the Constitution, which prohibited any religious test. Anti-Federalists in the 1788 North Carolina ratifying convention opposed the new constitution; one reason was the fear that some day Catholics or Muslims might be elected president. William Lancaster said: "Let us remember that we form a government for millions not yet in existence.... In the course of four or five hundred years, I do not know how it will work. This is most certain, that Papists may occupy that chair, and Mahometans may take it. I see nothing against it." *(See Ref 706, 707)*

Indeed, in 1788 many opponents of the Constitution pointed to the Middle East, especially the Ottoman Empire as a negative object lesson against standing armies and centralised state authority. However, Alexander Russell Webb is considered by historians to be the earliest prominent Anglo-American convert to Islam in 1888. In 1893 he was the only person representing Islam at the first Parliament for the World's Religions. *(See Ref 708)*

During the American Civil war, the "scorched earth" policy of the North destroyed churches, farms, schools, libraries, colleges, and a great deal of other property. The libraries at the University of Alabama managed to save one book from the debris of their library buildings. One morning, when Federal troops reached the campus with order to destroy the university, Andre Deloffre, a modern language professor and custodian of the library, appealed to the commanding officer to spare one of the finest libraries in the South. The officer, being sympathetic, sent a courier to General Croxton at his headquarters in Tuscaloosa asking permission to save the Rotunda. The general's reply was no. The officer reportedly said, "I will save one volume as a memento of this occasion". The volume selected was a rare copy of the Koran. *(See Ref 709)*

Many of the slaves brought to colonial America from Africa were Muslims. By 1800, some 500,000 Africans arrived in what became the United States. Historians estimate that between 15 to 30 percent of all enslaved African men, and less than 15 percent of the enslaved African women, were Muslims. These enslaved Muslims stood out from their compatriots because of their "resistance, determination and education". *(See Ref 696, 710)*

It is estimated that over 50% of the slaves imported to North America came from areas where regions influenced by Islam. Substantial numbers originated from Senegambia, a region with an established community of Muslim inhabitants extending to the 11th century. Michael A. Gomez speculated that Muslim slaves may have accounted for "thousands, if not tens of thousands", but does not offer a precise estimate. He also suggests many non-Muslim slaves were acquainted with some tenets of Islam, due to Muslim trading and proselytising activities.Historical records indicate many enslaved Muslims conversed in the Arabic language. Some even composed literature (such as autobiographies) and commentaries on the Koran. *(See Ref 711)*

Some newly arrived' Muslim slaves assembled for communal "Salat" (prayers). Some were provided a private praying area by their owner. The two best documented Muslim slaves were Ayuba Suleiman Diallo and Omar Ibn Said. Suleiman was brought to America in 1731 and returned to Africa in 1734. Like many Muslim slaves, he often encountered impediments when attempting to perform religious rituals and was eventually allotted a private location for prayer by his master.

Small-scale migration to the U.S. by Muslims began in 1840, with the arrival of Yemenites and Turks, and lasted until World War I. Most of the immigrants from Arab areas of the Ottoman Empire came with the purpose of making money and returning to their homeland. However, the economic hardships of 19th-Century America prevented them from prospering, and as a result the immigrants settled in the United States permanently. These immigrants settled primarily in Dearborn, Michigan; Quincy, Massachusetts; and Ross, North Dakota. Ross, North Dakota is the site of the first documented mosque and Muslim Cemetery, but it was abandoned and later torn down in the mid 1970s. A new mosque was built in its place in 2005. *(See Ref 708)*

In 1906 Bosnian Muslims in Chicago, Illinois started the Jamaat al-Hajrije (Assembly Society; a social service organisation devoted to Bosnian Muslims). This is the longest lasting incorporated Muslim community in the United States. They met in coffee houses and eventually opened the first Islamic Sunday School with curriculum and textbooks under Imam Kamil Avdih (a graduate of al-Azhar and author of Survey of Islamic Doctrines). Construction of mosques sped up in the 1920s and 1930s, and by 1952, there were over 20 mosques. Although the first mosque was established in the U.S. in 1915, relatively few mosques were founded before the 1960s. Eighty-seven percent of mosques in the U.S. were founded within the last three decades according to the Faith Communities Today (FACT) survey. California has more mosques than any other state. *(See Ref 712)*

Chinese Muslims have immigrated to the United States and lived within the Chinese community rather than integrating into other foreign Muslim communities. Two of the most prominent Chinese American Muslims are the Republic of China National Revolutionary Army General Ma Hongkui and his son Ma Dunjing who moved to Los Angeles, California after fleeing from China to Taiwan. Pai Hsien-yung, son of the Chinese Muslim General Bai Chongxi, is a Muslim writer who moved to Santa Barbara, California after fleeing from China to Taiwan.

During the first half of the 20th century few numbers of African Americans established groups based on Islamic and Black supremacist teachings. The first of such groups created was the Moorish Science Temple of America, founded by Timothy Drew (Drew Ali) in 1913. Drew taught that Black people were of Moorish origin but their Muslim identity was taken away through slavery and racial segregation, advocating the return to Islam of their Moorish ancestry. *(See Ref 713, 714)*

The Nation of Islam (NOI) was the largest organisation, created in 1930 by Wallace Fard Muhammad. It however taught a different form of Islam, promoting Black supremacy and labeling White people as "devils". Fard drew inspiration for NOI doctrines from those of Noble Drew Ali's Moorish Science Temple of America. He provided three main principles which serve as the foundation of the NOI: "Allah is God, the white man is the devil and the so called Negroes are the Asiatic Black People, the cream of the planet earth". In 1934 Elijah Muhammad became the leader of the NOI, he deified Wallace Fard, saying that he was an incarnation of God, and taught that he was a prophet who had been taught directly by God in the form of Wallace Fard. Although Elijah's message caused great concern among White Americans, it was effective among Blacks attracting mainly poor people including students and professionals. One of the famous people to join the NOI was Malcolm X, who was the face of the NOI in the media. Also boxing world champion Muhammad Ali. Malcolm X was one of the most influential leaders of the NOI; he advocated complete separation of Blacks between Whites. He left the NOI after being silenced for 90 days. He then formed his own Black Nationalist Movement, and made the pilgrimage to Mecca, converting to Sunni Islam. He is viewed as the first person to start the movement among African Americans towards Sunni Islam. *(See Ref 713, 715)*

After the death of Elijah Muhammad, he was succeeded by his son Warith Deen Muhammad. Warith Deen rejected many teachings of his father, such as the divinity of Fard Muhammad and saw a white person as also a worshipper. As he took control of the organisation, he quickly brought in new reforms. He renamed it as the World Community of al-Islam in the West, later it became the American Society of Muslims. It was estimated that there were 200,000 followers of W.D. Muhammad at the time. *(See Ref 716, 717)*

W.D. Muhammad introduced teachings which were based on orthodox Sunni Islam.He removed the chairs in temples with mosques, teaching how to pray the "salat", to observe the fasting of Ramadan, and to attend the pilgrimage to Mecca.It was the largest mass religious conversion in the 20th century, with thousands who had converted to orthodox Islam. A few number of Black Muslims however rejected these new reforms brought by Imam Muhammad, Louis Farrakhan who broke away from the organisation, re-established the Nation of Islam under the original Fardian doctrines, and remains its leader. As of today it is estimated there are at least 20,000 members. However, today the group has a wide influence in the African American community. The first Million Man March took place in Washington, D.C. 1995 and was followed later by another one in 2000 which was smaller in group sponsors cultural and academic education, economic independence, and personal and social responsibility. The Nation of Islam has received a great deal of criticism for its anti-white, anti-Christian, and anti-semitic teachings, and is listed as a hate group by the Southern Poverty Law Centre. *(See Ref 718, 719, 720)*

There is no accurate count of the number of Muslims in the United States, as the U.S. Census Bureau does not collect data on religious identification. There is an ongoing debate as to the true size of the Muslim population in the US. Various institutions and organisations have given widely varying estimates about how many Muslims live in the U.S. These estimates have been controversial, with a number of researchers being explicitly critical of the survey methodologies that have led to the higher estimates.

US Muslim Population Estimates

American Religious Identification Survey	**1.3 Million**	**(2008)**
Pew Research Center	**2.5 Millions**	**(2009)**
Encyclopeadia Britannica	**4.7 Millions**	**(2004)**
U.S. News And World Report	**5.0 Millions**	**(2008)**
Council Of American –Islamic Relations (CAIR)	**7.0 Millions**	**(2010)**

According to a 2007 religious survey, 72 percent of Muslims believe religion is very important, which is higher in comparison to the overall population of the United States at 59 percent. The frequency of receiving answers to prayers among Muslims was 31 percent at least once a week, and 12 percent once or twice a month. Nearly a quarter of the Muslims are converts to Islam (23 percent), mainly native-born. Of the total who had converted, 59 percent are African American and 34 percent white. Previous religions of those converted was Protestantism (67 percent), Roman Catholicism (10 percent) and 15 percent no religion. *(See Ref 721)*

Mosques are usually explicitly Sunni or Shia. There are 1,209 mosques in the United States and the nation's largest mosque, the Islamic Centre of America, is in Dearborn, Michigan. It caters mainly to the Shi'a Muslim congregation; however, all Muslims may attend this mosque. It was rebuilt in 2005 to accommodate over 3,000 people for the increasing Muslim population in the region. Muslim Americans are racially diverse communities in the United States, two-thirds are foreign-born. The majority, about three-fifths of Muslim Americans are of South Asian and Arab origin, a quarter of the population are recent converts of whites and indigenous African Americans, while the remaining are other ethnic groups which includes Turks, Iranians, Bosnians, Malays, Indonesians, West Africans, Somalis, and Kenyans, with also small but growing numbers of white and Hispanic converts. *(See Ref 722)*

A survey of ethnic comprehension by the Pew Forum survey in 2007 showed that 37 percent respondents viewed themselves white (mainly of Arab and South Asian origin), 24 percent were Africans and White converts in the ratio 2:1, 20 percent Asian (mainly South Asian origin), 15 percent other race (includes mixed Arabs or Asians) and 4 percent were of Hispanic descent. Since the arrival of South Asian and Arab communities during the 1990s there has been divisions with the African Americans due to the racial and cultural differences, however since post September 11, the two groups joined together when the immigrant communities looked towards the African Americans for advice on civil rights. *(See Ref 723)*

Remembering the fact that Arabs are generally counted among Whites, and majority of Arabs in U.S. are Christians; the more accurate figure would be 65-70% South Asians and Arabs in the ratio 1:1 to 2:1 (includes mixed Arabs and Asians which comprise a significant 25 percent of the total Asian population), 20-25 percent Blacks belonging to traditional and Nations Of Islam sect and 4 percent were of Hispanic descent. Only about a quarter of the Arab American population is Muslim. The 2000 census reported about 1.25 million Americans of Arab ancestry. Contrary to popular perceptions the condition of Muslims in U.S. is very good. Among South Asians in USA, the large Indian American community stands out as particularly well educated and prosperous, with education and income levels that exceed those of U.S.-born whites. Many are professionals, especially doctors, scientists, engineers, and financial analysts, and there are also a large number of entrepreneurs. The five urban areas with the largest Indian populations include the Washington/Baltimore metropolitan area as well as New York, Chicago, Los Angeles, and San Francisco. The 10 states with the largest Muslim populations are California, New York, Illinois, New Jersey, Indiana, Michigan, Virginia, Texas, Ohio, and Maryland. 45 percent of immigrant Muslims report annual household income levels of $50,000 or higher. This compares to the national average of 44 percent. Immigrant Muslims are well represented among higher-income earners, with 19 percent claiming annual household incomes of $100,000 or higher (compared to 16 percent for the Muslim population as a whole and 17 percent for the U.S. average). This is likely due to the strong concentration of Muslims in professional, managerial, and technical fields, especially in information technology, education, medicine, law, and the corporate world. *(See Ref 724)*

Approximately half (50 percent) of the religious affiliations of Muslims is Sunni, 16 percent Shi'a, 22 percent non-affiliated and 16 percent other/

non-response. Muslims of Arab descent are mostly Sunni (56 percent) with minorities who are Shia (19 percent). Pakistanis (62 percent) and Indians (82 percent) are mainly Sunni, while Iranians are mainly Shia (91 percent).Of African American Muslims, 48 percent are Sunni, 34 percent are unaffiliated, 2 percent Shia, the remaining are others. *(See Ref 725)*

In 2005, according to the New York Times, more people from Muslim countries became legal permanent United States residents -nearly 96,000- than in any year in the previous two decades. In addition to immigration, the state, federal and local prisons of the United States may be a contributor to the growth of Islam in the country. J. Michael Waller claims that Muslim inmates comprise 17-20 percent of the prison population, or roughly 350,000 inmates in 2003. He also claims that 80 percent of the prisoners who "find faith" while in prison convert to Islam.These converted inmates are mostly African American, with a small but growing Hispanic minority. Waller also asserts that many converts are radicalised by outside Islamist groups linked to terrorism, but other experts suggest that when radicalisation does occur it has little to no connection with these outside interests. *(See Ref 727, 728)*

After the 11 September 2001 attacks, America saw an increase in the number of hate crimes committed against people who were perceived to be Muslim, particularly those of Middle Eastern and South Asian descent. A publication in Journal of Applied Social Psychology found evidence that the number of anti-Muslim attacks in America in 2001 increased from 354 to 1,501 following September 11. The same year, the Arab American Institute reported an increase in anti-Muslim hate crimes ranging from discrimination and destruction of private property to violent threats and assaults, some of which resulted in deaths. *(See Ref 729, 730, 731, 732)*

In a 2007 survey, 53 percent of American Muslims reported that it was more difficult to be a Muslim after the September 11 attacks. Asked to name the most important problem facing them, the options named by more than ten percent of American Muslims were discrimination (19 percent), being viewed as a terrorist (15 percent), public's ignorance about Islam (13 percent), and stereotyping (12 percent). 54 percent believe that the U.S. government's anti-terrorism activities single out Muslims. 76 percent of surveyed Muslim Americans stated that they are very or somewhat concerned about the rise of Islamic extremism around the world, while 61 percent express a similar concern about the possibility of Islamic extremism in the United States. *(See Ref 725)*

On a small number of occasions Muslim women who wore distinctive hijab were harassed, causing some Muslim women to stay at home, while others temporarily abandoned the practice. In November 2009 Amal Abusumayah, a mother of four young girls, had her hijab pulled following derogatory comments while grocery shopping. In 2006, one Californian woman was shot dead as she walked her child to school; she was wearing a headscarf and relatives and Muslim leaders believe that the killing was religiously motivated.While 51 percent of American Muslims express worry that women wearing hijab will be treated poorly, 44 percent of American Muslim women who always wear hijab express a similar concern. *(See Ref 725)*

Some Muslim Americans have been criticised for letting their religious beliefs affect their ability to act within mainstream American value systems. Muslim cab drivers in Minneapolis, Minnesota have been criticised for refusing passengers for carrying alcoholic beverages or dogs, including disabled passengers with guide dogs. The Minneapolis-Saint Paul International Airport authority has threatened to revoke the operating authority of any driver caught discriminating in this manner.There are reported incidents in which Muslim cashiers have refused to sell pork products to their clientèle. *(See Ref 733, 734)*

Public institutions in the U.S. have also been criticised for accommodating Islam at the expense of taxpayers. The University of Michigan–Dearborn and a public college in Minnesota have been criticised for accommodating Islamic prayer rituals by constructing footbaths for Muslim students using tax-payers' money. Critics claim this special accommodation, which is made only to satisfy Muslims' needs, is a violation of Constitutional provisions separating church and state.Along the same constitutional lines, a San Diego public elementary school is being criticised for making special accommodations specifically for American Muslims by adding Arabic to its curriculum and giving breaks for Muslim prayers. Since these exceptions have not been made for any religious group in the past, some critics see this as an endorsement of Islam. *(See Ref 735, 736)*

The first American Muslim Congressman, Keith Ellison, created controversy when he compared President George W. Bush's actions after the 11 September 2001 attacks to Adolf Hitler's actions after the Nazi-sparked Reichstag fire, saying that Bush was exploiting the aftermath of 9/11 for political gain, as Hitler had exploited the Reichstag fire to suspend constitutional liberties.The United States Holocaust Memorial Museum and the Anti-Defamation League condemned Ellison's remarks. The congressman later retracted the statement, saying that it was "inappropriate" for him to have made the comparison. *(See Ref 737, 738)*

At Columbus Manor School, a suburban Chicago elementary school with a student body nearly half Arab American, school board officials have considered eliminating holiday celebrations after Muslim parents complained that their culture's holidays were not included. Local parent Elizabeth Zahd said broader inclusion, not elimination, was the group's goal: "I only wanted them modified to represent everyone", the Chicago Sun-Times quoted her as saying. "Now the kids are not being educated about other people". However, the district's superintendent, Tom Smyth, said too much school time was being taken to celebrate holidays already, and he sent a directive to his principals requesting that they "tone down" activities unrelated to the curriculum, such as holiday parties. *(See Ref 739)*

The 2007 Pew poll reported that 15 percent of American Muslims under the age of 30 supported suicide bombings against civilian targets in at least some circumstances, while a further 11 percent said it could be "rarely justified." Among those over the age of 30, just 6 percent expressed their support for the same. (9 percent of Muslims over 30 and 5 percent under 30 chose not to answer). Only 5 percent of American Muslims had a favourable view of al-Qa'ida. *(See Ref 725)*

While the strong religious attachments of Muslim Americans has been a source of concern for some in the U.S., who fear the spread of Islam, Pew statistics indicate that the prominence of religious identity amongst Muslim Americans reflects a broader trend in American society. Nearly half of Muslim Americans surveyed considered themselves to be Muslim before American, 28 percent of respondents consider themselves American first, and a significant 20 percent responded both American and Muslim to the question. These results compare with the Protestant response to this question, in which nearly half of the respondents said their religious identity takes precedent, while the other half said their American identity does. Finally, when Muslim Americans were asked questions on their political views, the Pew report concluded that they are "moderate with respect to many issues that have divided Muslims and Westerners around the world".

There is an openly anti-American Muslim group in the U.S. The Islamic Thinkers Society, found only in New York City, engages in leafleting and picketing to spread their viewpoint. Young, immigrant Muslims feel more frustrated and exposed to prejudice than their parents. Because most U.S. Muslims are raised conservatively, and won't consider rebelling through sex or drugs, many experiments with their faith shows a poll, dated 7 June 2007. *(See Ref 726, 727)*

There has been a marked increase in U.S. public affairs interest in Muslim Americans for two distinct, but not unrelated reasons: 1) connecting to the Muslim American population provides a possible bridge to building better international relations with the Muslim World, which will enhance the U.S.'s image overseas; and 2) working with Muslims has been crucial to U.S. domestic intelligence operations aimed at dealing with Muslims in the U.S. as a security threat. This latter tendency has in fact lead to increased tensions as the FBI seeks to establish operatives within mosques and carry out surveillance on Muslim communities around the country. These positions have lead to a dichotomy in reporting on Muslim Americans, who are portrayed sometimes as an important element of the religious and ethnic diversity of the U.S. But more often then not, Muslims in the U.S. are represented as a growing and constant danger within the national borders. *(See Ref 728, 729, 730)*

Indeed, a significant amount of post-September 11 reporting on Muslims and Islam in the mainstream media reveals intense discrimination against Muslims in the U.S. Media coverage of Muslims in the U.S. documents an increase in hate crimes against Muslims, which has also been noted by the Council on American Islamic Relations (CAIR) in its Civil Rights Report. But the media has also been a source of discriminatory practices, often employing stereotypes and caricatures of Muslims in its reporting. In a 2008 Newsweek article entitled "Today's Boo Radley: Muslim Americans", the author argues that the way in which both Republican and Democrat 2008 presidential candidates refused to court the Muslim American vote reflects the continuing prejudice that exists on both sides of the political spectrum towards this community. This tendency illustrates the persistent suspicion that many Americans feel towards their Muslim compatriots. In a 2007 Salon.com article, Paul Barrett analyses this suspicion. Barrett, who has interviewed many prominent Muslim Americans, is regularly asked by non-Muslims in the U.S. "why Muslim Americans don't seem to condemn outspokenly terrorism." His response, in essence, is that there is blame to be had on both sides. On the one hand, some leading Muslim American individuals and organisations have condemned terrorism, but have given ambiguous or much delayed responses. On the other hand, the mainstream American media has not been very receptive to those Muslim American voices which have unequivocally condemned terrorism from the start. By recognising shortcomings on both sides, Barrett's article offers a wider frame for understanding the media discourse on Muslim Americans.

So, are the American Muslims a danger within to U.S.A.?

This answer was the subject of the winter 2010 report of Rand Corporation which concluded that, between 11 September 2001, and the end of 2009, a total of 46 cases of domestic radicalisation and recruitment to jihadist terrorism were reported in the United States. In some of the cases, individuals living in the United States plotted to carry out terrorist attacks at home; some were accused of "providing material support to foreign terrorist organisations"; and some left the United States to join jihadist organisations abroad. All these individuals can be called "homegrown terrorists." *(See Ref 731)*

Forty-six cases of radicalisation in a period of little more than eight years may seem significant, but in each case, an average of only three people were accused - and half of the cases, including some of the fully formulated plots to carry out terrorist attacks in the United States, involved only a single individual. Only 125 persons were identified in the 46 cases.

Although the numbers are small, the 13 cases in 2009 did indicate a marked increase in radicalisation leading to criminal activity, up from an average of about four cases a year from 2002 to 2008. In 2009, there was also a marked increase in the number of individuals involved. Only 81 of the 125 persons identified were indicted for jihadist-related crimes between 2002 and 2008; in 2009 alone, 42 individuals were indicted. The remaining two individuals were indicted in January 2010 in connection with a plot uncovered in 2009.

Who are the recruits?

Most of America's homegrown terrorists are U.S. citizens. Information on national origin or ethnicity is available for 109 of the identified homegrown terrorists. The Arab and South Asian immigrant communities are statistically overrepresented in this small sample, but the number of recruits is still tiny. There are between 3 million to 7 million Muslims in the United States, and few more than 100 have joined jihad- about one out of every 30,000 to 70,000-suggesting an American Muslim population that remains hostile to jihadist ideology and its exhortations to violence. A mistrust of American Muslims by other Americans seems misplaced.

Many of the jihadist recruits in the United States began their journey on the Internet, where they could readily find resonance and reinforcement of their own discontents and people who would legitimate and direct their anger. Some of the recruits gained experience on the streets. At least 23 have criminal records - some of them very long records - for charges including aggravated assault, armed robbery, and drug dealing. A good percentage of those arrested could be described as having the experience and skills that would make them dangerous. But what is most at issue here are intentions, not ability. The 46 cases demonstrate earnest intent. The individuals were ready to be terrorists. Their ideological commitment was manifest. Some were naïve, some were adventurers, and others were misguided. But many were no doubt sincere in their anger and determination, having made the ideological leap to armed jihad. They came into contact with U.S. authorities when they tried to act on their beliefs. They had, in the words of one prosecutor, "jihadi hearts and jihadi minds," and juries convicted them on their intent.

Who are these homegrown terrorists?

As of January 2010, all but two of the U.S.- based perpetrators were men. The two exceptions are the ex-wife of one of the men arrested in the 2002 Portland Seven case and Colleen LaRose, the woman who called herself Jihad Jane.

Nearly all the domestically radicalized terrorists have been Muslims or converts to Islam. Those who claimed no ties to Islam include Ronald Grecula, who was angry at the U.S. government in connection with a dispute over child custody, and Michael Reynolds, who offered to blow up the Trans-Alaska Pipeline on behalf of an undercover agent he believed that he was an agent of al-Qa'ida. Reynolds was fascinated with explosives and wanted money. The Liberty City Seven, arrested for plotting to blow up buildings in Miami and Chicago, were members of the Seas of David, a splinter of the Moorish Science Temple of America. Their religion combined the teachings of Christianity and Islam, but one member also earned money by conducting voodoo ceremonies. *(See Ref 731)*

While the synergetic beliefs of the Liberty City Seven may be consigned to the category of the eccentric, few of America's accused terrorists seem to have arrived at jihadism through a process of profound spiritual discernment. There is no metric for measuring faith, but the attraction of the jihadists' extremist ideology for these individuals appears to have had more to do with participating in action than with religious instruction.

Beyond their common beliefs, America's homegrown terrorists are a diverse group. Information on national origin or ethnicity is available for 109 of the 125 individuals named in the radicalisation cases. Most are U.S. citizens. Sixteen of them come from Pakistani families, and 16 come from Somali families. Twenty are Yemenis, Jordanian (7), Egyptian (2), Iraqi (1), Lebanese (1), or Palestinian (1) origin. Seven come from the Muslim areas of the Balkans: Albania (3), Kosovo (2), and Bosnia (2). Twelve are native-born Caucasians, and 12 are African-Americans, seven of whom belong to the Seas of David, while five others are converts. Few of America's accused terrorists seem to have arrived at jihadism through a process of profound spiritual discernment...

While the Arab and South Asian communities are statistically overrepresented in this small sample, the number of terrorist recruits is still tiny.

The four cases involving Somalis in America who went to Somalia (Maldonado, Kazui, and the two Somali recruiting cases) indicate a continuing effort to radicalise and recruit Somali-American residents to join "a-Shabaab".

Three cases - the 2003 Northern Virginia cluster case, the 2005 Brent case, and the 2009 Headley case - were linked to the Pakistan-based terrorist group Lashkare-Taiba. Christopher Paul, Jose Padilla, Lyman Faris, Bryant Vinas, Sharif Mobley, and Najibullah Zazi are individuals who received training and instruction from al-Qa'ida. These 13 cases, which constitute one-fourth of the total, illustrate the ability of domestic extremists and prospective extremists to connect with foreign terrorist organisations, receive training, and become terrorist operatives in the United States. There is, however, no evidence of an organised terrorist underground in U.S.A. - no army of "sleepers," as some once feared. Most of these individuals recruited themselves into the role of terrorists in response to jihadist propaganda. Many of the jihadist recruits in the United States began their journey on the Internet, where they could readily find resonance and reinforcement of their own discontents and people who would legitimate and direct their anger. The dramatic growth in the number of jihadist websites and chat rooms, especially the significant increase in English-language sites from a handful to hundreds, has made the narrative and message of violent jihad more accessible and compelling to those who cannot read or speak Arabic. Native-born U.S. citizens, currently acting as spokespersons for the jihadist cause, have become motivators. *(See Ref 732)*

They include Adam Gadahn, a Californian who speaks on behalf of al-Qa'ida; Omar Hammami, who makes jihadist recruiting videos in Somalia; and Yemen-based Anwar al-Awlaki, who communicated with Nidal Hasan and Umar Farouk Abdulmutallab and who also inspired Michael Finton.

Given the direct American military involvement in Iraq, Afghanistan, and Pakistan and the growing indirect involvement in Somalia and Yemen, more jihadist echoes in the United States should probably be anticipated. Today's conflicts are not geographically confined. There are no frontiers, no front lines, and no home fronts. The battlefield is everywhere. There is no distinction between combatants and bystanders. It is also important to remember that these individuals believe that the entire Islamic community is the target of aggression by the United States, Israel, and other "infidel" powers. Armed defence, according to this view, is a necessary and personal duty. For some, the jihadist narrative can be compelling. *(See Ref 731)*

A mistrust of American Muslims by the American public seems misplaced, however. There are more than 3 million Muslims in the United States, and few more than 100 have joined jihad - about one out of every 30,000 - suggesting an American Muslim population that remains hostile to jihadist ideology and its exhortations to violence.

The homegrown jihadist threat in America today consists of tiny conspiracies, lone gunmen, and one-off attacks. The continued trust and cooperation of the Muslim community, tips to police from the family members and close acquaintances of those heading toward violence, alert citizens, and focused intelligence - collection efforts will remain essential components of the thus – far successful containment of domestic jihadist terrorism.

But prevention will not always work. More attempts will occur, and there will, on occasion, be bloodshed.

In addition to traditional law enforcement, police intelligence collection, and community policing, public reaction is an essential component of homeland defence. Needless alarm, exaggerated portrayals of the terrorist threat, unrealistic expectations of a risk-free society, and unreasonable demands for absolute protection will only encourage terrorists' ambitions to make America fibrillate in fear and bankrupt itself with security. As long as America's psychological vulnerability is on display, jihadists will find inspiration, and more recruitment and terrorism will occur. Panic is the wrong message to send America's terrorist foes.

CHAPTER FIFTEEN

CAN THE WEST CONTAIN ISLAMIC EXTREMISM?

The events of 11 September 2001, brutally announced the presence of an enemy seemingly distinct from any U.S.A. and the West had faced before. Unlike previous adversaries, such as Nazi Germany, Imperial Japan, or the Spanish monarchy, this new enemy was difficult to define, let alone understand. It was not motivated by causes that an avowedly secular government could easily comprehend, and it took an amorphous yet terrifying form with little historical precedent.

The West leaders and especially in Washington responded to this new threat with dramatic changes. In the largest government reorganisation of the past 50 years, the U.S. Department of Homeland Security lumbered into existence. A new U.S. Director of National Intelligence was named to oversee America's vast intelligence apparatus, and the defence of the homeland was made the military's top priority. Most dramatically, the United States announced - and then implemented - an aggressive new policy of pre-emptive war.

Yet, with about 10 years, it seems clear that policy makers have not responded particularly well. Islamic extremists are gaining strength, while America and its allies find themselves struggling to find a solution to defeat or to contain this new threat. The coalition of the willing, never overly robust, is now on life support. In the Middle East, the Islamist parties Hezbollah and Hamas have enough popular support to prosper in free and fair elections, and al-Qa'ida is adding franchise chapters in North Africa, the Levant, the Arabian Peninsula, and elsewhere. The West most prominent post- September 11 action remains the Afghanistan and Iraq wars, which have arguably failed to improve America's and the West's national security even as they have strengthened the position of the West sworn enemies in the government of Iran.

The question which comes to mind here: why the West has failed until now to contain the Islamic radicalism?

The September 11 Commission stressed that the term war on terrorism was misleading and recommended that it should be renamed to place greater ideological emphasis against Islam. In October 2001 U.S. General Wesley Clark, said that the U.S. war against terrorism "was a war over Islam" that would define Islam "as either a peaceful or militant" force in society. Yet others have argued that it should be appropriately labelled war against political Islam. *(See Ref 678)*

Whatever differences exist amongst America's political elite over the naming of the war, there are few to be found amongst ordinary Americans. Thanks to the "Islamaphobic" corporate media, most Americans irrespective of their political orientation view the war on terror as a fight against Islam.

The same milieu exists in Europe. The lack of boldness on part of the Europe's political class to confront former American President George W Bush on these questions together with the "Islamaphobic" media has convinced ordinary Europeans that their new enemy is Islam and Muslims who live in their midst.

Before September 11, a lot of Muslims long held the view that American intervention in their lands is part of the on-going struggle between Islam and the West. The aftermath of 9/11 only served to reinforce this view. Today an overwhelming majority of Muslims believe unequivocally that the war on terrorism is a war against Islam and Muslims.

So, why this conclusion by the majority of Muslims, and accordingly is Islam compatible with the West culture and values?

Samuel Huntington and Bernard Lewis both argue that Islam as a religion and a culture is incompatible with liberal, democratic and American values. *(See Ref 734, 735, 736, 737)*

Not only is Islam inconsistent with the West, but it poses a direct and significant conflict according to these scholars. This viewpoint has been popularised in American and European media and by government officials who declare fundamentalist Muslims as enemies of freedom and liberalism. In a U.S. Army War College strategic paper, Jack McClanahan in 2002 assessed, "failure of the US to resolutely answer the challenge in the war of ideas in the Muslim world will only result in increasing support for terrorism, leading to an escalation in terrorist attacks against the U.S.". However, it is not clear that the grounds of conflict are based on religious ideology. Are the most devout Muslims really opposed to political incorporation in the United States, or are other traditional non-religious factors such as socio-economic status and acculturation more important in understanding political alienation? To date, nearly every study of Islam and Western values has been qualitative, anecdotal or philosophical in nature, leaving most questions unanswered, at least empirically. In many ways, one of the most interesting, and also one of the most crucial political questions today remains: are Islamic principles compatible with the American political system? *(See Ref 738)*

To answer these questions, Professor Matt A Barreto and Professor Karam Dana of Washington University in Seattle fielded a public opinion survey of Muslim Americans (29/8/2008) to ask whether or not the teachings of Islam were compatible with participation in American democracy. In contrast to prevailing judgments, they found that more 'fundamentalist' or religiously devout Muslims are significantly more likely to support political participation in America. They argued that there is nothing inconsistent with Islam and liberal democracy, and to the contrary, the most religiously devoted Muslims are the most likely to support Western democratic and participatory values because of their knowledge of and adherence to the teachings of Islam. This idea, that Islam teaches compatibility with liberal democratic values has been established theoretically by Imam Faisel Abdul Rauf, Lucas Swaine, and Andrew March. However it has never been tested empirically. So Matt Barreto and Karam Dana essay offers the first empirical test, of arguably the most important cultural debate in the twenty-first century. *(See Ref 739, 740, 741, 742)*

Most political science research on racial and ethnic minorities in the United States tends to focus on African Americans and Latinos and to a lesser extent Asian Americans. Further, most studies of Muslims typically look at democratisation and political participation in the Middle East and Asia. Relatively few efforts have been made to understand the patterns of social, civic, and political participation among Muslims in the United States, despite great increases in their population, citizenship, and civic participation over recent decades. In their article, Barreto and Dana brought together scholarship on the politics of race and ethnicity with literature on Islam and the West, to offer a new theoretical perspective to understand the political position of Muslim Americans.

This theory has two principle components: (1) culturally and religiously, they argue that at its heart, the social contract of Islam encourages participation in democratic societies, so long as the participation does not prohibit the private expression of faith; (2) as a largely immigrant-based population in the United States, Muslim Americans can be understood through the lens of immigrant acculturation in which longer time/generations in the U.S. greatly increases political incorporation. *(See Ref 757)*

One of the most hotly debated topics on Sunday morning news programs is the perceived growth in "home-grown terrorists," yet only anecdotal evidence is presented by pundits. The reason is that little to no scholarly data and research exists to determine the path to political incorporation and efficacy on the one hand, and political alienation and isolation on the other among Muslim Americans. Despite the lack of reliable data, the media have regularly described home-grown terrorists as an evolution of al-Qa'ida "plotting to kill large numbers of their fellow citizens for reasons of religious zeal". Arrests in Buffalo, Toronto, and London of home-grown "Islamic terrorist cells" have called into question the allegiance of American, Canadian, and British citizens who practice Islam. In 2003, the U.S. Senate heard testimony stating, "the rise of militant Islamic leadership in the United States requires particular attention if we are to succeed in the War on Terror". *(See Ref 758, 759)*

In the United States, Muslims have faced various forms of discrimination especially after the events of 11 September 2001. Questions related to Muslims' loyalty to the US are repeatedly raised, and the idea of being a Muslim American is often considered to be somewhat contradictory. The debate has existed for a few decades and depicts the United States as a liberal, modern, western civilisation, and the envy of developing countries. In contrast, Islam is viewed as a traditional, conservative, and aggressive religious ideology whose roots are often described diametrically to all characteristics of western civilisation.

This idea of a cultural divide between the western tradition and Islamic thought was made obvious in political science in the early 1990s, though the cultural and religious debate is more than a century old. Samuel

Huntington's "The Clash of Civilization" set the stage for an argument that envisions conflict in the new world order based purely on cultural grounds. Huntington argues that the world will no longer witness conflicts around ideological and economic differences, but rather around cultural "fault lines," most notably Islam versus the West. *(See Ref 760, 761)*

Long before Huntington, Daniel Lerner wrote: "… the top policy problem, for three generations of Middle Eastern leaders, has been whether one must choose between 'Mecca or Mechanization,' or whether one can make them compatible". Lerner's contention of an inherent incompatibility between Islam and industrialisation has been prevalent, especially with the emergence of scholars studying the Middle East and Islamic history. *(See Ref 762)*

Though his argument is based more on political institutions and leadership styles in selected Middle Eastern nations, Lerner advances the position that Islam as a religion requires theocratic states which oppose social and political modernisation. Within Islam, secular Muslims are often described as the least worrisome while the most devout have been characterised as the main threat. This is best exemplified in the academy, in an article by David Zeidan published just after 9/11: "most fundamentalist movements are united in these goals of Islamising the total social and political system of their societies and of establishing a revived authentic world-wide Islamic state based on Shari'a (the all-encompassing law ordained by God for humans and based on Koran and Hadith)". To bolster his claims, Zeidan picks and chooses selected quotes from the Koran that match his thesis, ignoring any claims to the contrary which often appeared in adjacent paragraphs. *(See Ref 763)*

The underlying argument of Huntington and Lerner focuses on the religious tenets of Islam. Both authors suggest that the true and full interpretation of Islam calls for the expansion of Islamic ideology and the rejection of any non-Islamic worldviews that naturally hamper Islam's growth. The implication is that close followers of the religion are the greatest cause for concern. Indeed, many sociological studies of religion find fundamentalism (in Christianity) positively correlated with authoritarianism, prejudice, and in-group favouritism, though none of these studies are referenced in Huntington's volume, let alone replicated among Muslims. In fact, in a study of Catholic Croats and Muslim Bosnians, Robert Kunovich and Randy Hodson find no evidence that religiosity, is a motivator of intolerance, nor it is a motivator of ethnic conflict for Muslims. *(See Ref 764, 765, 766, 767)*

If Huntington has provided one anchor of the incompatibility thesis, historian Bernard Lewis has provided the second and more recent anchor. Lewis, influential in intensifying the debate between Islam and modernity, makes the argument that Muslims as both individuals and communities are incapable of modernisation, a process that is inherently western and non-Islamic. While Lewis provides no clear definition of modernity in his book "What Went Wrong" he did offer a definition in an earlier article: "in every era of human history, modernity…has meant the ways, norms, and standards of the dominant and expanding civilisation," . These ways, norms and standards are quite general and elusive, especially when making an argument that would define an incompatibility between Islam as a religion that does not have cultural and national boundaries, to a western civilisation that also transcends national boundaries and is now a mosaic of varying ethnic backgrounds and traditions. Further, Lewis uses broad generalisations when identifying problems in the "Islamic world." His theory clearly implies that all persons of Islamic faith, regardless of national origin, income or education are part of "what went wrong" – always in contrast to the West. For example, the opening sentence of his article in Atlantic Monthly previewing his book, is: "In the course of the twentieth century it became abundantly clear that things had gone badly wrong in the Middle East – and, indeed, in all lands of Islam". Part of the challenge according to Lewis is that Muslims are not capable of divorcing their religious practices from their political beliefs and political participation because "all problems are so to speak ultimately religious, and all final answers are therefore religious". According to Lewis' perspective, throughout history, "Muslims developed no secularist movement of their own" leaving them with no option but to join religion and politics. *(See Ref 750, 768)*

The argument that the practice of Islam is incompatible with western democratic values has received considerable attention among policy analysts and policy makers alike. In 2003, the United States Senate Subcommittee on Terrorism, Technology and Homeland Security heard testimony that linked religiously-minded Muslim Americans to terrorist. Matthew Epstein testified that "with deep pocketbooks, and religious conviction, the Saudi Wahhabists have bankrolled a series of Islamic institutions in the United States that actively seek to undermine U.S. counterterrorism policy at home and abroad," and argued that Islamic religious leaders in the U.S. instruct their followers to not cooperate with federal agents, posing a significant threat to national security. Likewise, the McClanahan report for the Army War College concludes that "America is in an ideological war with Islamism". *(See Ref 759, 769)*

While former President Bush routinely states that the United States "respects the vibrant faith of Islam" (2002) and that Islam is a "religion of peace" (2006), many prominent Pentagon officials have declared just the opposite. During a 2002 speech, then Deputy Secretary of Defence Paul Wolfowitz dismissed the viewpoint that poverty or other social factors were behind anti-Western sentiments, arguing instead religion is the underlying source, stating there is something "substantially Islamic about the form of terrorism that we're confronting today." Thus, the clash of civilisations argument and theory holds that significant religious ideological differences exist between Western Christian societies and Eastern Muslim peoples.

How accurate is the representation of Huntington, Lewis and other scholars about the incompatibility between Islam and democracy or liberalism? Matt A Barreto and Karam Dana consider "this question is central", especially when reflecting upon the idea of a "collective identity" that Muslims seem to share, according to these scholars. Dale Eickelman argues that "buzzwords such as 'fundamentalism,' and catchy phrases such as Samuel Huntington's rhyming 'West versus Rest' and Daniel Lerner's alliterative 'Mecca or mechanization,' are of little use in understanding this reformation. Indeed, they obscure or even distort the immense spiritual and intellectual ferment that is taking place today among the world's more than one billion Muslims, reducing it in most cases to a fanatical rejection of everything modern, liberal, or progressive". Rather than a source of opposition, the alternative viewpoint suggests that Islam is compatible with the core democratic values of the West. A more holistic or in-depth understanding of the Koran, Hadith and Islam provides for a convergence of civilisations, not a conflict. *(See Ref 770)*

First, the continued description of anti-American viewpoints as part of fundamentalist Islam inappropriately emphasises religiosity as problematic. Fundamentalist Islam is often interchanged with 'radical Islam,' 'militant Islam,' and depicted as an ultra-religious viewpoint within Islam. This is a mistake. According to Francis Robinson, "the term fundamentalist has been extensively misused by the media to refer to terrorists who happen to be Muslim, or who are anti-American Muslims. This is not accurate. Fundamentalist Islam is simply the conservative wing of Islam, just as fundamentalist Christians are the conservative wing of Christianity, (and just as the fundamentalist Jews who are the conservative wing of the Judaism). The vast majority of Muslim fundamentalists are pious individuals who strictly follow the teachings of Prophet Muhammad, promote regular attendance at mosques, and promote the reading of the Koran". Scholars who promote the incompatibility thesis have cast a misguidedly wide net over the sum of religious Muslims, without actually investigating the practices, theories and belief systems of religious Muslims. *(See Ref 757)*

According to Karel Steenbrink, those with a high sense of religiosity, also called "tadayyun" are likely to have a close and personal connection to Islam. "Tadayyun", an Arabic word meaning religiosity, is often equated with the degree of devoutness and practice of Islam. Those with a high sense of "tadayyun" are likely to be the most familiar with Hadith, most often read the Koran, regularly attend prayer services at the mosque, and have a strong sense of shared community with other Muslims. Nothing in Islam equates "tadayyun" with jihad. In contrast, Barrett and Dana argue that religiosity and Islamic faith are linked with a sense of respect for the codes and values of non-Muslim societies. Why? Because the Koran, Hadith, and the Prophet Muhammad ask Muslims to uphold the social contracts of non-Muslim societies, so long as they are free to practice their religion. In the West and especially in the United States, a country with little to no prohibitions on religious expression or practice, Islam suggests political incorporation is an acceptable, if not desirable outcome. This argument builds heavily on recent research by Andrew March who extends his theory more directly to political participation. *(See Ref 754, 755, 771, 772)*

March acknowledges that a cursory review of Islamic texts will reveal "prohibitions on submitting to the authority of non-Muslims states, serving in their armies, contributing to their strength or welfare, participating in their political systems". However, such a conclusion would not be based on a comprehensive review of Islamic doctrines, nor would it be based on an in-depth understanding of how Islam is interpreted and practiced by the most devout. In contrast, March argues that "even pre-modern Islamic legal discourses affirm a certain set of values and principles… chief among these is the insistence within Islamic jurisprudence on the inviolability of contracts," and he provides the example of the American social contract. *(See Ref 754, 755, 772)*

Many Muslim jurists and texts clearly state that it is reasonable for Muslims to reside in non-Muslims societies, so long as the non-Muslim society does not prevent the manifesting of Islam. Through an extensive review of Islamic texts, March concludes that "not only is it permitted to reside in a non-Muslim polity, but also it is permitted to do so while being subject to and obeying non-Muslim law". This obligation is rooted in a religious following of the spirit and letter of Islam. Among Muslims living in the U.S., we should expect then, the most religiously devout, those with a high degree of "tadayyun", to support and affirm the American social contract.

"We offer a significant challenge to conventional wisdom – religiosity may encourage Muslims to support the political system in America (and the West). The value and support for contracts is not a cultural but rather a religious notion rooted in many Islamic texts, Koranic verses, and fatawa", Tariq Ramadan explains that "contracts determine our status, fix our duties and rights and direct the nature and scope of our actions. Once agreed, the terms of a covenant should be respected and if there is a point which seems to work against Muslim rights - or even their conscience as Believers – this has to be discussed and negotiated because Muslims are, unilaterally, not allowed to breach a treaty". As a religious minority, Muslims greatly benefit by the guarantee of religious rights and freedoms in the United States and the West. *(See Ref 773)*

Feisal Abdul Rauf, a noted Imam and advocate of Muslim advancement in the United States argues that America is an ideal state to practice Islam. This may sound surprising if not absurd to many Americans, and Muslims outside America, but it is founded on the argument that the "American Constitution and system of governance uphold the core principles of Islamic Law". Writing as an Imam with expert knowledge of Islamic teachings and practices, Abdul Rauf argues that the principles of equality and the free exercise of religion, embedded in American legal and political history, provide Muslims with an open environment to practice their religion, and that in fact Prophet Muhammad instructed his followers to uphold the laws and practices of their host society, if they should find themselves in a majority non-Muslim state. *(See Ref 753)*

Returning to March, the theory that Islam is compatible with the West gains strength in his argument that "once a Muslim has accepted the security of a non-Muslim state he is bound to follow all of its laws, including paying taxes that contribute to general social welfare. Crucially, for most scholars this is a moral duty grounded in religion, and not a mere quietest exhortation to avoid punishment or other negative consequences for the Muslim community". March points to two significant Koranic verses (KV. 16:91 and KV. 17:34) which spell this out quite clearly. *(See Ref 755)*

Therefore, Barreto and Karam argument rests on the notion that the Muslim more knowledgeable of Islam, the Muslim who reads the Koran, the Muslim who knows the stories of the Prophets, is more likely to challenge the conflict hypothesis because conflict-based theories pick and choose sensational components of Islam, ignoring the full context, or full picture so to speak of Islam. In an earlier article, March (2005) argues that those with an in-depth knowledge, belief in, and understanding of Islam will frequently cite the story of Prophet Yusuf who served as an appointed minister to the non-Muslim Pharaoh of Egypt as support for compatibility. March cites a statement by Sheikh al-Shanqiti as evidence, "there is nothing prohibited in Muslims' participating in elections run in non-Muslim countries, especially when such participation accrues benefits to Muslims or wards off harm". More than not prohibiting political incorporation, some argue that the more religious Muslims would understand they have a duty to support the political system in America and in the West, and to participate themselves in order to show care for others, as well as to help improve the position of Muslims in society. *(See Ref 774, 775)*

Does one's Islamic way of life (or identity) conflict with being an American or European living in a largely non-Muslim society? Even though Bernard Lewis says that there is a conflict, he does not provide quantitative data that would support his claims. In contrast, Andrew March concludes that "culturally authentic Islamic values exist which can ground "Islamically" a social contract between Muslims and a non-Muslim liberal democracy".

While we believe that Islam is compatible with the West culture and values and there is no clash of civilisations and that Muslims in the West will integrate with time and can live without any problems, we don't believe that the extremist jihadi Muslims will be compatible with such culture and values or with any other culture and values including moderate Islam. So the question here what the West must do then to contain those radicals?

The United States and the West have yet to formulate a holistic strategy to guide the prosecution of the old-new war in Afghanistan. U.S.A. and NATO have not articulated a clear set of mutually reinforcing goals, and they have not undertaken a consistent set of actions designed to achieve their aims even as they demonstrate the West national values. Indeed, The West has not even managed to properly identify its enemies; despite the rhetoric of the past 10 years, America and the West are not at war with terror, because terror is not a foe but a tactic.

Blundering forward, U.S.A. have squandered the swell of global good will after September 11, punished its friends, and rewarded its enemies with short-sighted, even self-destructive, tactics.

Yet what The West face today is not wholly novel: It is a war of ideas, mirroring the Cold War. Like the Communists, violent Islamic extremists are trying to spread a worldview that denigrates personal liberty and demands submission to a narrow ideology. And, as with the Cold War, it must be The West and its allies in the world goal to stop them. The United States and its allies should therefore adopt a new version of the policy that served them so well during that last long war: containment.

Why?

The war against the Islamic militants needs the equivalent of the 1941 Atlantic Charter or the 1950 NSC-68 statement that successfully guided U.S. strategy during the Cold War. With a clear policy directive, officials might more effectively provide the public a clear and consistent goal outlining the war's aims and moral imperatives. Winston Churchill understood this when, in 1941, he commented on radio that, "It was necessary to give all peoples, and especially the oppressed and conquered peoples, a simple, rough and ready wartime statement of the goal towards which the British Commonwealth and the United States mean to make their way and thus make a way for others to march with them upon a road which will certainly be painful and may be long". *(See Ref 776, 777)*

According to U.S. Commander Philip Kapusta and his colleague Captain Donovan Campbell, a policy of "neo-containment", like 1950 NSC-68, is required because it would avoid self-defeating military confrontations in favour of an aggressive campaign to isolate the enemies. The modern equivalent of the Soviet Bloc, that geographic haven for a hostile ideology, is the arc of instability that extends from Central Asia west through Iran and the Arabian Peninsula and south across North Africa. The West should build a virtual wall of stable, moderate nations on the periphery of that arc, literally containing the spread of the hostile belief system. "More broadly, we must enter into - and prevail in - the war of ideas, winning the hearts and minds of both domestic and foreign audiences. We must pursue this goal not only in the mental arena - in what has been variously describe as political warfare, propaganda, or psychological operations - but also in the practical one, by consistently demonstrating our belief system in action. Our deeds are more important than anything we say, and in the aggressive prosecution of our war on terror, we have strayed from our core value of individual freedom". *(See Ref 778)*

The two American officers argued that, of course, neo-containment will have to address the important differences between the conflicts of today and yesterday. "Today's threat emanates not from a hyper-governed nation-state but from a loosely networked group of radicals based primarily in under-governed areas of the world - which makes carefully defining and targeting our true foes all the more important. Just as we strove to separate the Soviet elites from the people they repressively ruled, now we must separate the Islamic radicals from the vast majority of Muslims. We cannot, and should not, target an entire religion."

However, there is also a crucial difference in the danger's scale. For four decades, the USSR and its massive nuclear arsenal posed a clear existential threat to the United States and its allies. In contrast, today's extremists cannot eliminate the West. The West needs to ratchet down the doomsday rhetoric and the military-driven response. The West primary ideological export should not be fear; it should be hope. The war is with people and their belief systems, and ideas cannot be killed by bullets. They can only be killed by better ideas.

Furthermore, Kapusta and Campbell argue that after military theoreticians evaluate an opponent using ends, ways, and means analysis, they seek to determine the "centre of gravity", which military theory teaches is crucial to the development of a successful counterinsurgency strategy. The centre of gravity is the means or source of power that enemies use to accomplish their goals. If an adversary's centre of gravity is neutralised, then it cannot achieve its objective. U.S. and West military planners thus work to disrupt an opponent's Centre of gravity by targeting its critical requirements. *(See Ref 779, 780)*

In the Islamist jihadist's pre-revolutionary and revolutionary phases, there are two centres of gravity: Islamist cells and religious schools (madrassas). Among the critical requirements for these centres of gravity are an ideology to inspire recruits; a fertile environment in which to recruit; command and control leadership; legitimacy-providing sponsorship from either a state, political party, or media outlet; funding; sanctuary; and access to supplies, including everything from paper for pamphlets to C-4 plastic explosives. Damaging any of these weakens the centre of gravity. If the attacks are of sufficient quality, the centre of gravity deteriorates to the point that it ceases to function. In traditional military parlance, these critical requirements are the "fronts" or "lines of operation" in the war on terrorism. *(See Ref 779)*

Of these requirements, ideology is the most important according to the two American officers. Fortunately, it is also the most vulnerable. Discrediting Islamist ideology should be the main component of the U.S. and the West counterinsurgency plan. When Egypt was at the height of its Islamist insurgency in the mid-1990s, the Egyptian government subtly undercut the Muslim Brotherhood's ideology and legitimacy with a comedy that mocked the Islamists. The legendary Egyptian actor Adel Imam portrayed a naive, unmarried Islamist terrorist under the tutelage of a polygamist Machiavellian religious leader. Injured in a car accident, he is brought to a middle class household where he salivates over women in miniskirts and learns about soccer. More than a decade after its release, al-Irhabi (The Terrorist) remains among Egypt's most popular-and most effective-films. Much of the thought behind the U.S. government-funded Radio Sawa is that bombarding the Middle East with popular Western culture will more effectively win the hearts and minds of the masses than will dry recitation of news or analysis targeted more toward the elite. *(See Ref 781, 782)*

In the military struggle against Islamism, winning the war of ideas is crucial. This is nothing new. The Cold War was a struggle of ideologies. The United States did not rely on military action alone to counter the Soviet threat. Simultaneously, the U.S. government bestowed foreign aid upon African and Asian countries in order to make their local environments less fertile to Soviet subterfuge. With regard to the war against terrorism, former US Secretary of Defence Donald Rumsfeld accurately identified the core question when he was asked whether U.S. forces were killing terrorists faster than Islamists could produce them. *(See Ref 783)*

Centre-of-gravity analysis suggests that a successful strategy should focus upon the critical requirements of ideology and the environment. U.S. and NATO military force does have a role. But, swatting individual mosquitoes can only bring victory if the United States and its allies simultaneously work to drain the swamp. Victory requires an approach that leverages diplomacy, information operations, economic leverage, and military pressure in a focused and coordinated effort. For example, discrediting militant Islam's ideology, while both promoting tolerant interpretations of Islam and defending Western values, is an informational and diplomatic effort not suited for military action. *(See Ref 784)*

Rumsfeld also advocates a multidimensional approach. On September 7, 2004, he explained, [The war on terror] "is not a military problem alone, to be sure. It is clear that the political, the economic, and the military have to proceed apace ... I think that there's a better, deeper understanding of the fact that this is not a one-dimensional, military-only conflict; this is something that is multidimensional". *(See Ref 785)*

In the war against terrorism, it is not enough for the United States to have the best ideology. According to Kapusta and Campbell, it is not the best idea that wins, but rather the best-promoted one. Most Iraqis, for example, presumably would like to live in a country that is tolerant and democratic. But the inability of the U.S. government to establish an effective television network in Iraq ceded valuable momentum to al-Alam and al-Jazeera. Since Islamist jihadist ideology is the base of both the Shi'ite and Sunni insurgencies in Iraq, convincing the populace of the vacuity of the Islamist ideal provides the key to the movement's downfall. Promotion of the virtues of tolerance, moderation, freedom, and democracy, while discrediting militant Islamic ideology, is vital to U.S., the West, and the moderate Islam victory.

U.S. strategic communications, therefore, become essential to waging a battle of ideas, itself a major component of the global war on terrorism. In military parlance, strategic communication synchronises actions that include public diplomacy, public affairs, public relations, outreach, information operations, and psychological operations. Strategic communication is the overarching concept that unifies and focuses the right message to the right audience with the intent to shape perception. But are U.S. strategic communications working in the global war on terrorism? Not always. There have been a number of failures in strategic communications. Former Coalition Provisional Authority administrator L. Paul Bremer appeared frequently on television, for example, even though such exposure was counterproductive to the U.S. mission since it reinforced notions of occupation rather than liberation. *(See Ref 778)*

The Coalition Provisional Authority also bungled strategic communications during its daily press conferences. Coalition spokesmen-more often U.S. or British officials rather than Iraqis-would often refer to the threat posed by "foreign fighters" in Iraq. While such explanations were effective for an American and British constituency, their impact on an Iraqi audience was far different. After all, from an Iraqi perspective, coalition military forces were more foreign than the Syrian or Iranian fighters. With poor choice of words, coalition spokesman Dan Senor may have unintentionally established equivalency between coalition troops and enemy foreign fighters. A bit more cultural and linguistic care can go a long way. Retired Marine colonel Nick Pratt, director of the Program on Terrorism and Security at the George C. Marshall European Centre for Security Studies, had extensive experience both in the Middle East and with the Afghan's mujahideen at the time of the Soviet occupation. He suggested co-opting Arabic terms to better define the insurgents. For example, Pratt suggested that both the U.S. Marines and Iraqi forces "should refer to the so-called 'foreign fighters' who are killing increasing numbers of innocent Iraqis and our military personnel by the most appropriate Arabic and Islamic names possible, the al-Mufsid Usama, Osama's evildoers, [or] al-Mufsid Saddam". *(See Ref 786, 787)*

Bernard Lewis urges cultural considerations rather than direct translation in order to win the propaganda battle. In April 2004, a year after the fall of Baghdad, he told the Atlantic Monthly: "I see a failure of communication ... Simple translation isn't good enough. Even accurate translation may be misleading, because in different cultures we use the same word with different meanings. There is a great danger of misunderstanding ... I don't think the problem has improved-if anything it has gotten worse". *(See Ref 788)*

On the other hand, moderate interpretations of Islam provide a resource to erode such exclusivist interpretation. Moderate Islam, in brief, serves as an antidote to militant Islam among Sunnis and Shi'ites alike. "In the case of the Islamic Republic of Iran, for example, a small number of clerics adhering to a minority theological strain hold the reins of government. However, the majority of ayatollahs believe that secular power is by nature corrupt and that religious clerics might give advice but should remain separate from government. If the U.S. government and its Western allies facilitated the broadcast into Iran of traditional Shi'ite sermons, these might help undercut the religious legitimacy of the Islamic Republic". *(See Ref 789)*

As important as strategic communication is abroad, it is also necessary at home. Kapusta and Campbell state that failure to define the threat has undercut the U.S. response. An informal survey conducted in 2004 with the vice presidents of a major U.S. company illustrated such failures. Highly educated, worldly, and abreast of the news, they, nonetheless, believed that the only objective of the global war on terror was the capturing or killing of one person, Osama bin Laden. This is false: the first objective is to attack and destroy terrorist networks, not to focus on one person or organisation. More than three years at that time, after former president Bush declared war on terrorism, such misstated public perception shows the failure of U.S. strategic communications on the domestic front. *(See Ref 778, 790)*

Another example of the U.S. government's inability to effectively shape perception was the controversy surrounding the Pentagon's Office of Strategic Influence. Rumsfeld created the office in the aftermath of the September 11 attacks in response to concerns that the United States was losing international public support for the war on terrorism, particularly in Western Europe and the Middle East. Granted, the Pentagon may have been a poor place to locate such a public effort, but mischaracterisation of the office's mission led the administration to disband it, leaving vacant an important component of the fight against terrorism. *(See Ref 791)*

Without a coherent strategy, America's "war on terror" which now became with President Barack Obama "The struggle against militant Islamic radicalism is the great ideological conflict of the early years of the 21st century", has been tragically inconsistent. The West says that its mandate is to spread freedom and democracy, yet it tries to do so at the point of a gun. Washington says that the battle must be fought by a coalition of like-minded allies, but it eschews diplomacy and browbeat its friends when they disagree with its policy. America says that it stands for the highest human ideals, but the world harbours deep suspicions of the indefinite detentions at Guantanamo.

Those contradictory words and actions have alienated virtually the entire

Arab and Islamic nations. NATO remains fractured and largely ineffectual against the resurgent Taliban, and the Washington clock has run out on the Iraq war. The West have elevated al-Qa'ida's importance to nearly its own and U.S.A. moving into a deadly no-man's-land where America is neither respected nor feared. It is almost inconceivable, and yet it has come to this: the West is losing the global influence war to people who blow up women and children at kebab stands.

But if the West, especially US, can retool and take the long view, as the architects of Cold War containment did, "we will watch Islamic extremism collapse under the weight of its own contradictions - witness the recent grass-roots uprising against al-Qa'ida in Iraq. Like Marxism, militant Islam is long on promising the violent overthrow of the materialistic West and short on fashioning actual utopias." *(See Ref 778)*

The original doctrine of containment had its roots in a time of uncertainty much like U.S. itself. By the end of World War II, the United States was the dominant global power, and for a brief period there was hope that the world might fashion a lasting peace under the fledgling United Nations.

By 1949, however, it was clear that the world was bifurcating, and that this constituted a serious challenge to U.S. security. The Soviet Union became the second nuclear-armed superpower, China fell to Communism, and the proliferation of ballistic missiles threatened the American homeland. Coming on the heels of the decisive triumph of the war, the new Communist threat generated the same feelings of vulnerability and confusion that the September 11 attacks would foster decades later.

To respond to this changing world, senior national security officials writing for President Harry Truman articulated a new kind of policy. Drawing heavily from articles written by the American diplomat George Kennan, [the landmark National Security Council Report 68 (NSC-68)] outlined a strategy of containment that served as the core of American foreign policy for every president from Truman to Reagan.

Presciently, NSC-68 identified the essential clash between the United States and the Soviet Union as one between diametrically opposed ideologies. On the Soviet side was a dogmatic belief system that demanded absolute submission of individual freedom and sought to impose its authority over the rest of the world. On the American side was an ideology premised on the overriding value of freedom, a system founded upon the dignity and worth of the individual. This ideology relied upon its inherent appeal, and did not aim to bring other societies into conformity through force of arms.

Strikingly, officers Kapusta and Campbell argue that, if one replaces "communism" with "Islamic extremism" and "the Kremlin" with "al-Qa'ida", NSC-68 could have been written in 2002, not 1950. Like communism, Islamic extremism lusts for political power, in this case through the restoration of the caliphate and the imposition of Shari'a law on all peoples. Indeed, language from NSC-68 rings eerily true today - it described the Soviets as "animated by a new fanatic faith, antithetical to our own". Al-Qa'ida and its ilk are the latest in a long line of narrow ideologies that claim to provide the only true answer to life's existential questions. And as with Soviet communism, the idea has a geographic nucleus. *(See Ref 778)*

Washington and its allies' task now is to envelop this nucleus with prosperous, stable countries whose inhabitants are free to choose their own beliefs. Working from the outside in, the United States and the West must partner with nations on the periphery to help them build a stronger economy and stronger middle class, enhance their education systems, improve basic health, and lower government corruption. The West must help elected and unelected governments to allow greater empowerment of their citizens, whether through a slow march toward representative government or expanded economic opportunity for all classes.

The rise of Islamic fundamentalism is a problem for the Muslim populace as well. But they will not fight it with true conviction unless the United States and the West change their attitude toward Muslims and correct their past mistakes.

The objectives of Islamic resurgent movements have all been centred in Islam because this is their frame of reference and way of life, inclusive of political and socio-economic dispensations. To analyse the objectives of Islamic resurgent movements according to their violent manifestations only is to misunderstand their arguments. These movements are seeking a system inclusive of Islam simply because it is their way of life, their culture. Because Islam provides unity resurgent movements will always seek to overcome political and socio-economic exclusion and replace it with a system inclusive of all. However, Muslims will have to find a way of meeting their aims and objectives in a modern world. The outside world can facilitate but not dictate.

The manner in which the objectives of Islamic resurgent movements have been met has arguably manifested itself in violence as a modus operandi, but there has been another more important consequence. This has been the emergence of socio-economic organisations and infrastructure that have managed to entrench the significance of resurgent movements in broader society. Not only has the presence of these organisations provided a workable alternative for resurgent movements, but their popularity has shown what the true needs in society are and, more importantly, that these needs have not been addressed. The modi operandi of resurgent movements have been derived from the ideologies of mainly al-Banna and Qutb. They included the ideas and aspirations of past ideologies and formulated ideologies and modi operandi for their era. Since then very few have managed to come forward and capture an audience in the same manner. The problem is not centred in Islam but in the interpretation of the Koran. However, Muslims will have to take the opportunity to find different interpretations inclusive of Islam.

Furthermore, U.S.A. and NATO must institutionalise the lessons learned so painfully over 10 years of war. The military must dramatically improve its nation-building doctrine, capacity, and will, acknowledging that post-war stability is much more important in the long run than is dominating the active combat phase. The West remains unchallenged in its ability to win conventional military conflicts, but it must develop the language skills, cultural awareness, and civil-affairs specialists necessary to prevail in unconventional campaigns and in fighting's messy aftermath.

On the battlefield, it is at least as important to articulate what you are for as it is to define what you are against. In a war of ideas, this is even more critical. To do this across the world, nation by nation, will take time, and that does not come naturally to the West fast paced, results-oriented society. But the West, especially America, needs to muster the requisite patience. Untold numbers of lives hinge on it.

However, many in the West had taken lately comfort in al-Qa'ida's silence after the death of Osama bin Laden and in the wake of the uprisings in the Arab world this year, as secular, nonviolent protests, led by educated youth focused on redressing longstanding local grievances, showcased democracy's promise and seemed to leave al-Qa'ida and Islamists behind.

Indeed, the pristine spirit of the Arab Spring does represent an existential threat to al-Qa'ida and its affiliates' extremist ideology. But the organisation's new leaders also know that this is a strategic moment. They are banking on the disillusionment that inevitably follows revolutions to reassert their prominence in the region. And now al-Qa'ida is silent no more — and is taking the rhetorical offensive.

In recent statements, Ayman al-Zawahiri and al-Qa'ida surrogates have aligned themselves with the protesters in Libya, Egypt and elsewhere, while painting the West as an enemy of the Arab people.

In North Africa, al-Qa'ida in the Islamic Maghreb bombed on 28 April 2011 Argana restaurant in Marrakesh killing 14 tourists and claimed that while protesters flooded the streets of Tunis and Cairo, it had been fighting in the mountains against the same enemies. Anwar al-Awlaki, a Yemeni-American cleric affiliated with al-Qa'ida in the Arabian Peninsula, declared that in the wake of the revolutions, "our mujahedeen brothers ... will get a chance to breathe again after three decades of suffocation" and that "the great doors of opportunity would open up for the mujahedeen all over the world."

Al-Zawahiri has denounced democracy, arguing that toppling dictators is insufficient and that "justice, freedom, and independence" can be achieved only through "jihad and resistance until the Islamic regime rises."

The chaos and disappointment that follow revolutions will inevitably provide many opportunities for al-Qa'ida to spread its influence. Demographic pressures, economic woes and corruption will continue to bedevil even the best-run governments in the region. Divisions will beset the protest movements, and vestiges of the old regimes may re-emerge.

Al-Qa'ida and its allies don't need to win the allegiance of every protester to exert their influence; they have a patient view of history.

Although Washington must avoid tainting organic movements or being perceived as a central protagonist, the United States and its Western allies should not be shy about working with reformers and democrats to shape the region's trajectory — and ensuring al-Qa'ida's (and the Islamic radicals) irrelevance in the Middle East and the Arab world, the heart of its supposed constituency.

In countries where autocrats have been toppled (as in Egypt and Tunisia), the West must help shape the new political and social environment; in nondemocratic, allied states (like the region's monarchies), it needs to accelerate internal reform; and in repressive states (like Iran, Libya and Syria), it should challenge the legitimacy of autocratic regimes and openly assist dissidents and democrats.

This is not about military intervention or the imposition of American-style democracy. It is about using American and the Western power and influence to support organic reform movements.

The United States Agency for International Development and the West advocacy organisations can help civil society groups grow; human rights groups can organise and assist networks of dissidents; and Western women's groups and trade unions could support their counterparts throughout the Middle East. Wealthy philanthropists and entrepreneurs who are part of the Middle Eastern diaspora could make investments and provide economic opportunities for the region's youth, while technology companies interested in new markets could partner with anticorruption groups to aid political mobilisation and increase government accountability and transparency. Hollywood and Bollywood writers and producers should lionize the democratic heroes who took to the streets to challenge the orthodoxy of fear.

A focused campaign to shape the course of reform would align the Western and moderate Islamic values and interests with the aspirations of the protesters. More important, it would answer the challenge from al-Qa'ida to define what happens next and reframe the tired narratives of the past.

In 2005, al-Zawahiri anticipated this battle for reform and noted that "demonstrations and speaking out in the streets" would not be sufficient to achieve freedom in the Muslim world. If the West help the protesters succeed, it will not only serve long-term West national security interests but also mark the beginning of the end of the Islamic radicals including al-Qa'ida.

REFERENCES AND NOTES

1. *Auriana Ojeda, "Current Controversies: The Middle East", 2003*

2. *Tariq Modood: "Muslims In The West: A Positive Asset", 2001*

3. *Graham Fuller: Islam, A Force For Change", Le monde Diplomatique, Septembre 1999*

4. *Nazih N. Ayubi, "Political Islam, Religion and Politics in The Arab World", 1982, 1991*

5. *Nina Voges, "The Development of Islamic Esurgent Movements In Egypt", November 2006*

6. *Mehdi Mozaffari, "Authority in Islam: From Mohammed To Khomeini", 1987*

7. *Emmanuel Sivan, "Radical Islam Medieval Theology and Modern Politics", 1985*

8. *A. Thabet, Nikkie Keddie, Homa Pakdaman, and M. Black, "Perception of Islamic Militant Groups Toward the West", 2001*

9. *International Crisis Group (ICG), 20 April 2004; and David Sagiv, "Fundamentalism and Intellectuals in Egypt, 1973-1993", 1995*

10. *Olivier Roy, "L'echec De L'Islam Politique", 1992; and Olivier Roy, "The Failure of Political Islam", 1994.*

11. *Lisa M Farhamy, "Inside The New Terrorism", 2009*

12. *Charles Hill, "International Business: Competing In The Global Market Place", 2007*

13. *Dilip Hiro, "War Without End: The Rise Of Islamist Terrorism And Global Response", 2002*

14. *Nikki R Keddie, "Sayyid Jamal ad-Din al-Afghani an Islamic Response To Imperialism", 1968; and Homa A Pakdaman, "Djamal el-Din Assad Abadi Dit Afghani", 1969*

15. *Giles Kepel, "Muslim Extremism in Egypt: Prophet To Pharaoh", 1986*

16. *Kalim Siddiqui, "Stages of Islamic Revolution", 1996*

17. *John L Esposito, "Centraly War: Terror in The Name Of Islam", 2002*

18. *Kamran Bokhari, "Jihad & Jihadism: A Rendition of Transnational Militant Non-State Actors", 2004*

19. *John Calvert, "Sayyid Qutb And The Origins Of Radical Islam", October 2009.*

20. *Farih A. Noor, "The Evolution Of 'Jihad' in Islamic Political Discourse", 2002*

21. *Omar Bakri Muhammad, "The Islamic Verdict on Jihad as a Methodology to Establish the Khilafa", 2000*

22. *Paul Pillari, "Terrorism and U.S. Policy", 2001*

23. *Bruce Hoffman, "Inside Terrorism", 1968; and Paul Pillar, "Terrorism and US Foreign Policy", 2001; and Matthew Morgan, "The Origins Of The New Terrorism", 2004*

24. *Marc Sageman, "Leaderless Jihad: Terror Networks In The Twenty First Century", 2008*

25. *David Rapoport, "Terrorism", 2006*

26. *Nadine Gurr and Benjamin Cole, "The New Face of Terrorism: Threats From Weapons Of Mass Distruction", 2002*

27. *Mark Juergensmeyer, "Terror In The Mind Of God: The Global Rise Of Religious Violence", 2000, 2003*

28. *Peter Chalker et al, "Beyond al-Qaeda: The Global Jihadist Movement", 2006*

29. *Stephen Kinzer, The New York Times, 4/12/2006*

30. *Amer Ali, "Islamism: Emancipation, Protest and Identity", Journal of Muslim Minority Affairs, Vol. 20, No1, 2000*

31. *Russell D Howard, "understanding al-Qaeda's Aplication Of The New Terrorism The Key To Victory In The Current Campaign", 2004*

32. *Jon Elster, "Motivations and Beliefs in Suicide Missions", 2006*

33. *Benjamin T Acosta, "The Suicide Bomber As Sunni-Shi'i Hybrid", 2010*

34. *See David Cook, "Martyrdom in Islam", 2007*

35. *Salafi Manhaj, "Martyrdom in Islam VersusSuicide Bombing", 2007*

36. *Benjamin T. Acosta, "Palestinian Precedents: The Origins of Al-Qaeda's Use of Suicide Terrorism and Istishhad", in Joseph M. Skelly, ed., "Political Islam from Muhammad to Ahmadinejad: Defenders, Detractors, and Definitions", 2009*

37. *Joseph M Skelly, ed., "Political Islam From Muhammad To Ahmadinejad: Defenders, Detractors, and Definitions", 2009*

38. *Christopher Reuter, "My Life is A Weapon: A Modern History of Suicide Bombing", 2004*

39. *Al-Hayat interview with Rantissi conducted on 25/4/2001*

40. *Rashmi Singh, "The Efficacy of Terrorist Suicide Bombings and Other Tactics", 2007*

41. *William Spencer, "Global Studies: The Middle East", 1944; and Daniel C Diller, "The Middle East", English Edition,1994*

42. *Albert Hourani, "A History of The Arab Peoples", 1994*

43. *Randal James, "The Islamist Challenge in The Middle East and North Africa", 1996*

44. *Bernard Lewis, "The Political Language Of Islam", 1988*

45. *Mahmud A Faksh, "The Future Of Islam In The Middle East", 1997*

46. *Nina Voges, "The Development of Islamic Esurgent Movement In Egypt", 2007*

46a. *Reuters, 7/10/2003*

47. *David sagiv, "Fundamentalism and Intellectuals in Egypt, 1973-1993", 1995*

48. *Robert Springborg, "State, Politics and Islam", 1987*

49. *Richard P Mitchell, "The Society of Muslim Brotherhood", 1969*

50. *Ian Johnson, "A Mosque in Munich: Nazis, The CIA and Rise Of The Muslim Brotherhood in The West", 2010*

51. *Mathias Kuntzel, "Jihad and Jew Hatred: Islamism, Nazism and the Roots of 9/11", 2007*

52. *Jeffrey Herf, "Nazi Propaganda for the Arab World", 2009*

53. *Jebran Chamieh, "Traditionalists, Militants and Liberals In Present Islam", 1994*

54. *Giles Kepel, "Muslim Extremism in Egypt: The Prophet and the Pharaoh", 1984*

55. *Gabriel R Warburg, and Uri M Kupferschmidt, "Islam, Nationalism and Radicalism in Egypt and The Sudan", 1998*

56. *Richard P Mitchell, "The Society of Muslim Brotherhood", 1993*

57. *Carrie Rosefsky Wickam, "Mobilizing Islam: Religion, Activism, and Political Change in Egypt", 2002*

58. *Mark N Cooper, "The Transformation of Egypt", 1982*

59. *Asaf Hussain, "Islamic Movement in Egypt, Pakistan, and Iran", 1983*

60. *International Crisis Group (ICG), 20/4/2004*

61. *Michelle Poison, "The History of Muslim Brotherhood", 2008*

62. *Ray Takeyh and Nicolas K gvosdev, "The Rise and Fall of Radical Political Islam", 2004*

63. *Robert Springborg, "Mubarak's Egypt Fragmentation of the Political Order", 1989*

64. *Johannes J G Jansen, "The Neglected Duty- The Creed of Sadat's Assassins and Islamic Resurgent in the Middle East", 1986*

65. *Denis Joseph Sullivan and Sana Abed-Kotob, "Islam in Contemporary Egypt, Civil Society versus the State", 1999*

66. *Dr Israel Elad Altman, "Current Trends In The Ideology Of The Egyptian Muslim Brotherhood", January 2006*

67. *Quintan Wiktrowicz, "The Management of Islamic Activism", 2001*

68. *Mamoun Fandy, "Egypt's Islamic Group: Regional Revenge?" Middle East Journal, vol. 48, no. 4, Autumn 1994*

69. *Jeffrey Azava and Samuel Tadros, "The Problem of The Egyptian Brotherhood", Middle East Outlook, 30/11/2007*

70. *Steven Barraclough, "Al Azhar: Between the Government and the Islamists", The Middle East Journal, vol. 52, no. 2, Spring 1998*

71. *Wikipeadia*

72. *Arab Press Review Issue no. 1749, 11/9/2003*

73. *BBC News 29/11/2010, and 6/12/2010*

74. *Denis Joseph Sullivan and Sana Abed-Kotob, "Islam in Contemporary Egypt, Civil Society versus the State", 1999*

75. *Giles Kepel, "Jihad, The Trail of Political Islam", 2002*

76. *International Crisis Group (ICG), 30 September 2003*

77. *Hesham Al-Awadi, "Mubarak and The Islamists: Why Did The Honeymoon End", Middle East Journal, 1/1/2005*

78. *Damian Piretti, "Islamism and Democracy in Egypt: Converging Path", Washington Report on Middle East Affairs, March 2008*

79. *Olivier Roy, "The Failure of Political Islam", 1994*

80. *The US Library of Congress, Country Profile Saudi Arabia, Federal Research Division, March 2005*

81. *Philip Khuri Hitti, "History of the Arabs", revised 10th edition, 2002*

82. *Saudi Arabia: A country Study, By Federal Research Division, Kissinger Publishing 2004*

83. *David Commins: "The Wahhabi Mission and Saudi Arabia", 2006*

84. *"Alliance Of Muhammad Ibn Saud And Muhammad Ibn Abd al-Wahhab", King Abdul Aziz Ibn Saud Information Resource*

85. *"The Saud Family and Wahhabi Islam", Library of US Congress Country Studies*

86. *John Esposito, "The Oxford Dictionary Of Islam", 2003*

87. *Official Website of Saudi Arabia TV*

88. *Wikipaedia, "King Faisal Ibn Saud"*

89. *Alexei Vassiliev, "The History of Saudi Arabia", 1998*

90. *Official Saudi Government Journal Umm Al-Qura, Issue 2193, 20/10/1967*

91. *Joshua Tietelbaum, "A family Affair: Civil-Military Relations in The Kingdom Of Saudi Arabia"*

92. *Wikipaedia, "King Khalid Al Saud"*

93. *Anouar Boukhars, "At The Crossroads: Saudi Arabia's Dilemmas", Summer 2006*

94. *Stephen Schwartz, "Liberation, Not Containment: How to win the war on Wahhabism," The National Review, 30/11/ 2001*

95. *Michael Scott Doran, review of "The Two Faces of Islam: The House of Sa'ud From Tradition to Terror," Washington Post, 22/12/ 2002*

96. *Anthony H. Cordesman, "Saudi Government Counterterrorism-Counter Extremism Actions", Saudi-US Relations Information Service, 4/8/2003*

97. *"Saudi Arabia Backgrounder: Who are the Islamists?" ICG Middle East Report no. 31, 219/ 2004*

98. *Alain Gresh, "Saudi Arabia: Radical Islam or reform?", Le Monde Diplomatique, June 2003*

99. *Daniel Benjamin and Steven Simon, "The Age Of Secret Terror", 2002*

100. *Prince Bandar bin Sultan bin Abd al-Aziz Al Saud, "a Diplomat's Call for War", Washington Post, 6/6/2004*

101. *The Economist, "Reform in Saudi Arabia: At a Snail's Pace", 30/9/2010*

102. *Christpher Dicky, "The Monarch Who Declared His Own Revolution", Newsweek, 21/3/2009*

103. *Paul Handley, "Saudi Shake-Up Aims To Ease Islamist Hold", AFP, 19/2/2009*

104. *The Columbia Electronic Encyclopedia, 6th Edition, "Afghanistan Early History", 2007*

105. *The Afghans- Their History and Culture". United States: Centre For Applied Linguistics CAL), 30/6/2002*

106. *"Country Profile: Afghanistan", United States: Library of Congress Country Studies on Afghanistan, August 2001 & 2008*

107. *George Bruce Malleson, "History of Afghanistan, from the Earliest Period to the Outbreak of the War of 1878"*

108. *D. Balland, "Afghanistan x. Political History", Encyclopædia Iranica*

109. *Hector E Maletta, "Arable Land Tenure in Afghanistan in Post-Taliban Era", African and Asian Studies, Vol. 6, 2007*

110. *Christian Parenti, "Unnatural Borders, Open Wounds: The Human Landscape Of Pakistan", 2008*

111. *World Fact Book, CIA, 2010, Population of Afghanistan*

112. *Phil Gasper, "Afghanistan, The CIA, Bin Laden and The Taliban", International Social Review, Nov.-Dec., 2001*

113. *Barry Bearak, "Former King Of Afghanistan Dies at 92", The New York Times, 23/7/2007*

114. *Phil Gasper, "Afghanistan, The CIA, Bin Laden and The Taliban", International Social Review, Nov.-Dec., 2001*

115. *Amin Saikal, "Modern Afghanistan: A History of Struggle and Survival", 2006.*

116. *The Washington Post 14/2/1980*

117. *"How Jimmy Carter And I Started The Mujahideen", [in French], Le Nouvel Observateur, 15/1/1998*

118. *"How the CIA created Osama bin Laden", greenleft, 2001*

119. *Dilip Hiro, "War Without End: The Rise of Islamist Terrorism and Global Response", 2002*

120. *Ahmed Rashid, "Pakistan - Elite's Loss, Islamists Gain", Far Eastern Economic Review 05/01/2001*

121. *"Turning The Tide In Afghanistan As War Unfolded Strategy Evolved", Boston Globe, 31/12/2001*

122. *Human Rights Watsh, "Blood-Stained Hands, Past Atrocities In Kabul and Afghanistan's Legacy of Impunity", 6/7/2005*

123. *Barnett R Rubin, "Afghanistan Under Taliban", 1992*

124. *Aisha Ahmad, "Taliban and Islamic Courts Union: How They Changed The Game In Afghanistan and Somalia", Policy Perspectives, Vol. 6, No 2, July-December 2009*

125. *Alan F Fogelquist, "Al-Qaeda and The Question of State Sponsorship", 29/2/2002*

126. *Michael Griffin, "Reoping The Whirlwind"*

127. *Ahmed Rashid, "The Taliban - First, The War", Far Eastern Economic Review, 26/07/2001.*

128. *Anthony Davis, "Afghanistan Taliban", Janes' Intelligence Review, 1/7/1995*

129. *Ahmed Rashid, "Taliban Fighters Massacre 300 Shia Muslims", Daily Telegraph, 8/2/2001*

130. *Ahmed Rashid, "Going all the Way in Kabul", Far Eastern Economic Review, 14/6/2001*

131. *Giles Dorronsoro and Elizabeth Bumiller, "Stopping The Taliban's Momentum?", 23/9/2010*

132. *Hillary Clinton testimony before the US House Foreign Committee, 22/4/2009.*

133. *Fareed Zakaria, "Terrorism's Supermarket", Newsweek, 7/5/2010*

134. *Husain Haqqi, "Pakistan Between Mosque and Military", 2005*

135. *Selig S Harrison, "Nightmare in Balushistan", Foreign Policy, vol.22, fall 1978*

136. *Selig S Harrison, "In Afghanistan Shadow", 1978*

137. *Alan Campbell-Johnson, "Mission With Mountbatten", 1951*

138. *Tariq Ali, "Can Pakistan Survive?", 1983*

139. *Mujtaba Razvi, "The Frontiers of Pakistan", 1971*

140. *Rajat Ganguly, "Pakistan As A Rogue State", 2008*

141. *Yasmin Khan, "The Great Partition: The Making Of India and Pakistan", 2007*

142. *Bhimrao Ramji Ambedkar, "Pakistan, or Partition of India", 1946*

143. *Jyotindra Nalh Dixit, "India-Pakistan in War & Peace", 2002*

144. *Rajat Ganguly, "India, Pakistan and The Kashmir Dispute", 1994*

145. *The Columbia Electronic Encyclopedia, 2007*

146. *Alexander Evans, "Reducing Tensions is Not Enough", Washington Quarterly, spring 2001*

147. *Christopher Hitchens, "The Perils of Partition", The Atlantic Monthly, March 2003*

148. *Arundhali Roy, "The Cost of Living", New York, The Modern Library, 1999*

149. *Stanley A. Wolpert, "India", 1991*

150. *"An Indian Perestroika." Part 2 of Rajiv Gandhi's interview in Sunday, 19-25 August 1990*

151. *Chris Hedges, "Many Islamic Militants Trained in Afghan War", The New York Times, 28/3/1993*

152. *Shiraz Sidhva, "Days of Despair", Sunday, 16-22 June 1991*

153. *Sanjoy Hazarika, "Afghans Joining Rebels in Kashmir", The New York Times, 24/8/1993*

154. *Ahmed Rashid, "No Longer Welcome", Far Eastern Economic Review, 2/4/1992*

155. *Sumil Gangula, Devin T Hagerty, "Fearful symmetry: India-Pakistan crises in the shadow of nuclear weapons", 2005*

156. *Gregory Possehl, "Revolution in The Urban Revolution- The Emergence Of Indus Urbanization", Anuual Review of Anthropology, October 1990*

157. *Jonathan Mark Kenoyer, Kimberley Heuston, "The Ancient South Asian World", May 2005*

158. *"Palaeolithic and Pleistocene of Pakistan", Department of Archaeology, University of Sheffield*

159. *Sir Muhammad Iqbal's 1930 Presidential address*

160. *Qutubuddin Aziz, "Muslim's Struggle for Independent Statehood", Jang Group Newspaers*

161. *"2002 – Kashmir Crisis", GlobalSecurity.org*

162. *Hassan Abbas, "Pakistan's Troubled Frontiers", Asia Society, 15/3/2010*

163. *Greg Bruno, Jashree Bajoria, "Shared Goals for Pakistan's Militants", Council on Foreign Relations, 6/5/2010*

164. *Hassan Abbas, "Benazir's sacrifice may yet save Pakistan", The Guardian, 1/1/2008*

165. *Don Rassler, "al-Qa'ida Pakistan Strategy", CTC Sentinel, Vol. 2, Issue 6/6/2009*

166. *Brian Fishman, "The Battle for Pakistan: FATA and NWFP", 19/4/2010*

167. *Bernard Gwertzman, "The Danger of Delay in Afghan Policymaking", Council on Foreign Relations, 8/10/2009.*

168. *Ayesha Siddiqa, "Terror's Training Ground", Newsline, 9/9/2009*

169. *Jayree Bajoria, "Pakistan's New Generation of Terrorists", 7/10/2010*

170. *Steve Coll, "Globalization of Terror", 5/3/2010*

171. *Selig S Harrison, "Nightmare in Balushistan", Foreign Policy, Vol.22, fall 1978+*

172. *Mujtaba Razvi, "The Frontiers Of Pakistan: A Study Of Frontier Problems In Pakistan's Foreign Policy", 1971*

173. *Anthony Spaeth, "No Peace In The Valley: In Kasmir Deadly Disputes Continue To Divide And Multiply", Harper's Magazine, April, 1993*

174. *Amy Zalman, "What's So New About The 'New Terrorism'?", 1/3/2008*

175. *Robert Jay Lifton, "Destroying the World to Save It: Aum Shinrikyo, Apocalyptic Violence, and the New Global Terrorism", 1999*

176. *James F Rinehart, "Apocalyptic Faith and Political Violence: Prophets of Terror", 2006*

177. *Sayyid Qutb, "Islam: The Religion of the Future", Beirut, Lebanon: International Islamic Federation of Student Organisations, 1971*

178. *Wikipaedia, "Al-Qaeda"*

179. *Lawrence Wright, "The Looming Tower: Al-Qaeda and The Road To 9/11", 2006*

180. *FBI Agent Jack Clornan Frontline Interview, PBS, 13/7/2005*

181. *Marc Sageman, "Understanding Terror Networks", 2004*

182. *Peter L Bergen, "Holy war, Inc.: inside the secret world of Osama bin Laden", 2001*

183. *Interview with Alfred McCoy, 9/11/1991 by Paul DeRienzo*

184. *"The War on Terror and the Politics of Violence in Pakistan", Jamestown Foundation, 2/7/2004*

185. *Steve Emerson, "Abdullah Assam: The Man Before Osama Bin Laden"*

186. *"MIPT Terrorism Knowledge Base", Tkb.org*

187. *Rohan Gunaratna, "Inside Al Qaeda", 2002.*

188. *Richard Z. Chesnoff, Brian Duffy, and Louise Lief, "Bad Company in Khartoum", US News & World Report, 30/8/1993*

189. *"Is Sudan Terrorism's New Best Friend", Time, 30/8/1993*

190. *Alan F Fogelquist, "Al-Qaeda and The Question Of State Sponsorship", 29/8/2002*

191. *Simon Reeve, "The New Jackals: Ramzi Yousef, Osama Bin Laden and the Future of Terrorism", 1999*

192. *"Mubarak Survives Ambush", Minneapolis Star Tribune, 27/6/1995*

193. *"Sudan Denies Role in Mubarak attack", Jerusalem Post, 27/6/1995*

194. *"Ethiopia Assassins: Three Mubarak Ambush Suspects Arrested", Inter Press Service News Wire, 4/8/1995; and Raja Asghar, "Bomb Kills 15 at Egyptian Mission in Pakistan", News India, 24/11/1995*

195. *Mansoor Ijaz, "Clinton Let Bin Laden Slip Away and Metastasize", Los Angeles Times, 5/12/2001*

196. *Timothy Carney, Mansoor Ijaz, "Intelligence Failure? Let's Go Back to Sudan", The Washington Post, 30/6/2002*

197. *David Rose, "The Osama Files", Vanity Fair, January 2002*

198. *National Commission: Terrorist Attacks Upon The United States: Responses To Al Qaeda's Initial Assaults*

199. *Ahmed Rashid, "Taliban: Militant Islam, Oil and Fundamentalism in Central Asia", 2002*

200. *"Text of Fatwa Urging Jihad against Americans", al-Quds al-Arabi, 3/2/1998.*

201. *Yonah Alexander and Michael S. Setnam, "Usama Bin Laden's Al-Qaida: Profile of a Terrorist Network", 2001*

202. *Syed Saleem Shahzad, "Al-Qaida: the Unwanted Guests", Le Monde Diplomatique, July 2007*

203. *Marc Sageman, "Understanding Terror Networks", 2004*

204. *Yaroslav Trofimov, "Faith At War: A Journey On the Frontlines of Islam, From Baghdad to Timbuktu", 2006*

205. *Ivan Tulyakov, "Al-Qaeda Slowly Makes Its Way to Somalia and Yemen", Pravda, 15/9/2009*

206. *CBS News staff, "Did Abdulmutallab Talk to Radical Cleric?", CBS News, 29/12/2009*

207. *The full Text of the speech is available at www.cnn.com/2001/us/09/20/gen.bush.transcript/*

208. *Daniel L Byman, "Al-Qaida As An Adversary: Do We Understand Our Enemy?", 2004*

209. *Anonymous, "Through Our Enemies' Eyes: Osama Bin Ladin, Radical Islam, and the Future of America", 2002*

210. *Daniel Benjamin, and Steven Simon, "The Age of Sacred Terror", 2002*

211. *Gilles Kepel, "Jihad: The Trail of Political Islam", 2002*

212. *Jason Burke, "What Exactly Does Al-Qaeda Want?", The Guardian, 21/3/2204*

213. *Rohan Gunaratna, "Inside Al Qaeda", 2002*

214. *Adam Curtis, "The Power of Nightmares", BBC Documentary, 2004*

215. *"WMD Terrorism and Usama bin Laden", by the Centre of Nonproliferation Studies*

216. *"Witness: Bin Laden Planned Attack on US Embassy in Saudi Arabia", CNN, 13/2/2001*

217. *Johanna McGeany, "A Traitor's tale", Time, 19/2/2001*

218. *Curt Anderson, "New Al-Qaeda Leader Lived in US For Years", Associated Press, 6/8/2010*

219. *"Progress Report On The Global War On Terrorism", US State Department, 22/9/2003*

220. *Mark Basile, "Going To The Source: Why Al-Qaeda's Financial Network Is Likely To Withstand The Current War On Terrorist Financing", May 2004*

221. *Bruce Hoffman, "The Emergence of The New Terrorism", 2002*

222. *The text of the President's speech is available at http://usinfo.state.gov/usa/ islam/s.09.2001.htm*

223. *Samuel P Huntington, "The Clash Of Civilisations And The Remaking Of World Order", 1996*

224. *Douglas Frantz, et al., "The New Face of Al-Qaeda", Los Angeles Times, 26/9/2004*

225. *Derek Reveron, "Tuned to Fear", National Review Online, 13/1/2005*

226. *BBC News, 14/7/2004*

227. *Emily Hunt, "Virtual Incompetence", Daily Standard, Washington, D.C., 18/8/2006*

228. *Fareed Zakaria, "Osama Needs More Mud Huts", Newsweek, 8/5/2006*

229. *Jason Burke, "Al-Qaeda: The True Story of Radical Islam", 2004*

230. *Peter Bergen, "The Return of Al Qaeda", The New Republic, 29/1/2007; and The Washington Post, 30/5/2007*

231. *Michael Scheuer, "Al-Qaeda and Algeria's GSPC: Part of a Much Bigger Picture", Terrorism Focus, 3/4/2007*

232. *"Trends in Global Terrorism: Implications for the United States", National Intelligence Estimate, National Intelligence Council, Washington, D.C., Apr. 2006*

233. *"The Terrorist Threat to the US Homeland", National Intelligence Estimate, National Intelligence Council, Washington, D.C., July 2007*

234. *Abu Mus'ab al-Suri, "The Call for Global Islamic Resistance", Arlington, Va.: DCIA Counterterrorism Center, 2006*

235. *Abu Bakr Naji, "The Management of Savagery", West Point, N.Y.: Combating Terrorism Center, 2006*

236. *"9-11 Commission Report: Final Report of the National Commission on Terrorist Attacks upon the United State", released Feb. 14, 2006*

237. *Abdel Bari Atwan, "The Secret History of al Qaeda", 2006*

238. *NBC News, 24/6/2005*

239. *Petter Nesser, "Jihad in Europe: A Survey of the Motivations for Sunni Islamist Terrorism in Post-Millennium Europe", 2004*

240. *The Christian Science Monitor, 22/3/2004*

241. *Lawrence Wright, "The Terror Web",The New Yorker, 2/8/2004*

242. *"Iraq the Jihad: Expectations and Dangers", Center of Mujahideen Services, 2003*

243. *Report into the London Terrorist Attacks on 7 July 2005, Intelligence and Security Committee, The Stationery Office, London, 11/5/2006*

244. *Dan Darling and Steve Schippert, "British 7/7 Bombing Report Ignores Al-Qaeda", ThreatsWatch, 10/4/2006*

245. *CNN.com, 11/8/2004*

246. *Daveed Gartenstein and Kyle Dabruzzi, "Al-Qa'ida Central Leadership Relevant?", 1/4/2008*

247. *Steven Simon, "Al-Qaeda Takes it To The Streets", The Washington Post, 8/10/2010*

248. *Laurent Bonnefoy, "Varieties Of Islamism In Yemen: The Logic Of Integration Under Pressure", Middle East Review Of International Affairs, 13/1/2009*

249. *"Arabian Peninsula 1000B-1AD", Heilbrunn Timeline of Art History, The Metropolitan Museum Of Art*

250. *"Arabian Peninsula 200-1000BC", Heilbrunn Timeline of Art History, The Metropolitan Museum Of Art*

251. *Wikipedia, "Yemen History"*

252. *R. Lambert Playfair, "A History of Arabia Felix or Yemen: From The Commencement of The Christian Era To Present Time, Including An Account Of The British Settlement Of Aden Education Society's Press", 1859*

253. *Muhsin Ibn Ahmad Harrazi, "Fatrat al-Fawda Wa "awdat al-Atrak Ila San'a",[in Arabic] 1986*

254. *"History of Yemen", Universal Touring Company*

255. *The UN Refugee Agency, "Yemen: The Conflict in Saada Governate", 24/7/2008*

256. *Jane Merrick, Kim Sengupta, "Yemen The Land With More Guns Than People", The Independent, 20/9/2009*

257. *"Yemen", European Institute For Research on Mediterranean and Euro-Arab Cooperation*

258. *Bernard Haykel, "Revival and Reform: The Legacy of Muhammad al-Shawkani", 2003*

259. *Laurent Bonnefoy, "Les identités religieuses contemporaines au Yémen: convergence, résistances et instrumentalisations", Revue des mondes musulmans et de la Méditerranée, No. 121-122, 2008*

260. *François Burgat and Marie Camberlin, "Révolution mode d'emploi: Zubayri et les erreurs des libres", Chroniques yéménites, No. 9, 2002*

261. *Paul Dresch and Bernard Haykel, "Stereotypes and Political Styles: Islamists and Tribesfolk in Yemen", International Journal of Middle East Studies, No. 27, 1995*

262. *Abd al-Fattah al-Hakimi, "al-Islamiyyin wal-Siyyasa: Al-Ikhwan al-Muslimun Namudhajan", San'a: Al-Muntada al-Jami'i, 2003*

263. *Abdallah bin Husayn al-Ahmar," Mudhakira"t, San'a: al-Afaq, 2007*

264. *Helem Chapen Metz, "Persian Gulf States", Country Studies, Third Edition, Library of Congress-Federal Research Division, 1994*

265. *Fathel Abu Ghanem, Ali Ahmed, "The Tribal Structure in Yemen: Between Continuance and Change", [in Arabic], 1991*

266. *Elham M Manea, "Yemen, The Tribe and The State", 10/10/1998*

267. *Laurent Bonnefoy and Fayçal Ibn Cheikh, "Le Rassemblement yéménite pour la Réforme (al-Islah) face à la crise du 11 septembre et la guerre en Afghanistan," Chroniques yéménites, No. 9, 2002*

268. *Jamal al-Suwaidi (ed.), "The Yemeni War of 1994: Causes and Consequences, 1995*

269. *Michaelle Browers, "Origins and Architects of Yemen's Joint Meeting Parties", International Journal of Middle Eastern Studies, Vol. 39, No. 4, 2007*

270. *Marine Poirier, "Yémen nouveau, futur meilleur? Retour sur l'élection présidentielle de 2006", Chroniques yéménites, No. 15, 2009*

271. *Abd al-Karim Qasim Sa'id, "al-Ikhwan al-Muslimun wal-Haraka al-Usuliyya fil-Yaman", 1998*

272. *Mustafa Badi al-Lawjri, "Afghanistan: Ihtilal al-Dhakira", 2007*

273. *Sa'id Ubayd al-Jambi, "al-Qa'ida fi al-Yaman", 2008*

274. *Laurent Bonnefoy, "Les relations religieuses transnationales contemporaines entre le Yémen et l'Arabie Saoudite: un salafisme importé?", 2007*

275. *Muqbil al-Wadi'i (ed.), "Tarjamat Abi 'Abd al-Rahman Muqbil bin Hadi al-Wadi'I", 1999*

276. *Muqbil al-Wadi'i, "Tuhfat al-mujib ala as'ilat al-hadar wa al-gharib", San'a: Dar al-athar, 2005*

277. *Brynjar Lia, "'Destructive Doctrinarians': Abu Musab al-Suri's Critique of the Salafis in the Jihadi Current," Norwegian Defence Research Institute, 2007*

278. *Alexander Knysh, "Contextualizing the Salafi-Sufi Conflict: from the Northern Caucasus to Hadramawt", Middle Eastern Studies, Vol. 43, No. 3, 2007*

279. *Engeng Ho, "The Graves of Tarim: Genealogy and Mobility Across the Indian Ocean", 2006*

280. *Samy Dorlian, "Zaydisme et Modernisation: Émergence d'un Nouvel Universel Politique?", Chroniques Yéménites, No. 13, 2006*

281. *François Burgat, "Le Yémen après le 11 septembre 2001 : entre construction de l'Etat et rétrécissement du champ politique", Critique internationale, No. 32, 2006*

282. *Ludmila du Bouchet, "The State, Political Islam and Violence: The Reconfiguration of Yemeni Politics since 9/11," in Amélie Blom, Laetitia Bucaille, and Luis Martinez (eds.), The Enigma of Islamist Violence", 2007*

283. *Robert Burrowes, "Yemen: Political Economy and the Effort against Terrorism," in Robert Rotberg (ed.), Battling Terrorism in the Horn of Africa, 2005*

284. *"Profile: Al-Qaeda in the Arabian Peninsula", BBC News, 31/10/2010*

285. *Mohamed Sudam, "Qaeda Group Claims U.S. Jet Plot, Vows For More Attacks", Reuters 28/12/2009*

286. *Issues 1 to 24 of Mu'asker al-Battar are available online at http://www.e-prism.org/pages/5/index.htm*

287. *Al-Khansaa, a convert to Islam and a companion of the Prophet, is*

remembered for her eulogies, particularly the one written for her brother Sakhr who died in a tribal feud. She is considered "the mother of the Shaheeds (Martyrs)" because when her four sons died in the battle of Al-Qadasiyya (637), she did not mourn, but thanked Allah Who had "honoured her with their deaths"; see also Al-Khansaa, no. 1 (20 August 2004). Available at http://www.e-prism.org/images/kh01.pdf

288. *Haim Malka, "Must Innocents Die? The Islamic Debate over Suicide Attacks", The Middle East Quarterly X, no.2, 2003*

289. *Julie Cohn, "Islamist Radicalism in Yemen",, CFR, 29/6/2010*

290. *Gregory D Johnsen, "Ignoring Yemen At Our Peril", Foreign Policy, 31/10/2010*

291. *William R Brown, "The Yemeni Dilemma," Middle East Journal 17, no. 4, 1963*

292. *Paul K Dresch, "The Tribal Factor in the Yemeni Crisis" In "The Yemeni War of 1994: Causes and Consequences, ed. J al-Suwaidi, Emirates Centre for Strategic Studies and Research, 1995*

293. *Steven C Caton, "Yemen Chronicle: An Anthropology of War and Mediation", 2005*

294. *Sarah Phillips, "Yemen's Democracy Experiment in Regional Perspective: Patronage and Pluralized Authoritarianism", 2008*

295. *Christopher Boucek, "Yemen: Avoiding a Downward Spiral", 2009*

296. *Sarah Philps, "What Comes Next In Yemen? Al-Qaeda, The Tribes and State Building", March 2010*

297. *Ayman al-Zawahiri, "From Kabul to Mogadishu," statement released February 22, 2009*

298. *Brian O'Neill, "AQAP a Rising Threat in Yemen", CTC Sentinel, 2(4), 2009*

299. *Ken Menkhams, "Somalia After The Ethiopian Occupation: First Steps To End The Conflict And Combat Extremism", 9/2/2009*

300. *Julie Cohn, "Terrorism Havens: Somalia", Council On Foreign Relations, June 2010*

301. *Jeffrey Gettleman, "Situation in Somalia Seems About To Get Worse", New York Times, 6/12/2008*

302. *"Somali President Calls Emergency", BBC News, 22/6/2009*

303. *Ken Menkhause, "Somalia: A Country In Peril, A Policy Nightmare",*
     September 2009

304. *Ziauddin Sardar and Merryl Wyn Davies, "The No-nonsens Guide To*
     Islam", 2004

305. *Muhammad Fast, Ivan Hrbek, "Africa From The Seventh To The Eleventh*
     Century", 1988

306. *David D Laitin, Politics, Language, and Thought: The Somali Experience",*
     1977

307. *"Somalia A Country Study", Federal Research Division, Kissinger*
     Publishing, 2004

308. *Ken Menkhaus, "The Crisis in Somalia: A Tragedy in Five Acts," African*
     Affairs, Issue 106, 2007

309. *Lara Santoro, "Islamic Clerics Combat Lawlessness In Somalia", The*
     Christian Sciences Monitor, 31/1/1999

310. *John Prendergast, "15 Years After Black Hawk Down: Somalia's Chance?",*
     April 2008

311. *See the details of the Djibouti Agreement on http://unpos.unmissions.org/*
     Portals/UNPOS/Repository%20UNPOS/080818%20-%20Djibouti%20
     Agreement.pdf.

312. *Daveed Gartenstein-Ross, "The Strategic Challenge Of Somalia's al-*
     Shabaab: Dimension Of Jihad", Middle East Quarterly, fall 2009

313. *Daveed Gartenstein-Ross, "While Pakistan Burns", The Weekly Standard,*
     29/10/2007

314. *Karen A. Mingst and Margaret P. Karns, "The United Nations in the 21st*
     Century", 3rd ed., 2006

315. *Ken Menkhaus, "Somalia: State Collapse and the Threat of Terrorism",*
     2004

316. *Nick Grace, "Shabaab Reaches Out to al Qaeda Senior Leaders, Announces*
     Death of al Sudani", The Long War Journal, 2/9/2008

317. *Abdurahman M. Abdullahi, "Perspective on the State Collapse in*
     Somalia", in Abdullahi A. Osman and Issaka K. Souaré, eds., "Somalia
     at the Crossroads: Challenges and Perspectives on Reconstituting a Failed
     State", 2007

318. *Shaul Shay, "Somalia between Jihad and Restoration", 2008*

319. *"Somalia: Countering Terrorism in a Failed State", International Crisis Group (ICG), Africa Report, no. 45, 23/5/2002*

320. *Gregory Alonso Pirio and Hrach Gregorian, "Jihadist Threat in Africa", Middle East Times, 11/7/2006*

321. *Ken Menkhaus, "Somalia: State Collapse and the Threat of Terrorism", Adelphi Paper, 2004*

322. *Ameen Jan, "Somalia: Building Sovereignty or Restoring Peace?" in Elizabeth M. Cousens, et al. eds., "Peacebuilding as Politics: Cultivating Peace in Fragile Societies", 2000*

323. *"Somalia's al-Ittihad al-Islami", West Point Combating Terrorism Center*

324. *Amb. Robert Oakly, "Somalia: Is There a Light at the End of the Tunnel?", New York Times, 27/4/2001*

325. *Evan F. Kohlmann, "Shabaab al-Mujahideen: Migration and Jihad in the Horn of Africa", 2009*

326. *Taariikh Nololeedkii Macallin Aadan Xaashi Faarax Cayrow, Mar. 2009, posted on Al-Qimmah.net*

327. *The New York Times, 2/5/2008*

328. *"Somalia Civil War", GlobalSecurity.org*

329. *Asaf Maliach, "Somalia – Africa's Afghanistan?", International Policy Institute for Counter-Terrorism (ICT), 22/6/2006*

330. *SomaliNet, 9/8/2006*

331. *Sunguta West, "Somalia's ICU and Its Roots in al-Ittihad al-Islami", Terrorism Monitor, 4/8/2006*

332. *Executive Order 13224, U.S. Treasury Dept., 23/9/2001*

333. *Associated Press, 20/6/2006; and Associated Press, 5/7/2006*

334. *Michelle Shephard, "Back to Somalia: Asho's Sad End", The Toronto Star, 21/12/2008*

335. *Alex Wilner, "Is Somalia the Next Afghanistan?", Atlantic Institute for Market Studies, Halifax, 24/11/2006*

336. *CNN, 2/7/2006*

337. *BBC News, 5/7/2006*

338. *J. Peter Pham, "Financing Somalia's Islamist Warlords", World Defense Review, 21/9/2006*

339. *Schiemsky, et al., "Report of the Monitoring Group on Somalia"*

340. *Bill Roggio, "The Battle of Baidoa", The Long War Journal, 23/12/2006*

341. *Daveed Gartenstein-Ross, "Blackhawk Up", Weekly Standard, 29/1/2007*

342. *Abu Mansoor al-Amriki, "A Message to the Mujaahideen in Particular and Muslims in General", Jan. 2008*

343. *"Somalia: Al-Shabaab Leader Abu Mansur Addresses Rally in Southern City of Marka", Kataaib.net, 14/11/2008*

344. *The New York Post, 4/4/2009*

345. *"Somalia: Al-Shabaab Official Equates AU Peacekeepers with Ethiopian Troops", Kataaib.net, Open Source Center, trans., 17/1/2009*

346. *BBC News, 21/3/2008*

347. *The Sunday Independent (Johannesburg), Aug. 31/8/2008*

348. *"March Forth", Aug. 31/8/2008*

349. *"Somali Mujahideen Confirm al-Qaeda Suspect Abu Talha al-Sudani Killed Last Year", Terrorism Focus (Jamestown Foundation, Washington, D.C.), 10/9/2008*

350. *BBC News, 5/1/2007*

351. *"Al-Qa'ida Figure al-Libi Urges Somali 'Mujahidin' to Only Accept 'Islamic State'", Open Source Center Summary in Arabic, 22/6/2008*

352. *The Long War Journal, 22/3/2009*

353. *Osama bin Laden, "Fight on Champions of Somalia", Mar. 2009, Internet Archive, San Francisco*

354. *The Report To US Senate Committee On Foreign Relations, "Al-Qaeda In Yemen And Somalia", 21/1/2010*

355. *The Times, (London), 16/2/2009*

356. *Frederick Nzwili, "Leadership Profile: Somalia's Islamic Courts Union", Terrorism Focus, Jamestown Foundation, 16/2/2009, 13/6/2006*

357. *"The Rise of the Shabab", The Economist, 18/12/2008*

358. *Osama bin Laden's March 14, 2009 audiotape, entitled "Practical Steps to Liberate Palestine"*

359. *Daily Star [Beirut], 20/12/2005; and Jerusalem Post, 30/12/2005*

360. *Jerusalem Post, 30/12/2005*

361. *"Good Tidings for the Believers and Shattering Earthquakes for the Oppressors, Infidels, and Hypocrites: Second and Final Part of the Answers of the Arrowhead of the Mujahidin, Asad al-Jihad 2", Global Islamic Media Front, February 2009*

362. *See in particular the statements by Abu 'Umar al-Baghdadi, "Verily the Believers Are Brothers"; and Ayman al Zawahiri, "The Massacre of Gaza and the Siege of the Traitors"; and Osama bin Laden, "A Call to Jihad to Stop the Aggression against Gaza", released in quick succession in mid-January 2009 - many weeks after the start of the Gaza confrontation*

363. *Muhammad Ahmad Abd al-Ghani, "The Effects of Takfiri Thought on the Nahr al-Barid Refugee Camp", 2008*

364. *"Basha'ir li-l-mu'minin wa-zalzalah li-l-tawaghit wa-lkuffarwa-l-munafiqin: al-jiz' al-thani wa-l-akhir min ajwibatra's harbat al-mujahidin", Asad al-Jihad 2 [Good Tidings for the Believers and Shattering Earthquakes for the Oppressors, Infidels, and Hypocrites: Second and Final Part of the Answers of the Arrowhead of the Mujahidin, Asad al-Jihad 2] (Global Islamic Media Front, February 2009)*

365. *The complex treatment of the status of the question of Palestine in Salafist jihadism is exemplified in al-Difa' 'an Aradi al-Muslimin Aham Furud al-A'yan (standardized edition from Minbar al-Tawhid wa-l-Jihad website), by 'Abdallah 'Azzam, a principal advocate of jihadism, and bin Laden's mentor*

366. *The (positive) book review, and the enthusiastic viewer comments, at the Muslim Brethrenwebsite, available at www.ikhwanonline.com*

367. *Compare "Filistin, al-An Hamiya al-Watis," a 2009 video release in which Abu Yahya al-Libi highlights the importance of the Palestinian issue in the midst of the Israel-Hamas Gaza confrontation, to his Wasatiyyat al- Islam wa-Wasatiyyat al-Inhizam [Islamic Centrism versus Defeatist Centrism], As-Sahab Media, 2008*

368. *Hassan Mneimneh, "Al-Qaeda's Advance In The Levant", 2009*

369. *Sari Sammour, "Wujud Far' li-Tanzim al-Qa'idah fi Filistin, Mumkin aw*

Mustahil?" [Is the Existence of a Branch of al-Qa'ida in Palestine Possible or Impossible?], 2005

370. *www.alsoufia.org. Ahmad bin Hasan al-Mu'allim, "al-Quburiyyah, Nash'atuha, Atharuha, Mawqif al-'Ulama' Minha", [Shrine Worship: Origins, Sources, and Scholastic Assessment], Ta'iz: Dar ibn al-Jawzi, 2005, provides an overview of the doctrinal position of the Salafist critique and assessment of the current state of the confrontation in one part of Arabia*

371. *A description of the incremental "Salafization" of Al-Azhar was provided in 2006 by Nabil Sharaf al-Din in the web-based Arabic newspaper Elaph, available at www.elaph.com*

372. *The polemical character of the discussion on Shiite proselytism dominates the topic in Islamist forums. The Center for Belief Research (affiliated with the Iraqi Shiite leading cleric Grand Ayatollah Ali al-Sistani) maintains a section on converts to Shiism, available at www.aqaed.com*

373. *A compilation of many such fatwas, from a Salafist jihadist perspective, is available at www.muslm.net; and the influential mainline cleric Yusuf al-Qaradawi has also issued a fatwa endorsing suicide bombing operations. See www.qaradawi.net*

374. *www.ikhwanonline.com/Article.asp?ArtID=37377&SecID=343*

375. *Even Salafist complaints about the lack of implementation of Shari'a law in Gaza are countered with calls for patience and understanding. See http://alboraqforum.info*

376. *The response of Khalid Mish'al on the "advice" of Zawahiri, available at http://news.bbc.co.uk*

377. *Jaysh al-Islam was founded in 2006 by Palestinian militant Mumtaz Dughmush on Salafist-jihadist principles and consists mainly of militants of the Dughmush clan. See www.islamonline.net*

378. *"I'lan wa-Bayan li-Ummat al-Islam [A Proclamation for the Islamic Nation]," available at www.muslm.net; and See www.km-pal.ps; and www.moqawmh.com*

379. *Osama bin Laden, "al-Sabil li-Ihbat al-Mu'amarat" [The Way to Defeat Conspiracies], 29/12/2007*

380. *Abu 'Umar al-Baghdadi, "al-Din al-Nasihah" [Religion Is Advice], 14/3/2008*

381. Osama bin Laden, "al-Sabil li-Khalas Filistin" [The Way for the Salvation of Palestine]

382. www.ikhwan.net for a statement by the Iraqi Hamas

383. Asad al-Jihad 2, "Tabarru' Qadat al-Jihad al-Rasikhin min Qadat Hamas al-Mudhabdhibin, 22/3/2008

384. "The Cause Of The Conflict, on The Sixtieth Anniversary Of The Rise Of Israeli Occupation State", 15/5/2008

385. "Khutbat 'Eid al-Adha" [The Sermon of the Adha Feast], 9/11/2008

386. The (rhetorical) "declaration of allegiance" to al-Qa'ida by Abu 'Abir, a field commander of the al-Nasir Salahuddin Battalions, available at www.paldf.net

387. Bilal Y. Saab and Magnus Ranstrop, "Securing Lebanon from the Threat of Salafist Jihadism", 2007

388. Gabriel G Tabarani, "Israeli-Palestinian Conflict: From Balfour Promise To Bush Declaration - The Complications And The Road To A Lasting Peace",March 2008

389. Gary Gambill, "Ain al-Hilweh: Lebanon's 'Zone of Unlaw'", Middle East Intelligence Bulletin 5/6/2003

390. Rosemary Sayigh, "Palestinians in Lebanon: Harsh Present, Uncertain Future", Journal of Palestine Studies, Autumn 1995

391. Franklin Lamb, "Who's Behind the Fighting in North Lebanon: Inside Nahr al-Barid and Bedawi Refugee Camps", Counterpunch, 24/5/2007

392. Murad Batal al-Shishani, "Al-Qaeda Ideologue Describes Alleged Spread of Al-Qaeda in the Levant", Terrorism Monitor (Jamestown Foundation), March 2009

393. Omayma Abdel-Latif, "Cedar Jihadis", Al-Ahram, May 1-7, 2008

394. Fida Itani, "Arab Mujahadeen Bring Their Enthusiasm to Lebanon [in Arabic]", Al-Akhbar, 7/42008

395. Jonathan Schanzer, "Al-Qaeda's Armies", The Washington Institute for Near East Policy,2005

396. "Asbat al-Ansar", Jane's World Insurgency and Terrorism, 2008

397. Andrew Exum, "Return of the Jihadi", Democracy Journal, Summer 2008

398. Bilal Y. Saab, "Al-Qa'ida's Presence and Influence in Lebanon", CTC Sentinel (Combating Terrorism Center), November 2008

399. Abdulmajid al-Sabati, "Interview with Italian FM D'Alema", Al Watan, 13/1/2007

400. Marc Sageman, "Understanding terror networks", 2004

401. Audrey Kurth Cronin, "How al-Qaida Ends: The Decline and Demise of Terrorist Groups", International Security, Summer 2006

402. Marc Sageman, "Leaderless jihad: terror networks in the twenty-first century", 2008

403. Bruce Hoffman, "The Myth of Grass-Roots Terrorism: Why Osama bin Laden Still Matters", Foreign Affairs, May/June 2008

404. Bruce Riedel, "Al Qaeda Strikes Back", Foreign Affairs, May/June 2007

405. The 10 part series published in April 2007 in Al-Akhbar, a Lebanese daily newspaper. These series contain an unprecedented level of detail not found in English language sources and is considered a reputable and relatively impartial source on the question of al-Qa'ida in Lebanon

406. Jane's, "Al-Qaeda in Lebanon", Jane's Terrorism and Security Monitor, March 2006

407. Jane's, "Asbat al-Ansar"

408. U.S. Department of State, Country Reports on Terrorism: Chapter 6--Terrorist Organizations, Office of the Coordinator for Counterterrorism, 30/4/2008, http://www.state.gov

409. Fida Itani, "Thus Lebanon Entered the Era of Globalized Jihad [in Arabic]", Al Akhbar, 7/4/2008

410. Olga Mattera, "The Re-emergence of al-Qaeda in the Middle East [in Italian]", Osservatorio Strategico 8/4/2006

411. Alon Ben-David, "Al-Qaeda eyes options in Lebanon", Jane's Defense Weekly, February 2006

412. Olivier Guitta, "Al-Qaida's Opportunistic Strategy", Middle East Times, 18/8/2008

413. Emily Hunt, "Can al-Qaeda's Lebanese Expansion be Stopped?", Policy Watch, The Washington Institute for Near East Policy, 2006

414. Fida Itani, "Training and funding that paved the way for Fatah al-Islam

[in Arabic]", *Al-Akhbar*, *11/72008* and *Fida Itani*, *"Arab Mujahideen Bring Their Enthusiasm to Lebanon" [in Arabic]*

415. *Souad Mekhennet and Michael Moss, "Final in Lebanon Camp, a New Face of Jihad Vows Attacks on U.S.", The New York Times, 16/3/2007*

416. *Sami Moubayed, "Al-Qaeda sets Lebanon record straight", Asia Times, 15/9/2007*

417. *Will McCants, 24/5/2008, http://www.jihadica.com/bin-laden-statement-prompts-speculation-onaq-strategy-in-palestine-part-3*

418. *Andrew Exum, "Salafi-jihadism in Lebanon", Global Politician, March 2008*

419. *Bernard Rougier, "Everyday Jihad", 2007*

420. *Fida Itani, "Groups trained in Lebanon and launched worldwide" [in Arabic]", Al-Akhbar, 10/7/2008*

421. *Fida Itani, "Al-Qaida roots itself in Lebanon", Le Monde Diplomatique, February 4, 2008*

422. *Seymour M. Hersh, "The Redirection: Does the new policy benefit the real enemy?", The New Yorker, 5/3/2007*

423. *"March 14 denies charge of funding Fatah al-Islam",The Daily Star (Beirut), 8/11/2008*

424. *On February 13, 2007, al-Zawhiri said: "I call on the brothers of Islam and of jihad in Lebanon not to yield to resolution 1701 and not to accept. . . the presence of international and Crusader [Western] forces in south Lebanon". In December 2007, bin Laden described the UN peacekeeping force in south Lebanon as "Crusaders" sent to Lebanon "to protect the Jews" of Israel. On April 21, 2008, al-Zawhiri called upon jihadists to attack UNIFIL forces; see also Nicholas Blanford, "Was Al-Qaeda*

425. *Mahan Abedin, "A search for unity: interview with Omar Bakri Mohammed", Asia Times, 12/6/2008*

426. *"Al-Qaeda has Infiltrated Ain al-Hilway Camp", The Daily Star (Beirut), 13/9/2008*

427. *Muhammad Salah, "Ayn Al-Hilweh Trying to Avoid Fate of Al-Barid", Al-Safir, 10/11/2008*

428. *Nicholas Blanford, "In Lebanon, pragmatism tempers jihadist aims", Christian Science Monitor, 4/11/2008*

429. *Bilal Y. Saab and Magnus Ranstrop, "Fatah al Islam: How an Ambitious Jihadist Project Went Awry", Brookings Institution, 2007*

430. *"State Sponsors of Terrorism", U.S. State Department, Washington, D.C., 29/12/1979; and "Treasury Designates Members of Abu Ghadiyah's Network", U.S. Treasury Department, Washington, D.C., 28/2/2008*

431. *Associated Press, 29/10/2008*

432. *The Sunday Times (London), 2/11/2008*

433. *Abdallah Azzam, "al-Qai'ida al-Salbba" (the Solid Base), Jihad Magazine, Issue 41, April 1988*

434. *Al-Madi refers here to the Syrian Kurdish branch of the Naqshbandiyya Sufi order led by Ahmad al-Khaznawi. Al-Qubeisyat is a religiously conservative women's organisation. Muhammad Habash is director of the moderate Islamic Studies Center in Damascus. For the Abu Nur Institute, see Terrorism Monitor, The Jamestown Foundation, June 4, 2005*

435. *Murad Batal al-Shishani, "Jihadis Turn Their Eyes To Syria As A Post-Iraq Theater", The Jamestown Foundation, 20/8/2009*

436. *Beyond Political Islam in Syria: Abu Mus'ab al-Suri and the Third Generation of the Salafi-Jihadists), in Radwan Ziadeh (ed), "Muslim Brotherhood in Syria" [in Arabic], al-Misbar Studies and Research Center, Dubai, August 2009*

437. *Los Angeles Times, 28/4/2003*

438. *"Treasury Designates Individual Financially Fueling Iraqi Insurgency, al-Qaeda", U.S. Treasury Department, 25/1/2005*

439. *Associated Press, 6/12/2007*

440. *The New York Times, 28/10/2003*

441. *Caleb Temple, Defense Intelligence Agency, quoted in GlobalSecurity.org, 28/7/2005*

442. *Brian Fishman, "Bombers, Bank Accounts, and Bleedout", 2008*

443. *"Treasury Designates Individuals with Ties to Al Qaida, Former Regime", U.S. Treasury Department, 6/12/2007*

444. *"Letter from al-Zawahiri to al-Zarqawi", 9/11/2005, GlobalSecurity. org*

445. *Matthew Levitt, "Syria's Financial Support For Jihad", Middle East Quarterly, winter 2010*

446. *Quintan Wiktorowics, "Islamists, The State, and Cooperation in Jordan", Arab Studies Quarterly, Vol 21, No21, No 4, 1999*

447. *Marion Boulby, "The Muslim Brotherhood and The Kings Of Jordan", 1999*

448. *Curtis R Ryan, "Peace, Bread, And Riots: Jordan and The International Monetary Fund", Middle East Policy, Vol.6, No 2, fall 1998*

449. *Paul L Scham and Russel E Lucas, "'Normalization and Anti-Normalization' in Jordan: The Public Debate", Israel Affairs, Vol 9, No 3, 2003*

450. *The Saudi's Mufti at that time, Abd-al-Aziz bin Baz, issued a fatwa decreeing jihad in Afghanistan*

451. *Bernard Rougier, "Le Jihad en Afghanistan et la crise de l'islam Sunnite", Revue Afrique du Nord/Moyen Orient: Espace et Conflits, Edition 2005-2006*

452. *International Crisis Group Report "Jordan's 9/11: Dealing with Jihadi Islamism", 23/11/2005*

453. *Crisis Group Middle East/North Africa Report N°37, "Understanding Islamism", 2/3/2005*

454. *Vincenzo Olivetti, "Terror's sources: The ideology of Wahhabi-Salafism and its consequences", Birmingham, 2002*

455. *International Crisis Group interview with Samih Khreis, a trial lawyer involved in defending jihadis, Amman, 30 March 2005*

456. *Abdallah Abu Rumman spent three months in jail with Abu Mus'ab al-Zarqawi and Abu Muhammad al-Maqdisi in the mid-1990s on charges of publishing remarks critical of King Hussein. He was released on bail and eventually found "not responsible" for the alleged crime*

457. *International Crisis Group interview with Mohammad Abu Rumman, director of research at the daily Al-Ghad, Amman, 4 April 2005*

458. *Quintan Wiktorowicz, "The Management of Islamic Activism", New York, 2001*

459. *Al-Urdun al-Jedid Research Centre, "Islamic Movements in Jordan", Amman, 1997*

460. *Hazem al-Amin, "Zarqa Gave Birth"*

461. *International Crisis Group Middle East Briefing N°10, "The Challenge of Political Reform: Jordanian Democratisation and Regional Instability", 8/10/2003*

462. *Egbert Harmsen, "Islamic Voluntary Welfare Activism in Jordan", ISIM Newsletter, no. 13, December 2003*

463. *International Crisis Group Report, "Jordan's 9/11: Dealing With Jihadi Islamism", 23/11/2005*

464. *Hazem al-Amin, "Jordan's 'Zarqawists' Visit Their Sheikhs in Prison and Wait for the Opportunity to Join Abu Mus'ab in Iraq", Al-Hayat, 14/12/2004*

465. *Al-Ghad (Amman), 11/3/2005; and Associated Press, 14/4/2005. Al-Ghad's publisher promptly fired his editor-in-chief over the incident*

466. *Associated Press, Daily Star, 16/4/2005*

467. *Marc Sageman, "Presentation to the World Federation of Scientists Permanent Monitoring Panel on Terrorism", Erice (Sicily), 7/5/2005*

468. *Scott Atran, "The Virtual Hand of Jihad", Terrorism Monitor, vol. 3, no.10, 19 May 2005*

469. *Hazem al-Amin, "The Salafis of Salt Stage Weddings for Those Killed in Iraq and Urge Others to Leave and Fight", Al-Hayat, 16/12/2004*

470. *"Foreign pro-Taliban fighters inside Afghanistan (pre-hostilities)", Jane's World Armies, 8/10/2001*

471. *Kim Ghattas, "Afghanistan's Arab fighters", BBC News, 15/12/2001*

472. *David Benjamin, in charge of transnational threats at the White House at that time, commented, "We were astonished...at the amount of firepower that was involved...also the number of conspirators". CBS, "60 Minutes", 26/12/2001*

473. *Crisis Group Iraq Briefing N°4, "Radical Islam in Iraqi Kurdistan: The Mouse That Roared?", 7/2/2003*

474. *Gary Cambill, "Abu Musab al-Zarqawi: A Biographical Sketch", Terrorism Monitor, vol. 2, no. 24, 16/12/2004*

475. *Quoted in Reuven Paz, "Islamic Legitimacy for the London Bombings", Occasional Paper of the Project for the Research of Islamist Movements*

at the Global Research in International Affairs Centre (Israel), vol. 3, no. 4, July 2005

476. *Mohammed Ramahi and Faris Mehdawi, "Zarqawi declares war on Iraq Shi'ites", Reuters, 15/9/2005*

477. *Glenn Robinson, "Defensive Democratization in Jordan", International Journal of Middle East Studies, vol 30, No 3, 1998*

478. *For comparative analysis of the elections see Curtis R Ryan, "Elections and Parliamentary Democratization in Jordan", International Journal of Middle East Studies, vol 5, No 4, 1998*

479. *Curtis R Ryan, "Jordan in Transition For Hussein To Abdullah", 2002*

480. *Curtis R Ryan, "Islamist Political Activism in Jordan", 7 July 2008*

481. *Quintan Wiktorowics, "The Salafi Movement in Jordan", International Journal of Middle East Studies, vol 32, No 2, 2000*

482. *Fatima Mernissi, "Islam and Democracy: Fear Of The Modern World", 1982*

483. *Benedict Andrson, "Imagined Community", 1991*

484. *Mohamed el-Mansour, "Salafis and Modernist in Moroccan Nationalist Movement" in John Ruedy ed., "Islamism and Secularism in North Africa", 1994*

485. *Jamil M Abun-Nasr, "A History of the Maghreb in The Islamic Period", 1987*

486. *Remy Leveau, "Reflections on The Statein Maghreb", in George Joffe,ad., "North Africa Nation, State and Religion", 1993*

487. *Abdelbaki Hermassi, "State and Democratization in The Maghreb", in Ellis Goldberg Resat Kasalen and Joe Migdal, eds., "Rules and Rights in The Middle East", 1993*

488. *"Islam et Controle Politique au Maroc", cited in Francois Burgat and William Dowell, "The Islamic Movement in North Africa", 1993*

489. *Not to be confused with the Alawite in Syria*

490. *Rolli Lal, "The Muslim World After 9/11", Rand Corporation, 2004*

491. *Francois Burgat, "Face to face with the political Islam", 2003*

492. *Nizar al-Aly, "Morocco: Poverty Blamed for Terrorist Attack", May 19, 2003*

493. *"Moroccan Paper Views Recruitment Methods of Islamist Extremist Groups", Casablanca, Assabah, (in Arabic), 4/7/2003*

494. *Nicholas Marmie, "Moroccan Authorities Send Experts to Help With Madrid Bombing Identify Detainees", Associated Press, 13/3/2004*

495. *Sebastian Rotella, "Spain Hunts Fugitive Tied To al-Qaeda", Los Angeles Times, 14/7/2004*

496. *John Henly, "'Afghan Moroccans' Held in Casablanca Blast Enquiry", The Guardian (London), 6/4/2004*

497. *Nikki Keddie, "The Islamist Movement in Tunisia", The Maghreb Review, vol 2, No1, 1986*

498. *"Tunisian Now Says Explosion Was Terrorism", United Press International, 22/4/2002*

499. *"Madrid Ringleader Blew Self Up", CBCnews.com, 4/4/2004*

500. *"Witness incriminates al-Qa'ida Suspect at German Terror Trial", BBC Monitoring International Report, 11/5/2004*

501. *Yvonne Y Haddad, "Sayyid Qutb: Ideologue Of Islamic Revival" 1983*

502. *John L Espisoto, "Voices of Resurgence Islam", 1983*

503. *Norma Salem, "Tunisia", in Shireen T Hunter, ed., "The Politics Of Islamic Revivalism"*

504. *Rashed Ghannoushi, "Penseur et Tribun", Interview, Les Cahiers De L'orient, No 27, 1992*

505. *Khaled Elgindy, "The Rethoric of Rashid Ghannoushi", Arab Studies Journal, spring 1995*

506. *"Al-Shira", October 1994; and MSA News 8/7/1995*

507. *Mohammed Tozy, "Les Tendances De L'Islamisme en Algerie", Confluences Mediterranee, No 12, automne 1994*

508. *I. William Zartman, and William Mark Habeeb, "Polity and Society in Contemporary North Africa", 1993*

509. *Jean Claude Vatin, "Popular Puritanism versus State Reformism: Islam*

in Algeria", in James P Piscatori, ed. "Islamic Fundamentalism and the Gulf Crisis", 1991

510. *Rabia Bekkar, "Taking Up Space in Tlemcen: The Islamist Opposition In Urban Algeria", Middle East Report, Vol. 22, No 6, Nov/Dec 1992*

511. *Hugh Roberts, "A Trial Of Strength: Algerian Islamism", in James P Piscatori, ed., "Islamic Fundamentalism and The Gulf Crisis", 1991*

512. *Remy Leveau, "Le Sabre et Le Turban", 1993*

513. *Michael Willis, "The Islamist Challenge in Algeria: A Political History", 1996*

514. *Jonathan Schanzer, "Algeria's GSPC and America's War on Terror", Policy Watch, No 666, 2/10/2002*

515. *Brynjar Lia, "Architect Of Global Jihad: The Life Of Al-Qaeda Strategist Abu Mus'ab Al-Suri", 2008*

516. *Fred Burton and Scott Stewart, "Al-Qaeda in 2008, The Struggle For Relevance", 16/12/2008*

517. *Anthony N Celso, "Al-Qaeda in The Maghreb: The 'Newest' Front in The War on Terror", Mediterranean Quarterly, Vol 19, No1, winter 2008*

518. *Evan Kohlman, "Al-Qaeda Claims Suicide Attacks In Algeria, Possible Links in Morocco", 11/4/2007*

519. *"A Question of Colour, a Matter of Faith", Economist, 16/11/2002*

520. *Jean-Paul Gourévitch, "La France africaine: Islam, intégration, insécurité: infos et intox", 2000*

521. *Michel Gurfinkiel, "Islam in France: Is the French Way of Life in Danger?", Middle East Forum, March 1997*

522. *Rémy Leveau, "The Political Culture of the 'Beurs'", in "Islam in Europe: The Politics of Religion and Community", ed.Steven Vertovec and Ceri Peach, 1997*

523. *Suzanne Thave, "L'emploi des immgres en 1999", Paris: INSEE, 2000*

524. *Christopher Caldwell, "The Crescent and the Tricolor", Atlantic Monthly, 2000*

525. *Tariq Ramadan, "Muslims in France", Leicester, UK: Islamic Foundation, 1999*

526. *Catherine Wihtol de Wenden, "Muslims in France," in "Muslims in the Margin: Political Responses to the Presence of Muslims in Western Europe", ed. W.A.R. Shadid and P.S. Van Konigsveld, 1996*

527. *Chris Kutschera, "Murky Business Behind the 'Halal' Label in France", Middle East, 1996*

528. *Catherine Wihtol de Wenden, "Immigrants as Political Actors", 1994*

529. *Jocelyne Cesari, "Remarks on Political Participation of Muslims in Europe", Muslims in Europe Post-9/11 Conference, Oxford University, April 2003; and Omer Taspinar, "Europe's Muslim Street", Foreign Policy, 2003*

530. *Omer Taspinar, "Europe's Muslim Street", Foreign Policy, 2003*

531. *James Corbett, "Through French Windows: An Introduction to France in the Nineties", 1994*

532. *"Whose Fatherland? A Proposal to Grant Citizenship to Members of Germany's Vast Immigrant Community Stirs Passionate Debate", Time International, 25/1/1999*

533. *Ural Manco, "Turks in Europe: From a Garbled Image to the Complexity of Migrant Social Reality", Center for Islam in Europe, December 2000*

534. *German National Office of Statistics, Distribution of Foreigners According to Age Groups and Selected Nationalities, Berlin: German National Office of Statistics, 1992*

535. *Goldberg, "Status and Problems of Elderly Foreigners"*

536. *Jochen Mayer and Regina T. Riphahn, "Fertility Assimilation of Immigrants: Evidence from Count Data Models", Bonn, Germany: Institute for the Study of Labor, 1999*

537. *David Lawday, "The Germans: Multiculturalism Thrives in Germany", New Statesman, 17/7/2000*

538. *"Muslims in the European Union: Discrimination and Islamophobia", European Monitoring Center on Racism and Xenophobia, December 2006*

539. *Zehra Onder, "Muslim-Turkish Children in Germany: Sociocultural Problems", Migration World Magazine, 1996*

540. *See "New Data and Facts on the Islamic Associations in the Federal Republic of Germany", Muslim Review, 2000*

541. *Sigrid Bafekr and Johan Leman, "Highly-qualified Iranian Immigrants in Germany: The Roles of Ethnicity and Culture", Journal of Ethnic and Migration Studies, 1999*

542. *Robert J Pauly, "Islam In Europe: Assessing The Integration Challenges Facing Muslim Communities And Western European Governments", 2010*

543. *Deutsche Well, www.dw-world.de*

544. *William Drozdiak, "The New Year Brings a Wave of New Citizens in Germany: Law Eased to Fill Jobs with Foreign Workers", The Washington Post, 9/1/2000*

545. *Ruud Koopmans, "Germany and its Immigrants: An Ambivalent Relationship", Journal of Ethnic and Migration Studies, 1999*

546. *Christian Joppke, "Immigration and the Nation-State: The United States, Germany, and Great Britain, 2000*

547. *German Information Center, Citizenship Reform and Germany's Foreign Residents*

548. *British Office for National Statistics, "Census 2001: Ethnicity and Religion"; and General Register Office, Scotland, "Census 2001: Ethnicity and Religion"*

549. *Ceri Peach, "South Asian and Caribbean Ethnic Minority Housing Choice in Britain", Urban Studies, 1998*

550. *See Muhammad Anwar, "Muslims in Britain: Census and Other Statistical Sources", Birmingham, UK: Center for the Study of Christian-Muslim Relations, 1993*

551. *"Health Survey for England", 1999*

552. *Bhikhu Parekh, "South Asians in Britain",1997*

553. *Michael Banton, "Promoting Racial Harmony", 1985*

554. *Ian A. Macdonald, "Race Relations: The New Law", 1977*

555. *The Chicago Tribune, 19/9/2004*

556. *Daniel Pipes, "The Islamic States of America", Frontpagemagazine.com,/ 23/9/2004*

557. *Lorenzo Vidino, "The Muslim Brotherhood's Conquest Europe", Middle East Quarterly, winter 2005*

558. *Khalid Duran, "Jihadism in Europe", The Journal of Counterterrorism and Security International, Fall 2000*

559. *Richard Labeviere, "Dollars for Terror: The U.S. and Islam", 2000*

560. *Georges Lepre, "Himmler's Bosnian Division: The Waffen SS Handschar Division 1943-45", Schiffer Aviation History, Jan. 2000*

561. *M. H. Faruqi, "Les Frères Musulmans. Politique de 'rabbaniyya', les prières avant le pouvoir Dr. Saïd Ramadan, 1926-1995", Historique du Centre Islamique, Islamic Center of Geneva*

562. *"Prasidenten der IGD", Islamische Gemeinschaft in Deutschland*

563. *"Senators Request Tax Information on Muslim Charities for Probe", U.S. State Department news release, Jan. 14, 2004*

564. *Fouad Ajami, "Tariq Ramadan", The Wall Street Journal, 7/9/2004*

565. *Official dossier on Ahmed Nasreddin (hereafter Nasreddin dossier), Servizio per le Informazioni e la Sicurezza Democratica (Italian secret service, SISDE), 6/4/1996*

566. *Newsweek, 12/5/2004*

567. *"Recent OFAC Actions", U.S. Department of the Treasury, Office of Foreign Assets Control, 7/11/2001*

568. *"Islamische Gemeinschaft in Deutschland" Innenministerium, Nordrhein-Westfalen land website*

569. *"Islamismus", Landesamt fur Verfassungsschutz, Hessen website*

570. *"Official Guide to the Munich Mosque, Munich: The Islamic Center of Munich", the Milli Görüş' bookstore, Cologne*

571. *"Islamische Gemeinschaft in Deutschland" Innenministerium, Nordrhein-Westfalen land*

572. *Sueddeutsche Zeitung (Munich), July 29-30, 1967; and Nasreddin dossier*

573. *Report on radical Islam, Baden Württenberg state Verfassungsschutzbericht, 2003*

574. *"Koordination mit Zentren in folgenden Städten", Islamische Gemeinschaft in Deutschland website*

575. *Report on Ibrahim el-Zayat, Cologne police, 27/8/2003*

576. *David Kane, FBI senior special agent, affidavit in "Supplemental Declaration in Support of Pre-Trial Detention", United States of America v. Soliman S. Biheiri, U.S. District Court for the Eastern District of Virginia. The affidavit also details WAMY's links to the Palestinian organisation Hamas*

577. *The Wall Street Journal, 15/42003*

578. *Report on Ibrahim el-Zayat, Cologne police, 27/8/2003*

579. *Annual report of the Office for the Protection of the Constitution (Bundesverfassungsschutz), 2000, Cologne*

580. *Annual report of the Office for the Protection of the Constitution (Bundesverfassungsschutz), 1999, Cologne*

581. *Agence France De Presse, 16/1/1998*

582. *Mehmet Ülger, "Manifestatie Milli Görüş in Arnhem", De Humanist, July 2003*

583. *Udo Ulfkotte, "Der Krieg in unseren Staedten", Frankfurt: Eichborn Publishing, 2003*

584. *"Islamismus", Landesamt fur Verfassungsschutz, Hessen*

585. *"Christentum und Islam", German Association of Muslim Social Scientists (GMSG), Oct. 26/10/2002*

586. *"Anti-Semitism Worldwide 1998/9", Tel Aviv: Stephen Roth Institute, Tel Aviv University, 2000*

587. *Udo Ulfkotte, "Der Krieg in unseren Staedten"; and Annual report, Bundesverfassungsschutz, 2000*

588. *See Hartwig Mueller, head of the Verfassungsschutz of Nordrhein Westfahlen, interview on German television SWR, 21/3/2003*

589. *Die Welt (Berlin), 6/5/2003*

590. *Michael Waller, testimony before the Senate Judiciary Committee Subcommittee on Terrorism, Technology, and Homeland Security, 14/10/2003*

591. *The Wall Street Journal, 21/2/2003*

592. *Time Magazine, 2/11/2003*

593. *Time Magazine, 27/4/2003*

594. *Renzo Guolo, "Xenofobi e Xenofili. Gli Italiani e l'Islam", 2003*

595. *"The Global Community", MABOnline, Muslim Association of Britain, 20/12/2004*

596. *Forum of European Muslim Youth and Student Organisations, 2004*

597. *"L'Islam en Europe ou L'Islam d'Europe", conference program, European Parliament, Brussels, 11/12/2002*

598. *"Animosity toward the Jews", A Handy Encyclopedia of Contemporary Religions and Sects (WAMY), FBI translation from Arabic; Steven Emerson, statement to the National Commission on Terrorist Attacks upon the United States, July 9, 2003*

599. *David Kane, "Supplemental Declaration in Support of Pre-Trial Detention"*

600. *Bassam Tibi, Islamische Zuwanderung, Die gescheiterte Integration, Munich: DVA, 2002*

601. *Peter Nesser, "Ideological Influences and Patterns of Jihadism in Europe", 2009*

602. *The al-Muhajiroun organisation was formed in 1996, and focused primarily on supporting jihad in Kashmir. Despite strong circumstantial evidence, however, none of its members have been convicted for direct involvement in terrorist acts in Europe. Members of the group were rarely involved in terrorist acts before the early 2000s. After the invasion of Iraq, several people involved in terrorism in Europe (including the London bombers) had links to al-Muhajiroun*

603. *Omar Nasiri, "Inside the Jihad; My Life with Al Qaeda a Spy's Story", 2006*

604. *Omar Nasiri, "Inside the Jihad; My Life with Al Qaeda a Spy's Story", 2006*

605. *Apart from Europe based leaders and ideologues the sources correspond to material available on the Internet Library "Minbar al-Tawhid wa'l Jihad" analysed by the acknowledged Combating Terrorism Centre, consult "Militant Ideology Atlas, Executive Report", ed. William McCants, New York: Combating Terrorism Center, West Point, 2006; and "Militant Ideology Atlas, Research Compendium", ed. William McCants, New York: Combating terrorism Center, West Point, 2006*

606. *Kamil al-Tawil, "The Armed Islamic Movement in Algeria", (Al-Haraka*

Al-Islamiyya Al-Musallaha Fi'l-Jazai'r): From "The Salvation" To "The Group" [in Arabic], Beirut: Dar al-Nahar, 1998

607. *Indictment of the Unemployed Hairdresser and Asylum Applicant Shadi Moh,d Mustafa Abdalla Alias Emad Abdelhadie, 2003*

608. *Verdict in the Criminal Case against Mr Djilali Benali ("Aeurobui Beandali") Et Al [in German], 2003*

609. *Verdict regarding the permissibility of martyrdom operations by Sulayman Ibn Nasir Al-'Ulwan and The Clarification of what happened in America by Hamud Bin Uqla al-Shuaybi at http://tibyan.wordpress.com/*

610. *Proceedings 20/2004, Indictment al-Mallah of April 10 2006, Court of First Instance Number 6 of the Audencia National, "translation of the Indictment of the Madrid Bombers by Tine Gade", 2006*

611. *Helen Carter, "Beheading Plot Trial Told of Abu Hamza Material", The Guardian, 31/1/2008*

612. *Albert Benschop, "Chronicle of a Political Murder Foretold: Jihad in the Netherlands", University of Amsterdam, 2005*

613. *Rudolph Peters, "Dutch Extremist Islamism: Van Gogh's Murderer and His Ideas in Jihadi Terrorism and the Radicalization Challenge in Europe", ed. Rik Coolsaet, Aldershot: Ashgate, 2008*

614. *See http://tibyan.wordpress.com/*

615. *In the manifest for jihadism "Milestones", Qutb, called on Muslims to leave Muslim societies not governed by Islamic law (undertake hijra) and establish bases in which Muslims can prepare for war (fard ayn jihad) against their governments (like the Prophet and his Companions in Medina). Ideologically, many jihads perceive Europe to be the modern day Medina (for a vanguard of true believers aiming to restore the Caliphate), a base in which to prepare for violent Islamisation*

616. *Umar Abd al-Hakim, "A Summary of My Testimony on the Holy Struggle in Algeria, 1988-1996", 2004*

617. *Kamil al-Tawil, "Al-Qaida and Her Sisters, the Story of the Arab Jihadis", [in Arabic], Beirut: Dar al-Saqi, 2008*

618. *al-Ansar issues 1 through 158 with FFI's Terrorism Research Group; and Qatada defended his fatwa in a televised debate in November 2000 and in an interview with CNN in November 2001*

619. *"Abu Qatada Vs Secretary of State for the Home Department", Special Immigration Appeals Commission, 2007*

620. *Abu Qatada, "Globalization and the Troops of the Jihad" [Al-'Awlama Wa Siriyyiyyat Al-Jihad]", Minbar al-Tawhid wa'l Jihad: 2001*

621. *Jamil El-Banna Et Al Vs George W Bush President of the United States Et Al.*

622. *"Characteristics of the Victorious Party in the Foundation of the State of the Believers" [the Land of Ash-Sham], At-Tibyan Publications*

623. *Abu Abdulrahman Amin, "Open Letter to All Muslims" [English Translation], in Islam Report, American Islamic Group, 1995*

624. *The majority of the Council, especially the Jazairis, opposed Zaytuni's plan, on the grounds that it would divert resources from the war in Algeria and jeopardize the international support network, as by Kamil al-Tawil, "Al-Qaida and Her Sisters, the Story of the Arab Jihadis" [in Arabic]*

625. *Brynjar Lia, "Architect of Global Jihad: The Life of Al-Qaida Strategist Abu Mus'ab Al-Suri", 2007*

626. *Brynjar Lia and Ashid Kjøk, "Islamist Insurgencies, Diasporic Support Networks, and Their Host States: The Case of the Algerian GIA in Europe 1993-2000", 2001*

627. *Peter Nesser, "Jihad In Europe", 2004*

628. *John Hooper and Nick Hopkins, "Al-Qaida Cell in UK 'Planned Attack'", The Guardian, 26/10/2001*

629. *Verdict in the Criminal Case against Mr Djilali Benali, "Aeurobui Beandali" Et Al*

630. *Hanna Rogan, "Violent Trends in Algeria since 9/11", CTC Sentinel 1, no. 12, 2008*

631. *Peter Taylor, "Inside Story, a Jihad Warrior in London", The Guardian, 9/2/2004*

632. *Peter Taylor, "The Third World War: Al-Qaida, the Breeding Ground", BBC, 2004*

633. *Verbal Argument for Verdict: Part 1 "Verdict against Abu Dhess", 2005*

634. *Sean O'Neill, "Suicide Factory", 2008*

635. *Abu Hamza, "How to Live Islamically in the Land of the Kuffar", 1999*

636. *"The Preachings of Abu Hamza", The Guardian, 7/2/2006*

637. *The martyrdom testaments of the London bombers Mohammed Siddique Khan and Shehzad Tanweer, "Wasiyat Fursan Ghazwat London", [Testaments of the Knights of the London Attacks], al-Sahab Media Production 2006*

638. *Petter Nesser, "The Slaying of the Dutch Filmmaker: Religiously Motivated Violence or Islamist Terrorism in the Name of Global Jihad?", 2005*

639. *Thomas Hegghammer, "Documentation on Al-Qa'ida : Interviews, Communiqués and Other Primary Sources 1990-2002", 2002*

640. *"The Complete Archive of Speeches and Sermons by the Imam of the Mujahideen Usama Bin Muhammad Bin Laden", [in Arabic], Shabakat al-Buraq al-Islamiyya, 2007*

641. *"London Bomber: Text in Full", BBC News, 2/9/2005*

642. *"Headscarf Ban May Cause Attack on France" Daily Times, 26/2/2004*

643. *"May Our Mothers Be Bereaved If We Do Not Defend Our Prophet", al-Sahab, 2008*

644. *Abu Hamza mocked the principle of dar al-Aman in the 1999 speech, "How to Live Islamically in the Land of the Kuffar"*

645. *Omar Bakri Mohammed, "the World Is Divided into Two Camps..." Daar al-Kufr and Daar al-Islaam", 2004*

646. *Rosie Cowan, Richard Norton-Taylor, and Audrey Gillian, "Police Search Emails for Trail to Pakistan Canadian Accused of Aiding UK Suspects", The Guardian, 1/4/2004*

647. *Sean O'Neill and Yaakov Lappin, "Britain's Online Imam Declares War as He Calls Young to Jihad", The Times, 17/1/2005*

648. *"The British Plans for Islam & Muslims a Continuation of the Crusader Wars", Ad-Da'wah Publications, 2004*

649. *"Islamic Awakening", http://forums.islamicawakening.com/*

650. *"The Open Meeting with Shaykh Ayman Al-Zawahiri Part One", Al-Sahab Media Production, 2008*

651. *Ayman al-Zawahiri, "The Exoneration", al-Sahab Media, 2008*

652. *Vladimir C Nahirny, "Some Observations on Ideological Groups", American Journal of Sociology, vol. 67, 1961/62*

653. *Peter Waldmann, "The Radical Community: A Comparative Analysis of the Social Background of ETA, IRA, and Hizbollah", Sociologus, vol. 55, 2005*

654. *Paul B. Henze and S. Enders Wimbush "Russia's Encounter With Islam", The Wall Street Journal, April 14, 2010*

655. *Peter Waldmann, "Radikalisierung in der Diaspora: Wie Islamisten im Westen zu Terroristen Werden", Hamburg, 2009*

656. *Jan Assman: "Monotheimas und die Sprache der Gewalt", in P Walter ed., Das Gewalt potential des Monotheismus und der Dreieine Gott, Freiburg, 2005*

657. *Kabardino-Balkaria na puti k katastrofe: Predposylki vooruzhennogo vystupleniya v Nalchike 13-14 oktyabrya 2005 goda, Memorial Human Rights Center, 2008*

658. *John B Dunlop, "Russia Confronts Chechnya", 1998*

659. *"Extremists Declare 'Islamic State' in Dagestan", The Current Digest of Post-Soviet Press 31, no. 32, 1999*

660. *Edmund Spencer,"Travels in Circassia", Vol. II. London: Henry Colburn, 1839*

661. *David Damrel, "The Religious Roots Of Conflict: Russia and Chechnya", 1995*

662. *Richard D Lyons, "Explosive Mix in Chechnya: History, Hatred and Oil", NewYork Times, 14/12/1994*

663. *Alexandre Bennigsen and S. E. Wimbush, "Mystics and Commissars", 1985*

664. *A. Malashenko, "Islamic Fundamentalism in Russia" In "Muslim Eurasia: Conflicting Legacies", edited by Yaacov Ro'i, 1995*

665. *Mehrdad Haghayeghi's for a thorough discussion of the use of the term 'Wahhabi' Islam and Politics in Central Asia New York: St. Martin's Press, 1995*

666. *B. Pannier, "Wahhabism and the Cis (from Fergana to Chechnya)", 1997*

667. *Paul Henz 1995; and Sebastian Smith 1998*

668. *A.J. Lyon, "Separatism in Chechnya: The Role of the Jihad", in "Religion*

and Politics in the Developing World: Explosive Interactions", edited by Rolin G. Mainuddin. United Kingdom: Ashgate, 2001

669. *B.G. Williams, "Jihad and Ethnicity in Post Communist Eurasia. On the Trail of Trans-National Islamic Holy Warriors in Kashmir, Afghanistan, Central Asia, Chechnya and Kosovo", Journal of Ethnopolitics 2, no. 3-4, 2003*

670. *"Field Reports from 15 September - 31 October 1997." (1997): United Nations Inter-Agency Humanitarian Programme for Persons Displaced as a Result of the Emergency Situation in Chechnya.*

671. *Ana Matveeva, "The Islamist Challenge in Post-Soviet Eurasia" in "Political Islam and Conflicts in Russia and Central Asia", edited by Lena Jonson and Murad Esenov. Stockholm: The Swedish Institute of International Affairs, 1999*

672. *S. Isayev, "Chechen President Vows to Disband, Disarm Wahhabi Movement" Moscow, Interfax. 18/7/1998*

673. *Alynna J Lyon, "Transnational Mobilization Of Islamic Fundamentalism: Separatism In Chechnya And The Wahhabis", 2004*

674. *M. Reynolds, "Insurgents from Chechnya Seize 2 Towns in Dagestan", The Los Angeles Times, 8/8/1999*

675. *Ahmed Rashid, "The Taliban: Exporting Extremism", Foreign Affairs, no.November/December, 1999*

676. *"Extremists Declare 'Islamic State' in Dagestan", The Current Digest of Post-Soviet Press 31, no. 32, 1999*

677. *B. Akhmedkhanov, "Postwar Dagestan Torn by Inter-Ethnic Strife", Obshchaya Gazeta, 28/9/2000*

678. *B. G. Williams, "'Caucasus Belli' the Second Russo-Chechen War, 1999-2002: A Struggle for Freedom or Sub-Plot to the War on Terrorism?", Turkistan Newsletter, May 2002*

679. *"Russia Stirs up Religious Animosity in Chechnya", Network of East-West Women, 2000, available from http://lists.partners-intl.net/pipermail/women-inwar/2000-June/000077.html*

680. *N. Plotnikov, Nezavisimaya Gazette, 13/8/1999*

681. *F. Jean, "Chechnya: Moscow's Revenge", Harvard International Review 22, no. 3, 2000*

682. *B. Kipkeyev, March 25 2001, "Russia: Yastrzhembskiy Says Explosions in South Linked to Wahhabi Extremists." Moscow ITAR-TASS in Russian, 25/3/2001*

683. *M. Lanskoy, "Daghestan and Chechnya: The Wahhabi Challenge to the State", SAIS Review 22, no. 2, 2002*

684. *R. B. Ware et al., "Political Islam in Dagestan", Europe-Asia Studies, 2003*

685. *Charles King, Rajan Menon, "Prisoners To The Caucasus", Foreign Affairs, July/August, 2010*

686. *M. Agarkov, S. Burtin, and N. Silayev, "Udar v nervny uzel", Ekspert, 29/6/2009*

687. *V. Mukhin, "Boeviki nastupayut nevidimym frontom," Nezavisimaya gazeta, July 15, 2009*

688. *Alexey Malashenko, "Losing The Caucasus", August, 2009*

689. *"Strategicheskaya otsenka konfliktnosti", Severny Kavkaz, International Conflict and Security Consulting, 2009*

690. *A Ksilov and R Zemenkov, "USA and the Islamic World", 1984*

691. *The National Review, November 19, 1990; and US News and World Report, 22/3/1993*

692. *U.S. News and World Report, 22/3/1993*

693. *Bernard Lewis, "The Roots of Muslim Rage", The Atlantic Monthly, September 1990*

694. *Salim Kidwa, "United States And Islam", February 1999*

695. *Carla Power, "The New Islam", Span, May/June 1998*

696. *Edward Curtis, "Muslims In America ; A Short History", 2009*

697. *Jodi Wilgoren, "A Nation Challenged: American Muslims", New York Times, 22/10/2001*

698. *Mohamed Yunis, "Muslim Americans Exemplify Diversity, Potential", Gallup, 2/3/2009*

699. *Reuter, " Among US Religious Groups, Muslims Seen As Facing More Discrimination", Pew Forum On Religion & Public Life 9/11/2009*

700. *Charles D. Russell, "Islam as a Danger to Republican Virtue: Broadening Religious Liberty in Revolutionary Pennsylvania", Pennsylvania History, Summer 2009, Vol. 76 Issue 3*

701. *The Biography Of Benjamin Franklin, Published 1791, Chapter 10*

702. *Robert Battistini, "Glimpses of the Other before Orientalism: The Muslim World in Early American Periodicals, 1785-1800", Early American Studies Spring 2010, Vol. 8#2*

703. *Frank Lambert, "The Barbary Wars: American Independence in the Atlantic World", 2007*

704. *"US State Department Notes On Morocco"; and "The Avalon Yale Law Project, Article 11*

705. *http//etext.virginia.edu/Jefferson/quotations/jeff1650.htm;and http// www.state.gov/secretary/rm/2009a/09/129232.htm*

706. *Denise A. Spellberg, "Could a Muslim Be President? An Eighteenth-Century Constitutional Debate", Eighteenth-Century Studies 39#4, 2006*

707. *Robert J. Allison, "The Cresent Obscured: The United States and the Muslim World", 1776–1815, 1995*

708. *Amadou Mahtar M'bow;Ali Kettanii, "Islam and Muslims in the American continent", Beirut: Center of historical, economical and social studies, 2001*

709. *www.islam101.com/history*

710. *Samuel S. Hill, Charles H. Lippy, Charles Reagan Wilson "Encyclopedia of religion in the South", 2005*

711. *Michael A Gomez,"Muslims in Early America", "The Journal of Southern History" Nov. 1994*

712. *Abdul Sattar Ghazali, "The number of mosque attendants increasing rapidly in America" American Muslim perspective*

713. *Jacob Neusner, 2003*

714. *"Moorish Science Temple of America", Britannica Online Encyclopedia*

715. *"The Muslim Program"*

716. *John Esposito, "W.D. Muhammad: A Witness for True Islam", The Washington Post, 10/9/2008*

717. *"Imam W. Deen Muhammad 1933 ~ 2008", Chicago Tribune*

718. *"Farrakhan backs racial harmony", BBC News16/10/2000*

719. *http://religiousmovements.lib.virginia.edu/nrms/Nofislam.html*

720. *"Active U.S. Hate Groups in 2006", Southern Poverty Law Center*

721. *"Portrait of Muslims - Beliefs & Practices", Pew Research Center*

722. *"Being Muslim in America", United States Department of State*

723. *Andrea Elliot "Between Black and Immigrant Muslims, an Uneasy Alliance", 3/11/2007, The New York Times*

724. *http://www.america.gov/st/peopleplace,english/2008/December/2008122 2090246jmnamdeirf0.4547083.html*

725. *"Muslim Americans: Middle Class and Mostly Mainstream", Pew Research Center. 22/5/2007*

726. *Zogby phone survey, 2008*

727. *"Stars, Stripes, Crescent - A reassuring portrait of America's Muslims", The Wall Street Journal, 24/10/2005*

728. *"The Diversity of Muslims in the United States - Views as Americans", United States Institute of Peace, February 2006*

729. *Debra L. Oswald, "Understanding Anti-Arab Reactions Post-9/11: The Role of Threats, Social Categories, and Personal Ideologies", Journal of Applied Social Psychology, September 2005*

730. *http://www.humanitykingdom.com/library/general/arab-american*

731. *Evelyn Nieves, "Slain Arab-American May Have Been Hate-Crime Victim" The New York Times, 6/10/2001*

732. *http://usa.mediamonitors.net/content/view/full/12447/*

733. *Reuters, "Minnesota's Muslim cab drivers face crackdown", 17/4/2007*

734. *MSNBS "Target shifts Muslims who won't ring up pork products", 17/3/2007*

735. *http://www.startribune.com/kersten/story/1115081.htm*

736. *"Muslim prayers in school debated", The San Diego Union-Tribune*

737. *"Bush like Hitler, says first Muslim in Congress", The Telegraph 7/7/2007*

738. *"Congressman Admits 9/11 Error", Associated Press, 1/7/2007*

739. *Sun Times; and Fact Sheet: Department of Justice Anti-Terrorism Efforts Since Sept. 11, 2001, U.S. Department of Justice,5/11/2006*

740. *Migration Information Source, " The People Perceived as a Threat to Security: Arab Americans Since September 11"*

741. *http://judiciary.senate.gov/testimony.cfm?id=960&wit_id=2719*

742. *"Muslims Say FBI Tactics Sow Anger And Fear", New York Times, 2009*

743. *"The Expression Of Identity Through The Art Of Muslim American Women", New York Times, 2009*

744. *"US Sees Homegrown Muslim Extremism as a Rising Threat", Los Angeles Times, 2009*

745. *Michael Jenkins, "Would-Be Warriors, Incidents Of Jihadist Terrorist Radicalization in The United States Since September 11,2001", Rand Corporation, Winter 2010*

746. *Donna Abu-Nasr, and Lee Keath, "200 Websites Spread Al-Qaida's Message in English: Increasing Numbers of Radical Islamic Websites Are Spreading al-Qaida's Message in English," The Associated Press, 14/11/2009*

747. *Wesley K. Clarke speaking on BBC World's Hardtalk programme, 29/10/2001*

748. *Samuel Huntington, "The Clash Of Civilisations", Foreign Affairs, Summer 1993*

749. *Samuel Huntington, "Clash Of Civilisations", 1996*

750. *Bernard Lewis, "What went wrong?: Western impact and Middle Eastern response", 2002*

751. *Bernard Lewis, "From Babel to dragomans: interpreting the Middle East", 2004*

752. *In fact, there is only one empirical article published on Muslim Americans using public opinion data (Jamal 2005), and it does not take up the issue of compatibility between Islam and Western values. In her article Jamal explores the influence of mosque attendance on political participation among Black, Asian, and Arab Muslims in the New York City area*

451

753. *See Feisal Abdul Rauf, "What's right with Islam: a new vision for Muslims and the West", 2004*

754. *Andrew March, "Liberal Citizenship and the Search for an Overlapping Consensus: The Case of Muslim Minorities", 2006*

755. *Andrew March, "Islamic Foundations for a Social Contract in non-Muslim Liberal Democracies", American Political Science Review, Vol. 101, No. 2, May 2007*

756. *Lucas Swaine, "How Ought Liberal Democracies to Treat Theocratic Communities?", January 2001*

757. *Matt A Barreto and Karam Dana, "Is Islam Compatible With The West? Muslim American Political Participation In America", 29/8/2008*

758. *Aiden Kirby and Shawn Brimley, "Home-Grown Terrorosm", The Boston Globe, 8/6/2006*

759. *Matthew Epstein in his testimony to the US Senate in 2003*

760. *David Skidmore, "Huntington's Clash Revisited." Journal of World Systems Research, 1998*

761. *Antoine Abdel Nour, "Introduction a` l'histoire urbaine de la Syrie ottomane (XVIe-XVIIIe)", 1982*

762. *Daniel Lerner, "The passing of traditional society: modernizing the Middle East", 1958*

763. *David Zeidan, "The Islamic Fundamentalist View of Life as a Perennial Battle", Middle East Review of International Affairs, 5/12/2001*

764. *C. T. Burris and L.M. Jackson, "Hate the sin/love the sinner, or love the hater? Intrinsic religion and responses to partner abuse." Journal for the Scientific Study of Religion, 1999*

765. *R. J. Duck and B. Hunsberger, "Religious orientation and prejudice." International Journal for the Psychology of Religion, 1999*

766. *Robert M Kunovich and Randy Hodson. "Conflict, Religious Identity, and Ethnic Intolerance in Croatia" Social Force, Dec. 1999*

767. *C. D. Batson, P. Schoenrade, and W.L. Ventis. "Religion and the Individual : A Social-psychological perspective", 1993*

768. *Bernard Lewis, "What Went Wrong?", The Atlantic Monthly. January 2002*

769. *Jack McClanahan, "America's Information War on Terrorism: Winning Hearts and Minds in The Muslim World", Strategy Research Project, US Army War College, Carlisle Barrack, PA, March 2002*

770. *Dale F. Eickelman, "Inside the Islamic Reformation: Obscured by the media preoccupation with fanaticism and fundamentalism, a religious reformation not unlike that", The Wilson Quarterly, 1998*

771. *Karel A Steenbrink, "The Study of Comparative Religion by Indonesian Muslims: A Survey", Dec. 1990*

772. *Andrew March, "Dissertation Title", Doctoral dissertation, University, 2005*

773. *Tariq Ramadan, "To be a European Muslim: A Study of Islamic Sources in the European Context", 1999*

774. *Amir M. Ali, "A Case for Muslim Political Participation", Muslim Public Affairs Committee, UK, 2004*

775. *Sheikh Muhammad al-Mukhtar al-Shanqiti, "Muslims' Participation in US Elections", 2006*

776. *"NSC 68 United States Objectives and Programs for National Security", National Security Council, Washington, D.C., 14/4/1950*

777. *Joel H. Wiener, ed., Great Britain: Foreign Policy and the Span of Empire 1689-1971: A Documentary History, vol. 2, New York: Chelsea House/ McGraw-Hill, 1972*

778. *Commander Philip Kapusta and Captain Donovan Campbell, "How To Contain Radical Islam", 27/9/2008*

779. *Joe Strange, "Centres of Gravity and Critical Vulnerabilities", Second Edition, Marine Corps War College, 1996*

780. *"Doctrine for Joint Planning Operations", Second Draft, Washington, D.C.: Office of the Chairman, Joint Chiefs of Staff, 2002*

781. *The Observer (London), 24/4/1994*

782. *"U.S.-Funded Radio and Television Make Significant Gains in Middle East despite Anti-American Sentiments", Broadcasting Board of Governors, Washington, D.C., June 2004*

783. *The Boston Globe, 8/9/2004, "Rumsfeld Remarks at the International Institute for Strategic Studies"*

784. *"American Forces Information Service", The Boston Globe, 8/9/2004*

785. *The Boston Globe, Sept. 8, 2004*

786. *Brigadier General Mark Hertling, quoted in The Age (Melbourne), 29/10/2003*

787. *Paul Bremer, quoted in The Scotsman (Edinburgh), 16/2/2004*

788. *Bernard Lewis, "Islam Interpreter", interviewed in The Atlantic Monthly, April 2004*

789. *Dale Eikemeier, "How To Beat The Global Islamist Insurgency", Middle East Quarterly, winter 2005*

790. *"Progress Report on the Global War on Terrorism", the White House, Sept. 2003*

791. *The New York Times, 27/2/2002*

CPSIA information can be obtained at www.ICGtesting.com
Printed in the USA
BVOW010251110512

289952BV00005B/2/P